CASEBOOK ON EXISTENTIALISM 2

"Family Portrait" Woodcut 48" X 24"
Vincent Inconiglios

CASEBOOK ON EXISTENTIALISM 2

William V. Spanos
State University of New York,
Binghampton

Thomas Y. Crowell
Harper & Row, Publishers
New York Hagerstown Philadelphia San Francisco London

A CASEBOOK ON EXISTENTIALISM 2

Library of Congress Cataloging in Publication Data

Main entry under title:
Casebook on existentialism 2.

    Bibliography: p.
    1. Existentialism—Literary collections. 2. Existentialism in literature. 3. Existentialism.
I. Spanos, William V.
PN6071.E9C3 1976   808.8'038   75-44413
ISBN 0-690-00847-3

ACKNOWLEDGMENTS

    T. S. Eliot, excerpt from "The Dry Salvages" in *Four Quartets* in *The Complete Poems and Plays, 1909–1950* (New York: Harcourt Brace Jovanovich, 1952), p. 130. Reprinted by permission of Harcourt Brace Jovanovich, Inc., and Faber & Faber Ltd.
    David Ignatow, excerpt from "Rescue the Dead" in *Poems 1934–1969* (Middletown, Conn.: Wesleyan University Press, 1970), p. 209. Copyright © 1968 by David Ignatow. Reprinted by permission of Wesleyan University Press.
    William Butler Yeats, excerpt from "Sailing to Byzantium" in *Collected Poems of William Butler Yeats* (New York: Macmillan, 1952), pp. 191–192. Copyright 1928 by Macmillan Publishing Co., Inc., renewed 1956 by Georgie Yeats. Reprinted by permission of Macmillan Publishing Co., Inc., M. B. Yeats, Miss Anne Yeats, and The Macmillan Company of London & Basingstoke.
    _____, excerpt from "The Circus Animals' Desertion" in *Collected Poems of William Butler Yeats* (New York: Macmillan, 1952), p. 336. Copyright 1940 by Georgie Yeats, renewed 1968 by Bertha Georgie Yeats, Michael Butler Yeats, and Anne Yeats. Reprinted by permission of Macmillan Publishing Co., Inc., M. B. Yeats, Miss Anne Yeats, and The Macmillan Company of London & Basingstoke.

Old father, your blazing eye
melted our wings;
we plunged to zero
and the encounter
with the time
we'd fallen out of.

In the empty immensity of earth, sky, and water there she was, incomprehensible, firing into a continent. Pop, would go one of the six-inch guns . . . and nothing happened. . . . There was a touch of insanity in this proceeding. . . .

Joseph Conrad, Heart of Darkness

Now that my ladder's gone,

I must lie down where all the ladders start
In the foul rag-and-bone shop of the heart.

W. B. Yeats, "The Circus Animals' Desertion"

At last the horizon seems open once more, granting even that it is not bright; our ships can at last put out to sea in face of every danger; every hazard is again permitted to the discerner; the sea, *our* sea, again lies open before us; perhaps never before did such an "open sea" exist.

Friedrich Nietzsche, Joyful Wisdom

I feel along the edges of life
for a way
that will lead to open land.

David Ignatow, Rescue the Dead

Table of Contents

Preface

Ten years have gone by since the publication of *A Casebook on Existentialism*. Looked at superficially, it would seem that, in the process, Existentialism as a philosophical-theological movement, if it has not run its course, has at least been eclipsed as the governing thrust of modern thought in the academic world by new currents such as the various modes of Saussurian linguistics and structuralist anthropology. Thus, for example, in a seminar on "Postmodern" fiction I chaired at the Modern Language Association meetings of 1975, one of the panelists observed that he was "bored with the existential categories"—Anxiety, Nothingness, Despair, Care, Freedom, etc.—all of which had by this late date become for him worn-out clichés. The implication of putting it this way is, of course, that existentialism has been and continues to be simply a matter of words, that its categories are intellectual concepts in an intellectual system the fashionableness of which has abated. But, of course, this is not the case. On the contrary, as the cave paintings of Lascaux, the Book of Job, Ecclesiastes, *King Lear, Gulliver's Travels, Bleak House, The Trial,* Edvard Munch's painting "The Cry" or Giacommetti's sculpture "Head on a Rod" (to name but a few examples in the history of human "artistic" expression) will not let us forget, the existential standpoint—the standpoint of being-in-the-world—is precisely a profound human and thus transhistorical impulse to understand human being (Heidegger's term is *Dasein*), not a historical abstraction that is subject, ironically, to passing intellectual fashion. It is a human impulse especially strong, of course—indeed inescapable—in our time. For, as "Moderns" we have lost faith in and thus borne witness to the disintegration of traditional Systems of thought—theological, philosophical, and scientific (and their fictional paradigms)—Systems that tend to *see* human life *metaphysically* (*meta-ta-phusika*): from the end or, more specifically, from *beyond* or *above* existence. In other words, the catastrophes of modern history, not the least of which is the generation of ominous ecological imbalances in nature, have violently dislodged (in the sense of un-homed) us from the habitual safety of a familiar, a domesticated, universe—a universe conceived as a well-made fiction—and driven us, like it or not, into an anxious quest, not for a disinterested or objective understanding of existence, but an understanding *grounded* in immediate and interested or care-ful encounter with things as they are.

And so, despite the seeming eclipse of Existential*ism*, the existential impulse continues to manifest itself strongly in the *lived world*—which includes that part of the academy which insists that knowledge is integrally related to living. Here, the existential thinker—whether as philosopher, writer, artist or teacher—continues to speak and act as if he were *Homo Viator,* man on the way, an explorer, beyond boundaries, where learning is fraught with risk—and authentic possibilities.

Indeed, on closer examination, it becomes clear that the existential understanding of man has in fact deepened in the last decade. The existentialism of the postwar years had its center in the agonizing moral and political questions generated by the annunciation of "the death of God" at the end of the 19th century and brought to a climax in Europe by the historical catastrophe of Nazi totalitarianism (and in the United States, by the Vietnam War). Seen from the vantage point of 1975, this existentialism of "extreme situations," as Sartre called it in the late 1940s, was in fact, simply the most visible expression of a less dramatic but more fundamental and enduring and ultimately richer "center" of modern life: the quest —especially in theology, philosophy, and literature—for, as Edmund Husserl put it, "a new way of looking at things" based on a suspension of inherited (i.e. habitual) presuppositions about truth and a "return to the things themselves": *Zu dem Sachen selbst.* (This, I think, is what I was stumbling toward, when in the "Preface" to the earlier edition of *A Casebook* I wrote: "But existentialism is more than a philosophical movement. It has become *the* perspective from which the sensitive and concerned man looks at the world.") I am referring, of course, to the emergence of phenomenology, the unmethodological mode of knowing developed especially by Husserl, Martin Heidegger, and Maurice Merleau-Ponty, that has as its essential goal to bring the perceiver into a more immediate, or better, original, relationship to the lived world *(das Lebenswelt)* than the traditional methodological epistemologies, whether empirical or idealistic, allows.

This revision of *A Casebook on Existentialism* constitutes an effort to accommodate my recognition in the interim that the existentialism of the World War II period—the existentialism more or less embodied in the original edition—was in fact a particular expression of a much broader and more profound movement of the modern consciousness. It is also, therefore, an attempt to justify my faith in the enduring relevance and validity of the existential standpoint in the face of the equally enduring impulse of the Western consciousness to flee from the existential disclosures about the human predicament by naming them, by transforming them into clichés that "at-home" them or, better, that make them a habit—and by forgetting them.

The new anthology begins with the original introduction (slightly revised)—to which I have added a brief but important "Postscript" that extends the discussion of existential thematics to consider its relationship with phenomenology and the implications of an existential phenomenology for literary form. Unlike the earlier edition, this revised version is organized in a four-part structure. Part I presents a selection of fiction and drama that, in my opinion, best illustrates the various modes of the existential imagination. Part II contains critical commentary engaged in the task of elucidating the essential *thematic and formal* characteristics of existential literature and (what most modern critical theory tends to disregard) the kind of response it tries to generate. Part III presents what I take to be some of the most important and influential premodern expressions of the existential/phenomenological standpoint. And Part IV, finally, consists of a selection of representative statements by the major modern existential philosophers and theologians. Following the lead of the "Postscript," however, it will be noted that in revising I have shifted the emphasis in each section to create a more equitable balance between the imperatives of phenomenological existentialism for *literary form* and its imperatives for literary thematics. This shift "complicates" the literary issues informing the materials of the earlier edition, but does not reduce their accessibility. It simply opens out another, a deeper dimension of significance for those who want to pursue their investigations of the relationship between existentialism and literature beyond thematic boundaries. For those who wish to move even farther outward, I have added a brief but carefully selected annotated bibliography, subdivided into Philosophy, Theology, and Literary Criticism.

This revised edition of *A Casebook on Existentialism* has in a very real sense been in the making ever since the original was published. To acknowledge my debts to those scholars, critics, writers, students, and friends who have contributed to my developing understanding of the rich, inexhaustible, and important subject of this book would thus require an autobiographical account of the erratic and sometimes turbulent course of my intellectual life during the last ten years. I will, of course, spare the reader that ordeal. But I do wish to express my debt to all those recent literary critics like Nathan A. Scott, Stephen Crites, George Steiner, Harold Rosenberg, Murray Krieger, Frederic Jameson, Edward Said, Paul de Man, Geoffrey Hartman, Charles Altieri, Richard Wasson, and not the least, my student Paul Bové, who, despite the diversity of their approaches to the question, have recognized and insisted in one way or another that the literature of our time is fundamentally an expression of the same naked impulse that has evoked the great and profoundly moving existential diagnosis of the modern predicament and of human being at large, the diagnosis of Nietzsche, Husserl, Heidegger, Sartre, Buber, Jaspers, Merleau-Ponty, Derrida, Marcel, Unamuno, Ortega, Tillich, Bultmann, and others. I also wish to acknowledge a special debt to David Ignatow, whose poetry is, in my mind, the supreme expression of the existential imagination in America. Without realizing it, he gave me a deep insight into the existential literary imagination in the process of an extended "dialogue"

—part talk, part correspondence—which was eventually published in *boundary 2*, the journal of postmodern literature I co-edit with the novelist Robert Kroetsch.

On a more immediate level, I wish to thank Phillip Leininger of Thomas Y. Crowell for suggesting the project and for his encouragement and editorial help thereafter; Ms. Carol Horsburgh, for typing a great portion of the manuscript; Ms. Elizabeth Rankin, not only for assuming the onerous bibliographical tasks encumbent on putting this kind of book together, but also for enduring, graciously, my disquisitions every time a text in the anthology was mentioned; and finally—and again—my wife, Margaret, who has *shared* these ten more years with me.

William V. Spanos

Abraham, Sisyphus, and the Furies: Some Introductory Notes on Existentialism and a Postscript

> There are countless places of refuge, there is only one place of salvation; but the possibilities of salvation, again, are as numerous as all the places of refuge.
>
> Franz Kafka

The roots of existentialism extend deeply into Western history, even beyond St. Augustine to the pre-Socratic philosophers and the author of the Book of Job. But at no time in the past did the existential attitude (a term more appropriate, perhaps, than "philosophy") have the kind of relevance it has for modern man. In the past—as recently as Søren Kierkegaard's day—the existentialist philosopher or artist was an isolated voice asserting the precariousness of human life in the face of a community that largely ignored or refused to listen to him. As long as the community believed, or thought it believed, in the existence of a God who offered the reward of eternity as compensation for the suffering and anguish of temporal life, his warning went more or less unheard and the existential attitude thus remained marginal and undefined.

In the middle of the nineteenth century, however, after a long and inexorable process of secularization, God—at least the traditional image of God—expired and man was left naked to confront, in T. S. Eliot's great existential metaphor, "a heap of broken images." The proclamation by Nietzsche's madman of the death of God was the annunciation of the age of anxiety. After this, philosophers could no longer spin verbal webs in remote corners of the house of life without at least confronting the reality of Nothingness; nor could theologians build paper Gothic religious systems without confronting the very real absence of God; nor, for that matter, could artists project rationally unified and ordered microcosms without confronting the irrational macrocosm or, rather, multiverse.

Since Nietzsche, philosophy, religion, and the arts (especially on the European continent, but increasingly in England and America) have reflected in one way or another the existential crisis of unaccommodated man. Whether atheistic or theistic, the philosophy and art of the twentieth century constitutes largely an encounter with Nothingness and the effort to deal with the threat it poses to man's existence as man. Thus what was the attitude of the outsider is now that of everyman.

1

[II]

What specifically, then, is the existential attitude? Ultimately it is undefinable. Like the unicorn, whom legend endows with wondrous attributes, but whom the empirical eye has never calibrated, existentialism is a kind of antipoetic poetry of the philosophical imagination, defying rational systematization. Unlike traditional philosophies, existentialism is not a philosophy of essences, defining nature—including human nature—and imposing abstract structures upon it. It is, rather, a philosophy of existence, which attempts to view man in his immediate, his original, relationship to the universe, in all his concrete plentitude—and problematic ambiguity. Thus no two existentialists would have the same understanding of the human condition. Nevertheless the contemporary philosophical and literary existentialists, both atheistic (or humanistic) and theistic, address themselves to two broad alternatives facing man in a world in which God is dead: (1) the institutionalized and collectivized life on the analogy of the machinery of technology toward which modern man is drifting, and (2) the agonizingly difficult authentic existence of the individual who insists upon maintaining his unique consciousness in the face of the overwhelming pressures to conform—that is, on being a man-in-the-world.

Both humanistic and theistic existentialists recognize the threat of anonymity posed by the development of a mass technological society. They see the ultimate source of the threat, however, in man's real, if unconscious, obsession with order, which in the modern world has driven him into constructing rationally derived systems to replace the discredited Christian cosmology. Although the German idealist Hegel (whose "System" Kierkegaard felt it his life's mission to demolish) and, behind Hegel, the whole tradition of essentialist philosophy going back to Plato's and Aristotle's affirmation of the *logos* as eternal *presence*, come under the attack of existentialists, their more immediate philosophical *bête noire* is the scientific rationalism of the nineteenth-century utilitarian philosophers and their twentieth-century counterparts, the logical positivists.[1] For in the eyes of the existentialists this "scientism" stands as the fountainhead of the technological revolution which, in turn, has generated the worship of progress and consequently a materialistic utopianism that provides modern man with comfort and security but at the price of his freedom, his existential humanity, thus, as Dostoevski realized, reducing the human community to the level of an ant colony or, worse, as Ionesco puts it, transforming the human community into a herd of rhinoceroses.

1. Positivism is essentially a theory of meaning which holds that the meaningful is ultimately linked to the empirically verifiable—that which can be experienced by the senses. Unlike the existentialist, the positivist maintains that evaluative statements are not verifiable, and therefore are cognitively meaningless, though they express attitude.

According to the existentialists, scientific rationalism and its counter-part in practical life, the technological society, locate reality in the objec-tive realm of measurable matter, and value in the production and utilization of objects. In so doing, they subordinate man to the tool, con-sciousness to efficiency, and the individual to the social and productive organizations (including educational institutions). By the inescapable logic of this system of valuation, the individual becomes dehumanized. Defined according to his function and evaluated by the degree of his utility, he is reduced to the status of an object like other objects of nature, or, to use Martin Buber's term, a manipulable *It* (Jean-Paul Sartre's *l'en soi,* or the in-itself). Thus stripped of his subjectivity (his *Thou*ness) he is alienated from his authentic self and, like Ulrich in Robert Musil's novel *Der Mann ohne Eigenschaften,* becomes a "man without qualities," or, like the nar-rator of Ralph Ellison's novel, an "invisible man" or, like the American fliers—Aarfy, Milo, and so on—of Joseph Heller's *Catch 22,* a mindless and expendable instrument, and thus an easy, indeed willing, victim of a vast and insane efficient collective—a "Brotherhood," a "Catch 22"— grounded in objectivity and modeled after mass production processes, and often, as we have witnessed over and over again and everywhere in this century, a brutalized weapon in the arsenal of such a care-less collective in its effort to achieve universality.

Following Kierkegaard's violent denunciation of the crowd as "the untruth, by reason of the fact that it . . . weakens [the individual's] sense of responsibility by reducing it to a fraction," the condemnation of collecti-vism becomes a central preoccupation of existential philosophy and theology. From Nietzsche to Jaspers (though Sartre's Marxism constitutes a problematic ambiguity in his thought), existentialists have passionately expressed their horror of both the unconscious drift of democracies and the planned, that is, preestablished, advance of totalitarian societies to-ward the achievement of massive materialistic utopias. Perhaps no one, however, has put it so dramatically as Nicholas Berdyaev in *The End of Our Time:*

> Utopias appear to be far more possible than it was formerly thought. And we find ourselves confronting . . . a dreadful question: How to avoid their ulti-mate realization? . . . Utopias are possible. Life marches toward utopias. And perhaps a new century begins, a century in which the intellectuals and culti-vated class will imagine ways of avoiding utopias and of returning to a non-utopian society, less "perfect" and more free.

In the literature of existentialism this criticism of modern man's obses-sion with materialistic progress has taken the form of the antiutopian novel, which mercilessly satirizes his eagerness to relinquish the burden of his freedom to the collectivist state in return for the comforts and security of the easy life. Like its philosophical expression, the literary presentation of the theme of antiutopianism is first encountered in the nineteenth century, in fiction such as Dostoevski's *Notes from Underground* and "The Legend of the Grand Inquisitor," and in Dickens' *Hard Times.* But it was not until the mechanized brutality of World War I shook the modern artist into authentic awareness of the appallingly destructive potential of scientism that the form was fully defined in Eugene Zamiatin's novel *We* (1924). After this, the form achieved the status of something like a genre, a fact attested to by the successive appearance of such well-known antiutopian novels as Aldous Huxley's *Brave New World* (which, incidentally, as the epigraph from Berdyaev and the Dostoevskian echoes suggest, is more "existential" than hitherto realized), George Orwell's *1984*, Arthur Koestler's unjustifiably neglected *Arrival and Departure* and Virgil Gheorghiu's *The Twenty-fifth Hour.* Projecting a horribly "perfected" society into the future, that is, a society that represents a rigorously logical fulfillment of the present abdication of freedom implicit in the worship technological progress, this form, as Joseph Heller's absurdist *Catch 22* bears witness, has become a deadly satirical weapon in the existential assault upon contemporary utopianism, whether it be totalitarian, communistic, or capitalistic in design.[2]

It is primarily in their positive assertions about man and his relationship to the cosmos that humanistic and theistic existentialists differ. Nevertheless, there is enough agreement even in this area to warrant grouping them together. The acknowledgment of the death of God implies that man has no preordained purpose to fulfill in the universe, indeed, that he has been thrown (*geworfen*) into a multiverse he is not-at-home in. (For atheists such as Nietzsche, Sartre, Simone de Beauvoir, and Camus, the death of God means literally what it says; in the case of the early Heidegger, it implies radical uncertainty about God's existence; for theists such as Rudolph Bultmann, Paul Tillich, and Karl Jaspers, it means the death of the conventional gods of Christianity, above all, of the God who is the source of deterministic or idealistic theologies and the God "worshiped" on Sunday mornings by the complacent and self-satisfied middle class, the "solid" and "justified" citizens of Sartre's Bouville in *Nausea.*) Thus His demise opens up to the individual the dreadful need to choose between two broad alternative modes of existence. He can accept the definition of man posited by the behavioral sciences, which views him as another object

2. As I suggest in my essay "The Detective and the Boundary: Some Notes on the Postmodern Imagination," this antiutopian impulse of the existential imagination finds its most basic expression in the antidetective drama and fiction that pervades the literary scene in the post-World War II period. See the section "Literary Criticism."

among the objects and things in a rationally explicable universe, and thus submit to the same natural laws that govern stones. Or he can revolt against his predicament.

As a self-conscious—that is, free—creature, man constitutes a minority in a cosmos governed by natural law. From a rational point of view, then, he is by virtue of his consciousness an anomaly. As Zeus tells Orestes in Sartre's play *The Flies*, "You are not in your own home, intruder, you are a foreign body in the world, like a splinter in the flesh, or a poacher in his lordship's forest." All the empirical evidence (objects) in the universe leads to the inexorably logical conclusion that man ought to commit literal or at least spiritual suicide (that is, negate his consciousness) and thus become one with—a rationally understandable part of—the universe. This, without being aware of it, is what mass man does. But the existentialist, who passionately insists on the dignity and worth of human being, refuses to capitulate to the pressures of this kind of reason and the dehumanizing systems to which it gives rise. Despite the absence of rational justification, he irrationally affirms life against death. In this revolt against the cosmos, he becomes the absurd man. For the humanistic existentialist the mythic symbol of this man, according to Albert Camus, is Sisyphus, who, despite his being condemned to ceaselessly roll a rock to the top of a mountain only to have it fall back of its own weight, nevertheless not only endures but also finds joy in this task. For the theistic existentialist the mythic symbol of the absurd man, according to Kierkegaard, is the biblical Abraham, who although he cannot perceive God rationally, nevertheless chooses—"by virtue of the absurd"—to obey His terrible command to kill his beloved son Isaac, and discovers joy in the very agony of not knowing that he has decided rightly.

Put philosophically, the existential affirmation of man as opposed to the universe of things becomes the well-known formula of Jean-Paul Sartre, "Existence precedes essence," which means simply that a man, as opposed to a thing, *becomes* rather than merely *is:* he is a live (temporal) creature rather than an inanimate (spatial) object. As such, he does not have a universal and thus permanent and static *nature,* as, for example, a stone has (its "stoneness"). Unlike the stone, therefore, man cannot be abstracted and quantified, cannot, in other words, be placed in a system —a Euclidean space, as it were—which measures and classifies his attributes or properties and renders his behavior utterly predictable. To attempt to universalize man into Mankind, to posit that essence precedes existence, as essentialist philosophies and collectivist states do, is to reduce a unique and vital being to the level of an inert thing and to make the abstract whole greater than the sum or rather the process of its concrete parts. Put positively, "existence" refers to man (human being) and ultimately means that he is free; that, unlike objects, which merely *are* and thus are at the mercy of their preestablished essences, man alone is capable of choosing his own future—that is, of determining or discovering his own essence.

The concept of freedom, therefore, is the root principle of existential thought. But existential freedom has little to do with the rugged individualism of laissez faire, the right of economic man to pursue without constraint the pleasure principle or the profit motive, which is posited and defended by the capitalistic democracies of the West. On the contrary, existential freedom is grounded in the awareness of universal contingency and of the radical finality of man's middle state and, therefore, of his agonizing responsibility for choosing among complex alternatives concerning his existence. Stripped of the ethical guides deduced from theological or rational systems, the individual is left naked and alone to face in fear and trembling the great void and, to adapt King Lear's words, to decide whether to make something out of nothing.

Thus the existentialists refuse to allow man to take freedom for granted as he usually does. They reject the vague notion that it is a privilege that somehow renders life easier and happier. Rather, they assert its difficulty. As Sartre says, man "is *condemned* to freedom." Comfort (and security) and freedom are incompatible. The easy life, in fact, is the privilege of slaves, for whom all the painful decisions are made by others. The life of a truly free man is measured by the degree of his dread in the face of existence. In short, freedom, as the existentialists understand it, is, in the paradoxical words of Dostoevski's Grand Inquisitor, "a terrible gift."

The existentialists (who are as much moralists as they are philosophers) attempt to activate a genuine awareness of the difficult burden of freedom by means of their analysis of the fact of death. In their view, death is the one certain reality in man's life. Nevertheless, because it opens up the terrible possibility of the existence of the absurd, the possibility that life ends meaninglessly and is absorbed into the void of Nothingness, most men obsessively refuse to acknowledge the reality of death. The conventionally religious man uses the promise of eternal life made by traditional Christian theology to anesthetize the personal sting of death. In a similar way, the mass man of modern technological society immersed in the secular life evades the implications of death by a process of self-deception which takes the form of domesticating its terrible irrationality. As Heidegger, following Kierkegaard, puts it in *Being and Time:*

... death is "known" as a mishap which is constantly occurring—as a "case of death." ... The "they" [*das Man:* Heidegger's name for the man whose life is determined by public interpretations and imperatives] has already stowed away an interpretation for this event. It talks of it in a "fugitive" manner, either expressly or else in a way which is mostly inhibited, as if to say, "One of these days one will die too, in the end; but right now it has nothing to do with us."

...The expression "one dies" spreads abroad the opinion that what gets reached, as it were, by death, is the "they." ... Dying is leveled off to an occurrence which reaches *Dasein* [being there, that is, human being], to be sure, but belongs to nobody in particular.... Dying, which is essentially mine in such a way that no one can be my representative, is perverted into an event of public occurrence which the "they" encounters.... [Death's] character as a possibility gets concealed, and so are the other two items that belong to it —the fact that it is non-relational and that it is not to be outstripped.

The effort to socialize and thus to "outstrip" death, however, is inevitably unsuccessful. For the "fugitive" manner of speaking about death is a tacit awareness of the threat of personal annihilation. Eventually this uneasy awareness which, in T. S. Eliot's phrase "flickers in the corner of [one's] eye,"—this anxiety or dread of death and Nothingness—*Angst*, as the existentialists call it—drives the fugitive into a corner where there are no further avenues of escape. Here in "the place of origins," "the not-at-home," "the zero zone," "the alpha," or most appropriate in this context, "the precincts of his last evasions," as this primordial existential realm has been variously called, he must encounter his death, the apparent absurdity of existence, and the possibility of the palpable reality of Nothingness, and then, as a unique and solitary individual stripped of his protective social garments (including his public language), make a genuinely committed decision about his relationship to himself and to the world.

Thus, as Wallace Stevens says in his poem "Sunday Morning,"

Death is the mother of beauty; hence from her,
Alone, shall come fulfillment to our dreams
And our desires.[3]

As dreadful as the threat of annihilation is, for the existentialist it often becomes a paradoxically benign agent. For the face to face encounter with death clarifies the absurdity of the human condition and thus activates what Heidegger calls "care" (*Sorge*), or what might be called the interrogative mood—the mood that, in asking the Being question or, better, the question of what it means to be, distinguishes man from beast and stone. In other words, the confrontation *humanizes* the being who, like the biblical Job, and in a different way the classical Oedipus, or the Renaissance Hamlet, becomes perilously like the dead objects in the universe of things in his effort to escape his awareness of death and the absurd. Thus

3. From "Sunday Morning" by Wallace Stevens. In *The Collected Poems of Wallace Stevens* (New York: Alfred A. Knopf, 1954), pp. 68–69. Reprinted by permission of Random House, Inc.

Jaspers, echoing the Book of Job, writes in *The Way of Wisdom* that the authentic life can only spring from "the darkness in which the individual finds himself . . . from his sense of forlornness when he stares without love into the void, from his self-forgetfulness when he feels that he is being consumed by the busy-ness of the world, when suddenly he wakes up in terror and asks himself: What am I failing to do? What should I do?"

It is precisely at this point in the analysis of the human predicament —the moment of the individual's anxious confrontation with Nothingness —that the most significant difference between humanistic and theistic existentialists emerges. For the atheist, as we have seen, the alternative to physical or spiritual suicide is that of Sisyphus: a fully conscious, if agonized, acknowledgment of the irreconcilable nature of man's alienation from the universe and a rebellious, if precarious, assertion of the existential self against the discontinuities of the human predicament.[4] This is, as Paul Tillich puts it, the "courage of despair." For the theist, on the other hand, the alternative is that of Abraham: a leap of faith—not a rejection of the concrete world—a wager, to use Pascal's metaphor, concerning the truth of the existence of the absent God, or more specifically, the truth of the Incarnation, which reconciles time and eternity and thus infuses meaning into the apparently chaotic and fragmented temporal world.

As we have seen, the atheistic existentialist takes the death of God literally. Thus man is absolutely free to create his own essence. He becomes—from a Christian point of view at any rate—something like his own deity, and, along with the burden of responsibilities and risks, he also assumes the awesome creative potentialities generated by this situation. For the Christian, on the other hand, God is not dead; He is rationally incomprehensible; that is, He is absent, a *Deus absconditus.* Thus man's freedom becomes the dreadful awareness of the necessity to choose between a life of despair in the realm of Nothingness and a life of precarious joy in the realm which to the empirical eye appears meaningless, but to the eye of faith constitutes on the microcosmic level a reconciliation between existence and essence and on the macrocosmic level (in the words of T. S. Eliot's *Four Quartets*) an "intersection of the timeless with time," when "the past and future/Are conquered and reconciled." For the Christian existentialist, in other words, existence precedes essence only in the sense that man cannot know his divine essence and achieve an I-Thou relationship with God without immersion into the destructive element of existence.[5]

4. In the literature of atheistic existentialism, the rebellious affirmation is often nothing more positive than the stoic endurance of Nothingness. Occasionally, as in some of the dramas of the absurd, there is no suggestion of affirmation at all.
5. Occasionally, however, as in some of the writings of Kierkegaard and especially in the existential theology of Karl Barth, Christian existentialism interprets the leap of faith as a rejection of the things of this world for eternity.

For both atheistic and theistic existentialists, then, the royal way of "salvation" lies in the heart of darkness which is this world. Existential man, in Gabriel Marcel's metaphor, is *Homo Viator,* man on the way or man as explorer on uncharted and perilous seas. Thus Nietzsche says in *Joyful Wisdom* in response to the annunciation of the "death of God":

At last the horizon seems open once more, granting even that it is not bright; our ships can at last put out to sea in face of every danger; every hazard is again permitted to the discerner; the sea, *our* sea, again lies open before us; perhaps never before did such an "open sea" exist.—

Thus also Camus, after taking his readers to the edge of the bottomless void, writes, "This hell of the present is [man's] Kingdom at last." And echoing him, the Christian existentialist poet W. H. Auden concludes his Christmas oratorio *For the Time Being:*

He is the Truth
  Seek Him in the Kingdom of Anxiety;
You will come to a great city that has expected
    your return for years.

He is the Life
  Love Him in the World of the Flesh;
And at your marriage all its occasions shall dance
    for joy.[6]

But there remains the crucial difference. For Nietzsche and Camus, as for other humanistic existentialists, salvation is the humanizing awareness of the irreconcilable divorce between man and the world; for Auden, as for other theistic existentialists, it is a marriage of the individual and Christ —the Word made Flesh—and, through this, a reconciliation between man and the universe.

[III]

The existential literary imagination is as various as its philosophical counterpart. It employs all the genres of creative literature—autobiography, short and long fiction, drama, and poetry—and within each, a great variety of forms. Thus, for example, the forms of the drama of existential-

6. From "For the Time Being" by W. H. Auden. In *The Collected Poetry of W. H. Auden* (New York: Random House, 1945), p. 466. Copyright 1944 by W. H. Auden. Reprinted by permission of Random House, Inc., and Faber and Faber, Inc.

ism range from the traditional realism of Sartre's *Dirty Hands,* through the drama of ideas of Camus' *Caligula,* to the surrealist drama of the absurd of Eugène Ionesco, Harold Pinter, and Samuel Beckett. Like the thought of existentialist philosophers, therefore, the literature of existentialism is virtually impossible to classify in formal terms.

On the other hand, the metaphorical vehicles or myths that embody and express the existential predicament of modern man reveal a striking, and often illuminating, consistency. In *Modern Literature and the Religious Frontier,* Nathan Scott distinguishes four such pervasive myths or patterns of symbolic statement: the Myth of the Isolato, which presents the theme of isolation and estrangement (for example, Franz Kafka's novels *The Trial* and *The Castle*); the Myth of Hell, which embodies the theme of Nothingness, the disintegration of meaning in the modern world (William Faulkner's *The Sound and the Fury* and T. S. Eliot's *The Waste Land*); the Myth of Voyage, which projects the painful journey through the irrational self or world (James Joyce's *Ulysses* and Jean-Paul Sartre's *The Age of Reason*); and, finally, the Myth of Sanctity, which depicts the theme of reconciliation and salvation (T. S. Eliot's *The Family Reunion* and Graham Greene's *The End of the Affair*). These categories constitute a brilliant insight into the ways in which myth has been appropriated by the contemporary existential writer, but Scott's hint that the four myths, taken as a unit, resemble Dante's journey in *The Divine Comedy* through the Inferno and the Purgatorio to the Paradiso, coupled with Heidegger's analysis of death and Nothingness, suggests a more inclusive symbolic pattern to stand as the archetypal myth or, better perhaps, antimyth (if we see this as deconstructing the prevailing myths of universal order) of the existential imagination: the flight from a dark, threatening agent who pursues the fugitive protagonist into an isolated corner (often, the underground), where he must confront his relentless pursuer, whereupon, in a blinding moment of illumination he discovers the paradoxically benevolent aspect of his persecutor. This symbolic pattern, of course, is the Aeschylean "myth" of the Furies, in which the protagonist's (Orestes') face-to-face encounter with the pursuing *Erinyes* (The Angry Ones) activates their transfiguration into the *Eumenides* (the Kindly Ones).[7]

7. See William Barrett, "The Place of the Furies," *Irrational Man: A Study of Existential Philosophy* (Garden City, N.Y.: Doubleday, 1958), pp. 237–248, in which he uses Aeschylus' symbol of the Furies to define the existential diagnosis of modern man's flight from the irrational (including death) and to present the existential demand for authenticity. For the Christian existentialist, the figure of the pursuer takes the symbolic form of the hound of heaven, the archetypal projection of which occurs in that other ancient work which has been adopted by existentialists as a mythical construct of the human predicament: the Book of Job. The Old Testament myth can be interpreted as an analogy of the myth of the Furies presented by Aeschylus in *The Oresteia.* Just as the Furies pursue Orestes into perception of a different cosmos and thus of the positive side of his pursuers, so Satan, the symbol of the fallen world (that is, the world in which death holds sway) from which Job wishes to escape, drives Job into acceptance of its fallenness and thus into awareness of his pursuer as an agent of God. I have developed the formal implications of this thematic paradox of the existential imagination in some detail in my essay " 'Wanna Go Home Baby?': *Sweeney Agonistes* as Drama of the Absurd," *PMLA,* Vol. 85 (January 1970), 8–20.

This, for example, is precisely the symbolic pattern that Tolstoi discovers in "The Death of Ivan Ilych," a story William Barrett has called "something of a basic scripture for existential thought." The death—the "something new"—that Ivan, the archetypal functionary is trying desperately to evade is personified in the image of something closely resembling the *Erinyes*. Despite his bad faith—his effort to reestablish the old current of thought ("that had once screened the thought of death from him") by taking up again his duties in the law courts—the pain in his side

> ... would begin his own gnawing work. Ivan Ilych would turn his attention to it and try to drive the thought of it away, but without success. *It* would come and stand before him and look at him, and he would be petrified and the light would die out of his eyes, and he would again begin asking himself whether *It* alone was true. ... He would shake himself, try to pull himself together, manage somehow to bring the sitting to a close, and return home with the sorrowful consciousness that his judicial labours would not as formerly hide from him what he wanted them to hide, and could not deliver him from *It*. And what was worst of all was that *It* drew his attention to itself not in order to make him take some action but only that he should look at *It*, look it straight in the face: look at it and without doing anything, suffer inexpressibly.[8]

His flight away from death is presented as a paradoxical motion toward it: "What had happened to him was like the sensation one sometimes experiences in a railway carriage when one thinks one is going backwards while one is really going forward and suddenly becomes aware of the real direction." And finally, upon Ivan's authentic confrontation with his pursuer, death becomes a benign agent, or more precisely, a midwife who presides over a spiritual birth that Ivan perceives as his falling through the darkness of the womb into light ("In place of death there was light") and expresses in words that allude to Christ's final labor of creation that ends in the crucifixion ("Death is finished").[9]

In the literature of existentialism, the image of the pursuer often symbolizes something more than death. Nevertheless, its focal meaning is invariably a form or extension of death—the absurd, Nothingness, the fallen world, for example—and the pattern is invariably, if broadly, similar to that of "Ivan Ilych." Thus, in Jean-Paul Sartre's *The Flies*, the flies, which symbolize the agonizing remorse, or rather a view of death that demands remorse from the individual who breaks the dehumanizing eter-

8. The references to the gnawing in his side become pervasive after his accident, but only achieve a total identification with the *It*, the Fury figure, at the end of this section, when Ivan says to himself: "*It* sits there as before, gnawing just the same!"
9. See Eugène Ionesco's *Exit the King*, translated by Donald Watson (New York: Grove Press, 1963) for a version of Tolstoi's existential theme presented in the formal terms of the drama of the absurd.

nal order of the gods and the political order of the world's Grand Inquisitors, become in the end the humanizing burden of anguish that Orestes assumes when he rejects, first his rational Pangloss (the Tutor) and then Zeus and the eternal order for time, death, and freedom. Thus also, in T. S. Eliot's *The Family Reunion*, the Furies, symbolizing the nauseous meaninglessness of the fallen world—the world of death—become Harry's "bright angels" after they have pursued him into the "precincts of his last evasions."

There is, of course, in line with the philosophical distinction, a significant difference between the humanistic existentialist's treatment of the Furies and that of the Christian existentialist. For the former, the Furies activate an authenticity which is characterized by the protagonist's existential awareness of his thrownness, of his freedom, and of the abyss that separates him from the world, and which manifests itself in the courage to be in the face of despair. The humanistic Furies, in other words, symbolize things as they are in the natural world. They may appear to be demonic to the protagonist, but in reality there is no supernatural significance associated with them. For the Christian, on the other hand, the Furies activate an authenticity characterized by the protagonist's existential awareness of the possibility of ontological depth, a ground of Being that gives order and worth to the world. They constitute, that is, the incarnational principle, the hound of heaven, pursuing the protagonist, undermining his self-sufficient aesthetic, legalistic, or at best ethical, vision and driving him finally, through anguish and despair, to a recognition of at least the possibility of the coherent nature of existence, in which even death (or evil) itself is an organic part of the larger rhythm of creation. As the Skeleton or *figura rerum* (another Fury symbol) puts it in Charles Williams' neglected verse play *Thomas Cranmer of Canterbury*, this principle is "Christ's back" or again, "the Judas who betrays men to God." The difference, in other words, resides in the Christian existentialist's redemptive resolution. The journey activated by the Furies, which takes the protagonist to the edge of the abyss where the choice must be made, is fundamentally the same.

There are, of course, other myths and symbols that express the existential vision of the human predicament: the Underground Man (for example, in Dostoevski's *Notes from Underground* and Ralph Ellison's *The Invisible Man*), the Metamorphosis (in Franz Kafka's "Metamorphosis" and Eugène Ionesco's *Rhinoceros*), the Eternal Return (in Ionesco's *The Bald Soprano* and *The Lesson* and in Beckett's *Waiting for Godot* and *Endgame*), and the Grand Inquisitor (in such antiutopian novels as those of Aldous Huxley, George Orwell, Arthur Koestler, and Virgil Gheorghiu and, more subtly, in works such as Pirandello's *Six Characters in Search of an Author*, Sartre's *Nausea*, Ionesco's *Victims of Duty*, and Joseph

Heller's *Catch 22*). But none, it seems, is so pervasive and inclusive of the various facets of existentialism as the myth—or antimyth—of the Furies. It is discoverable in a great many other works besides those already mentioned. It can be seen in humanistic existential works such as Joseph Conrad's *Victory*, Kafka's *The Trial*, Albert Camus' *The Fall*, Archibald MacLeish's *J.B.*, Friedrich Dürrenmatt's *The Visit*, Harold Pinter's *The Birthday Party* and *A Slight Ache*, and Iris Murdoch's *A Severed Head*. It also informs such Christian existential works as Dostoevski's *Crime and Punishment*, Graham Greene's *The Power and the Glory*, T. S. Eliot's *Sweeney Agonistes* and *The Elder Statesman*, Charles Williams' *Cranmer of Canterbury*, and Christopher Fry's *A Sleep of Prisoners*.

This list could easily be extended, but these titles should be amply sufficient to suggest that the myth of the Furies (whether in the form given it by Aeschylus or the author of the Book of Job) constitutes something of an archetype in the literature of contemporary existentialism. This, however, should not be surprising. Far more than any other aspect of the human condition, the phenomenon of death, as the existentialists observe, has always been the closest intimate of mankind. No matter how obsessively men have striven to outstrip death by forgetting it, the effort has been futile. Death demands that each individual face and come to terms with his mortality. It is, therefore, not difficult to understand why the human imagination has always, especially in times of crisis like the present, mythologized, that is, made *something* of this terrible negation. What really counts is the kind of *something* the human imagination makes of *nothing*.

POSTSCRIPT

Since the publication of the first edition of *A Casebook on Existentialism*, I have become increasingly uneasy about the pervasive, and sometimes too easy, impulse on the part of students of literature to find existentialism everywhere in the literature of Western man, in works as different and as remote in time, as, say, Sophocles' *Oedipus the King* and Samuel Beckett's *Happy Days*. There is, of course, very real justification for this assumption, since, unlike the traditional philosopher or theologian, the traditional poet (I use the term in its generic sense) *presents* existence rather than *writing about* it. But with the emergent recognition that the existential attitude is itself grounded in a phenomenological mode of knowing, one begins to realize that an authentic existential literary text is defined as much by its formal character as by its content.

By "phenomenology"—to risk oversimplification—I mean the "unmethodical method" that (1) rejects or, rather, sets aside ("brackets") the

Western metaphysical frame of reference, which "understands" existence teleologically, that is, from the *end* (*meta-ta-phusika*), and, in the name of this "disinterested" or "objective" distance, transforms human (temporal) existence into an inanimate and quantifiable object or static *spatial configuration*. (This is the phenomenological reduction or *epoché*.) And it does this in order to achieve (2) a more primordial, which is to say, *temporal*, understanding of human existence, an understanding characterized by *interestedness* or, to use Heidegger's term, by *care* (*Sorge*). (This is the existential version of the principle the phenomenologists call the intentionality of consciousness.) It is, further, this originary interpretive methodology—this impulse to "return to the things themselves"— that lies behind the various existential philosophical and theological efforts to "Destruct" (Martin Heidegger) or "Demythologize" (Rudolph Bultmann) or "Deconstruct" (Jacques Derrida) the history of Western metaphysics and of Christian theology in order to regain authentic beginnings, *die Seinsfrage*, as Heidegger puts it: the primordial question of Being or, rather, the question of what it means to be. It is also this phenomenological interpretive methodology that lies behind the more recent analogous attempts in literary hermeneutics to deconstruct the Western literary tradition, the various historical versions of "Aristotelian" poetic form, and the critical concepts of the autonomy of art which they have nourished. I mean the *icon*-oclastic strategy to break-open (dis-close) their "closed," their "sealed-off," their "autotelic," their "bounded," structures in order to liberate and reveal the temporal or existential truth of be-ing (*a-letheia*: that which is brought out of hiddenness) which the teleological or spatial perspective closed off and concealed. To use another metaphor from the language of phenomenology—one that is made much of in the pages of this book on existentialism—the phenomenological standpoint, in returning to "the things themselves" or what is the same thing, to the place of origins, allows us to dis-cover what the habit of Western metaphysical thought and literary expression has covered up and, as the stem of the Greek word *a-letheia* also suggests, forgotten. In other words, it "retrieves" that history, renders it authentically relevant once more to man.

To return specifically to the relationship between phenomenology and literary form, the phenomenological standpoint, in other words, reveals that the traditional metaphysics of Western civilization has conditioned us to anthropomorphize existence, to perceive or to want to perceive the world as a well-made book (The Book of Nature). Indeed, we discover that we habitually perceive the temporal world as a *fiction* with a beginning, middle, and end or, at any rate, one in which the contradictions of existence are resolved "aesthetically" into a *significant form*, a "well wrought urn" (to use the metaphor that the American New Critics took from the "metaphysical" poet John Donne as their model for the authentically poetic modern poem). The phenomenological standpoint thus suggests, by analogy, that the Western literary tradition from Aristotle's *Poetics* on (with significant exceptions) had modeled the work of literary art on one or another version of this metaphysical order. It conceived the literary work, that is, as a microcosm, an instantaneously apprehensible ("graspable") picture or image or sculptured form of a teleological macrocosm in order to achieve (aesthetic) distance from and/or consolation for the dreadful—and painful—contradictions and discontinuities of man's temporal existence. This transcendence of the contingency of the temporal realm and the anxiety to which it gives rise is, of course, what Aristotle, in defining the effect of the well-made tragic action, calls *catharsis,* and what early Modernists like T. E. Hulme and James Joyce call "rest."

In the essay "Abraham, Sisyphus, and the Furies"—indeed, in the original *Casebook* at large—the operative definition of existential literature was more or less restricted to thematics. An existential work of literature was assumed to be one which attacks the metaphysical or, more generally, anthropomorphic world view of the Western tradition, especially its positivistic and linear version, and presents the existential vision of life primarily in its content or subject matter. I more or less disregarded in the works I referred to in the essay and in those I selected for inclusion, especially works which are precursors of existentialism, what should have been a signal: that in the most powerful and moving of these—works such as Dickens' *Bleak House,* Dostoevski's *Notes from Underground* and *Crime and Punishment,* Tolstoi's *The Death of Ivan Ilych,* Pirandello's *Six Characters in Search of an Author,* and Kafka's *The Trial*—the intensity of the author's felt expression of the "existential" theme disintegrates or at least distorts the traditional "Aristotelian" form, which in the beginning he too easily assumes can contain it. It breaks the whole picture, as it were.

At any rate, it is now my view that the existential/phenomenological effort to deconstruct the Western metaphysical tradition—the tradition, it must always be kept in mind, which posits a purposeful universe, a "world picture" in which the beginning and the process thereafter (middle) is rigorously determined from the end—has its counterpart in the authentic existential literature of our time. Though the impulse to deconstruct manifests itself in a variety of ways in contemporary literature, it is grounded essentially, I think, in a radical distrust of traditional *closed* forms (which may be broadly categorized as either "Aristotelian" or "symbolist") in favor of experiments in *open* forms. Whereas the former resolves the dramatic conflicts or brings them into aesthetic equilibrium at the end, the existential literature of open forms refuses to fulfill our expectation of resolution and our desire for the repose of *catharsis* and thus engages us as readers of a poem or a novel or as audience of a play, makes us authentically aware of the ambiguities of our Being-in-the-world. As Samuel Beckett put this impulse of the existential imagination in his famous interview with Tom Driver at the Madeleine: "It is all around us and our only chance now is to let it in. The only chance of *renovation is to open our eyes and see the mess.* . . . To find a form that accommodates the mess, that is the task of the artist now."

This amplification of the definition of existential literature to include literary form is the subject of my essay "The Detective and the Boundary: Some Notes on the Postmodern Imagination," which is reprinted in the section "Literary Criticism" of this second edition of *A Casebook on Existentialism.*

Literature

Fëdor Dostoevski
The Legend of the Grand Inquisitor

> The scene of this crucial selection from *The Brothers Karamazov* is set in a screened-off section of a room in a moscow tavern. Accompanied by the shouts for waiters, the popping of corks, the click of billiard balls, and the drone of an organ, Ivan Karamazov attempts to reveal his true self to his saintly brother Alyosha. Admitting the possibility of the existence of God, "the underlying order and meaning of life," and even the "eternal harmony" toward which existence is said to move, he nevertheless refuses to "accept this world of God's." For God's achievement of eternal harmony in the future is grounded on the senseless suffering of the innocent in the here and now. To Ivan the "higher harmony" is "not worth the tears of . . . one tortured child . . . because those tears are unatoned for." Nor will vengeance against the oppressors do, for that means greater suffering. He wants forgiveness, but "is there in the whole world a being who would have the right to forgive and could forgive?" Alyosha points to Christ, "who can forgive everything, all and for all, because He gave His innocent blood for all and everything." At this point Ivan recites his "poem in prose": The Legend of the Grand Inquisitor.

"Even this must have a preface—that is, a literary preface," laughed Ivan, "and I am a poor hand at making one. You see, my action takes place in the sixteenth century, and at that time, as you probably learnt at school, it was customary in poetry to bring down heavenly powers on earth. Not to speak of Dante, in France, clerks, as well as the monks in the monasteries, used to give regular performances in which the Madonna, the saints, the angels, Christ, and God himself were brought on the stage. In those days it was done in all simplicity. In Victor Hugo's 'Notre Dame de Paris' an edifying and gratuitous spectacle was provided for the people in the Hotel de Ville of Paris in the reign of Louis XI, in honour of the birth of the dauphin. It was called *Le bon judgment de la très sainte et gracieuse Vierge Marie,* and she appears herself on the stage and pronounces her *bon judgment.* Similar plays, chiefly from the Old Testament, were occasionally performed in Moscow too, up to the times of Peter the Great. But besides plays there were all sorts of legends and ballads scattered about

Source: Reprinted from *The Brothers Karamazov,* translated by Constance Garnett, Modern Library edition (Random House, Inc.).

the world, in which the saints and angels and all the powers of Heaven took part when required. In our monasteries the monks busied themselves in translating, copying, and even composing such poems—and even under the Tatars. There is, for instance, one such poem (of course, from the Greek), 'The Wanderings of Our Lady through Hell,' with descriptions as bold as Dante's. Our Lady visits Hell, and the Archangel Michael leads her through the torments. She sees the sinners and their punishment. There she sees among others one noteworthy set of sinners in a burning lake; some of them sink to the bottom of the lake so that they can't swim out, and 'these God forgets'—an expression of extraordinary depth and force. And so Our Lady, shocked and weeping, falls before the throne of God and begs for mercy for all in Hell—for all she has seen there, and indiscriminately. Her conversation with God is immensely interesting. She beseeches Him, she will not desist, and when God points to the hands and feet of her Son, nailed to the Cross, and asks, 'How can I forgive His tormentors?' she bids all the saints, all the martyrs, all the angels and archangels to fall down with her and pray for mercy on all without distinction. It ends by her winning from God a respite of suffering every year from Good Friday till Trinity day, and the sinners at once raised a cry of thankfulness from Hell, chanting, 'Thou art just, O Lord, in this judgment.' Well, my poem would have been of that kind if it had appeared at that time. He comes on the scene in my poem, but He says nothing, only appears and passes on. Fifteen centuries have passed since He promised to come in His glory, fifteen centuries since His prophet wrote, 'Behold, I come quickly'; 'Of that day and that hour knoweth no man, neither the Son, but the Father,' as He Himself predicted on earth. But humanity awaits him with the same faith and with the same love. Oh, with greater faith, for it is fifteen centuries since man has ceased to see signs from Heaven.

> *No signs from Heaven come to-day*
> *To add to what the heart doth say.*

There was nothing left but faith in what the heart doth say. It is true there were many miracles in those days. There were saints who performed miraculous cures; some holy people, according to their biographies, were visited by the Queen of Heaven herself. But the devil did not slumber, and doubts were already arising among men of the truth of these miracles. And just then there appeared in the north of Germany a terrible new heresy. 'A huge star like to a torch' (that is, to a church) 'fell on the sources of the waters and they became bitter.' These heretics began blasphemously denying miracles. But those who remained faithful were all the more ardent in their faith. The tears of humanity rose up to Him as before, awaiting His coming, loved Him, hoped for Him, yearned to suffer and die for Him as before. And so many ages mankind had prayed with faith and fervour, 'O Lord our God, hasten Thy coming,' so many ages called upon Him, that in His infinite mercy He deigned to come down to His servants. Before that day He had come down, He had visited some holy men, martyrs and hermits, as is written in their 'Lives.' Among us, Tyutchev, with absolute faith in the truth of his words, bore witness that

> Bearing the Cross, in slavish dress
> Weary and worn, the Heavenly King
> Our mother, Russia, came to bless,
> And through our land went wandering.

And that certainly was so, I assure you.

"And behold, He deigned to appear for a moment to the people, to the tortured, suffering people, sunk in iniquity, but loving Him like children. My story is laid in Spain, in Seville, in the most terrible time of the Inquisition, when fires were lighted every day to the glory of God, and 'in the splendid *auto da fé* the wicked heretics were burnt.' Oh, of course, this was not the coming in which He will appear according to His promise at the end of time in all His heavenly glory, and which will be sudden 'as lightning flashing from east to west.' No, He visited His children only for a moment, and there where the flames were crackling round the heretics. In His infinite mercy He came once more among men in that human shape in which He walked among men for three years fifteen centuries ago. He came down to the 'hot pavement' of the southern town in which on the day before almost a hundred heretics had, *ad majorem gloriam Dei,* been burnt by the cardinal, the Grand Inquisitor, in a magnificent *auto da fé,* in the presence of the king, the court, the knights, the cardinals, the most charming ladies of the court, and the whole population of Seville.

"He came softly, unobserved, and yet, strange to say, every one recognised Him. That might be one of the best passages in the poem. I mean, why they recognised Him. The people are irresistibly drawn to Him, they surround Him, they flock about Him, follow Him. He moves silently in their midst with a gentle smile of infinite compassion. The sun of love burns in His heart, light and power shine from His eyes, and their radiance, shed on the people, stirs their hearts with responsive love. He holds out His hands to them, blesses them, and a healing virtue comes from contact with Him, even with His garments. An old man in the crowd, blind from childhood, cries out, 'O Lord, heal me and I shall see Thee!' and, as it were, scales fall from his eyes and the blind man sees Him. The crowd weeps and kisses the earth under His feet. Children throw flowers before Him, sing, and cry hosannah. 'It is He—it is He!' all repeat. 'It must be He, it can be no one but Him!' He stops at the steps of the Seville cathedral at the moment when the weeping mourners are bringing in a little open white coffin. In it lies a child of seven, the only daughter of a prominent citizen. The dead child lies hidden in flowers. 'He will raise your child,' the crowd shouts to the weeping mother. The priest, coming to meet the coffin, looks perplexed, and frowns, but the mother of the dead child throws herself at His feet with a wail. 'If it is Thou, raise my child!' she cries, holding out her hands to Him. The procession halts, the coffin is laid on the steps at His feet. He looks with compassion, and His lips once more softly pronounce, 'Maiden, arise!' and the maiden arises. The little girl sits up in the coffin and looks around, smiling with wide-open wondering eyes, holding a bunch of white roses they had put in her hand.

"There are cries, sobs, confusion among the people, and at that moment the cardinal himself, the Grand Inquisitor, passes by the cathedral. He is an old man, almost ninety, tall and erect, with a withered face and sunken eyes, in which there is still a gleam of light. He is not dressed in his gorgeous cardinal's robes, as he was the day before, when he was burning the enemies of the Roman Church—at that moment he was wearing his coarse, old, monk's cassock. At a distance behind him come his gloomy assistants and slaves and the 'holy guard.' He stops at the sight of the crowd and watches it from a distance. He sees everything; he sees them set the coffin down at His feet, sees the child rise up, and his face darkens. He knits his thick grey brows and his eyes gleam with a sinister fire. He holds out his finger and bids the guards take Him. And such is his power, so completely are the people cowed into submission and trembling obedience to him, that the crowd immediately make way for the guards, and in the midst of deathlike silence they lay hands on Him and lead Him away. The crowd instantly bows down to the earth, like one man, before the old inquisitor. He blesses the people in silence and passes on. The guards lead their prisoner to the close, gloomy vaulted prison in the ancient palace of the Holy Inquisition and shut Him in it. The day passes and is followed by the dark, burning 'breathless' night of Seville. The air is 'fragrant with laurel and lemon.' In the pitch darkness the iron door of the prison is suddenly opened and the Grand Inquisitor himself comes in with a light in his hand. He is alone; the door is closed at once behind him. He stands in the doorway and for a minute or two gazes into His face. At last he goes up slowly, sets the light on the table and speaks.

" 'Is it Thou? Thou?' but receiving no answer, he adds at once, 'Don't answer, be silent. What canst Thou say, indeed? I know too well what Thou wouldst say. And Thou hast no right to add anything to what Thou hadst said of old. Why, then, art Thou come to hinder us? For Thou has come to hinder us, and Thou knowest that. But dost Thou know what will be to-morrow? I know not who Thou art and care not to know whether it is Thou or only a semblance of Him, but to-morrow I shall condemn Thee and burn Thee at the stake as the worst of heretics. And the very people who have to-day kissed Thy feet, to-morrow at the faintest sign from me will rush to heap up the embers of Thy fire. Knowest Thou that? Yes, maybe Thou knowest it,' he added with thoughtful penetration, never for a moment taking his eyes off the Prisoner."

"I don't quite understand, Ivan. What does it mean?" Alyosha, who had been listening in silence, said with a smile. "It is simply a wild fantasy, or a mistake on the part of the old man—some impossible *qui pro quo*?"

"Take it as the last," said Ivan, laughing, "if you are so corrupted by modern realism and can't stand anything fantastic. If you like it to be a case of mistaken identity, let it be so. It is true," he went on, laughing, "the old man was ninety, and he might well be crazy over his set idea. He might have been struck by the appearance of the Prisoner. It might, in fact, be simply his ravings, the delusion of an old man of ninety, over-excited by the *auto da fé* of a hundred heretics the day before. But does it matter to us after all whether it was a mistake of identity or a wild fantasy? All that matters is that the old man should speak out, should speak openly of what he has thought in silence for ninety years."

"And the Prisoner too is silent? Does He look at him and not say a word?"

"That's inevitable in any case," Ivan laughed again. "The old man has told Him He hasn't the right to add anything to what He has said of old. One may say it is the most fundamental feature of Roman Catholicism, in my opinion at least. 'All has been given by Thee to the Pope,' they say, 'and all, therefore, is still in the Pope's hands, and there is no need for Thee to come now at all. Thou must not meddle for the time, at least.' That's how they speak and write too—the Jesuits, at any rate. I have read it myself in the works of their theologians. 'Hast Thou the right to reveal to us one of the mysteries of that world from which Thou hast come?' my old man asks Him, and answers the question for Him. 'No, Thou hast not; that Thou mayest not add to what has been said of old, and mayest not take from men the freedom which Thou didst exalt when Thou wast on earth. Whatsoever Thou revealest anew will encroach on men's freedom of faith; for it will be manifest as a miracle, and the freedom of their faith was dearer to Thee than anything in those days fifteen hundred years ago. Didst Thou not often say then, "I will make you free"? But now Thou has seen these "free" men,' the old man adds suddenly, with a pensive smile. 'Yes, we've paid dearly for it,' he goes on, looking sternly at Him, 'but at last we have completed that work in Thy name. For fifteen centuries we have been wrestling with Thy freedom, but now it is ended and over for good. Dost Thou not believe that it's over for good? Thou lookest meekly at me and deignest not even to be wroth with me. But let me tell Thee that now, to-day, people are more persuaded than ever that they have perfect freedom, yet they have brought their freedom to us and laid it humbly at our feet. But that has been our doing. Was this what Thou didst? Was this Thy freedom?' "

"I don't understand again," Alyosha broke in. "Is he ironical, is he jesting?"

"Not a bit of it! He claims it as a merit for himself and his Church that at last they have vanquished freedom and have done so to make men happy. 'For now' (he is speaking of the Inquisition, of course) 'for the first time it has become possible to think of the happiness of men. Man was created a rebel; and how can rebels be happy? Thou wast warned,' he says to Him. 'Thou hast had no lack of admonitions and warnings, but Thou didst not listen to those warnings; Thou didst reject the only way by which men might be made happy. But, fortunately, departing Thou didst hand on the work to us. Thou hast promised, Thou has established by Thy word, Thou has given to us the right to bind and to unbind, and now, of course, Thou canst not think of taking it away. Why, then, hast Thou come to hinder us?' "

"And what's the meaning of 'no lack of admonitions and warnings'?" asked Alyosha.

"Why, that's the chief part of what the old man must say.

" 'The wise and dread Spirit, the spirit of self-destruction and nonexistence,' the old man goes on, 'the great spirit talked with Thee in the wilderness, and we are told in the books that he "tempted" Thee. Is that so? And could anything truer be said than what he revealed to Thee in three questions and what Thou didst reject, and what in the books is called "the temptation"? And yet if there has ever been on earth a real stupendous miracle, it took place on that day, on the day of the three temptations. The statement of those three questions was itself the miracle. If it were possible to imagine simply for the sake of argument that those three questions of the dread spirit had perished utterly from the books, and that we had to restore them and to invent them anew, and to do so had gathered together all the wise men of the earth—rulers, chief priests, learned men, philosophers, poets—and had set them the task to invent three questions, such as would not only fit the occasion, but express in three words, three human phrases, the whole future history of the world and of humanity—dost Thou believe that all the wisdom of the earth united could have invented anything in depth and force equal to the three questions which were actually put to Thee then by the wise and mighty spirit of the wilderness? From those questions alone, from the miracle of their statement, we can see that we have here to do not with the fleeting human intelligence, but with the absolute and eternal. For in those three questions the whole subsequent history of mankind is, as it were, brought together into one whole, and foretold, and in them are united all the unsolved historical contradictions of human nature. At the time it could not be so clear, since the future was unknown; but now that fifteen hundred years have passed, we see that everything in those three questions was so justly devined and foretold, and has been so truly fulfilled, that nothing can be added to them or taken from them.

" 'Judge Thyself who was right—Thou or he who questioned Thee then? Remember the first question; its meaning, in other words, was this: "Thou wouldst go into the world, and art going with empty hands, with some promise of freedom which men in their simplicity and their natural unruliness cannot even understand, which they fear and dread—for nothing has ever been more insupportable for a man and a human society than freedom. But seest Thou these stones in this parched and barren wilderness? Turn them into bread, and mankind will run after Thee like a flock of sheep, grateful and obedient, though for ever trembling, lest Thou withdraw Thy hand and deny them Thy bread." But Thou wouldst not deprive man of freedom and didst reject the offer, thinking what is that freedom worth, if obedience is bought with bread? Thou didst reply that man lives not by bread alone. But dost Thou know that for the sake of that earthly bread the spirit of the earth will rise up against Thee and will strive with Thee and overcome Thee, and all will follow him, crying, "Who can compare with this beast? He has given us fire from heaven!" Dost Thou know that the ages will pass, and humanity will proclaim by the lips of their sages that there is no crime, and therefore no sin; there is only hunger? "Feed men, and then ask of them virtue!" that's what they'll write on the banner, which they will raise against Thee, and with which they will destroy Thy temple. Where Thy temple stood will rise a new building; the terrible tower of Babel will be built again, and though, like the old of old, it will not be finished, yet Thou mightest have prevented that new tower and have cut short the sufferings of men for a thousand years; for they will come back to us after a thousand years of agony with their tower. They will seek us again, hidden underground in the catacombs, for we shall be again persecuted and tortured. They will find us and cry to us, "Feed us, for those who have promised us fire from heaven haven't given it!" And then we shall finish building their tower, for he finishes the building who feeds them. And we alone shall feed them in Thy name, declaring falsely that it is in Thy name. Oh, never, never can they feed themselves without us! No science will give them bread so long as they remain free. In the end they will lay their freedom at our feet, and say to us, "Make us your slaves, but feed us." They will understand themselves, at last, that freedom and bread enough for all are inconceivable together, for never, never will they be able to share between them! They will be convinced, too, that they can never be free, for they are weak, vicious, worthless and rebellious. Thou didst promise them the bread of Heaven, but, I repeat again, can it compare with earthly bread in the eyes of the weak, ever sinful and ignoble race of man? And if for the sake of the bread of Heaven thousands and tens of thousands shall follow Thee, what is to become of the millions and tens of thousands of millions of creatures who will not have the strength to forego the earthly bread for the sake of the heavenly? Or dost Thou care only for the tens of thousands of the great and strong, while the millions, numerous as the sands of the sea, who are weak but love Thee, must exist only for the sake of the great and strong? No, we care for the weak too. They are sinful and rebellious, but in the end they too will become obedient. They will marvel at us and look on us as gods, because we are ready to endure the freedom which they have found so dreadful and to rule over them—so awful it will seem to them to be free. But we shall tell them that we are Thy servants and rule them in Thy name. We shall deceive them again, for we will not let Thee come to us again. That deception will be our suffering, for we shall be forced to lie.

" 'This is the significance of the first question in the wilderness, and this is what Thou hast rejected for the sake of that freedom which Thou hast exalted above everything. Yet in this question lies hid the great secret of this world. Choosing "bread," Thou wouldst have satisfied the universal and everlasting craving of humanity—to find some one to worship. So long as man remains free he strives for nothing so incessantly and so painfully as to find some one to worship. But man seeks to worship what is established beyond dispute, so that all men would agree at once to worship it. For these pitiful creatures are concerned not only to find what one or the other can worship, but to find something that all would believe in and worship; what is essential is that all may be *together* in it. This craving for *community* of worship is the chief misery of every man individually and of all humanity from the beginning of time. For the sake of common worship they've slain each other with the sword. They have set up gods and challenged one another, "Put away your gods and come and worship ours, or we will kill you and your gods!" And so it will be to the end of the world, even when gods disappear from the earth; they will fall down before idols just the same. Thou didst know, Thou couldst not but have known, this fundamental secret of human nature, but Thou didst reject the one infallible banner which was offered Thee to make all men bow down to Thee alone—the banner of earthly bread; and Thou hast rejected it for the sake of freedom and the bread of Heaven. Behold what Thou didst further. And all again in the name of freedom! I tell Thee that man is tormented by no greater anxiety than to find some one quickly to whom he can hand over that gift of freedom with which the ill-fated creature is born. But only one who can appease their conscience can take over their freedom. In bread there was offered Thee an invincible banner; give bread, and man will worship Thee, for nothing is more certain than bread. But if some one else gains possession of his conscience—oh! then he will cast away Thy bread and follow after him who has ensnared his conscience. In that Thou wast right. For the secret of man's being is not only to live but to have something to live for. Without a stable conception of the object of life, man would not consent to go on living, and would rather destroy himself than remain on earth, though he had bread in abundance. That is true. But what happened? Instead of taking men's freedom from them, Thou didst make it greater than ever! Didst Thou forget that man prefers peace, and even death, to freedom of choice in the knowledge of good and evil? Nothing is more seductive for man than his freedom of conscience, but nothing is a greater cause of suffering. And behold, instead of giving a firm foundation for setting the conscience of man at rest for ever, Thou didst choose all that is exceptional, vague and enigmatic; Thou didst chose what was utterly beyond the strength of men, acting as though Thou didst not love them at all—Thou who didst come to give Thy life for them! Instead of taking possession of men's freedom, Thou didst increase it, and burden the spiritual kingdom of mankind with its sufferings for ever. Thou didst desire man's free love, that he should follow Thee freely, enticed and taken captive by Thee. In place of the rigid ancient law, man must hereafter with free heart decide for himself what is good and what is evil, having only Thy image before him as his guide. But didst Thou not know he would at last reject even Thy image and Thy truth, if he is weighed down with the fearful burden of free choice? They will cry aloud at last that the truth is not in Thee, for they could not have been left in greater confusion and suffering than Thou hast caused, laying upon them so many cares and unanswerable problems.

" 'So that, in truth, Thou didst Thyself lay the foundation for the destruction of Thy kingdom, and no one is more to blame for it. Yet what was offered Thee? There are three powers, three powers alone, able to conquer and to hold captive for ever the conscience of these impotent rebels for their happiness—those forces are miracle, mystery and authority. Thou hast rejected all three and hast set the example for doing so. When the wise and dread spirit set Thee on the pinnacle of the temple and said to Thee, "If Thou wouldst know whether Thou art the Son of God then cast Thyself down, for it is written: the angels shall hold him up lest he fall and bruise himself, and Thou shalt know then whether Thou art the Son of God and shalt prove then how great is Thy faith in Thy Father." But Thou didst refuse and wouldst not cast Thyself down. Oh! of course, Thou didst proudly and well like God; but the weak, unruly race of men, are they gods? Oh, Thou didst know then that in taking one step, in making one movement to cast Thyself down, Thou wouldst be tempting God and have lost all Thy faith in Him, and wouldst have been dashed to pieces against that earth which Thou didst come to save. And the wise spirit that tempted Thee would have rejoiced. But I ask again, are there many like Thee? And couldst Thou believe for one moment that men, too, could face such a temptation? Is the nature of men such, that they can reject miracle, and at the great moments of their life, the moments of their deepest, most agonising spiritual difficulties, cling only to the free verdict of the heart? Oh, Thou didst know that Thy deed would be recorded in books, would be handed down to remote times and the utmost ends of the earth, and Thou didst hope that man, following Thee, would cling to God and not ask for a miracle. But Thou didst not know that when man rejects miracle he rejects God too; for man seeks not so much God as the miraculous. And as man cannot bear to be without the miraculous, he will create new miracles of his own for himself, and will worship deeds of sorcery and witchcraft, though he might be a hundred times over a rebel, heretic and infidel. Thou didst not come down from the Cross when they shouted to Thee, mocking and reviling Thee, "Come down from the cross and we will believe that Thou art He." Thou didst not come down, for again Thou wouldst not enslave man by a miracle, and didst crave faith given freely, not based on miracle. Thou didst crave for free love and not the base raptures of the slave before the might that has overawed him for ever. But Thou didst think too highly of men therein, for they are slaves, of course, though rebellious by nature. Look round and judge; fifteen centuries have passed, look upon them. Whom hast Thou raised up to Thyself? I swear, man is weaker and baser by nature than Thou hast believed him! Can he, can he do what Thou didst? By showing him so much respect, Thou didst, as it were, cease to feel for him, for Thou didst ask far too much from him —Thou who hast loved him more than Thyself! Respecting him less, Thou wouldst have asked less of him. That would have been more like love, for his burden would have been lighter. He is weak and vile. What though he is everywhere now rebelling against our power, and proud of his rebellion? It is the pride of a child and a schoolboy. They are little children rioting and barring out the teacher at school. But there childish delight will end; it will cost them dear. They will cast down temples and drench the earth with blood. But they will see at last, the foolish children, that, though they are rebels, they are impotent rebels, unable to keep up their own rebellion. Bathed in their foolish tears, they will recognize at last that He who created them rebels must have meant to mock at them. They will say this in despair, and their utterance will be a blasphemy which will make them more unhappy still, for man's nature cannot bear blasphemy, and in the end always avenges it on itself. And so unrest, confusion and unhappiness—that is the present lot of man after Thou didst bear so much for their freedom! Thy great prophet tells in vision and in image, that he saw all those who took part in the first resurrection and that there were of each tribe twelve thousand. But if there were so many of them, they must have been not men but gods. They had borne Thy cross, they had endured scores of years in the barren, hungry wilderness, living upon locusts and roots—and Thou mayest indeed point with pride at those children of freedom, of free love, of free and splendid sacrifice for Thy name. But remember that they were only some thousands; and what of the rest? And how are the other weak ones to blame, because they could not endure what the strong have endured? How is the weak soul to blame that it is unable to receive such terrible gifts? Canst Thou have simply come to the elect and for the elect? But if so, it is a mystery and we cannot understand it. And if it is a mystery, we too have a right to preach a mystery, and to teach them that it's not the free judgment of their hearts, not love that matters, but a mystery which they must follow blindly, even against their conscience. So we have done. We have corrected Thy work and have founded it upon *miracle, mystery* and *authority.* And men rejoiced that they were again led like sheep, and that the terrible gift that had brought them such suffering, was, at last, lifted from their hearts. Were we right teaching them this? Speak! Did we not love mankind, so meekly acknowledging their feebleness, lovingly lightening their burden, and permitting their weak nature even sin with our sanction? Why hast Thou come now to hinder us? And why dost Thou look silently and search- ingly at me with Thy mild eyes? Be angry. I don't want Thy love, for I love Thee not. And what use is it for me to hide anything from Thee? Don't I know to Whom I am speaking? All that I can say is known to Thee already. And is it for me to conceal from Thee our mystery? Perhaps it is Thy will to hear it from my lips. Listen, then. We are not working with Thee, but with *him*—that is our mystery. It's long—eight centuries—since we have been on *his* side and not on Thine. Just eight centuries ago, we took from him what Thou didst reject with scorn, that last gift he offered Thee, showing Thee all the kingdoms of the earth. We took from him Rome and the sword of Caesar, and proclaimed ourselves sole rulers of the earth, though hitherto we have not been able to complete our work. But whose fault is that? Oh, the work is only beginning, but it has begun. It has long to await completion and the earth has yet much to suffer, but we shall triumph and shall be Caesars, and then we shall plan the universal happiness of man. But Thou mightest have taken even then the sword of Caesar. Why didst Thou reject that last gift? Hadst Thou accepted that last counsel of the mighty spirit, Thou wouldst have accomplished all that man seeks on earth—that is, some one to worship, some one to keep his con- science, and some means of uniting all in one unanimous and harmonious ant-heap, for the craving for universal unity is the third and last anguish of men. Mankind as a whole has always striven to organise a universal state. There have been many great nations with great histories, but the more highly they were developed the more unhappy they were, for they felt more acutely than other people the craving for worldwide union. The great conquerors, Timours and Ghenghis-Khans, whirled like hurricanes over the face of the earth striving to subdue its people, and they too were but the unconscious expression of the same craving for universal unity. Hadst Thou taken the world and Caesar's purple, Thou wouldst have founded the universal state and have given universal peace. For who can rule men if not he who holds their conscience and their bread in his hands. We have taken the sword of Caesar, and in taking it, of course, have rejected Thee and followed *him*. Oh, ages are yet to come of the confusion of free thought, of their science and cannibalism. For having begun to build their tower of Babel without us, they will end, of course, with cannibalism. But then the beast will crawl to us and lick our feet and spatter them with tears of blood. And we shall sit upon the beast and raise the cup, and on it will be written, "Mystery." But then, and only then, the reign of peace and happiness will come for men. Thou art proud of Thine elect, but Thou hast only the elect, while we give rest to all. And besides, how many of those elect, those mighty ones who could become elect, have grown weary waiting for Thee, and have transferred and will transfer the powers of their spirit and the warmth of their heart to the other camp, and end by raising their *free* banner against Thee. Thou didst Thyself lift up that banner. But with us all will be happy and will no more rebel nor destroy one another as under Thy freedom. Oh, we shall persuade them that they will only become free when they renounce their freedom to us and submit to us. And shall we be right or shall we be lying? They will be convinced that we are right, for they will remember the horrors of slavery and confusion to which Thy freedom brought them. Freedom, free thought and science, will lead them into such straits and will bring them face to face with such marvels and insoluble mysteries, that some of them, the fierce and rebellious, will destroy themselves, others, rebellious but weak, will destroy one another, while the rest, weak and unhappy, will crawl fawning to our feet and whine to us: "Yes, you were right, you alone possess His mystery, and we come back to you, save us from ourselves!"

" 'Receiving bread from us, they will see clearly that we take the bread made by their hands from them, to give it to them, without any miracle. They will see that we do not change the stones to bread, but in truth they will be more thankful for taking it from our hands than for the bread itself! For they will remember only too well that in old days, without our help, even the bread they made turned to stones in their hands, while since they have come back to us, the very stones have turned to bread in their hands. Too, too well they know the value of complete submission! And until men know that, they will be unhappy. Who is most to blame for their not knowing it, speak? Who scattered the flock and sent it astray on unknown paths? But the flock will come together again and will submit once more, and then it will be once for all. Then we shall give them the quiet humble happiness of weak creatures such as they are by nature. Oh, we shall persuade them at last not to be proud, for Thou didst lift them up and thereby taught them to be proud. We shall show them that they are weak, that they are only pitiful children, but that childlike happiness is the sweetest of all. They will become timid and will look to us and huddle close to us in fear, as chicks to the hen. They will marvel at us and will be awe-stricken before us, and will be proud at our being so powerful and clever, that we have been able to subdue such a turbulent flock of thousands of millions. They will tremble impotently before our wrath, their minds will grow fearful, they will be quick to shed tears like women and children, but they will be just as ready at a sign from us to pass to laughter and rejoicing, to happy mirth and childish song. Yes, we shall set them to work, but in their leisure hours we shall make their life like a child's game, with children's songs and innocent dance. Oh, we shall allow them even sin, they are weak and helpless, and they will love us like children because we allow them to sin. We shall tell them that every sin will be expiated, if it is done with our permission, that we allow them to sin because we love them, and the punishment for these sins we take upon ourselves. And we shall take it upon ourselves, and they will adore us as their saviour who have taken on themselves their sins before God. And they will have no secrets from us. We shall allow or forbid them to live with their wives and mistresses, to have or not to have children—according to whether they have been obedient or disobedient—and they will submit to us gladly and cheerfully. The most painful secrets of their conscience, all, all they will bring to us, and we shall have an answer for all. And they will be glad to believe our answer, for it will save them from the great anxiety and terrible agony they endure at present in making a free decision for themselves. And all will be happy, all the millions of creatures except the hundred thousand who rule over them. For only we, we who guard the mystery, shall be unhappy. There will be thousands of millions of happy babes, and a hundred thousand sufferers who have taken upon themselves the curse of the knowledge of good and evil. Peacefully they will die, peacefully they will expire in Thy name, and beyond the grave they will find nothing but death. But we shall keep the secret, and for their happiness we shall allure them with the reward of heaven and eternity. Though if there were anything in the other world, it certainly would not be for such as they. It is prophesied that Thou wilt come again in victory, Thou wilt come with Thy chosen, the proud and strong, but we will say that they have only saved themselves, but we have saved all. We are told that the harlot who sits upon the beast, and holds in her hands the *mystery,* shall be put to shame, that the weak will rise up again, and will rend her royal purple and will strip naked her loathsome body. But then I will stand up and point out to Thee the thousand millions of happy children who have known no sin. And we who have taken their sins upon us for their happiness will stand up before Thee and say: "Judge us if Thou canst and darest." Know that I fear Thee not. Know that I too have been in the wilderness, I too have lived on roots and locusts, I too prized the freedom with which Thou hast blessed men, and I too was striving to stand among Thy elect, among the strong and powerful, thirsting "to make up the number." But I awakened and would not serve madness. I turned back and joined the ranks of those *who have corrected Thy work.* I left the proud and went back to the humble, for the happiness of the humble. What I say to Thee will come to pass, and our dominion will be built up. I repeat, tomorrow Thou shalt see that obedient flock who at a sign from me will hasten to heap up the hot cinders about the pile on which I shall burn Thee for coming to hinder us. For if any one has ever deserved our fires, it is Thou. To-morrow I shall burn Thee. Dixi.' "

. . . . .

". . . When the Inquisitor ceased speaking he waited some time for his Prisoner to answer him. His silence weighed down upon him. He saw that the Prisoner had listened intently all the time, looking gently in his face and evidently not wishing to reply. The old man longed for Him to say something, however bitter and terrible. But He suddenly approached the old man in silence and softly kissed him on his bloodless aged lips. That was all his answer. The old man shuddered. His lips moved. He went to the door, opened it, and said to Him: 'Go, and come no more. . . . Come not at all, never, never!' And he let Him out into the dark alleys of the town. The Prisoner went away."

"And the old man?"

"The kiss glows in his heart, but the old man adheres to his idea."

"And you with him, you too?" cried Alyosha, mournfully.

Ivan laughed.

"Why, it's all nonsense, Alyosha. It's only a senseless poem of a senseless student, who could never write two lines of verse. Why do you take it so seriously? Surely you don't suppose I am going straight off to the Jesuits, to join the men who are correcting His work? Good Lord, it's no business of mine. I told you, all I want is to live on to thirty, and then . . . dash the cup to the ground!"

"But the little sticky leaves, and the precious tombs, and the blue sky, and the woman you love! How will you live, how will you love them?" Alyosha cried sorrowfully. "With such a hell in your heart and your head, how can you? No, that's just what you are going away for, to join them . . . if not, you will kill yourself, you can't endure it!"

"There is a strength to endure everything," Ivan said with a cold smile.

"What strength?"

"The strength of the Karamazovs—the strength of the Karamazov baseness."

"To sink into debauchery, to stifle your soul with corruption, yes?"

"Possibly even that ... only perhaps till I am thirty I shall escape it, and then."

"How will you escape it? By what will you escape it? That's impossible with your ideas."

"In the Karamazov way, again."

" 'Everything is lawful,' you mean? Everything is lawful, is that it?"

Ivan scowled, and all at once turned strangely pale.

"Ah, you've caught up yesterday's phrase, which so offended Miüsov —and which Dmitri pounced upon so naïvely and paraphrased!" he smiled queerly. "Yes, if you like, 'everything is lawful' since the word has been said. I won't deny it. And Mitya's version isn't bad."

Alyosha looked at him in silence.

"I thought that going away from here I have you at least," Ivan said suddenly, with unexpected feeling; "but now I see that there is no place for me even in your heart, my dear hermit. The formula, 'all is lawful,' I won't renounce—will you renounce me for that, yes?"

Alyosha got up, went to him and softly kissed him on the lips.

"That's plagiarism," cried Ivan, highly delighted. "You stole that from my poem. Thank you though. Get up, Alyosha, it's time we were going, both of us."

Ernest Hemingway
A Clean, Well-Lighted Place

It was late and every one had left the café except an old man who sat in the shadow the leaves of the tree made against the electric light. In the daytime the street was dusty, but at night the dew settled the dust and the old man liked to sit late because he was deaf and now at night it was quiet and he felt the difference. The two waiters inside the café knew that the old man was a little drunk, and while he was a good client they knew that if he became too drunk he would leave without paying, so they kept watch on him.

Source: "A Clean, Well-Lighted Place" (Copyright 1933 Charles Scribner's Sons:) is reprinted by permission of Charles Scribner's Sons from *Winner Take Nothing* by Ernest Hemingway.

"Last week he tried to commit suicide," one waiter said.

"Why?"

"He was in despair."

"What about?"

"Nothing."

"How do you know it was nothing?"

"He has plenty of money."

They sat together at a table that was close against the wall near the door of the café and looked at the terrace where the tables were all empty except where the old man sat in the shadow of the leaves of the tree that moved slightly in the wind. A girl and a soldier went by in the street. The street light shone on the brass number on his collar. The girl wore no head covering and hurried beside him.

"The guard will pick him up," one waiter said.

"What does it matter if he gets what he's after?"

"He had better get off the street now. The guard will get him. They went by five minutes ago."

The old man sitting in the shadow rapped on his saucer with his glass. The younger waiter went over to him.

"What do you want?"

The old man looked at him. "Another brandy," he said.

"You'll be drunk," the waiter said. The old man looked at him. The waiter went away.

"He'll stay all night," he said to his colleague. "I'm sleepy now. I never get into bed before three o'clock. He should have killed himself last week."

The waiter took the brandy bottle and another saucer from the counter inside the café and marched out to the old man's table. He put down the saucer and poured the glass full of brandy.

"You should have killed yourself last week," he said to the deaf man. The old man motioned with his finger. "A little more," he said. The waiter poured on into the glass so that the brandy slopped over and ran down the stem into the top saucer of the pile. "Thank you," the old man said. The waiter took the bottle back inside the café. He sat down at the table with his colleague again.

"He's drunk now," he said.

"He's drunk every night."

"What did he want to kill himself for?"

"How should I know."

"How did he do it?"

"He hung himself with a rope."

"Who cut him down?"

"His niece."

"Why did they do it?"

"Fear for his soul."

"How much money has he got?"

"He's got plenty."

"He must be eighty years old."

"Anyway I should say he was eighty."

"I wish he would go home. I never get to bed before three o'clock. What kind of hour is that to go to bed?"

"He stays up because he likes it."

"He's lonely. I'm not lonely. I have a wife waiting in bed for me."

"He had a wife once too."

"A wife would be no good to him now."

"You can't tell. He might be better with a wife."

"His niece looks after him."[1]

"I know. You said she cut him down."

"I wouldn't want to be that old. An old man is a nasty thing."

"Not always. This old man is clean. He drinks without spilling. Even now, drunk. Look at him."

"I don't want to look at him. I wish he would go home. He has no regard for those who must work."

The old man looked from his glass across the square, then over at the waiters.

"Another brandy," he said, pointing to his glass. The waiter who was in a hurry came over.

"Finished," he said, speaking with that omission of syntax stupid people employ when talking to drunken people or foreigners. "No more tonight. Close now."

"Another," said the old man.

"No. Finished." The waiter wiped the edge of the table with a towel and shook his head.

The old man stood up, slowly counted the saucers, took a leather coin purse from his pocket and paid for the drinks, leaving half a peseta tip.

The waiter watched him go down the street, a very old man walking unsteadily but with dignity.

"Why didn't you let him stay and drink?" the unhurried waiter asked. They were putting up the shutters. "It is not half-past two."

"I want to go home to bed."

"What is an hour?"

"More to me than to him."

1. The speaker of this line ought, it would seem, to be the older waiter, not the younger one. This confusion has been noted by several scholars, for example, F. P. Kroeger, "The Dialogue in A Clean, Well-Lighted Place," *College English* (February 1959), 240–241; and William E. Colburn, "Confusion in A Clean, Well-Lighted Place," *College English* (February 1959), 241–242—Ed.

"An hour is the same."

"You talk like an old man youself. He can buy a bottle and drink at home."

"It's not the same."

"No, it is not," agreed the waiter with a wife. He did not wish to be unjust. He was only in a hurry.

"And you? You have no fear of going home before your usual hour?"

"Are you trying to insult me?"

"No, hombre, only to make a joke."

"No," the waiter who was in a hurry said, rising from pulling down the metal shutters. "I have confidence. I am all confidence."

"You have youth, confidence, and a job," the older waiter said. "You have everything."

"And what do you lack?"

"Everything but work."

"You have everything I have."

"No. I have never had confidence and I am not young."

"Come on. Stop talking nonsense and lock up."

"I am of those who like to stay late at the café," the older waiter said. "With all those who do not want to go to bed. With all those who need a light for the night."

"I want to go home and into bed."

"We are of two different kinds," the older waiter said. He was now dressed to go home. "It is not only a question of youth and confidence although those things are very beautiful. Each night I am reluctant to close up because there may be some one who needs the café."

"Hombre, there are bodegas open all night long."

"You do not understand. This is a clean and pleasant café. It is well lighted. The light is very good and also, now, there are shadows of the leaves."

"Good night," said the younger waiter.

"Good night," the other said. Turning off the electric light he continued the conversation with himself. It is the light of course but it is necessary that the place be clean and pleasant. You do not want music. Certainly you do not want music. Nor can you stand before a bar with dignity although that is all that is provided for these hours. What did he fear? It was not fear or dread. It was a nothing that he knew too well. It was all a nothing and a man was nothing too. It was only that and light was all it needed and a certain cleanness and order. Some lived in it and never felt it but he knew it all was nada y pues nada y nada y pues nada. Our nada who art in nada, nada be thy name thy kingdom nada thy will be nada in nada as it is in nada. Give us this nada our daily nada and nada us our nada as we nada our nadas and nada us not into nada but deliver us from nada;

pues nada. Hail nothing full of nothing, nothing is with thee. He smiled and stood before a bar with a shining steam pressure coffee machine.

"What's yours?" asked the barman.

"Nada."

"Otro loco mas," said the barman and turned away.

"A little cup," said the waiter.

The barman poured it for him.

"The light is very bright and pleasant but the bar is unpolished," the waiter said.

The barman looked at him but did not answer. It was too late at night for conversation.

"You want another copita?" the barman asked.

"No, thank you," said the waiter and went out. He disliked bars and bodegas. A clean, well-lighted café was a very different thing. Now, without thinking further, he would go home to his room. He would lie in the bed and finally, with daylight, he would go to sleep. After all, he said to himself, it is probably only insomnia. Many must have it.

Franz Kafka

The Door of the Law

from *The Trial*

"Someone must have traduced Joseph K., for without having done anything wrong he was arrested one fine morning." This is how Franz Kafka begins his great existential novel of the absurd, *The Trial*. The "fine day" in the life of this ordinary, if exceptionally meticulous, bank clerk is, significantly, his thirtieth birthday—"Nel mezzo del cammin di nostra vita," when the distancing and comforting illusions of "civilized" existence inevitably begin to break down under the assaults of time. As the sentence makes clear, however, Joseph K. interprets this "unusual" happening—this inexplicable intrusion into or, better, this mysterious invasion of his regular and utterly predictable, that is,

Source: From *The Trial*, Definitive Edition, by Franz Kafka, translated by Willa and Edwin Muir. Copyright 1937, 1956, and renewed 1965 by Alfred A. Knopf, Inc. Reprinted by permission of Alfred A. Knopf, Inc., and of Shocken Books Inc.

domesticated, bourgeois world—in rational terms, though like his earlier counterparts, Job, Dante, Hamlet, and so on, he has deep intimations that these uncanny and disorienting powers that have come out of nowhere to call him to account cannot be objectified, named, and thus subdued. Nevertheless, in the course of the next year (the time of the novel) he will exhaust every rational means available to him in order to "prove" his innocence. To put it in another way, he will follow every lead, every thread to its source in his effort to get to the bottom (the ground, the center) of the proliferating mystery. The following excerpt is taken from the penultimate chapter of the novel, "In the Cathedral." The episode follows Joseph K.'s encounter with the servilely obedient tradesman Block, who in his own futile campaign to "win" his five-year-old case, has gone to the lengths of hiring five defense lawyers besides lawyer Huld to mediate for him before the enigmatic "court," and precedes K.'s terrible execution on his thirty-first birthday. Characteristically, K. has come punctually—"ten o'clock was striking just as he entered"—to the Cathedral, where he is to meet one of the bank's most influential clients, an Italian who wants to be "shown some of the town's art treasures and monuments." But the Italian visitor has not arrived.

Since he was tired he felt like sitting down, went into the Cathedral again, found on a step a remnant of carpetlike stuff, twitched it with his toe toward a near-by bench, wrapped himself more closely in his greatcoat, turned up his collar, and sat down. By way of filling in time he opened the album and ran idly through it, but he soon had to stop, for it was growing so dark that when he looked up he could distinguish scarcely a single detail in the neighboring aisle.

Away in the distance a large triangle of candle flames glittered on the high altar; K. could not have told with any certainty whether he had noticed them before or not. Perhaps they had been newly kindled. Vergers are by profession stealthy-footed, one never notices them. K. happened to turn round and saw not far behind him the gleam of another candle, a tall thick candle fixed to a pillar. It was lovely to look at, but quite inadequate for illuminating the altarpieces, which mostly hung in the darkness of the side chapels; it actually increased the darkness. The Italian was as sensible as he was discourteous in not coming, for he would have seen nothing, he would have had to content himself with scrutinizing a few pictures piecemeal by the light of K.'s pocket torch. Curious to see what effect it would have, K. went up to a small side chapel near by, mounted a few steps to a low balustrade, and bending over it shone his torch on the altarpiece. The light from a permanent oil-lamp hovered over it like an intruder. The first thing K. perceived, partly by guess, was a huge armored knight on the outermost verge of the picture. He was leaning on his sword, which was stuck into the bare ground, bare except for a stray blade of grass or two. He seemed to be watching attentively some event unfolding itself before his eyes. It was surprising that he should stand so still without approaching nearer to it. Perhaps he had been set there to stand guard. K., who had not seen any pictures for a long time, studied this knight for a good while, although the greenish light of the oil-lamp made his eyes blink. When he played the torch over the rest of the altarpiece he discovered that it was a portrayal of Christ being laid in the tomb, conventional in style and a fairly recent painting. He pocketed the torch and returned again to his seat.

In all likelihood it was now unnecessary to wait any longer for the Italian, but the rain was probably pouring down outside, and since it was not so cold in the Cathedral as K. had expected, he decided to stay there for the present. Quite near him rose the great pulpit, on its small vaulted canopy two plain golden crucifixes were slanted so that their shafts crossed at the tip. The outer balustrade and the stonework connecting it with the supporting column were wrought all over with foliage in which little angels were entangled, now vivacious and now serene. K. went up to the pulpit and examined it from all sides; the carving of the stonework was very carefully wrought, the deep caverns of darkness among and behind the foliage looked as if caught and imprisoned there; K. put his hand into one of them and cautiously felt the contour of the stone; he had never known that this pulpit existed. By pure chance he noticed a verger standing behind the nearest row of benches, a man in a loose-hanging black garment with a snuffbox in his left hand; he was gazing at K. "What's the man after?" thought K. "Do I look a suspicious character? Does he want a tip?" But when he saw that K. had become aware of him, the verger started pointing with his right hand, still holding a pinch of snuff in his fingers, in some vaguely indicated direction. His gestures seemed to have little meaning. K. hesitated for a while, but the verger did not cease pointing at something or other and emphasizing the gesture with nods of his head. "What does the man want?" said K. in a low tone, he did not dare to raise his voice in this place; then he pulled out his purse and made his way along the benches toward him. But the verger at once made a gesture of refusal, shrugged his shoulders, and limped away. With something of the same gait, a quick, limping motion, K. had often as a child imitated a man riding on horseback. "A childish old man," thought K., "with only wits enough to be a verger. How he stops when I stop and peers to see if I am following him!" Smiling to himself, K. went on following him through the side aisle almost as far as the high altar; the old man kept pointing at something, but K. deliberately refrained from looking round to see what he was pointing at, the gesture could have no other purpose than to shake K. off. At last he desisted from the pursuit, he did not want to alarm the old man too much; besides, in case the Italian were to turn up after all, it might be better not to scare away the verger.

As he returned to the nave to find the seat on which he had left the album, K. caught sight of a small side pulpit attached to a pillar almost immediately adjoining the choir, a simple pulpit of plain, pale stone. It was so small that from a distance it looked like an empty niche intended for a statue. There was certainly no room for the preacher to take a full step backward from the balustrade. The vaulting of the stone canopy, too, began very low down and curved forward and upward, although without ornamentation, in such a way that a medium-sized man could not stand upright beneath it, but would have to keep leaning over the balustrade. The whole structure was designed as if to torture the preacher; there seemed no comprehensible reason why it should be there at all while the other pulpit, so large and finely decorated, was available.

And K. certainly would not have noticed it had not a lighted lamp been fixed above it, the usual sign that a sermon was going to be preached. Was a sermon going to be delivered now? In the empty church? K. peered down at the small flight of steps which led upward to the pulpit, hugging the pillar as it went, so narrow that it looked like an ornamental addition to the pillar rather than a stairway for human beings. But at the foot of it, K. smiled in astonishment, there actually stood a priest ready to ascend, with his hand on the balustrade and his eyes fixed on K. The priest gave a little nod and K. crossed himself and bowed, as he ought to have done earlier. The priest swung himself right on to the stairway and mounted into the pulpit with short, quick steps. Was he really going to preach a sermon? Perhaps the verger was not such an imbecile after all and had been trying to urge K. toward the preacher, a highly necessary action in that deserted building. But somewhere or other there was an old woman before an image of the Madonna; she ought to be there too. And if it were going to be a sermon, why was it not introduced by the organ? But the organ remained silent, its tall pipes looming faintly in the darkness.

K. wondered whether this was not the time to remove himself quickly; if he did not go now he would have no chance of doing so during the sermon, he would have to stay as long as it lasted, he was already behindhand in the office and was no longer obliged to wait for the Italian; he looked at his watch, it was eleven o'clock. But was there really going to be a sermon? Could K. represent the congregation all by himself? What if he had been a stranger merely visiting the church? That was more or less his position. It was absurd to think that a sermon was going to be preached at eleven in the morning on a weekday, in such dreadful weather. The priest—he was beyond doubt a priest, a young man with a smooth, dark face—was obviously mounting the pulpit simply to turn out the lamp, which had been lit by mistake.

It was not so, however; the priest after examining the lamp screwed it higher instead, then turned slowly towad the balustrade and gripped the angular edge with both hands. He stood like that for a while, looking around him without moving his head. K. had retreated a good distance and was leaning his elbows on the foremost pew. Without knowing exactly where the verger was stationed, he was vaguely aware of the old man's bent back, peacefully at rest as if his task had been fulfilled. What stillness there was now in the Cathedral! Yet K. had to violate it, for he was not minded to stay; if it were this priest's duty to preach a sermon at a certain hour regardless of circumstances, let him do it, he could manage it without K.'s support, just as K.'s presence would certainly not contribute to its effectiveness. So he began slowly to move off, feeling his way along the pew on tiptoe until he was in the broad center aisle, where he advanced undisturbed except for the ringing noise that his lightest footstep made on the stone flags and the echoes that sounded from the vaulted roof faintly but continuously, in manifold and regular progression. K. felt a little forlorn as he advanced, a solitary figure between the rows of empty seats, perhaps with the priest's eyes following him; and the size of the Cathedral struck him as bordering on the limit of what human beings could bear. When he came to the seat where he had left the album he simply snatched the book up without stopping and took it with him. He had almost passed the last of the pews and was emerging into the open space between himself and the doorway when he heard the priest lifting up his voice. A resonant, well-trained voice. How it rolled through the expectant Cathedral! But it was no congregation the priest was addressing, the words were unambiguous and inescapable, he was calling out: "Joseph K.!"

K. paused and stared at the ground before him. For the moment he was still free, he could continue on his way and vanish through one of the small, dark, wooden doors that faced him at no great distance. It would simply indicate that he had not understood the call, or that he had understood it and did not care. But if he were to turn round he would be caught, for that would amount to an admission that he had understood it very well, that he was really the person addressed, and that he was ready to obey. Had the priest called his name a second time K. would certainly have gone on, but as everything remained silent, though he stood waiting a long time, he could not help turning his head a little just to see what the priest was doing. The priest was standing calmly in the pulpit as before, yet it was obvious that he had observed K.'s turn of the head. It would have been like a childish game of hide-and-seek if K. had not turned right round to face him. He did so, and the priest beckoned him to come nearer. Since there was now no need for evasion, K. hurried back—he was both curious and eager to shorten the interview—with long flying strides toward the pulpit. At the first rows of seats he halted, but the priest seemed to think the distance still too great; he stretched out an arm and pointed with sharply bent forefinger to a spot immediately before the pulpit. K. followed this direction too; when he stood on the spot indicated he had to bend his head far back to see the priest at all. "You are Joseph K.," said the priest, lifting one hand from the balustrade in a vague gesture. "Yes," said K., thinking how frankly he used to give his name and what a burden it had recently become to him; nowadays people he had never seen before seemed to know his name. How pleasant it was to have to introduce oneself before being recognized! "You are an accused man," said the priest in a very low voice. "Yes," said K., "so I have been informed." "Then you are the man I seek," said the priest. "I am the prison chaplain." "Indeed," said K. "I had you summoned here," said the priest, "to have a talk with you." "I didn't know that," said K. "I came here to show an Italian round the Cathedral." "That is beside the point," said the priest. "What is that in your hand? Is it a prayer book?" "No," replied K., "it is an album of sights worth seeing in the town." "Lay it down," said the priest. K. threw it away so violently that it flew open and slid some way along the floor with disheveled leaves. "Do you know that your case is going badly?" asked the priest. "I have that idea myself," said K. "I've done what I could, but without any success so far. Of course, my petition isn't finished yet." "How do you think it will end?" asked the priest. "At first I thought it must turn out well," said K., "but now I frequently have my doubts. I don't know how it will end. Do you?" "No," said the priest, "but I fear it will end badly. You are held to be guilty. Your case will perhaps never get beyond a lower Court. Your guilt is supposed, for the present, at least, to have been proved." "But I am not guilty," said K.; "it's a mistake. And, if it comes to that, how can any man be called guilty? We are all simply men here, one as much as the other." "That is true," said the priest, "but that's how all guilty men talk." "Are you prejudiced against me too?" asked K. "I have no prejudices against you," said the priest. "Thank you," said K.; "but all the others who are concerned in these proceedings are prejudiced against me. They are influencing outsiders too. My position is becoming more and more difficult." "You are misinterpreting the facts of the case," said the priest. "The verdict is not suddenly arrived at, the proceedings only gradually merge into the verdict." "So that's how it is," said K., letting his head sink. "What is the next step you propose to take in the matter?" asked the priest. "I'm going to get more help," said K., looking up again to see how the priest took his statement. "There are several possibilities I haven't explored yet." "You cast about too much for outside help," said the priest disapprovingly, "especially from women. Don't you see that it isn't the right kind of help?" "In some cases, even in many I could agree with you," said K., "but not always. Women have great influence. If I could move some women I know to join forces in working for me, I couldn't help winning through. Especially before this Court, which consists almost entirely of petticoat-hunters. Let the Examining Magistrate see a woman in the distance and he knocks down his desk and the defendant in his eagerness to get at her." The priest leaned over the balustrade, apparently feeling for the first time the oppressiveness of the canopy above his head. What fearful weather there must be outside! There was no longer even a murky daylight; black night had set in. All the stained glass in the great window could not illumine the darkness of the wall with one solitary glimmer of light. And at this very moment the verger began to put out the candles on the high altar, one after another. "Are you angry with me?" asked K. of the priest. "It may be that you don't know the nature of the Court you are serving." He got no answer. "These are only my personal experiences," said K. There was still no answer from above. "I wasn't trying to insult you," said K. And at that the priest shrieked from the pulpit: "Can't you see one pace before you?" It was an angry cry, but at the same time sounded like the unwary shriek of one who sees another fall and is startled out of his senses.

Both were now silent for a long time. In the prevailing darkness the priest certainly could not make out K.'s features, while K. saw him distinctly by the light of the small lamp. Why did he not come down from the pulpit? He had not preached a sermon, he had only given K. some information which would be likely to harm him rather than help him when he came to consider it. Yet the priest's good intentions seemed to K. beyond question, it was not impossible that they could come to some agreement if the man would only quit his pulpit, it was not impossible that K. could obtain decisive and acceptable counsel from him which might, for instance, point the way, not toward some influential manipulation of the case, but toward a circumvention of it, a breaking away from it altogether, a mode of living completely outside the jurisdiction of the Court. This possibility must exist, K. had of late given much thought to it. And should the priest know of such a possibility, he might perhaps impart his knowledge if he were appealed to, although he himself belonged to the Court and as soon as he heard the Court impugned had forgotten his own gentle nature so far as to shout K. down.

"Won't you come down here?" said K. "You haven't got to preach a sermon. Come down beside me." "I can come down now," said the priest, perhaps repenting of his outburst. While he detached the lamp from its hook he said: "I had to speak to you first from a distance. Otherwise I am too easily influenced and tend to forget my duty."

K. waited for him at the foot of the steps. The priest stretched out his hand to K. while he was still on the way down from a higher level. "Have you a little time for me?" asked K. "As much time as you need," said the priest, giving K. the small lamp to carry. Even close at hand he still wore a certain air of solemnity. "You are very good to me," said K. They paced side by side up and down the dusky aisle. "But you are an exception among those who belong to the Court. I have more trust in you than in any of the others, though I know many of them. With you I can speak openly." "Don't be deluded," said the priest. "How am I being deluded?" asked K. "You are deluding yourself about the Court," said the priest. "In the writings which preface the Law that particular delusion is described thus: before the Law stands a doorkeeper. To this doorkeeper there comes a man from the country who begs for admittance to the Law. But the doorkeeper says that he cannot admit the man at the moment. The man, on reflection, asks if he will be allowed, then, to enter later. 'It is possible,' answers the doorkeeper, 'but not at this moment.' Since the door leading into the Law stands open as usual and the doorkeeper steps to one side, the man bends down to peer through the entrance. When the doorkeeper sees that, he laughs and says: 'If you are so strongly tempted, try to get in without my permission. But note that I am powerful. And I am only the lowest doorkeeper. From hall to hall, keepers stand at every door, one more powerful than the other. And the sight of the third man is already more than even I can stand.' These are difficulties which the man from the country has not expected to meet, the Law, he thinks, should be accessible to every man and at all times, but when he looks more closely at the doorkeeper in his furred robe, with his huge pointed nose and long thin Tartar beard, he decides that he had better wait until he gets permission to enter. The doorkeeper gives him a stool and lets him sit down at the side of the door. There he sits waiting for days and years. He makes many attempts to be allowed in and wearies the doorkeeper with his importunity. The doorkeeper often engages him in brief conversation, asking him about his home and about other matters, but the questions are put quite impersonally, as great men put questions, and always conclude with the statement that the man cannot be allowed to enter yet. The man, who has equipped himself with many things for his journey, parts with all he has, however valuable, in the hope of bribing the doorkeeper. The doorkeeper accepts it all, saying, however, as he takes each gift: 'I take this only to keep you from feeling that you have left something undone.' During all these long years the man watches the doorkeeper almost incessantly. He forgets about the other doorkeepers, and this one seems to him the only barrier between himself and the Law. In the first years he curses his evil fate aloud; later, as he grows old, he only mutters to himself. He grows childish, and since in his prolonged study of the doorkeeper he has learned to know even the fleas in his fur collar, he begs the very fleas to help him and to persuade the doorkeeper to change his mind. Finally his eyes grow dim and he does not know whether the world is really darkening around him or whether his eyes are only deceiving him. But in the darkness he can now perceive a radiance that streams inextinguishably from the door of the Law. Now his life is drawing to a close. Before he dies, all that he has experienced during the whole time of his sojourn condenses in his mind into one question, which he has never yet put to the doorkeeper. He beckons the doorkeeper, since he can no longer raise his stiffening body. The doorkeeper has to bend far down to hear him, for the difference in size between them has increased very much to the man's disadvantage. 'What do you want to know now?' asks the doorkeeper, 'you are insatiable.' 'Everyone strives to attain the Law,' answers the man, 'how does it come about, then, that in all these years no one has come seeking admittance but me?' The doorkeeper perceives that the man is nearing his end and his hearing is failing, so he bellows in his ear: 'No one but you could gain admittance through this door, since this was intended for you. I am now going to shut it.'"

   "So the doorkeeper deceived the man," said K. immediately, strongly attracted by the story. "Don't be too hasty," said the priest, "don't take over someone else's opinion without testing it. I have told you the story in the very words of the scriptures. There's no mention of deception in it." "But it's clear enough," said K., "and your first interpretation of it was quite right. The doorkeeper gave the message of salvation to the man only when it could no longer help him." "He was not asked the question any earlier," said the priest, "and you must consider, too, that he was only a doorkeeper, and as such fulfilled his duty." "What makes you think he fulfilled his duty?" asked K. "He didn't fulfill it. His duty might have been to keep all strangers away, but this man, for whom the door was intended, should have been let in." "You have not enough respect for the written word and you are altering the story," said the priest. "The story contains two important statements made by the doorkeeper about admission to the Law, one at the beginning, the other at the end. The first statement is: that he cannot admit the man at the moment, and the other is: that this door was intended only for the man. If there was a contradiction between the two, you would be right and the doorkeeper would have deceived the man. But there is no contradiction. The first statement, on the contrary, even implies the second. One could almost say that in suggesting to the man the possibility of future admittance the doorkeeper is exceeding his duty. At that time his apparent duty is only to refuse admittance and indeed many commentators are surprised that the suggestion should be made at all, since the doorkeeper appears to be a precisian with a stern regard for duty. He does not once leave his post during these many years, and he does not shut the door until the very last minute; he is conscious of the importance of his office, for he says: 'I am powerful'; he is respectful to his superiors, for he says: 'I am only the lowest doorkeeper'; he is not garrulous, for during all these years he puts only what are called 'impersonal questions'; he is not to be bribed, for he says in accepting a gift: 'I take this only to keep you from feeling that you have left something undone'; where his duty is concerned he is to be moved neither by pity nor rage, for we are told that the man 'wearied the doorkeeper with his importunity'; and finally even his external appearance hints at a pedantic character, the large, pointed nose and the long, thin, black, Tartar beard. Could one imagine a more faithful doorkeeper? Yet the doorkeeper has other elements in his character which are likely to advantage anyone seeking admittance and which make it comprehensible enough that he should somewhat exceed his duty in suggesting the possibility of future admittance. For it cannot be denied that he is a little simple-minded and consequently a little conceited. Take the statements he makes about his power and the power of the other doorkeepers and their dreadful aspect which even he cannot bear to see—I hold that these statements may be true enough, but that the way in which he brings them out shows that his perceptions are confused by simpleness of mind and conceit. The commentators note in this connection: 'The right perception of any matter and a misunderstanding of the same matter do not wholly exclude each other.' One must at any rate assume that such simpleness and conceit, however sparingly manifest, are likely to weaken his defense of the door; they are breaches in the character of the doorkeeper. To this must be added the fact that the doorkeeper seems to be a friendly creature by nature, he is by no means always on his official dignity. In the very first moments he allows himself the jest of inviting the man to enter in spite of the strictly maintained veto against entry; then he does not, for instance, send the man away, but gives him, as we are told, a stool and lets him sit down beside the door. The patience with which he endures the man's appeals during so many years, the brief conversations, the acceptance of the gifts, the politeness with which he allows the man to curse loudly in his presence the fate for which he himself is responsible—all this lets us deduce certain feelings of pity. Not every doorkeeper would have acted thus. And finally, in answer to a gesture of the man's he bends down to give him the chance of putting a last question. Nothing but mild impatience—the doorkeeper knows that this is the end of it all—is discernible in the words; 'You are insatiable.' Some push this mode of interpretation even further and hold that these words express a kind of friendly admiration, though not without a hint of condescension. At any rate the figure of the doorkeeper can be said to come out very differently from what you fancied." "You have studied the story more exactly and for a longer time than I have," said K.

They were both silent for a little while. Then K. said: "So you think the man was not deceived?" "Don't misunderstand me," said the priest, "I am only showing you the various opinions concerning that point. You must not pay too much attention to them. The scriptures are unalterable and the comments often enough merely express the commentators' despair. In this case there even exists an interpretation which claims that the deluded person is really the doorkeeper." "That's a far-fetched interpretation," said K. "On what is it based?" "It is based," answered the priest, "on the simple-mindedness of the doorkeeper. The argument is that he does not know the Law from inside, he knows only the way that leads to it, where he patrols up and down. His ideas of the interior are assumed to be childish, and it is supposed that he himself is afraid of the other guardians whom he holds up as bogies before the man. Indeed, he fears them more than the man does, since the man is determined to enter after hearing about the dreadful guardians of the interior, while the doorkeeper has no desire to enter, at least not so far as we are told. Others again say that he must have been in the interior already, since he is after all engaged in the service of the Law and can only have been appointed from inside. This is countered by arguing that he may have been appointed by a voice calling from the interior, and that anyhow he cannot have been far inside, since the aspect of the third doorkeeper is more than he can endure. Moreover, no indication is given that during all these years he ever made any remarks showing a knowledge of the interior, except for the one remark about the doorkeepers. He may have been forbidden to do so, but there is no mention of that either. On these grounds the conclusion is reached that he knows nothing about the aspect and significance of the interior, so that he is in a state of delusion. But he is deceived also about his relation to the man from the country, for he is inferior to the man and does not know it. He treats the man instead as his own subordinate, as can be recognized from many details that must be still fresh in your mind. But, according to this view of the story, it is just as clearly indicated that he is really subordinated to the man. In the first place, a bondman is always subject to a free man. Now the man from the country is really free, he can go where he likes, it is only the Law that is closed to him, and access to the Law is forbidden him only by one individual, the doorkeeper. When he sits down on the stool by the side of the door and stays there for the rest of his life, he does it of his own free will; in the story there is no mention of any compulsion. But the doorkeeper is bound to his post by his very office, he does not dare go out into the country, nor apparently may he go into the interior of the Law, even should he wish to. Besides, although he is in the service of the Law, his service is confined to this one entrance; that is to say, he serves only this man for whom alone the entrance is intended. On that ground too he is inferior to the man. One must assume that for many years, for as long as it takes a man to grow up to the prime of life, his service was in a sense an empty formality, since he had to wait for a man to come, that is to say someone in the prime of life, and so he had to wait a long time before the purpose of his service could be fulfilled, and, moreover, had to wait on the man's pleasure, for the man came of his own free will. But the termination of his service also depends on the man's term of life, so that to the very end he is subject to the man. And it is emphasized throughout that the doorkeeper apparently realizes nothing of all this. That is not in itself remarkable, since according to this interpretation the doorkeeper is deceived in a much more important issue, affecting his very office. At the end, for example, he says regarding the entrance to the Law: 'I am now going to shut it,' but at the beginning of the story we are told that the door leading into the Law always stands open, and if it always stands open, that is to say at all times, without reference to the life or death of the man, then the doorkeeper cannot close it. There is some difference of opinion about the motive behind the doorkeeper's statement, whether he said he was going to close the door merely for the sake of giving an answer, or to emphasize his devotion to duty, or to bring the man into a state of grief and regret in his last moments. But there is no lack of agreement that the doorkeeper will not be able to shut the door. Many indeed profess to find that he is subordinate to the man even in knowledge, toward the end, at least, for the man sees the radiance that issues from the door of the Law while the doorkeeper in his official position must stand with his back to the door, nor does he say anything to show that he has perceived the change." "That is well argued," said K., after repeating to himself in a low voice several passages from the priest's exposition. "It is well argued, and I am inclined to agree that the doorkeeper is deceived. But that has not made me abandon my former opinion, since both conclusions are to some extent compatible. Whether the doorkeeper is clearsighted or deceived does not dispose of the matter. I said the man is deceived. If the doorkeeper is clear-sighted, one might have doubts about that, but if the doorkeeper himself is deceived, then his deception must of necessity be communicated to the man. That makes the doorkeeper not, indeed, a deceiver, but a creature so simple-minded that he ought to be dismissed at once from his office. You mustn't forget that the doorkeeper's deceptions do himself no harm but do infinite harm to the man." "There are objections to that," said the priest. "Many aver that the story confers no right on anyone to pass judgment on the doorkeeper. Whatever he may seem to us, he is yet a servant of the Law; that is, he belongs to the Law and as such is beyond human judgment. In that case one must not believe that the doorkeeper is subordinate to the man. Bound as he is by his service, even only at the door of the Law, he is incomparably greater than anyone at large in the world. The man is only seeking the

Law, the doorkeeper is already attached to it. It is the Law that has placed him at his post; to doubt his dignity is to doubt the Law itself." "I don't agree with that point of view," said K., shaking his head, "for if one accepts it, one must accept as true everything the doorkeeper says. But you yourself have sufficiently proved how impossible it is to do that." "No," said the priest," It is not necessary to accept everything as true, one must only accept it as necessary." "A melancholy conclusion," said K. "It turns lying into a universal principle."

K. said that with finality, but it was not his final judgment. He was too tired to survey all the conclusions arising from the story, and the trains of thought into which it was leading him were unfamiliar, dealing with impalpabilities better suited to a theme for discussion among Court officials than for him. The simple story had lost its clear outline, he wanted to put it out of his mind, and the priest, who now showed great delicacy of feeling, suffered him to do so and accepted his comment in silence, although undoubtedly he did not agree with it.

They paced up and down for a while in silence, K. walking close beside the priest, ignorant of his whereabouts. The lamp in his hand had long since gone out. The silver image of some saint once glimmered into sight immediately before him, by the sheen of its own silver, and was instantaneously lost in the darkness again. To keep himself from being utterly dependent on the priest, K. asked: "Aren't we near the main doorway now?" "No," said the priest, "we're a long way from it. Do you want to leave already?" Although at that moment K. had not been thinking of leaving, he answered at once: "Of course, I must go. I'm the Chief Clerk of a Bank, they're waiting for me, I only came here to show a business friend from abroad round the Cathedral." "Well," said the priest, reaching out his hand to K., "then go." "But I can't find my way alone in this darkness," said K. "Turn left to the wall," said the priest, "then follow the wall without leaving it and you'll come to a door." The priest had already taken a step or two away from him, but K. cried out in a loud voice, "Please wait a moment." "I am waiting," said the priest. "Don't you want anything more from me?" asked K. "No," said the priest. "You were so friendly to me for a time," said K., "and explained so much to me, and now you let me go as if you cared nothing about me." "But you have to leave now," said the priest. "Well, yes," said K., "you must see that I can't help it." "You must first see who I am," said the priest. "You are the prison chaplain," said K., groping his way nearer to the priest again; his immediate return to the Bank was not so necessary as he had made out, he could quite well stay longer. "That means I belong to the Court," said the priest. "So why should I want anything from you? The Court wants nothing from you. It receives you when you come and it dismisses you when you go."

Jean-Paul Sartre

Doctor Rogé and M. Achille: The Look

from *Nausea*

Jean-Paul Sartre's seminal novel of the postmodern imagination, *Nausea*, begins with Roquentin's entries in his diary about a disturbing occurrence that changes his life in a radical way. While walking along the seashore, he picks up a small stone to throw into the sea. Suddenly, having seen something in it "which disgusted [him]," he felt nauseated —and "without knowing what [he] was afraid of," became "afraid or had some other feeling of that sort." Following this intrusion of "[Something] new" into his life (it is reminiscent, incidentally, of the change that the radically "new thing"—the undiagnosable illness—brings into Ivan's life in Tolstoi's *The Death of Ivan Ilych* and prefigures the change of "existence off the ladder" felt by Watt when "Something slipped" in Samuel Beckett's *Watt*, Roquentin undergoes this dis-locating experience, this loss of the "feeble points of reference which men have traced on the surface [of things]," at increasingly shorter intervals and with increasingly greater intensity. And the process culminates in the famous scene in the public park of Bouville (the scene I have called "the Un-Naming" in one of the passages from *Nausea* included in the section on philosophy in this book). Here Roquentin is no longer able to fix, to stabilize, existence by naming things:

> In vain I tried to *count* the chestnut trees, to *locate* them by their relationship to the Velleda, to compare their height with the height of the plane trees: each of these escaped the relationship in which I tried to enclose it, isolated itself, and overflowed. Of these relations (which I insisted on maintaining in order to delay the crumbling of the human world, measures, quantities, and direction)—I felt myself to be the arbitrator; they no longer had their teeth into things. *In the way,* the chestnut tree there, opposite me, a little to the left. *In the way . . . .*

Here, in more familiar terms, Roquentin discovers the primordial existence which precedes essence.

Concurrent with and primarily because of these experiences of nausea, Roquentin also comes to discover the phenomenological

Source: Jean-Paul Sartre. *Nausea,* translated by Lloyd Alexander. Copyright © 1964 by New Directions Publishing Corporation. All Rights Reserved. Reprinted by permission of New Directions Publishing Corporation.

meaning of its opposite, especially in his encounters with the complacent and solid bourgeois merchants of Bouville, who feel secure because they believe "their existence is necessary": the coercive impulse
to impose fixed definitions on flux, which, when applied to other human
beings, Sartre calls "the look" *(le regard)*. The perceiving subject or
le pour soi (the for-itself), according to Sartre's phenomenological analysis of this metaphor in *Being and Nothingness,* fears the threatening
"unpredictability," the disruptive freedom, of the Other *(l'autrui)* and is
thus always tempted to transform him into *l'en soi* (the in-itself), that is,
to objectify his radical temporality, to impose a *Nature*—a fixed and
permanent name, or in more current language, a *finished image* on him,
thus "solidifying" his being. "The Other," Sartre says, turning the terms
around, "by rising up confers on the for-itself a being-in-itself-in-the-
midst-of-the-world as a thing among things. This petrifaction in in-itself
by the Other's look is the profound meaning of the myth of Medusa."
The following episode from *Nausea* takes place in Camille's, one of the
cafés which, until the intrusion of the new thing, "were [Roquentin's]
only refuge because they were full of people and well lighted." (The
reference to Hemingway's "A Clean, Well-Lighted Place" is evident.)
It is a powerful fictional expression of this phenomenological analysis
of "the look."

A man comes in, shivering.

"Messieurs, dames, bonjour."

He sits down without taking off his greenish overcoat. He rubs his long
hands, clasping and unclasping his fingers.

"What will you have?"

He gives a start, his eyes look worried:

"Eh? give me a Byrrh and water."

The waitress does not move. In the glass her face seems to sleep. Her
eyes are indeed open but they are only slits. That's the way she is, she is
never in a hurry to wait on customers, she always takes a moment to dream
over their orders. She must allow herself the pleasure of imagining: I
believe she's thinking about the bottle she's going to take from above the
counter, the white label and red letters, the thick black syrup she is going
to pour out: it's a little as though she were drinking it herself.

I slip Anny's letter back into my despatch case: she had done what she
could; I cannot reach the woman who took it in her hands, folded and put
it in the envelope. Is it possible even to think of someone in the past? As
long as we loved each other, we never allowed the meanest of our instants,
the smallest grief, to be detached and forgotten, left behind. Sounds,
smells, nuances of light, even the thoughts we never told each other; we
carried them all away and they remained alive: even now they have the
power to give us joy and pain. Not a memory: an implacable, torrid love,

without shadow, without escape, without shelter. Three years rolled into one. That is why we parted: we did not have enough strength to bear this burden. And then, when Anny left me, all of a sudden, all at once, the three years crumbled into the past. I didn't even suffer, I felt emptied out. Then time began to flow again and the emptiness grew larger. Then, in Saïgon when I decided to go back to France, all that was still left—strange faces, places, quays on the banks of long rivers—all was wiped out. Now my past is nothing more than an enormous vacuum. My present: this waitress in the black blouse dreaming near the counter, this man. It seems as though I have learned all I know of life in books. The palaces of Benares, the terrace of the Leper King, the temples of Java with their great broken steps, are reflected in my eyes for an instant, but they have remained there, on the spot. The tramway that passes in front of the Hotel Printania in the evening does not catch the reflection of the neon sign-board; it flames up for an instant, then goes on with black windows.

This little man has not stopped looking at me: he bothers me. He tries to give himself importance. The waitress has finally decided to serve him. She raises her great black arm lazily, reaches the bottle, and brings it to him with a glass.

"Here you are, Monsieur."

"Monsieur Achille," he says with urbanity.

She pours without answering; all of a sudden he takes his finger from his nose, places both hands flat on the table. He throws his head back and his eyes shine. He says in a cold voice:

"Poor girl."

The waitress gives a start and I start too: he has an indefinable expression, perhaps one of amazement, as if it were someone else who had spoken. All three of us are uncomfortable.

The fat waitress recovers first: she has no imagination. She measures M. Achille with dignity: she knows quite well that one hand alone would be enough to tear him from his seat and throw him out.

"And what makes you think I'm a poor girl?"

He hesitates. He looks taken aback, then he laughs. His face crumples up into a thousand wrinkles, he makes vague gestures with his wrist.

"She's annoyed. It was just to say something: I didn't mean to offend."

But she turns her back on him and goes behind the counter: she is really offended. He laughs again:

"Ha ha! You know that just slipped out. Are you cross? She's cross with me," he says, addressing himself vaguely to me.

I turn my head away. He raises his glass a little but he is not thinking about drinking: he blinks his eyes, looking surprised and intimidated; he looks as if he were trying to remember something. The waitress is sitting at the counter; she picks up her sewing. Everything is silent again: but it isn't the same silence. It's raining: tapping lightly against the frosted glass windows; if there are any more masked children in the street, the rain is going to spoil their cardboard masks.

The waitress turns on the lights: it is hardly two o'clock but the sky is all black, she can't see to sew. Soft glow: people are in their houses, they have undoubtedly turned on the lights too. They read, they watch the sky from the window. For them it means something different. They have aged differently. They live in the midst of legacies, gifts, each piece of furniture holds a memory. Clocks, medallions, portraits, shells, paperweights, screens, shawls. They have closets full of bottles, stuffs, old clothes, newspapers; they have kept everything. The past is a landlord's luxury.

Where shall I keep mine? You don't put your past in your pocket; you have to have a house. I have only my body: a man entirely alone, with his lonely body, cannot indulge in memories; they pass through him. I shouldn't complain: all I wanted was to be free.

The little man stirs and sighs. He is all wrapped in his overcoat but from time to time he straightens up and puts on a haughty look. He has no past either. Looking closely, you would undoubtedly find in a cousin's house a photograph showing him at a wedding, with a wing collar, stiff shirt and a slight, young man's moustache. Of myself I don't think that even that is left.

Here he is looking at me again. This time he's going to speak to me, and I feel all taut inside. There is no sympathy between us: we are alike, that's all. He is alone, as I am, but more sunken into solitude than I. He must be waiting for his own Nausea or something of that sort. Now there are still people who *recognize* me, who see me and think: "He's one of us." So? What does he want? He must know that we can do nothing for one another. The families are in their houses, in the midst of their memories. And here we are, two wanderers, without memory. If he were suddenly to stand up and speak to me, I'd jump into the air.

The door opens with a great to-do: it is Doctor Rogé.

"Good day everybody."

He comes in, ferocious and suspicious, swaying, swaying a little on his long legs which can barely support his body. I see him often, on Sundays, at the Brasserie Vézelise, but he doesn't know me. He is built like the old monitors at Joinville, arms like thighs, a chest measurement of 110, and he can't stand up straight.

"Jeanne, my little Jeanne."

He trots over to the coat rack to hang up his wide felt hat on the peg. The waitress has put away her sewing and comes without hurrying, sleep walking, to help the doctor out of his raincoat.

"What will you have, Doctor?"

He studies her gravely. That's what I call a handsome, masculine face. Worn, furrowed by life and passions. But the doctor has understood life, mastered his passions.

"I really don't know what I want," he says in a deep voice.

He has dropped onto the bench opposite me; he wipes his forehead. He feels at ease as soon as he gets off his feet. His great eyes, black and imperious, are intimidating.

"I'll have ... I'll have ... Oh, calvados. ..."

The waitress, without making a move, studies this enormous, pitted face. She is dreamy. The little man raises his head with a smile of relief. And it is true: this colossus has freed us. Something horrible was going to catch us. I breathe freely: we are among men now.

"Well, is that calvados coming?"

The waitress gives a start and leaves. He has stretched out his stout arms and grasped the table at both ends. M. Achille is joyful; he would like to catch the doctor's eye. But he swings his legs and shifts about on the bench in vain, he is so thin that he makes no noise.

The waitress brings the calvados. With a nod of her head she points out the little man to the doctor. Doctor Rogé slowly turns: he can't move his neck.

"So it's you, you old swine," he shouts, "aren't you dead yet?"

He addresses the waitress:

"You let people like that in here?"

He stares at the little man ferociously. A direct look which puts everything in place. He explains:

"He's crazy as a loon, that's that."

He doesn't even take the trouble to let on that he's joking. He knows that the loony won't be angry, that he's going to smile. And there it is: the man smiles with humility. A crazy loon: he relaxes, he feels protected against himself: nothing will happen to him today. I am reassured too. A crazy old loon: so that was it, so that was all.

The doctor laughs, he gives me an engaging, conspiratorial glance: because of my size, undoubtedly—and besides, I have a clean shirt on— he wants to let me in on his joke.

I do not laugh, I do not respond to his advances: then, without stopping to laugh, he turns the terrible fire of his eyes on me. We look at each other in silence for several seconds: he sizes me up, looking at me with half-closed eyes, up and down he places me. In the crazy loon category? In the tramp category?

Still, he is the one who turns his face away: allows himself to deflate before one lone wretch, without social importance, it isn't worth talking about—you can forget it right away. He rolls a cigarette and lights it, then stays motionless with his eyes hard and staring like an old man's.

The fine wrinkles; he has all of them: horizontal ones running across his forehead, crow's feet, bitter lines at each corner of the mouth, without counting the yellow cords depending from his chin. There's a lucky man:

as soon as you perceive him, you can tell he must have suffered, that he is someone who has lived. He deserves his face for he has never, for one instant, lost an occasion of utilizing his past to the best of his ability: he has stuffed it full, used his experience on women and children, exploited them.

M. Achille is probably happier than he has ever been. He is agape with admiration; he drinks his Byrrh in small mouthfuls and swells his cheeks out with it. The doctor knew how to take him! The doctor wasn't the one to let himself be hypnotized by an old madman on the verge of having his fit; one good blow, a few rough, lashing words, that's what they need. The doctor has experience. He is a professional in experience: doctors, priests, magistrates and army officers know men through and through as if they had made them.

I am ashamed for M. Achille. We are on the same side, we should have stood up against them. But he left me, he went over to theirs: he honestly believes in experience. Not in his, not in mine. In Doctor Rogé's. A little while ago M. Achille felt queer, he felt lonely: now he knows that there are others like him, many others: Doctor Rogé has met them, he could tell M. Achille the case history of each one of them and tell him how they ended up. M. Achille is simply a case and lets himself be brought back easily to the accepted ideas.

How I would like to tell him he's being deceived, that he is the butt of the important. Experienced professionals? They have dragged out their life in stupor and semi-sleep, they have married hastily, out of impatience, they have made children at random. They have met other men in cafés, at weddings and funerals. Sometimes, caught in the tide, they have struggled against it without understanding what was happening to them. All that has happened around them has eluded them; long, obscure shapes, events from afar, brushed by them rapidly and when they turned to look all had vanished. And then, around forty, they christen their small obstinacies and a few proverbs with the name of experience, they begin to simulate slot machines: put a coin in the left hand slot and you get tales wrapped in silver paper, put a coin in the slot on the right and you get precious bits of advice that stick to your teeth like caramels. As far as that goes, I too could have myself invited to people's houses and they'd say among themselves that I was a *"grand voyageur devant l'Eternel."* Yes: the Mohamedans squat to pass water; instead of ergot, Hindu midwives use ground glass in cow dung; in Borneo when a woman has her period she spends three days and nights on the roof of her house. In Venice I saw burials in gondolas, Holy Week festivals in Seville, I saw the Passion Play at Oberammergau. Naturally, that's just a small sample of all I know: I could lean back in a chair and begin amusement:

"Do you know Jihlava, Madame? It's a curious little town in Moravia where I stayed in 1924."

And the judge who has seen so many cases would add at the end of my story: "How true it is, Monsieur, how human it is. I had a case just like that at the beginning of my career. It was in 1902. I was deputy judge in Limoges ..."

But I was bothered too much by that when I was young. Yet I didn't belong to a professional family. There are also amateurs. These are secretaries, office workers, shopkeepers, people who listen to others in cafés: around forty they feel swollen, with an experience they can't get rid of. Luckily they've made children on whom they can pass it off. They would like to make us believe that their past is not lost, that their memories are condensed, gently transformed into Wisdom. Convenient past! Past handed out of a pocket! little gilt books full of fine sayings. "Believe me, I'm telling you from experience, all I know I've learned from life." Has life taken charge of their thoughts? They explain the new by the old—and the old they explain by the older still, like those historians who turn a Lenin into a Russian Robespierre, and a Robespierre into a French Cromwell: when all is said and done, they have never understood anything at all. ... You can imagine a morose idleness behind their importance: they see the long parade of pretences, they yawn, they think there's nothing new under the sun. "Crazy as a loon"—and Doctor Rogé vaguely recalls other crazy loons, not remembering any one of them in particular. Now, nothing M. Achille can do will surprise us: *because* he's a crazy loon!

He is not one: he is afraid. What is he afraid of? When you want to understand something you stand in front of it, alone, without help: all the past in the world is of no use. Then it disappears and what you wanted to understand disappears with it.

General ideas are more flattering. And then professionals and even amateurs always end up by being right. Their wisdom prompts them to make the least possible noise, to live as little as possible, to let themselves be forgotten. Their best stories are about the rash and the original, who were chastised. Yes, that's how it happens and no one will say the contrary. Perhaps M. Achille's conscience is not easy. Perhaps he tells himself he wouldn't be there if he had heeded his father's advice or his elder sister's. The doctor has the right to speak: he has not wasted his life; he has known how to make himself useful. He rises calm and powerful, above this flotsam and jetsam; he is a rock.

Doctor Rogé has finished his calvados. His great body relaxes and his eyelids droop heavily. For the first time I see his face without the eyes: like a cardboard mask, the kind they're selling in the shops today. His cheeks have a horrid pink colour. ... The truth stares me in the face: this man is going to die soon. He surely knows; he need only look in the glass: each day he looks a little more like the corpse he will become. That's what their experience leads to, that's why I tell myself so often that they smell of death: it is their last defence. The doctor would like to believe, he would like to hide out the stark reality; that he is alone, without gain, without a past, with an intelligence which is clouded, a body which is disintegrating. For this reason he has carefully built up, furnished, and padded his nightmare compensation: he says he is making progress. Has he vacuums in his thoughts, moments when everything spins round in his head? It's because his judgment no longer has the impulse of youth. He no longer understands what he reads in books? It's because he's so far away from books now. He can't make love any more? But he has made love in the past. Having made love is much better than still making it: looking back, he compares, ponders. And this terrible corpse's face! To be able to stand the sight of it in the glass he makes himself believe that the lessons of experience are graven on it.

The doctor turns his head a little. His eyelids are half-open and he watches me with the red eyes of sleep. I smile at him. I would like this smile to reveal all that he is trying to hide from himself. That would give him a jolt if he could say to himself: "There's someone who *knows* I'm going to die!" But his eyelids droop: he sleeps. I leave, letting M. Achille watch over his slumber.

The rain has stopped, the air is mild, the sky slowly rolls up fine black images: it is more than enough to frame a perfect moment; to reflect these images, Anny would cause dark little tides to be born in our hearts. I don't know how to take advantage of the occasion: I walk at random, calm and empty, under this wasted sky:

Wednesday:
I must not be afraid.

Nathalie Sarraute
from *Tropisms*: II, V, XII, XVIII, XX, XXII

Tropisms, Nathalie Sarraute's first work of fiction, initially appeared in 1939 and consists of twenty-four brief "scenes" from "ordinary" life such as those selected here. The term "tropism," a biological

Source: George Braziller, Inc.—from *Tropisms* by Nathalie Sarraute, translated by Maria Jolas; reprinted with the permission of the publisher. English translation copyright © 1963 by John Calder, Ltd.

metaphor referring to the reflexive movement of an organism in response to an external stimulus, points to the strange and often terrible primordial psychological origins of behavior hidden below the banal actions and clichés—the domesticated existence and language—of what Husserl would call man in the "natural attitude" and Heidegger, the "inauthentic they-self" *(das Man)*. These pieces, it might therefore be said, are fictional counterparts of the phenomenological reduction: the putting into parentheses of our habitual positivistic assumption about the identity of the self and its relation to others in order to reveal "the things themselves" in all their pristine and awful immediacy. In thus negating the distance that causal expectations generate, these pieces, which Sarraute also calls "sub-conversations" *(sous-conversations),* constitute a significant break from the traditional Western or humanistic concept of character that has informed fiction since Aristotle.

[II]

They tore themselves away from their wardrobe mirrors in which they were examining their faces. Sat up in their beds. "Dinner is ready, dinner is ready," she said. She rounded up the family, each one hiding in his lair, lonely, ill-tempered, exhausted. "What on earth is the matter with them, for them always to look so worn out?" she said when she talked to the cook.

She talked to the cook for hours, fussing about the table, always fussing about, preparing various medicines for them, or special dishes, she talked on and on, criticizing the people who came to the house, friends of theirs: "so-and-so's hair will darken, it will be like her mother's, and straight; people are lucky who don't need a permanent."—"Mademoiselle has pretty hair," said the cook, "it's thick and pretty, even if it doesn't curl." —"And so-and-so, I'm sure he didn't leave you a thing. They're stingy, they're all stingy, and they've got money, they've got money, it's revolting. And they're always economizing. Personally, that's something I don't understand."—"After all," said the cook, "after all, they can't take it with them. And that daughter of theirs, she's not married yet, and she's not bad, she has pretty hair, her nose is small, and her feet are pretty too."—"Yes, pretty hair, that's true," she said, "but, you know, nobody likes her, she's not attractive. It's really funny."

And he sensed percolating from the kitchen, humble, squalid, time-marking human thought, marking time in one spot, always in one spot, going round and round, in circles, as if they were dizzy but couldn't stop, as if they were nauseated but couldn't stop, the way we bite our nails, the way we tear off dead skin when we're peeling, the way we scratch ourselves when we have hives, the way we toss in our beds when we can't sleep, to give ourselves pleasure and make ourselves suffer, until we are exhausted, until we've taken our breath away. . . .

"But perhaps for them it was something else." This was what he thought, listening stretched out on his bed while, like some sort of sticky slaver, their thought filtered into him, lined him internally.

There was nothing to be done about it. Nothing to be done. To avoid it was impossible. Everywhere, in countless forms, "deception" ("The sun is deceptive today," the concierge said, "it's deceptive and you risk catching your death. That was how my poor husband . . . and yet he liked to take care of himself . . .") everywhere, in the guise of life itself, it caught hold of you as you went by, when you hurried past the concierge's door, when you answered the telephone, lunched with the family, invited your friends, spoke a word to anybody, whoever it might be.

You had to answer them and encourage them gently, and above all, above everything, not make them feel, not to make them feel a single second, that you think you're different. Be submissive, be submissive, be retiring: "Yes, yes, yes, yes, that's true, that's certainly true," that's what you should say to them, and look at them warmly, affectionately, otherwise a rending, an uprooting, something unexpected, something violent would happen, something that had never happened before, and which would be frightful.

It seemed to him that then, in a sudden surge of action, of power, with immense strength, he would shake them like old soiled rags, would wring them, tear them, destroy them completely.

But he also knew that this was probably a false impression. Before he would have time to leap at them—with that sure instinct, that instinct for defense, that easy vitality that constituted their disturbing force, they would turn on him and, all at once, he did not know how, they would knock him senseless.

[V]

On hot July days, the wall opposite cast a brilliant, harsh light into the damp little courtyard.

Underneath this heat there was a great void, silence, everything seemed in suspense: the only thing to be heard, aggressive, strident, was the creaking of a chair being dragged across the tiles, the slamming of a door. In this heat, in this silence, it was a sudden coldness, a rending.

And she remained motionless on the edge of her bed, occupying the least possible space, tense, as though waiting for something to burst, to crash down upon her in the threatening silence.

At times the shrill notes of locusts in a meadow petrified by the sun and as though dead, induce this sensation of cold, of solitude, of abandonment in a hostile universe in which something anguishing is impending.

In the silence, penetrating the length of the old blue-striped wallpaper in the hall, the length of the dingy paint, she heard the little click of the key in the front door. She heard the study door close.

She remained there hunched up, waiting, doing nothing. The slightest act, such as going to the bathroom to wash her hands, letting the water run from the tap, seemed like a provocation, a sudden leap into the void, an extremely daring action. In the suspended silence, the sudden sound of water would be like a signal, like an appeal directed towards them; it would be like some horrible contact, like touching a jellyfish with the end of a stick and then waiting with loathing for it suddenly to shudder, rise up and fall back down again.

She sensed them like that, spread out, motionless, on the other side of the walls, and ready to shudder, to stir.

She did not move. And about her the entire house, the street, seemed to encourage her, seemed to consider this motionlessness natural.

It appeared certain, when you opened the door and saw the stairway filled with relentless, impersonal, colorless calm, a stairway that did not seem to have retained the slightest trace of the persons who had walked on it, not the slightest memory of their presence, when you stood behind the dining room window and looked at the house fronts, the shops, the old women and little children walking along the street, it seemed certain that, for as long as possible, she would have to wait, remain motionless like that, do nothing, not move, that the highest degree of comprehension, real intelligence, was that, to undertake nothing, keep as still as possible, do nothing.

At the most, by being careful not to wake anybody, you could go down without looking at the dark, dead, stairway, and proceed unobtrusively along the pavements, along the walls, just to get a breath, to move about a bit, without knowing where you were going, without wanting to go anywhere, and then come back home, sit down on the edge of the bed and, once more, wait, curled up, motionless.

[XII]

During his very well attended lectures at the Collège de France, he amused himself with all that.

He enjoyed prying, with the dignity of professional gestures, with relentless, expert hands, into the secret places of Proust or Rimbaud, then, exposing their so-called miracles, their mysteries, to the gaze of his very attentive audience, he would explain their "case."

With his sharp, mischievous little eyes, his ready-tied necktie and his square-trimmed beard, he looked enormously like the gentleman in the advertisements who, with one finger in the air, smilingly recommends Saponite, the best of soap powders, or the model Salamander: economy, security, comfort.

"There is nothing," he said, "you see I went to look for myself, because I won't be bluffed; nothing that I myself have not already studied clinically countless times, that I have not catalogued and explained.

"They should not upset you. Look, in my hands they are like trembling, nude little children, and I am holding them up to you in the hollow of my hand, as though I were their creator, their father, I have emptied them for you of their power and their mystery. I have tracked down, harried what was miraculous about them.

"Now they hardly differ from the intelligent, curious and amusing eccentrics who come and tell me their interminable stories, to get me to help them, appreciate them, and reassure them.

"You can no more be affected than my daughters are when they entertain their girl friends in their mother's parlor, and chatter and laugh gaily without being concerned with what I am saying to my patients in the next room."

This was what he taught at the Collège de France. And in the entire neighborhood, in all the nearby Faculties, in the literature, law, history and philosophy courses, at the Institute and at the Palais de Justice, in the buses, the *métros,* in all the government offices, sensible men, normal men, active men, worthy, wholesome, strong men, triumphed.

Avoiding the shops filled with pretty things, the women trotting briskly along, the café waiters, the medical students, the traffic policemen, the clerks from notary offices, Rimbaud or Proust, having been torn from life, cast out from life and deprived of support, were probably wandering aimlessly through the streets, or dozing away, their heads resting on their chests, in some dusty public square.

[XVIII]

On the outskirts of London, in a little cottage with percale curtains, its little back lawn sunny and all wet with rain.

The big, wisteria-framed window in the studio, opens on to this lawn.

A cat with its eyes closed, is seated quite erect on the warm stone.

A spinster lady with white hair, and pink cheeks that tend towards purple, is reading an English magazine in front of the door.

She sits there, very stiff, very dignified, quite sure of herself and of others, firmly settled in her little universe. She knows that in a few moments the bell will ring for tea.

Down below, the cook, Ada, is cleaning vegetables at a table covered with white oilcloth. Her face is motionless, she appears to be thinking of nothing. She knows that it will soon be time to toast the buns, and ring the bell for tea.

[XX]

When he was little, he used to sit straight up in bed at night, call out. They would come running, light the light, they would take the white linens, the towels, the clothes, in their hands, and show them to him. There was nothing. In their hands the white linens became harmless, shrank, they became set and dead in the light.

Now that he was grown, he still made them come and look everywhere, hunt inside him, observe well and take in their hands the fears cowering in the nooks and corners inside him, and examine them in the light.

They were accustomed to coming in and looking, and he prepared the way for them, he himself lighted all the lights so as not to sense their hands groping about in the dark. They looked—he remained motionless, without daring to breathe—but there was nothing anywhere, nothing that could cause fear, everything seemed in good order, in place, they recognized everywhere familiar, well-known objects, and they showed them to him. There was nothing. What was he afraid of? At times, here or there, in a corner, something seemed to tremble vaguely, to waver slightly, but with a pat they set it straight again, it was nothing, one of his usual fears—they took it and showed it to him: his friend's daughter was already married? Was that it? Or else, so-and-so, who although he was a former classmate of his, had been promoted, was to be decorated? They repaired, they righted that, it was nothing. For a moment, he believed he felt stronger, propped up, patched up, but already he sensed his legs and arms grow heavy, lifeless, become numb with this solidified waiting, he had, as one has before losing consciousness, a tingling sensation in his nostrils: they saw him withdraw into himself all of a sudden, assume his strangely preoccupied, absent look: then, with little pats on his cheeks—the Windsors' travels, Lebrun, the quintuplets—they revived him.

But while he was coming to himself and when they left him finally mended, cleaned, repaired, all nicely seasoned and ready, fear formed in him again, at the bottom of the little compartments, of the little drawers they had just opened, in which they had seen nothing, and which they had closed.

[XXIII]

They were ugly, they were dull, commonplace, without personality, they were really too out-of-date, clichés, she thought, which she had already seen described everywhere, so many times, in the works of Balzac, of Maupassant, in *Madame Bovary,* clichés, copies, copies of copies, she decided.

She would have so liked to repulse them, seize them and hurl them away. But they stood quietly about her, they smiled at her, pleasantly, but dignifiedly, very decorously, they had been working all week, all their lives they had counted on nobody but themselves, they asked for nothing, except to see her from time to time; to rearrange a little the tie between them and her, feel that it was there, still in place, the tie that bound them to her. They wanted nothing more than to ask her—as was natural, as everybody did, when they went to call on friends, or on relatives—to ask her what she had been doing that was nice, if she had been reading a lot lately, if she had gone out often, if she had seen that, didn't she think those films were good ... They, themselves, had so enjoyed Michel Simon, Jouvet, they had laughed so hard, had had such a delightful evening ...

And as for all that, clichés, copies, Balzac, Flaubert, *Madame Bovary,* oh! they knew very well, they were acquainted with it all, but they were not afraid—they looked at her kindly, they smiled, they seemed to feel that they were safe with her, they seemed to know that they had been observed, depicted, described so often, been so sucked on, that they had become as smooth as pebbles, all shiny, without a nick, without a single hold. She could not get at them. They were safe.

They surrounded her, held out their hands to her: "Michel Simon ... Jouvet ... Ah! she had been obliged to book seats well ahead of time, had she not ... Later, there would have been no tickets to be had, except at exorbitant prices, nothing but boxes, or in the orchestra ..." They tightened the tie a little more, very gently, unobtrusively, without hurting her, they rearranged the slender tie, pulled ...

And little by little a certain weakness, a certain slackness, a need to approach them, to have them approach her, made her join in the game with them. She sensed how docilely (Oh! yes ... Michel Simon ... Jouvet ...) very docilely, like a good, amenable little girl, she gave them her hand and walked in a ring with them.

Ah! here we are at last all together, good as gold, doing what our parents would have approved of, here we all are then, well behaved, singing together like good little children that an invisible adult is looking after, while they walk gently around in a circle giving one another their sad, moist little hands.

Albert Camus

The Guest

The schoolmaster was watching the two men climb toward him. One was on horseback, the other on foot. They had not yet tackled the abrupt rise leading to the schoolhouse built on the hillside.. They were toiling onward, making slow progress in the snow, among the stones, on the vast expanse of the high, deserted plateau. From time to time the horse stumbled. Without hearing anything yet, he could see the breath issuing from the horse's nostrils. One of the men, at least, knew the region. They were following the trail although it had disappeared days ago under a layer of dirty white snow. The schoolmaster calculated that it would take them half an hour to get onto the hill. It was cold; he went back into the school to get a sweater.

He crossed the empty, frigid classroom. On the blackboard the four rivers of France, drawn with four different colored chalks, had been flowing toward their estuaries for the past three days. Snow had suddenly fallen in mid-October after eight months of drought without the transition of rain, and the twenty pupils, more or less, who lived in the villages scattered over the plateau had stopped coming. With fair weather they would return. Daru now heated only the single room that was his lodging, adjoining the classroom and giving also onto the plateau to the east. Like the class windows, his window looked to the south too. On that side the school was a few kilometers from the point where the plateau began to slope toward the south. In clear weather could be seen the purple mass of the mountain range where the gap opened onto the desert.

Somewhat warmed, Daru returned to the window from which he had first seen the two men. They were no longer visible. Hence they must have tackled the rise. The sky was not so dark, for the snow had stopped falling during the night. The morning had opened with a dirty light which had scarcely become brighter as the ceiling of clouds lifted. At two in the afternoon it seemed as if the day were merely beginning. But still this was better than those three days when the thick snow was falling amidst unbroken darkness with little gusts of wind that rattled the double door of the classroom. Then Daru had spent long hours in his room, leaving it only to go to the shed and feed the chickens or get some coal. Fortunately the delivery truck from Tadjid, the nearest village to the north, had

Source: From *Exile and the Kingdom* by Albert Camus, translated by Justin O'Brien. Copyright © 1957, 1958 by Alfred A. Knopf, Inc. Reprinted by permission of Alfred A. Knopf, Inc.

brought his supplies two days before the blizzard. It would return in forty-eight hours.

Besides, he had enough to resist a siege, for the little room was cluttered with bags of wheat that the administration left as a stock to distribute to those of his pupils whose families had suffered from the drought. Actually they had all been victims because they were all poor. Every day Daru would distribute a ration to the children. They had missed it, he knew, during these bad days. Possibly one of the fathers or big brothers would come this afternoon and he could supply them with grain. It was just a matter of carrying them over to the next harvest. Now shiploads of wheat were arriving from France and the worst was over. But it would be hard to forget that poverty, that army of ragged ghosts wandering in the sunlight, the plateaus burned to a cinder month after month, the earth shriveled up little by little, literally scorched, every stone bursting into dust under one's foot. The sheep had died then by thousands and even a few men, here and there, sometimes without anyone's knowing.

In contrast with such poverty, he who lived almost like a monk in his remote schoolhouse, nonetheless satisfied with the little he had and with the rough life, had felt like a lord with his whitewashed walls, his narrow couch, his unpainted shelves, his well, and his weekly provision of water and food. And suddenly this snow, without warning, without the foretaste of rain. This is the way the region was, cruel to live in, even without men —who didn't help matters either. But Daru had been born here. Everywhere else, he felt exiled.

He stepped out onto the terrace in front of the schoolhouse. The two men were now halfway up the slope. He recognized the horseman as Balducci, the old gendarme he had known for a long time. Balducci was holding on the end of a rope an Arab who was walking behind him with hands bound and head lowered. The gendarme waved a greeting to which Daru did not reply, lost as he was in contemplation of the Arab dressed in a faded blue jellaba, his feet in sandals but covered with socks of heavy raw wool, his head surmounted by a narrow, short *chèche*. They were approaching. Balducci was holding back his horse in order not to hurt the Arab, and the group was advancing slowly.

Within earshot, Balducci shouted: "One hour to do the three kilometers from El Ameur!" Daru did not answer. Short and square in his thick sweater, he watched them climb. Not once had the Arab raised his head. "Hello," said Daru when they got up onto the terrace. "Come in and warm up." Balducci painfully got down from his horse without letting go the rope. From under his bristling mustache he smiled at the schoolmaster. His little dark eyes, deep-set under a tanned forehead, and his mouth surrounded with wrinkles made him look attentive and studious. Daru took the bridle, led the horse to the shed, and came back to the two men, who were now waiting for him in the school. He led them into his room.

"I am going to heat up the classroom," he said. "We'll be more comfortable there." When he entered the room again, Balducci was on the couch. He had undone the rope tying him to the Arab, who had squatted near the stove. His hands still bound, the *chèche* pushed back on his head, he was looking toward the window. At first Daru noticed only his huge lips, fat, smooth, almost Negroid; yet his nose was straight, his eyes were dark and full of fever. The *chèche* revealed an obstinate forehead and, under the weathered skin now rather discolored by the cold, the whole face had a restless and rebellious look that struck Daru when the Arab, turning his face toward him, looked him straight in the eyes. "Go into the other room," said the schoolmaster, "and I'll make you some mint tea." "Thanks," Balducci said. "What a chore! How I long for retirement." And addressing his prisoner in Arabic: "Come on, you." The Arab got up and, slowly, holding his bound wrists in front of him, went into the classroom.

With the tea, Daru brought a chair. But Balducci was already enthroned on the nearest pupil's desk and the Arab had squatted against the teacher's platform facing the stove, which stood between the desk and the window. When he held out the glass of tea to the prisoner, Daru hesitated at the sight of his bound hands. "He might perhaps be untied." "Sure," said Balducci. "That was for the trip." He started to get to his feet. But Daru, setting the glass on the floor, had knelt beside the Arab. Without saying anything, the Arab watched him with his feverish eyes. Once his hands were free, he rubbed his swollen wrists against each other, took the glass of tea, and sucked up the burning liquid in swift little sips.

"Good," said Daru. "And where are you headed?"

Balducci withdrew his mustache from the tea. "Here, son."

"Odd pupils! and you're spending the night?"

"No. I'm going back to El Ameur. And you will deliver this fellow to Tinguit. He is expected at police headquarters."

Balducci was looking at Daru with a friendly little smile.

"What's this story?" asked the schoolmaster. "Are you pulling my leg?"

"No, son. Those are the orders."

"The orders? I'm not . . ." Daru hesitated, not wanting to hurt the old Corsican. "I mean, that's not my job."

"What! What's the meaning of that? In wartime people do all kinds of jobs."

"Then I'll wait for the declaration of war!"

Balducci nodded.

"O.K. But the orders exist and they concern you too. Things are brewing, it appears. There is talk of a forthcoming revolt. We are mobilized, in a way."

Daru still had his obstinate look.

"Listen, son," Balducci said. "I like you and you must understand. There's only a dozen of us at El Ameur to patrol throughout the whole territory of a small department and I must get back in a hurry. I was told to hand this guy over to you and return without delay. He couldn't be kept there. His village was beginning to stir; they wanted to take him back. You must take him to Tinguit tomorrow before the day is over. Twenty kilometers shouldn't faze a husky fellow like you. After that, all will be over. You'll come back to your pupils and your comfortable life."

Behind the wall the horse could be heard snorting and pawing the earth. Daru was looking out the window. Decidedly, the weather was clearing and the light was increasing over the snowy plateau. When all the snow was melted, the sun would take over again and once more would burn the fields of stone. For days, still, the unchanging sky would shed its dry light on the solitary expanse where nothing had any connection with man.

"After all," he said turning around toward Balducci, "what did he do?" And, before the gendarme had opened his mouth, he asked: "Does he speak French?"

"No, not a word. We had been looking for him for a month, but they were hiding him. He killed his cousin."

"Is he against us?"

"I don't think so. But you can never be sure."

"Why did he kill?"

"A family squabble, I think. One owed the other grain, it seems. It's not at all clear. In short, he killed his cousin with a billhook. You know, like a sheep, *kreezk!*"

Balducci made the gesture of drawing a blade across his throat and the Arab, his attention attracted, watched him with a sort of anxiety. Daru felt a sudden wrath against the man, against all men with their rotten spite, their tireless hates, their blood lust.

But the kettle was singing on the stove. He served Balducci more tea, hesitated, then served the Arab again, who, a second time, drank avidly. His raised arms made the jellaba fall open and the schoolmaster saw his thin, muscular chest.

"Thanks, kid," Balducci said. "And now, I'm off."

He got up and went toward the Arab, taking a small rope from his pocket.

"What are you doing?" Daru asked dryly.

Balducci, disconcerted, showed him the rope.

"Don't bother."

The old gendarme hesitated. "It's up to you. Of course, you are armed?"

"I have my shotgun."

"Where?"

"In the trunk."

"You ought to have it near your bed."

"Why? I have nothing to fear."

"You're crazy, son. If there's an uprising, no one is safe, we're all in the same boat."

"I'll defend myself. I'll have time to see them coming."

Balducci began to laugh, then suddenly the mustache covered the white teeth.

"You'll have time? O.K. That's just what I was saying. You have always been a little cracked. That's why I like you, my son was like that."

At the same time he took out his revolver and put it on the desk.

"Keep it; I don't need two weapons from here to El Ameur."

The revolver shone against the black paint of the table. When the gendarme turned toward him, the schoolmaster caught the smell of leather and horseflesh.

"Listen, Balducci," Daru said suddenly, "every bit of this disgusts me, and first of all your fellow here. But I won't hand him over. Fight, yes, if I have to. But not that."

The old gendarme stood in front of him and looked at him severely.

"You're being a fool," he said slowly. "I don't like it either. You don't get used to putting a rope on a man after years of it, and you're even ashamed—yes, ashamed. But you can't let them have their way."

"I won't hand him over," Daru said again.

"It's an order, son, and I repeat it."

"That's right. Repeat to them what I've said to you: I won't hand him over."

Balducci made a visible effort to reflect. He looked at the Arab and at Daru. At last he decided.

"No, I won't tell them anything. If you want to drop us, go ahead; I'll not denounce you. I have an order to deliver the prisoner and I'm doing so. And now you'll just sign this paper for me."

"There's no need. I'll not deny that you left him with me."

"Don't be mean with me. I know you'll tell the truth. You're from hereabouts and you are a man. But you must sign, that's the rule."

Daru opened his drawer, took out a little square bottle of purple ink, the red wooden penholder with the "sergeant-major" pen he used for making models of penmanship, and signed. The gendarme carefully folded the paper and put it into his wallet. Then he moved toward the door.

"I'll see you off," Daru said.

"No," said Balducci. "There's no use being polite. You insulted me."

He looked at the Arab, motionless in the same spot, sniffed peevishly, and turned away toward the door. "Good-by, son," he said. The door shut behind him. Balducci appeared suddenly outside the window and then disappeared. His footsteps were muffled by the snow. The horse stirred on the other side of the wall and several chickens fluttered in fright. A moment later Balducci reappeared outside the window leading the horse by the bridle. He walked toward the little rise without turning around and disappeared from sight with the horse following him. A big stone could be heard bouncing down. Daru walked back toward the prisoner, who, without stirring, never took his eyes off him. "Wait," the schoolmaster said in Arabic and went toward the bedroom. As he was going through the door, he had a second thought, went to the desk, took the revolver, and stuck it in his pocket. Then, without looking back, he went into his room.

For some time he lay on his couch watching the sky gradually close over, listening to the silence. It was this silence that had seemed painful to him during the first days here, after the war. He had requested a post in the little town at the base of the foothills separating the upper plateaus from the desert. There, rocky walls, green and black to the north, pink and lavender to the south, marked the frontier of eternal summer. He had been named to a post farther north, on the plateau itself. In the beginning, the solitude and the silence had been hard for him on these wastelands peopled only by stones. Occasionally, furrows suggested cultivation, but they had been dug to uncover a certain kind of stone good for building. The only plowing here was to harvest rocks. Elsewhere a thin layer of soil accumulated in the hollows would be scraped out to enrich paltry village gardens. This is the way it was: bare rock covered three quarters of the region. Towns sprang up, flourished, then disappeared; men came by, loved one another or fought bitterly, then died. No one in this desert, neither he nor his guest, mattered. And yet, outside his desert neither of them, Daru knew, could have really lived.

When he got up, no noise came from the classroom. He was amazed at the unmixed joy he derived from the mere thought that the Arab might have fled and that he would be alone with no decision to make. But the prisoner was there. He had merely stretched out between the stove and the desk. With eyes open, he was staring at the ceiling. In that position, his thick lips were particularly noticeable, giving him a pouting look. "Come," said Daru. The Arab got up and followed him. In the bedroom, the schoolmaster pointed to a chair near the table under the window. The Arab sat down without taking his eyes off Daru.

"Are you hungry?"

"Yes," the prisoner said.

Daru set the table for two. He took flour and oil, shaped a cake in a frying-pan, and lighted the little stove that functioned on bottled gas. While the cake was cooking, he went out to the shed to get cheese, eggs, dates, and condensed milk. When the cake was done he set it on the window sill to cool, heated some condensed milk diluted with water, and beat up the eggs into an omelette. In one of his motions he knocked against the revolver stuck in his right pocket. He set the bowl down, went into the classroom, and put the revolver in his desk drawer. When he came back to the room, night was falling. He put on the light and served the Arab. "Eat," he said. The Arab took a piece of the cake, lifted it eagerly to his mouth, and stopped short.

"And you?" he asked.

"After you. I'll eat too."

The thick lips opened slightly. The Arab hesitated, then bit into the cake determinedly.

The meal over, the Arab looked at the schoolmaster. "Are you the judge?"

"No, I'm simply keeping you until tomorrow."

"Why do you eat with me?"

"I'm hungry."

The Arab fell silent. Daru got up and went out. He brought back a folding bed from the shed, set it up between the table and the stove, perpendicular to his own bed. From a large suitcase which, upright in a corner, served as shelf for papers, he took two blankets and arranged them on the camp bed. Then he stopped, felt useless, and sat down on his bed. There was nothing more to do or to get ready. He had to look at this man. He looked at him, therefore, trying to imagine his face bursting with rage. He couldn't do so. He could see nothing but the dark yet shining eyes and the animal mouth.

"Why did you kill him?" he asked in a voice whose hostile tone surprised him.

The Arab looked away.

"He ran away. I ran after him."

He raised his eyes to Daru again and they were full of a sort of woeful interrogation. "Now what will they do to me?"

"Are you afraid?"

He stiffened, turning his eyes away.

"Are you sorry?"

The Arab stared at him openmouthed. Obviously he did not understand. Daru's annoyance was growing. At the same time he felt awkward and self-conscious with his big body wedged between the two beds.

"Lie down there," he said impatiently. "That's your bed."

The Arab didn't move. He called to Daru:

"Tell me!"

The schoolmaster looked at him.

"Is the gendarme coming back tomorrow?"

"I don't know."

"Are you coming with us?"

"I don't know. Why?"

The prisoner got up and stretched out on top of the blankets, his feet toward the window. The light from the electric bulb shone straight into his eyes and he closed them at once.

"Why?" Daru repeated, standing beside the bed.

The Arab opened his eyes under the blinding light and looked at him, trying not to blink.

"Come with us," he said.

In the middle of the night, Daru was still not asleep. He had gone to bed after undressing completely; he generally slept naked. But when he suddenly realized that he had nothing on, he hesitated. He felt vulnerable and the temptation came to him to put his clothes back on. Then he shrugged his shoulders; after all, he wasn't a child and, if need be, he could break his adversary in two. From his bed he could observe him, lying on his back, still motionless with his eyes closed under the harsh light. When Daru turned out the light, the darkness seemed to coagulate all of a sudden. Little by little, the night came back to life in the window where the starless sky was stirring gently. The schoolmaster soon made out the body lying at his feet. The Arab still did not move, but his eyes seemed open. A faint wind was prowling around the schoolhouse. Perhaps it would drive away the clouds and the sun would reappear.

During the night the wind increased. The hens fluttered a little and then were silent. The Arab turned over on his side with his back to Daru, who thought he heard him moan. Then he listened for his guest's breathing, become heavier and more regular. He listened to that breath so close to him and mused without being able to go to sleep. In this room where he had been sleeping alone for a year, this presence bothered him. But it bothered him also by imposing on him a sort of brotherhood he knew well but refused to accept in the present circumstances. Men who share the same rooms, soldiers or prisoners, develop a strange alliance as if, having cast off their armor with their clothing, they fraternized every evening, over and above their differences, in the ancient community of dream and fatigue. But Daru shook himself; he didn't like such musings, and it was essential to sleep.

A little later, however, when the Arab stirred slightly, the schoolmaster was still not asleep. When the prisoner made a second move, he stiffened, on the alert. The Arab was lifting himself slowly on his arms with almost the motion of a sleepwalker. Seated upright in bed, he waited motionless without turning his head toward Daru, as if he were listening attentively. Daru did not stir; it had just occurred to him that the revolver was still in the drawer of his desk. It was better to act at once. Yet he continued to observe the prisoner, who, with the same slithery motion, but his feet on the ground, waited again, then began to stand up slowly. Daru was about to call out to him when the Arab began to walk, in a quite natural but extraordinarily silent way. He was heading toward the door at the end of the room that opened into the shed. He lifted the latch with precaution and went out, pushing the door behind him but without shutting it. Daru had not stirred. "He is running away," he merely thought. "Good riddance!" Yet he listened attentively. The hens were not fluttering; the guest must be on the plateau. A faint sound of water reached him, and he didn't know what it was until the Arab again stood framed in the doorway, closed the door carefully, and came back to bed without a sound. Then Daru turned his back on him and fell asleep. Still later he seemed, from the depths of his sleep, to hear furtive steps around the schoolhouse. "I'm dreaming! I'm dreaming!" he repeated to himself. And he went on sleeping.

When he awoke, the sky was clear; the loose window let in a cold, pure air. The Arab was asleep, hunched up under the blankets now, his mouth open, utterly relaxed. But when Daru shook him, he started dreadfully, staring at Daru with wild eyes as if he had never seen him and such a frightened expression that the schoolmaster stepped back. "Don't be afraid. It's me. You must eat." The Arab nodded his head and said yes. Calm had returned to his face, but his expression was vacant and listless.

The coffee was ready. They drank it seated together on the folding bed as they munched their pieces of the cake. Then Daru led the Arab under the shed and showed him the faucet where he washed. He went back into the room, folded the blankets and the bed, made his own bed and put the room in order. Then he went through the classroom and out onto the terrace. The sun was already rising in the blue sky; a soft, bright light was bathing the deserted plateau. On the ridge the snow was melting in spots. The stones were about to reappear. Crouched on the edge of the plateau, the schoolmaster looked at the deserted expanse. He thought of Balducci. He had hurt him, for he had sent him off in a way as if he didn't want to be associated with him. He could still hear the gendarme's farewell and, without knowing why, he felt strangely empty and vulnerable. At that moment, from the other side of the schoolhouse, the prisoner coughed. Daru listened to him almost despite himself and then, furious, threw a pebble that whistled through the air before sinking into the snow. That man's stupid crime revolted him, but to hand him over was contrary to honor. Merely thinking of it made him smart with humiliation. And he cursed at one and the same time his own people who had sent him this Arab and the Arab too who had dared to kill and not managed to get away. Daru got up, walked in a circle on the terrace, waited motionless, and then went back into the schoolhouse.

The Arab, leaning over the cement floor of the shed, was washing his teeth with two fingers. Daru looked at him and said: "Come." He went back into the room ahead of the prisoner. He slipped a hunting-jacket on over his sweater and put on walking-shoes. Standing, he waited until the Arab had put on his *chèche* and sandals. They went into the classroom and the schoolmaster pointed to the exit, saying: "Go ahead." The fellow didn't budge. "I'm coming," said Daru. The Arab went out. Daru went back into the room and made a package of pieces of rusk, dates, and sugar. In the classroom, before going out, he hesitated a second in front of his desk, then crossed the threshold and locked the door. "That's the way," he said. He started toward the east, followed by the prisoner. But, a short distance from the schoolhouse, he thought he heard a slight sound behind them. He retraced his steps and examined the surroundings of the house; there was no one there. The Arab watched him without seeming to understand. "Come on," said Daru.

They walked for an hour and rested beside a sharp peak of limestone. The snow was melting faster and faster and the sun was drinking up the puddles at once, rapidly cleaning the plateau, which gradually dried and vibrated like the air itself. When they resumed walking, the ground rang under their feet. From time to time a bird rent the space in front of them with a joyful cry. Daru breathed in deeply the fresh morning light. He felt a sort of rapture before the vast familiar expanse, now almost entirely yellow under its dome of blue sky. They walked an hour more, descending toward the south. They reached a level height made up of crumbly rocks. From there on, the plateau sloped down, eastward, toward a low plain where there were a few spindly trees and, to the south, toward outcroppings of rock that gave the landscape a chaotic look.

Daru surveyed the two directions. There was nothing but the sky on the horizon. Not a man could be seen. He turned toward the Arab, who was looking at him blankly. Daru held out the package to him. "Take it," he said. "There are dates, bread, and sugar. You can hold out for two days. Here are a thousand francs too." The Arab took the package and the money but kept his full hands at chest level as if he didn't know what to do with what was being given him. "Now look," the schoolmaster said as he pointed in the direction of the east, "there's the way to Tinguit. You have a two-hour walk. At Tinguit you'll find the administration and the police. They are expecting you." The Arab looked toward the east, still holding the package and the money against his chest. Daru took his elbow and turned him rather roughly toward the south. At the foot of the height on which they stood could be seen a faint path. "That's the trail across the plateau. In a day's walk from here you'll find pasturelands and the first nomads. They'll take you in and shelter you according to their law." The Arab had now turned toward Daru and a sort of panic was visible in his expression. "Listen," he said. Daru shook his head: "No, be quiet. Now I'm leaving you." He turned his back on him, took two long steps in the direction of the school, looked hesitantly at the motionless Arab, and started off again. For a few minutes he heard nothing but his own step resounding on the cold ground and did not turn his head. A moment later, however, he turned around. The Arab was still there on the edge of the hill, his arms hanging now, and he was looking at the schoolmaster. Daru felt something rise in his throat. But he swore with impatience, waved vaguely, and started off again. He had already gone some distance when he again stopped and looked. There was no longer anyone on the hill.

Daru hesitated. The sun was now rather high in the sky and was beginning to beat down on his head. The schoolmaster retraced his steps, at first somewhat uncertainly, then with decision. When he reached the little hill, he was bathed in sweat. He climbed it as fast as he could and stopped, out of breath, at the top. The rock-fields to the south stood out sharply against the blue sky, but on the plain to the east a steamy heat was already rising. And in that slight haze, Daru, with heavy heart, made out the Arab walking slowly on the road to prison.

A little later, standing before the window of the classroom, the schoolmaster was watching the clear light bathing the whole surface of the plateau, but he hardly saw it. Behind him on the blackboard, among the winding French rivers, sprawled the clumsily, chalked-up words he had just read: "You handed over our brother. You will pay for this." Daru looked at the sky, the plateau, and, beyond, the invisible lands stretching all the way to the sea. In this vast landscape he had loved so much, he was alone.

Eugène Ionesco
Victims of Duty

A Pseudo-Drama

SET: A petit bourgeois *interior.* CHOUBERT *is sitting in an armchair near the table reading a newspaper.* MADELEINE, *his wife, is sitting at the table darning socks.*
[*Silence*]
MADELEINE: [*pausing in her work*]:   Any news in the paper?

Source: Eugène Ionesco, *Victims of Duty,* translated by Donald Watson. Copyright © 1958 by John Calder. Reprinted by permission of Grove Press, Inc.

CHOUBERT: Nothing ever happens. A few comets and a cosmic disturbance somewhere in the universe. Nothing to speak of. The neighbours have been fined for letting their dogs make a mess on the pavement . . .
MADELEINE: Serve them right. It's horrible when you step on it.
CHOUBERT: And think of the people on the ground floor, opening their windows in the morning to see *that!* Enough to put them in a bad mood for the rest of the day.
MADELEINE: They're *too* sensitive.
CHOUBERT: It's the times we live in; all nerves. Nowadays men have lost the peace of mind they had in the past. [*Silence*] Oh, and here's an official announcement.
MADELEINE: What's it say?
CHOUBERT: It's quite interesting. The Government's urging all the citizens of the big towns to cultivate detachment. According to this, it's our last hope of finding an answer to the economic crisis, the confusion of the spirit and the problems of existence.
MADELEINE: We've tried everything else, and it hasn't done any good, but I don't suppose it's anyone's fault.
CHOUBERT: For the time being the Government's merely recommending this ultimate solution in a friendly manner. They can't fool us; we know how a recommendation has a way of turning into an order.
MADELEINE: You're always so anxious to generalize!
CHOUBERT: We know how suggestions suddenly come to look like rules, like strict laws.
MADELEINE: Well, my dear, you know, the law *is* necessary, and what's necessary and indispensable is *good,* and everything that's good is *nice.* And it really is very nice indeed to be a good, law-abiding citizen and do one's duty and have a clear conscience! . . .
CHOUBERT: Yes, Madeleine. When one really thinks about it, you're right. There is something to be said for the law.
MADELEINE: Of course there is.
CHOUBERT: Yes, yes. Renunciation has one important advantage: it's political and mystical at the same time. It bears fruit on two levels.
MADELEINE: So you can kill two birds with one stone.
CHOUBERT: That's what's so interesting about it.
MADELEINE: You see!
CHOUBERT: Besides, if I remember rightly from my history lessons, this system of government, the "detachment system," has already been tried before, three centuries ago, and five centuries ago, nineteen centuries ago, too, and again last year . . .
MADELEINE: Nothing new under the sun!
CHOUBERT: . . . successfully too, on whole populations, in capital cities and in the countryside, [*He gets up.*] on nations, on nations like ours!

MADELEINE: Sit down. [CHOUBERT *sits down again.*]

CHOUBERT [*sitting*]:   Only, it's true, it *does* demand the sacrifice of some of our creature comforts. It's still rather a nuisance.

MADELEINE: Oh, not necessarily! ... Sacrifice isn't always so difficult. There's sacrifice *and* sacrifice. Even if it *is* a bit of a nuisance right at the start, getting rid of some of our habits, once we're rid of them, we're rid of them, and you never really give them another thought!

[*Silence*]

CHOUBERT: You're often going to the cinema; you must be very fond of the theatre.

MADELEINE: Of course I am, just like everyone else.

CHOUBERT: *More* than everyone else.

MADELEINE: Yes, more.

CHOUBERT: What do you think of the modern theatre? What are your ideas on the drama?

MADELEINE: You and your theatre! It's an obsession, you'll soon be a pathological case.

CHOUBERT: Do you really think something new can be done in the theatre?

MADELEINE: I've just told you there's nothing new under the sun. Even when there isn't any.

[*Silence*]

CHOUBERT: You're right. Yes, you're right. All the plays that have ever been written, from Ancient Greece to the present day, have never really been anything but thrillers. Drama's always been realistic and there's always been a detective about. Every play's an investigation brought to a successful conclusion. There's a riddle, and it's solved in the final scene. Sometimes earlier. You seek, and then you find. Might as well give the game away at the start.

MADELEINE: You ought to quote examples, you know.

CHOUBERT: I was thinking of the Miracle Play about the woman Our lady saved from being burned alive. If you forget that bit of divine intervention, which really has nothing to do with it, what's left is a newspaper story about a woman who has her son-in-law murdered by a couple of stray killers for reasons that are unmentioned ...

MADELEINE: And unmentionable ...

CHOUBERT: The police arrive, there's an investigation and the criminal is unmasked. It's a thriller. A naturalistic drama, fit for the theatre of Antoine.

MADELEINE: That's it.

CHOUBERT: Come to think of it, there's never been much evolution in the theatre.

MADELEINE: Pity.

CHOUBERT: You see, the theatre's a riddle, and the riddle's a thriller. It's always been that way.

MADELEINE: What about the classics?

CHOUBERT: Refined detective drama. Just like naturalism.

MADELEINE: You've got some original ideas. Perhaps there's something in them. Still, you ought to get an expert opinion on the subject.

CHOUBERT: Who from?

MADELEINE: Oh, there's bound to be someone, among the cinema enthusiasts, or the professors at the *Collège de France,* the influential members of the Agricultural School, the Norwegians or some of those veterinary surgeons . . . A vet, now there's someone who should have lots of ideas.

CHOUBERT: Everyone's got ideas. No shortage there. But it's facts that count.

MADELEINE: Facts, nothing but facts. Still, we could ask them what they think.

CHOUBERT: We'll *have* to ask them.

MADELEINE: We must give them the time to think about it. You've *got* the time . . .

CHOUBERT: It's a fascinating subject.

[*Silence.* MADELEINE *darns socks.* CHOUBERT *reads his paper. Someone is heard knocking at a door, but not one of the doors of the room they are in.* CHOUBERT, *however, raises his head.*]

MADELEINE: It's the other side, for the concierge. She's never there.

[*The knocking is heard again. The door of the concierge's place is probably on the same landing. Then:*]

DETECTIVE'S VOICE: Concierge! Concierge!

[*Silence. Again there is knocking, and again.*]

Concierge! Concierge!

MADELEINE: She's *never* there. We're so badly looked after!

CHOUBERT: A concierge ought to be chained to her room. I expect it's for one of the tenants. Shall I go and see?

[*He gets up and sits down again.*]

MADELEINE [*quite quietly*]: It's no business of ours. Neither of us is a concierge, you know. Everyone in society has his own special duty to perform!

[*Short silence.* CHOUBERT *reads his paper.* MADELEINE *darns her socks. Gentle tapping on the right-hand door.*]

CHOUBERT: This time, it's for us.

MADELEINE: You can go and see, dear.

CHOUBERT: I'll open the door.

[CHOUBERT *gets up, walks to the right-hand door and opens it. The* DETECTIVE *is seen in the doorway. He is very young, with a brief-case under one arm. He is wearing a beige overcoat and is hatless, a fair man, soft-spoken and excessively shy.*]

DETECTIVE [*in the doorway*]: Good evening, Monsieur. [*Then to* MADELEINE, *who has also risen and moved to the door:*] Good evening, Madame.

CHOUBERT: Good evening. [*To* MADELEINE:] It's the Detective.

DETECTIVE [*taking one short timid step forward*]: Forgive me, Madame, Monsieur, I wanted some information from the concierge, the concierge isn't there . . .

MADELEINE: Naturally.

DETECTIVE: . . . do you know where she is? Do you know if she'll soon be back? Oh, I'm so sorry, please forgive me, I . . . I'd never have knocked on your door, if I'd found the concierge, I wouldn't have dared to trouble you like this . . .

CHOUBERT: The concierge should soon be back, Monsieur. Theoretically she only goes out on Saturday nights. Goes dancing, you know, every Saturday night, since she married her daughter off. And as this is Tuesday night . . .

DETECTIVE: Thank you, Monsieur, thank you very much, I'll be going, Monsieur, I'll wait for her on the landing. You've really been very helpful. Glad to have had the privilege of making your acquaintance, Madame.

MADELEINE [*to* CHOUBERT]: What a polite young man! Such wonderful manners. Ask him what he wants to know, perhaps you could help him.

CHOUBERT [*to* DETECTIVE]: Can I help you, Monsieur? Perhaps I can tell you what you want to know?

DETECTIVE: I'm really very sorry to trouble you like this.

MADELEINE: It's no trouble at all.

DETECTIVE: It's really quite a simple matter . . .

MADELEINE [*to* CHOUBERT]: Why don't you ask him in?

CHOUBERT [*to* DETECTIVE]: Just step inside a minute, Monsieur.

DETECTIVE: Oh, Monsieur, really, I . . . I . . .

CHOUBERT: My wife would like you to step inside, Monsieur.

MADELEINE [*to* DETECTIVE]: My husband and I would both like you to step inside, dear Monsieur.

DETECTIVE [*consulting his wristlet watch*]: I don't really think I've enough time, I'm late already, you see!

MADELEINE [*aside*]: He's wearing a gold watch!

CHOUBERT [*aside*]: She's already noticed he's wearing a gold watch!

DETECTIVE: . . . well then, for five minutes, as you insist . . . but I shan't be able to . . . oh well . . . I'll come in if you like, on condition you let me go away again at once . . .

MADELEINE: Don't worry, dear Monsieur, we're not going to keep you here by force, but you can still come in and rest a moment.

DETECTIVE: Thank you, I'm very grateful to you. You're very kind.
[*The* DETECTIVE *takes another step into the room, stops and undoes his overcoat.*]
MADELEINE [*to* CHOUBERT]: What a lovely brown suit—brand new, too!
CHOUBERT [*to* MADELEINE]: What a wonderful pair of shoes!
MADELEINE [*to* CHOUBERT]: And what lovely fair hair! [*The* DETECTIVE *runs his fingers through his hair.*] Beautiful eyes, such a gentle look. Hasn't he?
CHOUBERT [*to* MADELEINE]: A nice man you feel you can trust. With the face of a child.
MADELEINE: Please don't stand, Monsieur. Do sit down.
CHOUBERT: Take a seat.
[*The* DETECTIVE *takes another step forward. He does not sit down.*]
DETECTIVE: You are Monsieur and Madame Choubert, aren't you?
MADELEINE: Why yes, Monsieur.
DETECTIVE [*to* CHOUBERT]: It seems you're fond of the theatre, Monsieur?
CHOUBERT: Er ... er ... yes ... I take an interest in it.
DETECTIVE: How right you are, Monsieur! I'm very fond of the theatre too, but unfortunately I hardly ever have the time to go.
CHOUBERT: And the sort of plays they put on!
DETECTIVE [*to* MADELEINE]: Monsieur Choubert does, I believe, also support the policy called "the detachment-system"?
MADELEINE [*showing little surprise*]: Yes, Monsieur, he does.
DETECTIVE [*to* CHOUBERT]: It's an honour for me to share your opinion, Monsieur. [*To both:*] I'm afraid I'm taking your time. I simply wanted to know about the name of the previous tenants of your flat: was it Mallot, with a t at the end, or Mallod with a d? That's all.
CHOUBERT [*without hesitation*]: Mallot, with a t.
DETECTIVE [*more coldly*]: Just as I thought. [*Without speaking, the* DETECTIVE *advances boldly into the room, with* MADELEINE *and* CHOUBERT *on either side, though half a pace behind. The* DETECTIVE *makes for the table, takes hold of one of the two chairs and sits down, while* MADELEINE *and* CHOUBERT *remain standing beside him. The* DETECTIVE *lays his brief case on the table and opens it. He takes a large cigarette-case from his pocket and, without offering any to his hosts, lights one in leisurely fashion, crosses his legs, takes a fresh puff and then:*] So you knew the Mallots?
[*As he asks this question he looks up, first at* MADELEINE, *then a little longer, at* CHOUBERT.]
CHOUBERT [*somewhat intrigued*]: No. I never knew them.
DETECTIVE: Then how do you know their name ends in a t?
CHOUBERT [*very surprised*]: Why yes, of course, you're right ... How

do I know? *How* do I know? . . . How do I *know?* . . . I don't know how I know!

MADELEINE [*to* CHOUBERT]: What's the matter with you? Answer him! When we're on our own you don't swallow your tongue. You talk so fast, you talk too much, such violent language too, and so loud. [*To the* DETECTIVE:] You don't know that side of him. He's a lot brighter than this, in private.

DETECTIVE: I'll make a note of that.

MADELEINE [*to* DETECTIVE]: Still, I'm quite fond of him. After all, he *is* my husband, isn't he? [*To* CHOUBERT:]: Oh, come on, now! Did we know the Mallots or not! Say something! Try and remember!

CHOUBERT [*after struggling silently with his memory for a few moments, while* MADELEINE *gets visibly more irritated and the* DETECTIVE *remains impassive*]: I can't remember! Did I know them or not!

DETECTIVE [*to* MADELEINE]: Take his tie off, Madame, perhaps it's worrying him. Then he'll do a bit better.

CHOUBERT [*to* DETECTIVE]: Thank you, Monsieur. [*To* MADELEINE, *who is taking his tie off:*] Thank you, Madeleine.

DETECTIVE [*to* MADELEINE]: The belt too, and his shoe-laces! [MADELEINE *removes them.*]

CHOUBERT [*to* DETECTIVE]: They were a bit too tight, Monsieur, very kind of you.

DETECTIVE [*to* CHOUBERT]: Well, Monsieur?

MADELEINE [*to* CHOUBERT]: Well?

CHOUBERT: It's much easier to breathe. And I feel freer in my movements. But I still can't remember.

DETECTIVE [*to* CHOUBERT]: Come along now, old chap, you're not a child any more.

MADELEINE [*to* CHOUBERT]: Come along, you're not a child. Did you hear what he said? . . . Oh, you're hopeless!

DETECTIVE [*tipping back on his chair, to* MADELEINE]: Will you make me some coffee?

MADELEINE: With pleasure, Monsieur, I'll go and get it ready. Mind you don't tip over, rocking about like that.

DETECTIVE [*still rocking his chair*]: Don't worry, Madeleine. [*With a mysterious smile, to* CHOUBERT:] That is her name, isn't it? [*To* MADELEINE:] Don't worry, Madeleine, I'm used to it . . . Really strong, the coffee, and plenty of sugar!

MADELEINE: Three lumps?

DETECTIVE: Twelve! And a calvados, a large one.

MADELEINE: Very well, Monsieur.

[MADELEINE *leaves the room through the left-hand door. From the wings can be heard the noise of coffee being ground, almost loud enough at the start to drown the voices of* CHOUBERT *and the* DETECTIVE, *and then gradually fading.*]

CHOUBERT: And so, Monsieur, you really are, like me, a firm believer in the "detachment-system," politically and mystically? And I'm pleased to hear we also have the same tastes in art: I'm sure you accept the principle that the art of drama should be revolutionary.

DETECTIVE: That is not the point we're discussing just now! [*The* DETECTIVE *takes a photo from his pocket and shows it to* CHOUBERT:] See if this photograph can jog your memory. Is *this* Mallot? [*The* DETECTIVE'S *tone becomes more and more sharp; after a pause:*] Is this Mallot?

[*At the extreme left of the forestage a spotlight should suddenly pick up a large portrait, not noticeable before in the shadows; it roughly resembles the man* CHOUBERT *is describing from the photograph he is looking at in his hand. The characters naturally pay no attention to the illuminated portrait—they appear not to realize it is there—and it disappears again into darkness as soon as the description has been made; it might be better to have an actor, instead of the illuminated portrait, who would stand motionless on the extreme left of the forestage, also looking like the man described; again it might be possible to have both the portrait and the actor, one on each side of the forestage.*]

CHOUBERT   [*after gazing at the photo for some time with great attention and describing the man's face*]:   It's a man of about fifty . . . yes . . . I see . . . he's got several days' growth of beard . . . and on his chest there's a card with the number 58614 . . . yes, it's 58614 all right . . .

[*The spotlight is cut out; the portrait or the actor is no longer visible on the forestage.*]

DETECTIVE: Is this Mallot? I'm being very patient.

CHOUBERT   [*after a moment's silence*]:   You know, Monsieur Inspector, I . . .

DETECTIVE: Chief Inspector!

CHOUBERT: I'm sorry, you know, Monsieur Chief Inspector, I can't really tell. Like that, without a tie, collar torn, a face all bruised and swollen, how can I recognize him? . . . And yet it seems to me, yes, it certainly seems it *could* be him. . . .

DETECTIVE: When did you know him and what did he talk to you about?

CHOUBERT   [*lowering himself onto a chair*]:   Forgive me, Monsieur Chief Inspector, I'm terribly tired! . . .

DETECTIVE: My question is: when did you know him and what did he talk to you about?

CHOUBERT: When did I know him? [*He holds his head in his hands.*] What did he *talk* about? What *did* he talk about? *What* did he talk about?

DETECTIVE: Answer!

CHOUBERT: What did he talk to me about? . . . What did he . . . But when on earth did I meet him? . . . When was the first time I saw him? When was the last time?

DETECTIVE: It's not my job to give the answers.

CHOUBERT: Where was it? Where? . . . Where? . . . In the garden? . . . The house I lived in as a child? . . . At school? . . . In the army? . . . On his wedding day? . . . *My* wedding day? . . . Was I his best man? . . . Was *he* my best man? . . . No.

DETECTIVE: You don't want to remember?

CHOUBERT: I can't . . . And yet I do recall . . . some place by the sea, at twilight, it was damp, a long time ago, and dark rocks . . . [*Turning his head to call after* MADELEINE:] Madeleine! Where's that coffee for Monsieur the Chief Inspector!

MADELEINE [*coming in*]: The coffee can grind itself.

CHOUBERT [*to* MADELEINE]: Really, Madeleine, you ought to be seeing to it.

DETECTIVE [*banging his fist on the table*]: All very considerate of you, I'm sure, but it's none of your business. Stick to your own affairs. You were telling me about some place by the sea . . . [CHOUBERT *is silent.*] Did you hear what I said?

MADELEINE [*overawed by the authoritative tone and gesture of the* DETECTIVE, *in a mixture of fear and admiration, to* CHOUBERT]: The gentleman's asking if you heard what he said? Tell him, can't you?

CHOUBERT: Yes, Monsieur.

DETECTIVE: Well? Well?

CHOUBERT: Yes, that's where I must have met him. We must have been very young! . . .

[*It is already obvious, since* MADELEINE *came back on the stage, that she has changed her walk and even her voice; now her old dress falls away and reveals one that is low-cut. She is a different person; her voice, too, has changed; now it is gentle and musical.*]

No, not there! I can't see him there . . .

DETECTIVE: You can't see him there! You can't see him there! Where can it have been then? In the local bistrot? Drunken sot! and he calls himself a married man!

CHOUBERT: When you come to think about it, I suppose, to find Mallot with a t, you must go down, right down . . .

DETECTIVE: Go on down, then.

MADELEINE [*in her musical voice*]: Right down, right down, right down, right down . . .

CHOUBERT: It must be dark down there, won't be able to see anything.

DETECTIVE: I'll show you the way. You've only got to follow my directions: it's not difficult, you just have to let yourself slide.

CHOUBERT: Oh, I'm quite a long way down already.

DETECTIVE [*harshly*]:   Not far enough!

MADELEINE: Not far enough, darling, my love, not far enough! [*She throws her arms around* CHOUBERT, *languorously, almost obscenely; then she is down on her knees before him, forcing him to bend his knees.*] Don't keep your legs so stiff! Mind you don't slip! the steps are greasy . . . [MADELEINE *has risen to her feet.*] Hold tight to the handrail . . . Down . . . go on down . . . if it's me you want!

[CHOUBERT *is holding on to* MADELEINE'S *arm, as if it were a handrail; he looks as though he were going downstairs;* MADELEINE *takes her arm away, but* CHOUBERT *does not notice and goes on clutching an imaginary handrail; he goes on down the stairs towards* MADELEINE. *The expression on his face is lustful; suddenly he stops, holding out an arm and looks at the floor, then all round him.*]

CHOUBERT: This must be it.

DETECTIVE: It'll do, for the moment.

CHOUBERT: Madeleine!

MADELEINE [*moving back towards the sofa as she intones, musically*]: I am here . . . I am here . . . Further down . . . A stair . . . A step . . . a stair . . . a step . . . a stair . . . a step . . . a stair . . . a step . . . a stair . . . Cuckoo . . . Cuckoo . . . [*She lies full-length on the sofa.*] Darling . . .

[CHOUBERT *moves towards her, laughing nervously. For a few moments* MADELEINE, *smiling erotically on the sofa with her arms stretched out to* CHOUBERT, *intones:*] La, la la la la . . .

[CHOUBERT, *although standing very close to the sofa, has his arms stretched out towards* MADELEINE *as if she were still a long way off; he laughs the same strange laugh and rocks slightly to and fro; for a few seconds they remain like this, with* MADELEINE *punctuating her singing with provocative laughter, and* CHOUBERT *calling her in a thick voice.*]

CHOUBERT: Madeleine! Madeleine! I'm coming . . . It's me, Madeleine! It's me . . . any minute now . . .

DETECTIVE: He's down the first steps all right. Now he must go right down. He's not doing so badly so far.

[*This erotic scene is broken by the* DETECTIVE'S *interruption;* MADELEINE *rises to her feet and makes for the back of the stage, at the same time moving a little nearer the detective; she still keeps her musical voice for a while, though it gradually becomes less sensual, but in the end it often takes on the shrewish note it had before;* CHOUBERT *lets his arms fall to his side, and with an expressionless face walks with slow mechanical steps towards the* DETECTIVE.]

You've got to go deeper.

MADELEINE [*to* CHOUBERT]:   Deeper, my love, deeper . . . deeper . . . deeper

CHOUBERT: It's so dark.

DETECTIVE: Think about Mallot and keep your eyes skinned. Look for Mallot ...

MADELEINE [*amost singing*]: Look for Mallot, Mallot, Mallot ...

CHOUBERT: I'm walking through the mud. It's sticking to the soles of my shoes ... my feet are so heavy! I'm afraid of slipping.

DETECTIVE: Don't be afraid. Go on down, till you come to the bottom, turn right, turn left.

MADELEINE [*to* CHOUBERT]: Down, deeper my darling, darling deeper down ...

DETECTIVE: Down, right, left, right, left.

[CHOUBERT *follows the* DETECTIVE'S *directions and goes on moving like a sleep-walker. Meanwhile* MADELEINE, *her back to the audience, has thrown her shawl over her shoulders: suddenly she is all hunched up, and from behind she looks very old. She is shaken by silent sobbing.*]

DETECTIVE: Straight in front of you ...

[CHOUBERT *turns to* MADELEINE *and speaks to her. His hands are clasped and his expression is sorrowful.*]

CHOUBERT: Is that you, Madeleine? Is it really you, Madeleine? What a terrible misfortune! How did it happen? How could it happen? We never noticed ... Poor old lady, poor little faded doll, it's you just the same, but how different you look! When did it happen? Why didn't we stop it? This morning our path was strewn with flowers. The sky was drenched in sunshine. Your laughter rang clear. Our clothes were brand new, and we were surrounded by friends. Nobody had died and you'd never shed a tear. Suddenly it was winter and now ours is an empty road. Where are all the others? In their graves, by the roadside. I want our happiness back again, we've been robbed and despoiled. Oh, when will the light be blue again? Madeleine, you must believe me, I swear it wasn't I who made you old! No ... I won't have it, I don't believe it, love is always young, love never dies. *I* haven't changed. Neither have you, you're pretending. Oh, but no! I can't deceive myself, you *are* old, so terribly old! Who made you old like that? Old, old, old, old, little old woman, old little doll. Our youth, on the road. Madeleine, little girl, I'll buy you a new dress, primroses, jewels. Your skin will find its bloom again. I want, I love you, I want, oh, please! We don't grow old when we're in love. I love you, grow young again, throw away that mask and look into my eyes. You must laugh, laugh, little girl! To smooth away the wrinkles. Oh, if only we could go singing and skipping and jumping again! I am young. We are young.

[*His back to the audience, he takes* MADELEINE *by the hand, and they both try to sing in a very old voice and skip about. Their voices are cracked and shaken with sobs.*] ·

CHOUBERT [*vaguely accompanied by* MADELEINE]: Fountains of spring ... and fresh young leaves ... The enchanted garden has folded into night, has sunk into the mud . . . Our love in the night, our love in the mud, in the night, in the mud . . . When our youth has flown, our tears are the pure water of the wells . . . the wells of life, of immortality . . . Do the flowers flower in the mud . . .

DETECTIVE: That's not it, it's not that at all. You're wasting your time, forgetting about Mallot, you stop and hang about, lazy beggar . . . and you're not going in the right direction. If you can't find Mallot in the leaves or the water of the wells, don't stop, keep going. We've no time to lose. While you stand still, he's running God knows where. You, you get soft and sentimental about yourself and stop; it never does to get sentimental; and you must never stop. [*During the* DETECTIVE'S *first words* MADELEINE *and* CHOUBERT *have slowly stopped singing. To* MADELEINE, *who has turned round and straightened up:*] As soon as he gets soft, he stops.

CHOUBERT: I won't get soft any more, Monsieur Chief Inspector.

DETECTIVE: That remains to be seen. Go down, turn, down, turn.

[CHOUBERT *has started walking again and* MADELEINE *has again become what she was in the previous scene.*]

CHOUBERT: Have I gone far enough, Monsieur Chief Inspector?

DETECTIVE: Not yet. Go further.

MADELEINE: Cheer up.

CHOUBERT [*his eyes closed, his arms outstretched*]: I've fallen down, but I'm getting up; I've fallen down, but I'm getting up . . .

DETECTIVE: Stay down.

MADELEINE: Stay down, my darling.

DETECTIVE: Look for Mallot, Mallot with a t. Can you see Mallot? Can you see Mallot? . . . Are you getting any nearer?

MADELEINE: Mallot . . . Mallo-o-o-o . . .

CHOUBERT [*still with his eyes shut*]: It doesn't help, however wide I open my eyes . . .

DETECTIVE: I'm not asking you to read with your eyes.

MADELEINE: Go on, let yourself slide, darling.

DETECTIVE: You've got to touch him, catch hold of him, stretch out your arms and grope . . . grope . . . nothing to be frightened of . . .

CHOUBERT: I'm trying . . .

DETECTIVE: He hasn't even got to a thousand metres below sea-level yet.

MADELEINE: Why don't you go further down? Don't be afraid.

CHOUBERT: The tunnel's blocked up.

DETECTIVE: Go straight down where you are, then.

MADELEINE: Go right in, my darling.

DETECTIVE: Can you still talk?

CHOUBERT: The mud's up to my chin.

DETECTIVE: You're not down far enough. Never mind the mud. You're still a long way from Mallot.

MADELEINE: Go right in, darling, go down where it's deepest.

DETECTIVE: Get your chin down, that's it ... now your mouth ...

MADELEINE: Your mouth, too. [CHOUBERT *utters stifled grunts.*] Go on, sink right in ... further, further in, still further ...

[*Grunts from* CHOUBERT.]

DETECTIVE: Now your nose ...

MADELEINE: Your nose ...

[*During all this time* CHOUBERT *is miming a descent into the deep, a drowning man.*]

DETECTIVE: His eyes ...

MADELEINE: He's opened one eye in the mud ... There's one eyelash showing ... [*To* CHOUBERT:] Bend your head lower, my love.

DETECTIVE: Why don't you shout louder? He can't hear ...

MADELEINE [*to* CHOUBERT, *very loud*]: Bend your head lower, my love! ... Go down! [*To the* DETECTIVE:] He always was hard of hearing.

DETECTIVE: You can still see the top of his ear sticking out.

MADELEINE [*shouting to* CHOUBERT]: Darling! ... Get your ear under!

CHOUBERT [*to* MADELEINE]: You can see his hair.

MADELEINE [*to* CHOUBERT]: You've still got some hair showing ... Go right under. Stretch out your arms in the mud, move your fingers about, swim through the deep and find Mallot, whatever you do ... Down ... Down ...

DETECTIVE: You've got to have depth. Of course. Your wife is right. You won't find Mallot until you touch rock bottom.

[*Silence.* CHOUBERT *has really gone very deep. He is advancing with difficulty, his eyes shut, as though on the bed of the ocean.*]

MADELEINE: You can't hear him any more.

DETECTIVE: He's passed the sound barrier.

[*Darkness. For the moment only the characters' voices are heard; they are no longer visible.*]

MADELEINE: Oh, poor darling! I'm frightened for him. I shall never hear it again, that voice I love so well ...

DETECTIVE [*harshly to* MADELEINE]: It'll come back to us, you'll only make things worse by whining and wailing.

[*Light. Only* MADELEINE *and the* DETECTIVE *are on stage.*]

MADELEINE: You can't see him any more.

DETECTIVE: He's passed the sight barrier.

MADELEINE: He's in danger! He's in danger! I ought never to have agreed to this little game.

DETECTIVE: He'll come back to you, Madeleine, your little treasure, he may be a bit late, but *he'll* be back! *He's* still got a trick or two up his sleeve. He's got the hide of a rhinoceros.

MADELEINE [*weeping*]: I shouldn't have done it. It was wrong of me. When I think of the state he must be in, poor darling ...

DETECTIVE [*to* MADELEINE]:   Be quiet, Madeleine! What are you fright-
ened of, you're with me ... we're alone, just the two of us, my beauty.
[*He puts his arms absent-mindedly round* MADELEINE, *then takes them
away again.*]
MADELEINE [*weeping*]:   What have we done! But we had to, didn't we?
It's all quite legal?
DETECTIVE: Why yes, of course, there's nothing to fear. He'll come back
to you. Cheer up. I'm quite fond of him, too.
MADELEINE: Are you really?
DETECTIVE: He'll come back to us, the long way round ... He'll live again
in us ... [*Groans coming from the wings.*] You hear ... It's him breath-
ing ...
MADELEINE: Yes, that breathing I love so well.
[*Darkness. Light.* CHOUBERT *passes right across the stage. The other two
characters are no longer there.*]
CHOUBERT: I can see ... I can see ...
[*His words are lost in groans. He goes out on the right, while* MADELEINE
and the DETECTIVE *come back from the left. They are transformed. The
actors who play the following scene have become two different char-
acters.*]
MADELEINE: You're a despicable creature! You've spent a whole lifetime
humiliating and torturing me. Morally you've disfigured me. You've made
me old before my time. You've destroyed me. I've finished with you.
DETECTIVE: And what do you think you're going to do?
MADELEINE: Kill myself, take poison.
DETECTIVE: You're free to do as you like, I'll not stop you.
MADELEINE: You'd be only too pleased to get rid of me! You'd *love* to be
rid of me, wouldn't you? I know you would!
DETECTIVE: I don't want to get rid of you at *any* price! But I can quite
easily get along without you. You and your complaining. It's just you're so
boring. You know nothing about life, you bore everyone stiff.
MADELEINE [*sobbing*]:   Brute!
DETECTIVE: Don't cry, it makes you even uglier than usual! ...
[CHOUBERT *has appeared again, and watches the scene from afar, without
a word, wringing his hands, as though powerless to intervene; at the most
he can be heard muttering: "Father, mother, father, mother ..."*]
MADELEINE[*beside herself*]:   Now you've gone too far. I can't bear it. [*She
takes from her bosom a small bottle she then carries to her lips.*]
DETECTIVE: You're mad, you're not going to do that! Stop it!
[*The* DETECTIVE *goes to* MADELEINE *and takes her by the arm to prevent
her swallowing the poison; then suddenly, as the expression on his face
changes, it is he who forces her to drink.*]
[CHOUBERT *utters a cry. Black-out. Lights again. He is alone on the
stage.*]

CHOUBERT: I am eight years old and its evening. My mother's holding me by the hand, in the rue Blomet after the bombing. We're walking along by the ruins. I'm frightened. My mother's hand is shaking in mine. There are shadowy figures looming in the gaps in the walls. The only light in the darkness comes from their eyes.

[MADELEINE *appears silently. She goes towards* CHOUBERT. *It's his mother.*]

DETECTIVE [*appearing at the other side of the stage and advancing with very slow steps*]:   Those shadowy figures, look, perhaps one of them is Mallot . . .

CHOUBERT: The light's gone from their eyes. Everything's returned to night, except for a skylight in the distance. It's so dark I can't see my mother any more. Her hand has melted away. I can hear her voice.

DETECTIVE: She must be talking about Mallot.

CHOUBERT: Sadly, very sadly she's saying: I'm going to leave you, and you'll have many a tear to shed, my child, my little lamb . . .

MADELEINE [*with great tenderness in her voice*]:   My child, my little lamb . . .

CHOUBERT: I shall be alone in the dark, in the mud . . .

MADELEINE: My poor child, in the dark, in the mud, all alone, little lamb . . .

CHOUBERT: There's only her voice, a whisper to guide me. She's saying . . .

MADELEINE: You must learn to forgive, my child, that's the hardest of all . . .

CHOUBERT: That's the hardest of all.

MADELEINE: That's the hardest of all.

CHOUBERT: And now she's saying . . .

MADELEINE: . . . The time for tears will come, the time for repentence and remorse, you must be good, you'll suffer for it if you're not and you never learn to forgive. When you see him, obey him, kiss him and forgive him.

[MADELEINE *goes out in silence.*

CHOUBERT *is in front of the* DETECTIVE, *who is sitting at the table facing the audience and holding his head in his hands, staying quite still.*]

CHOUBERT: Now the voice is silent. [CHOUBERT *addresses the* DETECTIVE:] Father, we never understood each other . . . Can you still hear me? I'll be obedient; forgive us as we forgave you . . . Let me see your face! [*The* DETECTIVE *does not move.*] You were hard, but perhaps you weren't too unkind. Perhaps it's not your fault. It's not you I hated. It was your selfishness and your violence. I had no pity for your frailties. You used to hit me. But I was stronger than you. My contempt hit you much harder. That was what killed you. Wasn't it? Listen . . . I had to avenge my mother

... I *had* to ... What *was* my duty? ... Did I really *have* to? ... She forgave you, but I went on and carried out *her* revenge myself ... What's the good of taking vengeance? It's always the avenger who suffers ... Do you hear me? Uncover your face. Give me your hand. We could have been good pals. I was far more unkind than you. You had your middle-class ways, but what did that matter? I was wrong to despise you. I'm no better than you are. What right had I to punish you? [*The* DETECTIVE *is still motionless.*] That's it, come with me and we'll go and find some of the boys! We'll all have a drink together. Look at me, look! I take after you. You don't want to ... If you would look at me, you'd see how alike we are. I've all the same faults as you. [*Silence. The* DETECTIVE'S *position does not change.*] Who will have mercy on me, I who have been unmerciful! Even if you did forgive me, I could never forgive myself!

[*While the* DETECTIVE'S *position remains unchanged, his recorded voice is heard coming from the opposite corner of the stage; during the ensuing monologue* CHOUBERT *stands quite still, arms hanging at his sides; his face expresses no emotion, but his body is occasionally shaken by shuddering despair.*][1]

DETECTIVE'S VOICE:[2]   My boy, I was a travelling salesman. My job sent me roving all over the globe. Unfortunately I always had to spend October to March in the northern hemisphere, and April to September in the southern, with the result that in my life it was winter all the time. My pay was wretched, my clothes were poor and my health was bad. I lived in a perpetual state of rage. My enemies grew richer and richer, and more and more powerful. Those who helped me went bankrupt and then they died, carried off, one after the other, by disreputable diseases or preposterous little accidents. I met nothing but disappointment. The good I did turned into evil, but the evil done to me never turned into good. Later I was a soldier, I was compelled, ordered to join in the massacre of tens of thousands of enemy soldiers, of whole communities of old men, women and children. Then the town where I was born, with all its suburbs, was utterly destroyed. In peacetime the misery went on, and I had a horror of mankind. I planned all kinds of horrible revenge. I loathed the earth, the sun and its satellites. I longed to go into voluntary exile, to another universe. But there *is* no other.

CHOUBERT [*in the same attitude*]:   He doesn't want to look at me ... to speak to me ...

DETECTIVE'S VOICE:[2] [*while the* DETECTIVE *himself is still in the same position*]:   You were born, my son, just when I was about to blow our planet up. It was only your arrival that saved it. At least, it was you who

1. Author's Note: During the actual performance the DETECTIVE raised his head and spoke directly. This seems the better solution.
2. Or the DETECTIVE himself.

stopped me from killing mankind in my heart. You reconciled me to the human race and bound me irrevocably to the history, the crimes and hopes, despairs and disasters of all men. I trembled for their fate . . . and for yours.

CHOUBERT [*he and the* DETECTIVE *as before*]:   So I shall never know . . .

DETECTIVE'S VOICE:[2]   Yes, you had hardly emerged from the void when I began to feel I'd lost my weapons; I was gasping with joy and sorrow, my stony heart had turned into a sponge, a rag; my head was spinning with unspeakable remorse to think I'd not wanted a family and had tried to stop you coming into the world. You might never have been, never have been! Only to think of it now, I still get a tremendous feeling of panic; heart-rending regret, too, for all those thousands of children who might have been born and who haven't, for those countless faces never to be caressed, those little hands that no father will ever hold in his, those lips that will never know prattling. I should have liked to fill the emptiness with life. I tried to imagine all those little beings who so nearly came into existence, I wanted to create them in my mind, so that I could at least weep for them, as I weep for those who are already dead.

CHOUBERT [*both he and the* DETECTIVE, *still in the same positions*]:   He'll never open his mouth!

DETECTIVE'S VOICE:[3]   Yet, at the same time, I was overcome with delirious joy, for you, dear child, existed, you, a flickering star in an ocean of darkness, an island of being surrounded by nothing, and your existence cancelled out the void. I wept as my lips brushed your eyes: "Oh God, oh God!" I sighed. I was grateful to God, because if the creation had never been, if the universe had never had a history, century after century, then *you* would never have been, my son, and all the history of the world really led up to you. You would never have been here, were it not for that endless chain of cause and effect, not forgetting all the floods, the wars and revolutions, and every social, geological and cosmic catastrophe that ever was: for everything in the universe is the result of a whole system of causation, not excepting you, my child. I was grateful to God for all my misery and for all the misery of centuries, for all the sorrow and all the joy, for the humiliation, for the horror and the anguish, for the great sadness, since at the end there was your birth, which justified and redeemed in my eyes all the disasters of History. I had forgiven the world, for love of you. Everything was saved, because now nothing could ever wipe out the fact of your birth into the living universe. Even when you are no more, I told myself, nothing can alter the fact that you *have been.* You were here, for ever inscribed in the archives of the universe, firmly fixed in the eternal memory of God.

3. Or the DETECTIVE himself.

CHOUBERT [*both he and the* DETECTIVE *still in the same positions*]: He'll never, never, never say . . .

DETECTIVE'S VOICE[4] [*change of tone*]: And you . . . The more proud I was of you, the more I loved you, the more you despised me, accused me of every crime, some I had committed, others I had not. Then there was your mother, poor soul. But who can tell what passed between us, whether it was her fault, or my fault, her fault or my fault . . .

CHOUBERT [*both as before*]: He'll never speak again, and it's all my fault, my fault! . . .

DETECTIVE'S VOICE:[4] You can reject me and blush for me and insult my memory as much as you like. I'll not blame you. I'm no longer capable of hate. I can't help forgiving. I owe you more than you owe me. I wouldn't want you to suffer, I want you to stop feeling guilty. Forget what you consider to be my faults.

CHOUBERT: Father, why don't you speak, why don't you answer me! . . . How sad to think that never, never again I shall hear your voice . . . Never, never, never, never . . . And I shall never know . . .

DETECTIVE [*abruptly, as he stands up, to* CHOUBERT]: In this country a father's heart's as soft as a mother's. Moaning won't do you any good. What's your personal life to do with us? You stick to Mallot! Keep on his tracks. Don't think about anything else. There's nothing in the whole business of any interest, except Mallot. Forget the rest of it, I tell you.

CHOUBERT: Monsieur Chief Inspector, you see, I really would have liked to know . . . Were they . . . After all they were my parents . . .

DETECTIVE: Oh, you and your complexes! Don't start worrying us with them! I don't give a damn for your daddy and your mummy and your filial affection! . . . That's not what I'm paid for. Get back on the road.

CHOUBERT: Have I really still got to go down, Monsieur Chief Inspector? . . .

[*He searches blindly with his foot.*]

DETECTIVE: You must describe everything you see!

CHOUBERT [*advancing hesitantly, like a blind man*]: . . . A step to the right . . . Step to the left . . . to the left . . . left . . .

DETECTIVE [*to* MADELEINE, *who comes back from the right*]: Mind the steps, Madame . . .

MADELEINE: Thank you so much, I could have fallen . . .

[*The* DETECTIVE *and* MADELEINE *have become theatre-goers.*]

DETECTIVE [*hurrying towards* MADELEINE]: Better take my arm . . .

[*The* DETECTIVE *and* MADELEINE *are finding their seats;* CHOUBERT *disappears for a moment in the semi-darkness, after walking away with the*

_____
4. Or the DETECTIVE himself.

same hesitant step; he is to reappear in a moment at the other side on a platform or small stage.]

DETECTIVE [*to* MADELEINE]: Shall we find our seats and sit down? It's going to begin. Every evening he shows himself off like this.

MADELEINE: I'm glad you booked the tickets.

DETECTIVE: Here we are.

[*He sets the two chairs down beside each other.*]

MADELEINE: Thank you, how kind. Are they good seats? Are they the best? Can we see everything? And hear everything? Have you any opera-glasses?

[CHOUBERT *has come into full view on the little stage, groping his way.*]

DETECTIVE: There he is . . .

MADELEINE: Oh, he makes quite an impression, quite a good actor! Is he really blind?

DETECTIVE: No way of knowing. But you'd think so.

MADELEINE: Poor man! They really ought to have given him a pair of white sticks, a small one, like a policeman's, so he could direct traffic all by himself, and a larger one, like a blind man's . . . [*To the* DETECTIVE:] Must I remove my hat? Oh no, I don't think so, do you? It's not in anyone's way. I'm not so tall as all that.

DETECTIVE: He's talking, be quiet, we can't hear him.

MADELEINE [*to* DETECTIVE]: Perhaps that's because he's deaf as well . . .

CHOUBERT [*on the platform*]: Where am I?

MADELEINE [*to* DETECTIVE]: Where is he?

DETECTIVE [*to* MADELEINE]: Don't be so impatient. He's going to tell you. It's all in his part.

CHOUBERT: . . . sorts of streets . . . sorts of roads . . . sorts of lakes . . . sorts of people . . . sorts of nights . . . sorts of skies . . . a sort of world . . .

MADELEINE [*to* DETECTIVE]: What's he say? . . . sorts of what?

DETECTIVE [*to* MADELEINE]: All sorts of sorts . . .

MADELEINE [*loudly to* CHOUBERT]: Louder!

DETECTIVE [*to* MADELEINE]: Be quiet, can't you? That's not allowed.

CHOUBERT: . . . Shades waking to life . . .

MADELEINE [*to* DETECTIVE]: What! . . . Is that all we're good for, just to pay up and applaud? [*Still louder, to* CHOUBERT:] Louder!

CHOUBERT [*still acting*]: . . . nostalgia, shreds and fragments of a universe . . .

MADELEINE [*to* DETECTIVE]: What does that mean?

DETECTIVE [*to* MADELEINE]: He said: fragments of a universe . . .

CHOUBERT [*as before*]: A yawning pit . . .

DETECTIVE [*whispering in* MADELEINE'S *ear*]: A yawning pit . . .

MADELEINE [*to* DETECTIVE]:   He's not normal. He must be ill. He ought to keep his feet on the ground.

DETECTIVE [*to* MADELEINE]:   He can't, he's underground.

MADELEINE [*to* DETECTIVE]:   Oh yes! That's true! [*Admiringly*] You're a wonderful man, so clever at understanding things!

CHOUBERT [*still acting*]:   Resign myself ... resign myself ... The light is dark ... the stars are dim ... I'm suffering from an unknown disease ...

MADELEINE [*to* DETECTIVE]:   What's the name of the actor playing this part?

DETECTIVE: Choubert.

MADELEINE [*to* DETECTIVE]:   Not the composer, I hope!

DETECTIVE [*to* MADELEINE]:   No fear.

MADELEINE [*very loud, to* CHOUBERT]:   Speak up!

CHOUBERT: My face is wet with tears. Where has beauty gone? And goodness? And love? I've lost my memory ...

MADELEINE: This is a fine time! Just when there isn't a prompter!

CHOUBERT [*in a tone of great despair*]:   My toys ... in pieces ... My toys are broken ... The toys I had as a child ...

MADELEINE: So childish!

DETECTIVE [*to* MADELEINE]:   Quite a pertinent remark!

CHOUBERT [*with the same intensity of despair*]:   I am old ... I am old ...

MADELEINE: Doesn't look as old as that. He's exaggerating. He wants us to pity him.

CHOUBERT: In days gone by ... gone by ...

MADELEINE: What's happening now?

DETECTIVE [*to* MADELEINE]:   He's remembering his past, I suppose, dear lady.

MADELEINE: If we all started reminiscing, where would it end ... We'd all have something to say. We take good care not to. We're too shy, too modest.

CHOUBERT: ... In days gone by ... A great wind arose ...

[*He groans loudly.*]

MADELEINE: He's crying ...

DETECTIVE [*to* MADELEINE]:   He's imitating the sound of the wind ... through the forest.

CHOUBERT [*continuing as before*]:   The wind shakes the forests, the lightning rends the thick gloom, and there on the horizon, behind the storm, a gigantic curtain of darkness is heavily lifting ...

MADELEINE: What's that? What's that?

CHOUBERT [*as before*]:   ... and there, appearing in the distance, gleaming through the shadows, still as a dream in the midst of the storm, a magic city ...

MADELEINE [*to* DETECTIVE]:   A what?

DETECTIVE: The city! The city!

MADELEINE: I see.

CHOUBERT [*as before*]:   ... or a magic garden, a bubbling spring and fountains and flowers of fire in the night ...

MADELEINE: And I bet you he thinks he's a poet! A lot of bad parnassian-symbolic-surrealism.

CHOUBERT [*as before*]:   ... a palace of icy flames, glowing statues and incandescent seas, continents blazing in the night, in oceans of snow!

MADELEINE: He's an old ham! It's ridiculous! Unthinkable! He's a liar!

DETECTIVE [*shouting to* CHOUBERT, *half of him becoming the* DETECTIVE *again, though the other half is still an astonished theatre-goer*]:   Can you see his dark shadow outlined against the light? Or is it a shining silhouette outlined against the dark?

CHOUBERT: The fire has lost its brightness, the palace its brilliance, it's getting darker.

DETECTIVE [*to* CHOUBERT]:   At least you can say what you feel! ... What *are* your feelings? Tell us!

MADELEINE [*to* DETECTIVE]:   My dear, we'd far better spend the rest of the evening at a cabaret ...

CHOUBERT [*as before*]:   ... Joy ... and pain ... tearing you ... healing you ... Fullness ... And emptiness ... Hopeless hope. I feel strong, I feel weak, I feel ill, I feel well, but I feel, above all, I feel myself, still, I feel myself ...

MADELEINE [*to* DETECTIVE]:   All he does is contradict himself.

DETECTIVE [*to* CHOUBERT]:   And then? And then? [*To* MADELEINE:] One minute, dear lady, forgive me ...

CHOUBERT [*with a great shout*]:   Is it all going out? It *is* going out. The night's all around me. Only one butterfly of light painfully rising ...

MADELEINE [*to* DETECTIVE]:   My dear man, he's a fraud ...

CHOUBERT: One last spark ...

MADELEINE [*applauding as the curtains of the small stage close*]:   So dull and ordinary. It could have been so much more amusing ... or at least instructive, couldn't it, but I suppose ...

DETECTIVE [*to* CHOUBERT *who is at this moment hidden by the curtains*]:   No, No! You've got to start walking. [*To* MADELEINE:] He's on the wrong road. We must put him back on the right one.

MADELEINE: We'll give him another round.

[*They clap.* CHOUBERT'S *head reappears for an instant between the curtains of the small stage, then disappears again.*]

DETECTIVE: Choubert, Choubert, Choubert. You must realize Mallot's got to be found again. It's a question of life and death. It's your duty. The fate of all mankind depends on you. It's not as difficult as that, you've only got to remember. Remember and then everything will come clear again . . . [*To* MADELEINE:] He'd gone too far down. He's got to come up again . . . A little . . . in our estimation.

MADELEINE [*timidly, to the* DETECTIVE]:   He felt all right, though.

DETECTIVE [*to* CHOUBERT]:   Are you there? Are you there?

[*The small stage has vanished.* CHOUBERT *appears again at another spot.*]

CHOUBERT: I'm turning my memories over.

DETECTIVE: Do it systematically, then.

MADELEINE [*to* CHOUBERT]:   Turn them over systematically. Listen and do what you're told.

CHOUBERT: I'm back on the surface again.

DETECTIVE: That's good, old chap, that's good . . .

CHOUBERT [*to* MADELEINE]:   Do *you* remember?

DETECTIVE [*to* MADELEINE]:   You see, he's getting on better already.

CHOUBERT: Honfleur . . . How blue the sea is . . . No . . . At Mont Saint-Michel . . . No . . . Dieppe . . . No, I've never been there . . . at Cannes . . . not there either.

DETECTIVE: Trouville, Deauville . . .

CHOUBERT: Never been there either.

MADELEINE: He's never been there either.

CHOUBERT: Collioure. Architects once built a temple there on the waving sea.

MADELEINE: He's raving!

DETECTIVE [*to* MADELEINE]:   Stop this silly playing with words!

CHOUBERT: No sign of Montbéliard . . .

DETECTIVE: It's true, Montbéliard, that was his nickname. And you pretended not to know him!

MADELEINE [*to* CHOUBERT]:   You see!

CHOUBERT [*very astonished*]:   Why yes, good Lord, yes . . . It's true . . . it's funny, it's true.

DETECTIVE: Look somewhere else. Come on, now, quick, the towns . . .

CHOUBERT: Paris, Palermo, Pisa, Berlin, New York . . .

DETECTIVE: The mountains and the gorges . . .

MADELEINE: Mountains, well there ought to be plenty of them about . . .

DETECTIVE: Why not in the Andes, in the Andes . . . have you been there?

MADELEINE [*to* DETECTIVE]:   Actually, Monsieur, he hasn't . . .

CHOUBERT: No, but I know enough geography to . . .

DETECTIVE: You mustn't invent. You must find him again. Come on, old chap, just a little effort . . .

CHOUBERT [*making a painful effort*]:   Mallot with a t, Montbéliard with a d, with a t, with a d . . .

[*If the producer so desires, the same character who appeared before can be spotlighted again at the other side of the stage: he still has his number and, in addition, an alpenstock, a rope or a pair of skis. Once again he vanishes after a few moments.*]

CHOUBERT: Swept along by the surface currents, I'm crossing the ocean. Landing in Spain. Making for France. The customs officials are touching their caps. Narbonne, Marsielle, Aix, the watery grave. Arles, Avignon, with its popes, its mules and its palaces. In the distance, Mont Blanc.

MADELEINE [*who is gradually beginning to object rather slyly to* CHOUBERT'S *latest itinerary, to* DETECTIVE]:   The forest's between you.

DETECTIVE: Go on just the same.

CHOUBERT: I'm going through the trees. How fresh it is! Is it evening?

MADELEINE: The forest is dense . . .

DETECTIVE: Don't be afraid.

CHOUBERT: I can hear the bubbling of the springs. Wings are brushing my face. Grass up to my waist. The tracks have finished. Madeleine, give me your hand.

DETECTIVE [*to* MADELEINE]:   Whatever you do, don't give him your hand.

MADELEINE [*to* CHOUBERT]:   Not my hand, he won't let me.

DETECTIVE [*to* CHOUBERT]:   You can find your own way through. Use your eyes! Look above you!

CHOUBERT: The sun's shining between the trees. Blue light. I'm advancing quickly, the branches are moving aside. Twenty feet away the wood-cutters are working and whistling . . .

MADELEINE: They may not be *real* woodcutters . . .

DETECTIVE [*to* MADELEINE]:   Quiet!

CHOUBERT: There's a bright light ahead. I'm coming out of the forest . . . into a pink village.

MADELEINE: My favourite colour . . .

CHOUBERT: Low cottages.

DETECTIVE: Can you see anyone?

CHOUBERT: It's too early. The shutters are closed. The square's empty. A fountain and a statue. I'm running, and the echo of my clogs . . .

MADELEINE [*shrugging her shoulders*]:   His clogs!

DETECTIVE: Keep going. You're nearly there . . . Keep moving.

MADELEINE: Moving, always moving, moving forward.

CHOUBERT: The land is flat, but gently rising. Another stretch and I'm at the foot of the mountain.

DETECTIVE: Up you go.

CHOUBERT: I'm climbing a steep path, have to hang on. I've left the forest behind me. The village is right down below. I'm getting higher. A lake on the right.

DETECTIVE: Go on up.

MADELEINE: He wants you to go on if you can. If you can!

CHOUBERT: It's so steep! Thorns and stones. The lake's behind me. I can see the Mediterranean.

DETECTIVE: Go on up, up.

MADELEINE: Up further, that's what he says.

CHOUBERT: A fox, last of the animals. A blind owl. Not another bird in sight. No more springs . . . No more tracks . . . No more echo. I'm sweeping the horizon.

DETECTIVE: Can you see *him*?

CHOUBERT: It's an empty waste.

DETECTIVE: Higher. Go on up.

MADELEINE: Up further, then, as it can't be helped.

CHOUBERT: I'm clinging to the stones, I'm slipping and clutching at thorns, crawling on all fours . . . Oh, the altitude's too much for me . . . Why do I always have to climb mountains . . . Why am I always the one who's made to do the impossible . . .

MADELEINE [*to* DETECTIVE]:   The impossible . . . He said it himself. [*To* CHOUBERT:] You ought to be ashamed.

CHOUBERT: I'm thirsty, I'm hot, I'm sweating.

DETECTIVE: Don't stop now to wipe your brow. You can do that later. Later. Go on up.

CHOUBERT: . . . So tired . . .

MADELEINE: Already! [*To* DETECTIVE:] Believe me, Monsieur Chief Inspector, it doesn't surprise me. He's quite incapable.

DETECTIVE [*to* CHOUBERT]:   Lazy devil!

MADELEINE [*to* DETECTIVE]:   He's always been lazy. Never gets anywhere.

CHOUBERT: Not a scrap of shade. The sun's enormous. A furnace. I'm stifling. Roasting.

DETECTIVE: You can't be far away now, you see, you're getting warm.

MADELEINE [*unheard by the* DETECTIVE]:   I could send someone else in your place . . .

CHOUBERT: Another mountain ahead of me. A wall without a crack. I'm out of breath.

DETECTIVE: Higher, higher.

MADELEINE [*very fast, now to the* DETECTIVE, *now to* CHOUBERT]:
Higher. He's out of breath. Higher. He mustn't rise too high above us. You'd better come down. Up higher. Down lower. Up higher.

DETECTIVE: Go on, higher.

MADELEINE: Up. Down.

CHOUBERT: My hands are bleeding.

MADELEINE [*to* CHOUBERT]:   Up. Down.

DETECTIVE: Hang on. Climb.

CHOUBERT [*quite still, continuing his ascent*]:   It's hard to be alone in the world! If only I'd had a son!

MADELEINE: I'd rather have had a girl. Boys are so ungrateful!

DETECTIVE [*tapping his foot*]: Kindly keep those observations for a different occasion. [*To* CHOUBERT:] Go on up, don't waste time.

MADELEINE: Up. Down.

CHOUBERT: After all, I'm only a man.

DETECTIVE: You must be a man to the bitter end.

MADELEINE [*to* CHOUBERT]: Be a man to the bitter end.

CHOUBERT: No-o-o! . . . No! . . . I can't lift my knees again. I can't bear it!

DETECTIVE: Come on now, one last effort.

MADELEINE: One last effort. Do try. No, don't. Do try.

CHOUBERT: I've done it. I've done it. I'm here. At the top! . . . You can see right through the sky, but there's no sign of Montbéliard.[5]

MADELEINE [*to* DETECTIVE]: He's going to escape us, Monsieur Chief Inspector.

DETECTIVE [*not hearing* MADELEINE, *to* CHOUBERT]: Look for him, look.

MADELEINE [*to* CHOUBERT]: Look, stop looking, look, stop looking. [*To* DETECTIVE:] He's going to escape you.

CHOUBERT: There's no more . . . No more . . . No more . . .

MADELEINE: No more what?

CHOUBERT: No more towns, or woods, or valleys, or sea, or sky. I'm alone.

MADELEINE: If you were down here, there'd be two of us.

DETECTIVE: What's he talking about? What does he mean? And what about Mallot and Montbéliard!

CHOUBERT: I can run without walking.

MADELEINE: He's going to take off . . . Choubert! Do you hear . . .

CHOUBERT: I'm alone. I've lost my footing. I'm not dizzy . . . I'm not afraid to die any more.

DETECTIVE: I couldn't care less about that.

MADELEINE: Think about us. It's not good to be alone. You can't leave us . . . Have pity, pity! [*She is a beggarwoman.*] I've no bread for my children. I've got four children. My husband's in prison. I'm just out of hospital. I'm sure you've a kind heart, Sir . . . [*To* DETECTIVE]: What I've had to put up with, with him! . . . You understand me now, Monsieur Chief Inspector?

DETECTIVE [*to* CHOUBERT]: Remember the solidarity of the human race. [*Aside*] I've driven him too far. Now he's getting away from us. [*Shouting*] Choubert, Choubert, Choubert . . . My dear old chap, we've both got on the wrong track.

MADELEINE [*to* DETECTIVE]: I told you so.

DETECTIVE [*slapping* MADELEINE'S *face*]: I didn't ask your opinion.

MADELEINE [*to* DETECTIVE]: I'm sorry, Monsieur Chief Inspector.

DETECTIVE [*to* CHOUBERT]: It's your duty to look for Mallot, your duty to

---

5. In Jacques Mauclair's production CHOUBERT'S ascent was made in the following manner: he first crawled under the table, climbed on to it and then stood on a chair that he had placed on the table. He started walking when he said: "I'm going through the trees." . . .

look for Mallot, you're not betraying your friends, Mallot, Montbéliard, Mallot, Montbéliard! Why don't you look, look! Can't you see you're not looking! What can you see? . . . Look in front of you. Answer me, do you hear? Answer . . .

MADELEINE: Why don't you answer?

[*To persuade* CHOUBERT *to come down,* MADELEINE *and the* DETECTIVE *draw a picture of the advantages of everyday life in society.* MADELEINE *and the* DETECTIVE *become more and more grotesque, until they are almost clowning.*]

CHOUBERT: It's a morning in June. The air I breathe is lighter than air. *I* am lighter than air. The sun's melting into light that's mightier than the sun. I can float through solid objects. All forms have disappeared. I'm going up . . . and up . . . shimmering light . . . and up . . .

MADELEINE: He's getting away! . . . I told you so, Monsieur Chief Inspector, I told you he would . . . I won't have it, I won't have it. [*Speaking in* CHOUBERT'S *direction:*] You might at least take me with you.

DETECTIVE [*to* CHOUBERT]: Hey! . . . You wouldn't do that to me . . . Eh? Would you? . . . Bastard . . .

CHOUBERT [*without mime, talking to himself*]: Can I . . . go through . . . over the top . . . can I . . . jump . . . one step . . . lightly . . . one . . .

DETECTIVE [*military march*]: One, two, One, two . . . I taught you your arms drill, you were a quartermaster's clerk . . . Don't pretend you can't hear me, you're not the type to desert . . . and don't be cheeky to your sergeant-major! . . . Discipline! [*A bugle sounds.*] . . . The country that bore you has need of you.

MADELEINE [*to* CHOUBERT]: You're all I've got to live for.

DETECTIVE [*to* CHOUBERT]: You've got your life, your career ahead of you! You'll be rich, happy and stupid, a chargé d'affaires! Here's your appointment! [*He holds out a paper that* CHOUBERT *ignores; this is really the time for* MADELEINE *and the* DETECTIVE *to give* their *show. To* MADELEINE:] There's still hope, all the time we can keep him from flying away . . .

MADELEINE [*to the still motionless* CHOUBERT]: Here's gold for you, and fruit . . .

DETECTIVE: The heads of your enemies will be served to you on a plate.

MADELEINE: You can take what revenge you like, be as sadistic as you want!

DETECTIVE: I'll make you archbishop.

MADELEINE: Pope!

DETECTIVE: If you like. [*To* MADELEINE:] Perhaps we wouldn't be able to . . . [*To* CHOUBERT:] If you like, you can start life afresh, learn to walk again . . . fulfill your ambitions.

CHOUBERT [*neither seeing nor hearing the others*]: I'm gliding over a rocky surface, ever so high. I can fly!

[*The* DETECTIVE *and* MADELEINE *hold on to* CHOUBERT.]

MADELEINE: Quick! . . . He needs some more ballast . . .

DETECTIVE [*to* MADELEINE]:   Mind your own business . . .

MADELEINE [*to* DETECTIVE]:   You're somewhat to blame for this, too, Monsieur Chief Inspector . . .

DETECTIVE [*to* MADELEINE]:   No, it's you. I wasn't properly backed up. You didn't understand. I was given a partner who's nothing but a clumsy little fool . . .

[MADELEINE *weeps.*]

DETECTIVE [*to* MADELEINE]:   A little fool! . . . Yes, a fool . . . fool . . . fool . . . [*Turning abruptly* to CHOUBERT:] It's lovely in our valleys in the spring, the winter's mild and it never rains in summer . . .

MADELEINE [*to* DETECTIVE, *snivelling*]:   I did my best, Monsieur Chief Inspector. I did all I could.

DETECTIVE [*to* MADELEINE]:   Silly little fool!

MADELEINE: You're quite right, Monsieur Chief Inspector.

DETECTIVE [*to* CHOUBERT *in a desperate voice*]:   And what of the huge reward for the man who finds Mallot? Even if you lose your honour, you realize you'll still have the money, the uniform and the honours that go with them! . . . What more do you want!

CHOUBERT: I can fly.

MADELEINE AND DETECTIVE [*clinging onto* CHOUBERT]:   No! No! No! Don't do that!

CHOUBERT: I'm bathing in the light. [*Total darkness on the stage.*] The light is seeping through me. I'm so surprised to be, surprised to be, surprised to be . . .

TRIUMPHANT VOICE OF DETECTIVE;   He'll never pass the surprise barrier.

VOICE OF MADELEINE: Be careful, Choubert . . . remember how giddy you get.

VOICE OF CHOUBERT: I am light! I'm flying!

VOICE OF MADELEINE: Well, why don't you fall and put yourself out!

VOICE OF DETECTIVE: That's the stuff, Madeleine!

VOICE OF CHOUBERT [*suddenly in distress*]:   Oh! . . . I don't dare . . . I feel ill . . . I'm going to jump! . . .

[CHOUBERT *is heard groaning. The stage is lit again.* CHOUBERT *is sprawling in a large waste-paper basket, with* MADELEINE *and the* DETECTIVE *standing over him. A new character, a* LADY, *who takes no notice at all of what is going on, is sitting on the left, near the wall, on a chair.*]

DETECTIVE [*to* CHOUBERT]:   Well, my lad?

CHOUBERT: Where am I?

DETECTIVE: Have a look round, fathead!

CHOUBERT: What! Were you still here, Monsieur Chief Inspector? How did you manage to find a way into my memories?

DETECTIVE: I followed you . . . every step. Luckily!

MADELEINE: Oh yes! It's lucky you did!

DETECTIVE [*to* CHOUBERT]: Right! On your feet! [*He pulls him up by his ears.*] If I'd not been here . . . If I'd not pulled you back . . . You're so light-headed you're practically disembodied, you've no memory, you forget everything, forget yourself, forget your duty. That's your great fault. You're either too heavy or too light.

MADELEINE: I think it's rather that he's too heavy.

DETECTIVE [*to* MADELEINE]: I don't like being contradicted! [*to* CHOUBERT:] I'll cure you all right . . . That's what I'm here for.

CHOUBERT: And *I* thought I'd reached the top. Higher even.

[CHOUBERT's *behaviour gets more and more babyish.*]

DETECTIVE: That's not what you were asked to do!

CHOUBERT: Oh . . . I took the wrong road . . . I'm cold . . . My feet are soaking . . . I've shivers down my spine. Have you got a nice dry sweater?

MADELEINE: Ah! He's got shivers down his spine, has he! . . .

DETECTIVE [*to* MADELEINE]: It's only because he wants to get his own back.

CHOUBERT [*like a child excusing himself*]: It's not my fault . . . I looked everywhere. I couldn't find him . . . It's not my fault. . . . You were watching me, you saw . . . I wasn't cheating.

MADELEINE [*to* DETECTIVE]: He's weak in the head. How could I ever have married such a man! He made far more impression when he was younger! [*To* CHOUBERT:] Do you hear? [*To* DETECTIVE;] He's an old fox, Monsieur Chief Inspector, I told you he was, and a sly one too! . . . But he's much too feeble . . . He wants fattening up, put some stuffing into him . . .

DETECTIVE [*to* CHOUBERT]: You're weak in the head! How could she ever have married such a man! You made far more impression when you were younger! Do you hear? You're an old fox, I told you you were, and a sly one too! . . . But you're much too feeble, and you need some stuffing . . .

CHOUBERT [*to* DETECTIVE]: Madeleine just said exactly the same. Monsieur Chief Inspector, you're a copy-cat!

MADELEINE [*to* CHOUBERT]: You ought to be ashamed of yourself, talking to Monsieur Chief Inspector like that!

DETECTIVE [*getting into a terrible rage*]: I'll teach you to be rude, you poor wretch, you . . . nonentity!

MADELEINE [*to* DETECTIVE, *who is not listening*]: And yet I *am* a good cook, Monsieur. And *he's* got a good appetite! . . .

DETECTIVE [*to* MADELEINE]: You can't teach me anything about medicine, Madame, I know my job. If your son's not falling on his nose, he's always wandering off on his own. He's just not strong enough! We've really got to fatten him up . . .

MADELEINE [*to* CHOUBERT]: You hear what the Doctor says? Think yourself lucky you only fell on your bottom!

DETECTIVE [*getting more and more furious*]:   We're no further forward than we were just now! We keep going from top to bottom, from bottom to top, from top to bottom, up and down, round and round, it's a vicious circle!

MADELEINE [*to* DETECTIVE]:   I'm afraid he's stuffed with vice! [*In an aggrieved voice, to the* LADY, *who has just come in and remains silent and impassive:*] Isn't he, Madame? [*To* CHOUBERT:] And now I suppose you're going to have the cheek to tell Monsieur Chief Inspector you're not trying to get your own back.

DETECTIVE: I told you before: he's heavy when he ought to be light, too light when he ought to be heavy, he's unbalanced, he's got no grip on reality!

MADELEINE [*to* CHOUBERT]:   You've no sense of reality.

CHOUBERT [*sniveling*]:   He's had other names too: Marius, Marin, Lougastec, Perpignan, Machecroche ... His last name was Machecroche! ...

DETECTIVE: You see, you liar, you're right up to date! But it's *him* we want, the rat. When you get your strength back you'll go and find him. You'll have to learn to go straight to the point. [*To the* LADY:] Won't he, Madame? [*The* LADY *does not reply; anyway, she is not expected to.*] I'll teach you how to avoid wasting time on the way.

MADELEINE [*to* CHOUBERT]:   Meanwhile, he's well away, old Machecroche ... He'll be first, he doesn't waste *his* time, *he's* not lazy.

DETECTIVE [*to* CHOUBERT]:   *I'll* give you strength. I'll teach you to do as you're told.

MADELEINE [*to* CHOUBERT]:   You must always do as you're told.

[*The* DETECTIVE *sits down again and rocks his chair.*]

MADELEINE [*to the* LADY]:   Mustn't he, Madame?

DETECTIVE [*shouting, very loud to* MADELEINE]:   Are you bringing me coffee, or aren't you?

MADELEINE: Of course I am, Monsieur Chief Inspector! [*She goes towards the kitchen.*]

DETECTIVE [*to* CHOUBERT]:   Now it's between us two!

[*At the same moment* MADELEINE *goes out; and at exactly the same time* NICOLAS *comes in through the glass door at the back:* NICOLAS *is tall, with a great black beard, his eyes bleary with sleep, his hair is tousled and his clothes well-worn; he looks like someone who has been asleep in his clothes and has just woken up.*]

NICOLAS [*coming in*]:   Hallo!

CHOUBERT [*in a voice that expresses neither hope, nor fear, nor surprise, but is simply a flat statement*]:   It's you, Nicolas! You've finished your poem!

[*The* DETECTIVE, *on the other hand, seems very put out by the arrival of this new character; he gives a jump, looks at* NICOLAS *anxiously with rounded eyes, raises himself from his chair and glances at the way out, as if he had a vague idea of flight.*]

CHOUBERT [*to* DETECTIVE]:   It's Nicolas d'Eu.

DETECTIVE [*looking rather wild*]: The Tsar of Russia?

CHOUBERT [*to* DETECTIVE]:   Oh no, Monsieur, D'Eu is his surname: d apostrophe, e, u. [*To the* LADY *who never replies:*] Isn't it, Madame?

NICOLAS [*with much gesticulation*]:   Carry on, carry on, don't let me interrupt you! Don't worry about me!

[*He goes and sits at one side, on the red sofa.* MADELEINE *comes in with a cup of coffee; she seems no longer quite sure who is present. She lays the cup down on the sideboard and goes out again. She repeats this manoeuvre several times, one after the other, without stopping, getting faster and faster and piling up the cups until they cover the whole sideboard. Pleased with* NICOLAS'S *attitude, the* DETECTIVE *utters a sigh of relief and starts smiling again as he calmly plays at opening and closing his briefcase during the next two short remarks.*]

CHOUBERT [*to* NICOLAS]:   Are you pleased with your poem?

NICOLAS [*to* CHOUBERT]:   I slept. It's more restful. [*To the imperturbable* LADY:] Isn't it, Madame?

[*The* DETECTIVE *fixes* CHOUBERT *with a stare, crumples a sheet of paper he has taken from his briefcase and throws it on the floor.* CHOUBERT *makes a movement to pick it up.*]

DETECTIVE [*coldly*]:   Doesn't matter. Don't pick it up. It's all right where it is. [*Their faces close together, he peers at* CHOUBERT:] I'll give you back your strength. You can't find Mallot, because you've gaps in your memory. We're going to plug those gaps!

NICOLAS [*slight cough*]:   Sorry!

DETECTIVE[*winks at* NICOLAS, *as if they were in league together, then says with servility*]:   Don't mention it. [*Humbly, still to* NICOLAS:] You're a poet, Monsieur? [*To the impassive* LADY:] He's a poet! [*Then, taking an enormous crust of bread from his briefcase, he offers it to* CHOUBERT:] Eat!

CHOUBERT: I've just had my dinner, Monsieur Chief Inspector, I'm not hungry, I don't eat very much in the evening . . .

DETECTIVE: Eat!

CHOUBERT: I don't feel like it. Really I don't.

DETECTIVE: I'm ordering you to eat, to build up your strength, to plug the gaps in your memory!

CHOUBERT [*plaintively*]:   Oh well, if you're going to make me . . .

[*Groaning and with a look of disgust he slowly brings the food to his lips*]

DETECTIVE: Faster, come on, faster, we've lost enough time like this already!

[CHOUBERT *bites, with great difficulty, into the wrinkled old crust.*]

CHOUBERT: It's the bark of a tree, an oak probably. [*To the impassive* LADY:] Isn't it, Madame?

NICOLAS [*without leaving his place, to the* DETECTIVE]:   What's your attitude, Monsieur Chief Inspector, to renunciation and detachment?

DETECTIVE [*to* NICOLAS]:   One moment . . . So sorry. [*To* CHOUBERT:] It's nice, it's very good for you. [*To* NICOLAS:] My duty, you know, my dear Sir, is simply to apply the system.

CHOUBERT: It's very tough!

DETECTIVE [*to* CHOUBERT]:   Come on, no nonsense, don't pull a face, quick, chew! NICOLAS [*to* DETECTIVE]:   You're not just a civil servant, you're also a thinking being! . . .Like the reed . . . You're an individual . . .

DETECTIVE: I am just a soldier, Monsieur . . .

NICOLAS [*without irony*]:   I congratulate you.

CHOUBERT [*groaning*]:   It's very tough!

DETECTIVE [*to* CHOUBERT]:   Chew!

[CHOUBERT *calls to* MADELEINE, *as she rushes in and out setting cups down on the sideboard.*]

CHOUBERT [*like a child*]:   Madeleine . . . Madelei-ei-ne . . .

[MADELEINE *goes on rushing in and out, in and out, without taking any notice.*]

DETECTIVE [*to* CHOUBERT]:   Leave her alone! [*Conducting the chewing operation by gesture from where he is.*] Can't you move your jaws? Get those jaws working properly!

CHOUBERT [*weeping*]:   I'm sorry, Monsieur Chief Inspector, I'm sorry. *Please* forgive me! . . . [*He chews.*]

DETECTIVE: Tears don't have any effect on me.

CHOUBERT [*continuously chewing*]:   I've broken my tooth, it's bleeding!

DETECTIVE: Faster, come on, hurry up, chew, chew, swallow!

NICOLAS: I've thought a great deal about the chances of reforming the theatre. Can there be anything new in the theatre? What do you think Monsieur Chief Inspector?

DETECTIVE [*to* CHOUBERT]:   Quick, come on! [*To* NICOLAS:] I don't understand your question.

CHOUBERT: Oouch!

DETECTIVE [*to* CHOUBERT]:   Chew!

[MADELEINE'S *entries and exits are getting faster and faster.*]

NICOLAS [*to* DETECTIVE]:   The theatre of my dreams would be irrationalist.

DETECTIVE [*to* NICOLAS, *while still keeping an eye on* CHOUBERT   Not Aristotelian, you mean?

NICOLAS: Precisely. [*To the impassive* LADY:] What do you say, Madame?

CHOUBERT: There's no skin left on my palate, and my tongue's all lacerated! . . .

NICOLAS: The contemporary theatre is, indeed, still a prisoner of out-

moded forms, it's never got beyond the psychology of a Paul Bourget ...
DETECTIVE: You've said it! A Paul Bourget! [*To* CHOUBERT:] Swallow!
NICOLAS: You see, my dear fellow, the contemporary theatre doesn't reflect the cultural tone of our period, it's not in harmony with the general drift of the other manifestations of the modern spirit ...
DETECTIVE [*to* CHOUBERT]: Chew! Swallow! ...
NICOLAS: It is, however, essential not to lose sight of the new logic, the contributions made by a new kind of psychology ... a psychology based on antagonism ...
DETECTIVE [*to* NICOLAS]: Psychology, yes, Monsieur!
CHOUBERT [*his mouth full*]: New ... Psycho ... Lo ... gy ...
DETECTIVE [*to* CHOUBERT]: Eat, you! You can talk when you've finished! [*To* NICOLAS:] I'm listening. Theatre that's surrealizing?
NICOLAS: In so far as surrealism is oneirical ...
DETECTIVE [*to* NICOLAS]: Oneirical? [*To* CHOUBERT:] Chew, swallow!
NICOLAS: Inspiring me ... [*To the impassive* LADY:] Right, Madame? [*To* CHOUBERT *again:*] Inspiring me with a different logic and a different psychology, I should introduce contradiction where there is no contradiction, and no contradiction where there is what common-sense usually calls contradiction ... We'll get rid of the principle of identity and unity of character and let movement and dynamic psychology take its place ... We are not ourselves ... Personality doesn't exist. Within us there are only forces that are either contradictory or not contradictory ... By the way, you'd be interested to read LOGIC AND CONTRADICTION, that excellent book by Lupasco ...
CHOUBERT [*still weeping*]: Ouch! Ouch! [*Still chewing and moaning, to* NICOLAS:] You'd get rid of ... unity ... like that ...
DETECTIVE [*to* CHOUBERT]: It's none of your business ... *Eat!* ...
NICOLAS: The characters lose their form in the formlessness of becoming. Each character is not so much himself as another. [*To the impassive* LADY:] Isn't he, Madame?
DETECTIVE [*to* NICOLAS]: So, he'd be more likely to be ... [To CHOUBERT:] Eat ... [*To* NICOLAS:] ... Another than himself?
NICOLAS: That's obvious. As for plot and motivation, let's not mention them. We ought to ignore them completely, at least in their old form, which was too clumsy, too obvious ... too phoney, like anything that's too obvious ... No more drama, no more tragedy: the tragic's turning comic, the comic is tragic, and life's getting more cheerful ... more cheerful ...
DETECTIVE [*to* CHOUBERT]: Swallow! Eat ... [*To* NICOLAS:] I can't say I entirely agree with you ... though I've a high appreciation for your brilliant ideas ... [*To* CHOUBERT:] Eat! Swallow! Chew! [*To* NICOLAS:] As for me I remain Aristotelically logical, true to myself, faithful to my duty and full of respect for my bosses ... I don't believe in the absurd, everything hangs together, everything can be comprehended in time ... [*To* CHOU-

BERT:] Swallow! [*To* NICOLAS:] . . . thanks to the achievements of human thought and science.

NICOLAS [*to the* LADY]:   What do you think, Madame?

DETECTIVE: I keep moving forward, Monsieur, one step at a time, tracking down the extraordinary . . . I want to find Mallot with a t at the end. [*To* CHOUBERT:] Quick, quick, another piece, come on, chew, swallow!

[MADELEINE'S *entries and exits with the cups get still faster.*]

NICOLAS: You don't agree with me. No hard feelings.

DETECTIVE [*to* CHOUBERT]:   Quick, swallow!

NICOLAS: I notice, however, to your credit, that your knowledge of the question is right up-to-date.

CHOUBERT: Madeleine! Madelei-eine!

[*His mouth full and choking, he calls out desperately.*]

DETECTIVE [*to* NICOLAS]:   Yes, it's one of my special objects of study. I'm deeply interested . . . But it tires me to think too much about it . . .

[CHOUBERT *bites into the bark again and takes a large piece into his mouth.*]

CHOUBERT: Ouch!

DETECTIVE: Swallow!

CHOUBERT [*his mouth full*]:   I'm trying . . . I'm doing . . . my . . . best . . . Can't. . . . do . . . more . . .

NICOLAS [*to the* DETECTIVE, *who is engrossed in his efforts to get* CHOUB-ERT *to eat*]:   Have you also thought about the practical problems of production in this new theatre?

DETECTIVE [*to* CHOUBERT]:   Yes, you can! You don't want to! Everybody can! You must *want* to, you can do it all right! [*To* NICOLAS:] I'm sorry, Monsieur, I can't talk about that just now, it's not allowed, I'm on duty!

CHOUBERT: Let me swallow it in little pieces!

DETECTIVE: All right, but faster, faster, faster! [*To* NICOLAS:] We'll discuss it later!

CHOUBERT [*his mouth full—he has the mental age of a baby of two; he is sobbing*]:   Ma-ma-ma-de-lei-lei-ne!!!

DETECTIVE: No nonsense, now! Be quiet! Swallow! [*To* NICOLAS, *who is no longer listening as he is lost in thought:*] He's suffering from anorexia. [*To* CHOUBERT:] Swallow!

CHOUBERT [*passing his hand across his brow to wipe off the sweat; his stomach is heaving*]:   Ma-a-de-leine!

DETECTIVE [*in a yapping voice*]:   Watch out, whatever you do, don't be sick, it wouldn't get you anywhere, I'd make you swallow it again!

CHOUBERT [*putting his hand over his ears*]:   You're splitting my eardrums, Monsieur Inspector . . .

DETECTIVE [*still shouting*]:   . . . Chief!

CHOUBERT [*his mouth full, hands over his ears*]:   . . . *Chief* Inspector!!

DETECTIVE: Now listen to me carefully, Choubert, listen, leave your ears alone, don't stop them up, or I'll stop them for you, with a clip over the earhole . . .

[*He pulls his hands away by force.*]

NICOLAS [*who has shown signs, during the last few remarks, of great interest in what is going on*]:   . . . But . . . but . . . what are you doing, what do you think you're doing?

DETECTIVE [*to* CHOUBERT]:   Swallow! Chew! Swallow! Chew! Swallow! Chew! Swallow! Chew! Swallow! Chew! Swallow!

CHOUBERT [*his mouth full, utters incomprehensible sounds*]:   Heu . . . glu . . . you . . . kno . . . clem . . . neeg . . . erls . . .

DETECTIVE [*to* CHOUBERT]:   What did you say?

CHOUBERT [*spitting into his hand what he has in his mouth*]:   I wonder if you know? How lovely the columns of the temples are, and the knees of the young girls!

NICHOLAS [*from his seat, to the* DETECTIVE, *who is still busy with his job and not listening*]:   But what are you doing to that child?

DETECTIVE [*to* CHOUBERT]:   All this fuss, instead of swallowing your food! Mustn't talk at table! Snotty-nosed rascal! Ought to be ashamed! Children should be seen and not heard! Eat it all up! Quickly!

CHOUBERT: Yes, Monsieur Chief Inspector . . . [*He puts back into his mouth what he had spat into his hand; then with his mouth full and his eyes fixed on the* DETECTIVE'S:] . . . Ah . . . ee . . . ay . . .!

DETECTIVE: And now this! . . . [*He stuffs another piece of bread in his mouth.*] Chew! . . . Swallow! . . .

CHOUBERT [*making fruitless and painful efforts to chew and swallow*]:   . . . oo . . . ire . . .

DETECTIVE: What?

NICOLAS [*to* DETECTIVE]:   He says it's wood, and iron. It'll never go down. Can't you see? [*To the impassive* LADY:] Will it, Madame?

DETECTIVE [*to* CHOUBERT]:   It's only because he wants his own back!

MADELEINE [*coming in for the last time to put some more cups on the table, cups that no one touches or pays any attention to*]:   Here's the coffee! Only it's tea!

NICOLAS [*to* DETECTIVE]:   The poor child's having a good try, anyway! Wood and iron, it's all jammed in his throat!

MADELEINE [*to* NICOLAS]:   Leave him alone! He can look after himself, if he wants to!

[CHOUBERT *tries to shout and can't; he is choking.*]

DETECTIVE [*to* CHOUBERT]:   Faster, Faster, I tell you, swallow it all at once!

[*Out of patience, the* DETECTIVE *goes to* CHOUBERT, *opens his mouth and prepares to thrust his fist down his throat; he has previously rolled up his sleeve.* NICOLAS *suddenly gets up and approaches the* DETECTIVE, *silently and threateningly, planting himself opposite. The* DETECTIVE *lets go of*

CHOUBERT'S *head and leaves him sitting down, gazing at the scene, still silent, still chewing; the* DETECTIVE *is dumbfounded by* NICOLAS'S *intervention, and in a voice that is suddenly quite different, quite shaky, he says to* NICOLAS, *almost blubbering:*]

DETECTIVE: Why, Monsieur Nicolas d'Eu, I'm only doing my duty! I didn't come here just to pester him! I've really got to find out where he's hiding, Mallot with a t at the end. There's no other way I can do it. I've no choice. As for your friend—and I hope one day he'll be mine ... [*He points to the seated* CHOUBERT, *who is looking at them, purple in the face and chewing steadily:*] ... I respect him sincerely I do! You, too, my dear Monsieur Nicolas d'Eu. I've often heard about you and your books ...

MADELEINE [*to* NICOLAS]: Monsieur respects you, Nicolas.

NICOLAS [*to* DETECTIVE]: You're lying!

DETECTIVE AND MADELEINE: Oh!!

NICOLAS [*to* DETECTIVE]: The truth is I'm *not* a writer, and I'm proud of it!

DETECTIVE [*crushed*]: Oh yes, Monsieur, you *do* write! [*In increasing terror:*] Everyone ought to write.

NICOLAS: No point. We've got Ionesco and Ionesco, that's enough!

DETECTIVE: But, Monsieur, there are always things to be said ... [*He is trembling with fright; to the* LADY:] Aren't there, Madame?

LADY: No! No! Not Madame; Mademoiselle! ...

MADELEINE [*to* NICOLAS]: Monsieur the Chief Inspector's right. There are always things to be said. Now the modern world's in a state of decay, you can always report on the process!

NICOLAS [*screaming*]: I don't give a damn! ...

DETECTIVE [*shaking more and more violently*]: But you should, Monsieur!

NICOLAS [*laughing contemptuously in the* DETECTIVE'S *face*]: I don't give a damn what you think of me! [*He grips the* DETECTIVE *by his lapels.*] Don't you realize you're mad?

[CHOUBERT *is heroically struggling to chew and swallow. He is contemplating the scene, terrified too. He looks rather guilty. His mouth is too full for him to be able to intervene.*]

MADELEINE: All right, that's enough now, come on ...

DETECTIVE [*reaching the limit of indignation and stupefaction, he sits down again, then gets up, knocking his chair over so that it smashes*]: Me? Me mad! ...

MADELEINE: Drink the coffee, then!

CHOUBERT [*shouting*]: I feel all right again! I've swallowed it all! Swallowed it all!

[*During the ensuing conversation, no attention is paid to* CHOUBERT.]

NICOLAS [*to* DETECTIVE]: Yes, you, I mean you! ...

DETECTIVE [*bursting into tears*]: Oh! ... It's too much ... [*Weeping, to*

MADELEINE, *who is arranging the cups on the table:*] Thank you, Madeleine, for the coffee? [*Fresh outbreak of tears.*] It's wicked, it's not fair! . . .

CHOUBERT: I'm all right again, I've swallowed it all! Swallowed it all!

[*He is on his feet, hopping and jumping happily round the stage.*]

DETECTIVE [*to* NICOLAS, *defending himself*]: I didn't want to upset your friend! . . . I swear I didn't! . . . It's *he* who forced *me* to come into this flat . . . *I* didn't want to, I was in a hurry . . . They insisted, both of them . . .

MADELEINE [*to* NICOLAS]: It's the truth!

CHOUBERT [*continuing as before*]: I'm all right now. I swallowed it all, I can go and play!

NICOLAS [*cruelly and coldly to the* DETECTIVE]: Don't deceive yourself. That's not the reason I've got it in for you!

[*This is said in such a tone that* CHOUBERT *stops his frolicking. All movement stops; the characters have their eyes fixed on* NICOLAS, *who is in control of the situation.*]

DETECTIVE [*articulating with difficulty*]: But why, then, in Heaven's name? I've done you no harm!

CHOUBERT: Nicolas, I should never have thought you could hate like this.

MADELEINE [*full of pity for the* DETECTIVE]: Poor boy, your big eyes are scorched by all the terror of the earth . . . How white you look . . . now your nice face has lost its composure . . . Poor boy, poor boy! . . .

DETECTIVE [*terror-stricken*]: Did I thank you, Madeleine, for the coffee? [*To* NICOLAS:] I'm only a pawn, Monsieur, a soldier tied to his orders, I'm respectable, honest, a decent chap! . . . And then . . . I'm only twenty, Monsieur! . . .

NICOLAS [*implacably*]: I don't care, I'm forty-five!

CHOUBERT [*counting on his fingers*]: More than twice as old . . .

[NICOLAS *takes out a huge knife.*]

MADELEINE: Nicolas, think before you act! . . .

DETECTIVE: Oh God, oh God . . . [*His teeth are chattering.*]

CHOUBERT: He's shivering, he must be cold!

DETECTIVE: Yes, I am cold . . . Ah!

[*He cries out, for* NICOLAS *suddenly brandishes his knife as he moves around him in a circle.*]

MADELEINE: But the radiators are wonderfully hot . . . Nicolas, behave! . . .

[*The* DETECTIVE, *on the point of collapse and in a paroxysm of fear, is making a strange noise.*]

CHOUBERT [*loudly*]: There's a nasty smell . . . [*To the* DETECTIVE:] It's not nice to do it in your trousers!

MADELEINE [*to* CHOUBERT]: But don't you realize what's happening? Put yourself in his place! [*She looks at* NICOLAS.] What a look in his eyes! He's not joking! [NICOLAS *raises his knife.*]

DETECTIVE: Help!

MADELEINE [*neither her so* CHOUBERT *moving a step*]: Nicolas, you've gone all red. Be careful or you'll have an apoplectic fit! Think, Nicolas, you could have been his father! [NICOLAS *strikes once with his knife and the* DETECTIVE *wheels round and round.*]

CHOUBERT: Too late to stop him . . .

DETECTIVE [*spinning round*]: Long live the white race!

[NICOLAS, *his mouth twisted fiercely, strikes a second time.*]

DETECTIVE [*still spinning round*]: I should like . . . a posthumous decoration.

MADELEINE [*to* DETECTIVE]: You shall have it, my pet. I'll phone the President . . .

[NICOLAS *strikes for the third time.*]

MADELEINE [*with a start*]: Stop it, stop it now! . . .

CHOUBERT [*reprovingly*]: Nicolas, really!

DETECTIVE [*spinning round for the last time, while* NICOLAS *stands still, his knife in his hand*]: I am . . . a victim . . . of duty! . . . [*Then he crumples into a bloody heap.*]

MADELEINE [*rushing to the* DETECTIVE'S *body to see if he is dead*]: Right through the heart, poor boy! [*To* CHOUBERT *and* NICOLAS:] Help me, then! [NICOLAS *throws aside his bloody knife, then all three, watched by the inscrutable* LADY, *lift the body onto the divan.*] It's such a pity it had to happen in our flat! [*The body is laid on the divan.* MADELEINE *raises the head and slips a pillow under it.*] That's the way! Poor lad . . . [*To* NICOLAS:] We're going to miss him now, this young man you killed . . . Oh, you and your crazy hatred of the police . . . What are we going to do? Who's going to help us find Mallot now? Who? Who?

NICOLAS: Perhaps I was too hasty . . .

MADELEINE: Now you're admitting it; you're all the same . . .

CHOUBERT: Yes, we're all the same . . .

MADELEINE: You act without thinking, and then you're sorry! . . . We've got to find Mallot! His sacrifice [*Indicating the* DETECTIVE:] shall not have been in vain! Poor victim of duty!

NICOLAS: I'll find Mallot for you.

MADELEINE: Well done, Nicolas!

NICOLAS [*to the* DETECTIVE'S *body*]: No, your sacrifice won't have been in vain. [*To* CHOUBERT:] You're going to help me.

CHOUBERT: Oh no, I'm not! I'm not starting that all over again!

MADELEINE [*to* CHOUBERT]: Haven't you any heart? Surely you can do something for him! [*She indicates the* DETECTIVE.]

CHOUBERT [*tapping his foot like a sulky child and snivelling*]: No! I won't! No! I wo-o-on't!

MADELEINE: I don't like husbands who won't do as they're told! What do you mean by it? You ought to be ashamed!

[CHOUBERT *is still weeping, but is beginning to look resigned.*]
NICOLAS: [*sits down in the* DETECTIVE'S *place and holds out to* CHOUBERT *a piece of bread*] Come on, eat, eat, to plug the gaps in your memory!
CHOUBERT: I'm not hungry!
MADELEINE: Haven't you any heart? Do as Nicolas says!
CHOUBERT [*takes the bread and bites into it*]:   It hu-u-urts!
NICOLAS [*in the* DETECTIVE'S *voice*]:   No nonsense! Swallow! Chew! Swallow! Chew!
CHOUBERT [*his mouth full*]:   I'm a victim of duty, too!
NICOLAS: So am I!
MADELEINE: We're all victims of duty! [*To* CHOUBERT:] Swallow! Chew!
NICOLAS: Swallow! Chew!
MADELEINE [*to* CHOUBERT *and* NICOLAS]:   Swallow! Chew! Chew! Swallow!
CHOUBERT [*to* MADELEINE *and* NICOLAS, *while chewing*]:   Chew! Swallow! Chew! Swallow!
NICOLAS [*to* CHOUBERT *and* MADELEINE]: Chew! Swallow! Chew! Swallow!
[*The* LADY *moves towards the other three.*]
LADY: Chew! Swallow! Chew! Swallow!
[*While all the characters are ordering one another to chew and swallow, the curtain falls.*]
Curtain

September 1952

Jean Tardieu
The Lock

Characters:
THE MADAME
THE CLIENT

A salon decorated and furnished in lavish bad taste: bad paintings on the walls, overstuffed chairs and a gilt pedestal table. To the left, where the wall angles obliquely, an ominous looking door. It is unusually large,

Source: "La Serrure" from *Théâtre de Chambre* I by Jean Tardieu. © Editions Gallimard 1955. Translated by Margaret P. Spanos and William V. Spanos. Reprinted by permission of Editions Gallimard.

painted a dirty white, and surrounded by a black door frame. Half-way up this door—that is, abnormally placed—there is a massive lock, much larger than ordinary. The keyhole is also of unusual size, though it has a classic key shape. It seems as if all the blackness of night is collected and concentrated in this keyhole. Across from it, on the right, another door, but the dimensions of this one are moderate, ordinary, human. At the back of the stage, a window, covered by thick floor-length drapes, closed. The room is lit electrically. As the curtain rises, the door on the right opens suddenly: THE CLIENT *enters, a little flustered, ushered in by* THE MADAME.

THE CLIENT *is a timid little man, in unfashionably tight-fitting clothes which cramp his movements;* THE MADAME *is a voluminous woman, well past her prime, with bleached hair. She is dressed flamboyantly, in garish colors. She holds a bunch of keys in her hand.*

THE MADAME [*Hurriedly*]:   Over there, there, sit down right there . . . and wait for me! [THE CLIENT *sits down.* THE MADAME *closes the door behind them, seems momentarily distracted by something which is happening behind it, then:*] They're gone. Good, I'll slip out. I'll be back in a moment. [*She treats him to a large "business" smile and disappears to the right, closing the door on* THE CLIENT. *Left alone, he settles down to wait. He coughs, checks his watch, keeps glancing toward the door on the right and is beginning to show signs of impatience when* THE MADAME *reappears, still bustling and solicitous.*] Dear! dear! My poor dear sir! I haven't kept you waiting too long have I? What a shame to keep such a nice young client waiting!

THE CLIENT [*Rising, very intimidated*]:   But Madame. . . . To tell you the truth, Madame. . . . My time is my own. But of course . . .

THE MADAME: Of course, of course. . . . You were beginning to get impatient, little fox! Come on now, admit it. You know, certain gentlemen who come here aren't always complaining about being kept waiting. Oh, no, they don't complain! I might even say that some of them get, how should I say, get a certain pleasure from it! [*She laughs knowingly.*] You see what I mean?

THE CLIENT [*Drawing himself up with dignity*]:   But for myself, Madame, it is a completely different matter that brings me here!

THE MADAME [*Ironically*]:   Oh, of course. Each of our gentlemen *always* comes here for some other reason. And you, my *dear* sir, you too, naturally, Oh, naturally!

THE CLIENT [*A little taken aback, but mastered by his passion*]:   Madame, you know very well what I come here for! Or rather, who!

THE MADAME: Come now, I was only joking! What a touchy little man you are! I *am* teasing you. But only a little bit, because I know what you're looking for. Because I know you're going to get it. [*In a crooning voice:*] You're going to get it, you'll get what you want, just what you want!

THE CLIENT [*Eagerly, in a hoarse voice*]:   Where is She? Tell me, where is She?

THE MADAME [*Still crooning*]:   There, there! Where is she now, the loveliest of ladies? Where is she, the loveliest of ladies for my little gentleman?

THE CLIENT: For God's sake, stop playing with me!

THE MADAME [*Resuming her normal tone:*]   What a nuisance [*Shrugging.*] All right, then, you know you haven't come here for nothing.

THE CLIENT: I'm asking you . . . I'm begging you to tell me: Where is She?

THE MADAME [*Pointing ceremoniously to the great ominous door*]:   There!

THE CLIENT [*Already glowing*]:   There, she is there? She's there behind that door?

THE MADAME: I've just told you so! [*Correcting herself.*] Or rather, perhaps she's not there *yet*, not at this very moment, but soon she'll *surely* be there.

THE CLIENT [*Deceived*]:   Oh? Only soon?

THE MADAME: Oh, come on now, be reasonable! You ought to know that nothing is going to happen in front of a third party! Even a third party in my profession, a party who is only there to "procure" what you want. . . . but soon, when you're alone . . . if you're very good, then . . . [*She makes a gesture suggesting something miraculous.*]

THE CLIENT [*With a deep sigh*]:   I have yearned for this moment so, Madame!

THE MADAME [*Laughing cynically*]:   There's no doubting that!

THE CLIENT: Why are you laughing? Because I call you Madame?

THE MADAME [*Cynically*]:   If you say so.

THE CLIENT: It's not funny, you know!

THE MADAME: Yes, I know, I know it all.

THE CLIENT: It's not amusing, a passion like this! For days and nights, for years, I haven't been able to think of anything but Her! . . . I used to tell myself: If I could only *see* her! . . . Just see her! Just for an instant! . . . To see her . . . even if she couldn't see me. Just a glimpse of her . . . through a torn curtain, at a half open door, down a spy glass! . . . I told myself that was all it would take to make me happy. And now, suddenly, it's here! The moment has arrived.

THE MADAME: Patience, my dear. Soon, very soon now.

THE CLIENT: After all, it doesn't really matter whether it's now or soon! I have reached my goal. . . . Am I dreaming? Tell me, am I dreaming?

THE MADAME: No, love, you're not dreaming! You're really here, and wide-awake! In the flesh. In flesh and bone. For Her! . . . and you shall have your fill of her.

THE CLIENT: I still can't believe it! Is it possible? All this happiness . . . mine?

THE MADAME: Yours, my dear sir, all yours! For you and you alone. And very soon. As soon as you hear the signal . . .

THE CLIENT: What? She will speak to me! Maybe she'll sing?

THE MADAME: Don't work yourself up like that! And let me finish my sentence. As I was saying, you should look, you *must* look . . . at the arranged signal. In other words, when you hear six o'clock strike on the clock in Her room, there, right over there. . . . Six o'clock *(Slowly)* Ding! . . . Ding! . . . Ding! . . .

THE CLIENT [*Finishing in ecstasy*]:   Ding! . . . Ding! . . . Ding! . . . Six o'clock! Six o'clock in Her room! She's really there, you say? [*He points to the black and white door.*]

THE MADAME: Yes. Right there, on the other side of that door.

THE CLIENT [*Suddenly uneasy*]:   And you're sure I'll hear it . . . I'll be able to hear the clock strike clearly?

THE MADAME: Very clearly. Very distinctly! The pretty little chime of a lady's clock . . . and what a pretty lady's clock!

THE CLIENT [*Feverishly*]:   A clock on Her night table, isn't it? That must be beside Her bed, isn't it? I mean . . . *right beside Her bed?* . . . Answer me, won't you?

THE MADAME: A bit of advice: Calm down! Don't get yourself in such a state . . . *too soon!*

THE CLIENT: And how long must I wait for this clock to strike?

THE MADAME [*Tempting*]:   Not long. A very little while. It won't harm you. You'll only be happier . . . *after!*

THE CLIENT: No one will come to . . . disturb me?

THE MADAME: No one at all. You'll be left in peace. Sly fox! You'll have nothing to envy the lords of the earth!

THE CLIENT: And *where* and *how* shall I see her?

THE MADAME [*Pointing to the keyhole*]:   Through there.

THE CLIENT [*Chagrined*]:   Through there?

THE MADAME: Precisely!

THE CLIENT: Oh! you mean . . .

THE MADAME: Now what?

THE CLIENT: You mean I have to look through . . . there?

THE MADAME: You certainly do! And let's say it right out: through the keyhole!

THE CLIENT [*Deceived*]:   Ah!

THE MADAME: And so what? I can't see that it's all that bad!

THE CLIENT: Oh, no . . . no . . . certainly . . . But I . . .

THE MADAME [*Irritably, mocking him*]:   Oh, come now, my dear sir! You told me just now that you wanted to see Her at any price! You'd be perfectly content to see your Beauty through a torn curtain, a door left ajar, anyway at all! And now, when I offer you the perfect vantage point, a fine big keyhole in a fine big door, you're not satisfied!

THE CLIENT: Don't be angry, Madame! Please don't be angry! I didn't say I wasn't satisfied! I meant ... I said ... I thought ...

THE MADAME [*Peevishly*]:   Go on, get it out, big oaf!

THE CLIENT [*Pitifully*]:   That's it then? I couldn't ... well ... see a little *more?* [*With his hands he brackets a circle in the air: first the size of a saucer; then the size of a man's head; finally the size of a porthole.*]

THE MADAME [*Like a mother scolding a spoiled child*]:   You know perfectly well that's not possible! Why do you ask such questions? ... After I've worked so hard to get you what you want! Everything's ready! Things have come to a head! And now my fine gentleman isn't satisfied! A keyhole isn't good enough for him! He wants a porthole, a window, a barn door! And who knows what else? [*She shrugs.*] You're really impossible! You're not worth the pains I've taken for you! ... You're insatiable, an absolute glutton! ... And what's more, you're wasting my time! I have other clients waiting. And they're less demanding than you, I'm sure ... [*She gives him a tap on the cheek.*]

THE CLIENT: Please forgive me, Madame. I didn't want to offend you. I know you've been very good to me. Thank you, Madame.

THE MADAME: Go on, now. I'll leave you alone. ... Alone with Her, you understand! ... Enjoy Yourself ... [*Suddenly severe.*] But remember our rules!

THE CLIENT [*Humbly*]:   Yes, Madame.

THE MADAME: Above all, don't try to open the door.

THE CLIENT [*Protesting indignantly*]:   No, of course not, Madame!

THE MADAME: Even if she seems to be beckoning you!

THE CLIENT [*Incorruptible*]:   I won't open it. Not even then!

THE MADAME: You'll content yourself with looking, then?

THE CLIENT: Yes, Madame.

THE MADAME: Remember this, now! And remember that you can't see her until it strikes six.

THE CLIENT: ... on the clock in her room. Yes, Madame!

THE MADAME: That's good. So long, then, my dear. I'll be leaving. Try to be a ... good boy. [*She laughs an equivocal, suggestive laugh.*] A good boy! So to speak! [*She leaves, laughing.* THE CLIENT *waits a moment, then walks around the room, inspects the furniture, and stops in front of the door.*]

THE CLIENT: Magnificent door! ... The very image of my love! Tall, imposing, silent ... in a word, worthy of her! [*Returning stage front and talking to himself.*] Tell me now, can you believe what's happening to you? ... Can you really? ... Is it really *you* it's happening to? ... Is it really today?

[*He takes a notebook out of his pocket and consults it.*] Yes, it seems to be.... Am I really here? [*He laughs.*] Stupid question! What's here is really here ... at least so it seems.... And you, my good man, are you really you? [*He pokes his arms and legs.*] Evidently, since you can feel your body with your hands! Let's settle down now! Here you are, you yourself, at Her place, near Her, just as if you were at home! Hmm ... Let's settle down! ... Should I undress? No, not right away.... Wait until She comes, until She's here.... But just the same, let's get comfortable.... At least a little. ... Just for the sake of moving freely.... Let's see ... [*He begins to empty his pockets.*] First my watch! ... [*He draws the watch from his watch pocket and puts it to his ear.*] How you've beaten, little heart, waiting for this moment! ... Well then, rest a little. You should rest a little, I should say. [*He puts it gently on the table.*] And then my billfold! [*He takes out his billfold.*] My billfold! All the proofs of my existence in there—birth certificate, social security, draft card, snapshots, fingerprints! Well, so much for all that! Here I become nothing. Nothing but a worshipper of the Fair Sex.... So, then, no more identity! [*He puts the billfold down. Speaking comically to himself.*] Indeed, sir, what's your name? Joseph? Elias? Caesar? Poof! Noman! Stripped bare! ... And faceless, Eh? [*He pulls a small mirror out of another pocket and looks at himself grimacing.*] Faugh! The simpleton! Out of my sight! [*He throws the mirror on the table.*] Behind me! You leave me alone, too, blind witness! You've nothing to offer me either ... you can only reflect what you see! But beauty, since I have loved her, beauty has become my ally! Have I not come here to worship her? [*Looking at the door.*] Ah, when will I hear the signal? ... But what an imbecile I am! Perhaps it's the sound of my own words that keeps me from hearing it! [*Listen.*] These clocks sometimes have such a faint chime, so distant! ... If I've missed the most beautiful, the most important moment of my life! ... No, that's impossible. I wouldn't have been brought here. Not just to trick me! [*Thinking he hears the clock.*] There it is! I hear it! The first strokes! ... [*Deceived.*] No, it's the blood in my head! I'm going mad with impatience! ... Come on, now, calm down. If I go on like this, I won't be able to tell the illusion from reality! A little quiet! ... A little rest! ... There ... sit down!

[*He takes a chair, sits down and forces himself to stretch out. Suddenly clear, antique chimes are heard at regular intervals: the clock in the next room slowly strikes six o'clock.* THE CLIENT *gets up, in the grip of a powerful excitement which he can hardly control.*]

THE CLIENT: Six o'clock! ... The signal! ... I ... I can ... I should ... I ... I should go ... I *must* look! ... That is.... How stupid ... I don't dare! My legs are like lead! ... But still, I must dare! I was told! It's necessary! ... To look, ... look through there. Too bad if it's so hard for you! Just consider that you're going to see *her*.... Come on now! Courage! ...

[*He rubs his eyes, making a violent effort, approaches the door, bends down, and looks through the keyhole. Throughout his monologue, he will look and describe what he sees, now bending to the height of the keyhole, now turning to speak directly to the audience.*]

THE CLIENT [*Carried away*]:   Yes, yes! . . . It's really She! . . . She! . . . Just as I've always seen her, just as she has appeared to me on a thousand different occasions! . . . She! . . . I'm struck dumb! . . . Again! . . . Let me see her again! . . . God, how beautiful she is! . . . Her large deep eyes! Her slow movements! And then those . . . those . . . those . . . *shapes!* [*Gripped by an erotic spell.*] Those full . . . round shapes hiding under her long dress. . . . [*He makes ecstatic but ludicrously exaggerated gestures as if he were stroking her body.*] It's impossible to weary of looking . . . you'd like to touch . . . like to *hold* . . . In your hands, in your arms, those lovely . . . those handsome . . . those . . . things . . . those . . . how do you say it . . . Oh! I can't find the words! Oh! What's it called then? . . . *Everything!* [*He makes grotesque gestures, sketching the curves of an imaginary woman in the air.*] But what's all this? Oh, come on now, what's this? I'm dreaming. I don't *see* all that! I've only caught a glimpse of her! I . . . I . . . I'm imagining it all. And under such fashionable clothes! . . . [*As if relieved to return to propriety, to innocence, mopping his forehead.*] You see, I was dreaming! Oh, how elegantly she walks! . . . She comes! She goes! She pirouettes! . . . She seems to be dancing. As if it were the most natural thing in the world! [*He himself comes forward, goes back, dances grotesquely.*] A miracle of grace! What lightness! . . . Not a sound, not a breath! [*He presses his ear to the door.*] You can't even hear her breathe . . . Nor the floor creaking under her feet! Not even the rustle of her dress! But . . . she's slipping away, she's losing herself in the dark, in the far end of that vast room! [*Pleading wretchedly.*] Oh! don't go! Turn, turn your eyes toward me, mirrors of my life! Please! Come back to me, come close to me! . . . At last! Here she comes again! As if she surges up in a fountain of water! Floating through mists, gliding through sunbeams! She smiles, she's coming, she's dancing! . . . There you are, my light! There you are, my luminous black sun! . . . But what is she doing? Is it possible? Is it really possible, such happiness for me, for your slave? Yes. . . . My eyes don't deceive me . . . she's pulling them off . . . one after the other, her heavy earrings; one after the other, her long jet pendants, so perfectly set in her hair. . . . And now, oh yes, yes . . . she's sliding her rings down her long fingers, where they end in pointed nails . . . What a marvel of elegance and dexterity! It's as if she's betwitched the metal, even the heavy stones: not a sound from them! And the white of her wrists springs from her bracelets! And her neck seems longer, and more regal. [*He continues to translate all that he sees by ludicrous gestures.*] Oh, and now, now, she's taking off that little jacket that showed off the rise of her breasts, her tiny waist, the swell of her hips! [*He takes off his own jacket and throws it from him.*] She's leaning over! ... bending down! ... Through the opening at her neckline I can almost see ... Ah, how beautiful! How beautiful! [*He clasps his hands.*] And now she's taking off her velvet slippers! She throws them, like that ... across the room, playfully! She.... Oh, I can hardly stand the beating of my heart! Now she has unfastened her dress ... and it slides all shimmering silk down the length of her thigh! [*He takes off his vest, and appears in shirt sleeves: his collar too large, his tie badly knotted, wearing suspenders.*] At her feet, all about her, the earth is strewn with a garland of leaves, petals fallen from the flowers! And surging up, still erect in the heart of the wilted petals, her slip, pink and black, shorter than the dress, stretches over the dusky flesh! [*He slides his suspenders off his shoulders, but his pants stay up, supported by a belt.*] God, what splendor! ... Openings! More and more of them! As if the earth were showing between tufts of grass under a gust of wind! ... Nothing left but the slightest of supports! Stretched over the welling flesh! Pressed in the folds! The satin glistening under the pressure of her breasts! ... One hand, then the other, unhooks it! The cloth flutters down like gulls, like doves! [*While speaking he pulls a handkerchief out of his pocket, which he tosses away, then he removes his tie, which he also throws away.*] Behold her flesh! Her very flesh! Even here. Here, there! On all sides! Breast, arms, light, shadow! And above her, around her, fly other birds! Truth! The goal of all life! The depths of man's soul. [*He throws himself on his knees, without taking his eye from the keyhole.*] At last, at last, these fabulous globes before which my very being kneels down in gratitude!

[*From this moment on, what has been ludicrous in his gestures gives way to a kind of frenzied grandeur.*]

THE CLIENT: Oh, don't stop now, crown of my life! Let your last garments fall away. ... Still more ... still more laid bare. Keep no more mystery from me! Open yourself completely to my gaze, to my hands, to my blood! ... Ah! ... It's as if she heard my prayer! Thank you, Oh, thank you, my beloved! For you shower the blessings of the earth upon me! No single secret place of your flesh, darker, more moist than a crypt, remains unrevealed to me! Nor any secret of our birth! ... I seem to hear eternal music prowling around me, in the distance, still unheard. Ah, longing! Ah, fulfillment! Shipwreck! The swell raises me! I will shatter on your shores! ... [*A short silence.*] What? You don't want it to stop there? You shake your head, as if you would say "no," as if you had heard me! Is it my own fever that grips you? How your hands tremble! The trembling ... little by little ... it spreads through your whole body! ... Are you possessed by one of those magic dances of ancient times? That one cannot witness without dying? A sensual quiver accents the flare of your nostrils, hollows your cheeks! Your eyes withdraw into their own deepening shadows! Your

breast heaves higher and higher, faster and faster! The shudder mounts
from your ankles to your loins, from your wrists to your shoulders, ah! how
it tempers your body! You grow, you are drawn out like a rod of steel in
the flames! . . . Your eyes are deep hollows, whose steady glitter fixes me!
Your jawbones start out of the shadow, clenched in fury, in madness! . . .
Oh, my beloved, what has become of you, here, before my eyes? Your
thighs, wracked by waves of suffering wrench your marvelous body! The
light, which a moment ago worshipped your full curves, stabs angles into
your body! Your knees, your elbows! Flints and knives! From your breast-
bone the ribs stand out like the braid on a uniform. How you have changed
in a few moments, my splendor!

[*The light begins to dim progressively. It will have completely disappeared by the end of the monologue, while only the enormous keyhole will
be brightly illuminated. At the same time that darkness takes over the
stage, a musical note is heard—sustained, strident, piercing. Faint at first,
it will become deafening and should last a brief moment after* THE
CLIENT *falls*].

THE CLIENT: But what is it? . . . What's happening? . . . That music! It beats
on me, it takes over my brain, not an appeal any longer . . . but an imperious order! [*He looks once more through the keyhole.*] Ah, help her! . . .
Help her! . . . She makes one final effort! She will strip even further! Even
further! Further than any woman ever stripped for her lover! Ha! Hi! She
turns, she turns, she strains, strains, strains! . . . Ha! Hi! She casts it off!
Throws it from her! Her cheeks! Her lips! Her breasts! All her flesh! She
tears herself in strips! Hop! For the dogs! Hop! For the Birds! Hop! For the
worms . . . for the jackals! Hop! Hop! Hop! Go! Go! Go! Go! . . . Nothing
more! Nothing! No muscle! No veins! No skin! Oh, my beauty, you stand
more naked still! More perfect and more beautiful than ever before! . . .
Not even your flesh for clothing! . . . The globes of your eyes hang down
over your cheekbones! Your last finery, the sweet warmth of your body lies
with your trinkets in the confusion of your room. And beyond your remains, across an empty cage, I see, I still see *your glittering bed*! . . . But
you, always erect, always erect and quick! Your mouth smiles at me without lips! Your hairless brow bends lovingly toward me! Your ivory hands,
your arms, dry and empty as twigs, reach tenderly toward me! Your marble vertebrae, your legs, thin and fragile as broken branches, advance to
meet me! Oh! Hollow bones! Shattering, elegant, appalling! I come, love
of my life! I come! I come! I come!

[*Arms stretched toward her, he throws himself at the door, smashes into
it, and falls backwards to the floor, lifeless.*]

   [*At this moment the darkness is absolute: Only the keyhole glows
brightly. The sustained note is at its loudest, and it lasts several more
seconds.*]

[*The door on the right opens slowly. In the luminous doorway the immense silhouette of* the MADAME *is recognizable.*]
THE MADAME [*In a very low voice, almost whispering*]:   I take it . . . that monsieur . . . is satisfied.
Curtain

Harold Pinter
A Slight Ache

A country house, with two chairs and a table laid for breakfast at the centre of the stage. These will later be removed and the action will be focused on the scullery on the right and the study on the left, both indicated with a minimum of scenery and props. A large well kept garden is suggested at the back of the stage with flower beds, trimmed hedges, etc. The garden gate, which cannot be seen by the audience, is off right.
FLORA *and* EDWARD *are discovered sitting at the breakfast table.* EDWARD *is reading the paper.*

FLORA: Have you noticed the honeysuckle this morning?
EDWARD: The what?
FLORA: The honeysuckle.
EDWARD: Honeysuckle? Where?
FLORA: By the back gate, Edward.
EDWARD: Is that honeysuckle? I thought it was . . . convolvulus, or something.
FLORA: But you know it's honeysuckle.
EDWARD: I tell you I thought it was convolvulus.
[*Pause.*]
FLORA: It's in wonderful flower.
EDWARD: I must look.
FLORA: The whole garden's in flower this morning. The clematis. The convolvulus. Everything. I was out at seven. I stood by the pool.
EDWARD: Did you say—that the convolvulus was in flower?
FLORA: Yes.

Source: Harold Pinter, *A Slight Ache.* In *Three Plays: A Slight Ache, the Collection, and the Dwarfs* (New York: Grove Press, 1961). Copyright © 1961 by Harold Pinter. Reprinted by permission of Grove Press, Inc.

EDWARD: But good God, you just denied there was any.

FLORA: I was talking about the honeysuckle.

EDWARD: About the what?

FLORA [*calmly*]:   Edward—you know that shrub outside the toolshed . . .

EDWARD: Yes, yes.

FLORA: That's convolvulus.

EDWARD: That?

FLORA: Yes.

EDWARD: Oh.

[*Pause.*]

I thought it was japonica.

FLORA: Oh, good Lord no.

EDWARD: Pass the teapot, please.

[*Pause. She pours tea for him.*]

I don't see why I should be expected to distinguish between these plants. It's not my job.

FLORA: You know perfectly well what grows in your garden.

EDWARD: Quite the contrary. It is clear that I don't.

[*Pause.*]

FLORA [*rising*]:   I was up at seven. I stood by the pool. The peace. And everything in flower. The sun was up. You should work in the garden this morning. We could put up the canopy.

EDWARD: The canopy? What for?

FLORA: To shade you from the sun.

EDWARD: Is there a breeze?

FLORA: A light one.

EDWARD: It's very treacherous weather, you know.

[*Pause.*]

FLORA: Do you know what today is?

EDWARD: Saturday.

FLORA: It's the longest day of the year.

EDWARD: Really?

FLORA: It's the height of summer today.

EDWARD: Cover the marmalade.

FLORA: What?

EDWARD: Cover the pot. There's a wasp. [*He puts the paper down on the table.*] Don't move. Keep still. What are you doing?

FLORA: Covering the pot.

EDWARD: Don't move. Leave it. Keep still.

[*Pause.*]

Give me the "Telegraph."

FLORA: Don't hit it. It'll bite.

EDWARD: Bite? What do you mean, bite? Keep still.

[*Pause.*]
It's landing.

FLORA: It's going in the pot.

EDWARD: Give me the lid.

FLORA: It's in.

EDWARD: Give me the lid.

FLORA: I'll do it.

EDWARD: Give it to me! Now ... Slowly ...

FLORA: What are you doing?

EDWARD: Be quiet. Slowly ... carefully ... on ... the ... pot! Ha-ha-ha. Very good.

[*He sits on a chair to the right of the table.*]

FLORA: Now he's in the marmalade.

EDWARD: Precisely.

[*Pause. She sits on a chair to the left of the table and reads the "Telegraph."*]

FLORA: Can you hear him?

EDWARD: Hear him?

FLORA: Buzzing.

EDWARD: Nonsense. How can you hear him? It's an earthenware lid.

FLORA: He's becoming frantic.

EDWARD: Rubbish. Take it away from the table.

FLORA: What shall I do with it?

EDWARD: Put it in the sink and drown it.

FLORA: It'll fly out and bite me.

EDWARD: It will not bite you! Wasps don't bite. Anyway, it won't fly out. It's stuck. It'll drown where it is, in the marmalade.

FLORA: What a horrible death.

EDWARD: On the contrary.

[*Pause.*]

FLORA: Have you got something in your eyes?

EDWARD: No. Why do you ask?

FLORA: You keep clenching them, blinking them.

EDWARD: I have a slight ache in them.

FLORA: Oh, dear.

EDWARD: Yes, a slight ache. As if I hadn't slept.

FLORA: Did you sleep, Edward?

EDWARD: Of course I slept. Uninterrupted. As always.

FLORA: And yet you feel tired.

EDWARD: I didn't say I felt tired. I merely said I had a slight ache in my eyes.

FLORA: Why is that, then?

EDWARD: I really don't know.

[*Pause.*]

FLORA: Oh goodness!

EDWARD: What is it?

FLORA: I can see it. It's trying to come out.

EDWARD: How can it?

FLORA: Through the hole. It's trying to crawl out, through the spoon-hole.

EDWARD: Mmmnn, yes. Can't do it, of course. [*Silent pause.*] Well, let's kill it, for goodness' sake.

FLORA: Yes, let's. But how?

EDWARD: Bring it out on the spoon and squash it on a plate.

FLORA: It'll fly away. It'll bite.

EDWARD: If you don't stop saying that word I shall leave this table.

FLORA: But wasps do bite.

EDWARD: They don't bite. They sting. It's snakes . . . that bite.

FLORA: What about horseflies?

[*Pause.*]

EDWARD [*to himself*]:   Horseflies suck.

[*Pause.*]

FLORA [*tentatively*]:   If we . . . if we wait long enough, I suppose it'll choke to death. It'll suffocate in the marmalade.

EDWARD [*briskly*]:   You do know I've got work to do this morning, don't you? I can't spend the whole day worrying about a wasp.

FLORA: Well, kill it.

EDWARD: You want to kill it?

FLORA: Yes.

EDWARD: Very well. Pass me the hot water jug.

FLORA: What are you going to do?

EDWARD: Scald it. Give it to me.

[*She hands him the jug. Pause.*]

Now . . .

FLORA [*whispering*]:   Do you want me to lift the lid?

EDWARD: No, no, no. I'll pour down the spoon hole. Right . . . down the spoon-hole.

FLORA: Listen!

EDWARD: What?

FLORA: It's buzzing.

EDWARD: Vicious creatures.

[*Pause.*]

Curious, but I don't remember seeing any wasps at all, all summer, until now. I'm sure I don't know why. I mean, there must have been wasps.

FLORA: Please.

EDWARD: This couldn't be the first wasp, could it?

FLORA: Please.

EDWARD: The first wasp of summer? No. It's not possible.

FLORA: Edward.

EDWARD: Mmmmnnn?

FLORA: Kill it.

EDWARD: Ah, yes. Tilt the pot. Tilt. Aah . . . down here . . . right down . . . blinding him . . . that's . . . it.

FLORA: Is it?

EDWARD: Lift the lid. All right, I will. There he is! Dead. What a monster. [*He squashes it on a plate.*]

FLORA: What an awful experience.

EDWARD: What a beautiful day it is. Beautiful. I think I shall work in the garden this morning. Where's that canopy?

FLORA: It's in the shed.

EDWARD: Yes, we must get it out. My goodness, just look at that sky. Not a cloud. Did you say it was the longest day of the year today?

FLORA: Yes.

EDWARD: Ah, it's a good day. I feel it in my bones. In my muscles. I think I'll stretch my legs in a minute. Down to the pool. My God, look at that flowering shrub over there. Clematis. What a wonderful . . . [*He stops suddenly.*]

FLORA: What?

[*Pause.*]

Edward, what is it?

[*Pause.*]

Edward . . .

EDWARD [*thickly*]: He's there.

FLORA: Who?

EDWARD [*low, murmuring*]: Blast and damn it, he's there, he's there at the back gate.

FLORA: Let me see.

[*She moves over to him to look. Pause.*]

[*Lightly.*] Oh, it's the matchseller.

EDWARD: He's back again.

FLORA: But he's always there.

EDWARD: Why? What is he doing there?

FLORA: But he's never disturbed you, has he? The man's been standing there for weeks. You've never mentioned it.

EDWARD: What is he doing there?

FLORA: He's selling matches, of course.

EDWARD: It's ridiculous. What's the time?

FLORA: Half past nine.

EDWARD: What in God's name is he doing with a tray full of matches at half past nine in the morning?

FLORA: He arrives at seven o'clock.

EDWARD: Seven o'clock?

FLORA: He's always there at seven.

EDWARD: Yes, but you've never ... actually seen him arrive?

FLORA: No, I ...

EDWARD: Well, how do you know he's ... not been standing there all night?

[*Pause.*]

FLORA: Do you find him interesting, Edward?

EDWARD [*casually*]:   Interesting? No. No, I ... don't find him interesting.

FLORA: He's a very nice old man, really.

EDWARD: You've spoken to him?

FLORA: No. No, I haven't spoken to him. I've nodded.

EDWARD [*pacing up and down*]:   For two months he's been standing on that spot, do you realize that? Two months. I haven't been able to step outside the back gate.

FLORA: Why on earth not?

EDWARD [*to himself*]:   It used to give me great pleasure, such pleasure, to stroll along through the long grass, out through the back gate, pass into the lane. That pleasure is now denied me. It's my own house, isn't it? It's my own gate.

FLORA: I really can't understand this, Edward.

EDWARD: Damn. And do you know I've never seen him sell one box? Not a box. It's hardly surprising. He's on the wrong road. It's not a road at all. What is it? It's a lane, leading to a monastery. Off everybody's route. Even the monks take a short cut to the village, when they want to go ... to the village. No one goes up it. Why doesn't he stand on the main road if he wants to sell matches, by the *front* gate? The whole thing's preposterous.

FLORA [*going over to him*]:   I don't know why you're getting so excited about it. He's a quiet, harmless old man, going about his business. He's quite harmless.

EDWARD: I didn't say he wasn't harmless. Of course he's harmless. How could he be other than harmless?

[*Fade out and silence.*]

[FLORA'S *voice, far in the house, drawing nearer.*]

FLORA [*off*]:   Edward, where are you? Edward? Where are you, Edward?

[*She appears.*]

Edward?

Edward, what are you doing in the scullery?

EDWARD [*looking through the scullery window*]:   Doing?

FLORA: I've been looking everywhere for you. I put up the canopy ages ago. I came back and you were nowhere to be seen. Have you been out?

EDWARD: No.

FLORA: Where have you been?

EDWARD: Here.

FLORA: I looked in your study. I even went into the attic.

EDWARD [*tonelessly*]:   What would I be doing in the attic?

FLORA: I couldn't imagine what had happened to you. Do you know it's twelve o'clock?

EDWARD: Is it?

FLORA: I even went to the bottom of the garden, to see if you were in the toolshed.

EDWARD [*tonelessly*]:   What would I be doing in the toolshed?

FLORA: You must have seen me in the garden. You can see through this window.

EDWARD: Only part of the garden.

FLORA: Yes.

EDWARD: Only a corner of the garden. A very small corner.

FLORA: What are you going in here?

EDWARD: Nothing. I was digging out some notes, that's all.

FLORA: Notes?

EDWARD: For my essay.

FLORA: Which essay?

EDWARD: My essay on space and time.

FLORA: But ... I've never ... I don't know that one.

EDWARD: You don't know it?

FLORA: I thought you were writing one about the Belgian Congo.

EDWARD: I've been engaged on the dimensionality and continuity of space ... and time ... for years.

FLORA: And the Belgian Congo?

EDWARD [*shortly*]:   Never mind about the Belgian Congo.

[*Pause.*]

FLORA: But you don't keep notes in the scullery.

EDWARD: You'd be surprised. You'd be highly surprised.

FLORA: Good Lord, what's that? Is that a bullock let loose? No. It's the matchseller! My goodness, you can see him ... through the hedge. He looks bigger. Have you been watching him? He looks ... like a bullock.

[*Pause.*]

Edward?

[*Pause.*]

[*Moving over to him.*] Are you coming outside? I've put up the canopy. You'll miss the best of the day. You can have an hour before lunch.

EDWARD: I've no work to do this morning.

FLORA: What about your essay? You don't intend to stay in the scullery all day, do you?

EDWARD: Get out. Leave me alone.

[*A slight pause.*]
FLORA: Really Edward. You've never spoken to me like that in all your life.
EDWARD: Yes, I have.
FLORA: Oh, Weddie. Beddie-Weddie ...
EDWARD: Do not call me that!
FLORA: Your eyes are bloodshot.
EDWARD: Damn it.
FLORA: It's too dark in here to peer ...
EDWARD: Damn.
FLORA: It's so bright outside.
EDWARD: Damn.
FLORA: And it's dark in here.
[*Pause.*]
EDWARD: Christ blast it!
FLORA: You're frightened of him.
EDWARD: I'm not.
FLORA: You're frightened of a poor old man. Why?
EDWARD: I am not!
FLORA: He's a poor, harmless old man.
EDWARD: Aaah my eyes.
EDWARD: Let me bathe them.
EDWARD: Keep away.
[*Pause.*]
[*Slowly.*] I want to speak to that man. I want to have a word with him.
[*Pause.*]
It's quite absurd, of course. I really can't tolerate something so ... absurd, right on my doorstep. I shall not tolerate it. He's sold nothing all morning. No one passed. Yes. A monk passed. A non-smoker. In a loose garment. It's quite obvious he was a non-smoker but still, the man made no effort. He made no effort to cinch a sale, to rid himself of one of his cursed boxes. His one chance, all morning, and he made no effort.
[*Pause.*]
I haven't wasted my time. I've hit, in fact, upon the truth. He's not a matchseller at all. The bastard isn't a matchseller at all. Curious I never realized that before. He's an impostor. I watched him very closely. He made no move towards the monk. As for the monk, the monk made no move towards him. The monk was moving along the lane. He didn't pause, or halt, or in any way alter his step. As for the matchseller—how ridiculous to go on calling him by that title. What a farce. No, there is something very false about that man. I intend to get to the bottom of it. I'll soon get rid of him. He can go and ply his trade somewhere else. Instead of standing like a bullock ... a bullock, outside my back gate.

FLORA: But if he isn't a matchseller, what is his trade?

EDWARD: We'll soon find out.

FLORA: You're going out to speak to him?

EDWARD: Certainly not! Go out to *him*? Certainly . . . not. I'll invite him in here. Into my study. Then we'll . . . get to the bottom of it.

FLORA: Why don't you call the police and have him removed?

[*He laughs. Pause.*]

Why don't you call the police, Edward? You could say he was a public nuisance. Although I . . . I can't say I find him a nuisance.

EDWARD: Call him in.

FLORA: Me?

EDWARD: Go out and call him in.

FLORA: Are you serious?

[*Pause.*]

Edward, I could call the police. Or even the vicar.

EDWARD: Go and get him.

[*She goes out. Silence.*]

[EDWARD *waits.*]

FLORA [*in the garden*]: Good morning.

[*Pause.*]

We haven't met. I live in this house here. My husband and I.

[*Pause.*]

I wonder if you could . . . would you care for a cup of tea?

[*Pause.*]

Or a glass of lemon? It must be so dry, standing here.

[*Pause.*]

Would you like to come inside for a little while? It's much cooler. There's something we'd very much like to . . . tell you, that will benefit you. Could you spare a few moments? We won't keep you long.

[*Pause.*]

Might I buy your tray of matches, do you think? We've run out, completely, and we always keep a very large stock. It happens that way, doesn't it? Well, we can discuss it inside. Do come. This way. Ah now, do come. Our house is full of curios, you know. My husband's been rather a collector. We have goose for lunch. Do you care for goose?

[*She moves to the gate.*]

Come and have lunch with us. This way. That's . . . right. May I take your arm? There's a good deal of *nettle* inside the gate. [*The* MATCHSELLER *appears.*] Here. This way. Mind now. Isn't it beautiful weather? It's the longest day of the year today.

[*Pause.*]

That's honeysuckle. And that's convolvulus. There's clematis. And do you see that plant by the conservatory? That's japonica.

[*Silence. She enters the study.*]

FLORA: He's here.

EDWARD: I know.

FLORA: He's in the hall.

EDWARD: I know he's here. I can smell him.

FLORA: Smell him?

EDWARD: I smelt him when he came under my window. Can't you smell the house now?

FLORA: What are you going to do with him, Edward? You won't be rough with him in any way? He's very old. I'm not sure if he can hear, or even see. And he's wearing the oldest—

EDWARD: I don't want to know what he's wearing.

FLORA: But you'll see for yourself in a minute, if you speak to him.

EDWARD: I shall.

[*Slight pause.*]

FLORA: He's an old man. You won't . . . be rough with him?

EDWARD: If he's so old, why doesn't he seek shelter . . . from the storm?

FLORA: But there's no storm. It's summer, the longest day . . .

EDWARD: There was a storm, last week. A summer storm. He stood without moving, while it raged about him.

FLORA: When was this?

EDWARD: He remained quite still, while it thundered all about him.

[*Pause.*]

FLORA: Edward . . . are you sure it's wise to bother about all this?

EDWARD: Tell him to come in.

FLORA: I . . .

EDWARD: Now.

[*She goes and collects the* MATCHSELLER.]

FLORA: Hullo. Would you like to go in? I won't be long. Up these stairs here.

[*Pause.*]

You can have some sherry before lunch.

[*Pause.*]

Shall I take your tray? No. Very well, take it with you. Just . . . up those stairs. The door at the . . .

[*She watches him move.*]

the door . . .

[*Pause.*]

the door at the top. I'll join you . . . later. [*She goes out.*]

[*The* MATCHSELLER *stands on the threshold of the study.*]

EDWARD [*cheerfully*]:   Here I am. Where are you?

[*Pause.*]

Don't stand out there, old chap. Come into my study. [*He rises.*] Come in.

[*The* MATCHSELLER *enters.*]
That's right. Mind how you go. That's . . . it. Now, make yourself comfortable. Thought you might like some refreshment, on a day like this. Sit down, old man. What will you have? Sherry? Or what about a double scotch? Eh?
[*Pause.*]
I entertain the villagers annually, as a matter of fact. I'm not the squire, but they look upon me with some regard. Don't believe we've got a squire here any more, actually. Don't know what became of him. Nice old man he was. Great chess-player, as I remember. Three daughters. The pride of the county. Flaming red hair. Alice was the eldest. Sit yourself down, old chap. Eunice I think was number two. The youngest one was the best of the bunch. Sally. No, no, wait a minute, no, it wasn't Sally, it was . . . Fanny. Fanny. A flower. You must be a stranger here. Unless you lived here once, went on a long voyage and have lately returned. Do you know the district?
[*Pause.*]
Now, now, you mustn't . . . stand about like that. Take a seat. Which one would you prefer? We have a great variety as you see. Can't stand uniformity. Like different seats, different backs. Often when I'm working, you know, I draw up one chair, scribble a few lines, put it by, draw up another, sit back, ponder, put it by . . . [*absently*] . . . sit back . . . put it by . . .
[*Pause.*]
I write theological and philosophical essays . . .
[*Pause.*]
Now and again I jot down a few observations on certain tropical phenomena—not from the same standpoint, of course. [*Silent pause.*] Yes. Africa, now. Africa's always been my happy hunting ground. Fascinating country. Do you know it? I get the impression that you've . . . been around a bit. Do you by any chance know the Membunza Mountains? Great range south of Katambaloo. French Equatorial Africa, if my memory serves me right. Most extraordinary diversity of flora and fauna. Especially fauna. I understand in the Gobi Desert you can come across some very strange sights. Never been there myself. Studied the maps though. Fascinating things, maps.
[*Pause.*]
Do you live in the village? I don't often go down, of course. Or are you passing through? On your way to another part of the country? Well, I can tell you, in my opinion you won't find many prettier parts than here. We win the first prize regularly, you know, the best kept village in the area. Sit down.
[*Pause.*]
I say, can you hear me?

[*Pause.*]
I said, I say, can you hear me?
[*Pause.*]
You possess most extraordinary repose, for a man of your age, don't you? Well, perhaps that's not quite the right word . . . repose. Do you find it chilly in here? I'm sure it's chillier in here than out. I haven't been out yet, today, though I shall probably spend the whole afternoon working, in the garden, under my canopy, at my table, by the pool.
[*Pause.*]
Oh, I understand you met my *wife?* Charming woman, don't you think? Plenty of grit there, too. Stood by me through thick and thin, that woman. In season and out of season. Fine figure of a woman she was, too, in her youth. Wonderful carriage, flaming red hair. [*He stops abruptly.*]
[*Pause.*]
Yes, I . . . I was in much the same position myself then as you are now, you understand. Struggling to make my way in the world. I was in commerce too. [*With a chuckle.*] Oh, yes, I know what it's like—the weather, the rain, beaten from pillar to post, up hill and down dale . . . the rewards were few . . . winters in hovels . . . up till all hours working at your thesis . . . yes, I've done it all. Let me advise you. Get a good woman to stick by you. Never mind what the world says. Keep at it. Keep your shoulder to the wheel. It'll pay dividends.
[*Pause.*]
[*With a laugh.*] You must excuse my chatting away like this. We have few visitors this time of the year. All our friends summer abroad. I'm a home bird myself. Wouldn't mind taking a trip to Asia Minor, mind you, or to certain lower regions of the Congo, but Europe? Out of the question. Much too noisy. I'm sure you agree. Now look, what will you have to drink? A glass of ale? Curaçao Fockink Orange? Ginger beer? Tia Maria? A Wachenheimer Fuchsmantel Reisling Beeren Auslese? Gin and it? Chateauneuf-du-Pape? A little Asti Spumante? Or what do you say to a straightforward Piesporter Goldtropfschen Feine Auslese (Reichsgraf von Kesselstaff)? Any preference?
[*Pause.*]
You look a trifle warm. Why don't you take off your balaclava? I'd find that a little itchy myself. But then I've always been one for freedom of movement. Even in the depth of winter I wear next to nothing.
[*Pause.*]
I say, can I ask you a personal question? I don't want to seem inquisitive but aren't you rather on the wrong road for matchselling? Not terribly busy, is it? Of course you may not care for petrol fumes or the noise of traffic. I can quite understand that.

[*Pause.*]

Do forgive me peering but is that a glass eye you're wearing?

[*Pause.*]

Do take off your balaclava, there's a good chap, put your tray down and take your ease, as they say in this part of the world. [*He moves towards him.*] I must say you keep quite a good stock, don't you? Tell me, between ourselves, are those boxes full, or are there just a few half-empty ones among them? Oh yes, I used to be in commerce. Well now, before the good lady sounds the gong for petit déjeuner will you join me in an apéritif? I recommend a glass of cider. Now ... just a minute ... I know I've got some—Look out! Mind your tray!

[*The tray falls, and the matchboxes.*]

Good God, what ... ?

[*Pause.*]

You've dropped your tray.

[*Pause. He picks the matchboxes up.*]

[*Grunts.*] Eh, these boxes are all wet. You've no right to sell wet matches, you know. Uuuuugggh. This feels suspiciously like fungus. You won't get very far in this trade if you don't take care of your goods. [*Grunts, rising.*] Well, here you are.

[*Pause.*]

Here's your tray.

[*He puts the tray into the* MATCHSELLER'S *hands, and sits. Pause.*]

Now listen, let me be quite frank with you, shall I? I really cannot understand why you don't sit down. There are four chairs at your disposal. Not to mention the hassock. I can't possibly talk to you unless you're settled. Then and only then can I speak to you. Do you follow me? You're not being terribly helpful. [*Slight pause.*] You're sweating. The sweat's pouring out of you. Take off that balaclava.

[*Pause.*]

Go into the corner then. Into the corner. Go on. Get into the shade of the corner. Back. Backward.

[*Pause.*]

Get back!

[*Pause.*]

Ah, you understand me. Forgive me for saying so, but I had decided that you had the comprehension of a bullock. I was mistaken. You understand me perfectly well. That's right. A little more. A little to the right. Aaah. Now you're there. In shade, in shadow. Good-o. Now I can get down to brass tacks. Can't I?

[*Pause.*]

No doubt you're wondering why I invited you into this house? You may think I was alarmed by the look of you. You would be quite mistaken. I

was not alarmed by the look of you. I did not find you at all alarming. No, no. Nothing outside this room has ever alarmed me. You disgusted me, quite forcibly, if you want to know the truth.
[*Pause.*]
Why did you disgust me to that extent? That seems to be a pertinent question. You're no more disgusting than Fanny, the squire's daughter, after all. In appearance you differ but not in essence. There's the same ...
[*Pause.*]
The same ...
[*Pause.*]
[*In a low voice.*] I want to ask you a question. Why do you stand outside my back gate, from dawn till dusk, why do you pretend to sell matches, why ... ? What is it, damn you. You're shivering. You're sagging. Come here, come here ... mind your tray! [EDWARD *rises and moves behind a chair.*] Come, quick quick. There. Sit here. Sit ... sit in this.
[*The* MATCHSELLER *stumbles and sits. Pause.*]
Aaaah! You're sat. At last. What a relief. You must be tired. [*Slight pause.*] Chair comfortable? I bought it in a sale. I bought all the furniture in this house in a sale. The same sale. When I was a young man. You too, perhaps. You too, perhaps.
[*Pause.*]
At the same time, perhaps!
[*Pause.*]
[*Muttering.*] I must get some air. I must get a breath of air.
[*He goes to the door.*]
Flora!
FLORA: Yes?
EDWARD [*with great weariness*]: Take me into the garden.
[*Silence. They move from the study door to a chair under a canopy.*]
FLORA: Come under the canopy.
EDWARD: Ah. [*He sits.*]
[*Pause.*]
The peace. The peace out here.
FLORA: Look at our trees.
EDWARD: Yes.
FLORA: Our own trees. Can you heard the birds?
EDWARD: No, I can't hear them.
FLORA: But they're singing, high up, and flapping.
EDWARD: Good. Let them flap.
FLORA: Shall I bring your lunch out here? You can have it in peace, and a quiet drink, under your canopy.
[*Pause.*]

How are you getting on with your old man?

EDWARD: What do you mean?

FLORA: What's happening? How are you getting on with him?

EDWARD: Very well. We get on remarkably well. He's a little . . . reticent. Somewhat withdrawn. It's understandable. I should be the same, perhaps, in his place. Though, of course, I could not possibly find myself in his place.

FLORA: Have you found out anything about him?

EDWARD: A little. A little. He's had various trades, that's certain. His place of residence is unsure. He's . . . he's not a drinking man. As yet, I haven't discovered the reason for his arrival here. I shall in due course . . . by nightfall.

FLORA: Is it necessary?

EDWARD: Necessary?

FLORA [*quickly sitting on the right arm of the chair*]: I could show him out now, it wouldn't matter. You've seen him, he's harmless, unfortunate . . . old, that's all. Edward—listen—he's not here through any . . . design, or anything, I know it. I mean, he might just as well stand outside our back gate as anywhere else. He'll move on. I can . . . make him. I promise you. There's no point in upsetting yourself like this. He's an old man, weak in the head . . . that's all.

[*Pause.*]

EDWARD: You're deluded.

FLORA: Edward—

EDWARD [*rising*]: You're deluded. And stop calling me Edward.

FLORA: You're not still frightened of him?

EDWARD: Frightened of him? Of *him*? Have you *seen* him?

[*Pause.*]

He's like jelly. A great bullockfat of jelly. He can't see straight. I think as a matter of fact he wears a glass eye. He's almost stone deaf . . . almost . . . not quite. He's very nearly dead on his feet. Why should he frighten me? No, you're a woman, you know nothing. [*Slight pause.*] But he possesses other faculties. Cunning. The man's an imposter and he knows I know it.

FLORA: I'll tell you what. Look. Let me speak to him. I'll speak to him.

EDWARD [*quietly*]: And I know he knows I know it.

FLORA: I'll find out all about him, Edward. I promise you I will.

EDWARD: And he knows I know.

FLORA: Edward! Listen to me! I can find out all about him, I promise you. I shall go and have a word with him now. I shall . . . get to the bottom of it.

EDWARD: You? It's laughable.

FLORA: You'll see—he won't bargain for me. I'll surprise him. He'll . . . he'll admit everything.

EDWARD [*softly*]:   He'll admit everything, will he?
FLORA: You wait and see, you just—
EDWARD: [*hissing*]:   What are you plotting?
FLORA: I know exactly what I shall—
EDWARD: What are you plotting?
[*He seizes her arms.*]
FLORA: Edward, you're hurting me!
[*Pause.*]
[*With dignity.*] I shall wave from the window when I'm ready. Then you can come up. I shall get to the truth of it, I assure you. You're much too heavy-handed, in every way. You should trust your wife more, Edward. You should trust her judgment, and have a greater insight into her capabilities. A woman ... a woman will often succeed, you know, where a man must invariably fail.
[*Silence. She goes into the study.*]
Do you mind if I come in?
[*The door closes.*]
Are you comfortable?
[*Pause.*]
Oh, the sun's shining directly on you. Wouldn't you rather sit in the shade?
[*She sits down.*]
It's the longest day of the year today, did you know that? Actually the year has flown. I can remember Christmas and that dreadful frost. And the floods! I hope you weren't here in the floods. We were out of danger up here, of course, but in the valleys whole families I remember drifted away on the current. The country was a lake. Everything stopped. We lived on our own preserves, drank elderberry wine, studied other cultures.
[*Pause.*]
Do you know, I've got a feeling I've seen you before, somewhere. Long before the flood. You were much younger. Yes, I'm really sure of it. Between ourselves, were you ever a poacher? I had an encounter with a poacher once. It was a ghastly rape, the brute. High up on a hillside cattle track. Early spring. I was out riding on my pony. And there on the verge a man lay—ostensibly injured, lying on his front, I remember, possibly the victim of a murderous assault, how was I to know? I dismounted, I went to him, he rose, I fell, my pony took off, down to the valley. I saw the sky through the trees, blue. Up to my ears in mud. It was a desperate battle.
[*Pause.*]
I lost.
[*Pause.*]
Of course, life was perilous in those days. It was my first canter unchaperoned.
[*Pause.*]

Years later, when I was a Justice of the Peace for the county, I had him in front of the bench. He was there for poaching. That's how I know he was a poacher. The evidence though was sparse, inadmissible, I acquitted him, letting him off with a caution. He'd grown a red beard, I remember. Yes. A bit of a stinker.

[*Pause.*]

I say, you are perspiring, aren't you? Shall I mop your brow? With my chiffon? Is it the heat? Or the closeness? Or confined space? Or . . . ? [*She goes over to him.*] Actually, the day is cooling. It'll soon be dusk. Perhaps it is dusk. May I? You don't mind?

[*Pause. She mops his brow.*]

Ah, there, that's better. And your cheeks. It is a woman's job, isn't it? And I'm the only woman on hand. There.

[*Pause. She leans on the arm of chair.*]

[*Intimately.*] Tell me, have you a woman? Do you like women? Do you ever . . . think about women?

[*Pause.*]

Have you ever . . . stopped a woman?

[*Pause.*]

I'm sure you must have been quite attractive once. [*She sits.*] Not any more, of course. You've got a vile smell. Vile. Quite repellent, in fact.

[*Pause.*]

Sex, I suppose, means nothing to you. Does it ever occur to you that sex is a very vital experience for other people? Really, I think you'd amuse me if you weren't so hideous. You're probably quite amusing in your own way. [*Seductively.*] Tell me all about love. Speak to me of love.

[*Pause.*]

God knows what you're saying at this very moment. It's quite disgusting. Do you know when I was a girl I loved . . . I loved . . . I simply adored . . . what *have* you got on, for goodness sake? A jersey? It's clogged. Have you been rolling in mud? [*Slight pause.*] You haven't been rolling in mud, have you? [*She rises and goes over to him.*] And what have you got under your jersey? Let's see. [*Slight pause.*] I'm not tickling you, am I? No. Good . . . Lord, is this a vest? That's quite original. Quite original. [*She sits on the arm of his chair.*] Hmmnn, you're a solid old boy, I must say. Not at all like a jelly. All you need is a bath. A lovely lathery bath. And a good scrub. A lovely lathery scrub. [*Pause.*] Don't you? It will be a pleasure. [*She throws her arms round him.*] I'm going to keep you. I'm going to keep you, you dreadful chap, and call you Barnabas. Isn't it dark, Barnabas? Your eyes, your eyes, your great big eyes.

[*Pause.*]

My husband would never have guessed your name. Never. [*She kneels at his feet. Whispering.*] It's me you were waiting for, wasn't it? You've been standing waiting for me. You've seen me in the woods, picking daisies, in my apron, my pretty daisy apron, and you came and stood, poor creature, at my gate, till death us do part. Poor Barnabas. I'm going to put you to bed. I'm going to put you to bed and watch over you. But first you must have a good whacking great bath. And I'll buy you pretty little things that will suit you. And little toys to play with. On your deathbed. Why shouldn't you die happy?

[*A shout from the hall.*]

EDWARD: Well?

[*Footsteps upstage.*]

Well?

FLORA: Don't come in.

EDWARD: Well?

FLORA: He's dying.

EDWARD: Dying? He's not dying.

FLORA: I tell you, he's very ill.

EDWARD: He's not dying! Nowhere near. He'll see you cremated.

FLORA: The man is desperately ill!

EDWARD: Ill! You lying slut. Get back to your trough!

FLORA: Edward . . .

EDWARD [*violently*]:   To your trough!

[*She goes out. Pause.*]

[*Coolly.*] Good evening to you. Why are you sitting in the gloom? Oh, you've begun to disrobe. Too warm? Let's open the windows, then, what?

[*He opens the windows.*]

Pull the blinds.

[*He pulls the blinds.*]

And close . . . the curtains . . . again.

[*He closes the curtains.*]

Ah. Air will enter through the side chinks. Of the blinds. And filter through the curtains. I hope. Don't want to suffocate, do we?

[*Pause.*]

More comfortable? Yes. You look different in darkness. Take off all your togs, if you like. Make yourself at home. Strip to your buff. Do as you would in your own house.

[*Pause.*]

Did you say something?

[*Pause.*]

Did you say something?

[*Pause.*]

Anything? Well then, tell me about your boyhood. Mmnn?

[*Pause.*]

What did you do with it? Run? Swim? Kick the ball? You kicked the ball? What position? Left back? Goalie? First reserve?

[*Pause.*]

I used to play myself. Country house matches, mostly. Kept wicket and batted number seven.
[*Pause.*]
Kept wicket and batted number seven. Man called—Cavendish, I think had something of your style. Bowled left arm over the wicket, always kept his cap on, quite a dab hand at solo whist, preferred a good round of prop and cop to anything else.
[*Pause.*]
On wet days when the field was swamped.
[*Pause.*]
Perhaps you don't play cricket.
[*Pause.*]
Perhaps you never met Cavendish and never played cricket. You look less and less like a cricketer the more I see of you. Where did you live in those days? God damn it, I'm entitled to know something about you! You're in my blasted house, on my territory, drinking my wine, eating my duck! Now you've had your fill you sit like a hump, a mouldering heap. In my room. My den. I can rem ... [*He stops abruptly.*]
[*Pause.*]
You find that funny? Are you grinning?
[*Pause.*]
[*In disgust.*] Good Christ, is that a grin on your face? [*Further disgust.*] It's lopsided. It's all—down on one side. You're grinning. It amuses you, does it? When I tell you how well I remember this room, how well I remember this den. [*Muttering.*] Ha. Yesterday now, it was clear, clearly defined, so clearly.
[*Pause.*]
The garden, too, was sharp, lucid, in the rain, in the sun.
[*Pause.*]
My den, too, was sharp, arranged for my purpose ... quite satisfactory.
[*Pause.*]
The house too, was polished, all the banisters were polished, and the stair rods, and the curtain rods.
[*Pause.*]
My desk was polished, and my cabinet.
[*Pause.*]
I was polished. [*Nostalgic.*] I could stand on the hill and look through my telescope at the sea. And follow the path of the three-masted schooner, feeling fit, well aware of my sinews, their suppleness, my arms lifted holding the telescope, steady, easily, no trembling, my aim was perfect, I could pour hot water down the spoon-hole, yes, easily, no difficulty, my grasp firm, my command established, my life was accounted for, I was ready for my excursions to the cliff, down the path to the back gate, through the long grass, no heed to watch for the nettles, my progress was

fluent, after my long struggling against all kinds of usurpers, disreputables, lists, literally lists of people anxious to do me down, and my reputation down, my command was established, all summer I would breakfast, survey my landscape, take my telescope, examine the overhanging of my hedges, pursue the narrow lane past the monastery, climb the hill, adjust the lens [*he mimes a telescope*], watch the progress of the three-masted schooner, my progress was as sure, as fluent . . .

[*Pause. He drops his arms.*]

Yes, yes, you're quite right, it is funny.

[*Pause.*]

Laugh your bloody head off! Go on. Don't mind me. No need to be polite.

[*Pause.*]

That's right.

[*Pause.*]

You're quite right, it is funny. I'll laugh with you!

[*He laughs.*]

Ha-ha-ha! Yes! You're laughing with me, I'm laughing with you, we're laughing together!

[*He laughs and stops.*]

[*Brightly.*] Why did I invite you into this room? That's your next question, isn't it? Bound to be.

[*Pause.*]

Well, why not, you might say? My oldest acquaintance. My nearest and dearest. My kith and kin. But surely correspondence would have been as satisfactory . . . more satisfactory? We could have exchanged postcards, couldn't we? What? Views, couldn't we? Of sea and land, city and village, town and country, autumn and winter . . . clocktowers . . . museums . . . citadels . . . bridges . . . rivers . . .

[*Pause.*]

Seeing you stand, at the back gate, such close proximity, was not at all the same thing.

[*Pause.*]

What are you doing? You're taking off your balaclava . . . you've decided not to. No, very well then, all things considered, did I then invite you into this room with express intention of asking you to take off your balaclava, in order to determine your resemblance to—some other person? The answer is no, certainly not, I did not, for when I first saw you you wore no balaclava. No headcovering of any kind, in fact. You looked quite different without a head—I mean without a hat—I mean without a head-covering, of any kind. In fact every time I have seen you you have looked quite different to the time before.

[*Pause.*]

Even now you look different. Very different.
[*Pause.*]
Admitted that sometimes I viewed you through dark glasses, yes, and sometimes through light glasses, and on other occasions bare eyed, and on other occasions through the bars of the scullery window, or from the roof, the roof, yes in driving snow, or from the bottom of the drive in thick fog, or from the roof again in blinding sun, so blinding, so hot, that I had to skip and jump and bounce in order to remain in one place. Ah, that's good for a guffaw, is it? That's good for a belly laugh? Go on, then. Let it out. Let yourself go, for God's ... [*He catches his breath.*] You're crying ...
[*Pause.*]
[*Moved.*] You haven't been laughing. You're crying.
[*Pause.*]
You're weeping. You're shaking with grief. For me. I can't believe it. For my plight. I've been wrong.
[*Pause.*]
[*Briskly.*] Come, come, stop it. Be a man. Blow your nose for goodness sake. Pull yourself together.
[*He sneezes.*]
Ah.
[*He rises. Sneeze.*]
Ah. Fever. Excuse me.
[*He blows his nose.*]
I've caught a cold. A germ. In my eyes. It was this morning. In my eyes. My eyes.
[*Pause. He falls to the floor.*]
Not that I had any difficulty in seeing you, no, no, it was not so much my sight, my sight is excellent—in winter I run about with nothing on but a pair of polo shorts—no, it was not so much any deficiency in my sight as the airs between me and my object—don't weep—the change of air, the currents obtaining in the space between me and my object, the shades they make, the shapes they take, the quivering, the eternal quivering—please stop crying—nothing to do with heat-haze. Sometimes, of course, I would take shelter, shelter to compose myself. Yes, I would seek a tree, a cranny of bushes, erect my canopy and so make shelter. And rest. [*Low murmur.*] And then I no longer heard the wind or saw the sun. Nothing entered, nothing left my nook. I lay on my side in my polo shorts, my fingers lightly in contact with the blades of grass, the earthflowers, the petals of the earthflowers flaking, lying on my palm, the underside of all the great foliage dark, above me, but it is only afterwards I say the foliage was dark, the petals flaking, then I said nothing, I remarked nothing, things happened upon me, then in my times of shelter, the shades, the

petals, carried themselves, carried their bodies upon me, and nothing entered my nook, nothing left it.
[*Pause.*]
But then, the time came. I saw the wind. I saw the wind, swirling, and the dust at my back gate, lifting, and the long grass, scything together . . .
[*Slowly, in horror.*] You *are* laughing. You're laughing. Your face. Your body. [*Overwhelming nausea and horror.*] Rocking . . . gasping . . . rocking . . . shaking . . . rocking . . . heaving . . . rocking . . . You're laughing at me! Aaaaahhhh!
[*The* MATCHSELLER *rises. Silence.*]
You look younger. You look extraordinarily . . . youthful.
[*Pause.*]
You want to examine the graden? It must be very bright, in the moonlight.
[*Becoming weaker.*] I would like to join you . . . explain . . . show you . . . the garden . . . explain . . . The plants . . . where I run . . . my track . . . in training . . . I was number one sprinter at Howells . . . when a stripling . . . no more than a stripling . . . licked . . . men twice my strength . . . when a stripling . . . like yourself.
[*Pause.*]
[*Flatly.*] The pool must be glistening. In the moonlight. And the lawn. I remember it well. The cliff. The sea. The three-masted schooner.
[*Pause.*]
[*With great, final effort—a whisper.*] Who are you?
FLORA [*off*]:   Barnabas?
[*Pause.*]
[*She enters.*]
Ah, Barnabas. Everything is ready.
[*Pause.*]
I want to show you my garden, your garden. You must see my japonica, my convolvulus . . . my honeysuckle, my clematis.
[*Pause.*]
The summer is coming. I've put up your canopy for you. You can lunch in the garden, by the pool. I've polished the whole house for you.
[*Pause.*]
Take my hand.
[*Pause. The* MATCHSELLER *goes over to her.*]
Yes. Oh, wait a moment.
[*Pause.*]
Edward. Here is your tray.
[*She crosses to* EDWARD *with the tray of matches, and puts it in his hands. Then she and the* MATCHSELLER *start to go out as the curtain falls slowly.*]

Samuel Beckett

Watt at the House of Knott

from *Watt*

In Samuel Beckett's novel, *Watt,* a contemporary everyman like Kafka's K. in *The Castle,* sets out on a journey—reminiscent of the romantic quest for spiritual certainty—to Knott's house, where apparently, he has been hired as a servant. Armed with the weapon of rationality, Watt hopes to find in the house of Knott a final refuge from the anxieties of existence. Upon his arrival, "in his midst at last, after so many tedious years spent clinging to the perimeter," the weary Watt experiences "irrefragable" "premonitions . . . of imminent harmony," premonitions "that all is well, or at least for the best." He conceives of Knott's "establishment" as the timeless and abiding center of a Leibnitzian universe and Knott as its *logos,* its Word, its unmoved mover. Then, as with Arsene, whom Watt has come to replace, "Something slips," and everything suddenly changes. It is a change similar to that ominous one recorded by Roquentin in the first entry of his diary *(Nausea):* "Something has happened to me. I can't doubt it any more. It came as an illness does, not like an ordinary certainty, not like anything evident. It came cunningly, little by little: I felt a little strange, a little put out, that's all. Once established it never moved, it stayed quiet, and I was able to persuade myself that nothing was the matter with me, that it was a false alarm. And now, it's blossoming." As Arsene puts it prophetically to Watt in recalling his own experience, "What was changed was existence off the ladder. Do not come down the ladder, Ifor, I haf taken it away. This I am happy to inform you is the reversed metamorphosis, the Laurel into Daphne. The old thing where it always was, back again." What Watt discovers at the "end" of his journey is that Knott is not an abiding presence but, like Godot in *Waiting for Godot,* a mysterious and elusive absence. The following episode from Section II of the novel, which describes Watt's service on the ground floor, presents the initial stages of his psychological disintegration, when his weapon against the absurdity of existence in Knott's house— the "objective" and object-ifying language of rational explanation (the "old words"), no longer works, no longer is capable of "making a pillow . . . for a head," of setting his mind *at rest.*

On only one occasion, during Watt's period of service on the ground floor, was the threshold crossed by a stranger, by other feet that is that Mr Knott's, or Erskine's, or Watt's, for all were strangers to Mr Knott's establishment, as far as Watt could see, with the exception of Mr Knott himself, and his personnel at any given moment.

This fugitive penetration took place shortly after Watt's arrival. On his answering the door, as his habit was, when there was a knock at the door, he found standing before it, or so he realized later, arm in arm, an old man and a middleaged man. The latter said:

We are the Galls, father and son, and we are come, what is more, all the way from town, to choon the piano.

They were two, and they stood, arm in arm, in this way, because the father was blind, like so many members of his profession. For if the father had not been blind, then he would not have needed his son to hold his arm, and guide him on his rounds, no, but he would have set his son free, to go about his own business. So Watt supposed, though there was nothing in the father's face to show that he was blind, nor in his attitude either, except that he leaned on his son in a way expressive of a great need of support. But he might have done this, if he had been halt, or merely tired, on account of his great age. There was no family likeness between the two, as far as Watt could make out, and nevertheless he knew that he was in the presence of a father and son, for had he not just been told so. Or were they not perhaps merely stepfather and stepson. We are the Galls, stepfather and stepson—those were perhaps the words that should have been spoken. But it was natural to prefer the others. Not that they could not very well be a true father and son, without resembling each other in the very least, for they could.

How very fortunate for Mr Gall, said Watt, that he has his son at his command, whose manner is all devotion and whose mere presence, when he might obviously be earning an honest penny elsewhere, attests an affliction characteristic of the best tuners, and justifies emoluments rather higher than the usual.

When he had led them to the music-room, and left them there, Watt wondered if he had done right. He felt he had done right, but he was not sure. Should he not perhaps rather have sent them flying about their business? Watt's feeling was that anyone who demanded, with such tranquil assurance, to be admitted to Mr Knott's house, deserved to be admitted, in the absence of precise instructions to the contrary.

The music-room was a large bare white room. The piano was in the window. The head, and neck, in plaster, very white, of Buxtehude, was on the mantelpiece. A ravanastron hung, on the wall, from a nail, like a plover.

After a short time Watt returned to the music-room, with a tray, of refreshments.

Not Mr Gall Senior, but Mr Gall Junior, was tuning the piano, to Watt's great surprise. Mr Gall Senior was standing in the middle of the room, perhaps listening. Watt did not take this to mean that Mr Gall Junior was the true piano-tuner, and Mr Gall Senior simply a poor blind old man, hired for the occasion, no. But he took it rather to mean that Mr Gall Senior, feeling his end at hand, and anxious that his son should follow in his footsteps, was putting the finishing touches to a hasty instruction, before it was too late.

While Watt looked round, for a place to set down his tray, Mr Gall Junior brought his work to a close. He reassembled the piano case, put back his tools in their bag, and stood up.

The mice have returned, he said.

The elder said nothing. Watt wondered if he had heard.

Nine dampers remain, said the younger, and an equal number of hammers.

Not corresponding, I hope, said the elder.

In one case, said the younger.

The elder had nothing to say to this.

The strings are in flitters, said the younger.

The elder had nothing to say to this either.

The piano is doomed, in my opinion, said the younger.

The piano-tuner also, said the elder.

The pianist also, said the younger.

This was perhaps the principal incident of Watt's early days in Mr Knott's house.

In a sense it resembled all the incidents of note proposed to Watt during his stay in Mr Knott's house, and of which a certain number will be recorded in this place, without addition, or subtraction, and in a sense not.

It resembled them in the sense that it was not ended, when it was past, but continued to unfold, in Watt's head, from beginning to end, over and over again, the complex connexions of its lights and shadows, the passing from silence to sound and from sound to silence, the stillness before the movement and the stillness after, the quickenings and retardings, the approaches and the separations, all the shifting detail of its march and ordinance, according to the irrevocable caprice of its taking place. It resembled them in the vigour with which it developed a purely plastic content, and gradually lost, in the nice processes of its light, its sound, its impacts and its rhythm, all meaning, even the most literal.

Thus the scene in the music-room, with the two Galls, ceased very soon to signify for Watt a piano tuned, an obscure family and professional relation, an exchange of judgments more or less intelligible, and so on, if indeed it had ever signified such things, and became a mere example of light commenting bodies, and stillness motion, and silence sound, and comment comment.

This fragility of the outer meaning had a bad effect on Watt, for it caused him to seek for another, for some meaning of what had passed, in the image of how it had passed.

The most meagre, the least plausible, would have satisfied Watt, who had not seen a symbol, nor executed an interpretation, since the age of fourteen, or fifteen, and who had lived, miserably it is true, among face values all his adult life, face values at least for him. Some see the flesh before the bones, and some see the bones before the flesh, and some never see the bones at all, and some never see the flesh at all, never never see the flesh at all. But whatever it was Watt saw, with the first look, that was enough for Watt, that had always been enough for Watt, more than enough for Watt. And he had experienced literally nothing, since the age of fourteen, or fifteen, of which in retrospect he was not content to say, That is what happened then. He could recall, not indeed with any satisfaction, but as ordinary occasions, the time when his dead father appeared to him in a wood, with his trousers rolled up over his knees and his shoes and socks in his hand; or the time when in his surprise at hearing a voice urging him, in terms of unusual coarseness, to do away with himself, he narrowly escaped being knocked down, by a dray; or the time when alone in a rowing-boat, far from land, he suddenly smelt flowering currant; or the time when an old lady of delicate upbringing, and advantageous person, for she was amputated well above the knee, whom he had pursued with his assiduities on no fewer than three distinct occasions, unstrapped her wooden leg, and laid aside her crutch. Here no tendency appeared, on the part of his father's trousers, for example, to break up into an arrangement of appearances, grey, flaccid and probably fistular, or of his father's legs to vanish in the farce of their properties, no, but his father's legs and trousers, as then seen, in the wood, and subsequently brought to mind, remained legs and trousers, and not only legs and trousers, but his father's legs and trousers, that is to say quite different from any of the legs and trousers that Watt had ever seen, and he had seen a great quantity, both of legs and of trousers, in his time. The incident of the Galls, on the contrary, ceased so rapidly to have even the paltry significance of two men, come to tune a piano, and tuning it, and exchanging a few words, as men will do, and going, that this seemed rather to belong to some story heard long before, an instant in the life of another, ill told, ill heard, and more than half forgotten.

So Watt did not know what had happened. He did not care, to do him justice, what had happened. But he felt the need to think that such and such a thing had happened then, the need to be able to say, when the scene began to unroll its sequences, Yes, I remember, that is what happened then.

This need remained with Watt, this need not always satisfied, during the greater part of his stay in Mr Knott's house. For the incident of the Galls father and son was followed by others of a similar kind, incidents that is to say of great formal brilliance and indeterminable purport.

Watt's stay in Mr Knott's house was less agreeable, on this account, than it would have been, if such incidents had been unknown, or his attitude towards them less anxious, that is to say, if Mr Knott's house had been another house, or Watt another man. For outside Mr Knott's house, and of course grounds, such incidents were unknown, or so Watt supposed. And Watt could not accept them for what they perhaps were, the simple games that time plays with space, now with these toys, and now with those, but was obliged, because of his peculiar character, to enquire into what they meant, oh no into what they really meant, his character was not so peculiar as all that, but into what they might be induced to mean, with the help of a little patience, a little ingenuity.

But what was this pursuit of meaning, in this indifference to meaning? And to what did it tend? These are delicate questions. For when Watt at last spoke of this time, it was a time long past, and of which his recollections were, in a sense, perhaps less clear than he would have wished, though too clear for his liking, in another. Add to this the notorious difficulty of recapturing, at will, modes of feeling peculiar to a certain time, and to a certain place, and perhaps also to a certain state of the health, when the time is past, and the place left, and the body struggling with quite a new situation. Add to this the obscurity of Watt's communications, the rapidity of his utterance and the eccentricities of his syntax, as elsewhere recorded. Add to this the material conditions in which these communications were made. Add to this the scant aptitude to receive of him to whom they were proposed. Add to this the scant aptitude to give of him to whom they were committed. And some idea will perhaps be obtained of the difficulties experienced in formulating, not only such matters as those here in question, but the entire body of Watt's experience, from the moment of his entering Mr Knott's establishment to the moment of his leaving it.

But before passing from the Galls father and son to matters less litigious, or less tediously litigious, it seems advisable that the little that is known, on this subject, should be said. For the incident of the Galls father and son was the first and type of many. And the little that is known about it has not yet all been said. Much has been said, but not all.

Not that many things remain to be said, on the subject of the Galls father and son, for they do not. For only three or four things remain to be said, in this connexion. And three or four things are not really many, in comparison with the number of things that might have been known, and said, on this subject, and now never shall.

What distressed Watt in this incident of the Galls father and son, and in subsequent similar incidents, was not so much that he did not know what had happened, for he did not care what had happened, as that nothing had happened, that a thing that was nothing had happened, with the utmost formal distinctness, and that it continued to happen, in his mind, he supposed, though he did not know exactly what that meant, and though it seemed to be outside him, before him, about him, and so on, inexorably to unroll its phases, beginning with the first (the knock that was not a knock) and ending with the last (the door closing that was not a door closing), and omitting none, uninvoked, at the most unexpected moments, and the most inopportune. Yes, Watt could not accept, as no doubt Erskine could not accept, and as no doubt Arsene and Walter and Vincent and the others had been unable to accept, that nothing had happened, with all the clarity and solidity of something, and that it revisited him in such a way that he was forced to submit to it all over again, to hear the same sounds, see the same lights, touch the same surfaces, and so on, as when they had first involved him in their unintelligible intricacies. If he had been able to accept it, then perhaps it would not have revisited him, and this would have been a great saving of vexation, to put it mildly. But he could not accept it, could not bear it. One wonders sometimes where Watt thought he was. In a culture-park?

But if he could say, when the knock came, the knock become a knock, or the door become a door, in his mind, presumably in his mind, whatever that might mean, Yes, I remember, that is what happened then, if then he could say that, then he thought that then the scene would end, and trouble him no more, as the appearance of his father with his trousers rolled up and his shoes and socks in his hands troubled him no more, because he could say, when it began, Yes, yes, I remember, that was when my father appeared to me, in the wood, dressed for wading. But to elicit something from nothing requires a certain skill and Watt was not always unsuccessful either, for he was not. For if he had been always unsuccessful, how would it have been possible for him to speak of the Galls father and son, and of the piano they had come all the way from town to tune, and of their tuning it, and of their passing the remarks they had passed, the one to the other, in the way he did? No, he could never have spoken at all of these things, if all had continued to mean nothing, as some continued to mean nothing, that is to say, right up to the end. For the only way one can speak of nothing is to speak of it as though it were something, just as the only way one can speak of God is to speak of him as though he were a man, which to be sure he was, in a sense, for a time, and as the only way one can speak of man, even our anthropologists have realised that, is to speak of him as though he were a termite. But if Watt was sometimes unsuccessful, and sometimes successful, as in the affair of the Galls father and son, in foisting a meaning there where no meaning appeared, he was most often neither the one, nor the other. For Watt considered, with reason, that he was successful, in this enterprise, when he could evolve, from the meticulous phantoms that beset him, a hypothesis proper to disperse them, as often as this might be found necessary. There was nothing, in this operation, at variance with Watt's habits of mind. For to explain had always been to exorcize, for Watt. And he considered that he was unsuccessful, when he failed to do so. And he considered that he was neither wholly successful, nor wholly unsuccessful, when the hypothesis evolved lost its virtue, after one or two applications, and had to be replaced by another, which in its turn had to be replaced by another, which in due course ceased to be of the least assistance, and so on. And that is what happened, in the majority of cases. Now to give examples of Watt's failures, and of Watt's successes, and of Watt's partial successes, in this connexion, is so to speak impossible. For when he speaks, for example, of the incident of the Galls father and son, does he speak of it in terms of the unique hypothesis that was required, to deal with it, and render it innocuous, or in terms of the latest, or in terms of some other of the series? For when Watt spoke of an incident of this kind, he did not necessarily do so in terms of the unique hypothesis, or of the latest, though this at first sight seems the only possible alternative, and the reason why he did not, why it is not, is this, that when one of the series of hypotheses, with which Watt laboured to preserve his peace of mind, lost its virtue, and had to be laid aside, and another set up in its place, then it sometimes happened that the hypothesis in question, after a sufficient period of rest, recovered its virtue and could be made to serve again, in the place of another, whose usefulness had come to an end, for the time being at least. To such an extent is this true, that one is sometimes tempted to wonder, with reference to two or even three incidents related by Watt as separate and distinct, if they are not in reality the same incident, variously interpreted. As to giving an example of the second event, namely the failure, that is clearly quite out of the question. For there we have to do with events that resisted all Watt's efforts to saddle them with meaning, and a formula, so that he could neither think of them, nor speak of them, but only suffer them, when they recurred, though it seems probable that they recurred no more, at the period of Watt's revelation, to me, but were as though they had never been.

Finally, to return to the incident of the Galls father and son, as related by Watt, did it have that meaning for Watt at the time of its taking place, and then lose that meaning, and then recover it? Or did it have some quite different meaning for Watt at the time of its taking place, and then lose that meaning, and then receive that, alone or among others, which it exhibited, in Watt's relation? Or did it have no meaning whatever for Watt at the moment of its taking place, were there neither Galls nor piano then, but only an unintelligible succession of changes, from which Watt finally extracted the Galls and the piano, in self-defence? These are most delicate questions. Watt spoke of it as involving, in the original, the Galls and the piano, but he was obliged to do this, even if the original had nothing to do with the Galls and the piano. For even if the Galls and the piano were long posterior to the phenomena destined to become them, Watt was obliged to think, and speak, of the incident, even at the moment of its taking place, as the incident of the Galls and the piano, if he was to think and speak of it at all, and it may be assumed that Watt would never have thought or spoken of such incidents, if he had not been under the absolute necessity of doing so. But generally speaking it seems probable that the meaning attributed to this particular type of incident, by Watt, in his relations, was now the initial meaning that had been lost and then recovered, and now a meaning that had been lost and then recovered, and now a meaning quite distinct from the initial meaning, and now a meaning evolved, after a delay of varying length, and with greater or less pains, from the initial absence of meaning.

One more word on this subject.

Watt learned towards the end of this stay in Mr Knott's house to accept that nothing had happened, that a nothing had happened, learned to bear it and even, in a shy way, to like it. But then it was too late.

That then is that in which the incident of the Galls father and son resembled other incidents, of which it was merely the first in time, other incidents of note. But to say, as has been said, that the incident of the Galls father and son had this aspect in common with all the subsequent incidents of note, is perhaps to go a little too far. For not all the subsequent incidents of note, with which Watt was called upon to deal, during his stay in Mr Knott's house, and of course grounds, presented this aspect, no, but some meant something from the very beginning, and continued to mean it, with all the tenacity of, for example, the flowering currant in the rowing-boat, or the capitulation of the one-legged Mrs Watson, right up to the end.

As to that in which the incident of the Galls father and son differed from the subsequent incidents of its category, that is no longer clear, and cannot therefore be stated, with profit. But it may be taken that the difference was so nice as with advantage to be neglected, in a synopsis of this kind.

Watt thought sometimes of Arsene. He wondered what had become of the duck. He had not seen her leave the kitchen with Arsene. But then he had not seen Arsene leave the kitchen either. And as the bird was nowhere to be found, in the house or in the garden, Watt supposed she must have slipped away, with her master. He wondered also what Arsene had meant, nay, he wondered what Arsene had said, on the evening of his departure. For his declaration had entered Watt's ears only by fits, and his understanding, like all that enters the ears only by fits, hardly at all. He had realised, to be sure, that Arsene was speaking, and in a sense to him, but something had prevented him, perhaps his fatigue, from paying attention to what was being said and from enquiring into what was being meant. Watt was now inclined to regret this, for from Erskine no information was to be obtained. Not that Wat desired information, for he did not. But he desired words to be applied to his situation, to Mr Knott, to the house, to the grounds, to his duties, to the stairs, to his bedroom, to the kitchen, and in a general way to the conditions of being in which he found himself. For Watt now found himself in the midst of things which, if they consented to be named, did so as it were with reluctance. And the state in which Watt found himself resisted formulation in a way no state had ever done, in which Watt had ever found himself, and Watt had found himself in a great many states, in his day. Looking at a pot, for example, or thinking of a pot, at one of Mr Knott's pots, of one of Mr Knott's pots, it was in vain that Watt said, Pot, pot. Well, perhaps not quite in vain, but very nearly. For it was not a pot, the more he looked, the more he reflected, the more he felt sure of that, that is was not a pot at all. It resembled a pot, it was almost a pot, but it was not a pot of which one could say, Pot, pot, and be comforted. It was in vain that it answered, with unexceptionable adequacy, all the purposes, and performed all the offices, of a pot, it was not a pot. And it was just this hairbreadth departure from the nature of a true pot that so excruciated Watt. For if the approximation had been less close, then Watt would have been less anguished. For then he would not have said, This is a pot, and yet not a pot, no, but then he would have said, This is something of which I do not know the name. And Watt preferred on the whole having to do with things of which he did not know the name, though this too was painful to Watt to having to do with things of which the known name, the proven name, was not the name, any more, for him. For he could always hope, of a thing of which he had never known the name, that he would learn the name, some day, and so be tranquillized. But he could not look forward to this in the case of a thing of which the true name had ceased, suddenly, or gradually, to be the true name for Watt. For the pot remained a pot, Watt felt sure of that, for everyone but Watt. For Watt alone it was not a pot, any more.

Then, when he turned for reassurance to himself, who was not Mr Knott's, in the sense that the pot was, who had come from without and whom the without would take again,[1] he made the distressing discovery that of himself too he could no longer affirm anything that did not seem as false as if he had affirmed it of a stone. Not that Watt was in the habit of affirming things of himself, for he was not, but he found it a help, from time to time, to be able to say, with some appearance of reason, Watt is a man, all the same, Watt is a man, or, Watt is in the street, with thousands of fellow-creatures within call. And Watt was greatly troubled by this tiny little thing, more troubled perhaps than he had ever been by anything, and Watt had been frequently and exceedingly troubled, in his time, by this imperceptible, no, hardly imperceptible, since he perceived it, by this indefinable thing that prevented him from saying, with conviction, and to his relief, of the object that was so like a pot, that it was a pot, and of the creature that still in spite of everything presented a large number of exclusively human characteristics, that it was a man. And Watt's need of semantic succour was at times so great that he would set to trying names on things, and on himself, almost as a woman hats. Thus of the pseudo-pot he would say, after reflection, It is a shield, or, growing bolder, It is a raven, and so on. But the pot proved as little a shield, or a raven, or any other of the things that Watt called it, as a pot. As for himself, though he could no longer call it a man, as he had used to do, with the intuition that he was perhaps not talking nonsense, yet he could not imagine what else to call it, if not a man. But Watt's imagination had never been a lively one. So he continued to think of himself as a man, as his mother had taught him, when she said, There's a good little man, or, There's a bonny little man, or, There's a clever little man. But for all the relief that this afforded him, he might just as well have thought of himself as a box, or an urn.

It was principally for these reasons that Watt would have been glad to hear Erskine's voice, wrapping up safe in words the kitchen space, the extraordinary newel-lamp, the stairs that were never the same and of which even the number of steps seemed to vary, from day to day, and from night to morning, and many other things in the house, and the bushes without and other garden growths, that so often prevented Watt from taking the air, even on the finest day, so that he grew pale, and con-

1. Watt, unlike Arsene, had never supposed that Mr Knott's house would be his last refuge. Was it his first? In a sense it was, but it was not the kind of first refuge that promised to be the last. It occurred to him, of course, towards the end of his stay, that it might have been, that he might have made it, this transitory refuge, the last, if he had been more adroit, or less in need of rest. But Watt was very subject to fancies, towards the end of his stay under Mr Knott's roof. And it was also under the pressure of a similar eleventh hour vision, of what might have been, that Arsene expressed himself on this subject, in the way he did, on the night of his departure. For it is scarcely credible that a man of Arsene's experience could have supposed, in advance, of any given halt, that it was to be the last halt.

stipated, and even the light as it came and went and the clouds that climbed the sky, now slow, now rapid, and generally from west to east, or sank down towards the earth on the other side, for the clouds seen from Mr Knott's premises were not quite the clouds that Watt was used to, and Watt had a great experience of clouds, and could distinguish the various sorts, the cirrhus, the stratus, the cumulus and the various other sorts, at a glance. Not that the fact of Erskine's naming the pot, or of his saying to Watt, My dear fellow, or, My good man, or, God damn you, would have changed the pot into a pot, or Watt into a man, for Watt, for it would not. But it would have shown that at least for Erskine the pot was a pot, and Watt a man. Not that the fact of the pot's being a pot, or Watt's being a man, for Erskine, would have caused the pot to be a pot, or Watt to be a man, for Watt, for it would not. But it would perhaps have lent a little colour to the hope, sometimes entertained by Watt, that he was in poor health, owing to the efforts of his body to adjust itself to an unfamiliar milieu, and that these would be successful, in the end, and his health restored, and things appear, and himself appear, in their ancient guise, and consent to be named, with the time-honoured names, and forgotten. Not that Watt longed at all times for this restoration, of things, of himself, to their comparative innocuousness, for he did not. For there were times when he felt a feeling closely resembling the feeling of satisfaction, at his being so abandoned, by the last rats. For after these there would be no more rats, not a rat left, and there were times when Watt almost welcomed this prospect, of being rid of his last rats, at last. It would be lonely, to be sure, at first, and silent, after the gnawing, the scurrying, the little cries. Things and himself, they had gone with him now for so long, in the foul weather, and in the less foul. Things in the ordinary sense, and then the emptinesses between them, and the light high up before it reached them, and then the other thing, the high heavy hollow jointed unstable thing, that trampled down the grasses, and scattered the sand, in its pursuits. But if there were times when Watt envisaged this dereliction with something like satisfaction, these were rare, particularly in the early stages of Watt's stay in Mr Knott's house. And most often he found himself longing for a voice, for Erskine's, since he was alone with Erskine, to speak of the little world of Mr Knott's establishment, with the old words, the old credentials. There was of course the gardener, to speak of the garden. But could the gardener speak of the garden, the gardener who went home every evening, before nightfall, and did not return next morning until the sun was well up, in the sky? No, the gardener's remarks were not evidence, in Watt's opinion. Only Erskine could speak of the garden, as only Erskine could speak of the house, usefully, to Watt. And Erskine never spoke, either of the one, or of the other. Indeed Erskine never opened his mouth, in Watt's presence, except to eat, or belch, or cough, or keck, or muse, or sigh, or sing, or sneeze. It is true that during the first week hardly a day passed that Erskine did not address himself to Watt, on the subject of Watt's duties. But in the first week Watt's words had not yet begun to fail him, or Watt's world to become unspeakable. It is true also that from time to time Erskine would come running to Watt, all in a fluster, with some quite ridiculous question, such as, Did you see Mr Knott?, or, Has Kate come? But this was much later. Perhaps some day, said Watt, he will ask, Where is thy pot?, or, Where did you put that pot? These questions, absurd as they were, constituted nevertheless an acknowledgement of Watt that Watt was not slow to appreciate. But he would have appreciated it more if it had come earlier, before he had grown used to his loss of species. . . .

Donald Barthelme
Kierkegaard Unfair to Schlegel

A: I use the girl on the train a lot. I'm on a train, a European train with compartments. A young girl enters and sits opposite me. She is blond, wearing a short-sleeved sweater, a short skirt. The sweater has white and blue stripes, the skirt is dark blue. The girl has a book, *Introduction to French* or something like that. We are in France but she is not French. She has a book and a pencil. She's extremely self-conscious. She opens the book and begins miming close attention, you know, making marks with the pencil at various points. Meanwhile I am carefully looking out of the window, regarding the terrain. I'm trying to avoid looking at her legs. The skirt has raised itself a bit, you see, there is a lot of leg to look at. I'm also trying to avoid looking at her breasts. They appear to be free under the white-and-blue sweater. There is a small gold pin pinned to the sweater on the left side. It has lettering on it. I can't make out what it says. The girl shifts in her seat, moves from side to side, adjusting her position. She's very very self-aware. All her movements are just a shade overdone. The book is in her lap. Her legs are fairly wide apart, very tanned, the color of—

Source: From Donald Barthelme, *City Life* (New York: Farrar, Straus & Giroux, Inc., 1970), pp. 89–100. Reprinted by permission of the publisher.

Q: That's a very common fantasy.
A: All my fantasies are extremely ordinary.
Q: Does it give you pleasure?
A: A poor ... A rather unsatisfactory ...
Q: What is the frequency?
A: Oh God who knows. Once in a while. Sometimes.
Q: You're not cooperating.
A: I'm not interested.
Q: I might do an article.
A: I don't like to have my picture taken.
Q: Solipsism plus triumphantism.
A: It's possible.

Q: You're not political?
A: I'm extremely political in a way that does no good to anybody.
Q: You don't participate?
A: I participate. I make demands, sign newspaper advertisements, vote. I make small campaign contributions to the candidate of my choice and turn my irony against the others. But I accomplish nothing. I march, it's ludicrous. In the last march, there were eighty-seven thousand people marching, by the most conservative estimate, and yet being in the midst of them, marching with them ... I wanted to march with the Stationary Engineers, march under their banner, but two cops prevented me, they said I couldn't enter at that point, I had to go back to the beginning. So I went back to the beginning and marched with the Food Handlers for Peace and Freedom.
Q: What sort of people were they?
A: They looked just like everybody else. It's possible they weren't real food handlers. Maybe just the two holding the sign. I don't know. There were a lot of girls in black pajamas and peasant straw hats, very young girls, high-school girls, running, holding hands in a long chain, laughing ...

Q: You've been pretty hard on our machines. You've withheld your enthusiasm, that's damaging ...
A: I'm sorry.
Q: Do you think your irony could be helpful in changing the government?
A: I think the government is very often in an ironic relation to itself. And that's helpful. For example: we're spending a great deal of money for this army we have, a very large army, beautifully equipped. We're spending something on the order of twenty billions a year for it. Now, the whole point of an army is—what's the word?—deterrence. And the nut of deter-

rency is credibility. So what does the government do? It goes and sells off its surplus uniforms. And the kids start wearing them, uniforms or parts of uniforms, because they're cheap and have some sort of style. And immediately you get this vast clown army in the streets parodying the real army. And they mix periods, you know, you get parody British grenadiers and parody World War I types and parody Sierra Maestra types. So you have all these kids walking around wearing these filthy uniforms with wound stripes, hash marks, Silver Stars, but also ostrich feathers, Day-Glo vests, amulets containing powdered rhinoceros horn ... You have this splendid clown army in the streets standing over against the real one. And of course the clown army constitutes a very serious attack on all the ideas which support the real army including the basic notion of having an army at all. The government has opened itself to all this, this undermining of its own credibility, just because it wants to make a few dollars peddling old uniforms. . . .

Q: How is my car?
Q: How is my nail?
Q: How is the taste of my potato?
Q: How is the cook of my potato?
Q: How is my garb?
Q: How is my button?
Q: How is the flower bath?
Q: How is the shame?
Q: How is the plan?
Q: How is the flue?
Q: How is my mad mother?
Q: How is the aphorism I left with you?

Q: You are an ironist.
A: It's useful.
Q: How is it useful?
A: Well, let me tell you a story. Several years ago I was living in a rented house in Colorado. The house was what is called a rancher—three of four bedrooms, knotty pine or some such on the inside, cedar shakes or something like that on the outside. It was owned by a ski instructor who lived there with his family in the winter. It had what seemed to be hundreds of closets and we immediately discovered that these closets were filled to overflowing with all kinds of play equipment. Never in my life had I seen so much play equipment gathered together in one place outside, say, Abercrombie's. There were bows and arrows and shuffleboard and croquet sets, putting greens and trampolines and things that you strapped to your feet and jumped up and down on, table tennis and jai alai and

poker chips and home roulette wheels, chess and checkers and Chinese checkers and balls of all kinds, hoops and nets and wickets, badminton and books and a thousand board games, and a dingus with cymbals on top that you banged on the floor to keep time to the piano. The merest drawer in a bedside table was choked with marked cards and Monopoly money.

Now, suppose I had been of an ironical turn of mind and wanted to make a joke about all this, some sort of joke that would convey that I had noticed the striking degree of boredom implied by the presence of all this impedimenta and one which would also serve to comment upon the particular way of struggling with boredom that these people had chosen. I might have said, for instance, that the remedy is worse than the disease. Or quoted Nietzsche to the effect that the thought of suicide is a great consolation and had helped him through many a bad night. Either of these perfectly good jokes would do to annihilate the situation of being uncomfortable in this house. The shuffleboard sticks, the barbells, balls of all kinds —my joke has, in effect, thrown them out of the world. An amazing magical power!

Now, suppose that I am suddenly curious about this amazing magical power. Suppose I become curious about how my irony actually works— how if functions. I pick up a copy of Kierkegaard's *The Concept of Irony* (the ski instructor is also a student of Kierkegaard) and I am immediately plunged into difficulties. The situation bristles with difficulties. To begin with, Kierkegaard says that the outstanding feature of irony is that it confers upon the ironist a subjective freedom. The subject, the speaker, is negatively free. If what the ironist says is not his meaning, or is the opposite of his meaning, he is free both in relation to others and in relation to himself. He is not bound by what he has said. Irony is a means of depriving the object of its reality in order that the subject may feel free.

Irony deprives the object of its reality when the ironist says something about the object that is not what he means. Kierkegaard distinguishes between the phenomenon (the word) and the essence (the thought or meaning). Truth demands an identity of essence and phenomenon. But with irony quote the phenomenon is not the essence but the opposite of the essence unquote page 264. The object is deprived of its reality by what I have said about it. Regarded in an ironical light, the object shivers, shatters, disappears. Irony is thus destructive and what Kierkegaard worries about a lot is that irony has nothing to put in the place of what it has destroyed. The new actuality—what the ironist has said about the object —is peculiar in that it is a comment upon a former actuality rather than a new actuality. This account of Kierkegaard's account of irony is grossly oversimplified. Now, consider an irony directed not against a given object but against the whole of existence. An irony directed against the whole of existence produces, according to Kierkegaard, estrangement and poetry. The ironist, serially successful in disposing of various objects of his irony, becomes drunk with freedom. He becomes, in Kierkegaard's words, lighter and lighter. Irony becomes an infinite absolute negativity. Quote irony no longer directs itself against this or that particular phenomenon, against a particular thing unquote. Quote the whole of existence has become alien to the ironic subject unquote page 276. For Kierkegaard, the actuality of irony is poetry. This may be clarified by reference to Kierkegaard's treatment of Schlegel.

Schlegel had written a book, a novel, called *Lucinde*. Kierkegaard is very hard on Schlegel and *Lucinde*. Kierkegaard characterizes this novel of Schlegel's as quote poetical unquote page 308. By which he means to suggest that Schlegel has constructed an actuality which is superior to the historical actuality and a substitute for it. By negating the historical actuality poetry quote opens up a higher actuality, expands and transfigures the imperfect into the perfect, and thereby softens and mitigates that deep pain which would darken and obscure all things unquote page 312. That's beautiful. Now this would seem to be a victory for Schlegel, and indeed Kierkegaard says that poetry is a victory over the world. But it is not the case that *Lucinde* is a victory for Schlegel. What is wanted, Kierkegaard says, is not a victory over the world but a reconciliation with the world. And it is soon discovered that although poetry is a kind of reconciliation, the distance between the new actuality, higher and more perfect than the historical actuality, and the historical actuality, lower and more imperfect than the new actuality, produces not a reconciliation but animosity. Quote so that it often becomes no reconciliation at all but rather animosity unquote same page. What began as a victory eventuates in animosity. The true task is reconciliation with actuality and the true reconciliation, Kierkegaard says, is religion. Without discussing whether or not the true reconciliation is religion (I have a deep bias against religion which precludes my discussing the question intelligently) let me say that I believe that Kierkegaard is here unfair to Schlegel. I find it hard to persuade myself that the relation of Schlegel's novel to actuality is what Kierkegaard says it is. I have reasons for this (I believe, for example, that Kierkegaard fastens upon Schlegel's novel in its prescriptive aspect—in which it presents itself as a text telling us how to live—and neglects other aspects, its objecthood for one) but my reasons are not so interesting. What is interesting is my making the statement that I think Kierkegaard is unfair to Schlegel. And that the whole thing it is nothing else but a damned shame and crime!

Because that is not what I think at all. We have to do here with my own irony. Because of course Kierkegaard was "fair" to Schlegel. In making a statement to the contrary I am attempting to . . . I might have several purposes—simply being provocative, for example. But mostly I am trying to annihilate Kierkegaard in order to deal with his disapproval.

Q: Of Schlegel?
A: Of me.

Q: What is she doing now?
A: She appears to be—
Q: How does she look?
A: Self-absorbed.
Q: That's not enough. You can't just say, "Self-absorbed." You have to give more . . . You've made a sort of promise which . . .
A:
Q: Are her eyes closed?
A: Her eyes are open. She's staring.
Q: What is she staring at?
A: Nothing that I can see.
Q: And?
A: She's caressing her breasts.
Q: Still wearing the blouse?
A: Yes.
Q: A yellow blouse?
A: Blue.

A: Sunday. We took the baby to Central Park. At the Children's Zoo she wanted to ride a baby Shetland pony which appeared to be about ten minutes old. Howled when told she could not. Then into a meadow (not a real meadow but an excuse for a meadow) for ball-throwing. I slept last night on the couch rather than in the bed. The couch is harder and when I can't sleep I need a harder surface. Dreamed that my father told me that my work was garbage. Mr. Garbage, he called me in the dream. Then, at dawn, the baby woke me again. She had taken off her nightclothes and climbed into a pillowcase. She was standing by the couch in the pillowcase, as if at the starting line of a sack race. When we got back from the park I finished reading the Hitchcock-Truffaut book. In the Hitchcock-Truffaut book there is a passage in which Truffaut comments on *Psycho*. "If I'm not mistaken, out of your fifty works, this is the only film showing . . ." Janet Leigh in a bra. And Hitchcock says: "But the scene would have been more interesting if the girl's bare breasts had been rubbing against the man's chest." *That's true.* H. and S. came for supper. Veal Scaloppine Marsala and very well done, with green noodles and salad. Buckets of vodka before and buckets of brandy after. The brandy depressed me. Some talk about the new artists' tenement being made out of an old warehouse building. H. said, "I hear it's going to be very classy. I hear it's going to have white rats." H. spoke about his former wife and toothbrushes: "She was always at it, fiercely, many hours a day and night." I don't know if this stuff is useful . . .

Q: I'm not your doctor.

A: Pity.

A: But I love my irony.

Q: Does it give you pleasure?

A: A poor . . . A rather unsatisfactory. . . .

Q: The unavoidable tendency of everything particular to emphasize its own particularity.

A: Yes.

Q: You could interest yourself in these interesting machines. They're hard to understand. They're time-consuming.

A: I don't like you.

Q: I sensed it.

A: These imbecile questions . . .

Q: Inadequately answered. . . .

A: . . . imbecile questions leading nowhere . . .

Q: The personal abuse continues.

A: . . . that voice, confident and shrill . . .

Q (aside): He has given away his gaiety, and now has nothing.

Q: But consider the moment when Pasteur, distracted, ashamed, calls upon Mme. Boucicault, widow of the department-store owner. Pasteur stammers, sweats; it is clear that he is there to ask for money, money for his Institute. He becomes more firm, masters himself, speaks with force, yet he is not sure that she knows who he is, that he is Pasteur. "The least contribution," he says finally. "But of course," she (equally embarrassed) replies. She writes a check. He looks at the check. One million francs. They both burst into tears.

A (bitterly): Yes, that makes up for everything, that you know that story. . . .

Literary Criticism

William V. Spanos

The Detective and the Boundary: Some Notes on the Postmodern Literary Imagination

. . . All the plays that have ever been written, from ancient Greece to the present day, have never really been anything but thrillers. Drama's always been realistic and there's always been a detective about. Every play's an investigation brought to a successful conclusion. There's a riddle, and it's solved in the final scene. Sometimes earlier. Might as well give the game away at the start.

Eugène Ionesco: Choubert, Victims of Duty

And any explanation will satisfy:
We only ask to be reassured
About the noises in the cellar
And the window that should not have been open.
  Why do we all behave as if the door might suddenly open, the curtain be drawn,
  The cellar make some dreadful disclosure, the roof disappear,
And we should cease to be sure of what is real or unreal?
Hold tight, hold tight, we must insist that the world is what we have always taken
it to be . . . .

T. S. Eliot: Chorus, The Family Reunion

"Elementary, my dear Watson. . . ."

Arthur Conan Doyle: Sherlock Holmes, passim

Dread strikes us dumb.

Martin Heidegger, "What is Metaphysics?"

Nilb, mun, mud.

Samuel Beckett: Watt, Watt

    The literary revolution called Modernism that occurred at the end of the nineteenth century in reaction against the positivistic ethos of the

Source: William V. Spanos, "The Detective and the Boundary: Some Notes on the Postmodern Literary Imagination," *boundary 2: a journal of postmodern literature* Vol. 1 (Fall 1972). Reprinted by courtesy of *boundary 2*. This essay is published here in a somewhat revised form.

European middle class and achieved its highest expression in the work of such writers as Marcel Proust, Stéphane Mallarmé, W. B. Yeats, Ezra Pound, James Joyce, T. S. Eliot, and Virginia Woolf (and in the American New Criticism) was, ideologically, a revolt against the Western humanistic tradition and, aesthetically, against the "Aristotelian" tradition.[1] The modern movement continues to the present to be characterized by its "anti-Westernism" and its "anti-Aristotelianism." But about the time of World War II, which witnessed—especially in the context of the Resistance—the emergence of existentialism not merely as a life philosophy but, more specifically, as an antimetaphysical mode of consciousness (for example, phenomenology), the "anti-Aristotelianism" of the modern literary movement underwent a metamorphosis so profound that it has become necessary, I submit, to differentiate between an early or symbolist Modernism and a later existentialist post-Modernism.

Broadly speaking, the anti-Westernism of the symbolists was above all an aesthetic reaction against the humanistic principle of utility, the imperative that man's role vis-à-vis the material world was to control or, more accurately, to manipulate nature (the word "manipulate" will assume a different significance for the existential imagination) in behalf of the material well-being of man. Analogously, the anti-Aristotelianism of the symbolists constituted a rejection of "prose" in favor of "poetry" or, as Henri Bergson observes in *Time and Free Will*, a rejection of language that solidifies "our conscious states" for the purposes of social action[2] in favor of a language that achieves an autonomous and something like autotelic status. On the level of *mimesis*, symbolist anti-Aristotelianism constituted a rejection of the primacy of linear and temporal plot in favor of the simultaneity of "spatial form." I will return to this all too brief definition of symbolist Modernism. What I wish to suggest at the outset is that, unlike the early modern imagination—indeed, in partial reaction against its refusal of historicity—the postmodern imagination, agonized as it has been by the ongoing boundary situation which is contemporary history, is fundamentally an existential imagination. Its anti-Aristotelianism—its refusal to fulfill causally oriented expectations, to create fictions (and in extreme cases, sentences) with beginnings, middles, and ends—has its source, not

---

1. In the *Poetics*, Aristotle says that "the first principle ... and to speak figuratively, the soul of tragedy is the plot" (*Poetics*, VI, 145a), by which I take him to mean a unified and whole action in which the *end* —not only in the sense of termination but, as his reference to *soul* suggests, of goal or final cause (*telos*)—determines the process. By the "Aristotelian" tradition, then, I am referring to the fundamentally "essentialist" tradition of the West, which assumes the linear plot—the sequence of events that develops causally from a beginning which generates discords through a middle which amplifies discords into crisis to an end which resolves the discords—to be the constitutive formal dimension of all literary genres.
2. *Time and Free Will: An Essay on the Immediate Data of Consciousness*, translated by F. L. Pogson (New York and London: Macmillan, 1910), p. 226.

so much in an aesthetic as in an existential critique of the traditional Western view of man-in-the-world, especially as it has been formulated by positivistic science and disseminated by the vested interests of the modern —technological—city. It is not, in other words, the ugliness, the busyness, the noisiness, of a world organized on the principle of utility that has called forth postmodern anti-Aristotelianism; it is rather, though the two are not mutually exclusive, the anthropomorphic objectification of a world in which God is dead or has withdrawn.

At the heart of the existential/phenomenological critique of positivistic humanism—indeed, at the heart of all existential/phenomenological philosophies as such—is the well known but too often misunderstood concept of dread or anxiety (*Angst*) or, rather, the distinction between dread and fear (*Furcht*). According to Martin Heidegger, for example, who, it should be remembered, derived his fundamental categories from Soren Kierkegaard, dread differs radically from fear. "We are always *afraid* of this or that definite thing, which threatens us in this or that definite way."[3] Fear, in other words, has an object which, as Tillich puts it with Kierkegaard and Heidegger clearly in mind, "can be faced, analyzed, attacked, endured."[4] That is, fear has no ontological status because, having an object that can, as it were, *be taken hold of*, one is certain that it can be dealt with—eliminated or neutralized or even used. (This obsessive need *to take hold of nothing,* it is worth observing, reminds us of Keats's implicit criticism of the kind of writer who, because he does not have Negative Capability, reaches irritably "after fact or reason.")[5]

Dread, on the other hand, has no thing or nothing as its object. This "indefiniteness of *what* we dread is not just lack of definition: it represents the essential impossibility of defining the 'what' " ("WM," p. 335). It is, in other words, an existential and ontological (as opposed to existential and ontic) structure of reality:

> In dread, as we say, "one feels something uncanny [*unheimlich*]." What is this "something" (*es*) and this "one"? We are unable to say what gives "one" that uncanny feeling. "One" just feels it generally (*im Ganzen*). All things, and we with them, sink into a sort of indifference. But not in the sense that everything disappears; rather, in the very act of drawing away from us everything turns toward us. This withdrawal of what-is-in-totality, which then crowds round us

---

3. "What Is Metaphysics?" *Existence and Being,* with an introduction by Werner Brock (Chicago: Regnery, 1949), p. 335. Further references will be abbreviated to "WM" and incorporated in the text in parentheses. For a full discussion of the distinction between fear and dread (or anxiety), see Heidegger, *Being and Time,* translated by John Macquarrie and Edward Robinson (New York, Harper & Row, 1962), pp. 228–235.
4. *The Courage to Be* (New Haven, Conn.: Yale University Press, 1952), p. 36.
5. Hyder Edward Rollins, ed. *The Letters of John Keats,* Vol. I (Cambridge, Mass.: Harvard University Press, 1958), pp. 192–194.

in dread, this is what oppresses us. There is nothing [as there is in fear] to hold
on to. The only thing that remains and overwhelms us whilst what-is slips
away, is this "nothing" ("WM," p. 336).

What is crucial to perceive in Heidegger's phenomenological example is
that dread generates a withdrawal of the world as homogeneous system
or grid of definite or defined objects ("what-is-in-totality") and discloses
itself in its primordial ontological state, which is oppressive not only because it "crowds round us"—invades, as it were, our formerly secure world
—but also because it provides us—like the chorus in my epigraph from
Eliot's *The Family Reunion*—with "nothing to hold on to." Following
Kierkegaard, whose existentialism exfoliates from his assertion that "Nothing begets dread,"[6] Heidegger concludes in a separate paragraph: "Dread
reveals Nothing" ("WM," p. 336). Put in the way suggested by his reference to the feeling of uncanniness (*Unheimlichkeit*), dread breaks open
the depthless (superficial) charted habitation of inauthentic man; it discloses Dasein's (human being's) primordial not-at-homeness in the world.
      Seen in the light of the existential distinction between dread and fear,
the Western perspective—by which I specifically mean the rational or
rather the positivistic structure of consciousness that views spatial and
temporal phenomena in the world as "problems" to be "solved"—expresses itself as a self-deceptive effort to find objects for dread in order to
domesticate—to at-home—the threatening realm of Nothingness, the profound not-at-home, into which Dasein is thrown (*geworfen*) as Being-in-
the-world. It is, in other words, a rigidified, evasive anthropomorphic or,
better, metaphysical consciousness, which obsessively attempts by coercion to fix and stabilize the elusive flux of existence from *meta-ta-phusika*
(after or beyond things-as-they-are), from the vantage point of a final
rational cause. By means of this coercive transformation, this *object*ifica-
tion of Nothing, the positivistic structure of consciousness is able not only
to manipulate, to lay hands on, the irrational world (including man, of
course) for the purpose of achieving what one important early spokesman
for this perspective (this "inquisition of things") referred to as "man's
empire over the universe" "for the benefit and use" of man's estate.[7] More
basically, according to the existentialists, it can also *justify* the absurdity
of human existence: it allows man, that is, to perceive the immediate,
uncertain, problematic, and thus dreadful psychic or historical present of
Dasein as a necessary part of a linear design, as a causal link between the

6. *The Concept of Dread,* translated by Walter Lowrie (Princeton, N.J.: Princeton University Press, 1959),
p. 38.
7. Francis Bacon, *Selected Writings,* edited by Hugh G. Dick (New York: Modern Library, 1955), pp. 441,
151 (see also p. 539), 437. See also Lewis Mumford, *The Pentagon of Power: The Myth of the Machine* (New
York: Harcourt Brace Jovanovich, 1970), pp. 105–126.

past and/or future determined from a rational end, a *logos*. The one thing needful to fill the gaps between apparent discontinuities in both the internal and external worlds (that is, memory and history) or, another way of putting it, to apprehend (the etymology is significant here) and to exploit this comforting linear design behind the absurd and dislocating or, better, *dis-lodging* appearances, is a "disinterested" or "objective"—and distanced—observer of the uniformity among diverse phenomena, that is, the positivistic scientist or, what is the same thing, the behaviorist psychoanalyst.

According to the implications of existential phenomenology, then, the problem-solution perspective of the "straightforward" Western man of action, as Dostoevski's denizen of the underground calls the exponents of the Crystal Palace, has its ground in more than merely a belief in the susceptibility of nature to rational explanation. It is based, rather, on seeing temporal experience at once (spatially), that is, on a monolithic certainty that immediate psychic or historical experience is part of a comforting, even exciting and suspenseful well-made cosmic drama or novel—more particularly, a detective story (the French term is *policière*) in the manner of Poe's *The Murders in the Rue Morgue* or Conan Doyle's *The Hound of the Baskervilles*, or Agatha Christie's *Murder on the Orient Express*. For just as the form of the detective story has its source in the comforting certainty that an acute and all-encompassing "eye," private or otherwise, can solve the crime with resounding finality by inferring causal relationships between clues which point to it (they are "leads," suggesting the primacy of rigid linear narrative sequence), so the "form" of the well-made positivistic universe is grounded in the equally comforting certainty that the scientist/psychoanalyst/social scientist can solve the immediate problem by the inductive method, a process involving the inference of relationships between discontinuous "facts" that point to or lead straight to an explanation of the "mystery," the "crime" of contingent existence. " 'This is most important,' said [Holmes in *The Hound of the Baskervilles*]. . . . 'It fills up the gap which I had been unable to bridge in this most complex affair.' "

Far from being arbitrary, this way of defining the structure of consciousness into which, according to the existentialists, modern Western man has coerced his humanistic inheritance from the Renaissance is, as we shall see, amply justified, especially by the evidence of his popular (mass media) arts and public-political life. Though, on the whole, scientists and psychologists no longer are inclined to view existence in this rigidly positivistic and deterministic way, it is nevertheless this "meta-physical" structure of consciousness, which assumes the universe, the "book of nature," to be a well-made cosmic drama, that determines the questions and thus the expectations and answers—in speech and writing and in action—of the "silent majority," *das Man* (the "they-self") of the modern technological city and of the political executors of its will.

[II]

As the profound influence of certain kinds of literature on existentialism and phenomenology suggests, the impulse of the contemporary Western writer to refuse to fulfill causal expectations, to refuse to provide "solutions" for the "crime" of existence, has literary precedents that are prior to the existential critique of Westernism. We discover versions of it in, say, Euripides' *Orestes,* Shakespeare's problem plays, the tragicomedies of the Jacobeans, Wycherley's *The Plain Dealer,* Dickens' *Edwin Drood,* and more recently in Tolstoi's *The Death of Ivan Ilych,* Dostoevski's *Notes from Underground,* Alfred Jarry's *Ubu Roi,* Kafka's *The Trial,* Pirandello's *Six Characters in Search of an Author,* and even in T. S. Eliot's *Sweeney Agonistes* and Graham Greene's *Brighton Rock.*[8] In *Notes from Underground,* for example, Dostoevski as editor "concludes" this precursor of the open-ended antinovel: "The 'notes' of this paradoxalist do not end here. However, he could not resist and concluded them. But it also seems to me that we may stop here." Fully conscious of the psychological need of the "straightforward" Gentleman of the hyper-Westernized St. Petersburg—the "most intentional city in the whole world"—Dostoevski refuses to transform the discordant experience of this terrible and disconcerting voice into a "sublime and beautiful," that is, "straightforward" and distancing *story.*[9] So also in *Six Characters in Search of an Author,* where, seeking relief from the agony of their ambiguous relationships, the characters express their need to give artistic shape to the "infinite absurdities" of their lives. The Director (I want to emphasize the coercive implications of the word)—who hates their "authorless," that is, inconclusive drama ("It seems to me," he says in a contemptuous reference to Pirandellian drama, "you are trying to imitate the manner of a certain author whom I heartily detest.")—tries to make a well-made play, a melodrama in the manner of Eugène Scribe or Alexander Dumas *fils* of their dreadful experience: "What we've got to do is to combine and group up all the facts in one simultaneous close-knit action." But when the characters sense his formal strategy, they refuse to be coerced into this comforting but fraudulent "arrangement." Similarly in *Sweeney Agonistes,* just as Sweeney will not allow his anxious listeners to package the terrible "anti-Aristotelian" mur-

8. These are works, it is worth observing, the radical temporality of which does not yield readily to the spatial interpretive methodology of the New Criticism, which has its source in the iconic art of symbolist Modernism.
9. As medieval and Elizabethan poetry and drama suggest, the traditional Western metaphysical fiction has one of its most paradigmatic models in the analogy of the hierarchical universe as orchestra, the music of which can be heard by the man who is in harmonious relationship with nature. See E. M. W. Tillyard, *The Elizabethan World Picture* (New York: Vintage Books, 1961).

der story he tells them ("Well here again that don't apply/But I've gotta use words when I talk to you"), so Eliot in his great antidetective play will not allow his audience, whom he sees as a collective of middle-class fugitives, to fulfill their positivistically conditioned need to experience the explanatory and cathartic conclusion. Rather, like Dostoevski, he "ends" the play inconclusively with the dreadful knocking at the door.[10]

But in each of these early modern works, one has the feeling that the writer has only reluctantly resisted the conventional ending. It is actually the unconscious pressure of the powerfully felt content—the recognition and acknowledgment of contingency, or what I prefer to call the ontological invasion—that has driven him against his will into undermining the traditional Aristotelian dramatic or fictional form. The existential/ phenomenological diagnosis and critique of the humanistic tradition had not yet emerged to suggest the formal implications of metaphysical disintegration. Only after the existentialist philosophers revealed that the obsessive perception of the universe as a well-made fiction is in reality a self-deceptive effort of the Western consciousness to evade the anxiety of contingent existence by objectifying and taking hold of "it," did it become clear to the modern writer that the ending-as-solution is the literary agency of this evasive objectification. And it is the discovery of the "antiformal" imperatives of absurd time for fiction and drama and poetry (though poetry, which in our time means lyric poetry, as Sartre has said in *What Is Literature?*, tends by its natural amenability to spatialization to be nonhistorical)[11] that constitutes the most dynamic thrust of the contemporary Western literary imagination and differentiates the new from symbolist Modernism. As Samuel Beckett put it in his famous interview with Tom Driver: "What I am saying does not mean that there will henceforth be no form in art. It only means that there will be new form, and that this form will be of such a type that it admits the chaos and does not try to say that the chaos is really something else. . . . To find a form that accommodates the mess, that is the task of the artist now."[12]

Taking their lead from the existentialists, the postmodern absurdists —writers like the Sartre of *Nausea* and *No Exit,* Beckett, Ionesco, Genet, Pinter, Frisch, Sarraute, Murdoch, Pynchon, Barth, and so on—thus all tend in some degree to view the well-made play or novel (*la pièce bien faite*), the post-Shakespearian allotrope of the Aristotelian form, as the inevitable analogue of the well-made positivistic universe delineated by

10. See my essay " 'Wanna Go Home, Baby?': *Sweeney Agonistes* as Drama of the Absurd," *PMLA,* Vol. 85 (January 1970), 8–20. The examples I have cited above are, of course, only extensions of Euripides' parodic use of the *deus ex machina* in, say, *Orestes* to point critically to the motive of consolation behind the well-made plot (the formal and aesthetically distancing order) of classical tragedy or, to refer to a later example, of Shakespeare's derisive strategy of ending well what the morally ambiguous and dislocating action of, say, the ironically titled *All's Well that Ends Well* clearly suggests cannot possibly end well.
11. *What Is Literature?* translated by Bernard Frechtman (New York: Harper & Row, 1965), pp. 1–14.
12. "Beckett by the Madeleine," *Columbia University Forum,* Vol. IV (Summer 1961), 23.

the post-Renaissance humanistic structure of consciousness. More specifically, they tend to view the rigid deterministic plot of the well-made
fiction, like that of its metaphysical counterpart, as having its source in bad
faith. I mean (to appropriate the metaphor Heidegger uses to remind us
of the archetypal flight of the Apollonian Orestes from the *Erinyes*) the
self-deceptive effort of the "fallen 'they' " (*das verfallene "Man"*) "to flee
in the face of death" and the ominous absurd by finding objects for the
dread of Nothing, that is, *by imposing coercively a distancing and tran-
quilizing ending or* telos *from the beginning on the invading contingencies of existence.* What Roquentin observes in Sartre's *Nausea* about
l'aventure (which is the aesthetic equivalent of the Bouville merchants'
arrogant positivism—their certain "right to exist") in distinguishing it
from *la vie* is precisely what the postmodern absurdists seem to imply in
their "de-composed" drama and fiction about the modern humanistic
structure of consciousness and its metaphysical and aesthetic paradigms:

> ... everything changes when you tell about life [*raconte la vie:* Sartre seems
> to be pointing here to the relationship between the mathematical associations
> of the etymology and the concept of story or well-made plot and, ultimately,
> the recounting of existence from the vantage point of the end]; it's a change
> no one notices: ... Things happen one way and we tell about them in the
> opposite sense. You seem to start at the beginning: "It was a fine autumn
> evening in 1922. I was a notary clerk in Marommes." And in reality you have
> started at the end. It was there, invisible and present, it is the one which gives
> to words the pomp and value of a beginning. "I was out walking, I had left
> the town without realizing it, I was thinking about my money troubles." This
> sentence, taken simply for what it is, means that the man was absorbed,
> morose, a hundred leagues from adventure, exactly in the mood to let things
> happen without noticing them. But the end is there, transforming everything.
> For us, the man is already the hero of the story. His moroseness, his money
> troubles are much more precious than ours, they are all gilded by the light
> of future passions. And the story goes on in the reverse: instants have stopped
> piling themselves in a lighthearted way one on top of the other [as in life],
> they are snapped up by the end of the story which draws them and each one
> of them in turn, draws out the preceding instant: "It was night, the street was
> deserted." *The phrase is cast out negligently, it seems superfluous [superflue:*
> an equivalent of *de trop,* Sartre's term for the condition of man in the primor-
> dial realm of existence which is prior to essence]; *but we do not let ourselves
> be caught and put it aside: this is a piece of information whose value we shall
> subsequently appreciate.* And we feel that the hero has lived all the details
> of this night like annunciations, promises, or even that he lives only those that
> were promises, blind and deaf to all that did not herald adventure. ...
>   I wanted the moment of my life to follow and order themselves like those
> of a life remembered. You might as well try and catch time by the tail. (My
> italics.)

In short, the postmodern absurdists interpret this obsession for what Roland Barthes, perhaps with Sartre in mind, calls the bourgeois fiction of "the preterite mode,"[13] for the rigidly causal plot of the well-made work of the humanistic tradition that begins with Defoe and, in another parallel way, with Fielding and extends through Balzac, Zola, Flaubert, Galsworthy, and Bennett, as catering to and thus further hardening the expectation of—and aggravating the need for—the rational solution generated by the scientific analysis of man-in-the-world. As the reference to the technique of the detective story in the passage from *Nausea* suggests, these expectations demand the kind of fiction and drama that achieves its absolute fulfillment in the utterly formularized and aesthetically distancing clockwork certainties of plot in the innumerable detective drama series—"Perry Mason," "The FBI," "Hawaii 5-O," "Mannix," "Mission Impossible," and so on—which use up, or rather, "kill" prime television time in America. Ultimately, the postmodern imagination implies, they also demand the kind of social and political organization that finds its fulfillment in the imposed and habituating certainties of the well-made world of the totalitarian state, where investigation or inquisition on behalf of the negation of *mystery,* of uncanniness, or to put it positively, on behalf of the achievement of a total, that is, preordained or teleologically determined structure—a "final solution"—is the defining activity. It is, therefore, no accident that the postmodern literary imagination at large insists on the *mystery*—the ominous and threatening uncanniness that resists naming—and that the paradigmatic literary archetype it has discovered is the antidetective story (and its antipsychoanalytical analogue), the formal purpose of which is to evoke the impulse to "detect" and/or to psychoanalyze in order to violently frustrate it by refusing to solve the crime (or find the cause of the neurosis). I am referring, for example, to works as apparently different in technique as well as in time and place as Kafka's *The Trial;* T. S. Eliot's *Sweeney Agonistes* (subtitled significantly *Fragments of an Aristophanic Melodrama*); Graham Greene's *Brighton Rock;* Arthur Koestler's *Arrival and Departure;* Beckett's *Watt* and *Molloy* (especially the Moran section), *Waiting for Godot,* and *All that Fall;* Ionesco's *Victims of Duty;* Robbe-Grillet's *The Erasers;* Nathalie Sarraute's *Portrait of a Man Unknown;* Marguerite Duras' novels; Iris Murdoch's *Under the Net* and *The Severed Head;* Pinter's *The Birthday Party* and *A Slight Ache;* Pynchon's *V;* and even John Barth's "Menelaiad," each of which, as the narrator of Iris Murdoch's *Under the Net* says of the existential experience that has deconstructed his causal fictions, "makes mock of our contrived finalities." What Sartre says in his characteristically seminal way about Nathalie Sarraute's *Portrait of a Man Unknown* applies

13. *Writing Degree Zero* and *Elements of Semiology,* translated by Annette Lavers and Colin Smith (Boston: Beacon, 1968), p. 30ff.

in some degree to all of these and many other important works of contemporary literature: It is "an anti-novel that reads like a detective story. In fact, it is a parody on the novel of "quest" into which the author has introduced a sort of impassioned amateur detective . . . who . . . doesn't find anything, or hardly anything, and he gives up his investigation as a result of a metamorphosis; just as though Agatha Christie's detective, on the verge of unmasking the villain, had himself suddenly turned criminal."[14]

In *Victims of Duty,* to take but one of these examples, the Detective, like Sherlock Holmes, is certain in the beginning that "everything hangs together, everything can be comprehended in time" and thus "keeps moving forward . . . one step at a time, tracking down the extraordinary": "Mallot, with a t at the end, or Mallod with a d." Holmes, of course, eventually *gets* his man (though the foregone certainty, especially of the monstrous evilness of the criminal, should not obscure the grimness of the metaphor—which includes the collage reminiscent of T. S. Eliot's Prufrock—that characterizes Conan Doyle's fictional and real universe): "This chance of the picture has supplied us with one of our most obvious missing links. We have him, Watson, we have him, and I dare swear that before tomorrow he will be fluttering in our net as helpless as one of his own butterflies. A pin, a cork, and a card, and we add him to the Baker Street collection!" But the Detective in the process of Ionesco's play cannot make Choubert "catch hold of" the Protean Mallot. Despite his brutal efforts to "plug the gaps [of his wayward memory]" by stuffing food down his throat, what he "finds" is only the bottomless hole of Choubert's elusive being: that is, Nothing. And so, instead of ending with "A Restrospective" that "sees the whole picture," "fits the pieces of the puzzle together," "ties everything up" (clarifies—and negates—the mystery) as in *The Hound of the Baskervilles, Victims of Duty* "ends" in verbal, formal, and, analogously, ontological disintegration. The dislocating mystery still survives the brutal coercion.[15]

What I am suggesting is that it was the recognition of the ultimately "totalitarian" implications of the Western structure of consciousness—of the expanding analogy that encompasses art, politics, and metaphysics in the name of the security of rational order—that compelled the postmodern imagination to undertake the deliberate and systematic subversion of plot—the beginning, middle, and end structure—which has enjoyed virtually unchallenged supremacy in the Western literary tradition ever since

14. "Nathalie Sarraute," *Situations,* translated by Benita Eisler (New York: Braziller, 1965), pp. 195–196.
15. For a fuller treatment of *Victims of Duty* as antidetective story, see my essay "Modern Drama and the Aristotelian Tradition: The Formal Imperatives of Absurd Time," *Contemporary Literature,* Vol. XII (Summer 1971), 346–372.

Aristotle or, at any rate, since the Renaissance interpreters of Aristotle, claimed it to be the most important of the constitutive elements of literature. In the familiar language of Aristotle's *Poetics,* then, the postmodern strategy of de-composition exists to generate rather than purge pity and terror; to disintegrate, to atomize rather than to create a community. In the more immediate language of existential phenomenology, its purpose is to generate rather than purge anxiety and dread: to "de-struct" (Heidegger) our metaphysical presuppositions and thus to dislodge our tranquilized selves from the superficial "at-home of publicness," the domesticated, the scientifically charted and organized world, into direct encounter with "the things themselves." To invoke Sartre's seminal antinovel, *Nausea,* once more, the open, or, better perhaps, dis-closive forms of the postmodern imagination exist to make us feel what Roquentin, after his agony in the public park (*jardin public*), experiences in an inverted epiphany from the top of a hill overlooking the now not so "solid, bourgeois city," Bouville:

> They come out of their offices after their day of work, they look at the houses and the squares with satisfaction, they think it is *their* city, a good, solid, bourgeois city. They aren't afraid, they feel at home. . . . They have proof, a hundred times a day, that everything happens mechanically, that the world obeys fixed, unchangeable laws. In a vacuum all bodies fall at the same rate of speed, the public park is closed at 4 P.M. in winter, at 6 P.M. in summer, lead melts at 335 degrees centigrade. . . . And all this time, great, vague nature has slipped into their city, it has infiltrated everywhere, in their house, in their office, in themselves. It doesn't move, it stays quietly and they are full of it inside, they breathe it, and they don't see it, they imagine it to be outside, twenty miles from the city. I *see* it, I *see* this nature. . . . I know that its obedience is idleness, I know it has no laws: what they take for constancy is only habit and it can change tomorrow.
>   What if something were to happen? What if something suddenly started throbbing? Then they would notice it was there and they'd think their hearts were going to burst. Then what good would their dykes, bulwarks, power houses, furnaces and pile drivers be to them?[16]

16. The motif of ontological invasion is pervasive in postmodern literature. Besides Sartre's *Nausea* (where it gets its definitive expression in the famous episode in the public park, when Roquentin experiences the un-Naming of the chestnut tree), it is also central, for example, in Beckett's *Watt,* especially in the section depicting Watt's sojourn in the "unutterable or ineffable" Knott's house, when he suddenly "found himself in the midst of things which, if they consented to be named, did as it were with reluctance;" in Ionesco's *Exit the King,* which ends with the following stage directions: "In the end, there is nothing but this grey light. The disappearance of the windows, the doors, wall, king, and throne ought to occur slowly, progressively, very perceptibly. The king seated on his throne ought to remain visible for some time before being engulfed in a kind of thick haze;" and in John Barth's "Menelaiad," where it achieves its most self-conscious expression in the relationship between the proliferation of quotation marks and the figure of Proteus. Earlier important works pointing directly in their temporal process to the emergence of the theme of ontological invasion in postmodern literature are Shakespeare's *King Lear,* Herman Melville's "Bartleby the Scrivener," Conrad's *Heart of Darkness,* and D. H. Lawrence's *The Rainbow.*

This aesthetics of de-composition or de-struction is not, as is too often protested, a purely negative one. For the *dépayesment*—the ejection from one's "homeland"—as Ionesco refers to it after Heidegger,[17] which is effected by the carefully articulated discontinuities of absurdist literary form, reveals the *Ur-grund*, the primordial not-at-home, where dread, as Kierkegaard and Heidegger and Sartre and Tillich tell us, becomes not just the agency of despair but also and simultaneously of hope, that is, of freedom and infinite possibility:

> [*If*] a man were a beast or an angel [Kierkegaard, echoing Pascal, writes in *The Concept of Dread*], he would not be able to be in dread. Since he is a synthesis he can be in dread, and the greater the dread, the greater the man. And no Grand Inquisitor has in readiness such terrible tortures as has dread, and no spy knows how to attack more artfully the man he suspects, choosing the instant when he is weakest, nor knows how to lay traps where he will be caught and ensnared as dread knows how, and no sharpwitted judge knows how to interrogate, to examine the accused, as dread does, which never lets him escape, neither by diversion nor by noise, neither at work nor at play, neither by day nor by night.
>
> Dread is the possibility of freedom. Only this dread is by the aid of faith absolutely educative, *laying bare as it does all finite aims and discovering all their deceptions. . . .*
>
> He who is educated by dread is educated by possibility, and only the man who is educated by possibility is educated in accordance with his infinity.[18]

Thus on the psychological level too this dislodgement—this phenomenological reduction by violence—not only undermines the confident positivistic structure of consciousness (and its derived language of assertion) that really demands answers (ends) it has from the beginning (that is, the expectation of *catharsis*). It also compels the new self to ask, like Orestes or Job—the Job who, against the certain advice of his comforters, the advocates of the Law, "spoke of God that which is right"—the ultimate, the authentically humanizing question: *die Seinfrage,* as Heidegger puts it, the Being question or, better, the question of what it means to be.

To discover the buried metaphor I have hinted at in the passage from *The Concept of Dread,* the postmodern antiliterature of the absurd exists to strip its audience of positivized fugitives of their protective and alienating garments of rational explanation and leave them standing naked and unaccommodated—poor, bare, forked animals—before the encroaching

17. *Notes and Counter Notes: Writing on the Theatre,* translated by Donald Watson (New York: Grove, 1964), p. 163.
18. *The Concept of Dread,* translated by Walter Lowrie (Princeton, N.J.: Princeton University Press), pp. 139–140. The parallel with Kafka's *The Trial,* especially the "Parable of the Door of the Law," should not be missed.

Nothingness. Here, to add another dimension to the metaphor, in the precincts of their last evasions, the language that objectifies (clothes), whether the syntax of sentence or plot, "don't apply" (*Sweeney Agonistes*), that is, the "old words" no longer make a "pillow for [one's] head" (*Watt*). Here, therefore, in the realm of silence, where naming does not work (is seen to be mere noise), they must choose authentically (*eigentlich:* in the context of the naked my-ownness of death and Nothingness) whether to succumb to Nothingness, to endure it (this is what Tillich calls the courage to be in the face of despair), to affirm the Somethingness of Nothingness "by virtue of the absurd," or to risk letting Being be. It is this divestment and silence before the unnameable mystery, which finds its most forceful premodern expression in such works as *King Lear, Fear and Trembling, Crime and Punishment, The Death of Ivan Ilych,* and "The Overcoat," that gives postmodern antinovels and antiplays like Sartre's *Nausea* and *No Exit;* Ionesco's *Victims of Duty;* Tardieu's *The Lock* (*La Serrure*); Murdoch's *Under the Net;* Beckett's *Watt* and *Molloy;* Genet's *The Maids;* Pinter's *The Homecoming;* Sarraute's *Tropisms;* Joseph Heller's *Catch 22;* and John Barth's *Lost in the Funhouse* their special ambience.

The modes of standing-in are various, ranging from Jake's brooding wonder before the uncanny "mess" in *Under the Net:*

> Events stream past us like these crowds, and the face of each is seen only for a minute. What is urgent is not urgent forever but only ephemerally. All work and all love, the search for wealth and fame, the search for truth, life itself, are made up of moments which pass and become nothing. Yet through this shaft of nothings, we drive onwards with miraculous vitality that creates our precarious habitations in the past and the future. So we live—a spirit that broods and hovers over the continual death of time, and the lost meaning, the unrecaptured moment, the unremembered fact, until the final chop-chop that ends all our moments and plunges that spirit back into the void from which it came.

to Watt's poignant endurance of this abysmal world in *Watt:*

> *Of nought. To the source. To the teacher. To the temple. To him I brought. This emptied heart. These emptied hands. This mind ignoring. This body homeless. To love him my little reviled. My little rejected to have him. My little to learn him forgot. Abandoned my little to find him.*[19]

19. Having suffered a "mental breakdown" at the house of Knott, Watt communicates his story to the narrator, Sam, in stages of increasingly complicated inversions. At this stage, he speaks the phrases in reversed order. To be understood, therefore, the passage must be read from the end.

and to John Barth's assent to the "felt ultimacies"[20]—the irreconcilable gaps, the unending labyrinthine way, the Protean elusiveness of existence: what Derrida calls la differ*a*nce[21]—as (unlike the "mythotherapist" narrators of his two first novels) he dances (plays) precariously on the fragments of narrative artifice that he floats over the void in *Lost in the Funhouse:*

Ambrose's heart shook. For the moment Scylla and Charybdis, the Occult Order, his brother Pete—all were forgotten. Peggy Robbins, too, though she did not vanish altogether from his mind's eye, was caught up into the greater vision, vague and splendrous, whereof the sea-wreathed bottle was an emblem. Westward it lay, to westward, where the tide ran from East Dorset. Past the river and the Bay, from continents beyond, this messenger had come. Borne by currents as yet uncharted, nosed by fishes as yet unnamed, it had bobbed for ages beneath strange stars. Then out of the oceans it had strayed; past cape and cove, black can, red nun, the word had wandered willy-nilly to his threshold.

"For pity's sake bust it!" Perse shouted.

Holding the bottle by the neck Ambrose banged it on a mossed and barnacled brickbat. Not hard enough. His face perspired. On the third swing the bottle smashed and the note fell out.

The paper was half a sheet of coarse ruled stuff, torn carelessly from a tablet and folded thrice. Ambrose uncreased it. On a top line was penned in deep red ink:

TO WHOM IT MAY CONCERN

On the next-to-bottom:

YOURS TRULY

The lines between were blank, as was the space beneath the complimentary close. In a number of places, owing to the coarseness of the paper, the ink spread from the lines of fibrous blots.

But the uncertain ground on which these stances are taken is common.

[III]

We have seen during the twentieth century the gradual emergence of an articulate minority point of view—especially in the arts—that interprets Western technological civilization as a progress not toward the

---

20. John Barth, "The Literature of Exhaustion," *Atlantic Monthly*, Vol. 220, No. 2 (August 1967), 29–34.
21. Jaque Derrida, "Differance," *Speech and Phenomena and Other Essays on Husserl's Theory of Signs*, translated by David B. Allison with "Preface" by Newton Garver (Evanston, Ill.: Northwestern University Press), pp. 129–160.

utopian *polis* idealized by the Greeks, but toward a rationally mass-produced city which, like the St. Petersburg of Dostoevski's and Tolstoi's novels, is a microcosm of universal madness. This point of view involves a growing recognition of one of the most significant paradoxes of modern life: that in the pursuit of order the positivistic structure of consciousness, having gone beyond the point of equilibrium, generates radical imbalances in nature which are inversely proportional to the intensity with which it is coerced. However, it has not been able to call the arrogant anthropomorphic Western mind and its well-made universe into serious question.

As I have suggested, this is largely because the affirmative formal strategy of symbolist Modernism was one of religio-aesthetic withdrawal from existential time into the eternal simultaneity of essential art. The symbolist movement, that is, tried to deconstruct language, to drive it out of its traditional temporal orbit—established by the humanistic commitment to *kinesis* and utility and given its overwhelming socioliterary authority, as Marshall McLuhan has shown, by the invention of the printing press—in order to achieve iconic (that is, spatial) values. Its purpose was to undermine its utilitarian function in order to disintegrate the reader's linear-temporal orientation and to make him *see* synchronically—as one sees a painting or, more inclusively, a circular mythological paradigm—what the temporal words express. In other words, its purpose was to *reveal* (in the etymological sense of "unveil") *the whole as resolved tensions* and by so doing raise the reader above the immediate discontinuities of temporal life—the messiness or, as Yeats calls the realm of existence in "Phases of the Moon," "that raving tide," into a higher and more permanent reality.[22]

This impulse to transcend the historicity of the human condition in the "allatonceness" (the term is McLuhan's) of the spatialized work of symbolist literary art is brought into remarkably sharp focus when, by way of a Heideggerian "destruction," one perceives the similarity between the poetic implicit in W. B. Yeats's "Sailing to Byzantium" with Stephen Dedalus' aesthetics of *stasis* in *Portrait of the Artist as a Young Man,* which has often been taken, especially by the New Critics, as a theoretical definition of modern symbolist literary form:

You see I use the word *arrest.* I mean that the tragic emotion is static. Or rather the dramatic emotion is. The feelings excited by improper art are

22. This distancing from the immediate contradictions of existence (the metamorphosis of the either/or into the neither/nor) by way of artistic ordering (recollecting experience from the end) is what Kierkegaard refers to variously as "perceiving *aeterno modo,*" "unmastered irony," "poetry," and, most basically, the act of man in the "aesthetic stage" on life's way. For his criticism of this mode of perception, see especially his discussion of Friedrich Schlegel's *Lucinde* in *The Concept of Irony,* translated by Lee M. Capel (Bloomington: Indiana University Press, 1971), pp. 302–316. See also John Barth's analogous critique of "Mythotherapy" in *The End of the Road* (Garden City, N.Y.: Doubleday, 1967).

kinetic, desire and loathing. Desire urges us to possess, to go to something; loathing urges us to abandon, to go from something. These are kinetic emotions. The arts which excite them, pornographical or didactic, are therefore improper arts. The esthetic emotion (I use the general term) is therefore static. The mind is arrested and raised above desire and loathing.

O sages standing in God's holy fire
As in the gold mosaic of a wall,
Come from the holy fire, perne in a gyre,
And be the singing-masters of my soul.
Consume my heart away; sick with desire
And fastened to a dying animal
It knows not what it is; and gather me
Into the artifice of eternity.

Once out of nature I shall never take
My bodily form from any natural thing,
But such a form as Grecian goldsmiths make
Of hammered gold and gold enamelling
To keep a drowsy Emperor awake;
Or set upon a golden bough to sing
To lords and ladies of Byzantium
Of what is past, or passing, or to come.

For Stephen, growing up has been a terrible process of discovering the paradox that the city—the image of beauty, of order, of repose, for Plato, for Virgil, for Augustine, for Justinian, for Dante, for Plethon, for Campanella—has become in the modern world the space of radical ugliness and disorder, an "immense panorama of futility and anarchy."[23] To put it in Heidegger's terms, it has been a process of discovering that the at-home of the modern world has in fact become the realm of the not-at-home. This process, that is, has been one of *dislocation.* Thus for Stephen the ugliness and disorder, the "squalor" and "sordidness," that assault his sensitive consciousness after his "Ptolemaic," his "logocentric," universe (which he diagrams on the flyleaf of his geography book) has been utterly shattered during the catastrophic and traumatic Christmas dinner, is primarily or, at any rate, ontologically, a matter of random motion:

He sat near them [his numerous brothers and sisters] at the table and asked where his father and mother were. One answered:
—Goneboro toboro lookboro atboro aboro houseboro.
Still another removal! A boy named Fallon in Belvedere had often asked him with a silly laugh why they moved so often. . . .

23. T. S. Eliot, "*Ulysses,* Order, and Myth," reprinted from *Dial* (1923) in William Van O'Connor, ed., *Forms of Modern Fiction* (Bloomington: Indiana University Press), p. 123.

He asked:

—Why are we on the move again, if it's a fair question?

The sister answered:

—Becauseboro theboro landboro lordboro willboro putboro usboro outboro. . . . He waited for some moments, listening [to the children sing "Oft in the Stilly Night"] before he too took up the air with them. He was listening with pain of spirit to the overtones of weariness behind their frail fresh innocent voices. Even before they set out on life's journey they seemed weary already of the way.

. . . All seemed weary of life even before entering upon it. And he remembered that Newman had heard this note also in the broken line of Virgil *giving utterance, like the voice of Nature herself, to that pain and weariness yet hope of better things which has been the experience of her children in every time.*

(Walter Pater too had heard this sad Virgilian note and in quoting the passage in *Marius the Epicurean,* another novel having its setting in a disintegrating "civilized" world, established the nostalgia for rest as the essential motive of the aesthetic movement in England.)

Seen in the light of his discovery that random motion is the radical mode of modern urban life—that existence is prior to essence, which the postmodern writer will later present as the Un-Naming in the Garden-City—Stephen's well-known aesthetic or rather (to clarify what persistent critical reference to Stephen's "aesthetic" has obscured) his iconic poetics of *stasis,* both its volitional source, and its formal character, becomes clear. He wants, like T. E. Hulme, like Proust, like Virginia Woolf and most other symbolists, a poetry the iconic—and autotelic—nature of which *arrests* the mind—neutralizes the anxiety, the schism in the spirit—and *raises* it above desire and loathing, which is to say, the realm of radical motion, of contingency, of historicity, in the distancing moment when the contradictory parts are seen simultaneously as a whole in balanced equilibrium.

The "epiphanic"—one is tempted to say "Oriental"—nature of this iconic poetic is further clarified in Stephen's amplification of the principle of *stasis* in terms of St. Thomas' *"ad pulcritudinem tria requiruntur, integritas, consonantia, claritas,"* especially the first and, above all, the most important third categories. *Integritas* or "wholeness," Stephen observes, is the apprehension of "a bounding line drawn about the object" no matter whether it is in space or in time: ". . . temporal or spatial, the esthetic image is first luminously apprehended as selfbounded and selfcontained upon the immeasurable background of space or time which is not it. You apprehend it as *one* thing. You see it as one whole." *Consonantia* or "harmony" is the apprehension of the "rhythm of its structure": the feeling that "it is a *thing,*" "complex, multiple, divisible, separable, made up of parts, the result of its parts and their sum, harmonious." Finally, and

most important for Stephen, *claritas* or "radiance" (the etymology of his
translation—"radiance" is the light emitted in rays from a center or *logos*
—and his analysis of the term clearly suggest its relation with revelation
in the ontotheological tradition) is the apprehension of "that thing which
it is and no other thing. The radiance of which [St. Thomas] speaks is the
scholastic *quidditas,* the *whatness* of a thing. This supreme quality is felt
by the artist when the esthetic image is first conceived in his imagination.
. . . The instant wherein that supreme quality of beauty, the clear radiance
of the esthetic image, is apprehended *luminously by the mind which has
been arrested by its wholeness* and fascinated by its harmony in the *luminous silent stasis of esthetic pleasure. . . .*" (My italics.)

So also in "Sailing to Byzantium"—though the context is more ontological than social in orientation—Yeats's speaker, like Stephen, is articulating, both in the content and form of the poem, an iconic poetic that
has its source in a yearning for epiphanic transcendence—what Wilhelm
Worringer (the proponent of "primitive" and oriental, including Byzan-
tine, artistic models who influenced T. E. Hulme) in *Abstraction and
Empathy* calls the "urge to abstraction." As fully, if more implicitly, conscious of the paradoxical horror of the modern Western city as Stephen,
the poet has come to the city of the iconic imagination—the city of Phase
15—to pray to his mosaic models to teach him *an art of poetry* that will
"consume my heart away"—a heart like Stephen's, which, "sick with de-
sire/And fastened to a dying animal/ . . . knows not what it is." Such a
heart is ignorant because, as Yeats says here and reiterates in innumerable
ways throughout his early and middle poetry, its *immediate* relationship
to history makes everything appear to be random motion, that is, absurd.
Clearly, to continue with the language of existential phenomenology, this
centerless heart which can never *be,* is a synecdoche for the dislodged and
thus anxiety-ridden Being-in-the-world, the alienated Dasein in the dreadful, the uncanny *(unheimlich),* realm of temporality, of Nothingness. And,
as in Stephen's iconic poetic, Yeats's moment of consummation (the parallel with "radiance" should not be overlooked) which negates the human
heart and neutralizes (arrests) its desire—the Western, the empathetic,
urge "to possess, to go to something"—is the consummation of the creative
act, the metamorphosis of *kinesis* into *stasis,* becoming into being, the
uncertain, and open-ended temporal life into assured and en-closed iconic
artifact, "selfbounded and selfcontained upon the immeasurable background of space or time which is not it." (Similarly, the image of a Byzan-
tine mosaic Panaghiá or Saint is sharply delineated upon a depthless and
vast gold space that suggests the absolute purity of eternity.) Like Stephen's "instant" of "luminous silent stasis," Yeats's moment of consummation is thus the distancing moment when all time can be seen
simultaneously. The real birds of the first stanza of "Sailing to Byzantium"

—"those dying generations"—know not what they are because they are "caught" *in* time. Having assumed the form "as Grecian goldsmiths make/Of hammered gold and gold enamelling," having achieved the "unity of Being" (As Yeats elsewhere calls the iconic work/city of art), the poet can now, in this moment of consummation, sing in *full knowledge sub specie aeternitatis*—from a perspective beyond or "out of nature"— of the world below, which is to say, of history *seen all at once,* that is, as logocentric spatial image:

Of what is past, or passing, or to come.

In the words that Yeats's inclusive myth or rather his "sacred book" insists on, this burning moment, like that of Joyce's "priest of the eternal imagination," and so many other symbolist poets and novelists, is, in Ortega's term, the "dehumanizing" epiphanic moment of transcendence when time returns to its genetic origin *(arché) in illo tempore;* that is, becomes circular, and liberates us from our temporal bondage.[24]

[IV]

Committed to an iconic poetic of transcendence, Modernist literature (the symbolist literature of the late nineteenth and early twentieth centuries) thus tended to refuse to engage itself in the history of modern man. Though the Modernists were able to reveal the squalor of the "Unreal City" of the West, where, as one of T. S. Eliot's Thames daughters puts it, "I can connect/Nothing with nothing," and even point with Dickens and Dostoevski and Tolstoi to the ontological imbalances (the invasion) that the excessive pursuit of causal order had already generated, it did not seriously challenge the positivistic structure of consciousness which organizes and sustains it. Despite, therefore, the terrible historical lessons of the twentieth century, especially of the genocidal holocaust perpetrated by Nazism in the name of "the final solution," and the diagnosis of the

24. According to Mircea Eliade, "primitive" societies annulled the sting of existential temporality by periodic ritual reenactments (based on the seasonal cycle) of "a celestial archetype," that is, by returning to the abiding "center." Referring to the construction of a temple or a city (analogues of a work or symbolist or mythic art) Eliade observes: "Through repetition of the cosmogonic act, concrete time . . . is projected into mythical time, *in illo tempore* [in that time] when the foundation of the world occurred. Thus the reality and the enduringness of a construction are assured not only by the transformation of profane space into a transcendent space (the center) but also by the transformation of concrete time into mythic [timeless] time. Any ritual whatever . . . unfolds not only in a consecrated space (i.e., one different in essence from profane space) but also in a 'sacred time,' 'once upon a time' *(in illo tempore, ab origine),* that is, when the ritual was performed for the first time by a god, an ancestor, or a hero." This imitation of archetypes and repetition of paradigmatic gestures results in the "abolition of profane time, of duration, of 'history'; and he who reproduces the exemplary gesture thus finds himself transported into the mythical epoch in which its revelation took place." *Cosmos and History: The Myth of the Eternal Return,* translated by Willard R. Trask (New York: Harper Torchbooks, 1959), pp. 20–21, 35.

existential phenomenologists, it is still the "disinterested" (Heidegger would say "care-less") positivistic frame of reference that determines the questions-and-answers, that delineates "everyday" Western man's image of the universe and creates his values. From the governing bodies and the scientific-industrial-military complex and even educational and religious institutions to the working class it is still this "well-made" world, the world pointing toward a materialist utopia, toward a Crystal Palace end, that appears real. And as Sartre suggests in his assault on *les salauds* in *Nausea* and "The Childhood of a Leader," it is the certainty of the *rightness* of this fictional image of the macrocosm that continues to justify the coercion of the unique and disturbing deviation—that is, differ*a*nce—into its pre-determined role—or its elimination ("liquidation" or "wasting")—when it does not fulfill the rigid and inexorable expectations established by an end conceived from the beginning. Indeed, this world-picture, as a book like Lewis Mumford's *The Pentagon of Power* suggests, becomes more rigid and inclusive—totalitarian—in proportion to the irrationality it generates. The investigator and monstrous proliferation: these are the *presences* of contemporary life. And this, as both the existential phenomenologists and their literary counterparts, especially the absurdists, suggest, is no accident.

As I have already suggested, my definition of the Western structure of consciousness as one which perceives the world as a well-made melodrama is not a tour de force of the critical imagination. It is discoverable as an unexamined assumption everywhere in the language and the shape of action of men from all social levels of the Western city. It is impossible in this limited space to provide detailed support for this claim. But perhaps a quotation from an editorial on the subject of literature that appeared some time ago in *The Daily News,* the New York tabloid with a circulation of over 2 million, may suggest how rooted and inclusive this perspective is:

Winner and Still Champ

For generations William Shakespeare has been recognized as the greatest English master of the drama, and quite possibly the greatest handler of the English language, that ever yet has trod this earthly ball. . . .

Shakespeare and Dickens had several things in common. They . . . composed stage or fictional pieces which had definite beginnings, unmistakable climaxes and positive endings.

Neither Dickens nor Shakespeare wrote so-what tripe that gets nowhere and is in some fashion nowadays. Nor did they glorify characters whom even the ablest of modern psychiatrists couldn't help.

End of today's discussion of matters literary.[25]

25. Quoted in *Time* (August 31, 1970), p. 37.

This unquestioned obsession for the "positive" and comforting *ending* in the face of Shakespeare's—and even Dickens'—disturbing ambiguities, to say nothing of the uncertainties of contingent existence, I submit, lies behind this newspaper's editorial support of all causes "grounded" in a storybook patriotism (such as the United States' involvement in Vietnam, Richard Nixon's invasion of Cambodia, Spiro Agnew's rhetoric of law and order) and vilification of all others "grounded" in storybook treachery (such as the peace movement, senatorial opposition to unilateral policy making by the executive branch, and even Scandinavian anti-Americanism). More pernicious, because its implications are harder to perceive, this structure of consciousness also lies behind this newspaper's *presentation* of the news, whether a tenement murder, a campus uprising, or an international incident, as sensational melodrama whose problem-solution form not only neutralizes the reader's anxieties but even makes him a voyeur. That these disclosures of this all too brief deconstruction of the editorial perspective of *The Daily News* are not isolated journalistic phenomena is clearly suggested by pointing to the obvious parallel with, say, *Time* or even *Newsweek*, where the narrative structure of every article is conceived as a well-made fiction, that is, written—manipulated—from the end.

Further, this positivistic structure of consciousness also lies behind the political actions that constitute the news. As even the most cursory examination of "The Pentagon Papers" clearly suggests, for example, this "politics of illusion," as Harold Rosenberg calls it,[26] governed the futile involvement of the United States in Vietnam from the overthrow of Diem, the Tonkin Bay incident, and the ensuing large-scale "retaliatory" bombing of North Vietnam to the Vietnamization—which meant the Americanization or rather the Westernization—of Vietnam.[27] It is, then, no accident

26. *Act and Actor: Making the Self* (New York: Meridian Books, 1972), p. xxii. Because it sheds further historical light on the above discussion, the passage from which the phrase is taken (originally published in a *Partisan Review* symposium on "What's Happening to America" conducted during the Johnson administration) is worth quoting at some length: "The United States today is governed by professional illusionists. Not only are officials elected through campaigns of image-building based on fiction and caricature, but once in office their actions are decided not by anticipating consequences to the nation and/or humanity but by the kind of image those actions will enable them to present to the public. Washington acts by putting on an act. The same is true of every state capitol and city hall. With sheriffs behaving like movie actors, movie actors aspire to the highest offices. Politics increasingly takes on the forms of mass culture, in which the picture of a thing, or the publicity about it, achieves precedence over the thing itself, since the latter is seen by considerably fewer people. . . . Events are contrived out of the whole cloth in order to provide occasions for actions or statements of policy. Events are made to happen for the sake of words, instead of words being used to give an account of events. History has been turned inside out; writing it takes place in advance of its occurrence, and every statesman is an author in embryo."
27. The original version of this essay was written before the Watergate investigations of 1973–1974. Even the slightest knowledge of the disclosures of these investigations or of the contents of "The Presidential Transcripts" will show the absolute similarity between the structure of consciousness presiding over the Watergate affair and that which developed the "scenario" for Vietnam. The key to this relationship is, of course, the Nixon administration's choice of a detective story writer (E. Howard Hunt) to "mastermind" and undertake the Watergate burglary, to initiate, that is, the process of coercing threatening potentiality into certainty in behalf of aggrandizing the power of the executive or, what is the same thing, of tightening its arrogant hold on national and international events: history.

that *everywhere* in these secret documents the Southeast Asian situation is seen by their American authors as a problem to be solved; that the planning to solve the problem—to achieve conclusive American objectives—is referred to in the metaphor of plotting a *scenario;* that the execution—the acting out—of the scenario in this recalcitrant theater of operations is to be accomplished, first, by the CIA—the international detective agency whose job it is, we are now beginning to see, to coerce the reality under investigation into conformity with a preconceived order—and, then, by the military arm by way of a massive assault on the "criminal" enemy. In short, what emerges in these disturbing documents, if we deconstruct the language (especially its habitual metaphors), is an image of an action in which virtually every American involved in this terrible human disaster—from the executive branch and its councils to the intelligence agencies and the military and the press and its public—speaks and acts unknowingly as if he is playing a role in a well-made fiction in the utterly dehumanized mode of a play by Eugène Scribe, a novel by Sir Arthur Conan Doyle, or closest of all, an episode of "Mission Impossible."

I will refer specifically to only one concrete but representative action of the war in Vietnam: the large-scale interservice rescue operation staged against the Son Tay prisoner-of-war camp in North Vietnam in December 1970. Seen in the light of my discussion, this melodramatic action constitutes an illuminating paradigm not only of the war that America has been waging against Southeast Asia since 1954, but also—and more fundamentally, for it is not so much politics as ontology that concerns me here—of the war that the West has been waging against the world, indeed against Nature itself, ever since the seventeenth century. It reveals, that is, how embedded—how *located*—as an unexamined metaphysical assumption in the Western consciousness is the metaphor of the well-made universe and how intense the conditioned psychological need behind it. This elaborately plotted action, the "scenario" of which, according to *The New York Times* report, "was rehearsed for months in a stage-set replica of [the] objective on the Florida Gulf Coast,"[28] did not achieve its objective, that is, did not end, because, despite the split-second timing with which all the roles were acted out, there was no one there to rescue at the climactic moment. "It was like hollering in an empty room," one of the bewildered actors in this dreadful experience put it. "When we realized that there was no one in the compound," said another—his language should be marked well—"I had the most horrible feeling of my life." And *Time* summed up the action: "All the courage, the long training, the perfectly executed

28. "The Week in Review," Section 4, *The New York Times,* (November 29, 1970), p. 1.

mission, had come to naught."[29] Seen in the light of my deconstruction of the Western structure of consciousness, this language recalls the remarkable parallel with Watt's agonized quest for or, rather, futile effort "to take hold of" the elusive Knott in Samuel Beckett's great postmodern novel and assumes a grimly ironic significance.

Despite this mockery "of our contrived finalities," these revelatory glimpses into the horror, the secretary of defense (Melvin Laird) was driven to declare reiteratively in the following days that the Son Tay affair was a successfully completed operation. It is this metamorphosis of the absurd into manageable object, into fulfilled objective, into an accomplishment, which is especially revealing. For the obvious incommensurability between the assertion of successful completion and the absurd and dreadful non-end constitutes a measure of the intensity of the need that the power complex and the people that depend on it feel for definite conclusions. Returning to the ontological level, it is a measure of modern Western man's need *to take hold of the Nothing* that despite, or perhaps because of, his technics is crowding in on him. To put it in the central metaphor of the existential imagination, it is the measure of his need to flee from the Furies of the not-at-home and its imperatives for freedom.

[V]

In the past decade or so there have emerged a variety of "postmodern" modes of writing and critical thought that, despite certain resemblances to aspects of the existential/phenomenological imagination, are in their essential thrust extensions of early iconic Modernism. I am referring, for example, to the structuralist criticism deriving primarily from the anthropology of Claude Levi-Strauss and practiced by such critics as Roland Barthes and Tzvetan Todorov and (in this country) Robert Scholes;[30] the criticism of consciousness (or identification) of Georges Poulet and the Geneva school; the neo-imagist thought of Marshall McLuhan; the "neo-gnosticism" of Ihab Hassan;[31] the ethnopoetics of Jerome Rothenberg, Gary Snyder, and the contributors to the influential American journal *Alcheringa* (though this poetry is authentically postmodern insofar as it calls for the recovery of oral/temporal expression); the concrete poetry of Pierre Garnier, Franz Mon, and Ferdinand Kriwet; the "depthless" *roman nouveau* of Robbe-Grillet and Michel Butor; the formalist fiction of Robert Coover, Ronald Sukenick, and Raymond Federman; the "happenings" of

29. *Time* (December 7, 1970), p. 16.
30. See *Structuralism: An Introduction* (New Haven, Conn.: Yale University Press, 1974).
31. Ihab Hassan, *Paracriticism: Seven Speculations of the Times* (Urbana: University of Illinois Press, 1975).

Allan Kaprow and Claes Oldenburg; and the pop art literature advocated by critics such as Leslie Fiedler. The latter, it is worth observing, wants to reconcile the sensibilities of Henry Wadsworth Longfellow and Stephen Foster with those of the Beatles, Bob Dylan, Leonard Cohen, and so on, all of whom have in common not only the clichés and the assertive end rhymes he admires for their expression of childlike innocence, but also, and in a way at the source of these characteristics, the desire to go home again: the nostalgia for the hearth.[32] These modes of creativity and critical speculation attest to the variety of experimentation on the postmodern scene, but this pluralism has also tended to hide the fact that, *in tendency,* these impulses of the contemporary imagination are all oriented beyond history or, rather, they all aspire to the spatialization of time. As a result the existential sources of the primary thrust of the postmodern literary imagination have been obscured, thus jeopardizing the encouraging post-World War II impulse—activated by existential phonomenology—to release the temporality of the literary medium from the prison house of the plastic arts, which is to say, to engage literature in an ontological dialogue with the world in behalf of dis-covering the authentic historicity of man.

In the light of this deconstruction, then, the "Pentagon Papers" and the "Watergate Tapes" not only emerge as stark reminders that the totalizing structure of consciousness of the "straightforward" gentlemen who built the modern city continues to coerce history with missionary certainty into well-made fictions. Because they resemble so closely the kind of fiction and drama associated with the rise of science, technology, and middle-class culture in the nineteenth century, these documents also emerge as a paradigm capable of teaching both the contemporary writer and critic a great deal about the Western mind and the popular arts and the media that nourish it. In so doing, finally, they suggest a way of discriminating between modernisms and of clarifying the direction that the main impulse of the postmodern sensibility has taken and, I think, should continue to take in the immediate future, in, that is, the boundary situation we continue to inhabit.

Ultimately, one would like a literature of generosity, a literature, like Chaucer's or Shakespeare's or Dickens' or George Eliot's or Tolstoi's, that acknowledges, indeed, celebrates, the "messiness" of existence, as Iris Murdoch puts it, in the context of discovered form.[33] But at the moment, Western man as a cultural community or rather as a public is simply incapable of responding to the generosity—the humane impulse, having its source in the humility of acknowledged uncertainty, to let Being be—that, on occasion, infuses Shakespeare's stage and his world as stage. (As

32. Leslie Fielder, "The Children's Hour or, the Return of the Vanishing Longfellow: Some Reflection of the Future of Poetry," in Ihab Hassan, ed., *Liberations: New Essays on the Humanities in Revolution* (Middletown, Conn.: Wesleyan University Press, 1971), pp. 149–175.
33. See especially "The Sublime and the Beautiful Revisited," *Yale Review,* Vol. 43 (December 1959), 247–271.

the editorial quoted above suggests, the ungenerous effort of the "Enlightenment" to rewrite the "endings" of Shakespeare's "inconclusive" plays
continues down to the present, though it takes the form of accepting the
rewritten version as myth while the plays themselves are "explicated" out
of existence in college and university classrooms.) For, to put the point in
the familiar language of the historical critical debate, unlike the Western
past, when Art (*The Odyssey,* for example) was justifiably a taxonomic
model for ordering a brutal and terrifying Nature (existence) or a mode
of psychological consolation in the face of its immediate catastrophic
power, the Western present, as the "Pentagon Papers" and the Son Tay
"scenario" and the Watergate and the "Mission Impossible" series and *The
Daily News* and *Time* suggest, is a time that bears witness to a Nature
whose brutal and terrifying forces have been coerced—and domesticated
—into a very well-made and therefore very dangerous work of Art.

The Western structure of consciousness is bent, however inadver-
tently, on unleashing chaos in the name of the order of a well-made world.
If this is true, contemporary literature cannot afford the luxury of the
symbolist, or, as I prefer to call it, the iconic literary aesthetic nor of its
"postmodern" variants. For ours is no time for psychic flights, for Deda-
lean "seraphic embraces," however enticing they may be.[34] Neither, for
that matter, despite its more compelling claim as an authentic possibility,
can it afford the luxury of the aesthetic implicit in the concept of the later
Heidegger's *Gelassenheit* (that receptivity which might disclose the Being
of not-being and thus the sacramental at-homeness of the not-at-home),
the aesthetic of "letting be" or, perhaps, of letting Being be, that Nathan
Scott seems to be recommending in his important recent books, *Negative
Capability* and *The Wild Prayer of Longing.*[35] For, in the monolithic
well-made world that the positivistic structure of consciousness perceives
—and perceiving, creates—it is the Detective who has usurped the place
not only of God but of Being too as the abiding presence and, therefore,
has first to be confronted.

In *Being and Time* (1927) Martin Heidegger, adapting Husserl's phenomenological reduction to his own existential-ontological purposes,
called for a Destruction *(Destruktion)* of the Western philosophical tradi-

34. The anti-Modernist critique of aesthetic distance is remarkable in the consistency with which it refers
to this movement as flight (ascent). Kierkegaard calls it "hovering"; Conrad in *Victory* refers to Axel
Heyst's effort to fulfill his Schopenhauerian father's advice to "Look on—make no sound" as "a floating
existence"; Sartre makes the detached and memoryless Orestes—the Orestes under the tutelage of his
aesthetic Pangloss—say in *The Flies:* "I'm light as gossamer and walk on air" (this is also how Sartre
describes Mathieu Delarue in *The Age of Reason*); and Joseph Heller, fully conscious of its epistemological
significance, says of Yossarian at the end of *Catch 22:* "It was funny how he had really come to detest
flying."
35. *Negative Capability: Studies in the New Literature and the Religious Situation* (New Haven, Conn.:
Yale University Press, 1969) and *The Wild Prayer of Longing: Poetry and the Sacred* (New Haven, Conn.:
Yale University Press, 1971). See also Martin Heidegger *Discourse on Thinking,* translated by John M.
Anderson and E. Hans Freund. Originally published under the title *Gelassenheit* (New York: Harper &
Row, 1966).

tion to *dis-cover* and *remember* the radical temporality of Being that its
logocentric or metaphysical (spatial) orientation—the orientation established by Plato and Aristotle—covered over, habitualized, and eventually
forgot in its effort to master existence.[36] What Heidegger says as a phenomenologist, T. S. Eliot—the Eliot constantly at war with his Modernist
self who seeks, through art, for "a way of ordering, of giving shape and a
significance to the immense panorama of futility and anarchy which is
contemporary history"[37]—says as a poet in one of the great passages of
Four Quartets:

> I do not know much about gods; but I think that the
>   river
> Is a strong brown god—sullen, untamed and intractable,
> Patient to some degree, at first recognised as a
>   frontier;
> Useful, untrustworthy, as a conveyor of commerce;
> Then only a problem confronting the builder of bridges.
> The problem once solved, the brown god is almost
>   forgotten
> By the dwellers in cities—ever, however, implacable,
> Keeping his seasons and rages, destroyer, reminder
> Of what men choose to forget. Unhonoured,
>   unpropitiated
> By worshippers of the machine, but waiting, watching
>   and waiting.

Our time, Heidegger and Eliot—and the existential writers to whom
I have referred throughout this essay—imply, calls for an existence-art,
one which, by refusing to resolve discords (the differ*a*nce, in Jacque Derrida's term) into the satisfying concordances of a *telos*, constitutes an
assault against an *art*-ificialized Nature in behalf of the recovery of its
primordial terrors. The most immediate task, therefore, in which the
contemporary writer must engage himself—it is, to borrow a phrase un-
gratefully from Yeats, the most difficult task not impossible—is that of
undermining the detectivelike expectations of the positivistic mind, of
unhoming Western man, by evoking rather than purging pity and terror
—anxiety. It must, that is, continue the *iconoclastic* revolution begun in
earnest after World War II to dislodge or, to be absolutely accurate, to
dis-occident, the objectified modern Western man, the weighty, the solid

36. Martin Heidegger, *Being and Time,* translated by John Macquarrie and Edward Robinson (New York:
Harper & Row, 1962), pp. 41–49.
37. Eliot, "*Ulysses,* Myth and Order," p. 123.

citizen, to drive him out of the fictitious well-made world, not to be gathered into the "artifice of eternity," but to be exposed to the existential realm of history, where Nothing is certain. As the great poet of the American city, David Ignatow expresses it in "The Sky Is Blue":

> Put things in their place,
> my mother shouts. I am looking
> out the window, my plastic soldier
> at my feet. The sky is blue
> and empty. In it floats
> the roof across the street.
> What place, I ask her.[38]

For only in the precincts of our last evasions, where "dread strikes us dumb," only in this silent realm of dreadful uncertainty, this "zero zone," are we likely to discover the ontological and aesthetic possibilities of generosity.

In this image-breaking enterprise, therefore, the contemporary writer is likely to find his "tradition," not in the "anti-Aristotelian" line that goes back from the concrete poets, Proust, Joyce, the Imagists, Mallarmé, Gautier, and Pater to Coleridge and his "esemplastic imagination" but in the "anti-Aristotelianism" that looks back from Heller, Pynchon, Ellison, Beckett, Ionesco, Ignatow,[39] and the Sartre of *Nausea* and *No Exit* through the Eliot of *Sweeney Agonistes,* some of the surrealists, Kafka, Pirandello, Dostoevski and the "loose, and baggy monsters" of his countrymen, Dickens, Wycherly, and—with all due respect to the editor of *The Daily News*—the Shakespeare of *King Lear, Measure for Measure,* and the ironically entitled *All's Well that Ends Well,* in which one of the characters says:

> They say miracles are past, and we have our philosophical persons to make modern and familiar things supernatural and causeless. Hence it is that we make trifles of terrors, ensconcing ourselves into seeming knowledge when we should submit ourselves to an unknown fear.

38. From "The Sky Is Blue" by David Ignatow. In *Poems 1934–1969* (Middletown, Conn.: Wesleyan University Press, 1970), p. 201. Copyright © 1964 by David Ignatow. Reprinted by permission of Wesleyan University Press. See also David Ignatow, "A Dialogue with William Spanos," *boundary 2,* Vol. 2 (Spring 1974), 443–481.

39. The American tradition that goes back from David Antin, Robert Creeley, Charles Olson, through W. C. Williams, the Ezra Pound of *The Cantos* to Walk Whitman constitutes a counterpart in poetry of this "anti-Aristotelian" line insofar as it is committed to the deconstruction of spatial (closed) in favor of temporal (open) forms and to the oral impulse, that is, "language as the act of the instant." Charles Olson, "Human Universe," in Robert Creeley, ed., *Selected Writings* (New York: New Directions, 1966), p. 53. Though David Ignatow is not immediately related to these poets, it is no accident that he claims both Williams and Whitman as his essential forebears.

Søren Kierkegaard
Friedrich Schlegel

from *The Concept of Irony*

This selection from Kierkegaard's astonishing M.A. thesis constitutes a severe critique of the "unmastered irony" of his contemporary,
Friedrich Schlegel's Romantic novel *Lucinde*. As such it is his first
phenomenological/existential description and critique of the "aesthetic
stage," or, as he calls it in *Either/Or,* the "perspective aeterno modo."
Since irony—that is, the balancing of opposite attitudes in equilibrium
to achieve aesthetic distance—is one of the essential strategies of early
modern (symbolist) literature and serves as the basis of New Critical
poetics, Kierkegaard's existential critique of unmastered irony sheds
significant light not only on Western art in general but more specifically
on the reaction of post-World War II existential literature—the literature
of engagement—against that of early Modernism. Donald Barthelme's
story 'Kierkegaard Unfair to Schlegel' can be profitably read in this
context.

Friedrich Schlegel's celebrated novel *Lucinde*,[1] which became the
gospel of the Young Germany and the system for its *Rehabilitation des
Fleisches,* and which was an abomination to Hegel, will here be the object
of investigation. This discussion is not without difficulties, however, for
Lucinde, as everyone knows, is a very obscene book, and by including
certain passages for closer examination I shall be incurring the risk of
making it impossible for even the purest reader to come away wholly
unscathed. I shall therefore be as provident and sparing as possible.

In order not to do Schlegel an injustice one must recall the numerous
errors which have crept into the many relationships in life, and in particular which have been relentless in making love as tame, well-behaved,
sluggish and apathetic, as utilitarian and serviceable as any other domesticated animal, in short, as unerotic as possible. To this extent one must be
extremely beholden to Schlegel should he succeed in finding a solution.
But alas, the only climate he discovers in which love can thrive is even
worse, not a climate somewhat further south in relation to our northern
climate, but an ideal climate that exists nowhere. Accordingly, it is not

Source: "Friedrich Schlegel" in *The Concept of Irony* by Søren Kierkegaard, translated by Lee M. Capel.
Copyright © 1965 in the English translation by William Collins Sons & Co., Ltd., London, and Harper &
Row, Publishers, Inc. By permission of Harper & Row, Publishers, Inc.
1. Friedrich Schlegel, *Lucinde,* second unabridged edition, Stuttgart, 1835.

only the tame ducks and geese of a domesticated love which beat their wings and utter a terrifying cry when they hear the wild birds of love whistling by overhead. No, it is every more deeply poetic person, whose longings are too strong to be bound by romantic cobwebs, whose demands on life are too great to be satisfied through writing a novel, who here, precisely on behalf of poetry, must lay down his protest and endeavour to show that it was not a solution Friedrich Schlegel discovered but a delusion he strayed into, must endeavour to show that to live is something different from to dream. When we consider more closely what Schlegel opposed with his irony, it will surely not be denied that there both was and is much in the ingress, progress, and egress of marriage deserving such a correction, and which makes it natural for the subject to seek to emancipate himself from such things. There is an extremely constricted seriousness, a purposiveness, a wretched teleology worshipped by many like an idol, which demands every infinite pursuit as its rightful sacrifice. Love is thus nothing in and through itself, but only becomes something through the purpose whereby it is accommodated to that pettiness whose success creates such a furore in the private theatre of the family. "To have purposes, to carry out purposes, to interweave purposes artfully with purposes into a new purpose: this ridiculous habit is so deeply rooted in the foolish nature of godlike man that if once he wishes to move freely without any purpose, on the inner stream of ever flowing images and feelings, he must actually resolve to do it and make it a set purpose (p. 153). . . . It is, to be sure, a different matter with people who love in the ordinary way. The man loves in his wife only the race, the woman in her husband only the degree of his natural qualities and social position, and both love in their children only their own creation and property (p. 55). . . . Oh, it is true, my friend, man is by nature a most serious animal (p. 57)." There is a moral prudishness, a strait-jacket in which no rational human being can move. In God's name let it be sundered! There is, on the other hand, the moonlit kind of theatre marriages of an overwrought romanticism for which nature, at least, has no purpose, and whose barren breezes and impotent embraces profit a Christian state no more than a pagan one. Against all these let irony rage! But it is not merely against untruths such as these that Schlegel directs his attack. There is a Christian view of marriage which, at the very hour of the nuptials, has had the audacity to proclaim the curse even before it pronounces the benediction. There is a Christian view that places all things under sin, that recognizes no exception, spares nothing, not the child in the womb nor the most beautiful among women. There is a seriousness in this view too high to be grasped by the harassed toilers of prosaic daily life, too severe to be mocked by marital improvisors.— Thus those times are now past when mankind lived so happily and innocently without sorrow and tribulation, when everything was so like man, when the gods themselves set the fashion and sometimes laid aside their heavenly dignity in order to steal the love of some earthly woman; when one who quietly, furtively sneaked away to a rendevous could fear or flatter himself by finding a god among his rivals; those times when the sky arched itself proudly and beautifully over happy love like a friendly witness, or with quiet gravity concealed it in the solemn peace of the night; when everything lived only for love, and everything was in turn only a myth about love for the happy lovers. But there lies the difficulty, and it is from this perspective that one must evaluate the efforts of Schlegel and all earlier and later romanticism: *those times are past,* and still the longing of romanticism draws back to them. But in so doing it undertakes no *peregrinationes sacras* but *profanus.* Were it possible to reconstruct a bygone age, one must reconstruct it in its purity, hence Hellenism in all its naïveté. But this is what romanticism refuses to do. It is not properly Hellenism it reconstructs, but an unknown continent it discovers. But what is more, its enjoyments are refined to a high degree; for it does not merely seek to enjoy naïvely, but in this enjoyment desires to become conscious of the destruction of the given ethic. This is just the point of its enjoyment, as it were, that it smiles at the ethic under which it believes others groan, and in this lies the free play of ironic arbitrariness. Christianity by means of the spirit has established a dissension between the spirit and the flesh,[2] and either the spirit must negate the flesh or the flesh negate the spirit. Romanticism desires the latter, and is different from Hellenism in that along with the enjoyment of the flesh it also enjoys the negation of spirit. This it claims is to live poetically. I trust it will become apparent, however, that poetry is precisely what it misses, for true inward infinity proceeds only from resignation, and only this inward infinity is in truth infinite and in truth poetic.

Schlegel's *Lucinde* seeks to suspend the established ethic, or as Erdmann not infelicitously expresses it: "All moral determinations are mere sport, and it is accidental to the lover whether marriage is monogamous or whether *en quartre,* etc."[3] Were it possible to imagine that the whole of *Lucinde* were merely a caprice, an arbitrarily fashioned child of whim and fancy gesticulating with both her legs like the little Wilhelmine without a care for her dress or the world's judgment; were it but a light-headed whimsicality that found pleasure in setting everything on its head, in turning everything upside down; were it merely a witty irony over the total ethic identified with custom and use: who then would be so ridiculous as not to laugh at it, who would be such a distempered grouch that he

2. Christianity in no wise seeks by this to destroy sensuousness, for it teaches that it is only in the resurrection that none shall be taken in marriage nor given in marriage. But it also calls to mind the man who had no time to attend the great marriage feast because he was holding his own.
3. J. E. Erdmann, *Vorlesungen über Glauben und Wissen,* Berlin, 1837, p. 86.

could not even gloat over it? But this is not the case. Quite the contrary, *Lucinde* has a most doctrinaire character and a certain melancholy seriousness pervading it which seems to derive from the fact that its hero has arrived at this glorious knowledge of the truth so late that a part of his life has gone unutilized. The audacity which this novel so often reverts to, which it clamours for, as it were, is therefore not a momentary whimsical suspension of that which is objectively valid, so that the expression "audacity" as used here would itself have been capricious in using so strong an expression with deliberate abandon. No, this audacity is just what one calls audacity, but which is so amiable and interesting that ethics, modesty, and decency, which at first glance have some attraction, seem rather insignificant entities by comparison. Surely everyone who has read *Lucinde* will agree that it does have such a doctrinaire character. But should anyone wish to deny it, I must then ask him to explain how the Young Germany could have been so completely mistaken about it; and should he succeed in answering this, I shall then remind him that it is well known that Schlegel later became a Catholic and as such discovered the Reformation to have been the second fall of man, a fact which sufficiently shows that *Lucinde* was seriously intended.

Lucinde seeks to abrogate all ethics, not simply in the sense of custom and usage, but that ethical totality which is the validity of mind, the dominion of the spirit over the flesh. Hence it corresponds fully to what we have previously designated as the special pursuit of irony: to cancel all actuality and set in its place an actuality that is no actuality. In the first place, therefore, it is quite in order that the girl, or rather, the wife in whose arms Julian finds repose, that Lucinde "was also one of those who have a decided inclination for the romantic, and who do not live in the ordinary world but in one self-created and self-conceived" (p. 90), one of those, therefore, who properly have no other actuality than the sensual; quite in order, secondly, that it is one of Julian's great tasks to bring before his imagination an eternal embrace—presumably as the only true actuality.

If we consider *Lucinde* as such a catechism of love, it requires of its disciples "what Diderot calls the perception of the flesh," "a rare gift," and pledges them to develop it into that higher sense of artistic voluptuousness (pp. 29, 30). Naturally, Julian appears as priest in this worship "not without unction," that is, as one "to whom the spirit itself spake through a voice from heaven, saying: "Thou art my beloved son in whom I am well pleased" " (p. 35); as one who cries out to himself and others: "Consecrate thyself and proclaim that only nature is venerable and only health agreeable" (p. 27). What it seeks is a naked sensuality in which the spirit is a negated moment; what it opposes is a spirituality in which sensuality is an assimilated moment. To this extent it is incorrect when it takes as its ideal the little two-year-old Wilhelmine, "for her years the most clever [*geistreichste*] person of her time" (p. 15), since in her sensuality the spirit is not negated because it is not yet present. It desires nakedness altogether and so despises the northern coldness, and it seeks to ridicule that narrowmindedness unable to tolerate nakedness. However, I shall not concern myself any further whether this is a narrowmindedness, or whether the veil of attire is still not a beautiful image of how all sensuality ought to be, since when sensuality is intellectually mastered it is never naked. Instead, I shall merely call attention to the fact that the world still forgives Archimedes for running stark naked through the streets of Syracuse, and this surely not because of the mild southern climate, but because his spiritual exaltation, his "eureka, eureka" was a sufficient attire.

The confusion and disorder that *Lucinde* seeks to introduce into the established order [*Bestaaende*] it illustrates itself by means of the most perfect confusion in its design and structure. At the very outset Julian explains that along with the other conventions of reason and ethics he has also dispensed with chronology (p. 3). He then adds: "For me and for this book, for my love of it and for its internal formation, there is no purpose more purposive than that right at the start I begin by abolishing what we call order, keep myself entirely aloof from it, and appropriate to myself in word and deed the right to a charming confusion" (p. 5). With this he seeks to attain what is truly poetical, and as he renounces all understanding and allows the phantasy alone to rule,[4] it may well be possible for him and the reader, should the latter wish to do likewise, to let the imagination maintain this confusion [*Mellemhverandre*] in a single perpetually moving image.—In spite of this confusion, however, I shall endeavour to bring a kind of order into my presentation and let the whole consolidate itself at one definite point.

Julian, the hero of this novel, is no Don Juan (who by his sensual genius casts a spell over everything like a sorcerer; who steps forth with an immediate authority showing himself lord and ruler, an authority which words cannot describe but of which some representation may be had from a few imperious bars of Mozart; a being who does not seduce but by whom all would like to be seduced, and were their innocence restored to them would desire nothing more than to be seduced again; a dæmon who has no past, no history of development, but springs forth at once fully en-

---

4. That the imagination alone rules is repeated throughout the whole of *Lucinde*. Now who is such a monster that he is unable to delight in the free play of the imagination? But it does not follow from this that the whole of life should be given over to imagination. When the imagination is allowed to rule in this way it prostrates and anæsthetizes the soul, robs it of all moral tension, and makes of life a dream. Yet this is exactly what *Lucinde* seeks to accomplish, and its standpoint is essentially designated as follows (p. 153): "The supreme insight of the understanding is to choose the role of silence, to restore the soul to imagination, and not to disturb the sweet cooings of the young mother with her child." This obviously means that when the understanding has reached its zenith, its formation must give way to the imagination, which shall then rule and no longer be an interlude in the enterprise of life.

dowed like Minerva), but a personality ensnared in reflection who develops only successively. In the "Apprenticeship of Manhood" we learn more of his history. "To play faro with the appearance of the most violent passion, and yet to be distracted and absent-minded; to venture everything in a heated instant and as soon as it is lost to turn away indifferently: this was just one of the vicious habits by which Julian fulminated away his youth" (p. 59). The author thinks that by this single characteristic he has adequately portrayed Julian's life. In this we fully agree. Julian is a young man who, intensely torn asunder within, has by this very sundering acquired a living idea of that sorcery which in a few moments is able to make a man many, many years older; a young man who by this very sundering is in apparent possession of an enormous power, just as surely as the excitement of desperation produces athletic prowess; a young man who long ago had already begun the grand finale, but who nevertheless flourishes the goblet with a certain dignity and grace, with an air of intellectual ease in the world, and now summons all his strength in a single breath in order by a brilliant exit to cast a glorifying nimbus over a life which has had no value and leaves no bereavement behind; a young man who has long been familiar with the thought of suicide, but whose stormy soul has begrudged him time to reach a decision. Surely love must be that which shall save him! After having been on the verge of seducing a young and innocent girl (a fairy-tale, however, which has no further significance for him, since she was obviously too innocent to satisfy his thirst for knowledge), he discovers in Lisette the very teacher he needs, an instructress who has long been initiated into the nocturnal mysteries of love, and whose public instruction Julian tries in vain to restrict to a private instruction for himself alone.

The portrait of Lisette is perhaps the most accomplished in the whole novel, and the author has treated her with a visible partiality and spared nothing in order to cast a poetic glow over her. As a child she was more melancholy [*tungsindig*] than light-minded [*letsindig*], but even then she had been daemonically excited by sensuality (p. 78). Later she had been an actress, but only for a short time, and she always poked fun at her lack of talent and at all the boredom she had endured. Finally, she had offered herself completely to the service of sensuality. Next to independence she had an immense love for money, which she nevertheless knew how to use with taste. Her favours she allowed to be repaid sometimes by sums of money, sometimes by the satisfaction of a whimsical infatuation for some particular person. Her boudoir was open and wholly without conventional furniture, for on every side there were large, expensive mirrors, and alternating with these superb paintings by Correggio and Titian. In place of chairs she had genuine oriental carpets and some groups of marble in half life-size. Here she often sat Turkish fashion the whole day long, alone, her hands folded idly in her lap, for she despised all womanly tasks. She refreshed herself from time to time with sweet-scented perfumes, and had stories, travelogues, and fairy-tales read to her by her jockey, a plastically fair youth whom she had seduced in his fourteenth year. But she paid little heed to what was read, except when there was something ridiculous or some platitude which she, too, found true; for she esteemed nothing but reality, had no sense for anything else, and found all poetry ridiculous. Such is Schlegel's portrayal of a life, which, however corrupt it may be, nevertheless seems to put forward the claim to be poetical. The thing particularly prominent here is the exclusive indolence which bothers about nothing, which cannot be bothered with working but despises every womanly pursuit, which cannot be bothered with occupying the mind but merely lets it be occupied, which dissolves and exhausts every power of the soul in enervating enjoyments and causes consciousness itself to evaporate in a nauseous twilight. But enjoyment it was nonetheless, and surely to enjoy is to live poetically. The author seems also to want to find something poetical in the fact that Lisette did not always consider only money when distributing her favours. At such moments he seems to want to illuminate her wretched love with a reflection of that devotion belonging to innocent love, as if it were more poetical to be a slave to one's caprice than to money. So there she sits in this luxurious room with external consciousness slipping away from her, the huge mirrors reflecting her image from every angle produce the only consciousness she has remaining. When referring to her own person she usually called herself "Lisette," and often said that were she able to write she would then treat her story as though it were another's, altogether preferring to speak of herself in third person. This, evidently, was not because of her earthly exploits were as world historical as a Caesar's, so that her life was not her own because it belonged to the world. It was simply because the weight of this *vita ante acta* was too heavy for her to bear. To come to herself concerning it, to allow its menacing shapes to pass judgment upon her, this would indeed be too serious to be poetical. But to allow this wretched life to dissolve itself in indefinite contours, to stare at it as though it were something indifferent to her, this she liked to do. She might grieve over this lost and unhappy girl, she might offer her a tear, perhaps, but that this girl was herself she wanted to forget. But it is weak to seek to forget, although on occasion there may be stirring in this an energy foreshadowing something better. But to seek to relive oneself poetically in such a way that remorse can have no sting because it concerns another, all the while allowing enjoyment to become intensified through a secret complicity, this is a most effeminate cowardice. Throughout the whole of *Lucinde,* however, it is this lapsing into an æsthetic stupor[5] which appears as the designation for what it is to live poetically, and which, since it lulls the deeper ego into a somnambulant state, permits the arbitrary ego free latitude in ironic self-satisfaction.

But let us examine this more closely. There have been many attempts to show that such books as *Lucinde* are immoral, and there have been frequent cries of shame and ignominy over them. But so long as the author is allowed overtly to claim and the reader covertly to believe that such works are poetical, there is not much to be gained by this, and this so much the less since man has as great a claim on the poetical as the moral has claim on him. Be it therefore said, as it shall also be shown, that they are not only immoral but unpoetical, and this because they are irreligious. Let it be said first and last that every man can live poetically who in truth desires to. If we next inquire what poetry is, we might answer with the general characterization that poetry is victory over the world. It is through a negation of the imperfect actuality that poetry opens up a higher actuality, expands and transfigures the imperfect into the perfect, and thereby softens and mitigates that deep pain which would darken and obscure all things. To this extent poetry is a kind of reconciliation, though not the true reconciliation; it does not reconcile me with the actuality in which I live, for no transubstantiation of the given actuality occurs. Instead, it reconciles me with the given actuality by giving me another actuality, a higher and more perfect. Indeed, the greater the opposition, so much the more imperfect is the reconciliation, so that it often becomes no reconciliation at all but rather animosity. Only the religious, therefore, is capable of effecting the true reconciliation, for it renders actuality infinite for me. The poetical may well be a sort of victory over actuality, but the process whereby it is rendered infinite is more like an abandonment of, than a continuation in, actuality. To live poetically is therefore to live infinitely. But infinity may be either an external or an internal infinity. The person

5. This is set forth especially in the section entitled "An Idyl of Idleness," where the highest perfection is posited as pure and unadulterated passivity. "The more beautiful the climate we live in, the more passive we are. Only the Italians know how to walk, only the Orientals how to recline, and where do we find the human spirit developed more delicately and lusciously than in India? It is the privilege of being idle which is the true principle of nobility, and which everywhere distinguishes the noble from the common" (p. 42). "The highest and most perfect life is simply to vegetate" (p. 43). Plant life is the ideal to which it aspires, and so Julian writes to Lucinde: "The time is coming when we two shall intuit in one mind that we are blossoms of one plant or petals of one flower. Then shall we know with laughter that what we now call only hope was properly recollection" (p. 11). Hence longing itself assumes the form of vegetative still life. " 'Julian,' asked Lucinde, "why do I feel a deep longing in this serene peace?" "Because it is only in longing that we find peace," answered Julian. "Yes, peace is only when the mind, being disturbed by nothing, is moved to long and seek itself, where it can find nothing higher than its own longing' " (p. 148). "*Julian:* Divine peace, dear friend, I have found only in this longing. *Lucinde:* And that divine longing I have found in this beautiful peace" (p. 150).

who would have an infinitely poetical enjoyment also has an infinity before him, but it is an external infinity. When I enjoy I am constantly outside myself in the "other." But such an infinity must cancel itself. Only if I am not outside myself in what I enjoy but in myself, only then is my enjoyment infinite, for it is inwardly infinite. He who enjoys poetically, were he to enjoy the whole world, would still lack one enjoyment: he does not enjoy himself. To enjoy oneself (naturally not in a Stoic or egotistical sense, for here again there is no true infinity, but in a religious sense) is alone the true infinity.

If after these considerations we return to the claim that to live poetically is the same as to enjoy (and this opposition between poetic actuality and the given actuality, precisely because our age is so deeply penetrated by reflection, must exhibit itself in a much deeper form than it has ever before appeared in the world; for previously the poetic development went hand in hand with the given actuality, but now it is in truth a matter of to be or not to be, now one is not satisfied to live poetically once in a while, but demands that the whole of life should be poetic), then it readily appears that this utterly fails to secure the highest enjoyment, the true happiness wherein the subject no longer dreams but possesses himself in infinite clarity, is absolutely transparent to himself. This is only possible for the religious individual who does not have his infinity outside himself but within himself. To revenge oneself is accordingly a poetic enjoyment, and the pagans believed that the gods had reserved all vengeance into themselves because it was sweet. But though I were to have my revenge absolutely sated, though I were a god in the pagan sense before whom all things trembled and whose fiery anger were able to consume everything, still, I would in revenge merely be enjoying myself egotistically, my enjoyment would be merely an external infinity. To this extent the simplest human being who did not permit his vengeance to rage but mastered his anger was much nearer to having overcome the world, and only he enjoyed himself in truth, only he possessed inward infinity, only he lived poetically. If from this standpoint we would consider the life set forth in *Lucinde* as a poetic life, then we might allow it every possible enjoyment —but the right to use one predicate in describing it will surely not be denied us: it is an infinitely cowardly life. And provided one will not claim that to be cowardly is to live poetically, it might well be possible for this poetic life to exhibit itself rather unpoetically, that is to say, wholly unpoetically. For to live poetically cannot mean to remain obscure to oneself, to work oneself up into a disgusting suggestiveness, but to become clear and transparent to oneself, not in finite and egotistical satisfaction, but in one's absolute and eternal validity. And if this be not possible for every human being then life is madness, in which case it is a matchless foolhardiness for the individual—though he be the most gifted who has ever lived in the world—to delude himself in thinking that what was denied all others was reserved for him alone. Either to be a human being is absolute, or the whole of life is nonsense—despair the only thing awaiting everyone not so demented, not so uncharitable and haughty, not so desperate as to believe himself the chosen one. Hence one should not restrict himself to reciting certain moralisms against the whole tendency after *Lucinde,* which, often with much talent and often enchantingly enough, has taken it upon itself not to lead but to lead astray. One must not allow it to deceive itself and others that it is poetic, or that it is through this way that one attains what every human being has an imperative demand for—to live poetically.

But let us return to Julian and Lisette. Lisette ends her life as she began it, fulfilling what Julian never had enough time to resolve, and through the act of suicide seeks to attain the goal of all her aspirations— to be rid of her self. However, she preserves her æsthetic tact to the very end, and the last words which, according to her servant, she pronounced in a shrill voice: "Lisette must die, must die now! An inexorable fate requires it!" must be regarded as a kind of dramatic silliness quite natural for one who had formerly been an actress on the stage and who subsequently became one in life as well.—Now the death of Lisette must naturally have made an impression on Julian. I shall let Schlegel speak for himself, however, lest anyone think I distort. "The first effect of the death of Lisette was that Julian idolized her memory with fanatical veneration" (p. 77). Yet not even this event was sufficient to develop Julian: "This exception to what Julian regarded as ordinary among the female sex (the average woman, according to Julian, did not possess the same "high energy" as Lisette) was too unique, and the circumstances in which he found her too sordid for him to acquire true perspective through this" (p. 78).

Julian, after withdrawing in loneliness for a time, is again allowed by Schlegel to come into contact with society, and in a more intellectual relation to certain of this life's feminine members once more runs through several love affairs, until he finally discovers in Lucinde the unity of all these discrete moments, discovers as much sensuousness as cleverness [*Aandrighed*]. But as this love affair has no deeper foundation than intellectual sensuousness, as it embraces no moment of resignation, in other words, since it is no marriage, and as it asserts the view that passivity and vegetating constitute perfection; so here again the ethical integrity is negated. Accordingly, this love affair can acquire no content, can achieve no history in a deeper sense; and so their amusements can only be the same *en deux* as those with which Julian had formerly occupied his loneliness, namely, in considering what some clever lady would say or reply on some piquant occasion. It is a love without real content, and the eternity so often mentioned is none other than what might be called the eternal pleasure instant, an infinity without infinity and as such unpoetic. One can hardly refrain from smiling, therefore, when such a frail and fragile love fancies itself able to withstand the storms of life, fancies itself in possession of a strength sufficient to look upon "the harshest whim of chance as an excellent jest and a frolicsome caprice" (p. 9). For this love is not a home in the actual world, but belongs to an imaginary world where the lovers are themselves lords over storms and hurricanes. Moreover, as everything in this alliance is calculated in terms of enjoyment, so naturally it conceives its relation to the generation deriving its existence [*Tilværelse*] from it equally egotistically (p. 11): "Thus the religion of love weaves our love ever more closely and firmly together, for the child doubles the happiness of its gentle parents like an echo." Occasionally, one comes across parents who with foolish seriousness wish to see their children well settled as soon as possible, perhaps even to see them well settled in the grave. Julian and Lucinde, on the other hand, seem to want to keep their offspring always at the same age as the little Wilhelmine so as to derive amusement from them.

Now what is problematic about *Lucinde* and the whole tendency connected with it is that although beginning with the freedom and constitutive authority of the ego, it does not go on to arrive at a still higher aspect of mind but instead at sensuality, and consequently at its opposite. Ethics imply a relation of mind to mind, but as the ego seeks a higher freedom, seeks to negate ethical mind, it thereby succumbs to the law of the flesh and the appetites. But as this sensuality is not naïve, it follows that the same arbitrariness that established sensuality in its supposed privileges may at the next moment pass over to assert an abstract and eccentric aspect of mind. These vibrations may be conceived partly as the play of the irony of the world with the individual, partly as an attempt by the individual to mimic the irony of the world.

Stephen Crites
from "Pseudonymous Authorship as Art and as Act"

4. KIERKEGAARD'S CONCEPTION OF A WORK OF ART

An aesthetic work, as Kierkegaard understood it,[1] is the embodiment of an ideal form, its presentation to consciousness in an appropriate sensu-

Source: "Pseudonymous Authorship as Art and as Act" by Stephen Crites from the book *Kierkegaard: A Collection of Critical Essays.* Copyright © 1972 by Josiah Thompson, editor. Reprinted by permission of Doubleday & Co., Inc.
1. For a more detailed treatment of Kierkegaard's aesthetics, I again refer the reader to my introduction to *Crisis in the Life of an Actress,* particularly pp. 28–36. An important critical work on the subject is that of Theodor Wiesengrund-Adorno, *Kierkegaard: Konstruktion des Ästhetischen* (Tübingen: Verlag von J. C. B. Mohr [Paul Siebeck], 1933).

ous medium. The appropriate medium is the one in which that particular ideal form can be brought to full manifestation.

An ideal form or an idea is a pure possibility, but it is not necessarily an intellectual object, i.e., it is not necessarily an object of pure thought. For example, in his celebrated essay on Don Juan, Kierkegaard argues that the Don Juan idea, the "sensuous-erotic," cannot be brought to expression in the more reflective media of literature and drama, and analyzes the alleged limitations of the versions by Byron and Molière to support his point.[2] However successful such works may have been in other respects, not even such masters of language could render the essential Don Juan idea, because language is too discursive a medium to embody the sensuous immediacy of this particular idea. Here, Kierkegaard argues, music is the appropriate medium. That does not mean merely that the Don Juan idea has been fully understood all the while, while artists tried it out in different media to see which might fit it best. Kierkegaard means that the Don Juan idea had never been fully grasped until it was rendered by Mozart. Until then people had only groped for it. Even after it has been rendered musically we cannot understand it reflectively, in thought or word. The idea and its medium remain inseparable. Kierkegaard can write about Don Juan, but he does not confuse this assignment with the actual rendering of Don Juan. In Mozart's opera we apprehend it in the only way we can, musically. That is why this opera is a classic: an idea comes fully to expression in its own medium, and music finds in this idea its own essential subject.

But there are of course other ideal forms that could only be rendered clumsily if at all in music or graphic art, because they require the reflective medium of language for their presentation to consciousness. Here Kierkegaard is in his own element. In conscious contrast to Don Juan, whom he could only talk about, is Johannes the Seducer, Kierkegaard's own poetic creation whom he could actually *present* within the pages of the same volume of *Either/Or.* For unlike the sensuous immediacy of the Don Juan idea, an eroticism that is a sheer force of nature, Johannes is a reflective seducer who strives with a certain fastidious craftiness to manipulate his Cordelia into a state of pure poetic lyricism. "Light have I made her, light as a thought, and now should this, my thought, not belong to me!" he exclaims as his project nears its consummation, worrying that some acci-

---

2. *Either/Or,* I, tr. by David F. Swenson and Lillian M. Swenson with revisions by Howard A. Johnson (Garden City, N.Y.: Anchor Books, 1959), pp. 102–14 (*SV,* II, pp. 98–109). [*SV* refers to *Samlede Vaerker* (Collected Works), 14 vols., ed. by A. B. Drochmann, J. L. Heiberg, and H. O. Lange (Copenhagen: Gyldendal, 1901–1906).] The long article on Don Juan from which this section is cited was Kierkegaard's most ambitious work on aesthetics proper. He later returned to the subject in a little essay entitled "A Passing Comment on a Detail in *Don Juan,*" one of the "other essays on drama" translated with *Crisis* etc.

dent may yet spoil the poem he has made of their love affair.[3] The idea of this sort of seducer can only be rendered in language, since a bizarre sort of poetic reflection is its essential meaning. Kierkegaard's "Diary of the Seducer" is its adequate presentation to consciousness, since it enables us to follow every turn in the mad dialectic of the seducer's devices, and that dialectic is his idea.

It is a matter of great importance to Kierkegaard's aesthetics that neither Don Juan nor Johannes is or can be a living personality. Each is a pure idea that has found its proper aesthetic medium, and its role reality is in that medium. That is not to say that aesthetic ideas have no relation to real life. The sensuous-erotic does, after all, inhere in everyday life and loin, but always compounded with complicated personal and social factors. What we do not experience every day or any day is pure sensuous eroticism with all extraneous factors pared away—except in Mozart's *Don Juan!* And there we experience it as listeners caught up in it musically, at a great distance from its twitches in our own lives. Similarly with Johannes' idea, which we can experience in its purity only through the words of his diary.

In a successful work of art the idea is presented to consciousness in its timeless ideality, its luminous clarity, and its completeness. That, on Kierkegaard's terms, is why it is so satisfying. For if the human condition is real life is anything like Kierkegaard conceived it, it is the opposite of art. In its normal experience consciousness finds everything to be fleeting, unclear, and incomplete. Nagged by gritty realities, baffled by the heady play of confused and contradictory possibilities, consciousness finds a profound rest in a work of art. Here possibilities achieve luminosity and closure. Here at last is a project brought to satisfying conclusion. One can repose in it, enjoy it, turn it round and round, for it is solid and whole.

This view of art is not as soporific as it may appear. There certainly is on Kierkegaard's terms a proper excitement to be found in art, and also a purified reflection of the reality we inhabit. Art is a source of insight in an otherwise confusing life. It may even horrify us, but there is satisfaction in the lucidity with which it enables us to confront even the tragic or the grotesque. Kierkegaard insists, in fact, that we can be excited or illuminated by a work of art only because we are first able to find repose in it. If an artist is not able to become so thoroughly the servant of his idea that we catch no glimpse of his private human frailty in his presentation, if we are allowed to sense that his achievement depends on a series of accidents that another accident may spoil, then according to Kierkegaard the aes-

3. *Either/Or,* I, p. 433 (*SV,* II, p. 404).

thetic experience is itself made too insecure for us to be either stirred or enlightened by it. He insists for instance that an actress who renders the idea of youthful exuberance on the stage must induce in her audience a sense of absolute trust that her vitality is boundless. That is of course an illusion, the illusion of the stage, that has nothing to do with the private feelings of the actress, who may be quite old and tired. To body forth her idea within the frame of that illusion she must project an exuberance that can never flag.

> Let us take an example from immediate comedy, from whimsey. On a night when you see Rosenkilde come on the stage, as if straight from the infinite and with its swiftness, possessed by all the whimsical muses, when at the first sight of him you find yourself saying, "Well, this evening he's blowing up a regular storm": then you feel *eo ipso* indescribably soothed. You heave a sigh and settle down to relax; you assume a comfortable posture, as if you intended to remain sitting for a long time in the same position; you almost regret not having brought some food along, because the situation induces such trust and assurance, and therefore such tranquility, that you forget that it is only a matter of an hour in the theater. . . . It is usually said that a comedian must be able to make the audience laugh, but it might be better to say that he must first and foremost be able absolutely to soothe, for then the laughter will follow of itself.[4]

The trust and repose induced by a work of art are necessary if it is to communicate any sort of ideal content, because without this tranquility the consciousness of the spectator cannot suspend its own fundamental restlessness. The ideal possibilities manifested in art are illuminating just because they contrast so sharply with our own fragmentary and entangled possibilities.

5. AESTHETIC REST VS. EXISTENTIAL MOVEMENT

The ideality bodied forth in a work of art is always an abstraction from experience. It arises out of the temporality of experience, but it achieves a purified form as a self-contained possibility, free of temporality. That is why both the artist and his audience are able to come to rest in it. At least for this ideal moment of experience a man achieves integration, his consciousness drawn together by its concentration on a single purified possi-

4. *Crisis in the Life of an Actress,* pp. 75–76; cf. pp. 89–91 (*SV,* XIV, pp. 112–13, 122–24). Cf. *Repetition,* pp. 54–55, 61–66 (*SV,* V, pp. 141, 145–47).

bility. Kierkegaard speaks of this moment of repose in ideal possibility as a recollection, in a sense of the term derived from Plato: here temporal reality is recollected, assimilated to atemporal forms that are logically prior to it. The recollected possibilities, are logically prior in the sense that they give intelligible meaning to the reality of experience.

This important function of art is also performed by other operations of the mind and the imagination. Therefore Kierkegaard sometimes employs the term "aesthetic" in an extended sense that includes science and philosophy as well as art. For the cognitive grasp of an object, whether a purified object of experience or an ideal, logico-mathematical object, also enables consciousness to suspend its bewildering temporal peregrinations and to come to a satisfying moment of clarity. All knowledge is recollection.

Now when Kierkegaard says that his pseudonymous writings are all aesthetic works, he means that they are all works of art and reflection. They are generally aesthetic in both the primary and the extended sense. Both his poetic gifts and his dialectical powers are exercised in each of these works, though one or the other usually predominates. In any case, consciousness is engaged recollectively by the work, is brought to rest in it, and only if it is engaged in this way can anything else follow.

But then Kierkegaard also uses the term "aesthetic" in another extended sense, to signify a particular way of life or a general outlook that may be realized in a number of specific life-styles. An artist or thinker is not necessarily an "aesthetic man" in this sense; the aesthetic repose afforded by knowledge and art is fortunately available to anyone able to master its disciplines and summon the concentration it requires, whatever his way of life. And on the other hand the aesthetic man is not necessarily an artist or thinker by profession. The aesthetic way of life is a strategy for giving life coherence of a sort. It is a strategy modeled on the work of art, extending that model so far as possible to one's experience as a whole. Here Kierkegaard has in mind the romantic ideal of making life into a work of art. One becomes a collector of interesting experiences, or a contriver of them, actively seeking them out, and one seeks to give them satisfying form in the way they are grasped by consciousness. Since recollection is the aesthetic category, one lives recollectively. Like a novelist who looks for adventures to provide him with material for his novels, the aesthete attempts to get the better of life's turmoils and traumas by transmuting his whole experience into the ideality of recollection. As we are told in one of the diapsalmata:

To live in recollection is the most complete life conceivable, recollection satisfies more richly than all reality, and has a security that no reality possesses. A recollected life-relation has already passed into eternity and has no more temporal interest.[5]

The aesthetic way of life is in fact a self-negating project, a project to end all projects: its aim is to overcome within consciousness the temporality of consciousness itself. For temporality is chaotic or boring or both. The aesthete pursues the "interesting," and to be interesting an experience or a reflection must be lifted out of the relentless movement of lived time. For the interesting attracts the aesthete's attention, allows his consciousness to come to rest in it in a way that integrates consciousness itself. Consciousness so concentrates its otherwise dispersed powers on the interesting object that its own temporality is suspended.

Two kinds of objects are interesting, the momentary and the timeless. What is momentary engages our interest because it affords an intensity of experience that blots the future and the past out of consciousness in the total demand of the moment. The self is momentarily integrated with maximum intensity, concentrated in its experience. One of the most lyrical of the diapsalmata evokes such a moment. Walking down the street on a winter's day we are suddenly brought up short by a strain from Mozart. It turns out that it is being played by a couple of blind street musicians, who are minutely observed in a single glance, raggedly bundled up against the cold.

A few of us who admired these strains gradually gathered, a postman with his mailbag, a little boy, a servant girl, a couple of roustabouts. Elegant carriages rolled noisily by, workingmen's wagons drowned out these strains, but they still glittered forth in snatches. Unlucky pair of artists, do you know that these tones have all the world's glories hidden away in them?—Was it not like a lovers' meeting![6]

But it is not only in such little momentary ecstasies that time is suspended for consciousness. At the other pole of the aesthetic is reflection, the contemplation of abstract possibility or logical necessity, or the contemplation of reality under the aspect of eternity. "It is not only in isolated

5. *Either/Or*, I, pp. 31–32 (*SV*, II, p. 35). This theme is developed poetically in *Repetition*, where its darker side is revealed: a young poet in love already "recollects" his whole future life with his sweetheart, imagining himself as an old man looking back and recalling these first days of his love. His "confidant," Constantine Constantius, remarks that "He was basically finished with the whole relationship. Just as he is beginning he has made such a tremendous stride that he has leaped over his whole life. Though the girl should die tomorrow it will produce no essential difference. . . . Recollection has the great advantage that it begins with the loss, and so it is secure, for it has nothing to lose." *Repetition*, p. 12; cf. pp. 90–93 (*SV*, V, pp. 119–20, 160–61). Recollection is developed as a philosophical theme in the *Fragments* and *Postscript*, where it is treated as the Socratic mode to which the Christian "leap" is counterposed.
6. *Either/Or*, I, pp. 29–30 (*SV*, II, pp. 32–33).

moments that I contemplate everything *aeterno modo,* as Spinoza says, but I am constantly *aeterno modo.*"[7] Again, "Tautology is and remains the highest principle, the highest axiom of thought. . . . It is not so poor but that it can fill out a whole lifetime."[8] Again, the point is to suspend the temporality of experience, and so the temporality of the conscious subject of experience. Immediacy and reflection, the momentary and the timeless, are at opposite poles, but both have the effect of lifting consciousness out of time. They are the aesthetic polarities, in which everyone can find occasional repose; but they are also the two modes of the aesthetic way of life, which pursues the interesting. Only what is atemporal is interesting. Love's momentary consummation is interesting, and the idea of the eternal feminine is interesting; but marriage, a constancy in time, is boring. A mystical ecstasy is interesting, and philosophical contemplation is interesting, but a vocation is another of those boring constancies in time that are to be avoided.

Kierkegaard's existential categories, however, the variously projected ethical and religious modes, deal in precisely those temporal constancies that are dismissed by the aesthete as boring. Furthermore, in the pseudonymous works the aesthetic functions primarily as the backdrop against which to manifest the existential categories. It is easy enough to define the resulting tension in general terms: *Like* the aesthetic repose, the existential movement aims at an integration of conscious life, deliverance from the "drunken" confusion of consciousness. But *unlike* the aesthetic, the existential integration occurs through a projection into temporality through action. That is, both the aesthetic strategy and the existential movement proceed from the impasse created by our peculiarly human temporality. The aesthetic strategy, however, proceeds by negating that temporality, the existential movement by intensifying it and through passion giving it a form that is itself temporalized. Hence the distinctions within the existential itself: the diverse existential movements are the different temporal forms into which the self's becoming can be projected. These forms of temporality therefore imply diverse kinds of individuality. The aesthete achieves a kind of integration of experience, but not an individuality, because he refuses to commit himself to a career in time. In the terms in which Judge William belabors the young aesthete, he does not choose to choose. He comes to *rest* in apprehending the immediate or the timeless, but he refuses to make the *movement* of self-formative act. Aesthetic apprehension wrests ideal possibility out of the actual through recollection. Existential movement projects a chosen possibility into the real world through action.

7. Ibid., pp. 37–38 (*SV,* II, p. 40).
8. Ibid., p. 37 (*SV,* II. p. 39).

It should now be clear why the pseudonymous authorship was such a paradoxical undertaking: in these aesthetic works Kierkegaard had to find a way of pointing to the existential movements. That would not have been so difficult if he had been content simply to offer a schematic account of the existential categories and to differentiate them from the aesthetic, as we have just done at a very general level. But his plan was much more ambitious. He wanted to reflect the existential character of those movements in the very form of presentation. Indirectly, telegraphically, he would communicate the existential movement itself to his reader by means of a medium alien to it, would communicate it not so much *in* as *through* the aesthetic work. By way of a timeless medium of art and reflection he would evoke the sense of living time. That creates the basic dialectical tension in each of these writings.

6. THE PSEUDONYMOUS THEATER

Kierkegaard steadily insists that his pseudonymous works teach no doctrines, impart no objective knowledge. It does not follow that they have no content. One finds philosophical arguments, the posing of dialectical puzzles, stories, lyrical flights, psychological investigations, spiritual inquisitions, and a constant counterpoint of wit. There seem to be a good many assertions and exhortations besides.

But each of these works is deliberately ambiguous, ironical. What it says is never simply what it means. In fact, what it says is above all negated by the fact that nobody says it.

For each work is a quasi-theatrical production. It takes place on a stage, an old-fashioned proscenium, as it were, a self-enclosed frame of aesthetic illusion from which no actor comes skipping out in the modern manner to nuzzle and harangue the audience or to assure it that there is after all a man under the greasepaint. The frame is the device of pseudonymity. Each writing is attributed to a Johannes de Silentio, a Constantine Constantius, a Vigilius Haufniensis. In some cases there is a pseudonymous editor as well, a Victor Eremita, a Hilarius Bookbinder, assembling the works of other pseudonyms. Each of them is a fantastic creature, a creature of fantasy, an evident fiction. This is not a "realistic" theater; its pseudonymous authors and actors are not copies of real men. To be sure, an illusion of individuality is to some extent sustained by the fact that each speaks with a distinctive voice. He not only represents a definite point of view but reflects his point of view in the style and tone of his language. That is the supreme achievement of Kierkegaard's poetic gift. Constantine Constantius chooses his words between thoughtful sips of good wine, his young poet declaims in fits of lyric desperation; Judge

William's tone is earnest, firm, good-natured but humorless, yet beneath the prosaic surface one senses a quiet and constant ardor; Vigilius Haufniensis writes the sort of prose one would expect to meet in an academic journal; Johannes de Silentio intones as if from the bottom of a deep well. Anyone who has lived with these authors for a while would recognize the voice of any of them after three sentences, in exactly the way that he would recognize Falstaff or Goethe's Mephistopheles. But he would not mistake them for the voices of real human beings. They are altogether theatrical creations. They are sheer personae, masks without actors underneath, voices. William Afham, who has recollected for us the symposium on love in Part I of the *Stages,* speaks for himself only at the end and only to request that nobody make any inquiries about him. But just in case anyone should ask, he explains in a little spoof of Hegel that

> I am pure being, and therefore almost less than nothing. I am the pure being that is along everywhere but am still not noticeable because I am constantly *aufgehoben.* I am like the line that has the mathematical problem above it and the answer below; who bothers about the line? Of myself I am not capable of anything at all. . . .[9]

That is essentially true of all the pseudonyms, though most of them are not so self-effacing about it.

For unlike William Afham, most of the pseudonyms are situated in definite points of view. They represent animated life-possibilities. But in every case the point of view from which the work is written is itself transcended within the work, *"aufgehoben"* or at least rendered problematical, its limitations revealed. And yet that *aufgehoben* point of view, the possibility represented by the pseudonymous author, is the standpoint from which the whole problem of the work is treated. Every pseudonym occupies a specific position which like a mirror reflects its problem according to its angle of vision. Hence the quite different ways of conceiving the stages themselves, as we have observed. Every scheme or problem treated earlier is transformed when Kierkegaard projects his imagination into the frame of another pseudonym. And any existential movement treated in a particular work is presented as it is viewed from the pseudonymous author's angle of vision, generally glimpsed as it moves out of his field of vision altogether.

Repetition is a clear example. The book is written from the point of view of the aesthete and "psychologist" Constantine Constantius. After recounting his own humorously futile efforts to achieve repetition, how-

9. *Stages on Life's Way,* p. 93 (*SV,* VII, pp. 79–80).

ever, he concludes that it is "too transcendent for me." Repetition "is and remains a transcendence," and "A religious movement I cannot make, it is against my nature."[10] But Constantine's young friend, the poet, does in some sense make this movement, so Constantine thinks at any rate, though it is always given an essentially poetic expression in the book. There are occasional hints about the meaning of repetition, but we are never permitted to see the movement itself except in the distorting mirror of the aesthetic. Constantine speaks of the affair as a "wrestling match" or a "breaking" (*brydning*): "the universal breaks with the exception, breaks with it in strife, and strengthens it by this breaking."[11] This break is what we are permitted to see in the book, but as it occurs the young man breaks out of the aesthetic frame of the book as well, and is lost from view. Constantine, who has supplied that frame, has functioned in a "purely aesthetic and psychological" way; and yet he has been a "serving spirit" in the enterprise.

> Every move I have made is purely to shed light on him; I have constantly had him *in mente*, every word of mine is either ventriloquism or is said in relation to him. Even where joking and playfulness seem to tumble heedlessly, they take heed of him; even where everything ends in melancholy, it is a signal concerning him. . . . So I have done for him what I could, just as I now strive to serve you, dear reader, by again being something else.[12]

The pseudonym and his book constitute a mirror reflecting from its angle and within its frame the existential movement as it breaks away. This mirror is also held up to the reader, who through the aesthetic medium is essentially left alone with the existential movement itself and whatever claim it may make on him. The aesthetic medium is purely dialectical: it is simultaneously presented and obliterated. Like William Afham's line between the problem and its sum, the pseudonymous work is nothing at all in itself, yet it serves to put the reader into touch with a possibility that cannot be directly presented because it can only come forth in its truth in an actual lifetime.

A similar self-negation occurs in all the pseudonymous works, pointing to the existential movement but letting it break out of its aesthetic frame. In *Fear and Trembling*, subtitled "A Dialectical Lyric," the dialectical and the poetic are indeed fused to the highest degree Kierkegaard ever achieved; in that respect it is the work that most perfectly expresses

---

10. *Repetition*, pp. 95–105 (*SV*, V, pp. 161–62). Cf. *In the Twilight of Christendom*, Chapter 3, where I have attempted to interpret the category of repetition in its contrast to recollection.
11. Ibid., p. 152 (*SV*, V, pp. 190–91).
12. Ibid., pp. 154–55 (*SV*, V, p. 192).

his special genius. Yet, as in *Repetition* and most of the other pseudony-mous works, his name does not even appear on the title page. It is another purely aesthetic work, but again the possibility it holds out is never di-rectly manifest in the way Kierkegaard thought an ideal possibility is normally manifest in a work of art. For again it is a possibility that can only be realized in a human lifetime, and not in a work of art. The possibility is faith. But while Abraham is the father of faith, he cannot be presented as an archetype or a paradigm of faith, one cannot become a knight of faith by doing what Abraham did. For faith is again a singularity that breaks with the universal. Johannes de Silentio, on the other hand, does represent a prototypical religiosity. He represents resignation as a universal or para-digmatic possibility. The book is written from his point of view, and within that point of view he celebrates Abraham, marvels at Abraham, whom he repeatedly confesses he cannot understand at all.

In the more strictly philosophical or psychological works this dialectic is still operative, except that a paradoxical category rather than a poeti-cally projected character is made to break away from the standpoint of the work. In *The Concept of Dread* the dogmatic category of sin is obliquely disclosed by dread, a psychological category, but it is disclosed only as it breaks out of dread. In *Philosophical Fragments* the terms signifying the Socratic mode continue to be employed in the paradoxical "thought ex-periment" until they turn into their opposites. For example, the idea of the Socratic teacher is straightforward, but in the experiment we project a teacher who himself is the teaching; error becomes a willful error; knowledge becomes, not the recollection of truth immanent in the learner, but a leap tantamount to being born a second time; eternal divinity becomes the God in time; and so on. The Socratic meaning of every term is strained until it breaks. Though the pseudonym, Johannes Climacus, conducts the whole experiment from a Socratic point of view, un-Socratic expressions keep breaking out of the Socratic terms he em-ploys: the savior, sin, faith, etc. The same is true in the *Postscript*, but in this case Johannes goes much further into the dialectics of the break and into the explication of the Christian categories, though still from a Socratic angle of vision. As for what Johannes himself may think of the results of his experiment, he has told us plainly in the preface to the *Fragments* that it is none of our business and makes no difference in our consideration of the problems raised. Certainly he has presented no defense of Chris-tianity, and Kierkegaard like to point out that the view of the Christian possibility presented in the *Fragments* and *Postscript* would provide at least as serviceable a basis for attacking it as defending it—an option that his modern readers have been quick to exercise. In any case, this Socratic analysis cannot be confused with an act of faith, as Johannes is at pains to point out: and nothing but the act of faith would be a Christian expression of Christianity. The *Fragments* and *Postscript* are simply the performances of Johannes Climacus in our little theater. When the curtain rings down Johannes disappears with his heavy philosophical books into the aesthetic aether, just as Constantine Constantius did with his slender bit of poetry. In an appendix to the *Postscript,* Johannes even declares that everything in the book "is to be understood in such a way that it is revoked; that the book has not only a conclusion but a revocation."[13] Of this revocation we shall have more to say presently. It is already extraordinary enough that Kierkegaard should have carried his ironical devices so far as to revoke his chief philosophical work. He could regard even this book as a veil of illusion through which something was being communicated that the book had to leave unsaid.

If we continued calling the role of the pseudonyms we would discover that the dialectic of revocation and breaking away takes diverse forms. But always the work is suffused with double meaning. Sometimes this double meaning is achieved by presenting two or more pseudonyms (*Either/Or, Stages*), each sustaining a point of view that is consistent and complete in itself, but letting them collide in irreconcilable conflict. Each can resolve the issue, but purely on his own terms, which are cast in doubt from the point of view of the other pseudonyms.[14] For with respect to existential conflicts Kierkegaard denies that there is a general, unsituated, "objective" standpoint from which the issue could be resolved. That is the point of his attack on Hegelian "mediation" as he understood it. So there are no really coercive conclusions in any of the pseudonymous works. Every apparent conclusion is merely that implied by the standpoint of the pseudonym, and even it is called into question within the work as a whole. Kierkegaard does not deny that reasonably secure conclusions can be reached regarding matters of fact, or regarding abstract logical or mathematical possibilities. But here the question concerns possible ways of life, the way a man should project his own future, and that is not an issue that can be settled within an aesthetic frame. Like a literary treatment of a musical idea, the medium would break down in the attempt. What takes place on the stage of our little theater is always "interesting," but to the extent that we do in fact become interested in it we discover that the essential action is being conducted offstage.

13. *Concluding Unscientific Postscript,* p. 547 (*SV,* X, p. 280).
14. If one supposes that Judge William necessarily wins the palm in *Either/Or,* it should be noted how often the Judge expresses his exasperation at the ability of the quick-witted young aesthete to turn every question around. Also perhaps relevant to the Judge's efforts is a little passage in "The Rotation Method," where the aesthete describes his strategy for enduring the tiresome philosophical lectures of a certain gentleman: since in the heat of these earnest lectures the gentleman always perspired copiously, the aesthete learned to divert himself by observing the beads of sweat coursing from the gentleman's brow to the tip of his nose. *Either/Or,* I, p. 295 (*SV,* II, p. 276). If the aesthetic and the ethical did not reach a standoff in the book, the reader would not be confronted with a genuine either/or, and that is the whole point!

7. THE AUTHOR'S ACT AND THE READER'S BURDEN

There is one document in which a pseudonym who may be presumed to represent a religious movement is allowed to speak entirely for himself. That is the long diary entitled " 'Guilty?/Not Guilty?' " that appears in the third part of *Stages on Life's Way*. As in other cases, the existential movement represented in the diary is also reflected off the points of view of other pseudonyms, including that of the "psychologist," Frater Taciturnus, whose commentary on the diary concludes the book. It is Frater T., in fact, who interprets the diary as clearly representing some sort of inchoate religious movement. But in this case the subject of the movement is not merely glimpsed as he disappears beyond the horizon of his commentator, as in *Repetition* and *Fear and Trembling*. He also speaks for himself, indeed speaks at length and in the sort of total intimacy that the diary format allows. In this one case we seem to be permitted an interior view of an existential movement, and from this vantage point the meaning of the movement is by no means as clear as the commentary makes it seem. As the title suggests, the young diarist is in a state of fundamental conflict about the meaning of what he has done, which his many anguished pages of reflection serve to clarify but which no amount of reflection can seem to resolve. Outwardly, his abandonment of his lady love would in many respect have resembled the conduct of that other diarist, Johannes the Seducer, whose diary this one is clearly intended to parallel. Inwardly the situation is totally different. The diarist behaved as he did out of an obscure sense of a kind of religious vocation that seemed to preclude marriage. But we leave him in a state of total uncertainty whether he has indeed received such a calling or whether he has been undone by some dark morbidity. He even keeps alive a strange hope that he may yet in some unimagined manner receive his beloved back again. It is possible that he is indeed embarked on a religious movement, as Frater T. insists, but if so it is clear that he offers the reader no simple paradigm of such a movement. Again, though in a new way, Kierkegaard has invested the existential movement with double meaning.

The closest the young diarist comes to a conclusion is expressed in this comment:

> I have never been able to understand it in any other way than this, that every man is essentially assigned to himself, and that apart from this there is either an authority such as that of an apostle—the dialectical determination of which I cannot comprehend, and meanwhile out of respect for what has been handed down to me as holy I refrain from concluding anything from my non-understanding—or there is chatter.[15]

15. *Stages on Life's Way*, p. 314 (*SV*, VIII, p. 148).

That, in the end, represents the standpoint of Kierkegaard's authorship as a whole. Some of the later works, written in his own name, do attempt to bring out what it would mean for an individual to live under apostolic authority. But the pseudonymous writings are designed to throw every reader back on his own resources. There is not even an actual author to lay any claim on him. They assign him to himself.

The pseudonymous works present their life-possibilities in this elusive form in order to evoke in the reader a movement that is entirely his own. They are not cookbooks that he could follow in concocting a novel but pretested pattern for his life, like an exotic soufflé. But each work is in its own way designed to create a quiet crisis in the life of a reader that can be resolved only by his own decision. To a reader bewildered by the riot of possibility they also offer an oblique aid in recognizing and nurturing a possibility that he might be able to make his own.

While these works may encourage a man in whom a decision may be stirring, it is obvious that no book can force a man to decide. Kierkegaard was not one to underestimate the potential complacency of a reader. The resources of human torpor seemed to him to be perfectly awesome. That is why he regularly distinguished between the "real reader" of his books and others who might chance to turn their pages. The page turners might scrutinize them either superficially or carefully. That was not the point of the distinction. The reason he regarded the professors as his particular nemesis was that they would perhaps be careful page turners, looking for ideas to merchandise in their own books and lectures, without ever being "real readers" at all. Kierkegaard found artful ways of distinguishing between the readers and the page turners. He quotes a motto from Lichtenberg as the superscription to the first part of *Stages on Life's Way:* "Such works are mirrors: when an ape peers in no apostle can look out." He frequently appends little letters to his "reader," as in *Repetition* where his pseudonym tells this reader that the book has been written after the manner of Clemens Alexandrinus, who wrote "in such a way that the heretics could not understand it."[16] That particular letter is preceded by a kind of envelope, taking up a whole page, addressed "To the Honorable Mr. N. N., this book's real reader."[17] When other works were addressed to "that individual" the intent was the same, for only the reader who permitted himself to be singled out by the book for a movement into individuality was its "real reader." For the books are so designed that their real resolution can only be carried out by the reader.

This way of presenting the existential categories, essentially shifting the burden of each book onto the reader, was not a mere literary conceit

16. *Repetition*, p. 149 (*SV,* V, p. 189).
17. Ibid., p. 147 (*SV,* V, p. 187).

on Kierkegaard's part. That was the way it had to be done, given his view of the existential categories. They refer to movements in existence. The attempt to describe them directly would falsify what is essential. For again, as in Kierkegaard's view of art, an idea can be brought forth only in its own medium. Only in this case the medium is the temporality of human existence itself: a lifetime. As the Don Juan idea can only be rendered in music, and not in poetry, an existential movement can only be realized in the life of an individual. One can talk *about* it, of course, and Kierkegaard devoted great ingenuity to finding ways to do so. But what is talked *about* never comes forth in its truth in the literary treatment. "Truth is subjectivity": the point of that much-misunderstood slogan is simply that an existential truth has a conscious human temporality for its medium, and not propositions, images, or any other aesthetic form. It is not an object of reflection, in which consciousness comes to rest, but the movement of a conscious life projected toward the future. Only in that medium can it come to clarity. To use one of Kierkegaard's favorite expressions, the idea becomes clear only when the individual becomes "transparent" to it.

We recall that Johannes Climacus concluded his big philosophical work, the very one in which he had enunciated the idea that "truth is subjectivity," by revoking the whole book. For to explain philosophically what was meant by this slogan was not the same as realizing a subjective truth! The revocation appears in an appendix significantly entitled "For an Understanding with the Reader." Johannes goes on to imagine the sort of reader who would fulfill his heart's desire, and even offers a eulogy for such an imaginary reader. He would read every line with care and would be able to "hold out just as long as the author." But then this reader

> can understand that understanding is revocation, understanding for him as a solitary reader is indeed precisely the book's revocation, he can understand that writing a book and revoking it is something different than not writing it at all.[18]

The reader who has absorbed the contents of the book will understand that the time has come for his move. That will be the real conclusion of the book, the only subjective truth it can have, and will be at the same time the revocation of the book as an aesthetic representation of existential movements. In other words, the contradiction between the aesthetic medium and the existential import of the book will be resolved when the reader is moved to act: then the book's idea will have found its own medium.

18. *Concluding Unscientific Postscript*, p. 548 (*SV*, X, p. 281).

The *Postscript* has another appendix, this one written in Kiekegaard's own name. He assumes legal responsibility for the whole pseudonymous authorship. But he makes it clear that he regards his position as author of these works as a kind of legal fiction, and insists that his only essential position is as one of the readers to whom they are addressed.

So in the pseudonymous books there is not a single word of my own; I have no opinion of them except as a third person, no knowledge of their meaning except as a reader, not the remotest private relation to them, since it would be impossible to have that toward a doubly-reflected communication. A single word from me personally in my own name would be a presumptuous self-forgetfulness, which by that one word would make me guilty, dialectically viewed, of essentially annihilating the pseudonyms.[19]

The detachment of these "communications" from any communicator had sometimes been reinforced within the works themselves by having a pseudonymous editor offer outlandish accounts of how he came upon these writings: he fished the box in which they were contained out of a lake, he found them accidentally in a secret drawer of an ancient desk, etc. Furthermore, Kierkegaard seems personally to have indulged in a good deal of ingenious if slightly ludicrous play acting in his public demeanor in order to disown them. For that seemed to him to be a way of supporting their essential function. He thrust the pseudonymous writings away from himself so that they could float as pure aesthetic objects, entirely at the reader's disposal.

That was what it meant for Kierkegaard to communicate "indirectly." He considered that these devices served, just by means of the great aesthetic distance they produced, to make this authorship a form of action on his part, in which his own lifetime telegraphically addressed the lifetime of the reader. The effect of this action depended entirely on the reader. But precisely by placing the burden on the reader in this way, Kierkegaard would fulfill his peculiar vocation as a writer: to communicate the sort of possibility that could only be forged out of a lifetime. Just this act of communication, however, precluded any personal connection between author and reader beyond the most polite tip of the author's tall hat by way of encouragement. The intentions of the author, and whatever use he himself might be able to make of these little theatrical productions in finding his way to some kind of individuality, were irrelevant to this act of communication.

19. "A First and Last Declaration," appended to the *Postscript*, p. 551 (*SV*, X, p. 286). The declaration as a whole is an excellent statement of Kierkegaard's design in the pseudonymous works, and has served as a guide to the interpretation offered in this essay.

What is indirect is to place dialectical contrasts together—and then not one word concerning [the author's] personal understanding.

What is more indulgent in the more direct communication is that there is in the communication a craving to be personally understood, a fear of being misunderstood. The indirect is sheer tension.[20]

The final irony of the pseudonymous writings is that Kierkegaard finally found himself unable to sustain this tension. In the end he did worry about being misunderstood, worried about it a great deal, and finally could not stand it. In his last years he kept interpreting the pseudonymous works, lest the reader miss the Christian point of the whole. *The Point of View for My Work as an Author,* subtitled "A Direct Communication" and "A Report to History," was only his most elaborate attempt to explain himself. And then he died leaving his journals and papers behind, deliberately addressed to posterity. Otherwise we surely would not understand Kierkegaard and his intentions as well as we do. But with these disclosures the whole delicate screen of indirect communication was torn aside. The author appears during each performance offered in his little theater, and his admirers hoist him on the stage to give a running explanation of the piece being performed. Despite his horror at the thought that his work would spawn a flourishing field of Kierkegaard scholarship, despite his clear sense that that would be the final misunderstanding, he brought it on himself, and made it almost impossible to read his works as he had intended.

But who knows? Perhaps when the possibilities of Kierkegaard scholarship have been exhausted, when the last detail of the affair between Søren and Regine has been ferreted out, when the Kierkegaard encyclopedias and concordances have been safely embalmed in the upper stacks and the dust has settled so thick on the multi-volume editions of the *Journals* that only archaeologists have access to them, when the American-Scandinavian Foundation is a thing of distant memory—perhaps then a young student, if there still are students, will chance to come upon *Either/Or* with his earphones off, or an older man still vigorous on early retirement and with time on his hands will chance to flip the wrong switch of his microfiche machine and find himself reading how Johannes Climacus, smoking his cigar in the Frediksberg Garden and wondering what to do with his life, decided to become an author who would make things difficult for people. And who knows? perhaps Kierkegaard will yet find his reader.

20. *Søren Kierkegaard's Journals and Papers,* Hong tr. (Bloomington and London: Indiana University Press, Vol. I, 1967), p. 318 (*Papirer,* X³ A 624).

Jean-Paul Sartre

François Mauriac and Freedom

The novel does not present things, but rather their signs.[1] How, with these mere signs, these words that are *indicaions* in a vacuum, are we to build a world that holds together? How does Stavrogin come alive? It would be an error to think that he draws his life from my imagination. When we muse over words, they beget images, but when I read, I am not musing; I am deciphering. I do not imagine Stavrogin; I wait for him; I wait expectantly for his acts, for the end of his adventure.

The thick substance I brew as I read *The Possessed* is my own expectancy, my own time. For a book is either a mere stack of dry leaves or else a great form in motion, in other words, the act of reading. The novelist takes hold of this movement, guides and inflects it, makes of it the stuff of his characters. A novel is a series of readings, of little parasitic lives, none of them longer than a dance. It swells and feeds on the reader's time. But in order for the duration of my impatience and ignorance to be caught and then moulded and finally presented to me as the flesh of these creatures of invention, the novelist must know how to draw it into the trap, how to hollow out in his book, by means of the signs at his disposal, a time resembling my own, one in which the future does not exist. If I suspect that the hero's future actions are determined in advance by heredity, social influence or some other mechanism, my own time ebbs back into me; there remains only myself, reading and persisting, confronted by a static book. Do you want your characters to live? See to it that they are free.

It is not a matter of defining passions and unpredictable acts, still less of explaining them (in novels, even the best psychological analyses have a mouldy smell), but rather of *presenting* them. Neither you nor I know what Rogogine is going to do. I know that he is going to see his guilty mistress again, but I cannot tell whether he will control himself or whether his anger will drive him to murder; he is free. I slip into his skin, and there he is, awaiting himself with my waiting. He is afraid of himself, *inside me;* he is alive.

Source: Reprinted by permission of S. G. Phillips from *Literary and Philosophical Essays* by Jean-Paul Sartre. Copyright © 1955 by S. G. Phillips, Inc.
1. The observations in the present essay might also have been based on M. Mauriac's more recent works, such as *Maimona* or *Plongées*. But his particular purpose in writing *La Fin de la Nuit* was to treat the problem of freedom. That is why I prefer to draw my examples from this book.

It occurred to me, as I was about to begin *La Fin de la Nuit*, that Christian writers, by the very nature of their belief, have the kind of mentality best suited to the writing of novels. The religious man is free. The supreme forbearance of the Catholic may irritate us, because it is an acquired thing. If he is a novelist, it is a great advantage. The fictional and the Christian man, who are both centres of indeterminacy, do have characters, but only in order to escape from them. They are free, above and beyond their natures, and if they succumb to their natures, here again, they do so freely. They may get caught up in psychological machinery, but they themselves are never mechanical.

Even the Christian conception of sin corresponds to one of the principles of the writing of fiction. The Christian sins, and the hero of the novel must err. If the existence of the error—which cannot be effaced and which must be redeemed—does not reveal to the reader the irreversibility of time, the substantial duration of the work of art lacks the urgency that gives it its necessity and cruelty. Thus, Dostoievsky was a Christian novelist. Not a novelist and a Christian, as Pasteur was a Christian *and* a scientist, but a novelist in the service of Christ.

M. Mauriac is also a Christian novelist, and his book, *La Fin de la Nuit*, tries to penetrate to the inmost depths of a woman's freedom. He tells us in his preface that he is trying to depict "the power accorded to creatures who have all the odds against them, the power to say *no* to the law that beats them down." Here we touch the heart of the art of fiction and the heart of faith. Nevertheless, I must admit that the book has disappointed me. Not for a moment was I taken in, never did I forget *my* time; I went on existing, I felt myself living. Occasionally I yawned. Now and then I said to myself, "Well done." I thought more often of M. Mauriac than of Thérèse Desqueyroux—of M. Mauriac, subtle, sensitive and narrow, with his immodest discretion, his intermittent good will, his nervous pathos, his bitter and fumbling poetry, his pinched style, his sudden vulgarity. Why was I unable to forget him or myself? And what had become of this Christian predisposition for the novel? We must go back to the question of freedom. What are the processes by which M. Mauriac reveals to us the freedom he has conferred upon his heroine?

Thérèse Desqueyroux struggles against her destiny. Well and good. There are thus two elements in her make-up. One part of her is entirely an element of Nature; we can say this of her as we would of a stone or log. But another whole side of her defies description or definition, because it is simply an absence. If freedom accepts Nature, the reign of fatality begins. If it rejects and resists it, Thérèse Desqueyroux is free, free to say no, or free, at least, not to say yes. ("All that is asked of them is that they not resign themselves to darkness.") This is Cartesian freedom, infinite, formless, nameless and without destiny, "forever starting anew," whose only power is that of sanction, but which is sovereign because it can refuse sanction. There it is—at least as we see it in the preface. Do we find it in the novel?

The first thing to be said is that this suspensive will seems more tragic than novelistic. Thérèse's oscillations between the impulses of her nature and the action of her will are reminiscent of Rotrou's stanzas. The real conflict in a novel is rather between freedom and itself. In Dostoievski, freedom is poisoned at its very source. It gets tangled up in the very time it wants to untangle. Dmitri Karamazov's pride and irascibility are as free as Aliosha's profound peace. The nature that stifles him and against which he struggles is not God-made but self-made; it is what he has sworn to be and what remains fixed because of the irreversibility of time. Alain says, in this connection, that a character is an oath. While reading M. Mauriac —and this may be to his credit—we dream of another Thérèse who might have been abler and greater. But it is the venerable antiquity and orthodoxy of this conflict between freedom and nature which finally commends it to us. It is the struggle of reason against the passions; the rebellion of the Christian soul, linked by the imagination to the body, against the body's appetites. Let us accept this theme provisionally, even though it may not seem true; it is enough that it be beautiful.

But is this "fatality" against which Thérèse must struggle merely the determinism of her inclinations? M. Mauriac calls it destiny. Let us not confuse destiny and character. Character is still ourselves; it is the combination of mild forces which insinuate themselves into our intentions and imperceptibly deflect our efforts, always in the same direction.

When Thérèse gets furious with Mondoux, who has humiliated her, M. Mauriac writes, "This time it was really she speaking, the Thérèse who was ready to tear things apart." Here it is really a question of Thérèse's character. But a little later, as she is leaving, after managing to make a wounding reply,[2] I read, "This sure-handed blow helped her to gauge her power, to become aware of her mission." What mission? Then I remember the following words from the preface: "the power given her to poison and corrupt." And there we have the destiny which envelops and prevails over the character and which represents, within Nature itself and in M. Mauriac's work, basely psychological as it sometimes is, the power of the Supernatural.

It is a fixed law, independent of Thérèse's will, that governs her acts as soon as they escape from her, and that leads them all, even the best-intentioned of them, to unhappy consequences. It reminds one of the fairy's punishment: "Every time you open your mouth, frogs will jump

---

2. I know of few scenes more vulgar than this one, and the curious thing is that this vulgarity must evidently be attributed to M. Mauriac himself.

out." If you do not believe, this spell will have no meaning for you. But the believer understands it very well. What is it, after all, but the expression of that other spell, Original Sin? I therefore grant that M. Mauriac is in earnest when he speaks of destiny as a Christian. But when he speaks as a novelist, I can no longer follow him. Thérèse Desqueyroux's destiny is composed, on the one hand, of a flaw in her character and, on the other, of a curse that hangs over her acts. But these two factors are incompatible. One of them is visible from the inside, to the heroine herself; the other would require an infinite number of observations made from the outside by an observer intent on following Thérèse's acts to their ultimate consequences.

M. Mauriac is so keenly aware of this that, when he wishes to show Thérèse as a predestined character, he resorts to an artifice; he shows her to us as she appears *to others.* "It was not surprising that people turned to look back as she passed; an evil-smelling animal betrays itself at once." Here, then, is the great hybrid presence we are made to see throughout the novel: Thérèse—though not limited to her pure freedom—Thérèse as she escapes from herself, to lose herself in a world of baleful fog. But how, then, can Thérèse know she has a destiny, if not because she already consents to it? And how does M. Mauraic know it? The idea of destiny is poetic and contemplative. But the novel is an action, and the novelist does not have the right to abandon the battlefield and settle himself comfortably on a hill as a spectator musing on The Fortunes of War.

But we must not think that M. Mauriac has accidentally surrendered for once to poetic temptation. This way of first identifying himself with his character and then abandoning her suddenly to consider her from the outside, like a judge, is characteristic of his art. He has, from the first, given us to understand that he was going to adopt Thérèse's point of view to tell the story, but, as a matter of fact, we immediately feel the translucent density of another consciousness between our eyes and Thérèse's room, her servant and the noises that rise from the street. But when, a few pages further on, we think we are still inside her, we have already left her; we are outside, with M. Mauriac, and we are looking at her.

The reason is that M. Mauriac makes use, for purposes of illusion, of the ambiguity of the "third person." In a novel, the pronoun "she" can designate *another,* that is, an opaque object, someone whose exterior is all we ever see—as when I write, for example, "I saw *that she* was trembling." But it also happens that this pronoun leads us into an intimacy which ought logically to express itself in the third person. "She was astounded to hear the echo of her own words." There is really no way of my knowing this unless I am in a position to say that I have heard the echo of my own words." In actual fact, novelists use this quite conventional mode of expression out of a kind of discretion, so as not to demand of the reader an unreserved complicity, so as to screen the dizzying intimacy of the *I*. The heroine's mind represents the opera-glass through which the reader can look into the fictional world, and the word "she" gives the illusion of the perspective of the opera-glass. It reminds us that this revealing consciousness is also a fictional creation; it represents a viewpoint on the privileged point of view and fulfills for the reader the fond desire of the lover to be both himself and someone else.

The same word has thus two opposing functions: "she-subject" and "she-object." M. Mauriac takes advantage of this indefiniteness in order to shift us imperceptibly from one aspect of Thérèse to another. "Thérèse was ashamed of her feelings." Very well. This Thérèse is a subject, that is, a *me*, kept at a certain distance from myself, and I experience this shame *inside Thérèse* because Thérèse herself knows that she feels it. But, in that case, since I read into her with her eyes, all I can ever know of her is what she knows—everything she knows, but nothing more.

In order to understand who Thérèse really *is*, I would have to break this complicity and close the book. All that would remain with me would be a memory of this consciousness, a consciousness still clear, but now hermetically closed, like all things of the past, and I would try to interpret it as though it were a fragment of my own earlier life. Now, at this point, while I am still in this absolute proximity with his characters, their dupe when they dupe themselves, their accomplice when they lie to themselves, M. Mauriac, suddenly and unbeknown to them, sends streaks of lightning through them, illuminating for me alone the essence of their beings, of which they are unaware and on which their characters have been struck as on a medal. "Never had the slightest relationship been established in Thérèse's mind between her unknown adventure and a criminal affair ... *at least, in her conscious* mind," etc. ... I find myself in a strange situation; I *am* Thérèse, and, at a certain aesthetic distance, she is myself. Her thoughts are my thoughts; as hers take shape, so do mine.

And yet I have insights into her which she does not have. Or else, seated in the centre of her consciousness, I help her lie to herself, and, at the same time, I judge and condemn her, I put myself inside her, as *another person*. "She could not help but be aware of her lie; she settled down into it, made her peace with it." This sentence gives a fair idea of the constant duplicity M. Mauriac requires of me. Thérèse lies to herself, reveals her lies and, nevertheless, tries to hide them from herself. This behaviour is something I have no way of knowing except through Thérèse herself. But the very way in which this attitude is revealed to me involves a pitiless judgment from without.

Besides, this uneasiness does not last long. Suddenly, by means of that "third person" whose ambiguity I have noted, M. Mauriac slips out, taking me along with him. " 'Make-up does wonders for you, my dear . . .' This was Thérèse's first remark, the remark of one woman to another." The flame of Thérèse's consciousness has gone out; this face, no longer lighted from within, has reassumed its compact opacity. But neither the name nor the pronoun which designates her, nor even the character of the narrative, has changed.

M. Mauriac finds this see-sawing so natural that he moves from Thérèse-subject to Thérèse-object within a single sentence. "She heard the clock strike nine. She had some time to kill, because it was still too early to take the pill which would assure her of a few hours' sleep; *not that such was the habit of this cautious and desperate woman*, but tonight she could not do without this aid." Who is judging Thérèse to be a "cautious and desperate woman"? It cannot be Thérèse herself. No, it is M. Mauriac, it is myself; we have the Desqueyroux record before us and we are pronouncing judgment.

But M. Mauriac plays other tricks as well. Like Asmodeus, that nosey and mischievous devil so dear to his heart, he likes to pry off the corners of roofs. When it suits his purpose, he leaves Thérèse and suddenly installs himself inside another character, whether it be Georges or Maria or Bernard Desqueyroux, or Anne the servant. He takes a look about and then trundles off, like a marionette. "Thérèse was unable to understand the meaning of that troubled look on the girl's face and *did not know* that the other was thinking, 'In all my life, I'll never live through half of what that old woman has been through in a few days.' " Didn't she know? It doesn't matter. M. Mauriac suddenly abandons her, leaves her to her ignorance, drops in on Marie and brings back a little snapshot for us.

On the other hand, at times he generously permits one of his creatures to share in the novelist's divine lucidity. "She stretched out her arms to draw him to her, but he drew violently away, and she *realized* that she had lost him." The indications are uncertain, and besides, they involve only the present. But what does it matter? M. Mauriac has decided that Georges is lost to Thérèse. He has decided, just as the ancient Gods decreed Oedipus' parricide and incest. Then, in order to inform us of his decree, he lends his creature, for a few moments, some of Tiresias' power of divination; have no fear; she will soon relapse into darkness. Besides, here is the curfew. The minds of all the characters go out. Tired, M. Mauriac suddenly withdraws from all of them. There remains only the façade of a world, a few puppets in a cardboard set:

The child spread the fingers that covered her eyes.
"I thought you were sleeping."
The voice begged her again, "Swear to me that you're happy."

There are gestures and sounds in the shadows. M. Mauriac is seated nearby, thinking, " 'How you must have suffered, Mummy!' 'Oh no, I didn't feel a thing . . .' What? Could it be that the rattling in her throat and her purple face had not been signs of suffering? Can a person go through a hell of pain and then forget about it completely?"

It is obvious to anyone familiar with Marie's character that the girl wastes no time in such reflections. No, what we have here is rather M. Mauriac resting from his labours on the seventh day and thrilled with his creation.

And now here is the real reason for his failure. He once wrote that the novelist is to his own creatures what God is to His. And that explains all the oddities of his technique. He takes God's standpoint on his characters. God sees the inside and outside, the depths of body and soul, the whole universe at once. In like manner, M. Mauriac is omniscient about everything relating to his little world. What he says about his characters is Gospel. He explains them, categorizes them and condemns them without appeal. If anyone were to ask him how he knows that Thérèse is a cautious and desperate woman he would probably reply, with great surprise, "Didn't I create her?"

No, he didn't! The time has come to say that the novelist is not God. We would do well to recall the caution with which Conrad suggests to us that Lord Jim may be "romantic." He takes great care not to state this himself; he puts the word into the mouth of one of his characters, a fallible being, who utters it hesitantly. The word "romantic," clear as it is, thereby acquires depth and pathos and a certain indefinable mystery. Not so with M. Mauriac. "A cautious and desperate woman" is no hypothesis; it is an illumination which comes to us from above. The author, impatient to have us grasp the character of his heroine, suddenly gives us the key. But what I maintain is precisely the fact that he has no right to make these absolute judgments. A novel is an action related from various points of view. And M. Mauriac is well aware of this, having written, in *La Fin de la Nuit*, that ". . . the most conflicting judgments about a single person can be correct; it is a question of lighting, and no one light reveals more than another." But each of these interpretations must be in motion, drawn along, so to speak, by the very action it interprets.

It is, in short, the testimony of a participant and should reveal the man who testifies as well as the event to which he testifies. It should arouse our impatience (will it be confirmed or denied by events?), and thus give us a feeling of the dragging of time. Thus, each point of view is relative, and the best one will be that which makes the reader feel most acutely the dragging of time. The participants' interpretations and explanations will all be hypothetical. The reader may have an inkling, beyond these conjectures, of the event's absolute reality, but it is for him alone to re-establish it. Should he care to try this sort of exercise, he will never get beyond the realm of likelihood and probability.

In any case, the introduction of absolute truth or of God's standpoint constitutes a twofold error of technique. To begin with, it presupposes a purely contemplative narrator, withdrawn from the action. This inevitably conflicts with Valéry's law of aesthetics, according to which any given element of a work of art ought always to maintain a plurality of relationships with the other elements. And besides, the absolute is nontemporal. If you pitch the narrative in the absolute, the string of duration snaps, and the novel disappears before your eyes. All that remains is a dull truth, *sub specie aeternitatis.*

But there is something even more serious. The definitive judgments with which M. Mauriac is always ready to intersperse the narrative prove that he does not conceive his characters as he ought. He fabricates their natures before setting them down, he decrees that they *will be* this or that. The essence of Thérèse, the evil-smelling animal, the desperate and cautious woman, is, I admit, complex, and not to be expressed in a single sentence. But what exactly is this essence? Her inmost depths? Let us look at it more closely. Conrad saw clearly that the word "romantic" had meaning when it expressed an aspect of character *for other people.* Such words as "desperate and cautious" and "evil-smelling animal" and "castaway" and other such neat phrases are of the same sort as the word that Conrad puts into the mouth of the merchant of the islands. When Thérèse resumes her story,

> For years she had been unaware that the pattern of her destiny had been a series of attempts to get out of a rut, each ending in failure. But now that she had emerged from the darkness, she saw clearly . . .

she is able to judge her past so easily only because she cannot return to it. Thus, when he thinks he is probing the hearts of his characters, M. Mauriac remains outside, at the door.

This would be quite all right if M. Mauriac were aware of it and wrote novels like Hemingway's, in which we hardly know the heroes except through their gestures and words, and the vague judgments they pass on each other. But when M. Mauriac, making full use of his creative authority, forces us to accept these exterior views as the inner stuff of his creatures, he is transforming his characters into *things.* Only things can simply *be;* they have only exteriors. Minds cannot simply be; they become. Thus, in shaping his Thérèse *sub specie aeternitatis,* M. Mauriac first makes of her a thing, after which he adds, on the sly, a whole mental thickness. But in vain. Fictional beings have their laws, the most rigorous of which is the following: the novelist may be either their witness or their accomplice, but never both at the same time. The novelist must be either inside or out. Because M. Mauriac does not observe these laws, he does away with his characters' minds.

We are now back at freedom, Thérèse's other dimension. What becomes of her in this darkened world? Until now, Thérèse has been a *thing,* an ordered succession of motives and patterns, of passions, habits and interests, a *story* one could sum up in a few maxims—a *fatality.* This witch, this possessed creature, is now presented to us as free. M. Mauriac takes pains to tell us what we are to understand by this freedom.

> But yesterday, in particular, when I decided to give up my fortune, I felt deep delight. I floated a thousand cubits *above my real self.* I climb, climb, climb . . . and then suddenly I slide back and find myself in that evil, cold, wilfulness, which is what I am when I make no effort, *which is what I fall back on when I fall back on myself.*[3]

Thus, freedom is not Thérèse's "real self" any more than consciousness is. This self, "what I fall back on when I fall back on myself," is a piece of data, a *thing.* Consciousness and freedom come later, consciousness as power to have illusions about oneself, and freedom as power to escape from oneself.

We must understand that for M. Mauriac, freedom cannot *construct.* A man, using his freedom, cannot create himself or forget his own history. Free will is merely a discontinuous force which allows for brief escapes, but which produces nothing, except a few short-lived events. Thus, *La Fin de la Nuit,* which, according to M. Mauriac, is the novel of someone's freedom, appears to be, above all, the story of an enslavement. So much so that the author, who, at first, wanted to show us "the stages of a spiritual ascension," confesses in his preface that Thérèse has led him, in spite of himself, into hell. "The finished work," he observes, not without regret, "disappoints in part the hopes contained in the title." But how could it have been otherwise?

Freedom, by the very fact of its having been thus tacked on to Thérèse's dense and fixed nature, loses its omnipotence and indeterminacy. Freedom itself is defined and characterized, since we know *in opposition to what* it is freedom. M. Mauriac goes even further and imposes a law

3. The italics are mine.

upon it. "I climb, climb, climb ... and then suddenly I slide back. ...."
Thus, it is decreed in advance that Thérèse will sink back again each time.
We are even informed in the preface that it would be indiscreet to ask
more of her. "She belongs to that race of beings who emerge from darkness only when they depart from life. All that is asked of them is that they
not resign themselves to darkness." It is Thérèse herself who speaks of the
"pattern of her destiny." Freedom is a phase of this pattern. Even in her
freedom, Thérèse is predictable. M. Mauriac has measured out with the
precision of a doctor's prescription or of a cooking recipe the little freedom he allows her. I expect nothing from her: I know everything. Her ups
and downs affect me little more than those of a cockroach climbing a wall
with stupid obstinacy.

The reason is that no allowance has been made for freedom. Because
Thérèse's freedom has been doled out with a dropper, it no more resembles real freedom than her mind resembles a real mind. And when M.
Mauriac, absorbed in describing Thérèse's psychological mechanisms,
wants us to feel that she is no longer a mechanism, he suddenly finds that
he lacks the necessary devices. Of course he shows us Thérèse struggling
against her evil inclinations. "Thérèse tightened her jaw. 'I won't talk
about Garcin to him,' she said to herself." But what proof have I that a
closer analysis would not reveal the deterministic links and reasons behind
this sudden revolt? M. Mauriac feels this so acutely that occasionally, in
desperation, he tugs at our sleeve and whispers, "Look! This time it's the
real thing! She's free!" As in the following passage: "She interrupted herself in the middle of a sentence (for she was being entirely honest)." I know
of no clumsier device than this parenthetical admonition, but the author
is obviously obliged to use it.

On the basis of this hybrid creature of M. Mauriac's begetting which
he calls Thérèse's nature, *there is no way of distinguishing between a free
action and a passion.* But perhaps there is: through a sort of evanescent
grace that plays over the features or the soul of a character fresh from a
victory over himself:

> The expression on her face was as beautiful as he had ever seen it.
> She did not feel herself suffering, she felt relieved, delivered of some
> nameless burden, as if she were no longer going round in circles, as if she were
> suddenly going forward.

But these moral recompenses are not enough to convince us. On the
contrary, they show us that, for M. Mauriac, freedom differs from slavery
in *value,* and not in nature. Any intention directed upwards, toward Good,
is free, and any will to Evil is fettered. It is needless for us to discuss the
intrinsic worth of this distinguishing principle. In any case, it stifles free-

dom in fiction and, with it, the immediate duration which is the substance of the novel.

How *could* Thérèse's story have duration? It involves the old theological conflict between divine omniscience and human freedom. Thérèse's "pattern of destiny," the graph of her ups and downs, resembles a fever curve; it is dead time, since the future is spread out like the past and simply repeats it. The reader of a novel does not want to be God. In order for my duration to be transfused into the veins of Thérèse and Marie Desqueyroux, I must, at least once, be unaware of their fate and impatient to know it. But M. Mauriac does not bother to play upon my impatience. His sole aim is to make me as knowing as himself. He showers me with information. No sooner do I feel my curiosity begin to stir than it is satisfied beyond measure. Dostoevsky would have surrounded Thérèse with dense and mysterious figures whose meaning would have been at the brink of surrender on every page, only to elude my grasp. But M. Mauriac places me straight away in the very depths of his characters' hearts. No one has any secrets; he spreads an even light over everyone.

Thus, even if I were ever curious about the development of events, I could not identify my own impatience with that of Thérèse, since we are not waiting for the same things and what she would like to know, I have known for a long time. To me, she is like one of those abstract partners in the explanation of a bridge game who are kept in hypothetical ignorance of the opposing hands and who plan in terms of that very ignorance, whereas I can see all the cards already and know the errors in their hopes and calculations.

It is plain to see, moreover, that M. Mauriac has no liking for time, no fondness for the Bergsonian necessity of waiting "for the sugar to melt." To him, his creature's time is a dream, an all-too-human illusion; he gets rid of it and resolutely sets himself up within the eternal. But this alone, to my way of thinking, should have deterred him from writing novels. The real novelist is stirred by things that offer resistance; he is excited by doors because they must be opened, by envelopes because they must be unsealed.

In Hemingway's admirable *A Farewell to Arms,* objects are time-traps; they fill the narrative with innumerable tiny, obstinate resistances which the hero must break down one after the other. But M. Mauriac detests these lowly barriers that deter him from his purpose; he speaks of them as little as possible. He even wants to economize on the time of his characters' conversations; he suddenly speaks up for them and summarizes, in a few words, what they are going to say.

> "Love," said Thérèse, "isn't everything in life—especially for men ..." She went off on this theme. She could have talked till dawn; the sensible remarks she was making out of duty and with an effort were not the kind ... etc.

There is, perhaps, no graver error in all the book than this stinginess. By cutting short the dialogue of his characters just when they begin to interest me, M. Mauriac projects me suddenly (and how can he fail to see this?) out of their time and out of their story. For these dialogues do not stop; I know they go on somewhere, but my right to sit in on them has been withdrawn. He would probably regard these sudden stops and sudden beginnings as "foreshortenings." I, for my part, prefer to regard them as breakdowns. Of course a novelist has to "foreshorten" now and then, but that does not in the least mean that he suddenly drains off the duration. In a novel, you must tell all or keep quiet; above all, you must not omit or skip anything. A foreshortening is simply a change of speed in the narration. M. Mauriac is in a hurry; he has probably sworn that no work of his will ever exceed the dimensions of a long short story.

I look in vain through *La Fin de la Nuit* for the long, stammering conversations, so frequent in English novels, in which the heroes are forever going over their stories, without managing to make them advance. I look in vain for the respites that suspend the action only to increase its urgency, the "between-times" in which, beneath a dark and cloudy sky, the characters busily absorb themselves in their familiar occupations. M. Mauriac treats only the essential passages, which he then joins together with brief summaries.

It is because of this taste for concision that his creatures talk as though they were in the theatre. M. Mauriac is interested only in getting them to say what they have to say as quickly and clearly as possible. Rejecting the superfluity, repetition and fumbling of actual speech, he gives to his heroes' remarks their naked power of significance. And since we must, nevertheless, be able to sense a difference between what he himself writes and what he makes them say, he imparts to these overclear speeches a sort of torrential speed which is that of the theatre. Listen, for example, to Thérèse:

"What? How dare you? Do you mean to say I didn't commit the act? But I did. Though it is nothing compared to my other more cowardly, more secret crimes—crimes that involved no risk."

This passage should be spoken aloud rather than read. Notice the oratorical movement of the beginning, and the question which swells with repetition. Doesn't it recall Hermione's jealous rages in *Andromaque?* I catch myself whispering the words aloud, struck by that rhetorical beginning typical of all good tragic dialogue. Now read this:

"However rash your friend may be, he cannot be so rash as to think you attractive. Had I meant to make him jealous, I should have taken more care to make the matter seem credible."

Doesn't the reader recognize the turn of phrase dear to the comic writers of the eighteenth century? The novel is not at all suited to graces of this kind, not because people ought to talk in the novel as they do in life, but because the novel has its own kind of stylization. The transition to dialogue ought to be marked by a kind of flickering of the lights. It is dark, the hero struggles to express himself; his words are not pictures of his soul, but rather free and clumsy acts, which say too much and too little. The reader gets impatient; he tries to see beyond these involved and fumbling statements. Dostoevsky, Conrad and Faulkner have known how to use this resistance of words, which is a source of endless misunderstandings and involuntary revelations, and thereby to make of dialogue "the fictional moment," the time when the sense of duration is richest. M. Mauriac's classicism is probably repelled by such woolly conversation. But everyone knows that French classicism is rhetorical and theatrical.

Nor is this all. M. Mauriac also insists that each of these conversations be effective and, consequently, he complies with another theatrical law— for it is only in the theatre that the dialogue must keep the action going forward. He therefore builds up "scenes." The entire novel is made up of four scenes each of which ends in a "catastrophe." Each scene is prepared exactly as in a tragedy.

Take, for example, the following: At Saint-Clair, Marie receives a letter from Georges, her fiancé, who backs out of his engagement. Convinced, through a misunderstanding, that her mother is responsible for the break, she leaves immediately for Paris. We know all about this turbulent, selfish, passionate, rather silly girl, who is also capable of good impulses. She is shown during this journey as being mad with rage, her claws bared, determined to fight, to wound, to pay back with interest the blows she has received. Thérèse's state is described with no less precision. We know that she has been consumed by suffering, that she is half out of her mind. Is it not obvious that the meeting of these two women is brought about as in a play? We know the forces present. The situation is rigorously defined? it is a confrontation. Marie does not know that her mother is mad. What will she do when she realizes it? The problem is clearly formulated.

We have only to leave everything to determinism, with its movements and counter-movements, its dramatic and anticipated reversals. It will lead us inevitably to the final catastrophe, with Marie playing the nurse and prevailing upon her mother to come back to the Desqueyroux home. Doesn't this recall Sardou or the great scene in Bernstein's *The Spy*, or the second act of *The Thief?* I quite understand M. Mauriac's being tempted by the theatre. While reading *La Fin de la Nuit*, I felt, time and again, as if I were reading the argument and chief passages of a four-act play.

Let us look at the passage in *Beauchamp's Career* where Meredith shows us the last meeting of Beauchamp and Renée. They are still in love and are within an ace of confessing their feelings, but they part. When they meet, *anything* is possible between them. The future does not yet exist. Gradually their little weaknesses and mistakes and resentments begin to get the better of their good will. They cease to see straight. Nevertheless, up to the very end, even when I begin to fear that they may break up, I still feel that *it may all still work out.* The reason is that they are free. Their final separation will be of their own making. *Beauchamp's Career* is a novel!

La Fin de la Nuit is not a novel. How can anyone call this angular, glacial book, with its analyses, theatrical passages and poetic meditations, a "novel"? How can anyone confuse these bursts of speed and violent jamming of the brakes, these abrupt starts and breakdowns, with the majestic flow of fictional time? How can anyone be taken in by this motionless narrative, which betrays its intellectual framework from the very start, in which the mute faces of the heroes are inscribed like angles in a circle? If it is true that a novel is a *thing,* like a painting or architectural structure, if it is true that a novel is made with time and free minds, as a picture is painted with oil and pigments, then *La Fin de la Nuit* is not a novel. It is, at most, a collection of signs and intentions. M. Mauriac is not a novelist.

Why? Why hasn't this serious and earnest writer achieved his purpose? Because, I think, of the sin of pride. Like most of our writers, he has tried to ignore the fact that the theory of relativity applies in full to the universe of fiction, that there is no more place for a privileged observer in a real novel than in the world of Einstein, and that it is no more possible to conduct an experiment in a fictional system[4] in order to determine whether the system is in motion or at rest than there is in a physical system. M. Mauriac has put himself first. He has chosen divine omniscience and omnipotence. But novels are written *by* men and *for* men. In the eyes of God, Who cuts through appearances and goes beyond them, there is no novel, no art, for art thrives on appearances. God is not an artist. Neither is M. Mauriac.

(February 1939.)

4. By fictional system, I mean the novel as a whole, as well as the partial systems that make it up (the minds of the characters, their combined psychological and moral judgments).

Nathan A. Scott, Jr.
The Literary Imagination in a Time of Dearth

The characteristic literature of the present time—which begins already to take us deeply into the post-modern phase of our culture—is ... a literature that may well be conceived as deserving the appellation Hunger-Art. For it is a literature that specializes in the art of abstention, the art of getting on without the consolations either of Reality or the Myth. Inheriting all the exactions entailed in the legacy of Flaubert, James, Conrad, and Joyce; of Baudelaire, Laforgue, Eliot, and Pound; of Ibsen, Strindberg, Chekhov, and Brecht, the writer of our period feels his principal obligation to be that of confronting the total reality of the contemporary scene. But the breadth and variousness, the indeterminateness and the immense multiformity of that scene are profoundly intimidating, and have the effect of convincing the literary imagination of the futility of any serious attempt to compete with the "new reality." The generation of 1914 could still conceive it to be the writer's vocation to forge in the smithy of his soul the uncreated conscience of his race, to master and somehow to subdue—at least by the formalizing power of art itself—the rampant disorder of the modern world. But ... increasingly it is the tendency of our novelists and playwrights and poets to feel that, late now in these post-modern days of our history, their only *donnée* (as one critic has remarked of Sartre) is that nothing is given, that there are no paradigms spacious enough to comprehend the human scene of our time, and that the work of art can therefore be little more than an illustration of the world's opaque mysteriousness and contingency. The kind of large reconstructive effort undertaken by a Proust, a Yeats, a Stevens, or a Joyce can no longer, it is supposed, prove itself on the pulse of what Susan Sontag calls "the new sensibility." "Everything," as Bishop Butler said, "is what it is and not another thing": things are just as they are, and the world is simply what it is—this, or something like it, seems more and more to be a basic assumption of the literature following in the wake of traditionalist modernism. "Man looks at the world," says Alain Robbe-Grillet, "and the world does not look back at him." So the extravagant *profondeur* is simply irrelevant. And one mark of the artist's authenticity will, therefore, be found in his forswearing any attempt at radically clarifying or transfiguring the human reality. A central impulse guiding the literary imagination

Source: Reprinted by permission of the Yale University Press from *Negative Capability* by Nathan A. Scott, Jr. Copyright © 1969 by Yale University.

today appears, indeed, to be a violently mythoclastic rejection of all schemes and stratagems whereby coherence and order may be conferred upon the weltered givens of experience.

Yet, strangely, the artist's refusal to replace Reality with Myth results in no significant enlargement of the grasp upon Reality. The great new commitment, to be sure, is to the concrete, not to some higher reality to which it affords access, not to some metaphysical meaning which it veils, not even to the volatile tropisms of one's own sensibility through which it may be filtered. What is rather being attempted is a return to things in themselves, for, as Nathalie Sarraute says (on behalf of a generation), "that's all that counts." The great flaw in the world is felt to be the flattening banality that is introduced by all the habits of the old "anthropomorphism" to which we have for so long been inured by a tradition that has encouraged us to take for granted a "metaphysical pact" between ourselves and "things." But, this pact being now at a discount, what is sought is an immediate encounter with things in themselves, as they exist before they are rendered spiritless and insipid by our codes and norms, by our concepts and values. Yet such a return to the concrete must, of course, inevitably be hung up on the fact that the actual human situation is never as Descartes imagined it, with consciousness and existence pitted against each other in radical duality. The world with which we have our actual transactions is never appropriable as something pristinely naked of human valuation: there is no such thing as " 'un-thought' reality."[1] And this may be partly why the new mystique of *l'actuelle* yields so imperfect a sense of the full, living historicity of the human life-world. The allegiance to a sceptical empiricism and the fascination with the contingent and the concrete are of a sort, in other words, that leave not only the Myth but also Reality itself behind.

So ours is a period-style that thrusts us into an "open situation,"[2] into that middle region between (as expressed in the mythography of the previous chapter) Antioch and Alexandria, the two great cities that polarize the world of the imagination. The literature that most clearly bears upon itself the stamp of contemporaneity seems to be making a double refusal, of both Reality and the Myth; and thus its precincts are those from within which the horizon of neither Antioch nor Alexandria is visible. Which is to say that the imagination of our period, as it finds reflection in the arts of the word, is without a "world," in something like Heidegger's

1. René Etiemble and Yassu Gauclère, *Rimbaud* (Paris, NRF, 1936), p. 141.
2. Though I make my own use of it, the term "open situation" I derive from Dietrich von Oppen; see his essay, "Man in the Open Situation," *Journal for Theology and the Church*, 2 ("Translating Theology into the Modern Age"), ed. Robert W. Funk (New York, Harper & Row, 1965), pp. 130–58. (This journal is an abbreviated English-language edition of the *Zertschrift für Theologie und Kirche*, edited by Gerhard Ebeling).

sense of the term. In the highly eccentric lexicon fashioned in his great book of 1927, *Being and Time,* the term *Dasein*—which means literally "to-be-there"—is the term which is reserved for the radically distinctive element in human existence. In Heidegger's vision, man is the creature whose unique vocation it is to be so much preoccupied with what it means to be that he deserves, therefore, himself to be conceived as *Dasein.* The essence of *Dasein* lies in its immitigable concern for the nature of its own reality. And "world," in the Heideggerian lexicon, is a characteristic of *Dasein.* For Heidegger the concept of "world" does not designate simply the total aggregate of everything present in the universe. It stands rather for that entire complex of unitive images and analogies and principles through which the whole welter of existence becomes the integral field of reality in which man actually dwells. It is in this way that the idea of "world" is considered to be inextricably involved in the idea of *Dasein.* And, preempting now this bit of Heidegger's rhetoric for another expository purpose, it may be said perhaps that, when the imagination can no longer enter either Antioch or Alexandria, its condition begins to be that of being unenclosed by any sort of "world"; its situation is an "open situation," and it finds itself committed to a time of dearth.

It is, then, through such a time that Martin Heidegger is today our great philosophic guide; and over many years, in the isolateness of his little mountain village of Todtnauberg in West Germany's Black Forest, he has been brooding, in a profoundly exciting way, on the shape that human life assumes in an open situation and on the peculiar vocation of the poet to venture out onto this uncertain terrain. The situation of man, at the end of the modern age, is, in Heidegger's reading of it, something open, in the sense of its being located in a great intervenient space, in a great *Between.* As he says, in the clumsy stiltedness of manner so typical of his strange rhetoric, ours "is the time of the gods that have fled *and* of the god that is coming. It is the time of *need,* because it lies under a double lack and a double Not: the No-more of the gods that have fled and the Not-yet of the god that is coming."[3]

The proposal that ours is a time of privation and dearth, of *need,* occurs, to be sure, towards the end of an essay on Hölderlin and reflects Heidegger's fascination with the special sort of eschatological sensibility controlling Hölderlin's poetry. But it also reflects, of course, his equal fascination with that other mad eschatologist in modern German tradition, born in the year following Hölderlin's death, who brusquely proclaimed the death of God (or at least of all the old names and

---

3. Martin Heidegger, "Hölderlin and the Essence of Poetry," in *Existence and Being,* ed. by Werner Brock and tr. by Douglas Scott (Chicago, Ill.: Henry Regnery, 1949), p. 313.

conceptualizations of God) in a book of 1882 curiously entitled *Die Frölīche Wissenschaft* (*The Gay Science*). Indeed, it is Friedrich Nietzsche who marks for Heidegger one of the great decisive turning points in the history of what he speaks of as "the humanization of truth."[4]

The humanization of truth—the doctrine that truth resides in some human perspective rather than in Being itself—is, for Heidegger, the great disaster involved in Western intellectual history, because it entails a sundering of the primordial bond between the human spirit and what (by adapting a phrase of Teilhard de Chardin) might be called the *milieu ontologique*. To be sure, in *Being and Time* he had declared "world" to be an achievement of *Dasein*, and such an epistemology would itself seem to have entailed a perspectivist concept of truth. Within a few years after the appearance of this book, however, he appears to have concluded that its account of the relation between *Dasein* and Being was applicable only in a very rough sort of way to the more perfunctory transactions of everyday that man has with reality; whereas, in the great decisive and extreme situations of human existence, it is not in man but in Being itself that truth is found to be resident. So, in a series of works belonging to the 1940s,[5] he began to launch a fierce polemic against the whole heresy of "humanism," wanting now most emphatically to insist upon the non-humanistic orientation of his own thought.

Heidegger's basic conviction now is that all encounters between the Self and the Not-self—the terms are not his—occur, inevitably, within the environing milieu of Being, and that all the referential thrusts of human intelligence outward beyond itself are confirmable only in consequence of this encompassing *Plenum* whose "unhiddenness" does indeed make it possible for the Self to meet the Not-self in an act of cognition. The locus of truth, in other words, is not in this or that perspective (or category, or proposition, or system) that may be imposed upon reality, but is rather in the "unhiddenness" or transparency of Being; which is to say that truth is not an achievement but a gift, something granted and received.

But, as Heidegger argues, the assumption perennially informing the Western tradition has been that truth is resident in the schemata of human intelligence. The project of "humanizing" truth was first launched by the Greeks, preeminently by Plato, whose theory of Ideas did in effect, he maintains, attribute ultimate reality to what were nothing more than projections of human reason. The traditional Platonist will no doubt be scandalized by Heidegger's insistence that the Platonic Idea is nothing more than a concept; but—conventional textbook scholarship to the con-

---

4. The view of Nietzsche is set forth in his *Nietzsche 1, 2* (Pfullingen, Günther Neske, 1961).

5. The principal documents in the case are perhaps *Platons Lehre von der Wahrheit* (Bern, Francke, 1942); *Vom Wesen der Wahrheit* (Frankfurt am Main, Klostermann, 1943); and *Über den Humanismus* (Frankfurt am Main, Klostermann, 1949). To these may be added the later works in which the critique of Kant is set forth—*Der Satz vom Grund* (Pfullingen, Günther Neske, 1957); *Die Frage nach dem Ding* (Tübingen, Max Niemeyer, 1962); and *Kants These über das Sein* (Frankfurt am Main, Klostermann, 1963).

trary (and he needs no instruction in this mode)—this, nevertheless, is his claim, that it is simply an audacious postulate, reified into Eternity. Thus the great bequest of Platonism to Western mentality has been the superstition that truth follows upon a proper deployment by the intellect of its own counters and that, in the ascending scale of ontological priority, certain human principles and idealities hold the sovereign place.

Heidegger finds an essentially identical error in medieval Scholasticism, where (as in Aquinas) truth is understood to consist in the "adequation" of the intellect to things as they are. This same view of truth as an achievement of human intelligence he finds being carried into the early modern period by Descartes, whose *Cogito* only signalized again how persistently the philosophic tradition remains (as Alfred Whitehead long ago remarked, though from a standpoint rather different from Heidegger's) but "a series of footnotes to Plato."

In Heidegger's reading of the Western tradition, this anthropocentric account of the world as an essentially human "project" gained even more emphatic expression in the critical philosophy of Kant which, after denying the possibility of our knowing things in themselves, went on to locate the ground of all objectivity in the synthetic categories with which the self orders its experience, thus making man himself the final and absolute measure of all truth. And so it comes to be that, for Heidegger, it is but a step from Kant to Nietzsche—and to the end of the whole Western experiment in humanization. For he who in 1882 announced the death of God was in effect embracing, in a violently strident way, what the whole antecedent tradition had been moving toward—the impertinence of regarding the world as itself simply an image of man. Nietzsche's according an ultimate status in reality to "the will to power"—to the principle of human assertiveness—did, in other words, entail, essentially, nothing more than a radicalization of what since Plato had been perennially inherent in the tradition; for the whole drive of the *philosophia perennis* is towards the assertion that man dwells, uncompanioned and alone, in a universe that is very largely of his own creation. Nor is this assessment of the meaning of our received tradition, for Heidegger, merely something which it is interesting for intellectual historicans to contemplate. On his account, it is precisely in the humanization of reality in the West that we may find the explanation of the great malaise that blights the world now, at the end of the modern period—which is a disquiet arising out of the discovery that the triumphs of our scientific technology have been purchased by such an unbridling of "the will to power" as has sundered our most elemental bonds with nature and resulted in a wholly artificial environment for human life.

At the heart of our culture there is, Heidegger suggests, a profound perversion, a great imbalance that needs correction. At the end now of (as he nominates it) the History of Being in the West, what is lost is simply

Being itself, and the great task awaiting the imagination is the recovery of a range of sympathy and conscience that will permit us to deal with the world in terms other than those simply of aggressive action. Our traditional habits of preference for what is assertive and bold and aggressive do indeed account for much that is distinctively a part of the impressive achievement of Western culture, but what Heidegger calls *the will to will* may also, as he sees, have the effect of so committing us to an essentially manipulative approach to reality that all attentiveness to the sheer ontological weight and depth of the world is lost. And this is precisely the sort of loss that he believes to threaten in such an advanced technological culture as our own, where our great temptation is to be so bent upon bringing the world to heel that we risk its becoming totally devoured by the engines of our science and ideology. In such a time our great need is somehow to bring the usual traffic of our acting and thinking to a stop, in order that we may deepen ourselves down into the kind of profound repose and expectancy that will permit our becoming permeable again by the integral reality of the world. When we have reentered those "quiet mysterious depths,"[6] where "all the forces of the soul [are] ... gathered together in quietude, ... in a state of virtuality and dormant energy,"[7] then the whole world of Creation seems to be resounding in ourselves, and we begin to be overtaken by a happy impulse (in Jonathan Edwards' phrase) simply to "consent to Being." Then it is at last that the truly human posture vis-à-vis the world is achieved, and the name which Heidegger gives to it is that which forms the title of his little book of 1959—*Gelassenheit:* submission, abandonment, surrender, acquiescence. It is, he maintains, only when *the will to will* has been thus subdued and when we have deeply surrendered to the unplumbed Mystery of Being that the Mystery begins to be transparent before the gaze of the mind; it is only when we have consented to be *stupid* before the absolute presence of Being that it begins, translucently and radiantly, to disclose itself.

But, after the long experiment of our culture in "humanization," by what means is it to be expected that we may overcome our "forgetfulness" of Being? This is for Heidegger, one feels, the central question needing to be raised in our own, late and problematic time, and it is just as the issue begins to be posed by the logic of his own thought that his answer begins already to be in view. For, untroubled by the sense of scandal that he may thereby give to his fellow philosophers, the remarkable position taken by this audacious thinker is that it is precisely the vocation of the poet to bring us once again into the region of fundamental reality.

6. Thomas Carlyle, "Characteristics," *Essays* (Boston, Brown and Taggard, 1860), *3, 9.*
7. Jacques Maritain, *Creative Intuition in Art and Poetry,* Bollingen Series, xxxv, 1 (New York, Pantheon Books, 1953), p. 242.

The epigones like now to make arcane distinctions between the earlier Heidegger (of *Being and Time*) and "the later Heidegger," between the phenomenologist of *Dasein* and the metaphysician for whom the primary reality is no longer *Dasein* but Being. For this later Heidegger the principal fact about our culture concerns its dominance by technology. In his view of the modern situation, the sovereign passion controlling our period is one which prompts an effort at winning mastery of the world: it is a passion to control and to manipulate both nature and human life itself, and this technological orientation is something long prepared for by a culture whose philosophic strategists so "humanized" the predominant conception of reality that Being came to be regarded as that which is to be grasped and manipulated and controlled. The consequence is that we now find ourselves enveloped by that desicating "second nature" comprised of the wholly artificial environment which technological enterprise throws round human life. In this extremity, any profound renewal of the human spirit will require that it unlearn its habit of approaching the world as something to be "attacked."[8] in the manner of a scientific experiment of technological project. What must be learned again is the discipline of "letting-be"[9] What Is, of throttling *the will to will* and of *surrendering* to the radically immanent presence of Being.

It is in just this discipline that the poet, as Heidegger maintains, offers a unique and an indispensable tutelage. His whole purpose is to stir and quicken within us an awareness of the irrevocability by which the things of this world are as they are. Much of Heidegger's writing of the last thirty years is integrally related to his theory of literature, even when, in a given work, his immediate theme may happen in no way to touch explicitly on the subject of poetry; but, for a reconstruction of this phase of his thought, the most crucial documents are two collections of essays, the *Interpretations of Hölderlin's Poetry (Erläuterungen zu Hölderlins Dichtung)*[10] and the book called *Paths in the Forest (Holzwege)*.[11] The language of these essays—like that of the entire *œuvre* to which they belong—is, in its obscurity and elusiveness, an achievement remarkable even in a tradition whose systematic thinkers have rarely been notable for their stylistic clarity. But, in so far as the true intention of this strange rhetoric is discernible at all, it would seem that, for Heidegger, it is most especially the distinctive office of the poet to make us look at the various concrete realities of experience with the kind of attentiveness that will permit their being

8. See Martin Heidegger, *Discourse on Thinking.* Originally published as *Gelassenheit,* tr. by John M. Anderson and E. Hans Freund (New York: Harper Torchbooks, 1966), p. 88.
9. See Martin Heidegger, "On the Essence of Truth," *Existence and Being,* pp. 319–51.
10. Frankfurt am Main, Klostermann, 1944.
11. Frankfurt am Main, Klostermann, 1950.

disclosed "in the starkness and strangeness of their being what they are."[12] The artist seeks to bring us into a relationship of intense intimacy with a given event, with some quite specific phenomenon. What he invites is an attitude of enthrallment before the sheer specificity of whatever may be the object which he is holding up for attention. The poetic world—that is, the world of literary art in general—is rooted in the concrete particularity of lived experience. Whereas the scientific view of the world is ultimately predatory, driving toward possession and mastery and control, "poetic art, in its deepest aspect, is a way of loving the concrete, the particular, the individual"[13]—a way, as Heidegger would say, of simply letting things be. The poet does not want, as it were, to put things on their good behavior by making them obedient to the well-driven machine of the Idea; rather, he wants to reconstitute our perceptual habits in a way that will restore to us the innocence which is simply enthralled by the bright actuality of the things of earth.

The poet, then, in Heidegger's view, might be said to be an adept in the art of "paying heed"—which is why he can say in the *Holzwege* that, in a work of art, "truth is at work" (p. 45). Truth is at work, because the carefulness with which the poet pays heed to the things of earth has the effect of bringing them "into the Open." Which is to say, in Heidegger's terminology, that the poet is he who "hails" Being, since Being itself is nothing other than "the Open"—that immediate and luminous presence constituting the inner cohesion whereby things are enabled simply to be what they are.

In the essay on "The Origin of a Work of Art" in the *Holzwege,* for example, Heidegger speaks of a Van Gogh painting of a pair of farm shoes, and he invites us to compare the artifact with the shoes themselves. The actual shoes are merely a piece of what he calls "equipment," and the "equipmental being" of the shoes consists, he says, in their "serviceability." The old peasant woman who uses them, who trudges in them day by day through the dampness of the soil and the furrows of her fields, knows these shoes in their equipmental being, and knows them without having to take thought. But we, as we look at the shoes, do not begin to comprehend their essential nature—how they vibrate with "the silent call of the earth," how they slide along "the loneliness of the field-path as evening declines," how they are pervaded by "the wordless joy" of "ripening corn" —until Van Gogh's painting opens them up out of their captivity unto themselves and into what they most emphatically are in their radical actuality. It is the work of art that brings into the open that which has "withdrawn" behind the shoes but which, once it is fully revealed, is seen

12. H. D. Lewis, "Revelation and Art," *Morals and Revelation* (London, Allen and Unwin, 1951), p. 212.
13. Nathan A. Scott, Jr., *The Broken Center: Studies in the Theological Horizon of Modern Literature* (New Haven, Yale University Press, 1966), p. 179.

to be that which in truth imparts "presence" to the shoes—and this is nothing other than Being itself whose location is necessarily always in finite things behind which it withdraws. When these things are truly paid heed to, so that they are brought into the open, what is then in view is nothing less than Being itself, for that is what Being is: it is simply that effulgence wherewith the things of earth are enabled to have an emphatic and persisting presence.

So poetic art, because it renders us alert to the concrete realities of the world in the dimension of presence, brings us into the region of Being, since Being itself is nothing other than Presence. But, in performing this kind of function, poetry is for Heidegger simply the crucial instance of language in general, since, as he says in the *Holzwege*, the primary task of language is not merely to be a technique of signification but "to bring beings as such for the first time into the Open" (p. 61). Indeed, man does not have a "world," does not have any sort of unified matrix of meanings and relations in which to dwell, unless he has a language, a way of declaring what things "appear to be as they come into the Open" (*Holzwege*, p. 61). This, one imagines, is the insight that he takes to be implicit in the saying of Hölderlin for which he has such a great liking, that "poetically,/-Man dwells upon the earth."[14] Man dwells upon the earth—in a really human way—only in so far as he transforms "earth" into "world," and he can have a world only if he has language, only if he has a way of being open to Being and of naming the things of earth in which Being resides: which is to say that he can have a world only as he manages in some manner to be a "poet."

But, of course, though our human situation requires us to dwell poetically on the earth, in the ordinary, day-to-day transactions of life, we become creatures of routinized modes of thought and feeling that permit only just so much attentiveness to reality as is requisite for the immediate fulfillment of our practical purposes. We hasten to and fro in the world, from day to day, from one occasion to another, hearing only so much of this and seeing only so much of that as the urgencies of our common affairs allow. "Just as meat to the dog is something to be eaten, and the cat simply something to be chased, so the chair to a tired man or an executive is simply something to be sat on; and to the thirsty man water, however lovely its flow or sparkle, simply something to be drunk."[15] So it is, ordinarily, throughout the whole gamut of our living: the environing world in which we are set is rarely perceived as anything primitively arresting or marvelous: things are merely cues for action or signals of desire—the bare minimum of all that would be there, were we to take the trouble of paying

14. See the essay on "Hölderlin and the Essence of Poetry" in *Erläuterungen zu Hölderlins Dichtung;* also in *Existence and Being*, pp. 293–315.
15. Irwin Edman, *Arts and the Man* (New York, W. W. Norton, 1939), p. 16.

heed. Thus our "experience is full of dead spots,"[16] everything, as it were, incidental and pragmatic, gross and philistine.

This impoverishment that is normally a part of ordinary experience is, however, in Heidegger's sense of things, very greatly deepened in a technological culture such as our own, where inorganic nature becomes merely an affair of pointer-readings and human biology itself becomes the experimental material of a casually deliberate medical science, and where a great screen is thrown up—by all our gadgets and artifacts—between man and the primitive realities of the earth. It is in such a climate that human life begins to descend into a most radical "godlessness."

Recurrently in his writings of the last thirty years, but most especially in the essays on Hölderlin, Heidegger has spoken in a curiously veiled and gnomic way about "the gods." He says, for example, that we dwell in a period between that in which the gods "fled" and that in which they will return, and he seems to regard it as one of the chief signs of the authentic poet that he should have a very profound sense of this present time as a time betwixt and between. Indeed, he defines the poet as "one who has been cast out . . . into [this] . . . Between, between gods and men."[17] He speaks of the poet as one who consents to take his stand in the presence of the gods and who names the gods. Similarly cryptic references to gods appear in various other contexts. But, ambiguously as the term behaves in the logic of Heidegger's thought, its effect has been sufficiently tantalizing to lead some of his theological interpreters apparently to assume that it is merely a somewhat eccentric locution carrying, at bottom, a traditionally monotheistic meaning.[18] Yet so to construe the import of his testimony is, I believe, to misconstrue it; for, despite the short shrift he gives any sort of conventional atheism and despite the deeply religious tenor of his entire work, his basic intentions are not those of Christian apologetics, as he has himself been at pains to remind us on more than one occasion. So it is surely an illicit maneuver to singularize Heidegger's "gods" and then to interpret what he says about their "return" as simply his figurative way of anticipating the coming end of Nietzschean nihilism, when the God of traditional Christian experience will no longer be absent and will once again return in power and glory.

But if the term "gods" is not translatable as God, how, then, is it to be understood within the framework of Heidegger's thought? The issue is not to be easily resolved, for the term does, of course, function figuratively and may not, therefore, be fully reducible at all to any definition of a univocal sort. But I would hazard the proposal that the basic consisten-

16. Ibid., p. 18.
17. "Hölderlin and the Essence of Poetry," Existence and Being, p. 312.
18. See, for example, two essays of Stanley Hopper's—"On the Naming of the Gods in Hölderlin and Rilke," Christianity and the Existentialists, ed. Carl Michalson (New York, Charles Scibner's Sons, 1956), pp. 148–90; and his Introduction, Interpretation: The Poetry of Meaning, ed. by Stanley Romaine Hopper and David L. Miller (New York, Harcourt, Brace and World, 1967), pp. ix-xxii.

cies of his vision are least violated when, by "gods," Heidegger is taken to mean whatever it is that holds the world together and "assembles" it into a stable unity. By "god" we may assume, I think, that he means that ultimate *power* of Being which permits things to sojourn on the earth and which guarantees to reality the character of permanence and stability and trustworthiness.[19] And his affirming it to be a part of the poet's office to *name* the gods is but his oblique manner of reasserting the radically cognitive way in which the literary experience thrusts outward, beyond itself, toward those realities that, in the most basic way, encompass the human enterprise.

So "godlessness" in Heidegger's lexicon is not properly equated with something like Nietzsche's "death of God"; it speaks, rather, of that profound inattentiveness to the essential fabric and texture of the things of earth which becomes epidemic in a technological culture, where everything that faces man is approached with an intention simply to control and manipulate and where, as a consequence, nothing is seen or experienced in the dimension of Holiness. The Holy (*das Heilige*) makes its way into Heidegger's thought through his meditation on that untitled poem of Hölderlin's which begins "Wie wenn am Feiertage . . ."—"As when on a holiday . . ."[20] He takes it to be a term required of Hölderlin himself by his fidelity to the sheer presence of Being in the finite realities of the earth. And this is precisely what Holiness means for Heidegger: it is that power and form wherewith a thing is what it is—whose penumbra of mystery naturally evokes an attitude of awe and astonishment.

Martin Buber reminds us that we may consider a tree as though it were merely a stiff column against a background of delicate blue and silver in a picture; or we can perceive it as an affair of vital movement, in its "ceaseless commerce with earth and air"; or we may simply regard a given tree, in its formation and structure, as an instance of a species; or we may "subdue its actual presence and form so sternly" as to recognize it only as an expression of certain laws governing the ways in which "the component substances mingle and separate"; or, again, the particular tree may be so subsumed under a given type that it is thought of only as belonging to some scheme of numerical relations. But, then, as he also reminds us, we may be so seized by "the power of exclusiveness" in the given tree that we find "everything, picture and movement, species and type, law and number, indivisibly united"[21] in the one tree that confronts the eye. Hei-

19. In his book *Earth and Gods: An Introduction to the Philosophy of Martin Heidegger* (The Hague, Martinus Nijhoff, 1961), Vincent Vycinas' interpretation of Heidegger's notion of "gods" soars off on a highly speculative flight (see chap. 5), and I remain unconvinced of its cogency or even that much of it has any clear relevance at all to what is actually being said in the Heideggerian texts. Nevertheless, my own "demythologization" has been influenced to some extent by his exegesis.
20. See *Erläuterungen zu Hölderlins Dichtung*, pp. 47–74.
21. Martin Buber, *I and Thou*, trans. Ronald Gregor Smith (Edinburgh, T. & T. Clark, 1937), p. 7.

degger would say, I think, that what, in this case, we are seized by is nothing other than the *presence of this* tree; it is simply that most primitive of all realities that we are claimed by—namely, the power of Being itself. And if we can manage not to regard the land on which the tree stands as merely a piece of real estate, to be cleared perhaps for a suburban housing development; if we can manage not to regard the tree as merely a piece of timber to be cut down and converted to some useful purpose; if we can manage so to subdue *the will to will* as to confront this tree in an attitude of "letting-be," so that we can really be laid hold of by the sheer presence of Being in the tree, then, Heidegger would say, we shall find that what indeed we are most essentially seized by is that which is Holy in the tree—for the Holy, he declares, is simply the "advent" (*Kommen*) of Being itself.

When man becomes so enrapt in the spirit of modern technological enterprise that he loses any capacity for reverential awe before the radical holiness of Creation, then human life begins to descend into the Profane. As the whole drift of the modern period reveals, it is possible for a culture to become so fixed in its lust for winning mastery of the things of earth that all appetite is lost for what Wordsworth in Book II of *The Prelude* calls "the sentiment of Being." That is to say, we can become so mesmerized by our own human purposes and so committed to an essentially manipulative and predatory attitude towards the world that we defraud ourselves of any capacity to marvel at the generosity with which things are steadied and supported by the power and presence of Being. To whatever extent, however, a man fails to be attentive to what Gerard Manley Hopkins called that "pitch of self" which distinguishes each bird, each tree, each flowing stream, each bit of Creation, then he is, of course, to that extent by way of losing any full sense of that pitch of self which distinguishes his own reality—as Hopkins put it, "that taste of myself, of *I* and *me* above and in all things, which is more distinctive than the taste of ale or alum, more distinctive than the smell of walnutleaf or camphor."[22] When there is no longer any sense of grandeur in the "shining from shook foil," or of splendor in "the ooze of oil/Crushed," when there is no longer any lively sense of "the dearest freshness deep down things,"[23] then a great descent has begun—into that deprived condition that Martin Heidegger would nominate as "godlessness."

In such a time—of dearth, of inanition, of godlessness—Heidegger believes that the vocation of the poet inevitably becomes something pastoral and priestly. It is most especially the mission of the poet to be a

22. *The Note-Books and Papers of Gerard Manley Hopkins,* ed. Humphry House (London and New York, Oxford University Press, 1937), p. 309.
23. Gerard Manley Hopkins, "God's Grandeur," *Poems of Gerard Manley Hopkins,* ed. Robert Bridges (London and New York, Oxford University Press, 1938), p. 26.

watchman (*Wächter*) or shepherd (*Hirt*) of Being, as it emerges in the things of earth.[24] And his meditations on the poems of Hölderlin that speak of the poet as a wanderer journeying homeward[25]— *"Heimkunft-/An die Verwandten"* ("Homecoming/To the Kinsmen") and *"An-denken"* ("Remembrance")—lead him to conclude that, when "forgetfulness" of Being has become the primary apostasy, then the poet must undertake to initiate in us a process of "remembrance" and to lead us homeward, back into "proximity to the Source"[26]

In the logic of Heidegger's metaphor, the process whereby the imagination recovers "the sentiment of Being" entails a "journey" because Being is "distant" and far away (*fern*).[27] It is far away simply because it is never to be encountered nakedly and in itself, but only in and through the things of earth which it supports and whose presence it establishes; which is to say, in the language of traditional philosophy, that Being is a transcendental, a reality which the imagination moves toward only by moving through the contingent and finite realities of immediate experience. Though Being is in this way "withdrawn," it is yet, paradoxically, also "near," since its presence in the things of our immediate experience is precisely that which enables them to *be*, and thus to be *near*. Hence it is, as Heidegger sees it, that, in a time of dearth the renewal of the life of the imagination can be conceived to involve a kind of journey. The journey is back to the "Source" (*Ursprung*), since that is what Being is; and to return into proximity to the Source is to be once again "at home," since Being is nothing other than the original and proper domain of the human spirit. And since to be brought back into the neighborhood of Being is to have been put in mind again of that which had been forgotten, the journey homewards is also conceived to be a process of remembrance or recollection.

In the contemporary world of Anglo-American poetics, given its empiricist sobriety and its impatience with any sort of Longinian aesthetic of elevation and transport, the whole tenor of Heidegger's reflections may seem excessively inflated and hyperbolic. But always, I think, he does in fact have in view the concrete actuality of *poiesis,* and everything that he has to say about the poet's openness to the Holy, about his "naming the gods" and his bringing us homeward to the Source is but his way of asserting that the poet supervises language with such cogency and adroit-

---

24. Though Heidegger's famous metaphor about the "shepherding" of Being is adumbrated at many points in his writings, its central locus is in the *Über den Humanismus* (*Letter on Humanism,* pp. 75, 90) —where he says, "Man is the shepherd of Being" (*"Der Mensch ist der Hirt des Seins."*). Though *man* is here said to bear this office, the *Letter on Humanism* implies that it is a vocation whose ideal exemplifications are to be seen most clearly in two special types of man—in "the thinker" (*der Denker*) and "the poet" (*der Dichter*).
25. *Erläuterungen zu Hölderlins Dichtung,* pp. 9–30, and pp. 75–143.
26. Ibid., p. 23.
27. Ibid., p. 138.

ness that we find ourselves being thrust onto new levels of heightened perception, where we no longer simply take for granted the common things of earth and where, performing again an act of genuine attention before the world that confronts us, we recover what is perhaps the most primitive of all sensations—the sense of astonishment that there is something rather than nothing, thus experiencing the "shock of Being."[28]

In his brilliant little book of thirty years ago, *Arts and the Man,* the late Irwin Edman recalls a story of Stephen Crane's about three shipwrecked men adrift in a small boat on an agitated sea. The opening sentence of the story, he reminds us, is, "They did not see the color of the sky." "So intent were they upon the possibilities of being saved that they had no time, interest, or impulse for seeing the color of the sky above them."[29] But what Heidegger wants to assert is that the whole job of the poet—in his office as priest—is so to intensify our awareness, our vision, of the concrete realities surrounding us that, instead of moving constantly "among the abstract possibilities of action,"[30] human sensibility may be reinstated into a kind of pure alertness to (as I spoke of it earlier) the sheer ontological weight and depth of the world. "I require of you only to look," says St. Theresa—and it is, says Heidegger, by making us gaze, by making us look, at the things of earth that the artist disarms us of that penchant for manipulation and use characteristic of the predatory spirit in which we normally approach the world; he invites us instead to approach it in the spirit of *letting-be,* to offer a kind of *Amen* to the various finite realities that make up the earth, since, in so far as they are truly present to us, their presence is seen to be consequent upon their being rooted in the creative Ground of Being itself. Using a phrase that John Crowe Ransom once bestowed upon a collection of his essays, we might say that Heidegger's testimony—and in this he surely adumbrates, in his own quite special way, a perennial axiom—is simply that it is the function of literary art to enliven and deepen our cognizance of "the world's body,"[31] to the point of enabling it to become for us a "glass of vision."[32] This, as he maintains, is what it is uniquely within the power of the literary imagination to confer upon us in a time of dearth.

Then, there is a final emphasis which deserves to be thought of as also a part of Heidegger's theory of literature, though, in his own writings, it actually figures not so much as a part of his account of *poiesis* as it does

---

28. The phrase derives from similar phrases of Paul Tillich's—"ontological shock" and "metaphysical shock"; see his *Systematic Theology, 1* (Chicago, University of Chicago Press, 1951), pp. 113, 163, 186. Tillich's concept of the "ontological shock" is, however, but one of many other usages in his work attesting to the probability of his having been far more profoundly influenced by Heidegger than he ever acknowledged or than his interpreters have thus far discerned.
29. Irwin Edman, p. 27.
30. Ibid., p. 29.
31. See John Crowe Ransom, *The World's Body* (New York, Charles Scribner's Sons, 1938).
32. See Austin Farrer, *The Glass of Vision* (Westminster, Dacre Press, 1948).

as a part of his account of the drama of *thought.* What is here in view is the duality in Heidegger's thought between the two great roles that are enacted in the adventure of man's encounter with Being—the role of the poet (*der Dichter*) and the role of the thinker (*der Denker*). That is to say, the path into Being may be by way either of poetic art or of systematic thought. But Heidegger's whole style of reflection tends so much, in effect, to convert the philosophic enterprise itself (*pace* contemporary positivism) into a kind of poetry that it is extremely difficult, therefore, to identify clearly the precise difference being drawn between poet and thinker. Presumably, of course, the task of the thinker *qua* thinker is to win as large a competence as possible in supervising the procedures of discursive reason and dialectical argument; whereas the task of the poet *qua* poet is that of winning the greatest possible precision and resourcefulness in those ways of metaphor and analogy that are most distinctively native to the creative imagination. But, like the poet, the thinker, too, does not possess any legislative prerogatives in regard to primal reality. Systematic thought is bound to be something crippled and misshapen unless it originates in a "willingness . . . to be the enemy of nothing that is,—actual or possible, contingent or necessary, animate or inanimate, natural, human, or divine."[33] In the presence of Being, the attitude of both the poet and the thinker needs to be that of docility and submissiveness, for that very presence is itself a gift. Unless it is patiently hearkened to, in a spirit of acquiescence and gratitude, there can be no good result for either poetry or thought; for vision, whether poetic or metaphysical, requires that there be something to be seen—and something which we consent to be reached by, which we consent to accept as a gift.[34]

At whatever point Heidegger launches into an analysis of the nature of thought—whether in the essay *On the Essence of Truth*[35] (*Vom Wesen der Wahrheit*) or the Postscript to the essay *What is Metaphysics?*[36] (*Was ist Metaphysik?*) or the book of 1954, *Was heisst Denken*[37] (*What Evokes Thought*)—he is to be found stressing the impertinence of any attempt on the part of the thinker to seize reality by direct assault, since, before the thinker can even begin to undertake his various labors, he must wait for the advent of Being, for the advent of the Holy. Though this theme figures most immediately in Heidegger's meditations on the nature of the philosophic enterprise, it is yet so integral to the whole body of his thought, and the line of demarcation between poet and thinker is everywhere so lightly drawn in his work that we may, therefore, consider all that he has to say

33. Robert Jordan, "Poetry and Philosophy: Two Modes of Revelation," *Sewanee Review, 67,* no. 1 (January–March, 1959), p. 13.
34. Ibid.
35. Trans. R. F. C. Hull and Alan Crick, *Existence and Being,* pp. 319–51.
36. Ibid., pp. 355–92.
37. Tübingen, Niemeyer.

in this connection as bearing just as immediately on his theory of poetry as on his theory of the philosophic act itself. Both the poet and the thinker, in other words, are adepts in the art of paying heed to Being, and both, therefore, teach us something about what is involved in the discipline of waiting.

It is in the book of 1957, *Der Satz vom Grund*[38] (*The Principle of Ground*) and the book of 1959, *Gelassenheit* (recently translated into English under the title *Discourse on Thinking*), that Heidegger presents some of his most suggestive statements on this issue. Since everything that he says here about the thinker as one who waits pertains equally as much to his understanding of the poet, the appropriate transposition is to be made, as though it had been explicitly made by Heidegger himself.

The basic presupposition of the little book of 1959 is—as it is said by the Teacher in his conversation with the Scholar and the Scientist—that "We are to do nothing but wait."[39] And nothing else is to be done, since, in all our transactions with the world, what comes *to* us is not a *re*-presentation of something which has already emerged out of ourselves; indeed, to suppose the contrary to be the case is to have submitted all over again to the old wrongheadedness of attempting to "humanize" reality. The basic ontological situation is simply that of man-in-the-neighborhood-of-Being, and, since Being is not a human property at man's disposal, there is nothing to be done but to await its coming-to-presence. And it is just here that we may identify the nature of the discipline which the poet enjoins upon us; for it is a great part of his distinctive office to teach us how to wait, to teach us how to approach the environing reality of the world in a spirit of meditative openness—in the spirit of *Gelassenheit,* of surrender, of abandonment to the influxions of Being. The poet—that is, the artist in words, whether in verse or drama or prose fiction—so deploys his sounds and images and dramatic situations that we are compelled to recognize how gross and inadequate are the various concepts and counters with which we customarily order and interpret experience, and how reductive and distorting they often are of our actual life-world. Thus, in effect, he invites us, as we approach the world, to hold these concepts and counters in a state of suspension, to "leave open what we are waiting for,"[40] in order that our waiting may release itself into the openness of Being without violating that openness. This is indeed, for Heidegger, the true meaning of *Gelassenheit;* it consists in nothing other than our consenting to let things be and to dwell on the earth without restlessly searching all the time for ways of domesticating reality within a framework of human design and purpose.

38. Pfullingen, Neske.
39. *Discourse on Thinking,* p. 62.
40. Ibid., p. 68.

Gelassenheit, in other words, is simply openness to the Mystery of Being. It is hinted in *Der Satz vom Grund* that, when *the will to will* in a man has been thus quietened and subdued, he may be found to be like that rose which is spoken of by the German mystical poet of the seventeenth century, Johannes Scheffler. Scheffler, generally known as Angelus Silesius (the name he gave himself after his conversion to the Roman Catholic Church), in one of the poems in his book *The Cherubinic Wanderer* (*Der Cherubinische Wandersmann*) declares:

> The rose is without why; it blooms because it blooms,
> It cares not for itself, asks not if it is seen.

This saying has very greatly fascinated Heidegger. For a rose that does not fret about the enabling conditions of its existence, that is not constantly attacking the world and seeking to contain it within some scheme of concepts and categories, that simply blooms because it blooms, being quite content to be "without why"—such a rose, in its undemanding openness to the Mystery, to the Ground of Being, becomes for Heidegger a kind of sign, an emblem of what man himself is like when he is most truly human. Because—like the rose, he, too, if he is to be *gelassen* before the spectacle of the world and thus genuinely open to the influx of Being, must learn to bloom simply for the sake of blooming, must learn to live without "care," without predatoriness, without anxiety, "without why." Which is to say that he must learn how to wait, and even how to wait without needing to know precisely what it is he waits for; since, if we are to "abandon ourselves to the game"[41] of existence, we must make up our minds to the fact that there is no way of aprioristically charting and conceptualizing the miracle of Being. "We are to do nothing but wait." And this is the great lesson that we are taught by poetry.

So, in a way, we are brought back now to the scene that was being scanned in the previous chapter. Which is not, of course, to say, in the conceit that was there being employed, that Heidegger's is a position outside both Antioch and Alexandria. But what deserves to be remarked is that it is often to be found that such a position is that of many of the writers today who express in the most interesting ways a major strain of contemporary sensibility. What ought perhaps primarily to concern us is not so much the logic or illogic of that position itself but, rather, what it would appear most basically to be prompted by—namely, the conviction that the burdened and perplexed people of our age are best served by being invited, in a time of dearth, to be patient—and to wait.

41. *Der Satz vom Grund*, p. 188.

Indeed, in many of the most representative plays and poems and novels of the immediate present, it is just at the point at which, apparently, a certain testimony is being tacitly made about waiting as the indispensable discipline to be undertaken by the human spirit in this late, bad time it is just at this point that Martin Heidegger may be conceived to be the great philosophic master of the literary imagination in our period. And to remark his presence as that which looms massively behind much of contemporary literature is already perhaps to have a way of identifying what is most deeply problematic in that literature; for it is, I believe, precisely the large unanswered question raised by the craggy magnificence of Heidegger's vision that points toward what remains in doubt in the account being given now of our human estate by those artists whose work, in its relation to the soulscape of the age, seems most emphatically to be marked by "the tone of the center."

In the case of Heidegger, it is, I think we may say, the large element of gratuitousness in his piety that makes it something problematic. Surely it is a mode of piety that is chiefly expressed by the kind of meditation he has sustained over the last forty years. For here, in one who is perhaps the last great seer of modern philosophy, what seems most notable is the immense sensitivity of ecological conscience which prompts this thinker to regard the whole of reality as sacramental, in the sense that the true identity of everything that exists is considered to reside in its way of showing forth the Mystery of Being. Everything is, therefore, instinct with holiness; so the man who has a proper awareness of the sacramental character of the things of earth does not attack them as if it were their final destiny simply to be dominated and raped by him. And he does not deal imperialistically with the world's resources, since he knows something like what Dylan Thomas says to be the case, that

> The force that through the green fuse drives the flower
> Drives my green age.
>
> . . . . .
>
> The force that drives the water through the rocks
> Drives my red blood.[42]

To move down, in other words, into the deep inwardness of things is to know that they are not just so many dead appurtenances of the human enterprise but that they are, rather, awakened into reality by a presence —the presence of Being itself. Thus the things of earth are to be approached in a spirit of homage, not aggressively or exploitatively but

42. *The Collected Poems of Dylan Thomas* (New York, New Directions, 1953), p. 10.

reverently, since it is in them and through them that the advent of Being becomes manifest—to him who waits.

This is a style of imagination that unquestionably bespeaks a very profound kind of piety toward all the wondrous works of Creation—toward the outgoings of the morning and evening, toward the north and the south, toward the lion and the adder and the children of men, toward all the round world and they that dwell therein; for, in all this, if we consent patiently and reverently to wait, the advent of Being may be descried. Yet in the Heideggerian *pietas* there is unavoidably to be felt something gratuitous, since the docile reverence with which we are invited to await this advent could only be "proved" by some persuasive testimony that, when this advent comes it will be found to bring an annunciation of something genuinely gracious—and, in behalf of such a possibility, Heidegger never submits any case.

If we undertake then to define what is ultimately problematic in Heidegger's whole vision, it must be said to be the large ambiguity that we are confronted by, when we find unanswered the question as to what it is in the character of Being that invites us, patiently and reverently (in Heidegger's sense of things), to await its advent. In this connection, it will be remembered with what stringency the late Albert Camus, in *Le Mythe de Sisyphe*, reproached those thinkers (like as he felt, Kierkegaard and Chestov and Jaspers) who "leap" into metaphysical affirmativeness. And one suspects that, had he ever looked closely at the later Heidegger, this "poet" of Being would not altogether have escaped his severity, for Heidegger, too, is an athlete—who takes a great leap.

In suggesting that Martin Heidegger may be regarded as the philosophic master of that whole tendency in contemporary literature which is being reviewed in the previous chapter, I am not, of course, intending to imply that the specific themes of his thought have somehow made their way into the poetry and fiction and drama that most fully exemplify the period-style of the present time; for it is not at all such a relationship that he bears to this literature. What I would rather remark is that—whether one turns to the novels of Alain Robbe-Grillet and John Hawkes, or to the theatre of Beckett and Pinter, or to the poetry of Charles Olson and John Ashberry—our literature today, in its way of handling the human reality, seems often disinclined to accept the kind of large reconstructive effort so characteristic of traditionalist modernism. *Dans le Labyrinthe, The Crying of Lot 49, Krapp's Last Tape, Naked Lunch,* and *Les Nègres* belong to a new tradition deeply informed by a sense of the world as so radically contingent and indeterminate as to prevent the artist's doing anything other than simply offering an illustration of the chaos. It is a tradition that wants to forswear the old *profondeurs;* and thus it is a tradition that has tended to sponsor a kind of ethos in which the artist becomes a specialist in Hunger-Art, an adept in the art of doing without—of waiting (as the language of Eliot's "East Coker" puts it) "without hope," since any kind of hope at all would be hope for that for which the human experience offers no sanction in an age which is, as Heidegger says, "the No-more of the gods that have fled and the Not-yet of the god that is coming."

Such a waiting differs, to be sure, from Heidegger's, for his—given the vision of Being, the expectation of its advent—is a waiting attached to a very great hopefulness. Yet whether one waits, as in the case of Heidegger, with reverence and in hope, or whether, as in the case of the Beckett of *Fin de Partie*, one simply waits, it would seem that the logic of the case requires some antecedent assurance that that for which one waits will not be found in any way to be essentially spendthrift of the human spirit itself, an assurance that it is indeed in some sense really gracious, that it is worth waiting for. Yet the kind of waiting frequently connoted by the testimony of our new literature not only seems generally to lack the empowerment that such an assurance might provide but also seems often to lack even any real specificity of intent or clear destination. It is, in other words, a waiting unprepared to give any cogent account of itself, and thus, in its gratuitous-ness, we may feel Martin Heidegger to be its great philosophic scholiast.

It is to be remembered, however, that this question as to what it means to wait has evoked still another body of contemporary testimony which is marked by that same austere religious grandeur so notably char-acteristic of Heidegger's meditations. It is indeed precisely "the ontology of the not yet" which constitutes the central issue of the massive and brilliant work of the distinguished East German Marxist philosopher Ernst Bloch, now living as an exile in West Germany. And I should not fail immediately to remark that my own misgivings about what is gratuitous in the kind of waiting enjoined today by the literary imagination would, in all likelihood, be responded to in an adverse way by Ernst Bloch, who would very probably assert that, in asking this waiting to clarify itself through some validating account of that for which it waits, I am in effect supposing that "confidence" is a necessary prerequisite for waiting. But, as he would doubtless argue, if one faces the future with confidence, then the future must itself be something already established and finished—in which case there can no longer be anything for which to wait.

In his great book of 1959, *Das Prinzip Hoffnung*, Bloch talks not about waiting but about hope, about that "infatuation with the possible" which he takes to be the basic principle of human existence and the fundamental theme for philosophic meditation. Man is indeed, in Bloch's anthropology, conceived to be a creature of hope, for he dwells intersti-tially—between what is and what is not yet, in the dimension of "not-yet-being" (*Noch-Nicht-Sein*). It is, in fact, just man's ineluctable orientation towards the future that leads Bloch, for all of his devotion to Feuerbach and Engels and Marx, very radically to revise the traditional Marxist critique of religion. He is himself, of course, an atheist who rejects any and every version of a substantialist metaphysical theism, with its vision of He-Who-Is; so it is not the *Deus absconditus,* it is not God, who lies ahead, and Bloch—unlike some of his theological disciples (say, the Germans Jürgen Moltmann and Wolfhart Pannenberg, or the American Harvey Cox)—does not want in any way theistically to conceive the idea of futurity; what lies ahead, indeed, is not the *Deus absconditus* but the *homo absconditus.* Nevertheless, he considers the real root of distinctively religious passion to be the longing for fulfillment, for "not-yet-being"— which leads, in St. Paul's phraseology, to "forgetting those things which are behind, and reaching forth unto those things which are before" (Philippians 3:13). However chimerical may be the anthropomorphic imagery whereby traditional theism objectifies the "things which are before," Bloch refuses to take the conventional Marxist line, that religion is simply a form of cultural pathology. In his hermeneutic, religion is hope—and hope originates in man's incorrigible fascination with the gap between what is and what is yet to be. So his is an "esoteric Marxism" which points toward "meta-religion."

Though Bloch's atheism is consistent and unremitting, his Principle of Hope, it is clear, does not refer to any particular finite projects or goals; it looks, rather, simply toward the "open space" of absolute futurity itself, towards that vacuum of "not-yet-being" which transcends all finite objectives, towards the unplumbable depths of *Noch-Nicht-Sein.* Yet, if it be suggested that steadily facing the openness of absolute futurity requires such an empowerment of the human spirit as can only be provided by the assurance that the future will itself be found in some way to be truly gracious—if it be suggested that waiting must, in the nature of the case, be grounded in faith, Bloch's immediate reply will be that hope is not "superstitious confidence."[43] Or, if it be asked what, then, it is that beckons the imagination out of the present and into the future, what it is that elicits hope, his answer will, in effect, be that hope posits itself and is grounded in nothing at all resembling a *promissio Dei,* but simply in the boundless possibility represented by man's historical future. So, on this reckoning, it would seem that it would in fact be precisely the gratuitousness of that waiting which figures so much in the literary ethos of our period that authenticates the spirituality it expresses.

We are here, then, in a strange land indeed where the imagination appears—like the heroine of Gabriel Marcel's play *Le Monde cassé*—to be listening "into the void." But, as Lao Tzu reminds us, it is precisely the hole in the middle—"the space where there is nothing"—that makes the

43. Ernst Bloch, *Das Prinzip Hoffnung* (Frankfurt am Main, Suhrkamp, 1959), p. 1523.

wheel.[44] And however gratuitous may seem a hearkening which is only to "the void," it may be that persistence in this mode of spirituality is, in our period, perhaps most especially for the artists of the word, the form which it is natural for the writer's fidelity to take—his fidelity, that is, to the uncreated Rock of reality. His business after all, as the English critic Frank Kermode has so finely said, "is not merly to satisfy the lovers of truth, but to make brilliant the poverty on which their thoughts dwell."[45] And in a time when to believe at all is, in Wallace Stevens' phrase, "to believe beyond belief," the poem will be

> the cry of its occasion,
> Part of the res itself and not about it.[46]

There is no way of guaranteeing, of course, that moving into the hole in the middle may prove to be a way of moving towards the wheel's periphery, but hoping that this may prove to be the case is, I believe, the central challenge presented to us by the literature of our time. For it is requiring us to explore anew, and deeply, the mystery of our privation and need—what Stevens called the mystery of "poverty."

44. Chap. 11 of *Tao Tê Ching*, trans. Arthur Waley in his *The Way and Its Power: A Study of the Tao Tê Ching and Its Place in Chinese Thought* (London, Allen and Unwin, 1934), p. 155.
45. Frank Kermode, *Wallace Stevens* (Edinburgh, Oliver & Boyd, 1960), p. 127.
46. Wallace Stevens, "An Ordinary Evening in New Haven," *Collected Poems* (New York: Alfred A. Knopf), p. 473.

Philosophical
and
Theological
Backgrounds

Blaise Pascal
from *Pensées*

[72]

Man's disproportion. (This is where our innate knowledge leads us. If it be not true, there is no truth in man; and if it be true, he finds therein great cause for humiliation, being compelled to abase himself in one way or another. And since he cannot exist without this knowledge, I wish that, before entering on deeper researches into nature, he would consider her both seriously and at leisure, that he would reflect upon himself also, and knowing what proportion there is . . .) Let man then contemplate the whole of nature in her full and grand majesty, and turn his vision from the low objects which surround him. Let him gaze on that brilliant light, set like an eternal lamp to illumine the universe; let the earth appear to him a point in comparison with the vast circle described by the sun; and let him wonder at the fact that this vast circle is itself but a very fine point in comparison with that described by the stars in their revolution round the firmament. But if our view be arrested there, let our imagination pass beyond; it will sooner exhaust the power of conception than nature that of supplying material for conception. The whole visible world is only an imperceptible atom in the ample bosom of nature. No idea approaches it. We may enlarge our conceptions beyond all imaginable space; we only produce atoms in comparison with the reality of things. It is an infinite sphere, the center of which is everywhere, the circumference nowhere. In short it is the greatest sensible mark of the almighty power of God, that imagination loses itself in that thought.

Returning to himself, let man consider what he is in comparison with all existence; let him regard himself as lost in this remote corner of nature; and from the little cell in which he finds himself lodged, I mean the universe, let him estimate at their true value the earth, kingdoms, cities, and himself. What is a man in the Infinite?

But to show him another prodigy equally astonishing, let him examine the most delicate things he knows. Let a mite be given him, with its minute body and parts incomparably more minute, limbs with their joints, veins in the limbs, blood in the veins, humors in the blood, drops in the

Source: From *Pensées* by Blaise Pascal, translated by W. F. Trotter. Dutton paperback edition published 1958. Reprinted by permission of the publishers, E. P. Dutton & Co., Inc., and of J. M. Dent & Sons Ltd.

humors, vapors in the drops. Dividing these last things again, let him exhaust his powers of conception, and let the last object at which he can arrive be now that of our discourse. Perhaps he will think that here is the smallest point in nature. I will let him see therein a new abyss. I will paint for him not only the visible universe, but all that he can conceive of nature's immensity in the womb of this abridged atom. Let him see therein an infinity of universes, each of which has its firmament, its planets, its earth, in the same proportion as in the visible world; in each earth animals, and in the last mites, in which he will find again all that the first had, finding still in these others the same thing without end and without cessation. Let him lose himself in wonders as amazing in their littleness as the others in their vastness. For who will not be astounded at the fact that our body, which a little while ago was imperceptible in the universe, itself imperceptible in the bosom of the whole, is now a colossus, a world, or rather a whole, in respect to the nothingness which we cannot reach? He who regards himself in this light will be afraid of himself, and observing himself sustained in the body given him by nature between those two abysses of the Infinite and Nothing, will tremble at the sight of these marvels; and I think that, as his curiosity changes into admiration, he will be more disposed to contemplate them in silence than to examine them with presumption.

For in fact what is man in nature? A Nothing in comparison with the Infinite, an All in comparison with the Nothing, a mean between nothing and everything. Since he is infinitely removed from comprehending the extremes, the end of things and their beginning are hopelessly hidden from him in an impenetrable secret; he is equally incapable of seeing the Nothing from which he was made, and the Infinite in which he is swallowed up.

What will he do then, but perceive the appearance of the middle of things, in an eternal despair of knowing either their beginning or their end. All things proceed from the Nothing, and are borne toward the Infinite. Who will follow these marvelous processes? The Author of these wonders understands them. None other can do so.

Through failure to contemplate these Infinites, men have rashly rushed into the examination of nature, as though they bore some proportion to her. It is strange that they have wished to understand the beginnings of things, and thence to arrive at the knowledge of the whole, with a presumption as infinite as their object. For surely this design cannot be formed without presumption or without a capacity infinite like nature.

If we are well informed, we understand that, as nature has graven her image and that of her Author on all things, they almost all partake of her double infinity. Thus we see that all the sciences are infinite in the extent of their researches. For who doubts that geometry, for instance, has an infinite infinity of problems to solve? They are also infinite in the multitude and fineness of their premises; for it is clear that those which are put forward as ultimate are not self-supporting, but are based on others which, again having others for their support, do not permit finality. But we represent some as ultimate for reason, in the same way as in regard to material objects we call that an indivisible point beyond which our senses can no longer perceive anything, although by its nature it is infinitely divisible.

Of these two Infinites, of course, that of greatness is the more palpable, and hence a few persons have pretended to know all things. "I will speak of the whole," said Democratus.

But the infinitely little is the least obvious. Philosophers have much oftener claimed to have reached it, and it is here they have all stumbled. This has given rise to such common titles as *First Principles, Principles of Philosophy,* and the like, as ostentatious in fact, though not in appearance, as that one which blinds us, *De omni scibili.*

We naturally believe ourselves far more capable of reaching the center of things than of embracing their circumference. The visible extent of the world visibly exceeds us; but as we exceed little things, we think ourselves more capable of knowing them. And yet we need no less capacity for attaining the Nothing than the All. Infinite capacity is required for both, and it seems to me that whoever shall have understood the ultimate principles of being might also attain to the knowledge of the Infinite. The one depends on the other, and one leads to the other. These extremes meet and reunite by force of distance, and find each other in God, and in God alone.

Let us then take our compass; we are something, and we are not everything. The nature of our existence hides from us the knowledge of first beginnings which are born of the Nothing; and the littleness of our being conceals from us the sight of the Infinite.

Our intellect holds the same position in the world of thought as our body occupies in the expanse of nature.

Limited as we are in every way, this state which holds the means between two extremes is present in all our impotence. Our senses perceive no extreme. Too much sound deafens us; too much light dazzles us; too great distance or proximity hinders our view. Too great length and too great brevity of discourse tend to obscurity; too much truth is paralyzing (I know some who cannot understand that to take four from nothing leaves nothing). First principles are too self-evident for us; too much pleasure disagrees with us. Too many concords are annoying in music; too many benefits irritate us; we wish to have the wherewithal to over-pay our debts. *Beneficia eo usque læta sunt dum videntur exsolvi posse; ubi multum antevenere, pro gratia odium redditur.* We feel neither extreme heat nor extreme cold. Excessive qualities are prejudicial to us and not perceptible by the senses; we do not feel but suffer them. Extreme youth and extreme age hinder the mind, as also too much and too little education. In short, extremes are for us as though they were not, and we are not within their notice. They escape us, or we them.

This is our true state; this is what makes us incapable of certain knowledge and of absolute ignorance. We sail within a vast sphere, ever drifting in uncertainty, driven from end to end. When we think to attach ourselves to any point and to fasten to it, it wavers and leaves us; and if we follow it, it eludes our grasp, slips past us, and vanishes forever. Nothing stays for us. This is our natural condition, and yet most contrary to our inclination; we burn with desire to find solid ground and an ultimate sure foundation whereon to build a tower reaching to the Infinite. But our whole groundwork cracks, and the earth opens to abysses.

Let us therefore not look for certainty and stability. Our reason is always deceived by fickle shadows; nothing can fix the finite between the two Infinites, which both enclose and fly from it.

If this be well understood, I think that we shall remain at rest, each in the state wherein nature has placed him. As this sphere which has fallen to us as our lot is always distant from either extreme, what does it matter that man should have a little more knowledge of the universe? If he has it, he but gets a little higher. Is he not always infinitely removed from the end, and is not the duration of our life equally removed from eternity, even if it lasts ten years longer?

In comparison with these Infinites all finites are equal, and I see no reason for fixing our imagination on one more than on another. The only comparison which we make of ourselves to the finite is painful to us.

If man made himself the first object of study, he would see how incapable he is of going further. How can a part know the whole? But he may perhaps aspire to know at least the parts to which he bears some proportion. But the parts of the world are all so related and linked to one another, that I believe it impossible to know one without the other and without the whole.

Man, for instance, is related to all he knows. He needs a place wherein to abide, time through which to live, motion in order to live, elements to compose him, warmth and food to nourish him, air to breathe. He sees light; he feels bodies; in short, he is in a dependent alliance with everything. To know man, then, it is necessary to know how it happens that he needs air to live, and, to know the air, we must know how it is thus related to the life of man, etc. Flame cannot exist without air; therefore to understand the one, we must understand the other.

Since everything then is cause and effect, dependent and supporting, mediate and immediate, and all is held together by a natural though imperceptible chain, which binds together things most distant and most different, I hold it equally impossible to know the parts without knowing the whole, and to know the whole without knowing the parts in detail.

(The eternity of things in itself or in God must also astonish our brief duration. The fixed and constant immobility of nature, in comparison with the continual change which goes on within us, must have the same effect.)

And what completes our incapability of knowing things is the fact that they are simple, and that we are composed of two opposite natures, different in kind, soul, and body. For it is impossible that our rational part should be other than spiritual; and if anyone maintain that we are simply corporeal, this would far more exclude us from the knowledge of things, there being nothing so inconceivable as to say that matter knows itself. It is impossible to imagine how it should know itself.

So if we are simply material, we can know nothing at all; and if we are composed of mind and matter, we cannot know perfectly things which are simple, whether spiritual or corporeal. Hence it comes that almost all philosophers have confused ideas of things, and speak of material things in spiritual terms, and of spiritual things in material terms. For they say boldly that bodies have a tendency to fall, that they seek their center, that they fly from destruction, that they fear the void, that they have inclinations, sympathies, antipathies, all of which attributes pertain only to mind. And in speaking of minds, they consider them as in a place, and attribute to them movement from one place to another; and these are qualities which belong only to bodies.

Instead of receiving the ideas of these things in their purity, we color them with our own qualities, and stamp with our composite being all the simple things which we contemplate.

Who would not think, seeing us compose all things of mind and body, but that this mixture would be quite intelligible to us? Yet it is the very thing we least understand. Man is to himself the most wonderful object in nature; for he cannot conceive what the body is, still less what the mind is, and least of all how a body should be united to a mind. This is the consummation of his difficulties, and yet it in his very being. *Modus quo corporibus adhærent spiritus comprehendi ab hominibus non potest, et hoc tamen homo est.* Finally, to complete the proof of our weakness, I shall conclude with these two considerations. . . .

[127]

Condition of man: inconstancy, weariness, unrest.

[128]

The weariness which is felt by us in leaving pursuits to which we are attached. A man dwells at home with pleasure; but if he sees a woman who charms him, or if he enjoys himself in play for five or six days, he is miserable if he returns to his former way of living. Nothing is more common than that.

[129]

Our nature consists in motion; complete rest is death.

[168]

Diversion.   As men are not able to fight against death, misery, ignorance, they have taken it into their heads, in order to be happy, not to think of them at all.

[172]

We do not rest satisfied with the present. We anticipate the future as too slow in coming, as if in order to hasten its course; or we recall the past, to stop its too rapid flight. So imprudent are we that we wander in the times which are not ours, and do not think of the only one which belongs to us; and so idle are we that we dream of those times which are no more, and thoughtlessly overlook that which alone exists. For the present is generally painful to us. We conceal it from our sight, because it troubles us; and if it be delightful to us, we regret to see it pass away. We try to sustain it by the future, and think of arranging matters which are not in our power, for a time which we have no certainty of reaching.

Let each one examine his thoughts, and he will find them all occupied with the past and the future. We scarcely ever think of the present; and if we think of it, it is only to take light from it to arrange the future. The present is never our end. The past and the present are our means; the future alone is our end. So we never live, but we hope to live; and, as we are always preparing to be happy, it is inevitable we should never be so.

[176]

Cromwell was about to ravage all Christendom; the royal family was undone, and his own forever established, but for a little grain of sand which formed in his bladder. Rome herself was trembling under him; but this small piece of gravel having formed there, he is dead, his family cast down, all is peaceful, and the king is restored.

[205]

When I consider the short duration of my life, swallowed up in the eternity before and after, the little space which I fill, and even can see, engulfed in the infinite immensity of spaces of which I am ignorant, and which know me not, I am frightened, and am astonished at being here rather than there; for there is no reason why here rather than there, why now rather than then. Who has put me here? By whose order and direction have this place and time been allotted to me? *Memoria hospitis unius diei præereuntis.*

[206]

The eternal silence of these infinite spaces frightens me.

[233]

Infinite—nothing. Our soul is cast into a body, where it finds number, time, dimension. Thereupon it reasons, and calls this nature, necessity, and can believe nothing else.

Unity joined to infinity adds nothing to it, no more than one foot to an infinite measure. The finite is annihilated in the presence of the infinite, and becomes a pure nothing. So our spirit before God, so our justice before divine justice. There is not so great a disproportion between our justice and that of God, as between unity and infinity.

The justice of God must be vast like His compassion. Now justice to the outcast is less vast, and ought less to offend our feelings than mercy toward the elect.

We know that there is an infinite, and are ignorant of its nature. As we know it to be false that numbers are finite, it is therefore true that there is an infinity in number. But we do not know what it is. It is false that it is even, it is false that it is odd; for the addition of a unit can make no change in its nature. Yet it is a number, and every number is odd or even (this is certainly true of every finite number). So we may well know that there is a God without knowing what He is. Is there not one substantial truth, seeing there are so many things which are not the truth itself?

We know then the existence and nature of the finite, because we also are finite and have extension. We know the existence of the infinite, and are ignorant of its nature, because it has extension like us, but not limits like us. But we know neither the existence nor the nature of God, because He has neither extension nor limits.

But by faith we know His existence; in glory we shall know His nature. Now, I have already shown that we may well know the existence of a thing, without knowing its nature.

Let us now speak according to natural lights.

If there is a God, He is infinitely incomprehensible, since, having neither parts nor limits, He has no affinity to us. We are then incapable of knowing either what He is or if He is. This being so, who will dare to undertake the decision of the question? Not we, who have no affinity to Him.

Who then will blame Christians for not being able to give a reason for their belief, since they profess a religion for which they cannot give a reason? They declare, in expounding it to the world, that it is a foolishness, *stultitiam,* and then you complain that they do not prove it! If they proved it, they would not keep their word; it is in lacking proofs, that they are not lacking in sense. "Yes, but although this excuses those who offer it as such, and takes away from them the blame or putting it forward without reason, it does not excuse those who receive it." Let us then examine this point, and say, "God is, or He is not." But to which side shall we incline? Reason can decide nothing here. There is an infinite chaos which separated us. A game is being played at the extremity of this infinite distance where heads or tails will turn up. What will you wager? According to reason, you can do neither the one thing nor the other; according to reason, you can defend neither of the propositions.

Do not then reprove for error those who have made a choice; for you know nothing about it. "No, but I blame them for having made, not this choice, but a choice; for again both he who chooses heads and he who chooses tails are equally at fault, they are both in the wrong. The true course is not to wager at all."

Yes; but you must wager. It is not optional. You are embarked. Which will you choose then? Let us see. Since you must choose, let us see which interests you least. You have two things to lose, the true and the good; and two things to stake, your reasons and your will, your knowledge and your happiness; and your nature has two things to shun, error and misery. Your reason is no more shocked in choosing one rather than the other, since you must of necessity choose. This is one point settled. But your happiness? Let us weigh the gain and the loss in wagering that God is. Let us estimate these two chances. If you gain, you gain all; if you lose, you lose nothing. Wager, then, without hesitation that He is. "That is very fine. Yes, I must wager; but I may perhaps wager too much." Let us see. Since there is an equal risk of gain and of loss, if you had only to gain two lives, instead of one, you might still wager. But if there were three lives to gain, you would have to play (since you are under the necessity of playing), and you would be imprudent, when you are forced to play, not to chance your life to gain three at a game where there is an equal risk of loss and gain. But there is an eternity of life and happiness. And this being so, if there were an infinity of chances, of which one only would be for you, you would still be right in wagering one to win two, and you would act stupidly, being obliged to play, by refusing to stake one life against three at a game in which out of an infinity of chances there is one for you, if there were an infinity of an infinitely happy life to gain. But there is here an infinity of an infinitely happy life to gain, a chance of gain against a finite number of chances of loss, and what you stake is finite. It is all divided; wherever the infinite is and there is not an infinity of chances of loss against that of gain, there is no time to hesitate, you must give all. And thus, when one is forced to play, he must renounce reason to preserve his life, rather than risk it for infinite gain, as likely to happen as the loss of nothingness.

For it is no use to say it is uncertain if we will gain, and it is certain that we risk, and that the infinite distance between the *certainty* of what is staked and the *uncertainty* of what will be gained, equals the finite good which is certainly staked against the uncertain infinite. It is not so, as every player stakes a certainty to gain an uncertainty, and yet he stakes a finite certainty to gain a finite uncertainty, without transgressing against reason. There is not an infinite distance between the certainty staked and the uncertainty of the gain; that is untrue. In truth, there is an infinity between the certainty of gain and the certainty of loss. But the uncertainty of the gain is proportioned to the certainty of the stake according to the proportion of the chances of gain and loss. Hence it comes that, if there are as many risks on one side as on the other, the course is to play even; and then the certainty of the stake is equal to the uncertainty of the gain, so far is it from fact that there is an infinite distance between them. And so our proposition is of infinite force, when there is the finite to stake in a game where there are equal risks of gain and of loss, and the infinite to gain. This demonstrable; and if men are capable of any truths, this is one.

"I confess it, I admit it. But, still, is there no means of seeing the faces of the cards?" Yes, Scripture and the rest, etc. "Yes, but I have my hands tied and my mouth closed; I am forced to wager, and am not free. I am not released, and am so made that I cannot believe. What, then, would you have me do?"

True. But at least learn your inability to believe, since reason brings you to this, and yet you cannot believe. Endeavor then to convince yourself, not by increase of proofs of God, but by the abatement of your passions. You would like to attain faith, and do not know the way; you would like to cure yourself of unbelief, and ask the remedy for it. Learn of those who have been bound like you, and who now stake all their possessions. These are people who know the way which you would follow, and who are cured of an ill of which you would be cured. Follow the way by which they began; by acting as if they believed, taking the holy water, having masses said, etc. Even this will naturally make you believe, and deaden your acuteness. "But this is what I am afraid of." And why? What have you to lose?

But to show you that this leads you there, it is this which will lessen the passions, which are your stumbling-blocks.

The end of this discourse.   Now, what harm will befall you in taking this side? You will be faithful, honest, humble, grateful, generous, a sincere friend, truthful. Certainly you will not have those poisonous pleasures, glory and luxury; but will you not have others? I will tell you that you will thereby gain in this life, and that, at each step you take on this road, you will see so great certainty of gain, so much nothingness in what you risk, that you will at last recognize that you have wagered for something certain and infinite, for which you have given nothing.

"Ah! This discourse transports me, charms me," etc.

If this discourse pleases you and seems impressive, know that it is made by a man who has knelt, both before and after it, in prayer to that Being, infinite and without parts, before whom he lays all he has, for you also to lay before Him all you have for your own good and for His glory, that so strength may be given to lowliness.

[242]

Preface to the second part.   To speak of those who have dealt with this matter.

I admire the boldness with which these persons undertake to speak of God. In addressing their argument to infidels, their first chapter is to prove Divinity from the works of nature. I should not be astonished at their enterprise, if they were addressing their argument to the faithful; for it is certain that those who have the living faith in their heart see at once that all existence is none other than the work of the God whom they adore. But for those in whom this light is extinguished, and in whom we purpose to rekindle it, persons destitute of faith and grace, who, seeking with all their light whatever they see in nature that can bring them to this knowledge, find only obscurity and darkness; to tell them that they have only to look at the smallest things which surround them, and they will see God openly, to give them, as a complete proof of this great and important matter, the course of the moon and planets, and to claim to have concluded the proof with such an argument, is to give them ground for believing that the proofs of our religion are very weak. And I see by reason and experience that nothing is more calculated to arouse their contempt.

It is not after this manner that Scripture speaks, which has a better knowledge of the things that are of God. It says, on the contrary, that God is a hidden God, and that, since the corruption of nature, He has left men in a darkness from which they can escape only through Jesus Christ, without whom all communion with God is cut off. *Nemo novit Patrem, nisi Filius, et cui voluerit Filius revelare.*

This is what Scripture points out to us, when it says in so many places that those who seek God find Him. It is not of that light, "like the noonday sun," that this is said. We do not say that those who seek the noonday sun, or water in the sea, shall find them; and hence the evidence of God must not be of this nature. So it tells us elsewhere: *Vere tu es Deus absconditus.*

[280]

The knowledge of God is very far from the love of Him.

[347]

Man is but a reed, the most feeble thing in nature; but he is a thinking reed. The entire universe need not arm itself to crush him. A vapor, a drop of water suffices to kill him. But, if the universe were to crush him, man would still be more noble than that which killed him, because he knows that he dies and the advantage which the universe has over him; the universe knows nothing of this.

All our dignity consists, then, in thought. By it we must elevate ourselves, and not by space and time which we cannot fill. Let us endeavor, then, to think well; this is the principle of morality.

[358]

Man is neither angel nor brute, and the unfortunate thing is that he who would act the angel acts the brute.

[373]

Skepticism. I shall here write my thoughts without order, and not perhaps in unintentional confusion; that is true order, which will always indicate my object by its disorder. I should do too much honor to my subject, if I treated it with order, since I want to show that it is incapable of it.

[397]

The greatness of man is great in that he knows himself to be miserable. A tree does not know itself to be miserable. It is then being miserable to know oneself to be miserable; but it is also being great to know that one is miserable.

[398]

All these same miseries prove man's greatness. They are the miseries of a great lord, of a deposed king.

[418]

It is dangerous to make man see too clearly his equality with the beasts without showing him his greatness. It is also dangerous to make him see his greatness too clearly, apart from his vileness. It is still more dangerous to leave him in ignorance of both. But it is very advantageous to show him both. Man must not think that he is on a level either with the beasts or with the angels, nor must he be ignorant of both sides of his nature; but he must know both.

[427]

Man does not know in what rank to place himself. He has plainly gone astray, and fallen from his true place without being able to find it again. He seeks it anxiously and unsuccessfully everywhere in impenetrable darkness.

Søren Kierkegaard

Is There Such a Thing as an Absolute Duty toward God?

from Fear and Trembling

In "Is There Such a Thing as a Teleological Suspension of the Ethical?" the chapter of Fear and Trembling preceding the selection below, Kierkegaard explicates the nature of faith and its relationship to the absurd by contrasting the tragic hero (who represents the "ethical" stage) and "the knight of faith" (who represents the "religious" stage). The tragic hero, such as Agamemnon or Brutus, sacrifices his child for a higher ethical law than that of "thou shalt love your son," for example, to reconcile the angry deities or to fulfill his duty to the state. That is, he does, through the mediation of the ethical law, a reasonable and therefore understandable act. He does not teleologically suspend the ethical. But Abraham, the knight of faith, who is called upon to sacrifice his son Isaac, teleologically suspends the ethical. He acts, not by virtue

Source: From *Fear and Trembling and the Sickness unto Death* by Søren Kierkegaard, translated with an Introduction and Notes, by Walter Lowrie (copyright 1941, 1954 by Princeton University Press; Princeton Paperback, 1968). Reprinted by permission of Princeton University Press.

of reason, but by "virtue of the absurd." He is confronted as a solitary individual by a voice that demands that he sacrifice Isaac. He cannot turn to universals, as the tragic hero can, to help him decide and to comfort him in his decision. He alone, in dread and anguish, must decide. And when he has acted, he does not know by virtue of reason that he has not perhaps committed a murder. When he acts, that is, he acts not by reason but by utter faith—by virtue of the absurd. The individual or "exception" thus becomes paradoxically superior to the universal. This selection and the one on Schlegel's *Lucinde* in the section "Literature" provide a good introduction to Kierkegaard's famous three stages on life's way. It is important to note, however, that *Fear and Trembling* is one of Kierkegaard's "pseudonymous" works, and that the speaker, Johannes de Silentio, is one of those narrators who are deeply disturbed by the existential "hero," but cannot themselves make the existential movement.

In the story of Abraham we find such a paradox. His relation to Isaac, ethically expressed, is this, that the father should love the son. This ethical relation is reduced to a relative position in contrast with the absolute relation to God. To the question, "Why?" Abraham has no answer except that it is a trial, a temptation (*Fristelse*)—terms which, as was remarked above, express the unity of the two points of view: that it is for God's sake and for his own sake. In common usage these two ways of regarding the matter are mutually exclusive. Thus when we see a man do something which does not comport with the universal, we say that he scarcely can be doing it for God's sake, and by that we imply that he does it for his own sake. The paradox of faith has lost the intermediate term, i.e. the universal. On the one side it has the expression for the extremest egoism (doing the dreadful thing it does for one's own sake); on the other side the expression for the most absolute self-sacrifice (doing it for God's sake). Faith itself cannot be mediated into the universal, for it would thereby be destroyed. Faith is this paradox, and the individual absolutely cannot make himself intelligible to anybody. People imagine maybe that the individual can make himself intelligible to another individual in the same case. Such a notion would be unthinkable if in our time people did not in so many ways seek to creep slyly into greatness. The one knight of faith can render no aid to the other. Either the individual becomes a knight of faith by assuming the burden of the paradox, or he never becomes one. In these regions partnership is unthinkable. Every more precise explication of what is to be understood by Isaac the individual can give only to himself. And even if one were able, generally speaking, to define ever so precisely what should be intended by Isaac (which moreover would be the most ludicrous self-contradiction, i.e. that the particular individual who definitely stands outside the universal is subsumed under universal categories precisely when he has to act as the individual who stands outside the universal), the individual nevertheless will never be able to assure himself by the aid of others that this application is appropriate, but he can do so only by himself as the individual. Hence even if a man were cowardly and paltry enough to wish to become a knight of faith on the responsibility of an outsider, he will never become one; for only the individual becomes a knight of faith as the particular individual, and this is the greatness of this knighthood, as I can well understand without entering the order, since I lack courage; but this is also its terror, as I can comprehend even better.

complete commitment to God

In Luke 14:26, as everybody knows, there is a striking doctrine taught about the absolute duty toward God: "If any man cometh unto me and hateth not his own father and mother and wife and children and brethren and sisters, yea, and his own life also, he cannot be my disciple." This is a hard saying, who can bear to hear it? For this reason it is heard very seldom. This silence, however, is only an evasion which is of no avail. Nevertheless, the student of theology learns to know that these words occur in the New Testament, and in one or another exegetical aid he finds the explanation that μισεῖν in this passage and a few others is used in the

contemplate the implications of your commitment

sense of μείσειν, signifying *minus diligo, posthabeo, non colo, nihili facio.* However, the context in which these words occur does not seem to strengthen this tasteful explanation. In the verse immediately following there is a story about a man who desired to build a tower but first sat down to calculate whether he was capable of doing it, lest people might laugh at him afterwards. The close connection of this story with the verse here cited seems precisely to indicate that the words are to be taken in as terrible a sense as possible, to the end that everyone may examine himself as to whether he is able to erect the building.

In case this pious and kindly exegete, who by abating the price thought he could smuggle Christianity into the world, were fortunate enough to convince a man that grammatically, linguistically and κατ' ἀναλογίαν [analogically] this was the meaning of that passage, it is to be hoped that the same moment he will be fortunate enough to convince the same man that Christianity is one of the most pitiable things in the world. For the doctrine which in one of its most lyrical outbursts, where the consciousness of its eternal validity swells in it most strongly, has nothing else to say but a noisy word which means nothing but only signifies that one is to be less kindly, less attentive, more indifferent; the doctrine which at the moment when it makes as if it would give utterance to the terrible ends by driveling instead of terrifying—that doctrine is not worth taking off my hat to.

The words are terrible, yet I fully believe that one can understand them without implying that he who understands them has courage to do them. One must at all events be honest enough to acknowledge what stands written and to admit that it is great, even though one has not the

courage for it. He who behaves thus will not find himself excluded from
having part in that beautiful story which follows, for after all it contains
consolation of a sort for the man who had not courage to begin the tower.
But we must be honest, and not interpret this lack of courage as humility,
since it is really pride, whereas the courage of faith is the only humble
courage.

One can easily perceive that if there is to be any sense in this passage,
it must be understood literally. God it is who requires absolute love. But
he who in demanding a person's love thinks that this love should be
proved also by becoming lukewarm to everything which hitherto was dear
—that man is not only an egoist but stupid as well, and he who would
demand such love signs at the same moment his own death-warrant,
supposing that his life was bound up with this coveted love. Thus a husband demands that his wife shall leave father and mother, but if he were
to regard it as a proof of her extraordinary love for him that she for his sake
became an indolent, lukewarm daughter etc., then he is the stupidest of
the stupid. If he had any notion of what love is, he would wish to discover
that as daughter and sister she was perfect in love, and would see therein
the proof that she would love him more than anyone else in the realm.
What therefore in the case of a man one would regard as a sign of egoism
and stupidity, that one is to regard by the help of an exegete as a worthy
conception of the Deity.

But how hate them? I will not recall here the human distinction
between loving and hating—not because I have much to object to in it (for
after all it is passionate), but because it is egoistic and is not in place here.
However, if I regard the problem as a paradox, then I understand it, that
is, I understand it in such a way as one can understand a paradox. The
absolute duty may cause one to do what ethics would forbid, but by no
means can it cause the knight of faith to cease to love. This is shown by
Abraham. The instant he is ready to sacrifice Isaac the ethical expression
for what he does is this: he hates Isaac. But if he really hates Isaac, he can
be sure that God does not require this, for Cain and Abraham are not
identical. Isaac he must love with his whole soul; when God requires Isaac
he must love him if possible even more dearly, and only on this condition
can he *sacrifice* him; for in fact it is this love for Isaac which, by its
paradoxical opposition to his love for God, makes his act a sacrifice. But
the distress and dread in this paradox is that, humanly speaking, he is
entirely unable to make himself intelligible. Only at the moment when his
act is in absolute contradiction to his feelings is his act a sacrifice, but the
reality of his act is the factor by which he belongs to the universal, and in
that aspect he is and remains a murderer.

Moreover, the passage in Luke must be understood in such a way as
to make it clearly evident that the knight of faith has no higher expression

of the universal (i.e. the ethical) by which he can save himself. Thus, for example, if we suppose that the Church requires such a sacrifice of one of its members, we have in this case only a tragic hero. For the idea of the Church is not qualitatively different from that of the State, in so far as the individual comes into it by a simple mediation, and in so far as the individual comes into the paradox he does not reach the idea of the Church; he does not come out of the paradox, but in it he must find either his blessedness or his perdition. Such an ecclesiastical hero expresses in his act the universal, and there will be no one in the Church—not even his father and mother etc.—who fails to understand him. On the other hand, he is not a knight of faith, and he has also a different answer from that of Abraham: he does not say that it is a trial or a temptation in which he is tested.

People commonly refrain from quoting such a text as this in Luke. They are afraid of giving men a free rein, are afraid that the worst will happen as soon as the individual takes it into his head to comport himself as the individual. Moreover, they think that to exist as the individual is the easiest thing of all, and that therefore people have to be compelled to become the universal. I cannot share either this fear or this opinion, and both for the same reason. He who has learned that to exist as the individual is the most terrible thing of all will not be fearful of saying that it is great, but then too he will say this in such a way that his words will scarcely be a snare for the bewildered man, but rather will help him into the universal, even though his words do to some extent make room for the great. The man who does not dare to mention such texts will not dare to mention Abraham either, and his notion that it is easy enough to exist as the individual implies a very suspicious admission with regard to himself; for he who has a real respect for himself and concern for his soul is convinced that the man who lives under his own supervision, alone in the whole world, lives more strictly and more secluded than a maiden in her lady's bower. That there may be some who need compulsion, some who, if they were free-footed, would riot in selfish pleasures like unruly beasts, is doubtless true; but a man must prove precisely that he is not of this number by the fact that he knows how to speak with dread and trembling; and out of reverence for the great one is bound to speak, lest it be forgotten for fear of the ill effect, which surely will fail to eventuate when a man talks in such a way that one knows it for the great, knows its terror—and apart from the terror one does not know the great at all.

Let us consider a little more closely the distress and dread in the paradox of faith. The tragic hero renounces himself in order to express the universal, the knight of faith renounces the universal in order to become the individual. As has been said, everything depends upon how one is placed. He who believes that it is easy enough to be the individual can always be sure that he is not a knight of faith, for vagabonds and roving geniuses are not men of faith. The knight of faith knows, on the other hand, that it is glorious to belong to the universal. He knows that it is beautiful and salutary to be the individual who translates himself into the universal, who edits as it were a pure and elegant edition of himself, as free from errors as possible and which everyone can read. He knows that it is refreshing to become intelligible to oneself in the universal so that he understands it and so that every individual who understands him understands through him in turn the universal, and both rejoice in the security of the universal. He knows that it is beautiful to be born as the individual who has the universal as his home, his friendly abiding-place, which at once welcomes him with open arms when he would tarry in it. But he knows also that higher than this there winds a solitary path, narrow and steep; he knows that it is terrible to be born outside the universal, to walk without meeting a single traveller. He knows very well where he is and how he is related to men. Humanly speaking, he is crazy and cannot make himself intelligible to anyone. And yet it is the mildest expression, to say that he is crazy. If he is not supposed to be that, then he is a hypocrite, and the higher he climbs on this path, the more dreadful a hypocrite he is.

The knight of faith knows that to give up oneself for the universal inspires enthusiasm, and that it requires courage, but he also knows that security is to be found in this, precisely because it is for the universal. He knows that it is glorious to be understood by every noble mind, so glorious that the beholder is ennobled by it, and he feels as if he were bound; he could wish it were this task that had been allotted to him. Thus Abraham could surely have wished now and then that the task were to love Isaac as becomes a father, in a way intelligible to all, memorable throughout all ages; he could wish that the task were to sacrifice Isaac for the universal, that he might incite the fathers to illustrious deeds—and he is almost terrified by the thought that for him such wishes are only temptations and must be dealt with as such, for he knows that it is a solitary path he treads and that he accomplishes nothing for the universal but only himself is tried and examined. Or what did Abraham accomplish for the universal? Let me speak humanly about it, quite humanly. He spent seventy years in getting a son of his old age. What other men get quickly enough and enjoy for a long time he spent seventy years in accomplishing. And why? Because he was tried and put to the test. Is not that crazy? But Abraham believed, and Sarah wavered and got him to take Hagar as a concubine —but therefore he also had to drive her away. He gets Isaac, then he has to be tried again. He knew that it is glorious to express the universal, glorious to live with Isaac. But this is not the task. He knew that it is a kindly thing to sacrifice such a son for the universal, he himself would have found repose in that, and all would have reposed in the commendation of his deed, as a vowel reposes in its consonant, but that is not the task—he is tried. That Roman general who is celebrated by his name of Cunctator checked the foe by procrastination—but what a procrastinator Abraham is in comparison with him! ... yet he did not save the state. This is the content of one hundred and thirty years. Who can bear it? Would not his contemporary age, if we can speak of such a thing, have said of him, "Abraham is eternally procrastinating. Finally he gets a son. That took long enough. Now he wants to sacrifice him. So is he not mad? And if at least he could explain why he wants to do it—but he always says that it is a trial." Nor could Abraham explain more, for his life is like a book placed under a divine attachment and which never becomes *publici juris*.

This is the terrible thing. He who does not see it can always be sure that he is no knight of faith, but he who sees it will not deny that even the most tried of tragic heroes walks with a dancing step compared with the knight of faith, who comes slowly creeping forward. And if he has perceived this and assured himself that he has not courage to understand it, he will at least have a presentiment of the marvellous glory this knight attains in the fact that he becomes God's intimate acquaintance, the Lord's friend, and (to speak quite humanly) that he says "Thou" to God in heaven, whereas even the tragic hero only addresses Him in the third person.

The tragic hero is soon ready and has soon finished the fight, he makes the infinite movement and then is secure in the universal. The knight of faith, on the other hand, is kept sleepless, for he is constantly tried, and every instant there is the possibility of being able to return repentantly to the universal, and this possibility can just as well be a temptation as the truth. He can derive evidence from no man which it is, for with that query he is outside the paradox.

So the knight of faith has first and foremost the requisite passion to concentrate upon a single factor the whole of the ethical which he transgresses, so that he can give himself the assurance that he really loves Isaac with his whole soul.[1] If he cannot do that, he is in temptation (*Anfech-*

---

1. I would elucidate yet once more the difference between the collisions which are encountered by the tragic hero and by the knight of faith. The tragic hero assures himself that the ethical obligation [i.e., the lower ethical obligation, which he puts aside for the higher; in the present case, accordingly, it is the obligation to spare his daughter's life] is totally present in him by the fact that he transforms it into a wish. Thus Agamemnon can say, "The proof that I do not offend against my parental duty is that my duty is my only wish." So here we have wish and duty face to face with one another. The fortunate chance in life is that the two correspond, that my wish is my duty and vice versa, and the task of most men in life is precisely to remain within their duty and by their enthusiasm to transform it into their wish. The tragic hero gives up his wish in order to accomplish his duty. For the knight of faith wish and duty are also identical, but he is required to give up both. Therefore when he would resign himself to giving up his wish he does not find repose, for that is after all his duty. If he would remain within his duty and his wish, he is not a knight of faith, for the absolute duty requires precisely that he should give them up. The tragic hero apprehended a higher expression of duty but not an absolute duty.

tung). In the next place, he has enough passion to make this assurance available in the twinkling of an eye and in such a way that it is as completely valid as it was in the first instance. If he is unable to do this, he can never budge from the spot, for he constantly has to begin all over again. The tragic hero also concentrated in one factor the ethical which he teleologically surpassed, but in this respect he had support in the universal. The knight of faith has only himself alone, and this constitutes the dreadfulness of the situation. Most men live in such a way under an ethical obligation that they can let the sorrow be sufficient for the day, but they never reach this passionate concentration, this energetic consciousness. The universal may in a certain sense help the tragic hero to attain this, but the knight of faith is left all to himself. The hero does the deed and finds repose in the universal, the knight of faith is kept in constant tension. Agamemnon gives up Iphigenia and thereby has found repose in the universal, then he takes the step of sacrificing her. If Agamemnon does not make the infinite movement, if his soul at the decisive instant, instead of having passionate concentration, is absorbed by the common twaddle that he had several daughters and *vielleicht* [perhaps] the *Ausserordentliche* [extraordinary] might occur—then he is of course not a hero but a hospital-case. The hero's concentration Abraham also has, even though in his case it is far more difficult, since he has no support in the universal; but he makes one more movement by which he concentrates his soul upon the miracle. If Abraham did not do that, he is only an Agamemnon—if in any way it is possible to explain how he can be justified in sacrificing Isaac when thereby no profit accrues to the universal.

Whether the individual is in temptation (*Anfechtung*) or is a knight of faith only the individual can decide. Nevertheless it is possible to construct from the paradox several criteria which he too can understand who is not within the paradox. The true knight of faith is always absolute isolation, the false knight is sectarian. This sectarianism is an attempt to leap away from the narrow path of the paradox and become a tragic hero at a cheap price. The tragic hero expresses the universal and sacrifices himself for it. The sectarian punchinello, instead of that, has a private theatre, i.e. several good friends and comrades who represent the universal just about as well as the beadles in *The Golden Snuffbox* represent justice. The knight of faith, on the contrary, is the paradox, is the individual, absolutely nothing but the individual, without connections or pretensions. This is the terrible thing which the sectarian manikin cannot endure. For instead of learning from this terror that he is not capable of performing the great deed and then plainly admitting it (an act which I cannot but approve, because it is what I do) the manikin thinks that by uniting with several other manikins he will be able to do it. But that is quite out of the question. In the world of spirit no swindling is tolerated.

A dozen sectaries join arms with one another, they know nothing whatever of the lonely temptations which await the knight of faith and which
he dares not shun precisely because it would be still more dreadful if he
were to press forward presumptuously. The sectaries deafen one another
by their noise and racket, hold the dread off by their shrieks, and such a
hallooing company of sportsmen think they are storming heaven and
think they are on the same path as the knight of faith who in the solitude
of the universe never hears any human voice but walks alone with his
dreadful responsibility.

The knight of faith is obliged to rely upon himself alone, he feels the
pain of not being able to make himself intelligible to others, but he feels
no vain desire to guide others. The pain is his assurance that he is in the
right way, this vain desire he does not know, he is too serious for that. The
false knight of faith readily betrays himself by this proficiency in guiding
which he has acquired in an instant. He does not comprehend what it is
all about, that if another individual is to take the same path, he must
become entirely in the same way the individual and have no need of any
man's guidance, least of all the guidance of a man who would obtrude
himself. At this point men leap aside, they cannot bear the martyrdom of
being uncomprehended, and instead of this they choose conveniently
enough the worldly admiration of their proficiency. The true knight of
faith is a witness, never a teacher, and therein lies his deep humanity,
which is worth a good deal more than this silly participation in others' weal
and woe which is honored by the name of sympathy, whereas in fact it is
nothing but vanity. He who would only be a witness thereby avows that
no man, not even the lowliest, needs another man's sympathy or should
be abased that another may be exalted. But since he did not win what he
won at a cheap price, neither does he sell it out at a cheap price, he is not
petty enough to take men's admiration and give them in return his silent
contempt, he knows that what is truly great is equally accessible to all.

Either there is an absolute duty toward God, and if so it is the paradox
here described, that the individual as the individual is higher than the
universal and as the individual stands in an absolute relation to the abso-
lute/or else faith never existed, because it has always existed, or, to put it
differently, Abraham is lost, or one must explain the passage in the fourteenth chapter of Luke as did that tasteful exegete, and explain in the
same way the corresponding passages and similar ones.

Søren Kierkegaard
Dread as a Saving Experience by Means of Faith

In one of Grimm's Fairy Tales there is the story of a youth who went out in search of adventures for the sake of learning what it is to fear or be in dread. We will let that adventurer go his way without troubling ourselves to learn whether in the course of it he encountered the dreadful. On the other hand I would say that learning to know dread is an adventure which every man has to affront if he would not go to perdition either by not having known dread or by sinking under it. He therefore who has learned rightly to be in dread has learned the most important thing. *combination of various + different parts*

If a man were a beast or an angel, he would not be able to be in dread. Since he is a synthesis he can be in dread, and the greater the dread, the greater the man. This, however, is not affirmed in the sense in which men commonly understand dread, as related to something outside a man, but in the sense that man himself produces dread. Only in this sense can we interpret the passage where it is said of Christ that he was in dread [*ængstes*] even unto death, and the place also where he says to Judas, "What thou doest, do quickly." Not even the terrible word upon which even Luther dreaded to preach, "My God, my God, why hast thou forsaken me?"—not even this expresses suffering so strongly. For this word indicates a situation in which Christ actually is; the former sayings indicate a relation to a situation which is not yet actual.

Dread is the possibility of freedom. Only this dread is by the aid of faith absolutely educative, laying bare as it does all finite aims and discovering all their deceptions. And no Grand Inquisitor has in readiness such terrible tortures as has dread, and no spy knows how to attack more artfully the man he suspects, choosing the instant when he is weakest, nor knows how to lay traps where he will be caught and ensnared, as dread knows how, and no sharp-witted judge knows how to interrogate, to examine the accused, as dread does, which never lets him escape, neither by diversion nor by noise, neither at work nor at play, neither by day nor by night.

Source: From *The Concept of Dread* by Søren Kierkegaard, translated by Walter Lowrie (copyright 1944, 1957 by Princeton University Press; Princeton Paperback, 1967). Reprinted by permission of Princeton University Press.

He who is educated by dread is educated by possibility, and only the man who is educated by possibility is educated in accordance with his infinity. Possibility is therefore the heaviest of all categories. One often hears, it is true, the opposite affirmed, that possibility is so light but reality is heavy. But from whom does one hear such talk? From a lot of miserable men who never have known what possibility is, and who, since reality showed them that they were not fit for anything and never would be, mendaciously bedizened a possibility which was so beautiful, so enchanting; and the only foundation of this possibility was a little youthful tomfoolery of which they might rather have been ashamed. Therefore by this possibility which is said to be light one commonly understands the possibility of luck, good fortune, etc. But this is not possibility, it is a mendacious invention which human depravity falsely embellishes in order to have reason to complain of life, of providence, and as a pretext for being self-important. No, in possibility everything is possible, and he who truly was brought up by possibility has comprehended the dreadful as well as the smiling. When such a person, therefore, goes out from the school of possibility, and knows more thoroughly than a child knows the alphabet that he can demand of life absolutely nothing, and that terror, perdition, annihilation, dwell next door to every man, and has learned the profitable lesson that every dread which alarms [*ængste*] may the next instant become a fact, he will then interpret reality differently, he will extol reality, and even when it rests upon him heavily he will remember that after all it is far, far lighter than the possibility was. Only thus can possibility educate; for finiteness and the finite relationships in which the individual is assigned a place, whether it be small and commonplace or world-historical, educate only finitely, and one can always talk them around, always get a little more out of them, always chaffer, always escape a little way from them, always keep a little apart, always prevent oneself from learning absolutely from them; and if one is to learn absolutely, the individual must in turn have the possibility in himself and himself fashion that from which he is to learn, even though the next instant it does not recognize that it was fashioned by him, but absolutely takes the power from him.

But in order that the individual may thus absolutely and infinitely be educated by possibility, he must be honest towards possibility and must have faith. By faith I mean what Hegel in his fashion calls very rightly "the inward certainty which anticipates infinity." When the discoveries of possibility are honestly administered, possibility will then disclose all finitudes and idealize them in the form of infinity in the individual who is overwhelmed by dread, until in turn he is victorious by the anticipation of faith.

What I say here appears perhaps to many an obscure and foolish saying, since they even boast of never having been in dread. To this I would reply that doubtless one should not be in dread of men, of finite things, but that only the man who has gone through the dread of possibility is educated to have no dread—not because he avoids the dreadful things of life, but because they always are weak in comparison with those of possibility. If on the other hand the speaker means that the great thing about him is that he has never been in dread, then I shall gladly initiate him into my explanation, that this comes from the fact that he is spirit-less.

If the individual cheats the possibility by which he is to be educated, he never reaches faith; his faith remains the shrewdness of finitude, as his school was that of finitude. But men cheat possibility in every way—if they did not, one has only to stick one's head out of the window, and one would see enough for possibility to begin its exercises forthwith. There is an engraving by Chodowiecki which represents the surrender of Calais as viewed by the four temperaments, and the theme of the artist was to let the various impressions appear mirrored in the faces which express the various temperaments. The most commonplace life has events enough, no doubt, but the question is whether the possibility in the individuality is honest towards itself. It is recounted of an Indian hermit who for two years had lived upon dew, that he came once to the city, tasted wine, and then became addicted to drink. This story, like every other of the sort, can be understood in many ways, one can make it comic, one can make it tragic; but the man who is educated by possibility has more than enough to occupy him in such a story. Instantly he is absolutely identified with that unfortunate man, he knows no finite evasion by which he might escape. Now the dread of possibility holds him as its prey, until it can deliver him saved into the hands of faith. In no other place does he find repose, for every other point of rest is mere nonsense, even though in men's eyes it is shrewdness. This is the reason why possibility is so absolutely educative. No man has ever become so unfortunate in reality that there was not some little residue left to him, and, as common sense observes quite truly, if a man is canny, he will find a way. But he who went through the curriculum of misfortune offered by possibility lost everything, absolutely everything, in a way that no one has lost it in reality. If in this situation he did not behave falsely towards possibility, if he did not attempt to talk around the dread which would save him, then he received everything back again, as in reality no one ever did even if he received everything double, for the pupil of possibility received infinity, whereas the soul of the other expired in the finite. No one ever sank so deep in reality that he could not sink deeper, or that there might not be one or another sunk deeper than he. But he who sank in the possibility has an eye too dizzy to see the measuring rod which Tom, Dick, and Harry hold out as a straw to the drowning man; his ear is closed so that he cannot hear what the market price for men is in his day, cannot hear that he is just as good as most of them. He sank absolutely, but then in turn he floated up from the depth of the abyss, lighter now than all that is oppressive and dreadful in life. Only I do not deny that he who is educated by possibility is exposed—not to the danger of bad company and dissoluteness of various sorts, as are those who are educated by the finite, but—to one danger of downfall, and that is self-slaughter. If at the beginning of his education he misunderstands the anguish of dread, so that it does not lead him to faith but away from faith, then he is lost. On the other hand, he who is educated by possibility remains with dread, does not allow himself to be deceived by its countless counterfeits, he recalls the past precisely; then at last the attacks of dread, though they are fearful, are not such that he flees from them. For him dread becomes a serviceable spirit which against its will leads him whither he would go. Then when it announces itself, when it craftily insinuates that it has invented a new instrument of torture far more terrible than anything employed before, he does not recoil, still less does he attempt to hold it off with clamor and noise, but he bids it welcome, he hails it solemnly, as Socrates solemnly flourished the poisoned goblet, he shuts himself up with it, he says, as a patient says to the surgeon when a painful operation is about to begin, "Now I am ready." Then dread enters into his soul and searches it thoroughly, constraining out of him all the finite and the petty, and leading him hence whither he would go.

When one or another extraordinary event occurs in life, when a world-historical hero gathers heroes about him and accomplishes heroic feats, when a crisis occurs and everything becomes significant, then men wish to be in it, for these are things which educate. Quite possibly. But there is a much simpler way of being educated much more fundamentally. Take the pupil of possibility, set him in the midst of the Jutland heath where nothing happens, where the greatest event is that a partridge flies up noisily, and he experiences everything more perfectly, more precisely, more profoundly, than the man who was applauded upon the stage of universal history, in case he was not educated by possibility.

Søren Kierkegaard

Existence and Reality

from *Concluding Unscientific Postscript*

The difficulty that inheres in existence, with which the existing individual is confronted, is one that never really comes to expression in the language of abstract thought, much less receives an explanation. Because abstract thought is *sub specie aeterni* it ignores the concrete and the temporal, the existential process, the predicament of the existing individual arising from his being a synthesis of the temporal and the eternal situated in existence.[1] Now if we assume that abstract thought is the highest manifestation of human activity, it follows that philosophy and the philosophers proudly desert existence, leaving the rest of us to face the worst. And something else, too, follows for the abstract thinker himself, namely, that since he is an existing individual he must in one way or another be suffering from absentmindedness.

The abstract problem of reality (if it is permissible to treat this problem abstractly, the particular and the accidental being constituents of the real, and directly opposed to abstraction) is not nearly so difficult a problem as it is to raise and to answer the question of what it means that this definite something is a reality. This definite something is just what abstract thought abstracts from. But the difficulty lies in bringing this definite something and the ideality of thought together, by penetrating the concrete particularity with thought. Abstract thought cannot even take cognizance of this contradiction, since the very process of abstraction prevents the contradiction from arising.

This questionable character of abstract thought becomes apparent especially in connection with all existential problems, where abstract thought gets rid of the difficulty by leaving it out, and then proceeds to

Source: From "Existence and Reality," in Søren Kierkegaard, *Concluding Unscientific Postscript*, translated by David Swenson and Walter Lowrie (copyright 1941 © 1969 by Princeton University Press; Princeton Paperback, 1968). Reprinted by permission of Princeton University Press and the American Scandinavian Foundation.
1. That Hegel in his *Logic* nevertheless permits himself to utilize a consciousness that is only too well informed about the concrete, and what it is that the professor needs next in spite of the necessary transition, is of course a fault, which Trendelenburg has very effectively called to our attention. To cite an example from the field of the subject immediately before us, how is the transition effected by which *die Existenz* becomes a plurality of existences? *"Die Existenz [?] die unmittelbare Einheit der Reflexion-in-sich und der Reflexion-in-anders. Sie ist daher [?] die unbestimmte Menge von Existierenden."* How does the purely abstract determination of existence come to be split up in this manner?

boast of having explained everything. It explains immortality in general, and all goes quite smoothly, in that immortality is identified with eternity, with the eternity which is essentially the medium of all thought. But whether an existing individual human being is immortal, which is the difficulty, abstract thought does not trouble to inquire. It is disinterested; but the difficulty inherent in existence constitutes the interest of the existing individual, who is infinitely interested in existing. Abstract thought thus helps me with respect to my immortality by first annihilating me as a particular existing individual and then making me immortal, about as when the doctor in Holberg killed the patient with his medicine—but also expelled the fever. Such an abstract thinker, one who neglects to take into account the relationship between his abstract thought and his own existence as an individual, not careful to clarify this relationship to himself, makes a comical impression upon the mind even if he is ever so distinguished, because he is in process of ceasing to be a human being. While a genuine human being, as a synthesis of the finite and the infinite, finds his reality in holding these two factors together, infinitely interested in existing—such an abstract thinker is a duplex being: a fantastic creature who moves in the pure being of abstract thought, and on the other hand, a sometimes pitiful professorial figure which the former deposits, about as when one sets down a walking stick. When one reads the story of such a thinker's life (for his writings are perhaps excellent), one trembles to think of what it means to be a man.[2] If a lacemaker were to produce ever so beautiful laces, it nevertheless makes one sad to contemplate such a poor stunted creature. And so it is a comical sight to see a thinker who in spite of all pretensions, personally existed like a nincompoop; who did indeed marry, but without knowing love or its power, and whose marriage must therefore have been as impersonal as his thought; whose personal life was devoid of pathos or pathological struggles, concerned only with the question of which university offered the best livelihood. Such an anomaly one would think impossible in the case of a thinker, to be met with only in the external world and its wretchedness, where one human being is the slave of another, and it is impossible to admire the laces without shedding tears for the lacemakers. But one would suppose that a thinker lived the richest human life—so at least it was in Greece.

It is different with the abstract thinker who without having understood himself, or the relationship that abstract thought bears to existence, simply follows the promptings of his talent or is made by training to become something of this sort. I am very well aware that one tends to admire an artistic career where the artist simply pursues his talent without

---

2. And when you read in his writings that thought and being are one, it is impossible not to think, in view of his own life and mode of existence, that the being which is thus identical with thought can scarcely be the being of a man.

at all making himself clear over what it means to be a human being, and that our admiration tends to forget the person of the artist over his artistry. But I also know that such a life has its tragedy in being a differential type of existence not personally reflected in the ethical; and I know that in Greece, at least, a thinker was not a stunted, crippled creature who produced works of art, but was himself a work of art in his existence. One would suppose that being a thinker was the last thing in the world to constitute a differential trait with respect to being human. If it is the case that an abstract thinker is devoid of a sensitiveness for the comical, this circumstance is in itself a proof that while his thought may be the product of a distinguished talent, it is not the thought of one who has in any eminent sense existed as a human being. We are told that thought is the highest stage of human life, that it includes everything else as subordinated to itself; and at the same time no objection is urged against the thinker failing to exist essentially *qua* human being, but only as a differential talent. That the pronouncement made concerning thought fails to be reduplicated in the concept of the thinker, that the thinker's existence contradicts his thought, shows that we are here dealing merely with professions. It is professed that thought is higher than feeling and imagination, and this is professed by a thinker who lacks pathos and passion. Thought is higher than irony and humor—this is professed by a thinker who is wholly lacking in a sense for the comical. How comical! Just as the whole enterprise of abstract thought in dealing with Christianity and with existential problems is an essay in the comical, so the so-called pure thought is in general a psychological curiosity, a remarkable species of combining and construing in a fantastic medium, the medium of pure being. The facile deification of this pure thought as the highest stage in life shows that the thinker who does it has never existed *qua* human being. It is evidence among other things that he has never willed in any eminent sense of the word; I do not mean willing in the sense of exploit, but from the standpoint of inwardness. But to have willed in this eminent sense is an absolute condition for having existed as a human being. Through having willed in this manner, through having ventured to take a decisive step in the utmost intensity of subjective passion and with full consciousness of one's eternal responsibility (which is within the capacity of every human being), one learns something else about life, and learns that it is quite a different thing from being engaged, year in and year out, in piecing together something for a system. And through thus existing essentially *qua* human being, one also acquires a sensitiveness for the comical. I do not mean that everyone who so exists is therefore a comic poet or a comic actor, but he will have a receptivity for the comical.

That the difficulty inherent in existence and confronting the existing individual never really comes to expression in the language of abstraction,

I shall proceed to illustrate by reference to a decisive problem, about which so much has been said and written. Everyone is familiar with the fact that the Hegelian philosophy has rejected the principle of contradiction. Hegel himself has more than once sat in solemn judgment upon those thinkers who remain in the sphere of reflection and understanding, and therefore insist that there is an either-or. Since his time it has become a favorite sport for some Hegelian, as soon as anyone lets fall a hint about an *aut-aut*, to come riding *trip trap trap*, like a gamekeeper in *Kallundsborgs-Krøniken*, and after gaining a victory to ride home again. Here in Denmark the Hegelians have several times been on the warpath, especially after Bishop Mynster, to gain the brilliant victory of speculative thought. Bishop Mynster has more than once become a vanquished standpoint, though as such he seems to be doing very well, and it is rather to be feared that the tremendous exertion incident to the winning of the victory has been too much for the unvanquished victors. And yet there is perhaps a misunderstanding at the root of the controversy and the victory. Hegel is utterly and absolutely right in asserting that viewed eternally, *sub specie aeterni*, in the language of abstraction, in pure thought and pure being, there is no either-or. How in the world could there be, when abstract thought has taken away the contradiction, so that Hegel and the Hegelians ought rather be asked to explain what they mean by the hocus-pocus of introducing contradiction, movement, transition, and so forth, into the domain of logic. If the champions of an either-or invade the sphere of pure thought and there seek to defend their cause, they are quite without justification. Like the giant who wrestled with Hercules, and who lost strength as soon as he was lifted from the ground, the either-or of contradiction is *ipso facto* nullified when it is lifted out of the sphere of the existential and introduced into the eternity of abstract thought. On the other hand, Hegel is equally wrong when, forgetting the abstraction of his thought, he plunges down into the realm of existence to annul the double *aut* with might and main. It is impossible to do this in existence, for in so doing the thinker abrogates existence as well. When I take existence away, i.e. when I abstract, there is no *aut-aut;* when I take this *aut-aut* away from existence I also take existence away, and hence I do not abrogate the *aut-aut* in existence. If it is an error to say that there is something that is true in theology which is not true in philosophy, it is at any rate quite correct to say that something is true for an existing individual which is not true in abstract thought. And it is also true that from the ethical point of view, pure being is a fantastic medium, and that it is forbidden to an existing individual to forget that he exists.

One must therefore be very careful in dealing with a philosopher of the Hegelian school, and, above all, to make certain of the identity of the being with whom one has the honor to discourse. Is he a human being, an existing human being? Is he himself *sub specie aeterni,* even when he sleeps, eats, blows his nose, or whatever else a human being does? Is he himself the pure "I am I"? This is an idea that has surely never occurred to any philosopher; but if not, how does he stand existentially related to this entity, and through what intermediate determinations is the ethical responsiblity resting upon him as an existing individual suitably respected? Does he in fact exist? And if he does, is he then not in process of becoming? And if he is in process of becoming, does he not face the future? And does he ever face the future by way of action? And if he never does, will he not forgive an ethical individuality for saying in passion and with dramatic truth, that he is an ass? But if he ever acts *sensu eminenti,* does he not in that case face the future with infinite passion? Is there not then for him an either-or? Is it not the case that eternity is for an existing individual not eternity, but the future, and that eternity is eternity only for the Eternal, who is not in process of becoming? Let him state whether he can answer the following question, i.e. if such a question can be addressed to him: "Is ceasing to exist so far as possible, in order to be *sub specie aeterni,* something that happens to him, or is it subject to a decision of the will, perhaps even something one ought to do?" For if I ought to do it, an *aut-aut* is established even with respect to being *sub specie aeterni.* Was he born *sub specie aeterni,* and has he lived *sub specie aeterni* ever since, so that he cannot even understand what I am asking about, never having had anything to do with the future, and never having experienced any decision? In that case I readily understand that it is not a human being I have the honor to address. But this does not quite end the matter; for it seems to me a very strange circumstance that such mysterious beings begin to make their appearance. An epidemic of cholera is usually signalized by the appearance of a certain kind of fly not otherwise observable; may it not be the case that the appearance of these fabulous pure thinkers is a sign that some misfortune threatens humanity, as for instance the loss of the ethical and the religious?

It is necessary to be thus careful in dealing with an abstract thinker who not only desires for himself to remain in the pure being of abstract thought, but insists that this is the highest goal for human life, and that a type of thought which leads to the ignoring of the ethical and a misunderstanding of the religious is the highest human thinking. But let us not on the other hand say that an *aut-aut* exists *sub specie aeterni,* where according to the Eleatic doctrine "everything is and nothing comes into being."[3] But where everything is in process of becoming, and only so much of eternity is present as to be a restraining influence in the passionate decision, where *eternity* is related as *futurity* to the individual in process of becoming, there the absolute disjunction belongs. When I put eternity and *becoming* together I do not get rest, but coming into being and futurity. It is undoubtedly for this reason that Christianity has announced eternity as the future life, namely, because it addresses itself to existing individuals, and it is for this reason also that it assumes an absolute either-or.

All logical thinking employs the language of abstraction, and is *sub specie aeterni.* To think existence logically is thus to ignore the difficulty, the difficulty, that is, of thinking the eternal as in process of becoming. But this difficulty is unavoidable, since the thinker himself is in process of becoming. It is easier to indulge in abstract thought than it is to exist, unless we understand by this latter term what is loosely called existing, in analogy with what is loosely called being a subject. Here we have again an example of the fact that the simplest tasks are the most difficult. Existing is ordinarily regarded as no very complex matter, much less an art, since we all exist; but abstract thinking takes rank as an accomplishment. But really to exist, so as to interpenetrate one's existence with consciousness, at one and the same time eternal and as if far removed from existence, and yet also present in existence and in the process of becoming: that is truly difficult. If philosophical reflection had not in our time become something queer, highly artificial, and capable of being learned by rote, thinkers would make quite a different impression upon people, as was the case in Greece, where a thinker was an existing individual stimulated by his reflection to a passionate enthusiasm; and as was also once the case in Christendom, when a thinker was a believer who strove enthusiastically to understand himself in the existence of faith. If anything of this sort held true of the thinkers of our own age, the enterprise of pure thought would have led to one suicide after the other. For suicide is the only tolerable existential consequence of pure thought, when this type of abstraction is

3. Misled by the constant reference to a continued process in which opposites are combined into a higher unity, and so again in a higher unity and so forth, a parallel has been drawn between Hegel's doctrine and that of Heraclitus, which asserts that everything is in a state of flux and nothing remains constant. But this is a misunderstanding, because everything said in Hegel's philosophy about process and becoming is illusory. This is why the System lacks an Ethic, and is the reason why it has no answer for the living when the question of becoming is raised in earnest, in the interest of action. In spite of all that Hegel says about process, he does not understand history from the point of view of becoming, but with the help of the illusion attaching to pastness understands it from the point of view of a finality that excludes all becoming. It is therefore impossible for a Hegelian to understand himself by means of his philosophy, for his philosophy helps him to understand only that which is past and finished, and a living person is surely not dead. He probably finds compensation in the thought that in comparison with an understanding of China and Persia and six thousand years of the world's history, a single individual does not much matter, even if that individual be himself. But it seems otherwise to me, and I understand it better conversely: when a man cannot understand himself, his understanding of China and Persia and the rest must surely be of a very peculiar kind.

not conceived as something merely partial in relation to being human, willing to strike an agreement with an ethical and religious form of personal existence, but assumes to be all and highest. This is not to praise the suicide, but to respect the passion. Nowadays a thinker is a curious creature who during certain hours of the day exhibits a very remarkable ingenuity, but has otherwise nothing in common with a human being.

To think existence *sub specie aeterni* and in abstract terms is essentially to abrogate it, and the merit of the proceeding is like the much trumpeted merit of abrogating the principle of contradiction. It is impossible to conceive existence without movement, and movement cannot be conceived *sub specie aeterni.* To leave movement out is not precisely a distinguished achievement, and to import it into logic in the form of the transition-category, and with it time and space, is only a new confusion. But inasmuch as all thought is eternal, there is here created a difficulty for the existing individual. Existence, like movement, is a difficult category to deal with; for if I think it, I abrogate it, and then I do not think it. It might therefore seem to be the proper thing to say that there is something which cannot be thought, namely, existence. But the difficulty persists, in that existence itself combines thinking with existing, in so far as the thinker exists.

Because Greek philosophy was not absent-minded, movement is perennially an object for its dialectical exertions. The Greek philosopher was an existing individual, and did not permit himself to forget that fact. In order that he might devote himself wholly to thought, he therefore sought refuge in suicide, or in a Pythagorean dying from the world, or in a Socratic form of philosopher's death. He was conscious of being a thinker, but he was also aware that existence as his medium prevented him from thinking continuously, since existence involved him in a process of becoming. In order to be able to think in very truth, therefore, he took his own life. Modern philosophy from its lofty height smiles at such childishness; for just as surely as every modern thinker knows that thought and being are one, so he also knows that it is not worth while to be what one thinks.

It is on this point about existence, and the demand which the ethical makes upon each existing individual, that one must insist when an abstract philosophy and a pure thought assume to explain everything by explaining away what is decisive. It is necessary only to have the courage to be human, and to refuse to be terrified or tricked into becoming a phantom merely to save embarrassment. It would be an altogether different thing if pure thought would accept the responsibility of explaining its own relation to the ethical, and to the ethically existing individual. But this it never does, nor does it even pretend; for in that case it would have to make terms with an entirely different dialectic, namely, the Greek or existential dialectic. The stamp of the ethical is what every existing individual has the right to expect of all that calls itself wisdom. If a beginning has already been made, if an unnoticed transition permits a man gradually to forget that he exists in order to think *sub specie aeterni,* the objection is of a different order. It is not impossible that within the sphere of pure thought many, many objections may be urged against the Hegelian philosophy; but this would leave everything essentially unaltered. Willing as I am to admire Hegel's *Logic* in the capacity of a humble reader, by no means aspiring to a critical judgment; willing as I am to admit that there may be much for me to learn when I return to a further reading of it, I shall be equally proud, insistent, fearless, and even defiant in standing by my thesis: that the Hegelian philosophy, by failing to define its relation to the existing individual, and by ignoring the ethical, confounds existence.

The most dangerous form of scepticism is always that which least looks like it. The notion that pure thought is the positive truth for an existing individual, is sheer scepticism, for this positiveness is chimerical. It is a glorious thing to be able to explain the past, the whole of human history; but if the ability to understand the past is to be the summit of attainment for a living individual, this positiveness is scepticism, and a dangerous form of it, because of the deceptive quantity of things understood. Hence the terrible thing can happen to Hegel's philosophy, that an indirect attack is most dangerous. Let a doubting youth, an existing doubter, imbued with a lovable and unlimited youthful confidence in a hero of thought, confidingly seek in Hegel's positive philosophy the truth, the truth for existence: he will write a formidable epigram over Hegel. Please do not misunderstand me. I do not mean that every youth can vanquish Hegel, far from it; if the youth is conceited and foolish enough to attempt it, his attack will be without significance. No, the youth must not even think of attacking Hegel. On the contrary, let him submit himself unconditionally, in feminine devotion, but with sufficient vigor of determination to hold fast to his problem: he will become a satirist without suspecting it. The youth is an existing doubter. Hovering in doubt and without a foothold for his life, he reaches out for the truth—in order to exist in it. He is negative and the philosophy of Hegel is positive—what wonder then that he seeks anchorage in Hegel. But a philosophy of pure thought is for an existing individual a chimera, if the truth that is sought is something to exist in. To exist under the guidance of pure thought is like travelling in Denmark with the help of a small map of Europe, on which Denmark shows no larger than a steel pen-point—aye, it is still more impossible. The admiration and enthusiasm of the youth, his boundless confidence in Hegel, is precisely the satire upon Hegel. This is something that would long ago have been perceived, if the prestige of pure thought had not been bolstered by an over-awing opinion, so that people have not dared to say that it is anything but excellent, and to avow that they have understood it—though this last is in a certain sense impossible, since this philosophy cannot help anyone to an understanding of himself, which is surely an absolute condition for all other kinds of understanding. Socrates said quite ironically that he did not know whether he was a human being or something else, but an Hegelian can say with due solemnity in the confessional: "I do not know whether I am a human being —but I have understood the System." I for my part would rather say: "I know that I am a human being, and I know that I have not understood the System." And having said so much quite simply, I will add that if any of our Hegelians will take pity on me and help me to an understanding of the System, there will be nothing in the way of hindrances interposed from my side. I shall strive to make myself as stupid as possible, so as not to have a single presupposition except my ignorance, only in order to be in a position to learn the more; and I shall strive to be as indifferent as possible over against every accusation directed against my lack of scientific training, merely to make sure of learning something.

It is impossible to exist without passion, unless we understand the word "exist" in the loose sense of a so-called existence. Every Greek thinker was therefore essentially a passionate thinker. I have often reflected how one might bring a man into a state of passion. I have thought in this connection that if I could get him seated on a horse and the horse made to take fright and gallop wildly, or better still, for the sake of bringing the passion out, if I could take a man who wanted to arrive at a certain place as quickly as possible, and hence already had some passion, and could set him astride a horse that can scarcely walk—and yet this is what existence is like if one is to become consciously aware of it. Or if a driver were otherwise not especially inclined toward passion, if someone hitched a team of horses to a wagon for him, one of them a Pegasus and the other a worn-out jade, and told him to drive—I think one might succeed. And it is just this that it means to exist, if one is to become conscious of it. Eternity is the winged horse, infinitely fast, and time is a worn-out jade; the existing individual is the driver. That is to say, he is such a driver when his mode of existence is not an existence loosely so called; for then he is no driver, but a drunken peasant who lies asleep in the wagon and lets the horses take care of themselves. To be sure, he also drives and is a driver; and so there are perhaps many who—also exist.

In so far as existence consists in movement there must be something which can give continuity to the movement and hold it together, for otherwise there is no movement. Just as the assertion that everything is true means that nothing is true, so the assertion that everything is in motion means that there is no motion.[4] The unmoved is therefore a con-

4. This was undoubtedly what the disciple of Heraclitus meant when he said that one could not pass through the same river even once. Johannes *de silentio* made a reference in *Fear and Trembling* to the remark of this disciple, but more with a rhetorical flourish than with truth.

stituent of the motion as its measure and its end. Otherwise the assertion that everything is in motion, and, if one also wishes to take time away, that everything is always in motion, is *ipso facto* the assertion of a state of rest. Aristotle, who emphasizes movement in so many ways, therefore says that God, Himself unmoved, moves all. Now while pure thought either abrogates motion altogether, or meaninglessly imports it into logic, the difficulty facing an existing individual is how to give his existence the continuity without which everything simply vanishes. An abstract continuity is no continuity, and the very existence of the existing individual is sufficient to prevent his continuity from having essential stability; while passion gives him a momentary continuity, a continuity which at one and the same time is a restraining influence and a moving impulse. The goal of movement for an existing individual is to arrive at a decision, and to renew it. The eternal is the factor of continuity; but an abstract eternity is extraneous to the movement of life, and a concrete eternity within the existing individual is the maximum degree of his passion. All idealizing passion[5] is an anticipation of the eternal in existence functioning so as to help the individual to exist.[6] The eternity of abstract thought is arrived at by abstracting from existence. The realm of pure thought is a sphere in which the existing individual finds himself only by virtue of a mistaken beginning; and this error revenges itself by making the existence of the individual insignificant, and giving his language a flavor of lunacy. This seems to be the case with almost the entire mass of men in our day, when you rarely or never hear a person speak as if he were an existing individual human being, but rather as one who sees everything in a dizzy pantheistic haze, forever talking about millions and whole nations and the historical evolution. But the passionate anticipation of the eternal is nevertheless not an absolute continuity for the existing individual; but it is the possibility of an approximation to the only true continuity that he can have. Here we are again reminded of my thesis that subjectivity is truth; for an objective truth is like the eternity of abstract thought, extraneous to the movement of existence.

Abstract thought is disinterested, but for an existing individual, existence is the highest interest. An existing individual therefore has always a *telos,* and it is of this *telos* that Aristotle speaks when he says (*De Anima,* III, 10, 2) that νοῦς θεωρέτικος differs from νοῦς πράκτικος τῷ τέλει. But pure thought is altogether detached, and not like the abstract thought which does indeed abstract from existence, but nevertheless preserves a relationship to it. This pure thought, hovering in mystic suspension be-

5. Earthly passion tends to prevent existence by transforming it into something merely momentary.
6. Art and poetry have been called anticipations of the external. If one desires to speak in this fashion, one must nevertheless note that art and poetry are not essentially related to an existing individual; for their contemplative enjoyment, the joy over what is beautiful, is disinterested, and the spectator of the work of art is contemplatively outside himself *qua* existing individual.

tween heaven and earth and emancipated from every relation to an existing individual, explains everything in its own terms but fails to explain
itself. It explains everything in such fashion that no decisive explanation
of the essential question becomes possible. Thus when an existing individual asks about the relationship between pure thought and an existing
individual, pure thought makes no reply, but merely explains existence
within pure thought and so confuses everything. It assigns to existence, the
category upon which pure thought must suffer shipwreck, a place within
pure thought itself; in this fashion everything that is said about existence
is essentially revoked. When pure thought speaks of the immediate unity
of reflection-in-self and reflection-in-other, and says that this immediate
unity is abrogated, something must of course intervene so as to divide the
two phases of this immediate unity. What can this something be? It is time.
But time cannot find a place within pure thought. What then is the meaning of the talk about abrogation and transition and the new unity? And in
general, what does it mean to think in such a manner as merely to pretend
to think, because everything that is said is absolutely revoked? And what
is the meaning of the refusal to admit that one thinks in this manner,
constantly blazoning forth this pure thought as positive truth?

Just as existence has combined thought and existence by making the
existing individual a thinker, so there are two media: the medium of
abstract thought, and the medium of reality. But pure thought is still a
third medium, quite recently discovered. It therefore begins, as the saying
is, after the most exhaustive abstraction. The relation which abstract
thought still sustains to that from which it abstracts, is something which
pure thought innocently or thoughtlessly ignores. Here is rest for every
doubt, here is the eternal positive truth, and whatever else one may be
pleased to say. That is, pure thought is a phantom. If the Hegelian philosophy has emancipated itself from every presupposition, it has won this
freedom by means of one lunatic postulate: the initial transition to pure
thought.

Existence constitutes the highest interest of the existing individual,
and his interest in his existence constitutes his reality. What reality is,
cannot be expressed in the language of abstraction. Reality is an *inter-esse*
between the moments of that hypothetical unity of thought and being
which abstract thought presupposes. Abstract thought considers both possibility and reality, but its concept of reality is a false reflection, since the
medium within which the concept is thought is not reality, but possibility.
Abstract thought can get hold of reality only by nullifying it, and this
nullification of reality consists in transforming it into possibility. All that
is said about reality in the language of abstraction and within the sphere
of abstract thought, is really said within the sphere of the possible. The

entire realm of abstract thought, speaking in the language of reality, sustains the relation of possibility to the realm of reality; but this latter reality is not one which is included within abstract thought and the realm of the possible. Reality or existence is the dialectical moment in a trilogy, whose beginning and whose end cannot be for the existing individual, since *qua* existing individual he is himself in the dialectical moment. Abstract thought closes up the trilogy. Just so. But how does it close the trilogy? Is abstract thought a mystic something, or is it not the act of the abstracting individual? But the abstracting individual is the existing individual, who is as such in the dialectical moment, which he cannot close or mediate, least of all absolutely, as long as he remains in existence. So that when he closes the trilogy, this closure must be related as a possibility to the reality or existence in which he remains. And he is bound to explain how he manages to do it, i.e. how he manages to do it as an existing individual; or else he must explain whether he ceases to be an existing individual, and whether he has any right to do this.

The moment we begin to ask this sort of question, we ask ethically, and assert the claim which the ethical has upon the existing individual. This claim is not that he should abstract from existence, but rather that he should exist; and this is at the same time his highest interest.

It is not possible for an existing individual, least of all *as* an existing individual, to hold fast absolutely a suspension of the dialectical moment, namely, existence. This would require another medium than existence, which is the dialectical moment. If an existing individual can become conscious of such a suspension, it can be only as a possibility. But this possibility cannot maintain itself when the existential interest is posited, for which reason the awareness of it can exist only in a state of disinterestedness. But the existing individual can never wholly attain this state *qua* existing individual; and ethically he is not justified even in trying to attain it *approximando,* since the ethical seeks contrariwise to make the existential interest infinite, so infinite that the principle of contradiction becomes absolutely valid.

Here again it appears, as was shown above, that the difficulty inherent in existence and confronting the existing individual is one which abstract thought does not recognize or treat. To think about the real in the medium of the possible does not involve the same difficulty as attempting to think it in the medium of existence, where existence and its process of becoming tend to prevent the individual from thinking, just as if existence could not be thought, although the existing individual is a thinker. In pure thought we are over our ears in profundity, and yet there is something rather absent-minded about it all, because the pure thinker is not clear about what it means to be a human being.

All knowledge about reality is possibility. The only reality to which an existing individual may have a relation that is more than cognitive, is his own reality, the fact that he exists; this reality constitutes his absolute interest. Abstract thought requires him to become disinterested in order to acquire knowledge; the ethical demand is that he become infinitely interested in existing.

The only reality that exists for an existing individual is his own ethical reality. To every other reality he stands in a cognitive relation; but true knowledge consists in translating the real into the possible.

The apparent trustworthiness of sense is an illusion. This was shown adequately as early as in Greek scepticism, and modern idealism has likewise demonstrated it. The trustworthiness claimed by a knowledge of the historical is also a deception, in so far as it assumes to be the very trustworthiness of reality; for the knower cannot know an historical reality until he has resolved it into a possibility. (On this point, more in what follows.) Abstract thought embraces the possible, either the preceding or the subsequent possibility; pure thought is a phantom.

The real subject is not the cognitive subject, since in knowing he moves in the sphere of the possible; the real subject is the ethically existing subject. An abstract thinker exists to be sure, but this fact is rather a satire on him than otherwise. For an abstract thinker to try to prove his existence by the fact that he thinks, is a curious contradiction; for in the degree that he thinks abstractly he abstracts from his own existence. In so far his existence is revealed as a presupposition from which he seeks emancipation; but the act of abstraction nevertheless becomes a strange sort of proof for his existence, since if it succeeded entirely his existence would cease. The Cartesian *cogito ergo sum* has often been repeated. If the "I" which is the subject of *cogito* means an individual human being, the proposition proves nothing: "I am thinking, *ergo* I am; but if I *am* thinking what wonder that I *am*:" the assertion has already been made, and the first proposition says even more than the second. But if the "I" in *cogito* is interpreted as meaning a particular existing human being, philosophy cries: "How silly; here there is no question of your self or my self, but solely of the pure ego." But this pure ego cannot very well have any other than a purely conceptual existence; what then does the *ergo* mean? There is no conclusion here, for the proposition is a tautology.

It has been said above that the abstract thinker, so far from proving his existence by his thought, rather makes it evident that his thought does not wholly succeed in proving the opposite. From this to draw the conclusion that an existing individual who really exists does not think at all, is an arbitrary misunderstanding. He certainly thinks, but he thinks everything in relation to himself, being infinitely interested in existing. Socrates was thus a man whose energies were devoted to thinking; but he reduced all other knowledge to indifference in that he infinitely accentuated ethical knowledge. This type of knowledge bears a relation to the existing subject who is infinitely interested in existing.

The attempt to infer existence from thought is thus a contradiction. For thought takes existence away from the real and thinks it by abrogating its actuality, by translating it into the sphere of the impossible. (Of this more in the following.) With respect to every reality other than the individual's own reality, the principle obtains that he can come to know it only by thinking it. With respect to his own reality, it is a question whether his thought can succeed in abstracting from it completely. This is what the abstract thinker aims at. But it avails him nothing, since he still exists; and this existential persistence, this sometimes pitiful professorial figure, is an epigram upon the abstract thinker, to say nothing of the insistent objection of the ethical.

In Greece, the philosopher was at any rate aware of what it means to exist. The so-called ataraxy of the sceptics was therefore an existential attempt to abstract from existence. In our time the process of abstracting from existence has been relegated to the printed page, just as the task of doubting everything is disposed of once for all on paper. One of the things that has given rise to so much confusion in modern philosophy is that the philosophers have so many brief sayings about infinite tasks, and respect this paper money among themselves, while it almost never occurs to anyone to try to realize the posited task. In this way everything is easily finished, and it becomes possible to begin without presuppositions. The presupposition of a universal doubt, for example, would require an entire human life; now, it is no sooner said than done.

Friedrich Nietzsche
from *Joyful Wisdom*

he only one sure enough to recognize something wrong — nissin

[125]

The madman: Have you ever heard of the madman who on a bright morning lighted a lantern and ran to the market-place calling out unceasingly: "I seek God! I seek God!"—As there were many people standing about who did not believe in God, he caused a great deal of amusement. Why! is he lost? said one. Has he strayed away like a child? said another. Or does he keep himself hidden? Is he afraid of us? Has he taken a sea-

Source: Friedrich Nietzsche, *The Joyful Wisdom*, translated by T. Common from *The Complete Works of Friedrich Nietzsche*, Oscar Levy, General Ed. (1909–1911) New York: Russell & Russell, 1964.
NOTE TO THE STUDENT: In documenting any part of this work of Nietzsche, it is customary to cite the number of the section rather than a page number.

voyage? Has he emigrated?—the people cried out laughingly, all in a hubbub. The insane man jumped into their midst and transfixed them with his glances. "Where is God gone?" he called out. "I mean to tell you! *We have killed him,*—you and I! We are all his murderers! But how have we done it? How were we able to drink up the sea? Who gave us the sponge to wipe away the whole horizon? What did we do when we loosened this earth from its sun? Whither does it now move? Whither do we move? Away from all suns? Do we not dash on unceasingly? Backwards, sideways, forewards, in all directions? Is there still an above and below? Do we not stray, as through infinite nothingness? Does not empty space breathe upon us? Has it not become colder? Does not night come on continually, darker and darker? Shall we not have to light lanterns in the morning? Do we not hear the noise of the grave-diggers who are burying God? Do we not smell the divine putrefaction?—for even Gods putrefy! God is dead! God remains dead! And we have killed him! How shall we console ourselves, the most murderous of all murderers? The holiest and the mightiest that the world has hitherto possessed, has bled to death under our knife,—who will wipe the blood from us? With what water could we cleanse ourselves? What lustrums, what sacred games shall we have to devise? Is not the magnitude of this deed too great for us? Shall we not ourselves have to become Gods, merely to seem worthy of it? There never was a greater event,—and on account of it, all who are born after us belong to a higher history than any history hitherto!"—Here the madman was silent and looked again at his hearers; they also were silent and looked at him in surprise. At last he threw his lantern on the ground, so that it broke in pieces and was extinguished. "I come too early," he then said, "I am not yet at the right time. This prodigious event is still on its way, and is travelling,—it has not yet reached men's ears. Lightning and thunder need time, the light of the stars needs time, deeds need time, even after they are done, to be seen and heard. This deed is as yet further from them than the furthest star,—*and yet they have done it!*"—It is further stated that the madman made his way into different churches on the same day, and there intoned his *Requiem aeternam deo*. When led out and called to account, he always gave the reply: "What are these churches now, if they are not the tombs and monuments of God?"—

[283]

Pioneers: I greet all the signs indicating that a more manly and warlike age is commencing, which will, above all, bring heroism again into honour! For it has to prepare the way for a yet higher age, and gather the force which the latter will one day require,—the age which will carry heroism into knowledge, and *wage war* for the sake of ideas and their consequences. For that end many brave pioneers are now needed, who, however, cannot originate out of nothing,—and just as little out of the sand and slime of present-day civilisation and the culture of great cities: men silent, solitary and resolute, who know how to be content and persistent in invisible activity: men who with innate disposition seek in all things that which is *to be overcome* in them: men to whom cheerfulness, patience, simplicity, and contempt of the great vanities belong just as much as do magnanimity in victory and indulgence of the trivial vanities of all the vanquished: men with an acute and independent judgment regarding all victors, and concerning the part which chance has played in the winning of victory and fame: men with their own holidays, their own work-days, and their own periods of mourning; accustomed to command with perfect assurance, and equally ready, if need be, to obey, proud in the one case as in the other, equally serving their own interests: men more imperilled, more productive, more happy! For believe me!—the secret of realising the largest productivity and the greatest enjoyment of existence is *to live in danger!* Build your cities on the slope of Vesuvius! Send your ships into unexplored seas! Live in war with your equals and with yourselves! Be robbers and spoilers, ye knowing ones, as long as ye cannot be rulers and possessors! The time will soon pass when you can be satisfied to live like timorous deer concealed in the forests. Knowledge will finally stretch out her hand for that which belongs to her:—she means to *rule* and *possess*, and you with her!

[296]

A fixed reputation: A fixed reputation was formerly a matter of the very greatest utility; and wherever society continues to be ruled by the herd-instinct, it is still most suitable for every individual *to give* to his character and business *the appearance* of unalterableness,—even when they are not so in reality. "One can rely on him, he remains the same"— that is the praise which has most significance in all dangerous conditions of society. Society feels with satisfaction that it has a reliable *tool* ready at all times in the virtue of this one, in the ambition of that one, and in the reflection and passion of a third one,—in honours this *tool-like nature*, this self-constancy, this unchangeableness in opinions, efforts, and even in faults, with the highest honours. Such a valuation, which prevails and has prevailed everywhere simultaneously with the morality of custom, edu- cates "characters," and brings all changing, re-learning, and self-trans- forming into *disrepute*. Be the advantage of this mode of thinking ever so great otherwise, it is in any case the mode of judging which is most injurious *to knowledge:* for precisely the good-will of the knowing one ever to declare himself hesitatingly as *opposed* to his former opinions, and in general to be distrustful of all that wants to be fixed in him—is here condemned and brought into disrepute. The disposition of the thinker, as incompatible with a "fixed reputation," is regarded as *dishonourable,* while the petrifaction of opinions has all the honour to itself:—we have at present still to live under the interdict of such rules! How difficult it is to live when one feels that the judgment of many millenniums is around one and against one. It is probable that for many millenniums knowledge was afflicted with bad conscience, and there must have been much self-contempt and secret misery in the history of the greatest intellects.

[343]

What our cheerfulness signifies: The most important of more recent events—that "God is dead," that the belief in the Christian God has become unworthy of belief—already begins to cast its first shadows over Europe. To the few at least whose eye, whose *suspecting* glance, is strong enough and subtle enough for this drama, some sun seems to have set, some old, profound confidence seems to have changed into doubt: our old world must seem to them daily more darksome, distrustful, strange and "old." In the main, however, one may say that the event itself is far too great, too remote, too much beyond most people's power of apprehension, for one to suppose that so much as the report of it could have *reached* them; not to speak of many who already knew *what* had taken place, and what must all collapse now that this belief had been undermined,—because so much was built upon it, so much rested on it, and had become one with it: for example, our entire European morality. This lengthy, vast and uninterrupted process of crumbling, destruction, ruin and overthrow which is now imminent: who has realised it sufficiently to-day to have to stand up as the teacher and herald of such a tremendous logic of terror, as the prophet of a period of gloom and eclipse, the like of which has probably never taken place on earth before? . . . Even we, the born riddle-readers, who wait as it were on the mountains posted 'twixt to-day and to-morrow, and engirt by their contradiction, we, the firstlings and premature children of the coming century, into whose sight especially the shadows which must forthwith envelop Europe *should* already have come—how it is that even we, without genuine sympathy for this period of gloom, contemplate its advent without any *personal* solicitude or fear? Are we still, perhaps, too much under the *immediate effects* of the event—and are these effects, especially as regards *ourselves,* perhaps the reverse of what was to be expected—not at all sad and depressing, but rather like a new and indescribable variety of light, happiness, relief, enlivenment, encouragement, and dawning day? . . . In fact, we philosophers and "free spirits" feel ourselves irradiated as by a new dawn by the report that the "old God is dead"; our hearts overflow with gratitude, astonishment, presentiment and expectation. At last the horizon seems open once more, granting even that it is not bright; our ships can at last put out to sea in face of every danger; every hazard is again permitted to the discerner; the sea, *our* sea, again lies open before us; perhaps never before did such an "open sea" exist. . . .

Friedrich Nietzsche
from *The Will to Power*

[430]

The great reasonableness underlying all moral education lay in the fact that it always attempted to attain to *the certainty of an instinct:* so that neither good intentions nor good means, as such, first required to enter consciousness. Just as the soldier learns his exercises, so should man learn how to act in life. In truth this unconsciousness belongs to every kind of perfection: even the mathematician carries out his calculations unconsciously. . . .

What, then, does Socrates' *reaction* mean, which recommended dialectics as the way to virtue, and which was amused when morality was unable to justify itself logically? But this is precisely what proves its *superiority*—without unconsciousness *it is worth nothing!*

In reality it means *the dissolution of Greek instincts,* when *demonstrability* is posited as the first condition of personal excellence in virtue. All these great "men of virtue" and of words are themselves types of dissolution.

In practice, it means that moral judgments have been torn from the conditions among which they grew and in which alone they had some sense, from their Greek and Græco-political soil, in order to be *denaturalised* under the cover of being *sublimated.* The great concepts "good" and "just" are divorced from the first principles of which they form a part, and,

Source: Friedrich Nietzsche, *The Will to Power,* translated by A. M. Ludovici, from *The Complete Works of Friedrich Nietzsche,* Oscar Levy, General Ed. (1909–1911) New York: Russell & Russell, 1964.

as "ideas" *become free,* degenerate into subjects for discussion. A certain truth is sought behind them; they are regarded as entities or as symbols of entities: a world is *invented* where they are "at home," and from which they are supposed to hail.

In short: the scandal reaches its apotheosis in Plato. . . . And then it was necessary to invent the *abstract perfect* man also:—good, just, wise, and a dialectician to boot—in short, the *scarecrow* of the ancient philosopher: a plant without any soil whatsoever; a human race devoid of all definite ruling instincts; a virtue which "justifies" itself with reasons. The perfectly absurd "individual" *per se!* the highest form of *Artificiability.* . . .

Briefly, the denaturalisation of moral values resulted in the creation of a degenerate *type of man*—"the good man," "the happy man," "the wise man."—Socrates represents a moment of the most *profound perversity* in the history of values.

[453]

The causes of error lie just as much in the *good* as in the *bad will* of man:—in an incalculable number of cases he conceals reality from himself, he falsifies it, so that he may not suffer from his good or bad will. God, for instance, is considered the shaper of man's destiny; he interprets his little lot as though everything were intentionally sent to him for the salvation of his soul,—this act of ignorance in "philology," which to a more subtle intellect would seem unclean and false, is done, in the majority of cases, with perfect *good faith.* Goodwill, "noble feelings," and "lofty states of the soul" are just as underhand and deceptive in the means they use as are the passions love, hatred, and revenge, which morality has repudiated and declared to be egotistic.

Errors are what mankind has had to pay for most dearly: and taking them all in all, the errors which have resulted from goodwill are those which have wrought the most harm. The illusion which makes people happy is more harmful than the illusion which is immediately followed by evil results: the latter increases keenness and mistrust, and purifies the understanding; the former merely narcoticises. . . .

Fine feelings and noble impulses ought, speaking physiologically, to be classified with the narcotics: their abuse is followed by precisely the same results as the abuse of any other opiate—*weak nerves.*

[521]

Concerning "logical appearance" The concept "individual" and the concept "species" are equally false and only apparent. "*Species*" only expresses the fact that an abundance of similar creatures come forth at the same time, and that the speed of their further growth and of their further transformation has been made almost imperceptible for a long time: so that the actual and trivial changes and increase of growth are of no account at all (—a stage of evolution in which the process of evolving is not visible, so that, not only does a state of equilibrium *seem* to have been reached, but the road is also made clear for the error of supposing *that an actual goal has been reached*—and that evolution had a goal . . .).

The form seems to be something enduring, and therefore valuable; but the form was invented merely by ourselves; and however often "the same form is attained," it does not signify that it *is the same form,—because something new always appears;* and we alone, who compare, reckon the new with the old, in so far as it resembles the latter, and embody the two in the unity of "form." As if a *type* had to be reached and were actually intended by the formative processes.

Form, species, law, idea, purpose—the same fault is made in respect of all these concepts, namely, that of giving a false realism to a piece of fiction: as if all phenomena were infused with some sort of obedient spirit —an artificial distinction is here made between that *which* acts and that *which* guides action (but both these things are only fixed in order to agree with our metaphysico-logical dogma: they are not "facts").

We should not interpret this *constraint* in ourselves, to imagine concepts, species, forms, purposes, and laws (*"a world of identical cases"*) as if we were in a position to construct a *real world;* but as a constraint to adjust a world by means of which *our existence* will be ensured: we thereby create a world which is determinable, simplified, comprehensible, etc., for us.

The very same constraint is active in *the functions of the senses* which support the reason—by means of simplification, coarsening, accentuation, and interpretation; whereon all "recognition," all the ability of making one's self intelligible rests. Our *needs* have made our senses so precise, that the "same world of appearance" always returns, and has thus acquired the semblance of *reality.*

Our subjective constraint to have faith in logic, is expressive only of the fact that long before logic itself became conscious in us, we did nothing *save introduce its postulates into the nature of things:* now we find ourselves in their presence,—we can no longer help it,—and now we would fain believe that this constraint is a guarantee of "truth." We it was who created the "thing," the "same thing," the subject, the attribute, the action, the object, the substance, and the form, after we had carried the process of equalising, coarsening, and simplifying as far as possible. The world *seems* logical to us, because we have already made it logical.

Fëdor Dostoevski

from *Notes from Underground*

It is important to point out that the disconcerting speaker of the following passages from *Notes from Underground* is not Dostoevski as such. As Part Two ("Apropos of the Wet Snow") of this proto-existential novel makes implicitly clear, the "confession/diatribe" in Part One of this alienated, and excessively individualistic irrationalist, is, in part, a neurotic rationalization—like that of Jean-Baptiste Clamence in Camus' *The Fall*—of his inability (out of fear) to offer love to Liza, the prostitute —another human being in need. To put it positively, it is a neurotic strategy to justify his impulse to neutralize the threat her existence poses for him by coercing, by subjugating, her unpredictable being within the rigid—and comforting—framework of a melodramatic or "well-made fiction" in which he is the guiding presence. " 'Real life,' " he says, "oppressed me with its novelty so much that I could hardly breathe."

But the speaker's powerful ironic argument against the Europeanized "straightforward gentlemen," who wish to build the Crystal Palace world on the foundation of causal logic, the logic of two plus two equals four, *is* Dostoevski's. It is worth noting, in this respect, that he had visited the Crystal Palace exhibition in London in 1862 and, despite a curious attraction, was appalled by its dehumanizing effects and by the ontological imbalances it threatened to generate:

> This city bustling day and night, unbounded like the sea, the whine and growl of the machines, the trains running over the houses (*and soon under the houses too*), this boldness of enterprise, this seeming disorder, which, in fact, is capitalist order of the highest degree, this polluted Thames, this air impregnated with coal fumes, these magnificent squares and parks, these terrible slums, like Whitechapel with its half-naked, savage and hungry population, the City with its millions and world trade, the Crystal Palace, the world exhibition. . . . Yes, the exhibition is amazing. You feel the terrible force which here unites all those numberless people from all over the world into one fold; you are conscious of some gigantic idea; you feel that here something has already been achieved, that here is victory, triumph. You even begin to fear something. However inde-

Source: From *Notes from Underground* by Fyodor Dostoyevsky. Translated by Ralph Matlaw. Translation © 1960 by E. P. Dutton & Co., Inc., and reprinted with their permission.

pendent you may be, you can't for some reason help feeling terrified. "Is this really 'the one fold'? Nill one really have to accept this as the final truth and fall down before it, mute and silent for ever?". . . . It's a kind of Biblical picture, something like Babylon, a kind of prophecy from the Apocalypse which is being fulfilled before our very eyes. [1]

And he was violently opposed to the "Westernization" of Russia begun by Peter the Great when he built St. Petersburg on the model of the rational European city. This explains the setting of *Notes* (as well as of *Crime and Punishment,* incidentally) and the speaker's ironic allusion to himself (a man suffering from "the disease of hyper-consciousness") in section II as "one who has the particular misfortune to inhibit Petersburg, the most abstract and intentional city in the whole world."

[V]

Come, can a man who even attempts to find enjoyment in the very feeling of self-degradation really have any respect for himself at all? I am not saying this now from any insipid kind of remorse. And, indeed, I could never endure to say, "Forgive me, Daddy, I won't do it again," not because I was incapable of saying it, but, on the contrary, perhaps just because I was too capable of it, and in what a way, too! As though on purpose I used to get into trouble on occasions when I was not to blame in the faintest way. That was the nastiest part of it. At the same time I was genuinely touched and repentant, I used to shed tears and, of course, tricked even myself, though it was not acting in the least and there was a sick feeling in my heart at the time. For that one could not even blame the laws of nature, though the laws of nature have offended me continually all my life more than anything. It is loathsome to remember it all, but it was loathsome even then. Of course, in a minute or so I would realize with spite that it was all a lie, a lie, an affected, revolting lie, that is, all this repentance, all these emotions, these vows to reform. And if you ask why I worried and tortured myself that way, the answer is because it was very dull to twiddle one's thumbs, and so one began cutting capers. That is really it. Observe yourselves more carefully, gentlemen, then you will understand that that's right! I invented adventures for myself and made up a life, so as to live at least in some way. How many times it has happened to me—well, for instance, to take offence at nothing, simply on purpose; and one knows oneself, of course, that one is offended at nothing, that one is pretending, but yet one brings oneself, at last, to the point of really being offended. All my life I have had an impulse to play such pranks, so that

1. "Winter Notes on Summer Impressions," quoted in David Magarshack, *Dostoevsky* (New York: Harcourt Brace Jovanovich, 1963), pp. 203–204.

in the end, I could not control it in myself. Another time, twice, in fact, I tried to force myself to fall in love. I even suffered, gentlemen, I assure you. In the depth of my heart I did not believe in my suffering, there was a stir of mockery, but yet I did suffer, and in the real, regular way I was jealous, I was beside myself, and it was all out of boredom, gentlemen, all out of boredom; inertia overcame me. After all, the direct, legitimate, immediate fruit of consciousness is inertia, that is, conscious thumb twiddling. I have referred to it already, I repeat, I repeat it emphatically: all straightforward persons and men of action are active just because they are stupid and limited. How can that be explained? This way: as a result of their limitation they take immediate and secondary causes for primary ones, and in that way persuade themselves more quickly and easily than other people do that they have found an infallible basis for their activity, and their minds are at ease and that, you know, is the most important thing. To begin to act, you know, you must first have your mind completely at ease and without a trace of doubt left in it. Well, how am I, for example, to set my mind at rest? Where are the primary causes on which I am to build? Where are my bases? Where am I to get them from? I exercise myself in the process of thinking, and consequently with me every primary cause at once draws after itself another still more primary, and so on to infinity. That is precisely the essence of every sort of consciousness and thinking. It must be a case of the laws of nature again. In what does it finally result? Why, just the same. Remember I spoke just now of vengeance. (I am sure you did not grasp that.) I said that a man revenges himself because he finds justice in it. Therefore he has found a primary cause, found a basis, to wit, justice. And so he is completely set at rest, and consequently he carries out his revenge calmly and successfully, as he is convinced that he is doing a just and honest thing. But, after all, I see no justice in it, I find no sort of virtue in it either, and consequently if I attempt to revenge myself, it would only be out of spite. Spite, of course, might overcome everything, all my doubts, and could consequently serve quite successfully in a place of a primary cause, precisely because it is not a cause. But what can be done if I do not even have spite (after all, I began with that just now)? Again, in consequence of those accused laws of consciousness, my spite is subject to chemical disintegration. You look into it, the object flies off into air, your reasons evaporate, the criminal is not to be found, the insult becomes fate rather than an insult, something like the toothache, for which no one is to blame, and consequently there is only the same outlet left again—that is, to beat the wall as hard as you can. So you give it up as hopeless because you have not found a fundamental cause. And try letting yourself be carried away by your feelings, blindly, without reflection, without a primary cause, repelling consciousness at least for a time; hate or love, if only not to sit and twiddle your thumbs.

The day after tomorrow, at the latest, you will begin despising yourself for having knowingly deceived yourself. The result—a soap-bubble and inertia. Oh, gentlemen, after all, perhaps I consider myself an intelligent man only because all my life I have been able neither to begin nor to finish anything. Granted, granted I am a babbler, a harmless annoying babbler, like all of us. But what is to be done if the direct and sole vocation of every intelligent man is babble, that is, the intentional pouring of water through a sieve?

[VII]

But these are all golden dreams. Oh, tell me, who first declared, who first proclaimed, that man only does nasty things because he does not know his own real interests; and that if he were enlightened, if his eyes were opened to his real normal interests, man would at once cease to do nasty things, would at once become good and noble because, being enlightened and understanding his real advantage, he would see his own advantage in the good and nothing else, and we all know that not a single man can knowingly act to his own disadvantage. Consequently, so to say, he would begin doing good through necessity. Oh, the babe! Oh, the pure, innocent child! Why, in the first place, when in all these thousands of years has there ever been a time when man has acted only for his own advantage? What is to be done with the millions of facts that bear witness that men, *knowingly*, that is, fully understanding their real advantages, have left them in the background and have rushed headlong on another path, to risk, to chance, compelled to this course by nobody and by nothing, but, as it were, precisely because they did not want the beaten track, and stubbornly, wilfully, went off on another difficult, absurd way seeking it almost in the darkness. After all, it means that this stubbornness and wilfulness were more pleasant to them than any advantage. Advantage! What is advantage? And will you take it upon yourself to define with perfect accuracy in exactly what the advantage of man consists of? And what if it so happens that a man's advantage *sometimes* not only may, but even must, consist exactly in his desiring under certain conditions what is harmful to himself and not what is advantageous. And if so, if there can be such a condition then the whole principle becomes worthless. What do you think—are there such cases? You laugh; laugh away, gentlemen, so long as you answer me: have man's advantages been calculated with perfect certainty? Are there not some which not only have not been included but cannot possibly be included under any classification? After all, you, gentlemen, so far as I know, have taken your whole register of human advantages from the average of statistical figures and scientific-economic formulas. After all, your advantages are prosperity, wealth, freedom, peace—and so on, and so on. So that a man who, for instance, would openly and knowingly oppose that whole list would, to your thinking, and indeed to mine too, of course, be an obscurantist or an absolute madman, would he not? But, after all, here is something amazing: why does it happen that all these statisticians, sages and lovers of humanity, when they calculate human advantages invariably leave one out? They don't even take it into their calculation in the form in which it should be taken, and the whole reckoning depends upon that. There would be no great harm to take it, this advantage, and to add it to the list. But the trouble is, that this strange advantage does not fall under any classification and does not figure in any list. For instance, I have a friend. Bah, gentlemen! But after all he is your friend, too; and indeed there is no one, no one, to whom he is not a friend! When he prepares for any undertaking this gentleman immediately explains to you, pompously and clearly, exactly how he must act in accordance with the laws of reason and truth. What is more, he will talk to you with excitement and passion of the real normal interests of man; with irony he will reproach the short-sighted fools who do not understand their own advantage, nor the true significance of virtue; and, within a quarter of an hour, without any sudden outside provocation, but precisely through that something internal which is stronger than all his advantages, he will go off on quite a different tack—that is, act directly opposite to what he has just been saying himself, in opposite to the laws of reason, in opposition to his own advantage—in fact, in opposition to everything. I warn you that my friend is a compound personality, and therefore it is somehow difficult to blame him as an individual. The fact is, gentlemen, it seems that something that is dearer to almost every man than his greatest advantages must really exist, or (not to be illogical) there is one most advantageous advantage (the very one omitted of which we spoke just now) which is more important and more advantageous than all other advantages, for which, if necessary, a man is ready to act in opposition to all laws, that is, in opposition to reason, honor, peace, prosperity—in short, in opposition to all those wonderful and useful things if only he can attain that fundamental, most advantageous advantage which is dearer to him than all.

"Well, but it is still advantage just the same," you will retort. But excuse me, I'll make the point clear, and it is not a case of a play on words, but what really matters is that this advantage is remarkable from the very fact that it breaks down all our classifications, and continually shatters all the systems evolved by lovers of mankind of the happiness of mankind. In short, it interferes with everything. But before I mention this advantage to you, I want to compromise myself personally, and therefore I boldly declare that all these fine systems—all these theories for explaining to mankind its real normal interests, so that inevitably striving to obtain these interests, it may at once become good and noble—are, in my opinion, so far, mere logical exercises! Yes, logical exercises. After all, to maintain even this theory of the regeneration of mankind by means of its own advantage, is, after all, to my mind almost the same thing as—as to claim, for instance, with Buckle, that through civilization mankind becomes softer, and consequently less bloodthirsty, and less fitted for warfare. Logically it does not seem to follow from his arguments. But man is so fond of systems and abstract deductions that he is ready to distort the truth intentionally, he is ready to deny what he can see and hear just to justify his logic. I take this example because it is the most glaring instance of it. Only look about you: blood is being spilled in streams, and in the merriest way, as though it were champagne. Take the whole of the nineteenth century in which Buckle lived. Take Napoleon—both the Great and the present one. Take North America—the eternal union. Take farcical Schleswig-Holstein. And what is it that civilization softens in us? Civilization only produces a greater variety of sensations in man—and absolutely nothing more. And through the development of this variety, man may even come to find enjoyment in bloodshed. After all, it has already happened to him. Have you noticed that the subtlest slaughterers have almost always been the most civilized gentlemen, to whom the various Attilas and Stenka Razins could never hold a candle, and if they are not so conspicuous as the Attilas and Stenka Razins it is precisely because they are so often met with, are so ordinary and have become so familiar to us. In any case if civilization has not made man more bloodthirsty, it has at least made him more abominably, more loathsomely bloodthirsty than before. Formerly he saw justice in bloodshed and with his conscience at peace exterminated whomever he thought he should. And now while we consider bloodshed an abomination, we nevertheless engage in this abomination and even more than ever before. Which is worse? Decide that for youselves. It is said that Cleopatra (pardon the example from Roman history) was fond of sticking gold pins into her slave-girls' breasts and derived enjoyment from their screams and writhing. You will say that that occurred in comparatively barbarous times; that these are barbarous times too, because (also comparatively speaking) pins are stuck in even now; that even though man has now learned to see more clearly occasionally than in barbarous times, he is still far from having *accustomed* himself to act as reason and science would dictate. But all the same you are fully convinced that he will inevitably accustom himself to it when he gets completely rid of certain old bad habits, and when common sense and science have completely re-educated human nature and turned it in a normal direction. You are confident that man will then refrain from erring *intentionally*, and will, so to say, willy-nilly, not want to set his will against his normal interests. More than that: then, you say, science itself will teach man (though to my mind that is a luxury) that he does not really have either caprice or will of his own and that he has never had it, and that he himself is something like a piano key or an organ stop, and that, moreover, laws of nature exist in this world, so that everything he does is not done by his will at all, but is done by itself, according to the laws of nature. Consequently we have only to discover these laws of nature, and man will no longer be responsible for his actions and life will become exceedingly easy for him. All human actions will then, of course, be tabulated according to these laws, mathematically, like tables of logarithms up to 108,000, and entered in a table; or, better still, there would be published certain edifying works like the present encyclopedic lexicons, in which everything will be so clearly calculated and designated that there will be no more incidents or adventures in the world.

Then—it is still you speaking—new economic relations will be established, all ready-made and computed with mathematical exactitude, so that every possible question will vanish in a twinkling, simply because every possible answer to it will be provided. Then the crystal palace will be built. Then—well, in short, those will be halcyon days. Of course there is no guaranteeing (this is my comment now) that it will not be, for instance, terribly boring then (for what will one have to do when everything is calculated according to the table?) but on the other hand everything will be extraordinarily rational. Of course boredom may lead you to anything. After all, boredom even sets one to sticking gold pins into people, but all that would not matter. What is bad (this is my comment again) is that for all I know people will be thankful for the gold pins then. After all, man is stupid, phenomenally stupid. Or rather he is not stupid at all, but he is so ungrateful that you could not find another like him in all creation. After all, it would not surprise me in the least, if, for instance, suddenly for no reason at all, a gentleman with an ignoble, or rather with a reactionary and ironical, countenance were to arise and, putting his arms akimbo, say to us all: "What do you think, gentlemen, hadn't we better kick over all that rationalism at one blow, scatter it to the winds, just to send these logarithms to the devil, and to let us live once more according to our own foolish will!" That again would not matter; but what is annoying is that after all he would be sure to find followers—such is the nature of man. And all that for the most foolish reason, which, one would think, was hardly worth mentioning: that is, that man everywhere and always, whoever he may be, has preferred to act as he wished and not in the least as his reason and advantage dictated. Why, one may choose what is contrary to one's own interests, and sometimes one *positively ought* (that is my idea). One's own free unfettered choice, one's own fancy, however wild it may be, one's own fancy worked up at times to frenzy—why that is that very "most advantageous advantage" which we have overlooked, which comes under no classification and through which all systems and theories are continually being sent to the devil. And how do these sages know that man must necessarily need a rationally advantageous choice? What man needs is simply *independent* choice, whatever that independence may cost and wherever it may lead. Well, choice, after all, the devil only knows . . .

[VIII]

"Ha! ha! ha! But after all, if you like, in reality, there is no such thing as choice," you will interrupt with a laugh. "Science has even now succeeded in analyzing man to such an extent that we know already that choice and what is called freedom of will are nothing other than—"

Wait, gentlemen, I meant to begin with that myself. I admit that I was even fightened. I was just going to shout that after all the devil only knows what choice depends on, and that perhaps that was a very good thing, but I remembered the teaching of science—and pulled myself up. And here you have begun to speak. After all, really, well, if some day they truly discover a formula for all our desires and caprices—that is, an explanation of what they depend upon, by what laws they rise, just how they develop, what they are aiming at in one case or another and so on, and so on, that is, a real mathematical formula—then, after all, man would most likely at once stop to feel desire, indeed, he will be certain to. For who would want to choose by rule? Besides, he will at once be transformed from a human being into an organ stop or something of the sort? for what is a man without desire, without free will and without choice, if not a stop in an organ? What do you think? Let us consider the probability—can such a thing happen or not?

"H'm!" you decide. "Our choice is usually mistaken through a mistaken notion of our advantage. We sometimes choose absolute nonsense because in our stupidity we see in that nonsense the easiest means for attaining an advantage assumed beforehand. But when all that is explained and worked out on paper (which is perfectly possible, for it is contemptible and senseless to assume in advance that man will never understand some laws of nature), then, of course, so-called desires will not exist. After all, if desire should at any time come to terms completely with reason, we shall then, of course, reason and not desire, simply because, after all, it will be impossible to retain reason and *desire* something senseless, and in that way knowingly act against reason and desire to injure ourselves. And as all choice and reasoning can really be calculated, because some day they will discover the laws of our so-called free will—so joking aside, there may one day probably be something like a table of desires so that we really shall choose in accordance with it. After all, if, for instance, some day they calculate and prove to me that I stuck my tongue out at someone because I could not help sticking my tongue out at him and that I had to do it in that particular way, what sort of *freedom* is left me, especially if I am a learned man and have taken my degree somewhere? After all, then I would be able to calculate my whole life for thirty years in advance. In short, if that comes about, then, after all, we could do nothing about it. We would have to accept it just the same. And, in fact, we ought to repeat to ourselves incessantly that at such and such a time and under such and such circumstances, Nature does not ask our leave; that we must accept her as she is and not as we imagine her to be, and if we really aspire to tables and indices and well, even—well, let us say to the chemical retort, then it cannot be helped. We must accept the retort, too, or else it will be accepted without our consent."

Yes, but here I come to a stop! Gentlemen, you must excuse me for philosophizing; it's the result of forty years underground! Allow me to indulge my fancy for a minute. You see, gentlemen, reason, gentlemen, is an excellent thing, there is no disputing that, but reason is only reason and can only satisfy man's rational faculty, while will is a manifestation of all life, that is, of all human life including reason as well as all impulses. And although our life, in this manifestation of it, is often worthless, yet it is life nevertheless and not simply extracting square roots. After all, here I, for instance, quite naturally want to live, in order to satisfy all my faculties for life, and not simply my rational faculty, that is, not simply one-twentieth of all my faculties for life. What does reason know? Reason only knows what it has succeeded in learning (some times it will perhaps never learn; while this is nevertheless no comfort, why not say so frankly?) and human nature acts as a whole, with everything that is in it, consciously or unconsciously, and, even if it goes wrong, it lives. I suspect, gentlemen, that you are looking at me with compassion; you repeat to me that an enlightened and developed man, such, in short, as the future man will be, cannot knowingly desire anything disadvantageous to himself, that this can be proved mathematically. I thoroughly agree, it really can—by mathematics. But I repeat for the hundredth time, there is one case, one only, when man may purposely, consciously, desire what is injurious to himself, what is stupid, very stupid—simply in order *to have the right* to desire for himself even what is very stupid and not to be bound by an obligation to desire only what is rational. After all, this very stupid thing, after all, this caprice of ours, may really be more advantageous for us, gentlemen, than anything else on earth, especially in some cases. And in particular it may be more advantageous than any advantages even when it does us obvious harm, and contradicts the soundest conclusions of our reason about our advantage—because in any case it preserves for us what is most precious and most important—that is, our personality, our individuality. Some, you see, maintain that this really is the most precious thing for man; desire can, of course, if it desires, be in agreement with reason; particularly if it does not abuse this practice but does so in moderation, it is both useful and sometimes even praiseworthy. But very often, and even most often, desire completely and stubbornly opposes reason, and ... and ... and do you know that that, too, is useful and sometimes even praiseworthy? Gentlemen, let us suppose that man is not stupid. (Indeed, after all, one cannot say that about him anyway, if only for the one consideration that, if man is stupid, then, after all, who is wise?) But if he is not stupid, he is just the same monstrously ungrateful! Phenomenally ungrateful. I even believe that the best definition of man is—a creature that walks on two legs and is ungrateful. But that is not all, that is not his worst defect; his worst defect is his perpetual immorality, perpetual—from the days of the Flood to the Schleswig-Holstein period of human destiny. Immorality, and consequently lack of good sense; for it has long been accepted that lack of good sense is due to no other cause than immorality. Try it, and cast a look upon the history of mankind. Well, what will you see? Is it a grand spectacle? All right, grand, if you like. The Colossus of Rhodes, for instance, that is worth something. Mr. Anaevsky may well testify that some say it is the work of human hands, while others maintain that it was created by Nature herself. Is it variegated? Very well, it may be variegated too. If one only took the dress uniforms, military and civilian, of all peoples in all ages— that alone is worth something, and if you take the undress uniforms you will never get to the end of it; no historian could keep up with it. Is it monotonous? Very well. It may be monotonous, too; they fight and fight; they are fighting now, they fought first and they fought last—you will admit that it is almost too monotonous. In short, one may say anything about the history of the world—anything that might enter the most disordered imagination. The only thing one cannot say is that it is rational. The very word sticks in one's throat. And, indeed, this is even the kind of thing that continually happens. After all, there are continually turning up in life moral and rational people, sages, and lovers of humanity, who make it their goal for life to live as morally and rationally as possible, to be, so to speak, a light to their neighbors, simply in order to show them that it is really possible to live morally and rationally in this world. And so what? We all know that those very people sooner or later toward the end of their lives have been false to themselves, playing some trick, often a most indecent one. Now I ask you: What can one expect from man since he is a creature endowed with such strange qualities? Shower upon him every earthly blessing, drown him in bliss so that nothing but bubbles would dance on the surface of his bliss, as on a sea; give him such economic prosperity that he would have nothing else to do but sleep, eat cakes and busy himself with ensuring the continuation of world history and even then man, out of sheer ingratitude, sheer libel, would play you some loathsome trick. He would even risk his cakes and would deliberately desire the most fatal rubbish, the most uneconomical absurdity, simply to introduce into all this positive rationality his fatal fantastic element. It is just his fantastic dreams, his vulgar folly, that he will desire to retain, simply in order to prove to himself (as though that were so necessary) that men still are men and not piano keys, which even if played by the laws of nature themselves threaten to be controlled so completely that soon one will be able to desire nothing but by the calendar. And, after all, that is not all: even if man really were nothing but a piano key, even if this were proved to him by natural science and mathematics, even then he would not become reasonable, but would purposely do something perverse out of sheer ingratitude, simply to have his own way. And if he does not find any means he will devise destruction and chaos, will devise sufferings of all sorts, and will thereby have his own way. He will launch a curse upon the world, and, as only man can curse (it is his privilege, the primary distinction between him and other animals) then, after all, perhaps only by his curse will he attain his object, that is, really convince himself that he is a man and not a piano key! If you say that all this, too, can be calculated and tabulated, chaos and darkness and curses, so that the mere possibility of calculating it all beforehand would stop it all, and reason would reassert itself—then man would purposely go mad in order to be rid of reason and have his own way! I believe in that, I vouch for it, because, after all, the whole work of man seems really to consist in nothing but proving to himself continually that he is a man and not an organ stop. It may be at the cost of his skin! But he has proved it; he may become a caveman, but he will have proved it. And after that can one help sinning, rejoicing that it has not yet come, and that desire still depends on the devil knows what!

You will shout at me (that is, if you will still favor me with your shout) that, after all, no one is depriving me of my will, that all they are concerned with is that my will should somehow of itself, of its own free will, coincide with my own normal interests, with the laws of nature and arithmetic.

Bah, gentlemen, what sort of free will is left when we come to tables and arithmetic, when it will all be a case of two times two makes four? Two times two makes four even without my will. As if free will meant that!

[IX]

Gentlemen, I am joking, of course, and I know myself that I'm joking badly, but after all you know, one can't take everything as a joke. I am, perhaps, joking with a heavy heart. Gentlemen, I am tormented by questions; answer them for me. Now you, for instance, want to cure men of their old habits and reform their will in accordance with science and common sense. But how do you know, not only that it is possible, but also that it is *desirable,* to reform man in that way? And what leads you to the conclusion that it is so *necessary* to reform man's desires? In short, how do you know that such a reformation will really be advantageous to man? And to go to the heart of the matter, why are you *so sure* of your conviction that not to act against his real normal advantages guaranteed by the conclusions of reason and arithmetic is always advantageous for man and must be a law for all mankind? After all, up to now it is only your supposition. Let us assume it to be a law of logic, but perhaps not a law of humanity at all. You gentlemen perhaps think that I am mad? Allow me to defend myself. I agree that man is preeminently a creative animal, predestined to strive consciously toward a goal, and to engage in engineering; that is, eternally and incessantly, to build new roads, *wherever they may lead.* But the reason why he sometimes wants to swerve aside may be precisely that he is *forced* to make that road, and perhaps, too, because however stupid the straightforward practical man may be in general, the thought nevertheless will sometimes occur to him that the road, it would seem, almost always does lead *somewhere,* and that the destination it leads to is less important than the process of making it, and that the chief thing is to save the well-behaved child from despising engineering, and so giving way to the fatal idleness, which, as we all know, is the mother of all vices. Man likes to create and build roads, that is beyond dispute. But why does he also have such a passionate love for destruction and chaos? Now tell me that! But on that point I want to say a few special words myself. May it not be that he loves chaos and destruction (after all, he sometimes unquestionably likes it very much, that is surely so) because he is instinctively afraid of attaining his goal and completing the edifice he is constructing? How do you know, perhaps he only likes that edifice from a distance, and not at all at close range, perhaps he only likes to build it and does not want to live in it, but will leave it, when completed, *aux animaux domestiques* —such as the ants, the sheep, and so on, and so on. Now the ants have quite a different taste. They have an amazing edifice of that type, that endures forever—the anthill.

With the anthill, the respectable race of ants began and with the anthill they will probably end, which does the greatest credit to their perseverance and staidness. But man is a frivolous and incongruous creature, and perhaps, like a chessplayer, loves only the process of the game, not the end of it. And who knows (one cannot swear to it), perhaps the only goal on earth to which mankind is striving lies in this incessant process of attaining, or in other words, in life itself, and not particularly in the goal which of course must always be two times two makes four, that is a formula, and after all, two times two makes four is no longer life, gentlemen, but is the beginning of death. Anyway, man has always been somehow afraid of this two times two makes four, and I am afraid of it even now. Granted that man does nothing but seek that two times two makes four, that he sails the oceans, sacrifices his life in the quest, but to succeed, really to find it—he is somehow afraid, I assure you. He feels that as soon as he has found it there will be nothing for him to look for. When workmen have finished their work they at least receive their pay, they go to the tavern, then they wind up at the police station—and there is an occupation for a week. But where can man go? Anyway, one can observe a certain awkwardness about him every time he attains such goals. He likes the process of attaining, but does not quite like to have attained, and that, of course, is terribly funny. In short, man is a comical creature; there seems to be a kind of pun in it all. But two times two makes four is, after all, something insufferable. Two times two makes four seems to me simply a piece of insolence. Two times two makes four is a fop standing with arms akimbo barring your path and spitting. I admit that two times two makes four is an excellent thing, but if we are going to praise everything, two times two makes five is sometimes also a very charming little thing.

And why are you so firmly, so triumphantly convinced that only the normal and the positive—in short, only prosperity—is to the advantage of man? Is not reason mistaken about advantage? After all, perhaps man likes something besides prosperity? Perhaps he likes suffering just as much? Perhaps suffering is just as great an advantage to him as prosperity? Man is sometimes fearfully, passionately in love with suffering and that is a fact. There is no need to appeal to universal history to prove that; only ask yourself, if only you are a man and have lived at all. As far as my own personal opinion is concerned, to care only for prosperity seems to me somehow even ill-bred. Whether it's good or bad, it is sometimes very pleasant to smash things, too. After all, I do not really insist on suffering or on prosperity either. I insist on my caprice, and its being guaranteed to me when necessary. Suffering would be out of place in vaudevilles, for instance; I know that. In the crystal palace it is even unthinkable; suffering means doubt, means negation, and what would be the good of a crystal palace if there could be any doubt about it? And yet I am sure man will never renounce real suffering, that is, destruction and chaos. Why, after all, suffering is the sole origin of consciousness. Though I stated at the beginning that consciousness, in my opinion, is the greatest misfortune for man, yet I know man loves it and would not give it up for any satisfaction. Consciousness, for instance, is infinitely superior to two times two makes four. Once you have two times two makes four, there is nothing left to do or to understand. There will be nothing left but to bottle up your five senses and plunge into contemplation. While if you stick to consciousness, even though you attain the same result, you can at least flog yourself at times, and that will, at any rate, liven you up. It may be reactionary, but corporal punishment is still better than nothing.

Phenomenology
and
Existentialism

Maurice Merleau-Ponty

Preface

from *The Phenomenology of Perception*

What is phenomenology? It may seem strange that this question has still to be asked half a century after the first works of Husserl. The fact remains that it has by no means been answered. Phenomenology is the study of essences; and according to it, all problems amount to finding definitions of essences: the essence of perception, or the essence of consciousness, for example. But phenomenology is also a philosophy which puts essences back into existence, and does not expect to arrive at an understanding of man and the world from any starting point other than that of their "facticity." It is a transcendental philosophy which places in abeyance the assertions arising out of the natural attitude, the better to understand them; but it is also a philosophy for which the world is always "already there" before reflection begins—as an inalienable presence; and all its efforts are concentrated upon re-achieving a direct and primitive contact with the world, and endowing that contact with a philosophical status. It is the search for a philosophy which shall be a "rigorous science," but it also offers an account of space, time and the world as we 'live' them. It tries to give a direct description of our experience as it is, without taking account of its psychological origin and the causal explanations which the scientists, the historian or the sociologist may be able to provide. Yet Husserl in his last works mentions a "genetic phenomenology,"[1] and even a "constructive phenomenology."[2] One may try to do away with these contradictions by making a distinction between Husserl's and Heidegger's phenomenologies; yet the whole of *Sein und Zeit* springs from an indication given by Husserl and amounts to no more than an explicit account of the "natürlicher Weltbegriff" or the "Lebenswelt" which Husserl, towards the end of his life, identified as the central theme of phenomenology, with the result that the contradiction reappears in Husserl's own philosophy. The reader pressed for time will be inclined to give up the idea of covering

Source: Maurice Merleau-Ponty, *The Phenomenology of Perception*, translated by Colin Smith (New York: Humanities Press, 1962), pp. vii–xxi. Reprinted by permission of Humanities Press, Inc. & Routledge & Kegan Paul Ltd.
1. *Méditations cartésiennes*, pp. 120 ff.
2. See the umpublished *6th Méditation cartésienne*, edited by Eugen Fink, to which G. Berger has kindly referred us.

a doctrine which says everything, and will wonder whether a philosophy which cannot define its scope deserves all the discussion which has gone on around it, and whether he is not faced rather by a myth or a fashion.

Even if this were the case, there would still be a need to understand the prestige of the myth and the origin of the fashion, and the opinion of the responsible philosopher must be that *phenomenology can be practised and identified as a manner or style of thinking, that it existed as a movement before arriving at complete awareness of itself as a philosophy.* It has been long on the way, and its adherents have discovered it in every quarter, certainly in Hegel and Kierkegaard, but equally in Marx, Nietzsche and Freud. A purely linguistic examination of the texts in question would yield no proof; we find in texts only what we put into them, and if ever any kind of history has suggested the interpretations which should be put on it, it is the history of philosophy. We shall find in ourselves, and nowhere else, the unity and true meaning of phenomenology. It is less a question of counting up quotations than of determining and expressing in concrete form this *phenomenology for ourselves* which has given a number of presentday readers the impression, on reading Husserl or Heidegger, not so much of encountering a new philosophy as of recognizing what they had been waiting for. Phenomenology is accessible only through a phenomenological method. Let us, therefore, try systematically to bring together the celebrated phenomenological themes as they have grown spontaneously together in life. Perhaps we shall then understand why phenomenology has for so long remained at an initial stage, as a problem to be solved and a hope to be realized.

It is a matter of describing, not of explaining or analysing. Husserl's first directive to phenomenology, in its early stages, to be a "descriptive psychology," or to return to the "things themselves," is from the start a rejection of science. I am not the outcome or the meeting-point of numerous causal agencies which determine my bodily or psychological make-up. I cannot conceive myself as nothing but a bit of the world, a mere object of biological, psychological or sociological investigation. I cannot shut myself up within the realm of science. All my knowledge of the world, even my scientific knowledge, is gained from my own particular point of view, or from some experience of the world without which the symbols of science would be meaningless. The whole universe of science is built upon the world as directly experienced, and if we want to subject science itself to rigorous scrutiny and arrive at a precise assessment of its meaning and scope, we must begin by reawakening the basic experience of the world of which science is the second-order expression. Science has not and never will have, by its nature, the same significance *qua* form of being as the world which we perceive, for the simple reason that it is a rationale or explanation of that world. I am, not a "living creature" nor even a "man," nor again even "a consciousness" endowed with all the characteristics which zoology, social anatomy or inductive psychology recognize in these various products of the natural or historical process—I am the absolute source, my existence does not stem from my antecedents, from my physical and social environment; instead it moves out towards them and sustains them, for I alone bring into being for myself (and therefore into being in the only sense that the word can have for me) the tradition which I elect to carry on, or the horizon whose distince from me would be abolished— since that distance is not one of its properties—if I were not there to scan it with my gaze. Scientific points of view, according to which my existence is a moment of the world's, are always both naïve and at the same time dishonest, because they take for granted, without explicitly mentioning it, the other point of view, namely that of consciousness through which from the outset a world forms itself round me and begins to exist for me. To return to things themselves is to return to that world which precedes knowledge, of which knowledge always *speaks,* and in relation to which every scientific schematization is an abstract and derivative sign-language, as is geography in relation to the countryside in which we have learnt beforehand what a forest, a prairie or a river is.

This move is absolutely distinct from the idealist return to consciousness, and the demand for a pure description excludes equally the procedure of analytical reflection on the one hand, and that of scientific explanation on the other. Descartes and particularly Kant *detached* the subject, or consciousness, by showing that I could not possibly apprehend anything as existing unless I first of all experienced myself as existing in the act of apprehending it. They presented consciousness, the absolute certainty of my existence for myself, as the condition of there being anything at all; and the act of relating as the basis of relatedness. It is true that the act of relating is nothing if divorced from the spectacle of the world in which relations are found; the unity of consciousness in Kant is achieved simultaneously with that of the world. And in Descartes methodical doubt does not deprive us of anything, since the whole world, at least in so far as we experience it, is reinstated in the *Cogito,* enjoying equal certainty, and simply labelled "thought about. . . ." But the relations between subject and world are not strictly bilateral: if they were, the certainty of the world would, in Descartes, be immediately given with that of the *Cogito,* and Kant would not have talked about his "Copernican revolution." Analytical reflection starts from our experience of the world and goes back to the subject as to a condition of possibility distinct from that experience, revealing the all-embracing synthesis as that without which there would be no world. To this extent it ceases to remain part of our experience and offers, in place of an account, a reconstruction. It is understandable, in view of this, that Husserl, having accused Kant of adopting a "faculty psychologism,"[3] should have urged, in place of a noetic analysis which bases the world on the synthesizing activity of the subject, his own *"noematic reflection"* which remains within the object and, instead of begetting it, brings to light its fundamental unity.

The world is there before any possible analysis of mine, and it would be artificial to make it the outcome of a series of syntheses which link, in the first place sensations, then aspects of the object corresponding to different perspectives, when both are nothing but products of analysis, with no sort of prior reality. Analytical reflection believes that it can trace back the course followed by a prior constituting act and arrive, in the "inner man"—to use Saint Augustine's expression—at a constituting power which has always been identical with that inner self. Thus reflection itself is carried away and transplanted in an impregnable subjectivity, as yet untouched by being and time. But this is very ingenuous, or at least it is an incomplete form of reflection which loses sight of its own beginning. When I begin to reflect my reflection bears upon an unreflective experience; moreover my reflection cannot be unaware of itself as an event, and so it appears to itself in the light of a truly creative act, of a changed structure of consciousness, and yet it has to recognize, as having priority over its own operations, the world which is given to the subject, because the subject is given to himself. The real has to be described, not constructed or formed. Which means that I cannot put perception into the same category as the syntheses represented by judgements, acts or predications. My field of perception is constantly filled with a play of colours, noises and fleeting tactile sensations which I cannot relate precisely to the context of my clearly perceived world, yet which I nevertheless immediately "place" in the world, without ever confusing them with my daydreams. Equally constantly I weave dreams round things. I imagine people and things whose presence is not incompatible with the context, yet who are not in fact involved in it: they are ahead of reality, in the realm of the imaginary. If the reality of my perception were based solely on the intrinsic coherence of "representations," it ought to be for ever hesitant and, being wrapped up in my conjectures on probabilities, I ought to be ceaselessly taking apart misleading syntheses, and reinstating in reality stray phenomena which I had excluded in the first place. But this does not happen. The real is a closely woven fabric. It does not await our judgement before incorporating the most surprising phenomena, or before rejecting the most plausible figments of our imagination. Perception is not a science of the world, it is not even an act, a deliberate taking up of a position; it is the background from which all acts stand out, and is presupposed by

3. *Logische Untersuchungen, Prolegomena zur reinen Logik*, p. 93.

them. The world is not an object such that I have in my possession the law of its making; it is the natural setting of, and field for, all my thoughts and all my explicit perceptions. Truth does not "inhabit" only "the inner man,"[4] or more accurately, there is no inner man, man is in the world and only in the world does he know himself. When I return to myself from an excursion into the realm of dogmatic common sense or of science, I find, not a source of intrinsic truth, but a subject destined to be in the world.

All of which reveals the true meaning of the famous phenomenological reduction. There is probably no question over which Husserl has spent more time—or to which he has more often returned, since the "problematic of reduction" occupies an important place in his unpublished work. For a long time, and even in recent texts, the reduction is presented as the return to a transcendental consciousness before which the world is spread out and completely transparent, quickened through and through by a series of apperceptions which it is the philosopher's task to reconstitute on the basis of their outcome. Thus my sensation of redness is *perceived as* the manifestation of a certain redness experienced, this in turn as the manifestation of a red surface, which is the manifestation of a piece of red cardboard, and this finally is the manifestation or outline of a red thing, namely this book. We are to understand, then, that it is the apprehension of a certain *hylè,* as indicating a phenomenon of a higher degree, the *Sinngebung,* or active meaning-giving operation which may be said to define consciousness, so that the world is nothing but "world-as-meaning," and the phenomenological reduction is idealistic, in the sense that there is here a transcendental idealism which treats the world as an indivisible unity of value shared by Peter and Paul, in which their perspectives blend. "Peter's consciousness" and "Paul's consciousness" are in communication, the perception of the world "by Peter" is not Peter's doing any more than its perception "by Paul" is Paul's doing; in each case it is the doing of pre-personal forms of consciousness, whose communication raises no problem, since it is demanded by the very definition of consciousness, meaning or truth. In so far as I am a consciousness, that is, in so far as something has meaning for me, I am neither here nor there, neither Peter nor Paul; I am in no way distinguishable from an "other" consciousness, since we are immediately in touch with the world and since the world is, by definition, unique, being the system in which all truths cohere. A logically consistent transcendental idealism rids the world of its opacity and its transcendence. The world is precisely that thing of which we form a representation, not as men or as empirical subjects, but in so far as we are all one light and participate in the One without destroying its unity. Analytical reflection knows nothing of the problem of other minds, or of

4. In te redi; in interiore homine habitat veritas (Saint Augustine).

that of the world, because it insists that with the first glimmer of consciousness there appears in me theoretically the power of reaching some universal truth, and that the other person, being equally without thisness, location or body, the Alter and the Ego are one and the same in the true world which is the unifier of minds. There is no difficulty in understanding how *I* can conceive the Other, because the I and consequently the Other are not conceived as part of the woven stuff of phenomena; they have validity rather than existence. There is nothing hidden behind these faces and gestures, no domain to which I have no access, merely a little shadow which owes its very existence to the light. For Husserl, on the contrary, it is well known that there is a problem of other people, and the *alter ego* is a paradox. If the other is truly for himself alone, beyond his being for me, and if we are for each other and not both for God, we must necessarily have some appearance for each other. He must and I must have an outer appearance, and there must be, besides the perspective of the For Oneself —my view of myself and the other's of himself—a perspective of For Others—my view of others and theirs of me. Of course, these two perspectives, in each one of us, cannot be simply juxtaposed, *for in that case it is not I that the other would see, nor he that I should see.* I must be the exterior that I present to others, and the body of the other must be the other himself. This paradox and the dialectic of the Ego and the Alter are possible only provided that the Ego and the Alter Ego are defined by their situation and are not freed from all inherence; that is, provided that philosophy does not culminate in a return to the self, and that I discover by reflection not only my presence to myself, but also the possibility of an "outside spectator"; that is, again, provided that at the very moment when I experience my existence—at the ultimate extremity of reflection—I fall short of the ultimate density which would place me outside time, and that I discover within myself a kind of internal weakness standing in the way of my being totally individualized: a weakness which exposes me to the gaze of others as a man among men or at least as a consciousness among consciousnesses. Hitherto the *Cogito* depreciated the perception of others, teaching me as it did that the I is accessible only to itself, since it defined *me* as the thought which I have of myself, and which clearly I am alone in having, at least in this ultimate sense. For the "other" to be more than an empty word, it is necessary that my existence should never be reduced to my bare awareness of existing, but that it should take in also the awareness that *one* may have of it, and thus include my incarnation in some nature and the possibility, at least, of a historical situation. The *Cogito* must reveal me in a situation, and it is on this condition alone that transcendental subjectivity can, as Husserl puts it,[5] *be* an intersubjectivity.

---

5. *Die Krisis der europäischen Wissenschaften und die transzendentale Phänomenologie,* III (unpublished).

As a meditating Ego, I can clearly distinguish from myself the world and things, since I certainly do not exist in the way in which things exist. I must even set aside from myself my body understood as a thing among things, as a collection of physico-chemical processes. But even if the *cogitatio*, which I thus discover, is without location in objective time and space, it is not without place in the phenomenological world. The world, which I distinguished from myself as the totality of things or of processes linked by causal relationships, I rediscover "in me" as the permanent horizon of all my *cogitationes* and as a dimension in relation to which I am constantly situating myself. The true *Cogito* does not define the subject's existence in terms of the thought he has of existing, and furthermore does not convert the indubitability of the world into the indubitability of thought about the world, nor finally does it replace the world itself as an inalienable fact, and does away with any kind of idealism in revealing me as "being-in-the-world."

It is because we are through and through compounded of relationships with the world that for us the only way to become aware of the fact is to suspend the resultant activity, to refuse it our complicity (to look at it *ohne mitzumachen*, as Husserl often says), or yet again, to put it "out of play." Not because we reject the certainties of common sense and a natural attitude to things—they are, on the contrary, the constant theme of philosophy—but because, being the presupposed basis of any thought, they are taken for granted, and go unnoticed, and because in order to arouse them and bring them to view, we have to suspend for a moment our recognition of them. The best formulation of the reduction is probably that given by Eugen Fink, Husserl's assistant, when he spoke of "wonder" in the face of the world.[6] Reflection does not withdraw from the world towards the unity of consciousness as the world's basis; it steps back to watch the forms of transcendence fly up like sparks from a fire; it slackens the intentional threads which attach us to the world and thus brings them to our notice; it alone is consciousness of the world because it reveals that world as strange and paradoxical. Husserl's transcendental is not Kant's and Husserl accuses Kants's philosophy of being "worldly," because it *makes use* of our relation to the world, which is the motive force of the transcendental deduction, and makes the world immanent in the subject, instead of *being filled with wonder* at it and conceiving the subject as a process of transcendence towards the world. All the misunderstandings with his interpreters, with the existentialist "dissidents" and finally with himself, have arisen from the fact that in order to see the world and grasp it as paradoxical, we must break with our familiar acceptance of it and, also, from the fact that from this break we can learn nothing but the

6. *Die phänomenologische Philosophie Edmund Husserls in der gegenwärtigen Kritik*, pp. 331 and ff.

unmotivated upsurge of the world. The most important lesson which the reduction teaches us is the impossibility of a complete reduction. This is why Husserl is constantly re-examining the possibility of the reduction. If we were absolute mind, the reduction would present no problem. But since, on the contrary, we are in the world, since indeed our reflections are carried out in the temporal flux on to which we are trying to seize (since they *sich einströmen*, as Husserl says), there is no thought which embraces all our thought. The philosopher, as the unpublished works declare, is a perpetual beginner, which means that he takes for granted nothing that men, learned or otherwise, believe they know. It means also that philosophy itself must not take itself for granted, in so far as it may have managed to say something true; that it is an ever-renewed experiment in making its own beginning; that it consists wholly in the description of this beginning, and finally, that radical reflection amounts to a consciousness of its own dependence on an unreflective life which is its initial situation, unchanging, given once and for all. Far from being, as has been thought, a procedure of idealistic philosophy, phenomenological reduction belongs to existential philosophy: Heidegger's "being-in-the-world" appears only against the background of the phenomenological reduction.

A misunderstanding of a similar kind confuses the notion of the "essences" in Husserl. Every reduction, says Husserl, as well as being transcendental is necessarily eidetic. That means that we cannot subject our perception of the world to philosophical scrutiny without ceasing to be identified with that act of positing the world, with that interest in it which delimits us, without drawing back from our commitment which is itself thus made to appear as a spectacle, without passing from the *fact* of our existence to its *nature,* from the Dasein to the Wesen. But it is clear that the essence is here not the end, but a means, that our effective involvement in the world is precisely what has to be understood and made amenable to conceptualization, for it is what polarizes all our conceptual particularizations. The need to proceed by way of essences does not mean that philosophy takes them as its object, but, on the contrary, that our existence is too tightly held in the world to be able to know itself as such at the moment of its involvement, and that it requires the field of ideality in order to become acquainted with and to prevail over its facticity. The Vienna Circle, as is well known, lays it down categorically that we can enter into relations only with meanings. For example, "consciousness" is not for the Vienna Circle identifiable with what we are. It is a complex meaning which has developed late in time, which should be handled with care, and only after the many meanings which have contributed, throughout the word's semantic development, to the formation of its present one have been made explicit. Logical positivism of this kind is the antithesis of Husserl's thought. Whatever the subtle changes of meaning which have ultimately brought us, as a linguistic acquisition, the word and concept of consciousness, we enjoy direct access to what it designates. For we have the experience of ourselves, of that consciousness which we are, and it is on the basis of this experience that all linguistic connotations are assessed, and precisely through it that language comes to have any meaning at all for us. "It is that as yet dumb experience . . . which we are concerned to lead to the pure expression of its own meaning."[7] Husserl's essences are destined to bring back all the living relationships of experience, as the fisherman's net draws up from the depths of the ocean quivering fish and seaweed. Jean Wahl is therefore wrong in saying that "Husserl separates essences from existence."[8] The separated essences are those of language. It is the office of language to cause essences to exist in a state of separation which is in fact merely apparent, since through language they still rest upon the ante-predicative life of consciousness. In the silence of primary consciousness can be seen appearing not only what words mean, but also what things mean: the core of primary meaning round which the acts of naming and expression take shape.

Seeking the essence of consciousness will therefore not consist in developing the *Wortbedeutung* of consciousness and escaping from existence into the universe of things said; it will consist in rediscovering my actual presence to myself, the fact of my consciousness which is in the last resort what the word and the concept of consciousness mean. Looking for the world's essence is not looking for what it is as an idea once it has been reduced to a theme of discourse; it is looking for what it is as a fact for us, before any thematization. Sensationalism "reduces" the world by noticing that after all we never experience anything but states of ourselves. Transcendental idealism too "reduces" the world since, in so far as it guarantees the world, it does so by regarding it as thought or consciousness of the world, and as the mere correlative of our knowledge, with the results that it becomes immanent in consciousness and the aseity of things is thereby done away with. The eidetic reduction is, on the other hand, the determination to bring the world to light as it is before any falling back on ourselves has occurred, it is the ambition to make reflection emulate the unreflective life of consciousness. I aim at and perceive a world. If I said, as do the sensationalists, that we have here only "states of consciousness," and if I tried to distinguish my perceptions from my dreams with the aid of "criteria," I should overlook the phenomenon of the world. For if I am able to talk about "dreams" and "reality," to bother my head about the

7. *Méditations cartésiennes*, p. 33.
8. Réalisme, dialectique et mystère, l'Arbalète, Autumn, 1942, unpaginated.

distinction between imaginary and real, and cast doubt upon the "real," it is because this distinction is already made by me before any analysis; it is because I have an experience of the real as of the imaginary, and the problem then becomes one not of asking how critical thought can provide for itself secondary equivalents of this distinction, but of making explicit our primordial knowledge of the "real," of describing our perception of the world as that upon which our idea of truth is for ever based. We must not, therefore, wonder whether we really perceive a world, we must instead say: the world is what we perceive. In more general terms we must not wonder whether our self-evident truths are real truths, or whether, through some perversity inherent in our minds, that which is self-evident for us might not be illusory in relation to some truth in itself. For in so far as we talk about illusion, it is because we have identified illusions, and done so solely in the light of some perception which at the same time gave assurance of its own truth. It follows that doubt, or the fear of being mistaken, testifies as soon as it arises to our power of unmasking error, and that it could never finally tear us away from truth. We are in the realm of truth and it is "the experience of truth" which is self-evident.[9] To seek the essence of perception is to declare that perception is, not presumed true, but defined as access to truth. So, if I now wanted, according to idealistic principles, to base this *de facto* self-evident truth, this irresistible belief, on some absolute self-evident truth, that is, on the absolute clarity which my thoughts have for me; if I tried to find in myself a creative thought which bodied forth the framework of the world or illuminated it through and through, I should once more prove unfaithful to my experience of the world, and should be looking for what makes the experience possible instead of looking for what it is. The self-evidence of perception is not adequate thought or apodeictic self-evidence.[10] The world is not what I think, but what I live through. I am open to the world, I have no doubt that I am in communication with it, but I do not possess it; it is inexhaustible. "There is a world," or rather: "There is the world"; I can never completely account for this ever-reiterated assertion in my life. This facticity of the world is what constitutes the *Weltlichkeit der Welt*, what causes the world to be the world; just as the facticity of the *cogito* is not an imperfection in itself, but rather what assures me of my existence. The eidetic method is the method of a phenomenological positivism which bases the possible on the real.

We can now consider the notion of intentionality, too often cited as the main discovery of phenomenology, whereas it is understandable only

9. *Das Erlebnis der Wahrheit (Logische Untersuchungen, Prolegomena zur reinen Logik)* p. 190.
10. There is no apodeictic self-evidence, the *Formale und transzendentale Logik* (p. 142) says in effect.

through the reduction. "All consciousness is consciousness of something"; there is nothing new in that. Kant showed, in the *Refutation of Idealism,* that inner perception is impossible without outer perception, that the world, as a collection of connected phenomena, is anticipated in the consciousness of my unity, and is the means whereby I come into being as a consciousness. What distinguishes intentionality from the Kantian relation to a possible object is that the unity of the world, before being posited by knowledge in a specific act of identification, is "lived" as ready-made or already there. Kant himself shows in the *Critique of Judgment* that there exists a unity of the imagination and the understanding and a unity of subjects *before the object,* and that, in experiencing the beautiful, for example, I am aware of a harmony between sensation and concept, between myself and others, which is itself without any concept. Here the subject is no longer the universal thinker of a system of objects rigorously interrelated, the positing power who subjects the manifold to the law of the understanding, in so far as he is to be able to put together a world—he discovers and enjoys his own nature as spontaneously in harmony with the law of the understanding. But if the subject has a nature, then the hidden art of the imagination must condition the categorial activity. It is no longer merely the aesthetic judgment, but knowledge too which rests upon this art, an art which forms the basis of the unity of consciousness and of consciousnesses.

Husserl takes up again the *Critique of Judgement* when he talks about a teleology of consciousness. It is not a matter of duplicating human consciousness with some absolute thought which, from outside, is imagined as assigning to it its aims. It is a question of recognizing consciousness itself as a project of the world, meant for a world which it neither embraces nor possesses, but towards which it is perpetually directed—and the world as this pre-objective individual whose imperious unity decrees what knowledge shall take as its goal. This is why Husserl distinguishes between intentionality of act, which is that of our judgements and of those occasions when we voluntarily take up a position—the only intentionality discussed in the *Critique of Pure Reason*—and operative intentionality (*fungierende Intentionalität*), or that which produces the natural and antepredicative unity of the world and of our life, being apparent in our desires, our evaluations and in the landscape we see, more clearly than in objective knowledge, and furnishing the text which our knowledge tries to translate into precise language. Our relationship to the world, as it is untiringly enunciated within us, is not a thing which can be any further clarified by analysis; philosophy can only place it once more before our eyes and present it for our ratification.

Through this broadened notion of intentionality, phenomenological "comprehension" is distinguished from traditional "intellection," which is confined to "true and immutable natures," and so phenomenology can become a phenomenology of origins. Whether we are concerned with a thing perceived, a historical event or a doctrine, to "understand" is to take in the total intention—not only what these things are for representation (the "properties" of the thing perceived, the mass of "historical facts," the "ideas" introduced by the doctrine)—but the unique mode of existing expressed in the properties of the pebble, the glass or the piece of wax, in all the events of a revolution, in all the thoughts of a philosopher. It is a matter, in the case of each civilization, of finding the Idea in the Hegelian sense, that is, not a law of the physico-mathematical type, discoverable by objective thought, but that formula which sums up some unique manner of behavior towards others, towards Nature, time and death: a certain way of patterning the world which the historian should be capable of seizing upon and making his own. These are the *dimensions* of history. In this context there is not a human word, not a gesture, even one which is the outcome of habit or absent-mindedness, which has not some meaning. For example, I may have been under the impression that I lapsed into silence through weariness, or some minister may have thought he had uttered merely an appropriate platitude, yet my silence or his words immediately take on a significance, because my fatigue or his falling back upon a ready-made formula are not accidental, for they express a certain lack of interest, and hence some degree of adoption of a definite position in relation to the situation.

When an event is considered at close quarters, at the moment when it is lived through, everything seems subject to chance: one man's ambition, some lucky encounter, some local circumstance or other appears to have been decisive. But chance happenings offset each other, and facts in their multiplicity coalesce and show up a certain way of taking a stand in relation to the human situation, reveal in fact an *event* which has its definite outline and about which we can talk. Should the starting-point for the understanding of history be ideology, or politics, or religion, or economics? Should we try to understand a doctrine from its overt content, or from the psychological make-up and the biography of its author? We must seek an understanding from all these angles simultaneously, everything has meaning, and we shall find this same structure of being underlying all relationships. All these views are true provided that they are not isolated, that we delve deeply into history and reach the unique core of existential meaning which emerges in each perspective. It is true, as Marx says, that history does not walk on its head, but it is also true that it does not think with its feet. Or one should say rather that it is neither its "head" not its "feet" that we have to worry about, but its body. All economic and psychological explanations of a doctrine are true, since the thinker never thinks from any starting-point but the one constituted by what he is. Reflection even on a doctrine will be complete only if it succeeds in linking up with the doctrine's history and the extraneous explanations of it, and in putting back the causes and meaning of the doctrine in an existential structure. There is, as Husserl says, a "genesis of meaning" (*Sinngenesis*),[11] which alone, in the last resort, teaches us what the doctrine "means." Like understanding, criticism must be pursued at all levels, and naturally, it will be insufficient, for the refutation of a doctrine, to relate it to some accidental event in the author's life: its significance goes beyond, and there is no pure accident in existence or in coexistence, since both absorb random events and transmute them into the rational.

Finally, as it is indivisible in the present, history is equally so in its sequences. Considered in the light of its fundamental dimensions, all periods of history appear as manifestations of a single existence, or as episodes in a single drama—without our knowing whether it has an ending. Because we are in the world, we are *condemned to meaning,* and we cannot do or say anything without its acquiring a name in history.

Probably the chief gain from phenomenology is to have united extreme subjectivism and extreme objectivism in its notion of the world or of rationality. Rationality is precisely measured by the experiences in which it is disclosed. To say that there exists rationality is to say that perspectives blend, perceptions confirm each other, a meaning emerges. But it should not be set in a realm apart, transposed into absolute Spirit, or into a world in the realist sense. The phenomenological world is not pure being, but the sense which is revealed where the paths of my various experiences intersect, and also where my own and other people's intersect and engage each other like gears. It is thus inseparable from subjectivity and intersubjectivity, which find their unity when I either take up my past experiences in those of the present, or other people's in my own. For the first time the philosopher's thinking is sufficiently conscious not to anticipate itself and endow its own results with reified form in the world. The philosopher tries to conceive the world, others and himself and their interrelations. But the meditating Ego, the "impartial spectator" (*uninteressierter Zuschauer*)[12] do not rediscover an already given rationality, they "establish themselves,"[13] and establish it, by an act of initiative which has no guarantee in being, its justification resting entirely on the effective power which it confers on us of taking our own history upon ourselves.

The phenomenological world is not the bringing to explicit expression of a pre-existing being, but the laying down of being. Philosophy is not the

11. The usual term in the unpublished writings. The idea is already to be found in the *Formale und transzendentale Logik,* pp. 184 and ff.
12. *6th Méditation cartésienne* (unpublished).
13. Ibid.

reflection of a pre-existing truth, but, like art, the act of bringing truth into being. One may well ask how this creation is *possible,* and if it does not recapture in things a pre-existing Reason. The answer is that the only pre-existent Logos is the world itself, and that the philosophy which brings it into visible existence does not begin by being *possible;* it is actual or real like the world of which it is a part, and no explanatory hypothesis is clearer than the act whereby we take up this unfinished world in an effort to complete and conceive it. Rationality is not a *problem.* There is behind it no unknown quantity which has to be determined by deduction, or, beginning with it demonstrated inductively. We witness every minute the miracle of related experiences, and yet nobody knows better than we do how this miracle is worked, for we are ourselves this network of relationships. The world and reason are not problematical. We may say, if we wish, that they are mysterious, but their mystery defines them: there can be no question of dispelling it by some "solution," it is on the hither side of all solutions. True philosophy consists in relearning to look at the world, and in this sense a historical account can give meaning to the world quite as "deeply" as a philosophical treatise. We take our fate in our hands, we become responsible for our history through reflection, but equally by a decision on which we stake our life, and in both cases what is involved is a violent act which is validated by being performed.

Phenomenology, as a disclosure of the world, rests on itself, or rather provides its own foundation.[14] All knowledge is sustained by a "ground" of postulates and finally by our communication with the world as primary embodiment of rationality. Philosophy, as radical reflection, dispenses in principle with this resource. As, however, it too is in history, it too exploits the world and constituted reason. It must therefore put to itself the question which it puts to all branches of knowledge, and so duplicate itself infinitely, being, as Husserl says, a dialogue or infinite meditation, and, in so far as it remains faithful to its intention, never knowing where it is going. The unfinished nature of phenomenology and the inchoative atmosphere which has surrounded it are not to be taken as a sign of failure, they were inevitable because phenomenology's task was to reveal the mystery of the world and of reason.[15] If phenomenology was a movement before becoming a doctrine or a philosophical system, this was attributable neither to accident, nor to fraudulent intent. It is as painstaking as the works of Balzac, Proust, Valéry or Cézanne—by reason of the same kind of attentiveness and wonder, the same demand for awareness, the same will to seize the meaning of the world or of history as that meaning comes into being. In this way it merges into the general effort of modern thought.

14. "Rückbeziehung der Phänomenologie auf sich selbst," say the unpublished writings.
15. We are indebted for this last experssion to G. Gusdorf, who may well have used it in another sense.

Maurice Natanson
Being-in-Reality

from *Literature, Philosophy and the Social Sciences:*
Essays in Existentialism and Phenomenology

[I]

In Joyce's *A Portrait of the Artist as a Young Man,* the boy here, we are told, "turned to the flyleaf of the geography and read what he had written there: himself, his name and where he was.

Stephen Dedalus
Class of Elements
Clongowes Wood College
Sallins
County Kildare
Ireland
Europe
The World
The Universe"[1]

Self-placement through listings of this sort is common, and we may attach to them no more significance than the desire of the child to find a primitive order in his world, or, perhaps, to approach what transcends him by pointing to it. But the very ordering arrangement may be a clue to a still different problem: the location and realization of the primal situation of the self in reality. Tentatively, it might be suggested that the ordering procedure is a way of securing the self against the initial lack of placement, a way of avoiding the ranges of experience that defy full comprehension, and a way of establishing the self as knowable, comprehensible, and controllable in a world in which knowing, comprehending, and controlling are ultimately ambiguous and fragmentary structures.

Transposed to the adult and philosophical level, it might be suggested that each of Stephen Dedalus' regions or realms could be fully explored in terms of a naturalistic position; that, for example, understanding of Stephen himself is possible through an empirical psychology developed to

Source: Reprinted from Maurice Natanson, *Literature, Philosophy and the Social Sciences: Essays in Existentialism and Phenomenology* (The Hague: Martinus Nijhoff, 1962) with the permission of Martinus Nijhoff.
1. Joyce, J., *A Portrait of the Artist as a Young Man,* New York, 1956, 15–16.

its mature form, that a thorough knowledge of place and county and country may be achieved through a coalescence of information gained from a dozen disciplines ranging from geography to political science; that, finally, knowledge of "world" and "universe" can be gained through the method of inquiry characteristic of the sciences. If the kind of naturalism involved here be of a sort similar to that of John Dewey, the underlying attitude might be summarized in the familiar recommendation that there is a qualitative continuity between the problems of the natural sciences and those of the cultural sciences, that scientific method is adequate, in principle, to resolve the problems of man and nature, and that progress is made through a reasoned effort to advance the possibilities inherent in a rational, scientific view of the world. Man, in this view, is fundamentally at home in the natural world, able to control crucial aspects of his environment and advance his cause over the opposition of superstition, ignorance, and prejudice.

Were this a full account of the matter, there would be little more to what we are calling the problem of placement in the world than awaiting definitive scientific answers to questions of a limited sort. But if there is any truth in suggesting that the problem of placement in reality goes beyond scientific questions and answers, then it is necessary to put the naturalistic position in question in order to see our problem. Just as Stephen Dedalus' primitive cosmology can be understood as a way of finding himself in the labyrinth of the world, so the categories and methods of naturalism may be treated as markers set up to map an otherwise wild terrain. So long as mapping the world is an ongoing affair, the original status of the mapper does not arise; so long as we are doing, making, acting in the world, our being in the world is unproblematic. Dewey's idea that a problem arises always within a context which is unproblematic is completely germane here, for being in the world, original placement in reality, is taken by the naturalist as the unproblematic context of his actions in the world. As long as we remain in the naturalist's standpoint, the very techniques of inquiry predicate a world and man in that world, the fundamental character of both being taken for granted, or, if placed in question, reduced to piecemeal problems. We suggest that the very articulation of the problem of being-in-reality requires a departure from the naturalistic position, or more generally, a disconnection from what Husserl calls the "natural attitude." The statement of our problem, therefore, requires a phenomenological transposition.

[II]

Within the natural attitude I act in a world which is real, a world that existed before I was born and which I think will continue to exist after I die. This world is inhabited not only by me, but also by my fellow men, who are human beings with whom I can and do communicate meaningfully. This world has familiar features which have been systematically described through the genetic-causal categories of science. The world of daily life is lived within this natural attitude, and as long as things go along smoothly and reasonably well, there arises no need to call this attitude into question. But even if I do occasionally ask whether something is "really real," whether the world is "really" as it appears to be, these questions are still posed in such a way that they are my questions about the natural world in which I live. I do not really scrutinize my natural attitude in any rigorous manner: I merely mark off a bit of it for more careful study. And so I continue to be a real being in the real world of real things sharing real experiences with other real companions and living a real life.

If I am questioned about my "identity" in my natural attitude, my answers are ready: I can give my name, validated by birth certificate, my age, place of birth, parents' names, address, occupation, and, if necessary, a list of my hobbies. These "vital statistics" summate my position within the natural attitude, though a full examination of that attitude would require an exhaustive analysis of common-sense reality. The problem of being-in-reality does not and cannot arise within the natural attitude for the essential reason that the natural attitude is at its root founded on the assumption that the individual is, *of course*, already in the world when we interrogate him about his history and interests. Being in reality here can mean no more than psychophysical presence. The person is in the world in much the same way that a marble is in the bag, that a cat is in the house, that a teacher is in the classroom. But it is at this point that a kind of rebellion takes place: the full reality of the individual is surely not exhausted in statistics, and the identity of the person demands an appreciation of *his* situation in the world as distinct from *one's* situation in the world. I am forced to the question of the true character of my placement in the world, of the signification of name, place, and realm, of the credentials of the natural attitude itself. It is Kierkegaard who leads the revolt. He writes in *Repetition:*

> One sticks one's finger into the soil to tell by the smell in what land one is: I stick my finger into existence—it smells of nothing. Where am I? Who am I? How came I here? What is this thing called the world? What does this word mean? Who is it that has lured me into the thing, and now leaves me there? Who am I? How did I come into the world? Why was I not consulted, why not made acquainted with its manners and customs . . .? How did I obtain an interest in this big enterprise they call reality? Why should I have an interest in it? Is it not a voluntary concern? And if I am to be compelled to take part in it, where is the director? I should like to make a remark to him.[2]

2. Kierkegaard, S., *Repetition*, Princeton, 1941, 114.

But to place the natural attitude in question is not only to declare in favour of an existential awareness of reality; it is also, in phenomenological terms, to try to get the meaning or sense of that awareness. Therefore, the disconnection from the natural attitude that leads in the direction of existential philosophy may itself be examined and made the object of scrutiny. A phenomenological description of being-in-reality turns first of all to the initial disconnection from the natural attitude that is at the root of existential awareness of what it means to be in the world. What is the character of this disconnection? Unfortunately, the celebrated theory of reduction in Husserl's phenomenology is a much misunderstood topic, and so it is not possible to answer our question by merely invoking the procedure of "bracketing." It is first necessary to clarify what is meant by phenomenological reduction.

" 'The' world is as fact-world always there," Husserl writes, "at the most it is at odd points 'other' than I supposed, this or that under such names as 'illusion,' 'hallucination,' and the like, must be struck *out of it,* so to speak; but the 'it' remains ever, in the sense of the general thesis, a world that has its being out there."[3] The radical "alteration" of the natural thesis requires a continuing procedure of disconnection or bracketing which transposes the naively experienced world into the intentional field of world-for-me. To bracket the world is neither to deny its reality nor to change its reality in any way; rather, it is to effect a change in my way of regarding the world, a change that turns my glance from the "real" object to the object as I take it, treat it, interpret it as real. Within the natural attitude I attend to the object; in the phenomenological attitude I attend to the object as known, as meant, as intended. The reality of the object is bracketed only in the sense that I attend to what presents itself to me immediately, whether really real or not, and seize the reality of the object as the object of my intentional acts. The object continues to be in the real world, as I do, but what now interests me, phenomenologically, is my awareness, my sense of its being in the real world. The object I reflect upon in the reduced sphere is the real thing as I've taken it to be real. Thus, "the" world is replaced by "my" world, not in any solipsistic sense, but only in the sense that "mine" indicates an intentional realm constituted by my own acts of seeing, hearing, remembering, imagining, and so on.

If I wish, phenomenologically, to refer to "the" world, I must attend to the world I take to be "the" world, i.e., world taken as "the" world. Placement *in* "the" world in the natural attitude presupposes the nature of that "in" structure, and the presupposition is not self-consciously considered. Husserl writes, "The General Thesis according to which the real world about me is at all times known not merely in a general way as

3. Husserl, E., *Ideas,* 106.

something apprehended, but as a fact-world *that has its being out there,* does *not* consist of course *in an act proper,* in an articulated judgment *about* existence. It is and remains something all the time the standpoint is adopted, that is, it endures persistently during the whole course of our life of natural endeavour."[4] The disconnection or bracketing in phenomenological reduction is an alteration of this General Thesis which, for methodological reasons, I suspend. My being in the natural attitude, of course, continues. I remain in the natural attitude at the very time I disconnect myself from it in terms of judgment and description. This means only that my being in the natural attitude becomes the theme of my phenomenological consideration, but that my physical bodily existence continues in commonsense fashion.

With the transposition to the intentional realm, my being in the world, or more generally, my being in reality, may now be expressed through the hyphenation given in the title of my paper: being-in-reality; and we understand by this hyphenation that disconnection from the natural attitude permits the originally taken for granted placement in the world to become the intentional object of phenomenological examination. Whereas unhyphenated being in reality is the unconscious basis of all our predications and actions, hyphenated being-in-reality involves the self-conscious reflection on the signification and structure of the General Thesis of the natural attitude. The relationship between the natural attitude and intentional consciousness may be restated in still a different way by referring back to our discussion of the Deweyan position.

To say, with Dewey, that every problem presupposes an unproblematic context within which, against which it arises, is to leave unexamined and unclarified the very meaning of "context." Whatever interpretation of "situation" Dewey presents is already founded on the assumption that we have, are *in,* or find or locate such a context. This assumption is proper to empirical science; in fact, it is its point of departure. But if part of the task of philosophy is to consider the foundational concepts and presuppositions of the sciences, it is necessary to start at the beginning and place in question what it means to take something as unproblematic. To do this is to shift from the natural standpoint to a reflective one; and to attempt to take the reflective standpoint itself as the object of scrutiny is to search for phenomenological roots. The effecting of the transposition from the natural to the phenomenological standpoint in no way alters or disregards any structure located or experienced in the natural attitude; in placing the natural attitude in suspension, the phenomenologist only tries to comprehend the meaningful structure of the Lifeworld as it reveals itself in intentional consciousness. Properly understood,

---

4. ibid., 107.

then, there is no disagreement between the natural attitude and the phenomenological standpoint or between natural science and phenomenological philosophy; the latter is nothing more than a systematic, sustained, but completely radical endeavour to illuminate our being-in-reality in its full intentional structure.

[III]

We are now prepared for a closer examination of our theme. My being-in-reality always presents itself to me within a horizon of relatedness to more or less determinate surroundings. My "being-in" is in a more or less circumscribed situation. Each concrete event in experience is, Husserl says, "partly pervaded, partly girt about with a *dimly apprehended depth or fringe of indeterminate reality.*"[5] Every "this" is a "this" within a context, clearly or dimly grasped, of a "more-than-this." And if I follow the horizontal character of the presentation involved, I am led to the vague "form" of a total inclusiveness. Husserl, describing the movement from limitation to form, writes:

Determining representations, dim at first, then livelier, fetch me something out, a chain of such recollections takes shape, the circle of determinancy extends ever farther, and eventually so far that the connexion with the actual field of perception as the *immediate* environment is established. But in general the issue is a different one: an empty mist of dim indeterminacy gets studded over with intuitive possibilities or presumptions, and only the "form" of the world as "world" is foretokened. Moreover, the zone of indeterminacy is infinite. The misty horizon that can never be completely outlined remains necessarily there.[6]

When I move, then, from a "this" to the vague form of "world" surrounding and including that "this," I explore the phenomenological horizon of my immediate placement in reality. The "in" of hyphenated "being-in-reality" is then, I would suggest, the horizontal directedness which attends and defines every act of placement. The "in" is therefore not the "in" of class inclusion or of physical habitation, but the radically different and unique structure of horizontal projection; i.e., the fluid movement from being "in" a concrete situation to being "in" the world as such. Reality, in this sense, is the form of the widest generality, the horizon of all horizons the indeterminate penumbra that surrounds our farthest reach of intention and presents itself as transcendence. To complete the clarification of terms, "being" may now be understood as the life of consciousness

5. ibid., 102.
6. ibid.

involved and engaged in intentional activity. Fully translated now, the title of our paper comes out from behind its hyphens: As a thinking, willing, perceiving, feeling, imagining consciousness, my intentions are directed to the concrete situations in which I live. The elements of these situations are not the objective things of the natural attitude, but the phenomenological objects of my intentional acts: I live within a world of my own attitudes and interpretations. But each act of consciousness intends some object within a concrete situation which itself finds placement in the world I think is "out there." When I carry out my intention to its farthest limit, I end with the strangeness, the uncanniness of reality taken as transcendent. *Being-in-reality is consciousness moving toward a horizon of transcendence.*

The suspension of the natural attitude alone makes possible the exploration of our theme. As long as we start with man naively existent in the world, the meaning of "man-in-the-world" cannot be explored. Phenomenology is an effort to overcome this naturalistic impasse by opening up for inspection the region of intentional consciousness. The point of this paper has not been to attempt a phenomenological study of "being-in-reality," but to try to show in what sense that structure is a valid philosophical problem, and to indicate the *kind* of approach a phenomenologist makes to such a root-problem. Since the very statement of the problem requires phenomenological disconnection from the General Thesis of the natural attitude, it has been necessary to move within the problem rather than commence with a direct statement of it. Instead of beginning with definitions, I have tried to end with them. But I think that this reflexive mode of thought, if circular, is not vicious. As Husserl says, "Philosophy can take root only in radical reflexion upon the meaning and possibility of its own scheme."

Martin Heidegger
from *Being and Time*

According to Martin Heidegger's de-struction *(Destruktion)* of the Western onto-theo-logical tradition, the fatal error it has persistently made in its investigations of Being is to assume that the word *logos* in the sentence, "Man is the animal who has *logos*," means "reason" or "judgment" (the adequation of intellect and thing) rather than "the ability to speak." Thus, by extension, it has persistently conceived of Being logocentrically: as an abiding *presence,* a final cause, an un-moved mover, that determines *existence* metaphysically (*meta-ta-phusika:* from after or beyond things-as-they-are), that is, from the distance of an end, or, what is the same, "spatially." *Being and Time* constitutes, above all, Heidegger's iconoclastic effort to break the West-ern habit of thinking of Being as a thing or bounded image (a world picture) to disclose the *temporality* contained and, in the process, for-gotten in it: to bring out of hiddenness (*a-letheia:* truth) the temporality of be-ing. The agency of this disclosure is Dasein (there- or human-being), the entity which, above all other entities, is characterized radi-cally by temporality and, accordingly, whose authentic stance in the world is *Care*-fulness, not the dis-interest—the Care-lessness—that modern Western technological man idealizes. The following selections from *Being and Time* can be read as existential/phenomenological statements about the human predicament. But they assume their deepest meaning when interpreted with Heidegger's ontological pur-poses in mind.

40. THE BASIC STATE-OF-MIND OF ANXIETY AS A DISTINCTIVE WAY IN WHICH DASEIN IS DISCLOSED

One of Dasein's possibilities of Being is to give us ontical "informa-tion" about Dasein itself as an entity. Such information is possible only in that disclosedness which belongs to Dasein and which is grounded in state-of-mind and understanding. How far is anxiety a state-of-mind which is distinctive? How is it that in anxiety Dasein gets brought before itself

Source: From *Being and Time* by Martin Heidegger, translated by John Macquarrie and Edward Robin-son: "The Basic State-of-Mind of Anxiety as a Distinctive Way in which Dasein Is Disclosed" #40 (pp. 228–235), "Being-towards-Death and the Everydayness of Dasein" #51 (pp. 296–299), "Existential Pro-jection of an Authentic Being-towards-Death" #53 (pp. 304–311), "Conscience as the Call of Care" #57 (pp. 319–325). Copyright © 1962 by SCM Press. By permission of Harper & Row, Publishers, Inc., and Basil Blackwell & Mott Ltd.

through its own Being, so that we can define phenomenologically the character of the entity disclosed in anxiety, and define it as such in its Being, or make adequate preparations for doing so?

Since our aim is to proceed towards the Being of the totality of the structural whole, we shall take as our point of departure the concrete analyses of falling which we have just carried through. Dasein's absorption in the "they" and its absorption in the "world" of its concern, make manifest something like a *fleeing* of Dasein in the face of itself—of itself as an authentic potentiality-for-Being-its-Self.[1] This phenomenon of Dasein's fleeing *in the face of itself* and in the face of its authenticity, seems at least a suitable phenomenal basis for the following investigation. But to bring itself face to face with itself, is precisely what Dasein does *not* do when it thus flees. It turns *away from* itself in accordance with its ownmost inertia [Zug] of falling. In investigating such phenomena, however, we must be careful not to confuse ontico-existentiell characterization with ontologico-existential Interpretation nor may we overlook the positive phenomenal bases provided for this Interpretation by such a characterization.

From an existentiell point of view, the authenticity of Being-one's-Self has of course been closed off and thrust aside in falling; but to be thus closed off is merely the *privation* of a disclosedness which manifests itself phenomenally in the fact that Dasein's fleeing is a fleeing *in the face of* itself. That in the face of which Dasein flees, is precisely what Dasein comes up "behind."[2] Only to the extent that Dasein has been brought before itself in an ontologically essential manner through whatever disclosedness belongs to it, *can* it flee *in the face of* that in the face of which it flees. To be sure, that in the face of which it flees is *not grasped* in thus turning away [Abkehr] in falling; nor is it experienced even in turning thither [Hinkehr]. Rather, in turning away *from* it, it is disclosed "there." This existentiell-ontical turning-away, by reason of its character as a disclosure, makes it phenomenally possible to grasp existential-ontologically that in the face of which Dasein flees, and to grasp it as such. Within the ontical "away-from" which such turning-away implies, that in the face of which Dasein flees can be understood and conceptualized by "turning thither" in a way which is phenomenologically Interpretative.

So in orienting our analysis by the phenomenon of falling, we are not in principle condemned to be without any prospect of learning something

1. "... offenbart so etwas wie eine *Flucht* des Daseins vor ihm selbst als eigentlichem Selbst-sein-können." The point of this paragraph is that if we are to study the totality of Dasein, Dasein must be brought "*before* itself" or "face to face with itself" ("*vor* es selbst"); and the fact that Dasein flees "*from* itself" or "in the face of itself" ("*vor ihm selbst*"), which may seem at first to lead us off the track, is actually very germane to our inquiry.
2. "Im Wovor der Flucht kommt das Dasein gerade "hinter" ihm her."

ontologically about the Dasein disclosed in that phenomenon. On the contrary, here, least of all, has our Interpretation been surrendered to an artificial way in which Dasein grasps itself; it merely carries out the explication of what Dasein itself ontically discloses. The possibility of proceeding towards Dasein's Being by going along with it and following it up [Mit- und Nachgehen] Interpretatively with an understanding and the state-of-mind that goes with it, is the greater, the more primordial is that phenomenon which functions methodologically as a disclosive state-of-mind. It might be contended that anxiety performs some such function.

We are not entirely unprepared for the analysis of anxiety. Of course it still remains obscure how this is connected ontologically with fear. Obviously these are kindred phenomena. This is betokened by the fact that for the most part they have not been distinguished from one another: that which is fear, gets designated as "anxiety," while that which has the character of anxiety, gets called "fear." We shall try to proceed towards the phenomenon of anxiety step by step.

Dasein's falling into the "they" and the "world" of its concern, is what we have called a "fleeing" in the face of itself. But one is not necessarily fleeing whenever one shrinks back in the face of something or turns away from it. Shrinking back in the face of what fear discloses—in the face of something threatening—is founded upon fear; and this shrinking back has the character of fleeing. Our interpretation of fear as a state-of-mind has shown that in each case that in the face of which we fear is a detrimental entity within-the-world which comes from some definite region but is close by and is bringing itself close, and yet might stay away. In falling, Dasein turns away from itself. That in the face of which it thus shrinks back must, in any case, be an entity with the character of threatening; yet this entity has the same kind of Being as the one that shrinks back: it is Dasein itself. That in the face of which it thus shrinks back cannot be taken as something "fearsome," for anything "fearsome" is always encountered as an entity within-the-world. The only threatening which can be "fearsome" and which gets discovered in fear, always comes from entities within-the-world.

Thus the turning-away of falling is not a fleeing that is founded upon a fear of entities within-the-world. Fleeing that is so grounded is still less a character of this turning-away, when what this turning-away does is precisely to *turn thither* towards entities within-the-world by absorbing itself in them. *The turning-away of falling is grounded rather in anxiety, which in turn is what first makes fear possible.*

To understand this talk about Dasein's fleeing in the face of itself in falling, we must recall that Being-in-the-world is a basic state of Dasein. *That in the face of which one has anxiety [das Wovor der Angst] is Being-in-the-world as such.* What is the difference phenomenally between that in the face of which anxiety is anxious [sich ängstet] and that in the face of which fear is afraid? That in the face of which one has anxiety is not an entity within-the-world. Thus it is essentially incapable of having an involvement. This threatening does not have the character of a definite detrimentality which reaches what is threatened, and which reaches it with definite regard to a special factical potentiality-for-Being. That in the face of which one is anxious is completely indefinite. Not only does this indefiniteness leave factically undecided which entity within-the-world is threatening us, but it also tells us that entities within-the-world are not "relevant" at all. Nothing which is ready-to-hand or present-at-hand within the world functions as that in the face of which anxiety is anxious. Here the totality of involvements of the ready-to-hand and the present-at-hand discovered within-the-world, is, as such, of no consequence; it collapses into itself; the world has the character of completely lacking significance. In anxiety one does not encounter this thing or that thing which, as something threatening, must have an involvement.

Accordingly, when something threatening brings itself close, anxiety does not "see" any definite "here" or "yonder" from which it comes. That in the face of which one has anxiety is characterized by the fact that what threatens is *nowhere*. Anxiety "does not know" what that in the face of which it is anxious is. "Nowhere," however, does not signify nothing: this is where any region lies, and there too lies any disclosedness of the world for essentially spatial Being-in. Therefore that which threatens cannot bring itself close from a definite direction within what is close by; it is already "there," and yet nowhere; it is so close that it is oppressive and stifles one's breath, and yet it is nowhere.

In that in the face of which one has anxiety, the "It is nothing and nowhere" becomes manifest. The obstinacy of the "nothing and nowhere within-the-world" means as a phenomenon that *the world as such is that in the face of which one has anxiety.* The utter insignificance which makes itself known in the "nothing and nowhere," does not signify that the world is absent, but tells us that entities within-the-world are of so little importance in themselves that on the basis of this *insignificance* of what is within-the-world, the world in its worldhood is all that still obtrudes itself.

What oppresses us is not this or that, nor is it the summation of everything present-at-hand; it is rather the *possibility* of the ready-to-hand in general; that is to say, it is the world itself. When anxiety has subsided, then in our everyday way of talking we are accustomed to say that "it was really nothing." And *what* it was, indeed, does get reached ontically by such a way of talking. Everyday discourse tends towards concerning itself with the ready-to-hand and talking about it. That in the face of which anxiety is anxious is nothing ready-to-hand within-the-world. But this "nothing ready-to-hand," which only our everyday circumspective discourse understands, is not totally nothing.[3] The "nothing" of readiness-to-hand is grounded in the most primordial "something"—in the *world*. Ontologically, however, the world belongs essentially to Dasein's Being as Being-in-the-world. So if the "nothing"—that is, the world as such —exhibits itself as that in the face of which one has anxiety, this means that *Being-in-the-world itself is that in the face of which anxiety is anxious.*

Being-anxious discloses, primordially and directly, the world as world. It is not the case, say, that the world first gets thought of by deliberating about it, just by itself, without regard for the entities within-the-world, and that, in the face of this world, anxiety then arises; what is rather the case is that the *world as world* is disclosed first and foremost by anxiety, as a mode of state-of-mind. This does not signify, however, that in anxiety the worldhood of the world gets conceptualized.

Anxiety is not only anxiety in the face of something, but, as a state-of-mind, it is also *anxiety about* something. That which anxiety is profoundly anxious [sich abängstet] about is not a *definite* kind of Being for Dasein or a *definite* possibility for it. Indeed the threat itself is indefinite, and therefore cannot penetrate threateningly to this or that factically concrete potentiality-for-Being. That which anxiety is anxious about is Being-in-the-world itself. In anxiety what is environmentally ready-to-hand sinks away, and so, in general, do entities within-the-world. The "world" can offer nothing more, and neither can the Dasein-with of others. Anxiety thus takes away from Dasein the possibility of understanding itself, as it falls, in terms of the "world" and the way things have been publicly interpreted. Anxiety throws Dasein back upon that which it is anxious about —its authentic potentiality-for-Being-in-the-world. Anxiety individualizes Dasein for its ownmost Being-in-the-world, which as something that understands, projects itself essentially upon possibilities. Therefore, with that which it is anxious about, anxiety discloses Dasein *as Being-possible*, and indeed as the only kind of thing which it can be of its own accord as something individualized in individualization [vereinzeltes in der Vereinzelung].

Anxiety makes manifest in Dasein its *Being towards* its ownmost potentiality-for-Being—that is, its *Being-free for* the freedom of choosing itself and taking hold of itself. Anxiety brings Dasein face to face with its *Being-free for* (*propensio in . . .*) the authenticity of its Being, and for this authenticity as a possibility which it always is.[4] But at the same time, this is the Being to which Dasein as Being-in-the-world has been delivered over.

---

3. "Allein dieses Nichts von Zuhandenem, das die alltägliche umsichtige Rede einzig versteht, ist kein totales Nichts." This sentence is grammatically ambiguous.
4. "Die Angst bringt das Dasein vor sein *Freisein für . . .* (*propensio in . . .*) die Eigentlichkeit seines Seins als Möglichkeit, die es immer schon ist."

That *about which* anxiety is anxious reveals itself as that *in the face of which* it is anxious—namely, Being-in-the-world. The selfsameness of that in the face of which and that about which one has anxiety, extends even to anxiousness [Sichängsten] itself. For, as a state-of-mind, anxiousness is a basic kind of Being-in-the-world. *Here the disclosure and the disclosed are existentially selfsame in such a way that in the latter the world has been disclosed as world, and Being-in has been disclosed as a potentiality-for-Being which is individualized, pure, and thrown; this makes it plain that with the phenomenon of anxiety a distinctive state-of-mind has become a theme for Interpretation.* Anxiety individualizes Dasein and thus discloses it as *"solus ipse."* But this existential "solipsism" is so far from the displacement of putting an isolated subject-Thing into the innocuous emptiness of a worldless occurring, that in an extreme sense what it does is precisely to bring Dasein face to face with its world as world, and thus bring it face to face with itself as Being-in-the-world.

Again everyday discourse and the everyday interpretation of Dasein furnish our most unbiased evidence that anxiety as a basic state-of-mind is disclosive in the manner we have shown. As we have said earlier, a state-of-mind makes manifest "how one is." In anxiety one feels *"uncanny."*[5] Here the peculiar indefiniteness of that which Dasein finds itself alongside in anxiety, comes proximally to expression: the "nothing and nowhere." But here "uncanniness" also means "not-being-at-home" [das Nicht-zuhause-sein]. In our first indication of the phenomenal character of Dasein's basic state and in our clarification of the existential meaning of "Being-in" as distinguished from the categorial signification of "insideness," Being-in was defined as "residing alongside ...," "Being-familiar with. ..." This character of Being-in was then brought to view more concretely through the everyday publicness of the "they," which brings tranquillized self-assurance—"Being-at-home," with all its obviousness—into the average everydayness of Dasein. On the other hand, as Dasein falls, anxiety brings it back from its absorption in the "world." Everyday familiarity collapses. Dasein has been individualized, but individualized *as* Being-in-the-world. Being-in enters into the existential 'mode' of the *"not-at-home."* Nothing else is meant by our talk about "uncanniness."

By this time we can see phenomenally what falling, as fleeing, flees in the face of. It does not flee *in the face of* entities within-the-world; these are precisely what it flees *towards*—as entities alongside which our concern, lost in the "they," can dwell in tranquillized familiarity. When in falling we flee *into* the "at-home" of publicness, we flee *in the face of* the "not-at-home"; that is, we flee in the face of the uncanniness which lies in

5. "Befindlichkeit, so wurde früher gesagt, macht offenbar, 'wie einem ist.' In der Angst ist einem ' *unheimlich.*' " While "unheimlich" is here translated as "uncanny," it means more literally "unhomelike," as the author proceeds to point out.

Dasein—in Dasein as thrown Being-in-the-world, which has been delivered over to itself in its Being. This uncanniness pursues Dasein constantly, and is a threat to its everyday lostness in the "they," though not explicitly. This threat can go together factically with complete assurance and self-sufficiency in one's everyday concern. Anxiety can arise in the most innocuous situations. Nor does it have any need for darkness, in which it is commonly easier for one to feel uncanny. In the dark there is emphatically "nothing" to see, though the very world is *still* "there," and "there" *more obtrusively.*

If we interpret Dasein's uncanniness from an existential-ontological point of view as a threat which reaches Dasein itself and which comes from Dasein itself, we are not contending that in factical anxiety too it has always been understood in this sense. When Dasein "understands" uncanniness in the everyday manner, it does so by turning away from it in falling; in this turning-away, the "not-at-home" gets "dimmed down." Yet the everydayness of this fleeing shows phenomenally that anxiety, as a basic state-of-mind, belongs to Dasein's essential state of Being-in-the-world, which, as one that is existential, never present-at-hand but *is* itself always in a mode of factical Being-there[6]—that is, in the mode of a state-of-mind. That kind of Being-in-the-world which is tranquillized and familiar is a mode of Dasein's uncanniness, not the reverse. *From an existential-ontological point of view, the "not-at-home" must be conceived as the more primordial phenomenon.*

And only because anxiety is always latent in Being-in-the-world, can such Being-in-the-world, as Being which is alongside the "world" and which is concernful in its state-of-mind, ever be afraid. Fear is anxiety, fallen into the "world," inauthentic, and, as such, hidden from itself.

After all, the mood of uncanniness remains, factically, something for which we mostly have no existentiell understanding. Moreover, under the ascendancy of falling and publicness, "real" anxiety is rare. Anxiety is often conditioned by "physiological" factors. This fact, in its facticity, is a problem *ontologically*, not merely with regard to its ontical causation and course of development. Only because Dasein is anxious in the very depths of its Being, does it become possible for anxiety to be elicited physiologically.

Even rarer than the existentiell Fact of "real" anxiety are attempts to Interpret this phenomenon according to the principles of its existential-ontological Constitution and function. The reasons for this lie partly in the general neglect of the existential analytic of Dasein, but more particularly in a failure to recognize the phenomenon of state-of-mind. Yet the factical rarity of anxiety as a phenomenon cannot deprive it of its fitness to take

6. Here we follow the earlier editions in reading "Da-seins." In the later editions the hyphen appears ambiguously at the end of a line.

over a methodological function *in principle* for the existential analytic. On the contrary, the rarity of the phenomenon is an index that Dasein, which for the most part remains concealed from itself in its authenticity because of the way in which things have been publicly interpreted by the "they," becomes disclosable in a primordial sense in this basic state-of-mind.

Of course it is essential to every state-of-mind that in each case Being-in-the-world should be fully disclosed in all those items which are constitutive for it—world, Being-in, Self. But in anxiety there lies the possibility of a disclosure which is quite distinctive; for anxiety individualizes. This individualization brings Dasein back from its falling, and makes manifest to it that authenticity and inauthenticity are possibilities of its Being. These basic possibilities of Dasein (and Dasein is in each case mine) show themselves in anxiety as they are in themselves—undisguised by entities within-the-world, to which, proximally and for the most part, Dasein clings.

How far has this existential Interpretation of anxiety arrived at a phenomenal basis for answering the guiding question of the Being of the totality of Dasein's structural whole?

51. BEING-TOWARDS-DEATH AND THE EVERYDAYNESS OF DASEIN

In setting forth average everyday Being-towards-death, we must take our orientation from those structures of everydayness at which we have earlier arrived. In Being-towards-death, Dasein comports itself *towards itself* as a distinctive potentiality-for-Being. But the Self of everydayness is the "they." The "they" is constituted by the way things have been publicly interpreted, which expresses itself in idle talk.[7] Idle talk must accordingly make manifest the way in which everyday Dasein interprets for itself its Being-towards-death. The foundation of any interpretation is an act of understanding, which is always accompanied by a state-of-mind, or, in other words, which has a mood. So we must ask how Being-towards-death is disclosed by the kind of understanding which, with its state-of-mind, lurks in the idle talk of the "they." How does the "they" comport itself understandingly towards that ownmost possibility of Dasein, which is non-relational and is not to be outstripped? What state-of-mind discloses to the "they" that it has been delivered over to death, and in what way?

In the publicness with which we are with one another in our everyday manner, death is "known" as a mishap which is constantly occurring—as

7. "... das sich in der öffentlichen Ausgelegtheit konstituiert, die sich im Gerede ausspricht." The earlier editions have "... konstituiert. Sie spricht sich aus im Gerede."

a "case of death."[8] Someone or other "dies," be he neighbour or stranger [Nächste oder Fernerstehende]. People who are no acquaintances of ours are "dying" daily and hourly. "Death" is encountered as a well-known event occurring within-the-world. As such it remains in the inconspicuousness characteristic of what is encountered in an everyday fashion. The "they" has already stowed away [gesichert] an interpretation for this event. It talks of it in a "fugitive" manner, either expressly or else in a way which is mostly inhibited, as if to say, "One of these days one will die too, in the end; but right now it has nothing to do with us."[9]

The analysis of the phrase 'one dies' reveals unambiguously the kind of Being which belongs to everyday Being-towards-death. In such a way of talking, death is understood as an indefinite something which, above all, must duly arrive from somewhere or other, but which is proximally *not yet present-at-hand* for oneself, and is therefore no threat. The expression 'one dies' spreads abroad the opinion that what gets reached, as it were, by death, is the "they." In Dasein's public way of interpreting, it is said that "one dies," because everyone else and oneself can talk himself into saying that "in no case is it I myself," for this "one" is *the "nobody."*[10] "Dying" is levelled off to an occurrence which reaches Dasein, to be sure, but belongs to nobody in particular. If idle talk is always ambiguous, so is this manner of talking about death. Dying, which is essentially mine in such a way that no one can be my representative, is perverted into an event of public occurrence which the "they" encounters. In the way of talking which we have characterized, death is spoken of as a "case" which is constantly occurring. Death gets passed off as always something "actual"; its character as a possibility gets concealed, and so are the other two items that belong to it—the fact that it is non-relational and that it is not to be outstripped. By such ambiguity, Dasein puts itself in the position of losing itself in the "they" as regards a distinctive potentiality-for-Being which belongs to Dasein's ownmost Self. The "they" gives its approval, and aggravates the *temptation* to cover up from oneself one's ownmost Being-towards-death. This evasive concealment in the face of death dominates everydayness so stubbornly that, in Being with one another, the "neighbours" often still keep talking the "dying person" into the belief that he will escape death and soon return to the tranquillized everydayness of the world of his concern. Such "solicitude" is meant to "console" him. It insists upon bringing him back into Dasein, while in addition it

8. "Die Öffentlichkeit des alltäglichen Miteinander 'kennt' den Tod als ständig vorkommendes Begegnis, als 'Todesfall.' "
9. ". . . man stirbt am Ende auch einmal, aber zunächst bleibt man selbst unbetroffen."
10. "Die öffentliche Daseinsauslegung sagt: 'man stirbt,' weil damit jeder andere und man selbst sich einreden kann: je nicht gerade ich; denn dieses Man ist das *Niemand.*" While we have usually followed the convention of translating the indefinite pronoun "man" as "one" and the expression "das Man" "the 'they,' " to do so here would obscure the point.

helps him to keep his ownmost non-relational possibility-of-Being completely concealed. In this manner the "they" provides [besorgt] a *constant tranquillization about death*. At bottom, however, this is a tranquillization not only for him who is "dying" but just as much for those who "console" him. And even in the case of a demise, the public is still not to have its own tranquillity upset by such an event, or be disturbed in the carefreeness with which it concerns itself.[11] Indeed the dying of Others is seen often enough as a social inconvenience, if not even a downright tactlessness, against which the public is to be guarded.

But along with this tranquillization, which forces Dasein away from its death, the "they" at the same time puts itself in the right and makes itself respectable by tacitly regulating the way in which *one* has to comport oneself towards death. It is already a matter of public acceptance that "thinking about death" is a cowardly fear, a sign of insecurity on the part of Dasein, and a sombre way of fleeing from the world. *The "they" does not permit us the courage for anxiety in the face of death.* The dominance of the manner in which things have been publicly interpreted by the "they," has already decided what state-of-mind is to determine our attitude towards death. In anxiety in the face of death, Dasein is brought face to face with itself as delivered over to that possibility which is not to be outstripped. The "they" concerns itself with transforming this anxiety into fear in the face of an oncoming event. In addition, the anxiety which has been made ambiguous as fear, is passed off as a weakness with which no self-assured Dasein may have any acquaintance. What is "fitting" [Was sich ... "gehört"] according to the unuttered decree of the "they," is indifferent tranquillity as to the "fact" that one dies. The cultivation of such a "superior" indifference *alienates* Dasein from its ownmost nonrelational potentiality-for-Being.

But temptation, tranquillization, and alienation are distinguishing marks of the kind of Being called *"falling."* As falling, everyday Being-towards-death is a constant *fleeing in the face of death*. Being-*towards*-the-end has the mode of *evasion in the face of it*—giving new explanations for it, understanding it inauthentically, and concealing it. Factically one's own Dasein is always dying already; that is to say, it is in a Being-towards-its-end. And it hides this Fact from itself by recoiling "death" as just a "case of death" in Others—an everyday occurrence which, if need be, gives us the assurance still more plainly that "oneself" is still "living." But in thus falling and fleeing *in the face of* death, Dasein's everydayness attests that the very "they" itself already has the definite character of *Being-towards-death*, even when it is not explicitly engaged in "thinking

11. Und selbst im Falle des Ablebens noch soll die Öffentlichkeit durch das Ereignis nicht in ihrer besorgten Sorglosigkeit gestört und beunruhigt werden."

about death." *Even in average everydayness, this ownmost potentiality-for-Being, which is non-relational and not to be outstripped, is constantly an issue for Dasein. This is the case when its concern is merely in the mode of an untroubled indifference* **towards** *the uttermost possibility of existence.* [12]

In setting forth everyday Being-towards-death, however, we are at the same time enjoined to try to secure a full existential conception of Being-towards-the-end, by a more penetrating Interpretation in which falling Being-towards-death is taken as an evasion *in the face of death. That in the face of which one flees* has been made visible in a way which is phenomenally adequate. Against this it must be possible to project phenomenologically the way in which evasive Dasein itself understands its death.

53. EXISTENTIAL PROJECTION OF AN AUTHENTIC BEING-TOWARDS-DEATH

Factically, Dasein maintains itself proximally and for the most part in an inauthentic Being-towards-death. How is the ontological possibility of an *authentic* Being-towards-death to be characterized "Objectively," if, in the end, Dasein never comports itself authentically towards its end, or if, in accordance with its very meaning, this authentic Being must remain hidden from the Others? Is it not a fanciful undertaking, to project the existential possibility of so questionable an existentiell potentiality-for-Being? What is needed, if such a projection is to go beyond a merely fictitious arbitrary construction? Does Dasein itself give us any instructions for carrying it out? And can any grounds for its phenomenal legitimacy be taken from Dasein itself? Can our analysis of Dasein up to this point give us any prescriptions for the ontological task we have now set ourselves, so that what we have before us may be kept on a road of which we can be sure?

The existential conception of death has been established; and therewith we have also established what it is that an authentic Being-towards-the-end should be able to comport itself towards. We have also characterized inauthentic Being-towards-death, and thus we have prescribed in a negative way [prohibitiv] how it is possible for authentic Being-towards-death *not* to be. It is with these positive and prohibitive instructions that the existential edifice of an authentic Being-towards-death must let itself be projected.

12. *"... wenn auch nur im Modus des Besorgens einer unbehelligten Gleichgültigkeit* **gegen** *die äusserste Möglichkeit seiner Existenz."* Ordinarily the expression "Gleichgültigkeit gegen" means simply "indifference towards." But Heidegger's use of boldface type suggests that here he also has in mind that "gegen" may mean "against" or "in opposition to."

Dasein is constituted by disclosedness—that is, by an understanding with a state-of-mind. *Authentic* Being-towards-death can *not evade* its ownmost non-relational possibility, or *cover up* this possibility by thus fleeing from it, or *give a new explanation* for it to accord with the common sense of the "they." In our existential projection of an authentic Being-towards-death, therefore, we must set forth those items in such a Being which are constitutive for it as an understanding of death—and as such an understanding in the sense of Being towards this possibility without either fleeing it or covering it up.

In the first instance, we must characterize Being-towards-death as a *Being towards a possibility*—indeed, towards a distinctive possibility of Dasein itself. "Being towards" a possibility—that is to say, towards something possible—may signifiy "Being out for" something possible, as in concerning ourselves with its actualization. Such possibilities are constantly encountered in the field of what is ready-to-hand and present-at-hand—what is attainable, controllable, practicable, and the like. In concernfully Being out for something possible, there is a tendency to *annihilate the possibility* of the possible by making it available to us. But the concernful actualization of equipment which is ready-to-hand (as in producing it, getting it ready,·readjusting it, and so on) is always merely relative, since even that which has been actualized is still characterized in terms of some involvements—indeed this is precisely what characterizes its Being. Even though actualized, it remains, as actual, something possible for doing something; it is characterized by an "in-order-to." What our analysis is to make plain is simply how Being out for something concernfully, comports itself towards the possible: it does so not by the theoretico-thematical consideration of the possible as possible, and by having regard for its possibility as such, but rather by looking *circumspectively away* from the possible and looking at that for which it is possible [das Wofür-möglich].

Manifestly Being-towards-death, which is now in question, cannot have the character of concernfully Being out to get itself actualized. For one thing, death as possible is not something possible which is ready-to-hand or present-at-hand, but a possibility of *Dasein's* Being. So to concern oneself with actualizing what is thus possible would have to signify, "bringing about one's demise." But if this were done, Dasein would deprive itself of the very ground for an existing Being-towards-death.

Thus, if by "being towards death" we do not have in view an "actualizing" of death, neither can we mean "dwelling upon the end in its possibility." This is the way one comports oneself when one "thinks about death," pondering over when and how this possibility may perhaps be actualized. Of course such brooding over death does not fully take away from it its character as a possibility. Indeed, it always gets brooded over as something that is coming; but in such brooding we weaken it by calculating how we are to have it at our disposal. As something possible, it is to show as little as possible of its possibility. On the other hand, if Being-towards-death has to disclose understandingly the possibility which we have characterized, and if it is to disclose it *as a possibility*, then in such Being-towards-death this possibility must not be weakened: it must be understood *as a possibility*, it must be culitivated *as a possibility*, and we must *put up with* it *as a possibility*, in the way we comport ourselves towards it.

However, Dasein comports itself towards something possible in its possibility by *expecting* it [im *Erwarten*]. Anyone who is intent on something possible, may encounter it unimpeded and undiminished in its "whether it comes or does not, or whether it comes after all."[13] But with this phenomenon of expecting, has not our analysis reached the same kind of Being towards the possible to which we have already called attention in our description of "Being out for something" concernfully? To expect something possible is always to understand it and to "have" it with regard to whether and when and how it will be actually present-at-hand. Expecting is not just an occasional looking-away from the possible to its possible actualization, but is essentially a *waiting for that actualization* [ein *Warten auf diese*]. Even in expecting, one leaps away from the possible and gets a foothold in the actual. It is for its actuality that what is expected is expected. By the very nature of expecting, the possible is drawn into the actual, arising out of the actual and returning to it.[14]

But being towards this possibility, as Being-towards-death, is so to comport ourselves towards *death* that in this Being, and for it, death reveals itself *as a possibility*. Our terminology for such Being towards this possibility is *"anticipation" of this possibility*.[15] But in this way of behaving does there not lurk a coming-close to the possible, and when one is close to the possible, does not its actualization emerge? In this kind of coming close, however, one does not tend towards concernfully making available something actual; but as one comes closer understandingly, the possibility of the possible just becomes "greater." *The closest closeness which one may have in Being towards death as a possibility, is as far as possible from anything actual.* The more unveiledly this possibility gets understood, the more purely does the understanding penetrate into it *as the possibility of the impossibility of any existence at all.* Death, as possi-

---

13. "Für ein Gespanntsein auf es vermag ein Mögliches in seinem 'ob oder nicht oder schliesslich doch' ungehindert und ungeschmälert zu begegnen."

14. "Auch im Erwarten liegt ein Abspringen vom Möglichen und Fussfassen im Wirklichen, dafür das Erwartete erwartet ist. Vom Wirklichen aus und auf es zu wird das Mögliche in das Wirkliche erwartungsmässig hereingezogen."

15. "... *Vorlaufen in die Möglichkeit.*" While we have used "anticipate" to translate "vorgreifen," which occurs rather seldom, we shall also use it—less literally—to translate "vorlaufen," which appears very often in the following pages, and which has the special connotation of "running ahead." But as Heidegger's remarks have indicated, the kind of "anticipation" which is involved in Being-towards-death, does not consist in "waiting for" death or "dwelling upon it" or "actualizing" it before it normally comes; nor does "running ahead into it" in this sense mean that we "rush headlong into it."

bility, gives Dasein nothing to be "actualized," nothing which Dasein, as actual, could itself *be*. It is the possibility of the impossibility of every way of comporting oneself towards anything, of every way of existing. In the anticipation of this possibility it becomes "greater and greater"; that is to say, the possibility reveals itself to be such that it knows no measure at all, no more or less, but signifies the possibility of the measureless impossibility of existence. In accordance with its essence, this possibility offers no support for becoming intent on someting, "picturing" to oneself the actuality which is possible, and so forgetting its possibility. Being-towards-death, as anticipation of possibility, is what first *makes* this possibility *possible,* and sets it free as possibility.

Being-towards-death is the anticipation of a potentiality-for-Being of that entity whose kind of Being is anticipation itself.[16] In the anticipatory revealing of this potentiality-for-Being, Dasein discloses itself to itself as regards its uttermost possibility. But to project itself on its ownmost potentiality-for-Being means to be able to understand itself in the Being of the entity so revealed—namely, to exist. Anticipation turns out to be the possibility of understanding one's *ownmost* and uttermost potentiality-for-Being—that is to say, the possibility of *authentic existence.* The ontological constitution of such existence must be made visible by setting forth the concrete structure of anticipation of death. How are we to delimit this structure phenomenally? Manifestly, we must do so by determining those characteristics which must belong to an anticipatory disclosure so that it can become the pure understanding of that ownmost possibility which is non-relational and not to be outstripped—which is certain and, as such, indefinite. It must be noted that understanding does not primarily mean just gazing at a meaning, but rather understanding oneself in that potentiality-for-Being which reveals itself in projection.

Death is Dasein's *ownmost* possibility. Being towards this possibility discloses to Dasein its *ownmost* potentiality-for-Being, in which its very Being is the issue. Here it can become manifest to Dasein that in this distinctive possibility of its own self, it has been wrenched away from the "they." This means that in anticipation any Dasein can have wrenched itself away from the "they" already. But when one understands that this is something which Dasein "can" have done, this only reveals its factical lostness in the everydayness of the they-self.

The ownmost possibility is *non-relational.* Anticipation allows Dasein to understand that that potentiality-for-being in which its ownmost Being is an issue, must be taken over by Dasein alone. Death does not just 'belong' to one's own Dasein in an undifferentiated way; death *lays claim* to it as an *individual* Dasein. The non-relational character of death, as

16. "... dessen Seinsart das Vorlaufen selbst ist." The earlier editions have "hat" instead of "ist."

understood in anticipation, individualizes Dasein down to itself. This individualizing is a way in which the "there" is disclosed for existence. It makes manifest that all Being-alongside the things with which we concern ourselves, and all Being-with Others, will fail us when our ownmost potentiality-for-Being is the issue. Dasein can be *authentically itself* only if it makes this possible for itself of its own accord. But if concern and solicitude fail us, this does not signify at all that these ways of Dasein have been cut off from its authentically Being-its-Self. As structures essential to Dasein's constitution, these have a share in conditioning the possibility of any existence whatsoever. Dasein is authentically itself only to the extent that, *as* concernful Being-alongside and solicitous Being-with, it projects itself upon its ownmost potentiality-for-Being rather than upon the possibility of the they-self. The entity which anticipates its non-relational possibility, is thus forced by that very anticipation into the possibility of taking over from itself its ownmost Being, and doing so of its own accord.

The ownmost, non-relational possibility is *not to be outstripped.* Being towards this possibility enables Dasein to understand that giving itself up impends for it as the uttermost possibility of its existence. Anticipation, however, unlike inauthentic Being-towards-death, does not evade the fact that death is not to be outstripped; instead, anticipation frees itself *for* accepting this. When, by anticipation, one becomes free *for* one's own death, one is liberated from one's lostness in those possibilities which may accidentally thrust themselves upon one; and one is liberated in such a way that for the first time one can authentically understand and choose among the factical possibilities lying ahead of that possibility which is not to be outstripped.[17] Anticipation discloses to existence that its uttermost possibility lies in giving itself up, and thus it shatters all one's tenaciousness to whatever existence one has reached. In anticipation, Dasein guards itself against falling back behind itself, or behind the potentiality-for-Being which it has understood. It guards itself against "becoming too old for its victories" (Nietzsche). Free for its ownmost possibilities, which are determined by the *end* and so are understood as *finite* [*endliche*], Dasein dispels the danger that it may, by its own finite understanding of existence, fail to recognize that it is getting outstripped by the existence-possibilities of Others, or rather that it may explain these possibilities wrongly and force them back upon its own, so that it may divest itself of its ownmost factical existence. As the non-relational possibility, death individualizes— but only in such a manner that, as the possibility which is not to be outstripped, it makes Dasein, as Being-with, have some understanding of the potentiality-for-Being of Others. Since anticipation of the possibility which is not to be outstripped discloses also all the possibilities which lie

17. "... die der unüberholbaren vorgelagert sind." ...

ahead of that possibility, this anticipation includes the possibility of taking the *whole* of Dasein in advance [Vorwegnehmens] in an existentiell manner; that is to say, it includes the possibility of existing as a *whole potentiality-for-Being*.

The ownmost, non-relational possibility, which is not to be outstripped, is *certain*. The way *to be* certain of it is determined by the kind of truth which corresponds to it (disclosedness). The certain possibility of death, however, discloses Dasein as a possibility, but does so only in such a way that, in anticipating this possibility, Dasein *makes* this possibility *possible* for itself as its ownmost potentiality-for-Being.[18] The possibility is disclosed because it is made possible in anticipation. To maintain oneself in this truth—that is, to be certain of what has been disclosed—demands all the more that one should anticipate. We cannot compute the certainty of death by ascertaining how many cases of death we encounter. This certainty is by no means of the kind which maintains itself in the truth of the present-at-hand. When something present-at-hand has been uncovered, it is encountered most purely if we just look at the entity and let it be encountered in itself. Dasein must first have lost itself in the factual circumstances [Sachverhalte] (this can be one of care's own tasks and possibilities) if it is to obtain the pure objectivity—that is to say, the indifference—of apodictic evidence. If Being-certain in relation to death does not have this character, this does not mean that it is of a lower grade, but that *it does not belong at all to the graded order of the kinds of evidence we can have about the present-at-hand.*

Holding death for true (death *is* just one's own) shows another kind of certainty, and is more primordial than any certainty which relates to entities encountered within-the-world, or to formal objects; for it is certain of Being-in-the-world. As such, holding death for true does not demand just *one* definite kind of behaviour in Dasein, but demands Dasein itself in the full authenticity of its existence. In anticipation Dasein can first make certain of its ownmost Being in its totality—a totality which is not to be outstripped. Therefore the evidential character which belongs to the immediate givenness of Experiences, of the "I," or of consciousness, must necessarily lag behind the certainty which anticipation includes. Yet this is not because the way in which these are grasped would not be a rigorous one, but because in principle such a way of grasping them cannot hold *for true* (disclosed) something which at bottom it insists upon "having

18. "Die gewisse Möglichkeit des Todes erschliesst das Dasein aber als Möglichkeit nur so, dass es vorlaufend zu ihr diese Möglichkeit als eigenstes Seinkönnen für sich *ermöglicht.*" While we have taken "Die gewisse Möglichkeit des Todes" as the subject of this puzzling sentence, "das Dasein" *may* be the subject instead. The use of the preposition "zu" instead of the usual "in" after "vorlaufend" suggests that in "anticipating" the possibility of death, Dasein is here thought of as "running ahead" *towards* it or *up to* it rather than *into* it. When this construction occurs in later passages, we shall indicate it by subjoining "zu" in brackets.

there" as true: namely, Dasein itself, which I myself *am*, and which, as a potentiality-for-Being, I can be authentically only by anticipation.

The ownmost possibility, which is non-relational, not to be out-stripped, and certain, is *indefinite* as regards its certainty. How does anticipation disclose this characteristic of Dasein's distinctive possibility? How does the anticipatory understanding project itself upon a potentiality-for-Being which is certain and which is constantly possible in such a way that the "when" in which the utter impossibility of existence becomes possible remains constantly indefinite? In anticipating [zum] the indefinite certainty of death, Dasein opens itself to a constant *threat* arising out of its own "there." In this very threat Being-towards-the-end must maintain itself. So little can it tone this down that it must rather cultivate the indefiniteness of the certainty. How is it existentially possible for this constant threat to be genuinely disclosed? All understanding is accompanied by a state-of-mind. Dasein's mood brings it face to face with the thrownness of its "that it is there." *But the state-of-mind which can hold open the utter and constant threat to itself arising from Dasein's ownmost individualized Being, is anxiety.*[19] *In this state-of-mind, Dasein finds itself face to face with the "nothing" of the possible impossibility of its existence. Anxiety is anxious about the potentiality-for-Being of the entity so destined [des so bestimmten Seienden], and in this way it discloses the uttermost possibility. Anticipation utterly individualizes Dasein, and allows it, in this individualization of itself, to become certain of the totality of its potentiality-for-Being. For this reason, anxiety as a basic state-of-mind belongs to such a self-understanding of Dasein on the basis of Dasein itself.*[20] *Being-towards-death is essentially anxiety. This is attested unmistakably, though "only" indirectly, by Being-towards-death as we have described it, when it perverts anxiety into cowardly fear and, in surmounting this fear, only makes known its own cowardliness in the face of anxiety.*

We may now summarize our characterization of authentic Being-towards-death as we have projected it existentially: *anticipation reveals to Dasein its lostness in the they-self, and brings it face to face with the possibility of being itself, primarily unsupported by concernful solicitude, but of being itself, rather, in an impassioned* **freedom towards death** *—a freedom which has been released from the Illusions of the "they," and which is factical, certain of itself, and anxious.*

19. *"Die Befindlichkeit aber, welche die ständige und schlechthinnige, aus dem eigensten vereinzelten Sein des Daseins aufsteigende Bedrohung seiner selbst offen zu halten vermag, ist die Angst."* Notice that *"welche"* may be construed either as the subject or as the direct object of the relative clause.
20. *"... gehört zu diesem Sichverstehen des Daseins aus seinem Grunde die Grundbefindlichkeit der Angst."* It is not grammatically clear whether "seinem" refers to "Sichverstehen" or to "Daseins."

All the relationships whch belong to Being-towards-death, up to the full content of Dasein's uttermost possibility, as we have characterized it, constitute an anticipation which they combine in revealing, unfolding, and holding fast, as that which makes this possibility possible. The existential projection in which anticipation has been delimited, has made visible the *ontological* possibility of an existentiell Being-towards-death which is authentic. Therewith, however, the possibility of Dasein's having an authentic potentiality-for-Being-a-whole emerges, *but only as an ontological possibility.* In our existential projection of anticipation, we have of course clung to those structures of Dasein which we have arrived at earlier, and we have, as it were, let Dasein itself project itself upon this possibility, without holding up to Dasein an ideal of existence with any special "content," or forcing any such ideal upon it "from outside." Nevertheless, this existentially "possible" Being-towards-death remains, from the existentiell point of view, a fantastical exaction. The fact that an authentic potentiality-for-Being-a-whole is ontologically possible for Dasein, signifies nothing, so long as a corresponding ontical potentiality-for-Being has not been demonstrated in Dasein itself. Does Dasein ever factically throw itself into such a Being-towards-death? Does Dasein *demand,* even by reason of its ownmost Being, an authentic potentiality-for-Being determined by anticipation?

Before answering these questions, we must investigate whether to *any* extent and in any way Dasein *gives testimony,* from its ownmost potentiality-for-Being, as to a possible *authenticity* of its existence, so that it not only makes known that in an existentiell manner such authenticity is possible, but *demands* this of itself.

The question of Dasein's authentic Being-a-whole and of its existential constitution still hands in mid-air. It can be put on a phenomenal basis which will stand the test only if it can cling to a possible authenticity of its Being which is attested by Dasein itself. If we succeed in uncovering that attestation phenomenologically, together with what it attests, then the problem will arise anew as to *whether the anticipation of* [*zum*] *death, which we have hitherto projected only in its* **ontological** *possibility, has an essential connection with that authentic potentiality-for-Being which has been* **attested.**

57. CONSCIENCE AS THE CALL OF CARE

Conscience summons Dasein's Self from its lostness in the "they." The Self to which the appeal is made remains indefinite and empty in its "what." When Dasein interprets itself in terms of that with which it concerns itself, the call passes over *what* Dasein, proximally and for the most part, understands itself as. And yet the Self has been reached, un-equivocally and unmistakably. Not only is the call meant for him to whom the appeal is made "without regard for person," but even the caller main-tains itself in conspicuous indefiniteness. If the caller is asked about its name, status, origin, or repute, it not only refuses to answer, but does not even leave the slightest possibility of one's making it into something with which one can be familiar when one's understanding of Dasein has a "worldly" orientation. On the other hand, it by no means disguises itself in the call. That which calls the call, simply holds itself aloof from any way of becoming well-known, and this belongs to its phenomenal character. To let itself be drawn into getting considered and talked about, goes against its kind of Being.[21] The peculiar indefiniteness of the caller and the impos-sibility of making more definite what this caller is, are not just nothing; they are distinctive for it in a *positive* way. They make known to us that the caller is solely absorbed in summoning us to something, that it is *heard only as such,* and furthermore that it will not let itself be coaxed. But if so, is it not quite appropriate to the phenomenon to leave unasked the question of what the caller is? Yes indeed, when it comes to listening to the factical call of conscience in an existentiell way, but not when it comes to analysing existentially the facticity of the calling and the existentiality of the hearing.

But is it at all necessary to keep raising explicitly the question of *who* does the calling? Is this not answered for Dasein just as unequivocally as the question of to whom the call makes its appeal? *In conscience Dasein calls itself.* This understanding of the caller may be more or less awake in the factical hearing of the call. Ontologically, however, it is not enough to answer that Dasein is *at the same time* both the caller and the one to whom the appeal is made. When Dasein is appealed to, *is* it not "there" in a different way from that in which it does the calling? Shall we say that its ownmost potentiality-for-Being-its-Self functions as the caller?

Indeed the call is precisely something which *we ourselves* have nei-ther planned nor prepared for nor voluntarily performed, nor have we ever done so. "It" calls,[22] against our expectations and even against our will. On the other hand, the call undoubtedly does not come from some-one else who is with me in the world. The call comes *from* me and yet *from beyond me and over me.*[23]

These phenomenal findings are not to be explained away. After all, they have been taken as a starting-point for explaining the voice of con-science as an alien power by which Dasein is dominanted. If the interpre-tation continues in this direction, one supplies a possessor for the power

---

21. "Es geht wider die Art seines Seins, sich in ein Betrachten und Bereden ziehen zu lassen."
22. " "Es" ruft . . ." Here the pronoun "es" is used quite impersonally, and does not refer back to "the call" itself ("Der Ruf").
23. "Der Ruf kommt *aus* mir und doch *über* mich."

thus posited,[24] or one takes the power itself as a person who makes himself known—namely God. On the other hand one may try to reject this explanation in which the caller is taken as an alien manifestation of such a power, and to explain away the conscience "biologically" at the same time. Both these explanations pass over the phenomenal findings too hastily. Such procedures are facilitated by the unexpressed but ontologically dogmatic guiding thesis that what *is* (in other words, anything so factual as the call) must be *present-at-hand*, and that what does not let itself be Objectively demonstrated as *present-at-hand*, just *is not* at all.

But methodologically this is too precipitate. We must instead hold fast not only to the phenomenal finding that I receive the call as coming both from me and from beyond me, but also to the implication that this phenomenon is here delineated ontologically as a phenomenon of *Dasein*. Only the existential constitution of *this* entity can afford us a clue for Interpreting the kind of Being of the "it" which does the calling.

Does our previous analysis of Dasein's state of Being show us a way of making ontologically intelligible the kind of Being which belongs to the caller, and, along with it, that which belongs to the calling? The fact that the call is not something which is explicitly performed *by me*, but that rather "it" does the calling, does not justify seeking the caller in some entity with a character other than that of Dasein. Yet every Dasein always exists factically. It is not a free-floating self-projection; but its character is determined by thrownness as a Fact of the entity which it is; and, as so determined, it has in each case already been delivered over to existence, and it constantly so remains. Dasein's facticity, however, is essentially distinct from the factuality of something present-at-hand. Existent Dasein does not encounter itself as something present-at-hand within-the-world. But neither does thrownness adhere to Dasein as an inaccessible characteristic which is of no importance for its existence. As something thrown, Dasein has been thrown *into existence*. It exists as an entity which has to be as it is and as it can be.

That is is factically, may be obscure and hidden as regards the *"why"* of it; but the *"that-it-is"* has *itself* been disclosed to Dasein.[25] The thrownness of this entity belongs to the disclosedness of the 'there' and reveals itself constantly in its current state-of-mind. This state-of-mind brings Dasein, more or less explicitly and authentically, face to face with the fact "that it is, and that it has to be something with a potentiality-for-Being as the entity which it is."[26] For the most part, however, its mood is such that its thrownness gets *closed off*. In the face of its thrownness Dasein flees

24. "... unterlegt man der festgelegten Macht einen Bestizer ..."
25. "*Dass* es faktisch ist, mag hinsichtlich des *Warum* verborgen sein, das *'Dass' selbst* jedoch ist dem Dasein erschlossen. ..."
26. "Diese bringt das Dasein mehr oder minder ausdrücklich und eigentlich vor sein "dass es ist und als das Seiende, das es ist, seinkönnend zu sein hat.'"

to the relief which comes with the supposed freedom of the they-self. This fleeing has been described as a fleeing in the face of the uncanniness which is basically determinative for individualized Being-in-the-world. Uncanniness reveals itself authentically in the basic state-of-mind of anxiety; and, as the most elemental way in which thrown Dasein is disclosed, it puts Dasein's Being-in-the-world face to face with the "nothing" of the world; in the face of this "nothing," Dasein is anxious with anxiety about its ownmost potentiality-for-Being. *What if this Dasein, which finds itself [sich befindet] in the very depths of its uncanniness, should be the caller of the call of conscience?*

Nothing speaks against this; but all those phenomena which we have hitherto set forth in characterizing the caller and its calling speak for it.

In its "who," the caller is definable in a "worldly" way by *nothing* at all. The caller is Dasein in its uncanniness: primordial, thrown Being-in-the-world as the "not-at-home"—the bare "that-it-is" in the "nothing" of the world. The caller is unfamiliar to the everyday they-self; it is something like an *alien* voice. What could be more alien to the "they," lost in the manifold "world" of its concern, than the Self which has been individualized down to itself in uncanniness and been thrown into the "nothing"? "It" calls, even though it gives the concernfully curious ear nothing to hear which might be passed along in further retelling and talked about in public. But what is Dasein even to report from the uncanniness of its thrown Being? *What* else remains for it than its own potentiality-for-Being as revealed in anxiety? How else is "it" to call than by summoning Dasein towards this potentiality-for-Being, which alone is the issue?

The call does not report events; it calls without uttering anything. The call discourses in the uncanny mode of *keeping silent.* And it does this only because, in calling the one to whom the appeal is made, it does not call him into the public idle talk of the "they," but *calls* him *back* from this *into the reticence of his existent* potentiality-for-Being. When the caller reaches him to whom the appeal is made, it does so with a cold assurance which is uncanny but by no means obvious. Wherein lies the basis for this assurance if not in the fact that when Dasein has been individualized down to itself in its uncanniness, it is for itself something that simply cannot be mistaken for anything else? What is it that so radically deprives Dasein of the possibility of misunderstanding itself by any sort of alibi and failing to recognize itself, if not the forsakenness [Verlassenheit] with which it has been abandoned [Überlassenheit] to itself?

Uncanniness is the basic kind of Being-in-the-world, even though in an everyday way it has been covered up. Out of the depths of this kind of Being, Dasein itself, as conscience, calls. The "it calls me" ["es ruft mich"] is a distinctive kind of discourse for Dasein. The call whose mood has been attuned by anxiety is what makes it possible first and foremost for Dasein to project itself upon its ownmost *potentiality-for-Being.* The call of conscience, existentially understood, makes known for the first time what we have hitherto merely contended: that uncanniness pursues Dasein and is a threat to the lostness in which it has forgotten itself.

The proposition that Dasein is at the same time both the caller and the one to whom the appeal is made, has now lost its empty formal character and its obviousness. *Conscience manifests itself as the call of care:* the caller is Dasein, which, in its thrownness (in its Being-already-in), is anxious[27] about its potentiality-for-Being. The one to whom the appeal is made is this very same Dasein, summoned to its ownmost potentiality-for-Being (ahead of itself . . .). Dasein is falling into the "they" (in Being-already-alongside the world of its concern), and it is summoned out of this falling by the appeal. The call of conscience—that is, conscience itself—has its ontological possibility in the fact that Dasein, in the very basis of its Being, is care.

So we need not resort to powers with a character other than that of Dasein; indeed, recourse to these is so far from clarifying the uncanniness of the call that instead it annihilates it. In the end, does not the reason why "explanations" of the conscience have gone off the track, lie in the fact that we have not looked *long enough* to establish our phenomenal findings as to the call, and that Dasein has been presupposed as having some kind of ontological definiteness or indefiniteness, whichever it may chance? Why should we look to alien powers for information before we have made sure that in starting our analysis we have not given *too low* an assessment of Dasein's Being, regarding it as an innocuous subject endowed with personal consciousness, somehow or other occurring?

And yet, if the caller—who is "nobody," when seen after the manner of the world—is interpreted as a power, this seems to be a dispassionate recognition of something that one can "come across Objectively." When seen correctly, however, this interpretation is only a fleeing in the face of the conscience—a way for Dasein to escape by slinking away from that thin wall by which the "they" is separated, as it were, from the uncanniness of its Being. This interpretation of the conscience passes itself off as recognizing the call in the sense of a voice which is "universally" binding, and which speaks in a way that is "not just subjective." Furthermore, the "universal" conscience becomes exalted to a "world-conscience," which still has the phenomenal character of an "it" and "nobody," yet which speaks—there in the individual 'subject'—as this indefinite something.

But this "public conscience"—what else is it than the voice of the "they"? A "world-conscience" is a dubious fabrication, and Dasein can

27. ". . . sich ängstigend . . ." The older editions have "sich ängstend," which has virtually the same meaning, and is more characteristic of Heidegger's style.

come to this only *because* conscience, in its basis and its essence, *is in each case mine*—not only in the sense that in each case the appeal is to one's ownmost potentiality-for-Being, but because the call comes from that entity which in each case I myself am.

With this Interpretation of the caller, which is purely in accord with the phenomenal character of the calling, the "power" of conscience is not diminished and rendered "merely subjective." On the contrary, only in this way do the inexorability and unequivocal character of the call become free. This Interpretation does justice to the "Objectivity" of the appeal for the first time by leaving it its "subjectivity," which of course denies the they-self its dominion.

Nevertheless, this Interpretation of the conscience as the call of care will be countered by the question of whether any interpretation of the conscience can stand up if it removes itself so far from "natural experience." How is the conscience to function as that which *summons* us to our ownmost potentiality-for-Being, when proximally and for the most part it merely *warns* and *reproves?* Does the conscience speak in so indefinite and empty a manner about our potentiality-for-Being? Does it not rather speak definitely and concretely in relation to failures and omissions which have already befallen or which we still have before us? Does the alleged appeal stem from a *"bad"* conscience or from a *"good"* one? Does the conscience give us anything positive at all? Does it not function rather in just a critical fashion?

Such considerations are indisputably within their rights. We can, however, demand that in any Interpretation of conscience "one" should recognize in it the phenomenon in question as it is experienced in an everyday manner. But satisfying this requirement does not mean in turn that the ordinary ontical way of understanding conscience must be recognized as the first court of appeal [erste Instanz] for an ontological Interpretation. On the other hand, the considerations which we have just marshalled remain premature as long as the analysis of conscience to which they pertain falls short of its goal. Hitherto we have merely tried to trace back conscience *as a phenomenon of Dasein* to the ontological constitution of that entity. This has served to prepare us for the task of making the conscience intelligible as *an attestation of Dasein's ownmost potentiality-for-Being*—an attestation which lies in Dasein itself.

But what the conscience attests becomes completely definite only when we have delimited plainly enough the character of the *hearing* which genuinely corresponds to the calling. The *authentic* understanding which "follows" the call is not a mere addition which attaches itself to the phenomenon of conscience by a process which may or may not be forthcoming. Only *from* an understanding of the appeal and together *with* such an understanding does the *full* Experience of conscience let itself be grasped. If in each case the caller and he to whom the appeal is made are *at the same time* one's own Dasein *themselves,* then in any failure to hear the call or any incorrect hearing of *oneself,* there lies a *definite kind* of Dasein's *Being.* A free-floating call from which "nothing ensues" is an impossible fiction when seen existentially. With regard to Dasein, "that *nothing* ensues" signifies something *positive.*

So then, only by analysing the way the appeal is understood can one be led to discuss explicitly *what the call gives one to understand.* But only with our foregoing general ontological characterization of the conscience does it become possible to conceive existentially the conscience's call of "Guilty!"[28] All experiences and interpretations of the conscience are at one in that they make the "voice" of conscience speak somehow of "guilt."

Martin Heidegger
What Is Metaphysics?

"What is metaphysics?" The question leads one to expect a discussion about metaphysics. Such is not our intention. Instead, we shall discuss a definite metaphysical question, thus, as it will appear, landing ourselves straight into metaphysics. Only in this way can we make it really possible for metaphysics to speak for itself.

Our project begins with the presentation of a metaphysical question, then goes on to its development and ends with its answer.

THE PRESENTATION OF A METAPHYSICAL QUESTION

Seen from the point of view of sound common sense, Philosophy, according to Hegel, is the "world stood on its head." Hence the peculiar nature of our task calls for some preliminary definition. This arises out of the dual nature of metaphysical questioning.

28. . . . das im Gewissen gerufene "schuldig" existentzial zu begreifen." As Heidegger will point out, the words "schuldig," "Schuld" and their derivatives have many different meanings, corresponding not only to "indebtedness," . . . , but also to "guilt" and "responsibility." In the present chapter we shall translate them by "guilty" and "guilt" whenever possible, even though these expressions will not always be entirely appropriate.

Source: Martin Heidegger, "What Is Metaphysics?" *Existence and Being,* translated by R. F. C. Hull and Alan Crick (Chicago: Henry Regnery Gateway Editions, 1960), pp. 325–349. © 1949 by Vision Press, London. Reprinted by permission of the publishers.

Firstly, every metaphysical question always covers the whole range of metaphysical problems. In every case it is itself the whole. Secondly, every metaphysical question can only be put in such a way that the questioner as such is by his very questioning involved in the question.

From this we derive the following pointer: metaphysical questioning has to be put as a whole and has always to be based on the essential situation of existence, which puts the question. We question here and now, on our own account. Our existence—a community of scientists, teachers and students—is ruled by science. What essential things are happening to us in the foundations of our existence, now that science has become our passion?

The fields of sciences lie far apart. Their methodologies are fundamentally different. This disrupted multiplicity of disciplines is today only held together by the technical organisation of the Universities and their faculties, and maintained as a unit of meaning by the practical aims of those faculties. As against this, however, the root of the sciences in their essential ground has atrophied.

And yet—insofar as we follow their most specific intentions—in all the sciences we are related to what-is. Precisely from the point of view of the sciences no field takes precedence over another, neither Nature over History nor vice versa. No one methodology is superior to another. Mathematical knowledge is no stricter than philological or historical knowledge. It has merely the characteristic of "exactness," which is not to be identified with strictness. To demand exactitude of history would be to offend against the idea of the kind of strictness that pertains to the humanistic sciences. The world-relationship which runs through all the sciences as such constrains them to seek what-is *in itself,* with a view to rendering it, according to its quiddity (*Wasgehalt*) and its modality (*Seinsart*), an object of investigation and basic definition. What the sciences accomplish, ideally speaking, is an approximation to the essential nature of all things.

This distinct world-relationship to what-is in itself is sustained and guided by a freely chosen attitude on the part of our human existence. It is true that the pre-scientific and extra-scientific activities of man also relate to what-is. But the distinction of science lies in the fact that, in an altogether specific manner, it and it alone explicitly allows the object itself the first and last word. In this objectivity of questioning, definition and proof there is a certain limited submission to what-is, so that this may reveal itself. This submissive attitude taken up by scientific theory becomes the basis of a possibility: the possibility of science acquiring a leadership of its own, albeit limited, in the whole field of human existence. The world-relationship of science and the attitude of man responsible for it can, of course, only be fully understood when we see and understand what is going on in the world-relationship so maintained. Man—one entity

(*Seiendes*) among others—"pursues" science. In this "pursuit" what is happening is nothing less than the irruption of a particular entity called "Man" into the whole of what-is, in such a way that in and through this irruption what-is manifests itself *as* and *how* it is. The manner in which the revelatory irruption occurs is the chief thing that helps what-is to become what it is.

This triple process of world-relationship, attitude, and irruption—a radical unity—introduces something of the inspiring simplicity and intensity of *Da-sein* into scientific existence. If we now explicitly take possession of scientific *Da-sein* as clarified by us, we must necessarily say:

That to which the world-relationship refers is what-is—and nothing else.

That by which every attitude is moulded is what-is—and nothing more.

That with which scientific exposition effects its "irruption" is what-is —and beyond that, nothing.

But it is not remarkable that precisely at that point where scientific man makes sure of his surest possession he should speak of something else? What is to be investigated is what-is—and nothing else; only what-is—and nothing more; simply and solely what-is—and beyond that, nothing.

But what about this "nothing"? Is it only an accident that we speak like that quite naturally? Is it only a manner of speaking—and nothing more?

But why worry about this Nothing? "Nothing" is absolutely rejected by science and abandoned as null and void (*das Nichtige*). But if we abandon Nothing in this way are we not, by that act, really admitting it? Can we, though, speak of an admission when we admit Nothing? But perhaps this sort of cross-talk is already degenerating into an empty wrangling about words.

Science, on the other hand, has to assert its soberness and seriousness afresh and declare that it is concerned solely with what-is. Nothing—how can it be for science anything other than a horror and a phantasm? If science is right then one thing stands firm: science wishes to know nothing of Nothing. Such is after all the strictly scientific approach to Nothing. We know it by wishing to know nothing of Nothing.

Science wishes to know nothing of Nothing. Even so the fact remains that at the very point where science tries to put its own essence in words it invokes the aid of Nothing. It has recourse to the very thing it rejects. What sort of schizophrenia is this?

A consideration of our momentary existence as one ruled by science has landed us in the thick of an argument. In the course of this argument a question has already presented itself. The question only requires putting specifically: What about Nothing?

THE DEVELOPMENT OF THE QUESTION

The development of our enquiry into Nothing is bound to lead us to a position where either the answer will prove possible or the impossibility of an answer will become evident. "Nothing" is admitted. Science, by adopting an attitude of superior indifference, abandons it as that which "is not."

All the same we shall endeavour to enquire into Nothing. What is Nothing? Even the initial approach to this question shows us something out of the ordinary. So questioning, we postulate Nothing as something that somehow or other "is"—as an entity (*Seiendes*). But it is nothing of the sort. The question as to the what and wherefore of Nothing turns the thing questioned into its opposite. The question deprives itself of its own object.

Accordingly, every answer to this question is impossible from the start. For it necessarily moves in the form that Nothing "is" this, that or the other. Question and answer are equally nonsensical in themselves where Nothing is concerned.

Hence even the rejection by science is superfluous. The commonly cited basic rule of all thinking—the proposition that contradiction must be avoided—and common "logic" rule out the question. For thinking, which is essentially always thinking about something, would, in thinking of Nothing, be forced to act against its own nature.

Because we continually meet with failure as soon as we try to turn Nothing into a subject, our enquiry into Nothing is already at an end— always assuming, of course, that in this enquiry "logic" is the highest court of appeal, that reason is the means and thinking the way to an original comprehension of Nothing and its possible revelation.

But, it may be asked, can the law of "logic" be assailed? Is not reason indeed the master in this enquiry into Nothing? It is in fact only with reason's help that we can define Nothing in the first place and postulate it as a problem—though a problem that consumes only itself. For Nothing is the negation (*Verneinung*) of the totality of what-is: that which is absolutely not. But at this point we bring Nothing into the higher category of the Negative (*Nichthaftes*) and therefore of what is negated. But according to the overriding and unassailable teachings of "logic" negation is a specific act of reason. How, then, in our enquiry into Nothing and into the very possibility of holding such an enquiry can we dismiss reason? Yet is it so sure just what we are postulating? Does the Not (*das Nicht*), the state of being negated (*die Verneintheit*) and hence negation itself (*Verneinung*), in fact represent that higher category under which Nothing takes its place as a special kind of thing negated? Does Nothing "exist" only because the Not, i.e. negation exists? Or is it the other way about? Does negation and the Not exist only because Nothing exists? This has not been decided—indeed, it has not even been explicitly asked. We assert: "Nothing" is more original than the Not and negation.

If this thesis is correct then the very possibility of negation as an act of reason, and consequently reason itself, are somehow dependent on Nothing. How, then, can reason attempt to decide this issue? May not the apparent nonsensicality of the question and answer where Nothing is concerned only rest, perhaps, on the blind obstinacy of the roving intellect?

If, however, we refuse to be led astray by the formal impossibility of enquiry into Nothing and still continue to enquire in the face of it, we must at least satisfy what remains the fundamental pre-requisite for the full pursuit of any enquiry. If Nothing as such is still to be enquired into, it follows that it must be "given" in advance. We must be able to encounter it.

Where shall we seek Nothing? Where shall we find Nothing? In order to find something must we not know beforehand that it is there? Indeed we must! First and foremost we can only look if we have presupposed the presence of a thing to be looked for. But here the thing we are looking for is Nothing. Is there after all a seeking without pre-supposition, a seeking complemented by a pure finding?

However that may be, we do know "Nothing" if only as a term we bandy about every day. This ordinary hackneyed Nothing, so completely taken for granted and rolling off our tongue so casually—we can even give an off-hand "definition" of it:

Nothing is the complete negation of the totality of what-is.

Does not this characteristic of Nothing point, after all, in the direction from which alone it may meet us?

The totality of what-is must be given beforehand so as to succumb as such to the negation from which Nothing is then bound to emerge.

But, even apart from the questionableness of this relationship between negation and Nothing, how are we, as finite beings, to render the whole of what-is in its totality accessible *in itself*—let alone to ourselves? We can, at a pinch, think of the whole of what-is as an "idea" and then negate what we have thus imagined in our thoughts and "think" it negated. In this way we arrive at the formal concept of an imaginary Nothing, but never Nothing itself. But Nothing is nothing, and between the imaginary and the "authentic" (*eigentlich*) Nothing no difference can obtain, if Nothing represents complete lack of differentiation. But the "authentic" Nothing—is this not once again that latent and nonsensical idea of a Nothing that "is"? Once again and for the last time rational objections have tried to hold up our search, whose legitimacy can only be attested by a searching experience of Nothing.

As certainly as we shall never comprehend absolutely the totality of what-is, it is equally certain that we find ourselves placed in the midst of what-is and that this is somehow revealed in totality. Ultimately there is an essential difference between comprehending the totality of what-is and finding ourselves in the midst of what-is-in-totality. The former is absolutely impossible. The latter is going on in existence all the time.

Naturally enough it looks as if, in our everyday activities, we were always holding on to this or that actuality (*Seiendes*), as if we were lost in this or that region of what-is. However fragmentary the daily round may appear it still maintains what-is, in however shadowy a fashion, within the unity of a "whole." Even when, or rather, precisely when we are not absorbed in things or in our own selves, this "wholeness" comes over us —for example, in real boredom. Real boredom is still far off when this book or that play, this activity or that stretch of idleness merely bores us. Real boredom comes when "one is bored." This profound boredom, drifting hither and thither in the abysses of existence like a mute fog, draws all things, all men and oneself along with them, together in a queer kind of indifference. This boredom reveals what-is in totality.

There is another possibility of such revelation, and this is in the joy we feel in the presence of the being—not merely the person—of someone we love.

Because of these moods in which, as we say, we "are" this or that (i.e. bored, happy, etc.) we find ourselves (*befinden uns*) in the midst of what-is-in-totality, wholly pervaded by it. The affective state in which we find ourselves not only discloses, according to the mood we are in, what-is in totality, but this disclosure is at the same time far from being a mere chance occurrence and is the ground-phenomenon of our *Da-sein.*

Our "feelings," as we call them, are not just the fleeting concomitant of our mental or volitional behaviour, nor are they simply the cause and occasion of such behavior, nor yet a state that is merely "there" and in which we come to some kind of understanding with ourselves.

Yet, at the very moment when our moods thus bring us face to face with what-is-in-totality they hide the Nothing we are seeking. We are now less than ever of the opinion that mere negation of what-is-in-totality as revealed by these moods of ours can in fact lead us to Nothing. This could only happen in the first place in a mood so peculiarly revelatory in its import as to reveal Nothing itself.

Does there ever occur in human existence a mood of this kind, through which we are brought face to face with Nothing itself?

This may and actually does occur, albeit rather seldom and for moments only, in the key-mood of dread (*Angst*). By "dread" we do not mean "anxiety" (*Aengstlichkeit*), which is common enough and is akin to nervousness (*Furchtsamkeit*)—a mood that comes over us only too easily. Dread differs absolutely from fear (*Furcht*). We are always *afraid* of this or that definite thing, which threatens us in this or that definite way. "Fear of" is generally "fear about" something. Since fear has this characteristic limitation—"of" and "about"—the man who is afraid, the nervous man, is always bound by the thing he is afraid of or by the state in which he finds himself. In his efforts to save himself from this "something" he becomes uncertain in relation to other things; in fact, he "loses his bearings" generally.

In dread no such confusion can occur. It would be truer to say that dread is pervaded by a peculiar kind of peace. And although dread is always "dread of," it is not dread of this or that. "Dread of" is always a dreadful feeling "about"—but not about this or that. The indefiniteness of *what* we dread is not just lack of definition: it represents the essential impossibility of defining the "what." The indefiniteness is brought out in an illustration familiar to everybody.

In dread, as we say, "one feels something uncanny." What is this "something" (*es*) and this "one"? We are unable to say what gives "one" that uncanny feeling. "One" just feels it generally (*im Ganzen*). All things, and we with them, sink into a sort of indifference. But not in the sense that everything simply disappears; rather, in the very act of drawing away from us everything turns towards us. This withdrawal of what-is-in-total-ity, which then crowds round us in dread, this is what oppresses us. There is nothing to hold on to. The only thing that remains and overwhelms us whilst what-is slips away, is this "nothing."

Dread reveals Nothing.

In dread we are "in suspense" (*wir schweben*). Or, to put it more precisely, dread holds us in suspense because it makes what-is-in-totality slip away from us. Hence we too, as existents in the midst of what-is, slip away from ourselves along with it. For this reason it is not "you" or "I" that has the uncanny feeling, but "one." In the trepidation of this suspense where there is nothing to hold on to, pure *Da-sein* is all that remains.

Dread strikes us dumb. Because what-is-in-totality slips away and thus forces Nothing to the fore, all affirmation (lit. "Is"-saying: *"Ist"-Sagen*) fails in the face of it. The fact that when we are caught in the uncanniness of dread we often try to break the empty silence by words spoken at random, only proves the presence of Nothing. We ourselves confirm that dread reveals Nothing—when we have got over our dread. In the lucid vision which supervenes while yet the experience is fresh in our memory we must needs say that what we were afraid of was "actually" (*eigentlich:* also "authentic") Nothing. And indeed Nothing itself, Nothing as such, was there.

With this key-mood of dread, therefore, we have reached that event in our *Da-sein* which reveals Nothing, and which must therefore be the starting-point of our enquiry.

What about Nothing?

THE ANSWER TO THE QUESTION

The answer which alone is important for our purpose has already been found if we take care to ensure that we really do keep to the problem of Nothing. This necessitates changing man into his *Da-sein*—a change always occasioned in us by dread—so that we may apprehend Nothing as and how it reveals itself in dread. At the same time we have finally to dismiss those characteristics of Nothing which have not emerged as a result of our enquiry.

"Nothing" is revealed in dread, but not as something that "is." Neither can it be taken as an object. Dread is not an apprehension of Nothing. All the same, Nothing is revealed in and through dread, yet not, again, in the sense that Nothing appears as if detached and apart from what-is-in-totality when we have that "uncanny" feeling. We would say rather: in dread Nothing functions as if *at one with* what-is-in-totality. What do we mean by "at one with"?

In dread what-is-in-totality becomes untenable (*hinfällig*). How? What-is is not annihilated (*vernichtet*) by dread, so as to leave Nothing over. How could it, seeing that dread finds itself completely powerless in face of what-is-in-totality! What rather happens is that Nothing shows itself as essentially belonging to what-is while this is slipping away in totality.

In dread there is no annihilation of the whole of what-is in itself; but equally we cannot negate what-is-in-totality in order to reach Nothing. Apart from the fact that the explicitness of a negative statement is foreign to the nature of dread as such, we would always come too late with any such negation intended to demonstrate Nothing. For Nothing is anterior to it. As we said, Nothing is "at one with" what-is as this slips away in totality.

In dread there is a retreat from something, though it is not so much a flight as a spell-bound (*gebannt*) peace. This "retreat from" has its source in Nothing. The latter does not attract: its nature is to repel. This "repelling from itself" is essentially an "expelling into": a conscious gradual relegation to the vanishing what-is-in-totality (*das entgleitenlassende Verweisen auf das versinkende Seiende im Ganzen*). And this total relegation to the vanishing what-is-in-totality—such being the form in which Nothing crowds round us in dread—is the essence of Nothing: nihilation. Nihilation is neither an annihilation (*Vernichtung*) of what-is, nor does it spring from negation (*Verneinung*). Nihilation cannot be reckoned in terms of annihilation or negation at all. Nothing "nihilates" (*nichtet*) of itself.

Nihilation is not a fortuitous event; but, understood as the relegation to the vanishing what-is-in-totality, it reveals the latter in all its till now undisclosed strangeness as the pure "Other"—contrasted with Nothing.

Only in the clear night of dread's Nothingness is what-is as such revealed in all its original overtness (*Offenheit*): that it "is" and is not Nothing. This verbal appendix "and not Nothing" is, however, not an *a posteriori* explanation but an *a priori* which alone makes possible any revelation of what-is. The essence of Nothing as original nihilation lies in this: that it alone brings *Da-sein* face to face with what-is as such.

Only on the basis of the original manifestness of Nothing can our human *Da-sein* advance towards and enter into what-is. But insofar as *Da-sein* naturally relates to what-is, as that which it is not and which itself is, Da-sein *qua Da-sein* always proceeds from Nothing as manifest.

Da-sein means *being projected into* Nothing (*Hineingehaltenheit in das Nichts*).

Projecting into Nothing, *Da-sein* is already beyond what-is-in-totality. This "being beyond" (*Hinaussein*) what-is we call Transcendence. Were *Da-sein* not, in its essential basis, transcendent, that is to say, were it not projected from the start into Nothing, it could never relate to what-is, hence could have no self-relationship.

Without the original manifest character of Nothing there is no self-hood and no freedom.

Here we have the answer to our question about Nothing. Nothing is neither an object nor anything that "is" at all. Nothing occurs neither by itself nor "apart from" what-is, as a sort of adjunct. Nothing is that which makes the revelation of what-is as such possible for our human existence. Nothing not merely provides the conceptual opposite of what-is but is also an original part of essence (*Wesen*). It is in the Being (*Sein*) of what-is that the nihilation of Nothing (*das Nichten des Nichts*) occurs.

But now we must voice a suspicion which has been withheld far too long already. If it is only through "projecting into Nothing" that our *Da-sein* relates to what-is, in other words, has any existence, and if Nothing is only made manifest originally in dread, should we not have to be in a continual suspense of dread in order to exist at all? Have we not, however, ourselves admitted that this original dread is a rare thing? But above all, we all exist and are related to actualities which we ourselves are not and which we ourselves are—without this dread. Is not this dread, therefore, an arbitrary invention and the Nothing attributed to it an exaggeration?

Yet what do we mean when we say that this original dread only occurs in rare moments? Nothing but this: that as far as we are concerned and, indeed, generally speaking, Nothing is always distorted out of its original state. By what? By the fact that in one way or another we completely lose ourselves in what-is. The more we turn to what-is in our dealings the less we allow it to slip away, and the more we turn aside from Nothing. But all the more certainly do we thrust ourselves into the open superficies of existence.

And yet this perpetual if ambiguous aversion from Nothing accords, within certain limits, with the essential meaning of Nothing. It—Nothing in the sense of nihilation—relegates us to what-is. Nothing "nihilates" unceasingly, without our really knowing what is happening—at least, not with our everyday knowledge.

What could provide more telling evidence of the perpetual, far-reaching and yet ever-dissimulated overtness of Nothing in our existence, than negation? This is supposed to belong to the very nature of human thought. But negation cannot by any stretch of imagination produce the Not out of itself as a means of distinguishing and contrasting given things, thrusting this Not between them, as it were. How indeed could negation produce the Not out of itself, seeing that it can only negate when something is there to be negated? But how can a thing that is or ought to be negated be seen as something negative (*nichthaft*) unless all thinking as such is on the look-out for the Not? But the Not can only manifest itself when its source—the nihilation of Nothing and hence Nothing itself—is drawn out of concealment. The Not does not come into being through negation, but negation is based on the Not, which derives from the nihilation of Nothing. Nor is negation only a mode of nihilating behaviour, i.e. behaviour based *a priori* on the nihilation of Nothing.

Herewith we have proved the above thesis in all essentials: Nothing is the source of negation, not the other way about. If this breaks the sovereignty of reason in the field of enquiry into Nothing and Being, then the fate of the rule of "logic" in philosophy is also decided. The very idea of "logic" disintegrates in the vortex of a more original questioning.

However often and however variously negation—whether explicit or not—permeates all thinking, it cannot *of itself* be a completely valid witness to the manifestation of Nothing as an essential part of *Da-sein*. For negation cannot be cited either as the sole or even the chief mode of nihilation, with which, because of the nihilation of Nothing, *Da-sein* is saturated. More abysmal than the mere propriety of rational negation is the harshness of opposition and the violence of loathing. More responsible the pain of refusal and the mercilessness of an interdict. More oppressive the bitterness of renunciation.

These possible modes of nihilating behaviour, through which our *Da-sein* endures, even if it does not master, the fact of our being thrown upon the world are not modes of negation merely. That does not prevent them from expressing themselves in and through negation. Indeed, it is only then that the empty expanse of negation is really revealed. The permeation of *Da-sein* by nihilating modes of behaviour points to the perpetual, ever-dissimulated manifestness of Nothing, which only dread reveals in all its originality. Here, of course, we have the reason why original dread is generally repressed in *Da-sein*. Dread is there, but sleeping. All *Da-sein* quivers with its breathing: the pulsation is slightest in beings that are timorous, and is imperceptible in the "Yea, yea!" and "Nay, nay!" of busy people; it is readiest in the reserved, and surest of all in the courageous. But this last pulsation only occurs for the sake of that for which it expends itself, so as to safeguard the supreme greatness of *Da-sein*.

The dread felt by the courageous cannot be contrasted with the joy or even the comfortable enjoyment of a peaceable life. It stands—on the hither side of all such contrasts—in secret union with the serenity and gentleness of creative longing.

Original dread can be awakened in *Da-sein* at any time. It need not be awakened by any unusual occurrence. Its action corresponds in depth to the shallowness of its possible cause. It is always on the brink, yet only seldom does it take the leap and drag us with it into the state of suspense.

Because our *Da-sein* projects into Nothing on this basis of hidden dread, man becomes the "stand-in" (*Platzhalter*) for Nothing. So finite are we that we cannot, of our own resolution and will, bring ourselves originally face to face with Nothing. So bottomlessly does finalisation (*Verendlichung*) dig into existence that our freedom's peculiar and profoundest finality fails.

This projection into Nothing on the basis of hidden dread is the overcoming of what-is-in-totality: Transcendence.

Our enquiry into Nothing will, we said, lead us straight to metaphysics. The name "metaphysics" derives from the Greek $\tau \grave{\alpha} \ \mu \epsilon \tau \grave{\alpha} \ \tau \grave{\alpha} \ \phi \upsilon \sigma \iota \kappa \acute{\alpha}$ This quaint title was later interpreted as characterising the sort of enquiry which goes $\mu \epsilon \tau \acute{\alpha}$—trans, beyond—what-is as such.

Metaphysics is an enquiry over and above what-is, with a view to winning it back again as such and in totality for our understanding.

In our quest for Nothing there is similar "going beyond" what-is, conceived as what-is-in-totality. It therefore turns out to be a "metaphysical" question. We said in the beginning that such questioning had a double characteristic: every metaphysical question at once embraces the whole of metaphysics, and in every question the being (*Da-sein*) that questions is himself caught up in the question.

To what extent does the question about Nothing span and pervade the whole of metaphysics?

Since ancient times metaphysics has expressed itself on the subject of Nothing in the highly ambiguous proposition: *ex nihilo nihil fit*—nothing comes from nothing. Even though the proposition as argued never made Nothing itself the real problem, it nevertheless brought out very explicitly, from the prevailing notions about Nothing, the over-riding fundamental concept of what-is.

Classical metaphysics conceives Nothing as signifying Not-being (*Nichtseiendes*), that is to say, unformed matter which is powerless to form itself into "being" and cannot therefore present an appearance (εἶδος). What has "being" is the self-creating product (*Gebilde*) which presents itself as such in an image (*Bild*), i.e. something seen (*Anblick*). The origin, law and limits of this ontological concept are discussed as little as Nothing itself.

Christian dogma, on the other hand, denies the truth of the proposition *ex nihilo nihil fit* and gives a twist to the meaning of Nothing, so that it now comes to mean the absolute absence of all "being" outside God: *ex nihilo fit—ens creatum:* the created being is made out of nothing. "Nothing" is now the conceptual opposite of what truly and authentically (*eigentlich*) "is"; it becomes the *summum ens,* God as *ens increatum.* Here, too, the interpretation of Nothing points to the fundamental concept of what-is. Metaphysical discussion of what-is, however, moves on the same plane as the enquiry into Nothing. In both cases the questions concerning Being (*Sein*) and Nothing as such remain unasked. Hence we need not be worried by the difficulty that if God creates "out of nothing" he above all must be able to relate himself to Nothing. But if God is God he cannot know Nothing, assuming that the "Absolute" excludes from itself all nullity (*Nichtigkeit*).

This crude historical reminder shows Nothing as the conceptual opposite of what truly and authentically "is," i.e. as the negation of it. But once Nothing is somehow made a problem this contrast not only undergoes clearer definition but also arouses the true and authentic metaphysical question regarding the Being of what-is. Nothing ceases to be the vague opposite of what-is: it now reveals itself as integral to the Being of what-is.

"Pure Being and pure Nothing are thus one and the same." This proposition of Hegel's ("The Science of Logic," I, WW III, p. 74) is correct. Being and Nothing hang together, but not because the two things—from the point of view of the Hegelian concept of thought—are one in their indefiniteness and immediateness, but because Being itself is finite in essence and is only revealed in the Transcendence of *Da-sein* as projected into Nothing.

If indeed the question of Being as such is the all-embracing question of metaphysics, then the question of Nothing proves to be such as to span the whole metaphysical field. But at the same time the question of Nothing pervades the whole of metaphysics only because it forces us to face the problem of the origin of negation, that is to say, forces a decision about the legitimacy of the rule of "logic" in metaphysics.

The old proposition *ex nihilo nihil fit* will then acquire a different meaning, and no one appropriate to the problem of Being itself, so as to run: *ex nihilo omne ens qua ens fit:* every being, so far as it is a being, is made out of nothing. Only in the Nothingness of *Da-sein* can what-is-in-totality—and this in accordance with its peculiar possibilities, i.e. in a finite manner—come to itself. To what extent, then, has the enquiry into Nothing, if indeed it be a metaphysical one, included our own questing *Da-sein?*

Our *Da-sein* as experienced here and now is, we said, ruled by science. If our *Da-sein,* so ruled, is put into this question concerning Nothing, then it follows that it must itself have been put in question by this question.

The simplicity and intensity of scientific *Da-sein* consist in this: that it relates in a special manner to what-is and to this alone. Science would like to abandon Nothing with a superior gesture. But now, in this question of Nothing, it becomes evident that scientific *Da-sein* is only possible when projected into Nothing at the outset. Science can only come to terms with itself when it does not abandon Nothing. The alleged soberness and superiority of science becomes ridiculous if it fails to take Nothing seriously. Only because Nothing is obvious can science turn what-is into an object of investigation. Only when science proceeds from metaphysics can it conquer its essential task ever afresh, which consists not in the accumulation and classification of knowledge but in the perpetual discovery of the whole realm of truth, whether of Nature or of History.

Only because Nothing is revealed in the very basis of our *Da-sein* is it possible for the utter strangeness of what-is to dawn on us. Only when the strangeness of what-is forces itself upon us does it awaken and invite our wonder. Only because of wonder, that is to say, the revelation of Nothing, does the "Why?" spring to our lips. Only because this "Why?" is possible as such can we seek for reasons and proofs in a definite way. Only because we can ask and prove are we fated to become enquirers in this life.

The enquiry into Nothing puts us, the enquirers, ourselves in question. It is a metaphysical one.

Man's *Da-sein* can only relate to what-is by projecting into Nothing. Going beyond what-is is of the essence of *Da-sein.* But this "going beyond" is metaphysics itself. That is why metaphysics belongs to the nature of man. It is neither a department of scholastic philosophy nor a field of chance ideas. Metaphysics is the ground-phenomenon of *Da-sein.* It is *Da-sein* itself. Because the truth of metaphysics is so unfathomable there is always the lurking danger of profoundest error. Hence no scientific discipline can hope to equal the seriousness of metaphysics. Philosophy can never be measured with the yard-stick of the idea of science.

Once the question we have developed as to the nature of Nothing is really asked by and among our own selves, then we are not bringing in metaphysics from the outside. Nor are we simply "transporting" ourselves into it. It is completely out of our power to transport ourselves into metaphysics because, in so far as we exist, we are already there. Φύσει γάρ, ὦ φίλει, ἔνεστί τις φιλοσοφία τῇ τοῦ ἀνδρὸς διανοία (Plato: Phaedrus 279a). While man exists there will be philosophising of some sort. Philosophy, as we call it, is the setting in motion of metaphysics; and in metaphysics philosophy comes to itself and sets about its explicit tasks. Philosophy is only set in motion by leaping with all its being, as only it can, into the ground-possibilities of being as a whole. For this leap the following things are of crucial importance: firstly, leaving room for what-is-in-totality; secondly, letting oneself go into Nothing, that is to say, freeing oneself from the idols we all have and to which we are wont to go cringing; lastly, letting this "suspense" range where it will, so that it may continually swing back again to the ground-question of metaphysics, which is wrested from Nothing itself:

Why is there any Being at all—why not far rather Nothing?

Jean-Paul Sartre
from *Nausea*

The following selections from Sartre's seminal novel *Nausea* all have to do with the fundamental existential/phenomenological priority of existence over essence. The distinction that Roquentin makes between adventure and life in the first, suggests some implications of existential phenomenology for literary form. For a brief introduction to *Nausea* that provides the context for these selections, see page 50 of this book.

Adventure versus Life

Saturday noon:

. . . . .

I have reconsidered my thoughts of yesterday. I was completely dry: it made no difference to me whether there had been no adventures. I was only curious to know whether there could *never be any.*

Source: Jean-Paul Sartre, *Nausea*, translated by Lloyd Alexander. Copyright © 1964 by New Directions Publishing Corporation. All Rights Reserved. Reprinted by permission of New Directions Publishing Corporation.

This is what I thought: for the most banal even to become an adventure, you must (and this is enough) begin to recount it. This is what fools people: a man is always a teller of tales, he lives surrounded by his stories and the stories of others, he sees everything that happens to him through them; and he tries to live his own life as if he were telling a story.

But you have to choose: live or tell. For example, when I was in Hamburg, with that Erna girl I didn't trust and who was afraid of me, I led a funny sort of life. But I was in the middle of it, I didn't think about it. And then one evening, in a little café in San Pauli, she left me to go to the ladies' room. I stayed alone, there was a phonograph playing "Blue Skies." I began to tell myself what had happened since I landed. I told myself, "The third evening, as I was going into a dance hall called *La Grotte Bleue,* I noticed a large woman, half seas over. And that woman is the one I am waiting for now, listening to 'Blue Skies,' the woman who is going to come back and sit down at my right and put her arms around my neck." Then I felt violently that I was having an adventure. But Erna came back and sat down beside me, she wound her arms around my neck and I hated her without knowing why. I understand now: one had to begin living again and the adventure was fading out.

Nothing happens while you live. The scenery changes, people come in and go out, that's all. There are no beginnings. Days are tacked on to days without rhyme or reason, an interminable, monotonous addition. From time to time you make a semi-total: you say: I've been traveling for three years, I've been in Bouville for three years. Neither is there any end: you never leave a woman, a friend, a city in one go. And then everything looks alike: Shanghai, Moscow, Algiers, everything is the same after two weeks. There are moments—rarely—when you make a landmark, you realize that you're going with a woman, in some messy business. The time of a flash. After that, the procession starts again, you begin to add up hours and days: Monday, Tuesday, Wednesday. April, May, June. 1924, 1925, 1926.

That's living. But everything changes when you tell about life; it's a change no one notices: the proof is that people talk about true stories. As if there could possibly be true stories; things happen one way and we tell about them in the opposite sense. You seem to start at the beginning: "It was a fine autumn evening in 1922. I was a notary's clerk in Marommes." And in reality you have started at the end. It was there, invisible and present, it is the one which gives to words the pomp and value of a beginning. "I was out walking, I had left the town without realizing it, I was thinking about my money troubles." This sentence, taken simply for what it is, means that the man was absorbed, morose, a hundred leagues from an adventure, exactly in the mood to let things happen without noticing them. But the end is there, transforming everything. For us, the

man is already the hero of the story. His moroseness, his money troubles
are much more precious than ours, they are all gilded by the light of future
passions. And the story goes on in the reverse: instants have stopped piling
themselves in a lighthearted way one on top of the other, they are snapped
up by the end of the story which draws them and each one of them in turn,
draws out the preceding instant: "It was night, the street was deserted."
The phrase is cast out negligently, it seems superfluous; but we do not let
ourselves be caught and we put it aside: this is a piece of information
whose value we shall subsequently appreciate. And we feel that the hero
has lived all the details of this night like annunciations, promises, or even
that he lived only those that were promises, blind and deaf to all that did
not herald adventure. We forget that the future was not yet there; the man
was walking in a night without forethought, a night which offered him a
choice of dull rich prizes, and he did not make his choice.

I wanted the moments of my life to follow and order themselves like
those of a life remembered. You might as well try and catch time by the
tail.

The Un-Naming

Wednesday:

. . . . .

I lean my hand on the seat but pull it back hurriedly: it exists. This
thing I'm sitting on, leaning my hand on, is called a seat. They made it
purposely for people to sit on, they took leather, springs and cloth, they
went to work with the idea of making a seat and when they finished, *that*
was what they had made. They carried it here, into this car and the car
is now rolling and jolting with its rattling windows, carrying this red thing
in its bosom. I murmur: "It's a seat," a little like an exorcism. But the word
stays on my lips: it refuses to go and put itself on the thing. It stays what
it is, with its red plush, thousands of little red paws in the air, all still, little
dead paws. This enormous belly turned upward, bleeding, inflated—
bloated with all its dead paws, this belly floating in this car, in this grey
sky, is not a seat. It could just as well be a dead donkey tossed about in the
water, floating with the current, belly in the air in a great grey river, a
river of floods; and I could be sitting on the donkey's belly, my feet dan-
gling in the clear water. Things are divorced from their names. They are
there, grotesque, headstrong, gigantic and it seems ridiculous to call them
seats or say anything at all about them: I am in the midst of things,
nameless things. Alone, without words, defenceless, they surround me, are
beneath me, behind me, above me. They demand nothing, they don't

impose themselves: they are there. Under the cushion on the seat there is a thin line of shadow, a thin black line running along the seat, mysteriously and mischievously, almost a smile. I know very well that it isn't a smile and yet it exists, it runs under the whitish windows, under the jangle of glass, obstinately, obstinately behind the blue images which pass in a throng, like the inexact memory of a smile, like a half forgotten word of which you can only remember the first syllable and the best thing you can do is turn your eyes away and think about something else, about that man half-lying down on the seat opposite me, there. His blue-eyed, terra cotta face. The whole right side of his body has sunk, the right arm is stuck to the body, the right side barely lives, it lives with difficulty, with avarice, as if it were paralysed. But on the whole left side there is a little parasitic existence, which proliferates; a chance: the arm begins to tremble and then is raised up and the hand at the end is stiff. Then the hand begins to tremble too and when it reaches the height of the skull, a finger stretches out and begins scratching the scalp with a nail. A sort of voluptuous grimace comes to inhabit the right side of the mouth and the left side stays dead. The windows rattle, the arm shakes, the nail scratches, scratches, the mouth smiles under the staring eyes and the man tolerates, hardly noticing it, this tiny existence which swells his right side, which has borrowed his right arm and right cheek to bring itself into being. The conductor blocks my path.

"Wait until the car stops."

But I push him aside and jump out of the tramway. I couldn't stand any more. I could no longer stand things being so close. I push open a gate, go in, airy creatures are bounding and leaping and perching on the peaks. Now I recognize myself, I know where I am: I'm in the park. I drop onto a bench between great black tree-trunks, between the black, knotty hands reaching toward the sky. A tree scrapes at the earth under my feet with a black nail. I would so like to let myself go, forget myself, sleep. But I can't, I'm suffocating: existence penetrates me everywhere, through the eyes, the nose, the mouth. . . .

And suddenly, suddenly, the veil is torn away, I have understood, I have *seen.*

6.00 P.M.

I can't say I feel relieved or satisfied; just the opposite, I am crushed. Only my goal is reached: I know what I wanted to know; I have understood all that has happened to me since January. The Nausea has not left me and I don't believe it will leave me so soon; but I no longer have to bear it, it is no longer an illness or a passing fit: it is I.

So I was in the park just now. The roots of the chestnut tree were sunk in the ground just under my bench. I couldn't remember it was a root any more. The words had vanished and with them the significance of things, their methods of use, and the feeble points of reference which men have traced on their surface. I was sitting, stooping forward, head bowed, alone in front of this black, knotty mass, entirely beastly, which frightened me. Then I had this vision.

It left me breathless. Never, until these last few days, had I understood the meaning of "existence." I was like the others, like the ones walking along the seashore, all dressed in their spring finery. I said, like them, "The ocean *is* green; that white speck up there *is* a seagull," but I didn't feel that it existed or that the seagull was an "existing seagull"; usually existence hides itself. It is there, around us, in us, it is *us*, you can't say two words without mentioning it, but you can never touch it. When I believed I was thinking about it, I must believe that I was thinking nothing, my head was empty, or there was just one word in my head, the word "to be." Or else I was thinking . . . how can I explain it? I was thinking of *belonging*, I was telling myself that the sea belonged to the class of green objects, or that the green was a part of the quality of the sea. Even when I looked at things, I was miles from dreaming that they existed: they looked like scenery to me. I picked them up in my hands, they served me as tools, I foresaw their resistance. But that all happened on the surface. If anyone had asked me what existence was, I would have answered, in good faith, that it was nothing, simply an empty form which was added to external things without changing anything in their nature. And then all of a sudden, there it was, clear as day: existence had suddenly unveiled itself. It had lost the harmless look of an abstract category: it was the very paste of things, this root was kneaded into existence. Or rather the root, the park gates, the bench, the sparse grass, all that had vanished: the diversity of things, their individuality, were only an appearance, a veneer. This veneer had melted, leaving soft, monstrous masses, all in disorder—naked, in a frightful, obscene nakedness.

I kept myself from making the slightest movement, but I didn't need to move in order to see, behind the trees, the blue columns and the lamp posts of the bandstand and the Velleda, in the midst of a mountain laurel. All these objects . . . how can I explain? They inconvenienced me; I would have liked them to exist less strongly, more dryly, in a more abstract way, with more reserve. The chestnut tree pressed itself against my eyes. Green rust covered it half-way up; the bark, black and swollen, looked like boiled leather. The sound of the water in the Masqueret Fountain sounded in my ears, made a nest there, filled them with signs; my nostrils overflowed with a green, putrid odour. All things, gently, tenderly, were letting themselves drift into existence like those relaxed women who burst out laughing and say: "It's good to laugh," in a wet voice; they were parading, one in front of the other, exchanging abject secrets about their existence. I realized that there was no half-way house between non-existence and this flaunting abundance. If you existed, you had to *exist all the way*, as far as mouldiness, bloatedness, obscenity were concerned. In another world, circles, bars of music keep their pure and rigid lines. But existence is a deflection. Trees, night-blue pillars, the happy bubbling of a fountain, vital smells, little heat-mists floating in the cold air, a red-haired man digesting on a bench: all this somnolence, all these meals digested together, had its comic side. . . . Comic . . . no: it didn't go as far as that, nothing that exists can be comic; it was like a floating analogy, almost entirely elusive, with certain aspects of vaudeville. We were a heap of living creatures, irritated, embarrassed at ourselves, we hadn't the slightest reason to be there, none of us, each one, confused, vaguely alarmed, felt in the way in relation to the others. *In the way:* it was the only relationship I could establish between these trees, these gates, these stones. In vain I tried to *count* the chestnut trees, to *locate* them by their relationship to the Velleda, to compare their height with the height of the plane trees: each of them escaped the relationship in which I tried to enclose it, isolated itself, and overflowed. Of these relations (which I insisted on maintaining in order to delay the crumbling of the human world, measures, quantities, and directions)—I felt myself to be the arbitrator; they no longer had their teeth into things. *In the way,* the chestnut tree there, opposite me, a little to the left. *In the way,* the Velleda. . . .

And I—soft, weak, obscene, digesting, juggling with dismal thoughts —I, too, was *In the way.* Fortunately, I didn't feel it, although I realized it, but I was uncomfortable because I was afraid of feeling it (even now I am afraid—afraid that it might catch me behind my head and lift me up like a wave). I dreamed vaguely of killing myself to wipe out at least one of these superfluous lives. But even my death would have been *In the way. In the way,* my corpse, my blood on these stones, between these plants, at the back of this smiling garden. And the decomposed flesh would have been *In the way* in the earth which would receive my bones, at last, cleaned, stripped, peeled, proper and clean as teeth, it would have been *In the way:* I was *In the way* for eternity.

The word absurdity is coming to life under my pen; a little while ago, in the garden, I couldn't find it, but neither was I looking for it, I didn't need it: I thought without words, *on* things, *with* things. Absurdity was not an idea in my head, or the sound of a voice, only this long serpent dead at my feet, this wooden serpent. Serpent or claw or root or vulture's talon, what difference does it make. And without formulating anything clearly, I understood that I had found the key to Existence, the key to my Nauseas, to my own life. In fact, all that I could grasp beyond that returns to this fundamental absurdity. Absurdity: another word; I struggle against words; down there I touched the thing. But I wanted to fix the absolute character of this absurdity here. A movement, an event in the tiny coloured world of men is only relatively absurd: by relation to the accompanying circumstances. A madman's ravings, for example, are absurd in relation to the situation in which he finds himself, but not in relation to his delirium. But a little while ago I made an experiment with the absolute or the absurd. This root—there was nothing in relation to which it was absurd. Oh, how can I put it in words? Absurd: in relation to the stones, the tufts of yellow grass, the dry mud, the tree, the sky, the green benches. Absurd, irreducible; nothing—not even a profound, secret upheaval of nature—could explain it. Evidently I did not know everything, I had not seen the seeds sprout, or the tree grow. But faced with this great wrinkled paw, neither ignorance nor knowledge was important: the world of explanations and reasons is not the world of existence. A circle is not absurd, it is clearly explained by the rotation of a straight segment around one of its extremities. But neither does a circle exist. This root, on the other hand, existed in such a way that I could not explain it. Knotty, inert, nameless, it fascinated me, filled my eyes, brought me back unceasingly to its own existence. In vain to repeat: "This is a root"—it didn't work any more. I saw clearly that you could not pass from its function as a root, as a breathing pump, *to that*, to this hard and compact skin of a sea lion, to this oily, callous, headstrong look. The function explained nothing: it allowed you to understand generally that it was a root, but not *that one* at all. This root, with its colour, shape, its congealed movement, was . . . below all explanation. Each of its qualities escaped it a little, flowed out of it, half solidified, almost became a thing; each one was *In the way* in the root and the whole stump now gave me the impression of unwinding itself a little, denying its existence to lose itself in a frenzied excess. I scraped my heel against this black claw: I wanted to peel off some of the bark. For no reason at all, out of defiance, to make the bare pink appear absurd on the tanned leather: to *play* with the absurdity of the world. But, when I drew my heel back, I saw that the bark was still black.

Black? I felt the word deflating, emptied of meaning with extraordinary rapidity. Black? The root *was not* black, there was no black on this piece of wood—there was . . . something else: black, like the circle, did not exist. I looked at the root: was it *more than* black or *almost* black? But I soon stopped questioning myself because I had the feeling of knowing where I was. Yes, I had already scrutinized innumerable objects, with deep uneasiness. I had already tried—vainly—to think something *about* them: and I had already felt their cold, inert qualities elude me, slip through my fingers. Adolphe's suspenders, the other evening in the "Railwaymen's Rendezvous." They *were not* purple. I saw the two inexplicable stains on the shirt. And the stone—the well-known stone, the origin of this whole business: it was not . . . I can't remember exactly just what it was that the stone refused to be. But I had not forgotten its passive resistance.

And the hand of the Self-Taught Man; I held it and shook it one day in the library and then I had the feeling that it wasn't quite a hand. I had thought of a great white worm, but that wasn't it either. And the suspicious transparency of the glass of beer in the Café Mably. Suspicious: that's what they were, the sounds, the smells, the tastes. When they ran quickly under your nose like startled hares and you didn't pay too much attention, you might believe them to be simple and reassuring, you might believe that there was real blue in the world, real red, a real perfume of almonds or violets. But as soon as you held on to them for an instant, this feeling of comfort and security gave way to a deep uneasiness: colours, tastes, and smells were never real, never themselves and nothing but themselves. The simplest, most idefinable quality had too much content, in relation to itself, in its heart. That black against my foot, it didn't look like black, but rather the confused effort to imagine black by someone who had never seen black and who wouldn't know how to stop, who would have imagined an ambiguous being beyond colours. It *looked* like a colour, but also . . . like a bruise or a secretion, like an oozing—and something else, an odour, for example, it melted into the odour of wet earth, warm, moist wood, into a black odour that spread like varnish over this sensitive wood, in a flavour of chewed, sweet fibre. I did not simply *see* this black: sight is an abstract invention, a simplified idea, one of man's ideas. That black, amorphous, weakly presence, far surpassed sight, smell and taste. But this richness was lost in confusion and finally was no more because it was too much.

This moment was extraordinary. I was there, motionless and icy, plunged in a horrible ecstasy. But something fresh had just appeared in the very heat of this ecstasy; I understood the Nausea, I possessed it. To tell the truth, I did not formulate my discoveries to myself. But I think it would be easy for me to put them in words now. The essential thing is contingency. I mean that one cannot define existence as necessity. To exist is simply *to be there;* those who exist let themselves be encountered, but you can never deduce anything from them. I believe there are people who have understood this. Only they tried to overcome this contingency by inventing a necessary, causal being. But no necessary being can explain existence: contingency is not a delusion, a probability which can be dissipated; it is the absolute, consequently, the perfect free gift. All is free, this park, this city and myself. When you realize that, it turns your heart upside down and everything begins to float, as the other evening at the "Railwaymen's Rendezvous": here is Nausea; here there is what those bastards—the ones on the Coteau Vert and others—try to hide from themselves with their idea of their rights. But what a poor lie: no one has any rights; they are entirely free, like other men, they cannot succeed in not feeling superfluous. And in themselves, secretly, they are *superfluous*, that is to say, amorphous, vague, and sad.

How long will this fascination last? I *was* the root of the chestnut tree. Or rather I was entirely conscious of its existence. Still detached from it —since I was conscious of it—yet lost in it, nothing but it. An uneasy conscience which, notwithstanding, let itself fall with all its weight on this piece of dead wood. Time had stopped: a small black pool at my feet; it was impossible for something to come *after* that moment. I would have liked to tear myself from that atrocious joy, but I did not even imagine it would be possible; I was inside; the black stump did *not move,* it stayed there, in my eyes, as a lump of food sticks in the windpipe. I could neither accept nor refuse it. At what a cost did I raise my eyes? Did I raise them? Rather did I not obliterate myself for an instant in order to be reborn in the following instant with my head thrown back and my eyes raised upward? In fact, I was not even conscious of the transformation. But suddenly it became impossible for me to think of the existence of the root. It was wiped out, I could repeat in vain: it exists, it is still there, under the bench, against my right foot, it no longer meant anything. Existence is not something which lets itself be thought of from a distance: it must invade you suddenly, master you, weigh heavily on your heart like a great motion-less beast—or else there is nothing more at all.

There was nothing more, my eyes were empty and I was spellbound by my deliverance. Then suddenly it began to move before my eyes in light, uncertain motions: the wind was shaking the top of the tree.

It did not displease me to see a movement, it was a change from these motionless beings who watched me like staring eyes. I told myself, as I followed the swinging of the branches: movements never quite exist, they are passages, intermediaries between two existences, moments of weak-ness, I expected to see them come out of nothingness, progressively ripen, blossom: I was finally going to surprise beings in the process of being born.

No more than three seconds, and all my hopes were swept away. I could not attribute the passage of time to these branches groping around like blind men. This idea of passage was still an invention of man. The idea was too transparent. All these paltry agitations, drew in on themselves, isolated. They overflowed the leaves and branches everywhere. They whirled about these empty hands, enveloped them with tiny whirlwinds. Of course a movement was something different from a tree. But it was still an absolute. A thing. My eyes only encountered completion. The tips of the branches rustled with existence which unceasingly renewed itself and which was never born. The existing wind rested on the tree like a great bluebottle, and the tree shuddered. But the shudder was not a nascent quality, a passing from power to action; it was a thing; a shudder-thing flowed into the tree, took possession of it, shook it and suddenly abandoned it, going further on to spin about itself. All was fullness and all was active, there was no weakness in time, all, even the least perceptible stirring, was made of existence. And all these existents which bustled about this tree came from nowhere and were going nowhere. Suddenly they existed, then suddenly they existed no longer: existence is without memory; of the vanished it retains nothing—not even a memory. Existence everywhere, infinitely, in excess, for ever and everywhere; existence—which is limited only by existence. I sank down on the bench, stupefied, stunned by this profusion of beings without origin: everywhere blossomings, hatchings out, my ears buzzed with existence, my very flesh throbbed and opened, abandoned itself to the universal burgeoning. It was repugnant. But why, I thought, why so many existences, since they all look alike? What good are so many duplicates of trees? So many existences missed, obstinately begun again and again missed—like the awkward efforts of an insect fallen on its back? (I was one of those efforts.) That abundance did not give the effect of generosity, just the opposite. It was dismal, ailing, embarrassed at itself. Those trees, those great clumsy bodies. ... I began to laugh because I suddenly thought of the formidable springs described in books, full of cracklings, burstings, gigantic explosions. There were those idiots who came to tell you about will-power and struggle for life. Hadn't they ever seen a beast or a tree? This plane-tree with its scaling bark, this half-rotten oak, they wanted me to take them for rugged youthful endeavour surging towards the sky. And that root? I would have undoubtedly had to represent it as a voracious claw tearing at the earth, devouring its food?

Impossible to see things that way. Weaknesses, frailties, yes. The trees floated. Gushing towards the sky? Or rather a collapse; at any instant I expected to see the tree-trunks shrivel like weary wands, crumple up, fall on the ground in a soft, folded, black heap. *They did not want* to exist, only they could not help themselves. So they quietly minded their own business; the sap rose up slowly through the structure, half reluctant, and the roots sank slowly into the earth. But at each instant they seemed on the verge of leaving everything there and obliterating themselves. Tired and old, they kept on existing, against the grain, simply because they were too weak to die, because death could only come to them from the outside: strains of music alone can proudly carry their own death within themselves like an internal necessity: only they don't exist. Every existing thing is born without reason, prolongs itself out of weakness and dies by chance. I leaned back and closed my eyes. But the images, forewarned, immediately leaped up and filled my closed eyes with existences: existence is a fullness which man can never abandon.

Strange images. They represented a multitude of things. Not real things, other things which looked like them. Wooden objects which looked like chairs, shoes, other objects which looked like plants. And then two faces: the couple who were eating opposite to me last Sunday in the

Brasserie Vézelise. Fat, hot, sensual, absurd, with red ears. I could see the woman's neck and shoulders. Nude existence. Those two—it suddenly gave me a turn—those two were still existing somewhere in Bouville; somewhere—in the midst of smells?—this soft throat rubbing up luxuriously against smooth stuffs, nestling in lace; and the woman picturing her bosom under her blouse, thinking: "My titties, my lovely fruits," smiling mysteriously, attentive to the swelling of her breasts which tickled . . . then I shouted and found myself with my eyes wide open.

Had I dreamed of this enormous presence? It was there, in the garden, toppled down into the trees, all soft, sticky, soiling everything, all thick, a jelly. And I was inside, I with the garden. I was frightened, furious, I thought it was so stupid, so out of place, I hated this ignoble mess. Mounting up, mounting up as high as the sky, spilling over, filling everything with its gelatinous slither, and I could see depths upon depths of it reaching far beyond the limits of the garden, the houses, and Bouville, as far as the eye could reach. I was no longer in Bouville, I was nowhere, I was floating. I was not surprised, I knew it was the World, the naked World suddenly revealing itself, and I choked with rage at this gross, absurd being. You couldn't even wonder where all that sprang from, or how it was that a world came into existence, rather than nothingness. It didn't make sense, the World was everywhere, in front, behind. There had been nothing *before* it. Nothing. There had never been a moment in which it could not have existed. That was what worried me: of course there was no *reason* for this flowing larva to exist. *But it was impossible* for it is not to exist. It was unthinkable: to imagine nothingness you had to be there already, in the midst of the World, eyes wide open and alive; nothingness was only an idea in my head, an existing idea floating in this immensity: this nothingness had not come *before* existence, it was an existence like any other and appeared after many others. I shouted "filth! what rotten filth!" and shook myself to get rid of this sticky filth, but it held fast and there was so much, tons and tons of existence, endless: I stifled at the depths of this immense weariness. And then suddenly the park emptied as through a great hole, the World disappeared as it had come, or else I woke up—in any case, I saw no more of it; nothing was left but the yellow earth around me, out of which dead branches rose upward.

I got up and went out. Once at the gate, I turned back. Then the garden smiled at me. I leaned against the gate and watched for a long time. The smile of the trees, of the laurel, *meant* something; that was the real secret of existence. I remembered one Sunday, not more than three weeks ago, I had already detected everywhere a sort of conspiratorial air. Was it in my intention? I felt with boredom that I had no way of understanding. No way. Yet it was there, waiting, looking at one. It was there on the trunk of the chestnut tree . . . it was *the* chestnut tree. Things—you might have called them thoughts—which stopped halfway, which were forgotten, which forgot what they wanted to think and which stayed like that, hanging about with an odd little sense which was beyond them. That little sense annoyed me: I *could not* understand it, even if I could have stayed leaning against the gate for a century; I had learned all I could know about existence. I left, I went back to the hotel and I wrote.

Bouville: Nature and the City

Sunday

. . . . .

I am afraid of cities. But you mustn't leave them. If you go too far you come up against the vegetation belt. Vegetation has crawled for miles towards the cities. It is waiting. Once the city is dead, the vegetation will cover it, will climb over the stones, grip them, search them, make them burst with its long black pincers; it will blind the holes and let its green paws hang over everything. You must stay in the cities as long as they are alive, you must never penetrate alone this great mass of hair waiting at the gates; you must let it undulate and crack all by itself. In the cities, if you know how to take care of yourself, and choose the times when all the beasts are sleeping in their holes and digesting, behind the heaps of organic debris, you rarely come across anything more than minerals, the least frightening of all existants.

I am going back to Bouville. The vegetation has only surrounded three sides of it. On the fourth side there is a great hole full of black water which moves all by itself. The wind whistles between the houses. The odours stay less time there than anywhere: chased out to sea by the wind, they race along the surface of the black water like playful mists. It rains. They let plants grow between the gratings. Castrated, domesticated, so fat that they are harmless. They have enormous, whitish leaves which hang like ears. When you touch them it feels like cartilage, everything is fat and white in Bouville because of all the water that falls from the sky. I am going back to Bouville. How horrible!

I wake up with a start. It is midnight. Anny left Paris six hours ago. The boat is already at sea. She is sleeping in a cabin and, up on deck, the handsome bronze man is smoking cigarettes.

Tuesday, in Bouville:
Is that what freedom is? Below me, the gardens go limply down towards the city, and a house rises up from each garden. I see the ocean, heavy, motionless, I see Bouville. It is a lovely day.

the condemnation of freedom

I am free: there is absolutely no more reason for living, all the ones I have tried have given way and I can't imagine any more of them. I am still fairly young, I still have enough strength to start again. But do I have to start again? How much, in the strongest of my terrors, my disgusts, I had counted on Anny to save me I realized only now. My past is dead. The Marquis de Rollebon is dead, Anny came back only to take all hope away. I am alone in this white, garden-rimmed street. Alone and free. But this freedom is rather like death.

Today my life is ending. By tomorrow I will have left this town which spreads out at my feet, where I have lived so long. It will be nothing more than a name, squat, bourgeois, quite French, a name in my memory, not as rich as the names of Florence or Bagdad. A time will come when I shall wonder: whatever could I have done all day long when I was in Bouville? Nothing will be left of this sunlight, this afternoon, not even a memory.

My whole life is behind me. I see it completely, I see its shape and the slow movements which have brought me this far. There is little to say about it: a lost game, that's all. Three years ago I came solemnly to Bouville. I had lost the first round. I wanted to play the second and I lost again: I lost the whole game. At the same time, I learned that you always lose. Only the rascals think they win. Now I am going to be like Anny, I am going to outlive myself. Eat, sleep, sleep, eat. Exist slowly, softly, like these trees, like a puddle of water, like the red bench in the streetcar.

The Nausea has given me a short breathing spell. But I know it will come back again: it is my normal state. Only today my body is too exhausted to stand it. Invalids also have happy moments of weakness which take away the consciousness of their illness for a few hours. I am bored, that's all. From time to time I yawn so widely that tears roll down my cheek. It is a profound boredom, profound, the profound heart of existence, the very matter I am made of. I do not neglect myself, quite the contrary: this morning I took a bath and shaved. Only when I think back over those careful little actions, I cannot understand how I was able to make them: they are so vain. Habit, no doubt, made them for me. They aren't dead, they keep on busying themselves, gently, insidiously weaving their webs, they wash me, dry me, dress me, like nurses. Did they also lead me to this hill? I can't remember how I came any more. Probably up the Escalier Dautry: did I really climb up its hundred and ten steps one by one? What is perhaps more difficult to imagine is that I am soon going to climb down again. Yet I know I am: in a moment I shall find myself at the bottom of the Coteau Vert, if I raise my head, see in the distance the lighting windows of these houses which are so close now. In the distance. Above my head; above my head; and this instant which I cannot leave, which locks me in and limits me on every side, this instant I am made of will be no more than a confused dream.

I watch the grey shimmerings of Bouville at my feet. In the sun they look like heaps of shells, scales, splinters of bone, and gravel. Lost in the midst of this debris, tiny glimmers of glass or mica intermittently throw off light flames. In an hour the ripples, trenches, and thin furrows which run between these shells will be streets, I shall walk in these streets, between these walls. These little black men I can just make out in the Rue Boulibet—in an hour I shall be one of them.

I feel so far away from them, on the top of this hill. It seems as though I belong to another species. They come out of their offices after their day of work, they look at the houses and the squares with satisfaction, they think it is *their* city, a good, solid, bourgeois city. They aren't afraid, they feel at home. All they have ever seen is trained water running from taps, light which fills bulbs when you turn on the switch, half-breed, bastard trees held up with crutches. They have proof, a hundred times a day, that everything happens mechanically, that the world obeys fixed, unchangeable laws. In a vacuum all bodies fall at the same rate of speed, the public park is closed at 4 P.M. in winter, at 6 P.M. in summer, lead melts at 335 degrees centigrade, the last streetcar leaves the Hotel de Ville at 11:05 P.M. They are peaceful, a little morose, they think about Tomorrow, that is to say, simply, a new today; cities have only one day at their disposal and every morning it comes back exactly the same. They scarcely doll it up a bit on Sundays. Idiots. It is repugnant to me to think that I am going to see their thick, self-satisfied faces. They make laws, they write popular novels, they get married, they are fools enough to have children. And all this time, great, vague nature has slipped into their city, it has infiltrated everywhere, in their house, in their office, in themselves. It doesn't move, it stays quietly and they are full of it inside, they breathe it, and they don't see it, they imagine it to be outside, twenty miles from the city. I *see* it, I *see* this nature . . . I know that its obedience is idleness, I know it has no laws: what they take for constancy is only habit and it can change tomorrow.

What if something were to happen? What if something suddenly started throbbing? Then they would notice it was there and they'd think their hearts were going to burst. Then what good would their dykes, bulwarks, power houses, furnaces and pile drivers be to them? It can happen any time, perhaps right now: the omens are present. For example, the father of a family might go out for a walk, and, across the street, he'll see something like a red rag, blown towards him by the wind. And when the rag has gotten close to him he'll see that it is a side of rotten meat, grimy with dust, dragging itself along by crawling, skipping, a piece of writhing flesh rolling in the gutter, spasmodically shooting out spurts of blood. Or a mother might look at her child's cheek and ask him: "What's that—a pimple?" and see the flesh puff out a little, split, open, and at the bottom of the split an eye, a laughing eye might appear. Or they might feel things gently brushing against their bodies, like the caresses of reeds to swimmers in a river. And they will realize that their clothing has become living things. And someone else might feel something scratching in his mouth. He goes to the mirror, opens his mouth: and his tongue is an enormous, live centipede, rubbing its legs together and scraping his palate. He'd like to spit it out, but the centipede is a part of him and he will have to tear it out with his own hands. And a crowd of things will appear for which people will have to find new names—stone-eye, great three-cornered arm, toe-crutch, spider-jaw. And someone might be sleeping in his comfortable bed, in his quiet, warm room, and wake up naked on a bluish earth, in a forest of rustling birch trees, rising red and white towards the sky like the smokestacks of Jouxtebouville, with big bumps half-way out of the ground, hairy and bulbous like onions. And birds will fly around these birch trees and pick at them with their beaks and make them bleed. Sperm will flow slowly, gently, from these wounds, sperm mixed with blood, warm and glassy with little bubbles. Or else nothing like that will happen, there will be no appreciable change, but one morning people will open their blinds and be surprised by a sort of frightful sixth sense, brooding heavily over things and seeming to pause. Nothing more than that: but for the little time it lasts, there will be hundreds of suicides. Yes! Let it change just a little, just to see, I don't ask for anything better. Then you will see other people, suddenly plunged into solitude. Men all alone, completely alone with horrible monstrosities, will run through the streets, pass heavily in front of me, their eyes staring, fleeing their ills yet carrying them with them, open-mouthed, with their insect-tongue flapping its wings. Then I'll burst out laughing even though my body may be covered with filthy, infected scabs which blossom into flowers of flesh, violets, buttercups. I'll lean against a wall and when they go by I'll shout: "What's the matter with your science? What have you done with your humanism? Where is your dignity?" I will not be afraid—or at least no more than now. Will it not still be existence, variations on existence? All these eyes which will slowly devour a face—they will undoubtedly be too much, but no more so than the first two, Existence is what I am afraid of.

Evening falls, the first lamps are lit in the city. My God! How *natural* the city looks despite all its geometries, how crushed it looks in the evening. It's so . . . so evident, from here; could I be the only one to see it? Is there nowhere another Cassandra on the summit of a hill watching a city engulfed in the depths of nature? But what difference does it make? What could I tell her?

My body slowly turns eastward, oscillates a little and begins to walk.

Jean-Paul Sartre
Existentialism

I should like on this occasion to defend existentialism against some charges which have been brought against it.

First, it has been charged with inviting people to remain in a kind of desperate quietism because, since no solutions are possible, we should have to consider action in this world as quite impossible. We should then end up in a philosophy of contemplation; and since contemplation is a luxury, we come in the end to a bourgeois philosophy. The communists in particular have made these charges.

On the other hand, we have been charged with dwelling on human degradation, with pointing up everywhere the sordid, shady, and slimy, and neglecting the gracious and beautiful, the bright side of human nature; for example, according to Mlle. Mercier, a Catholic critic, with forgetting the smile of the child. Both sides charge us with having ignored human solidarity, with considering man as an isolated being. The communists say that the main reason for this is that we take pure subjectivity, the *Cartesian I think,* as our starting point; in other words, the moment in which man becomes fully aware of what it means to him to be an isolated being; as a result, we are unable to return to a state of solidarity with the men who are not ourselves, a state which we can never reach in the *cogito.*

From the Christian standpoint, we are charged with denying the reality and seriousness of human undertakings, since, if we reject God's commandments and the eternal verities, there no longer remains anything but pure caprice, with everyone permitted to do as he pleases and incapable, from his own point of view, of condemning the points of view and acts of others. ↳ *sudden when or fancy*

I shall try today to answer these different charges. Many people are going to be surprised at what is said here about humanism. We shall try to see in what sense it is to be understood. In any case, what can be said from the very beginning is that by existentialism we mean a doctrine which makes human life possible and, in addition, declares that every truth and every action implies a human setting and a human subjectivity.

Source: Jean-Paul Sartre, *Existentialism,* translated by Bernard Frechtman (New York: Philosophical Library, 1947). Reprinted with the permission of Philosophical Library. This essay first appeared under the title "Existentialism Is a Humanism."

As is generally known, the basic charge against us is that we put the emphasis on the dark side of human life. Someone recently told me of a lady who, when she let slip a vulgar word in a moment of irritation, excused herself by saying, "I guess I'm becoming an existentialist." Consequently, existentialism is regarded as something ugly; that is why we are said to be naturalists; and if we are, it is rather surprising that in this day and age we cause so much more alarm and scandal than does naturalism, properly so called. The kind of person who can take in his stride such a novel as Zola's *The Earth* is disgusted as soon as he starts reading an existentialist novel; the kind of person who is resigned to the wisdom of the ages—which is pretty sad—finds us even sadder. Yet, what can be more disillusioning than saying "true charity begins at home" or "a scoundrel will always return evil for good"?

We know the commonplace remarks made when this subject comes up, remarks which always add up to the same thing: we shouldn't struggle against the powers-that-be; we shouldn't resist authority; we shouldn't try to rise above our station; any action which doesn't conform to authority is romantic; any effort not based on past experience is doomed to failure; experience shows that man's bent is always toward trouble, that there must be a strong hand to hold him in check, if not, there will be anarchy. There are still people who go on mumbling these melancholy old saws, the people who say, "It's only human!" whenever a more or less repugnant act is pointed out to them, the people who glut themselves on *chansons réalistes;* these are the people who accuse existentialism of being too gloomy, and to such an extent that I wonder whether they are complaining about it, not for its pessimism, but much rather its optimism. Can it be that what really scares them in the doctrine I shall try to present here is that it leaves to man a possibility of choice? To answer this question, we must re-examine it on a strictly philosophical plane. What is meant by the term *existentialism?*

Most people who use the word would be rather embarrassed if they had to explain it, since, now that the word is all the rage, even the work of a musician or painter is being called existentialist. A gossip collumnist in *Clartés* signs himself *The Existentialist,* so that by this time the word has been so stretched and has taken on so broad a meaning, that it no longer means anything at all. It seems that for want of an advance-guard doctrine analogous to surrealism, the kind of people who are eager for scandal and flurry turn to this philosophy which in other respects does not at all serve their purposes in this sphere.

Actually, it is the least scandalous, the most austere of doctrines. It is intended strictly for specialists and philosophers. Yet it can be defined easily. What complicates matters is that there are two kinds of existentialist, first, those who are Christian, among whom I would include Jaspers and Gabriel Marcel, both Catholic; and on the other hand the atheistic existentialists, among whom I class Heidegger, and then the French existentialists and myself. What they have in common is that they think that existence precedes essence, or, if you prefer, that subjectivity must be the starting point.

Just what does that mean? Let us consider some object that is manufactured, for example, a book or a paper-cutter: here is an object which has been made by an artisan whose inspiration came from a concept. He referred to the concept of what a paper-cutter is and likewise to a known method of production, which is part of the concept, something which is, by and large, a routine. Thus, the paper-cutter is at once an object produced in a certain way and, on the other hand, one having a specific use; and one can not postulate a man who produces a paper-cutter but does not know what it is used for. Therefore, let us say that, for the paper-cutter, essence—that is, the ensemble of both the production routines and the properties which enable it to be both produced and defined—precedes existence. Thus, the presence of the paper-cutter or book in front of me is determined. Therefore, we have here a technical view of the world whereby it can be said that production precedes existence.

When we conceive God as the Creator, He is generally thought of as a superior sort of artisan. Whatever doctrine we may be considering, whether one like that of Descartes or that of Leibnitz, we always grant that will more or less follows understanding or, at the very least, accompanies it, and that when God creates He knows exactly what He is creating. Thus, the concept of man in the mind of God is comparable to the concept of paper-cutter in the mind of the manufacturer, and, following certain techniques and a conception, God produces man, just as the artisan, following a definition and a technique, makes a paper-cutter. Thus, the individual man is the realisation of a certain concept in the divine intelligence.

In the eighteenth century, the atheism of the *philosophes* discarded the idea of God, but not so much for the notion that essence precedes existence. To a certain extent, this idea is found everywhere; we find it in Diderot, in Voltaire, and even in Kant. Man has a human nature; this human nature, which is the concept of the human, is found in all men, which means that each man is a particular example of a universal concept, man. In Kant, the result of this universality is that the wild-man, the natural man, as well as the bourgeois, are circumscribed by the same definition and have the same basic qualities. Thus, here too the essence of man precedes the historical existence that we find in nature.

Atheistic existentialism, which I represent, is more coherent. It states that if God does not exist, there is at least one being in whom existence precedes essence, a being who exists before he can be defined by any concept, and that this being is man, or, as Heidegger says, human reality. What is meant here by saying that existence precedes essence? It means that, first of all, man exists, turns up, appears on the scene, and, only afterwards, defines himself. If man, as the existentialist conceives him, is indefinable, it is because at first he is nothing. Only afterward will he be something, and he himself will have made what he will be. Thus, there is no human nature, since there is no God to conceive it. Not only is man what he conceives himself to be, but he is also only what he wills himself to be after his thrust toward existence.

Man is nothing else but what he makes of himself. Such is the first principle of existentialism. It is also what is called subjectivity, the name we are labeled with when charges are brought against us. But what do we mean by this, if not that man has a greater dignity than a stone or table? For we mean that man first exists, that is, that man first of all is the being who hurls himself toward a future and who is conscious of imagining himself as being in the future. Man is at the start a plan which is aware of itself, rather than a patch of moss, a piece of garbage, or a cauliflower; nothing exists prior to this plan; there is nothing in heaven; man will be what he will have planned to be. Not what he will want to be. Because by the word "will" we generally mean a conscious decision, which is subsequent to what we have already made of ourselves. I may want to belong to a political party, write a book, get married; but all that is only a manifestation of an earlier, more spontaneous choice that is called "will." But if existence really does precede essence, man is responsible for what he is. Thus, existentialism's first move is to make every man aware of what he is and to make the full responsibility of his exixtence rest on him. And when we say that a man is responsible for himself, we do not only mean that he is responsible for his own individuality, but that he is responsible for all men.

The word subjectivism has two meanings, and our oponents play on the two. Subjectivism means, on the one hand, that an individual chooses and makes himself; and, on the other, that it is impossible for man to transcend human subjectivity. The second of these is the essential meaning of existentialism. When we say that man chooses his own self, we mean that every one of us does likewise; but we also mean by that that in making this choice he also chooses all men. In fact, in creating the man that we want to be, there is not a single one of our acts which does not at the same time create an image of man as we think he ought to be. To choose to be this or that is to affirm at the same time the value of what we choose, because we can never choose evil. We always choose the good, and nothing can be good for us without being good for all.

If, on the other hand, existence precedes essence, and if we grant that we exist and fashion our image at one and the same time, the image is valid for everybody and for our whole age. Thus, our responsibility is much greater than we might have supposed, because it involves all mankind. If I am a workingman and choose to join a Christian trade-union rather than be a communist, and if by being a member I want to show that the best thing for man is resignation, that the kingdom of man is not of this world, I am not only involving my own case—I want to be resigned for everyone. As a result, my action has involved all humanity. To take a more individual matter, if I want to marry, to have children; even if this marriage depends solely on my own circumstances or passion or wish, I am involving all humanity in monogamy and not merely myself. Therefore, I am responsible for myself and for everyone else. I am creating a certain image of man of my own choosing. In choosing myself, I choose man.

This helps us understand what the actual content is of such rather grandiloquent words as anguish, forlorness, despair. As you will see, it's all quite simple.

First, what is meant by anguish? The existentialists say at once that man is anguish. What that means is this: the man who involves himself and who realizes that he is not only the person he chooses to be, but also a law-maker who is, at the same time, choosing all mankind as well as himself, can not help escape the feeling of his total and deep responsibility. Of course, there are many people who are not anxious; but we claim that they are hiding their anxiety, that they are fleeing from it. Certainly, many people believe that when they do something, they themselves are the only ones involved, and when someone says to them, "What if everyone acted that way?" they shrug their shoulders and answer, "Everyone doesn't act that way." But really, one should always ask himself, "What would happen if everybody looked at things that way?" There is no escaping this disturbing thought except by a kind of double-dealing. A man who lies and makes excuses for himself by saying "not everybody does that," is someone with an uneasy conscience, because the act of lying implies that a universal value is conferred upon the lie.

Anguish is evident even when it conceals itself. This is the anguish that Kierkegaard called the anguish of Abraham. You know the story: an angel has ordered Abraham to sacrifice his son; if it really were an angel who has come and said, "You are Abraham, you shall sacrifice your son," everything would be all right. But everyone might first wonder, "Is it really an angel, and am I really Abraham? What proof do I have?"

There was a madwoman who had hallucinations; someone used to speak to her on the telephone and give her orders. Her doctor asked her, "Who is it who talks to you?" She answered, "He says it's God." What proof did she really have that it was God? If an angel comes to me, what proof is there that it's an angel? And if I hear voices, what proof is there that they come from heaven and not from hell, or from the subconscious, or a pathological condition? What proves that they are addressed to me? What proof is there that I have been appointed to impose my choice and my conception of man on humanity? I'll never find any proof or sign to convince me of that. If a voice addresses me, it is always for me to decide that this is the angel's voice; if I consider that such an act is a good one, it is I who will choose to say that it is good rather than bad.

Now, I'm not being singled out as an Abraham, and yet at every moment I'm obliged to perform exemplary acts. For every man, everything happens as if all mankind had its eyes fixed on him and were guiding itself by what he does. And every man ought to say to himself, "Am I really the kind of man who has the right to act in such a way that humanity might guide itself by my actions? And if he does not say that to himself, he is masking his anguish.

There is no question here of the kind of anguish which would lead to quietism, to inaction. It is a matter of a simple sort of anguish that anybody who has had responsibilities is familiar with. For example, when a military officer takes the responsibility for an attack and sends a certain number of men to death, he chooses to do so, and in the main he alone makes the choice. Doubtless, orders come from above, but they are too broad; he interprets them, and on this interpretation depend the lives of ten or fourteen or twenty men. In making a decision he can not help having a certain anguish. All leaders know this anguish. That doesn't keep them from acting; on the contrary, it is the very condition of their action. For it implies that they envisage a number of possibilities, and when they choose one, they realize that it has value only because it is chosen. We shall see that this kind of anguish, which is the kind that existentialism describes, is explained, in addition, by a direct responsibility to the other men whom it involves. It is not a curtain separating us from action, but is part of action itself.

When we speak of forlornness, a term Heidegger was fond of, we mean only that God does not exist and that we have to face all the consequences of this. The existentialist is strongly opposed to a certain kind of secular ethics which would like to abolish God with the least possible expense. About 1880, some French teachers tried to set up a secular ethics which went something like this: God is a useless and costly hypothesis; we are discarding it; but, meanwhile, in order for there to be an ethics, a society, a civilization, it is essential that certain values be taken seriously and that they be considered as having an *a priori* existence. It must be obligatory, *a priori,* to be honest, not to lie, not to beat your wife, to have children, etc., etc. So we're going to try a little device which will make it possible to show that values exist all the same, inscribed in a heaven of ideas, though otherwise God does not exist. In other words—and this, I believe, is the tendency of everything called reformism in France—nothing will be changed if God does not exist. We shall find ourselves with the same norms of honesty, progress, and humanism, and we shall have made of God an outdated hypothesis which will peacefully die off by itself.

The existentialist, on the contrary, thinks it very distressing that God does not exist, because all possibility of finding values in a heaven of ideas disappears along with Him; there can no longer be an *a priori* Good, since there is no infinite and perfect consciousness to think it. Nowhere is it written that the Good exists, that we must be honest, that we must not lie; because the fact is we are on a plane where there are only men. Dostoevsky said, "If God didn't exist, everything would be possible." That is the very starting point of existentialism. Indeed, everything is permissible if God does not exist, and as a result man is forlorn, because neither within him nor without does he find anything to cling to. He can't start making excuses for himself.

If existence really does precede essence, there is no explaining things away by reference to a fixed and given human nature. In other words, there is no determinism, man is free, man is freedom. On the other hand, if God does not exist, we find no values or commands to turn to which legitimize our conduct. So, in the bright realm of values, we have no excuses behind us, nor justification before us. We are alone, with no excuses.

That is the idea I shall try to convey when I say that man is condemned to be free. Condemned, because he did not create himself, yet, in other respects is free; because, once thrown into the world, he is responsible for everything he does. The existentialist does not believe in the power of passion. He will never agree that a sweeping passion is a ravaging torrent which fatally leads a man to certain acts and is therefore an excuse. He thinks that man is responsible for his passion.

The existentialist does not think that man is going to help himself by finding in the world some omen by which to orient himself. Because he thinks that man will interpret the omen to suit himself. Therefore, he thinks that man, with no support and no aid, is condemned every moment to invent man. Ponge, in a very fine article, has said, "Man is the future of man." That's exactly it. But if it is taken to mean that this future is recorded in heaven, that God sees it, then it is false, because it would really no longer be a future. If it is taken to mean that, whatever a man may be, there is a future to be forged, a virgin future before him, then this remark is sound. But then we are forlorn.

To give you an example which will enable you to understand forlornness better, I shall cite the case of one of my students who came to see me under the following circumstances: his father was on bad terms with his mother, and, moreover, was inclined to be a collaborationist; his older brother had been killed in the German offensive of 1940, and the young man, with somewhat immature but generous feelings, wanted to avenge him. His mother lived alone with him, very much upset by the half-treason of her husband and the death of her older son; the boy was her only consolation.

The boy was faced with the choice of leaving for England and joining the Free French Forces—that is, leaving his mother behind—or remaining with his mother and helping her to carry on. He was fully aware that the woman lived only for him and that his going-off—and perhaps his death—would plunge her into despair. He was also aware that every act that he did for his mother's sake was a sure thing, in the sense that it was helping her to carry on, whereas every effort he made toward going off and fighting was an uncertain move which might run aground and prove completely useless; for example, on his way to England he might, while passing through Spain, be detained indefinitely in a Spanish camp; he might reach England or Algiers and be stuck in an office at a desk job. As a result, he was faced with two very different kinds of action: one, concrete, immediate, but concerning only one individual; the other concerned an incomparably vaster group, a national collectivity, but for that very reason was dubious, and might be interrupted en route. And, at the same time, he was wavering between two kinds of ethics. On the one hand, an ethics of sympathy, of personal devotion; on the other, a broader ethics, but one whose efficacy was more dubious. He had to choose between the two.

Who would help him choose? Christian doctrine? No. Christian doctrine says, "Be charitable, love your neighbor, take the more rugged path, etc., etc." But which is the more rugged path? Whom should he love as a brother? The fighting man or his mother? Which does the greater good, the vague act of fighting in a group, or the concrete one of helping a particular human being to go on living? Who can decide *a priori?* Nobody. No book of ethics can tell him. The Kantian ethics says, "Never treat any person as a means, but as an end." Very well, if I stay with my mother, I'll treat her as an end and not as a means; but by virtue of this very fact, I'm running the risk of treating the people around me who are fighting, as means; and, conversely, if I go to join those who are fighting, I'll be treating them as an end, and, by doing that, I run the risk of treating my mother as a means.

If values are vague, and if they are always too broad for the concrete and specific case that we are considering, the only thing left for us is to trust our instincts. That's what this young man tried to do; and when I saw him, he said, "In the end, feeling is what counts. I ought to choose whichever pushes me in one direction. If I feel that I love my mother enough to sacrifice everything else for her—my desire for vengeance, for action, for adventure—then I'll stay with her. If, on the contrary, I feel that my love for my mother isn't enough, I'll leave."

But how is the value of a feeling determined? What gives his feeling for his mother value? Precisely the fact that he remained with her. I may say that I like so-and-so well enough to sacrifice a certain amount of money for him, but I may say so only if I've done it. I may say "I love my mother well enough to remain with her" if I have remained with her. The only way to determine the value of this affection is, precisely, to perform an act which confirms and defines it. But, since I require this affection to justify my act, I find myself caught in a vicious circle.

On the other hand, Gide has well said that a mock feeling and a true feeling are almost indistinguishable; to decide that I love my mother and will remain with her, or to remain with her by putting on an act, amount somewhat to the same thing. In other words, the feeling is formed by the acts one performs; so, I can not refer to it in order to act upon it. Which means that I can neither seek within myself the true condition which will impel me to act, nor apply to a system of ethics for concepts which will permit me to act. You will say, "At least, he did go to a teacher for advice." But if you seek advice from a priest, for example, you have chosen this priest; you already knew, more or less, just about what advice he was going to give you. In other words, choosing your adviser is involving yourself. The proof of this is that if you are a Christian, you will say, "Consult a priest." But some priests are collaborating, some are just marking time, some are resisting. Which to choose? If the young man chooses a priest who is resisting or collaborating, he has already decided on the kind of advice he's going to get. Therefore, in coming to see me he knew the answer I was going to give him, and I had only one answer to give: "You're free, choose, that is, invent." No general ethics can show you what is to be done; there are no omens in the world. The Catholics will reply, "But there are." Granted—but, in any case, I myself choose the meaning they have.

When I was a prisoner, I knew a rather remarkable young man who was a Jesuit. He had entered the Jesuit order in the following way: he had had a number of very bad breaks; in childhood, his father died, leaving him in poverty, and he was a scholarship student at a religious institution where he was constantly made to feel that he was being kept out of charity; then, he failed to get any of the honors and distinctions that children like; later on, at about eighteen, he bungled a love affair; finally, at twenty-two, he failed in military training, a childish enough matter, but it was the last straw.

This young fellow might well have felt that he had botched everything. It was a sign of something, but of what? He might have taken refuge in bitterness or despair. But he very wisely looked upon all this as a sign that he was not made for secular triumphs, and that only the triumphs of religion, holiness, and faith were open to him. He saw the hand of God in all this, and so he entered the order. Who can help seeing that he alone decided what the sign meant?

Some other interpretation might have been drawn from this series of setbacks; for example, that he might have done better to turn carpenter or revolutionist. Therefore, he is fully responsible for the interpretation. Forlornness implies that we ourselves choose our being. Forlornness and anguish go together.

As for despair, the term has a very simple meaning. It means that we shall confine ourselves to reckoning only with what depends upon our will, or on the ensemble of probabilities which make our action possible. When we want something, we always have to reckon with probabilities. I may be counting on the arrival of a friend. The friend is coming by rail or street-car; this supposes that the train will arrive on schedule, or that the street-car will not jump the track. I am left in the realm of possibility; but possibilities are to be reckoned with only to the point where my action comports with the ensemble of these possibilities, and no further. The moment the possibilities I am considering are not rigorously involved by my action, I ought to disengage myself from them, because no God, no scheme, can adapt the world and its possibilities to my will. When Descartes said, "Conquer yourself rather than the world," he meant essentially the same thing.

The Marxists to whom I have spoken reply, "You can rely on the support of others in your action, which obviously has certain limits because you're not going to live forever. That means: rely on both what others are doing elsewhere to help you, in China, in Russia, and what they will do later on, after your death, to carry on the action and lead it to its fulfillment, which will be the revolution. You even *have* to rely upon that, otherwise you're immoral." I reply at once that I will always rely on fellow-fighters insofar as these comrades are involved with me in a common struggle, in the unity of a party or a group in which I can more or less make my weight felt; that is, one whose ranks I am in as a fighter and whose movements I am aware of at every moment. In such a situation, relying on the unity and will of the party is exactly like counting on the fact that the train will arrive on time or that the car won't jump the track. But, given that man is free and that there is no human nature for me to depend on, I can not count on men whom I do not know by relying on human goodness or man's concern for the good of society. I don't know what will become of the Russian revolution; I may make an example of it to the extent that at the present time it is apparent that the proletariat plays a part in Russia that it plays in no other nation. But I can't swear that this will inevitably lead to a triumph of the proletariat. I've got to limit myself to what I see.

Given that men are free and that tomorrow they will freely decide what man will be, I can not be sure that, after my death, fellow-fighters will carry on my work to bring it to its maximum perfection. Tomorrow, after my death, some men may decide to set up Fascism, and the others may be cowardly and muddled enough to let them do it. Fascism will then be the human reality, so much the worse for us.

Actually, things will be as man will have decided they are to be. Does that mean that I should abandon myself to quietism? No. First, I should involve myself; then, act on the old saw, "Nothing ventured, nothing gained." Nor does it mean that I shouldn't belong to a party, but rather that I shall have no illusions and shall do what I can. For example, suppose I ask myself, "Will socialization, as such, ever come about?" I know nothing about it. All I know is that I'm going to do everything in my power to bring it about. Beyond that, I can't count on anything. Quietism is the attitude of people who say, "Let others do what I can't do." The doctrine I am presenting is the very opposite of quietism, since it declares, "There is no reality except in action." Moreover, it goes further, since it adds, "Man is nothing else than his plan; he exists only to the extent that he fulfills himself; he is therefore nothing else than the ensemble of his acts, nothing else than his life."

According to this, we can understand why our doctrine horrifies certain people. Because often the only way they can bear their wretchedness is to think, "Circumstances have been against me. What I've been and done doesn't show my true worth. To be sure, I've had no great love, no great friendship, but that's because I haven't met a man or woman who was worthy. The books I've written haven't been very good because I haven't had the proper leisure. I haven't had children to devote myself to because I didn't find a man with whom I could have spent my life. So there remains within me, unused and quite viable, a host of propensities, inclinations, possibilities, that one wouldn't guess from the mere series of things I've done."

Now, for the existentialist there is really no love other than one which manifests itself in a person's being in love. There is no genius other than one which is expressed in works of art; the genius of Proust is the sum of Proust's works; the genius of Racine is his series of tragedies. Outside of that, there is nothing. Why say that Racine could have written another tragedy, when he didn't write it? A man is involved in life, leaves his impress on it, and outside of that there is nothing. To be sure, this may seem a harsh thought to someone whose life hasn't been a success. But, on the other hand, it prompts people to understand that reality alone is what counts, that dreams, expectations, and hopes warrant no more than to define a man as a disappointed dream, as miscarried hopes, as vain expectations. In other words, to define him negatively and not positively. However, when we say, "You are nothing else than your life," that does not imply that the artist will be judged solely on the basis of his works of art; a thousand other things will contribute toward summing him up. What we mean is that a man is nothing else than a series of undertakings, that he is the sum, the organization, the ensemble of the relationships which make up these undertakings.

When all is said and done, what we are accused of, at bottom, is not our pessimism, but an optimistic toughness. If people throw up to us our works of fiction in which we write about people who are soft, weak, cowardly, and sometimes even downright bad, it's not because these people are soft, weak, cowardly, or bad; because if we were to say, as Zola did, that they are that way because of heredity, the workings of environment, society, because of biological or psychological determinism, people would be reassured. They would say, "Well, that's what we're like, no one can do anything about it." But when the existentialist writes about a coward, he says that his coward is responsible for his cowardice. He's not like that because he has a cowardly heart or lung or brain; he's not like that on account of his physiological make-up; but he's like that because he has made himself a coward by his acts. There's no such thing as a cowardly constitution; there are nervous constitutions; there is poor blood, as the common people say, or strong constitutions. But the man whose blood is poor is not a coward on that account, for what makes cowardice is the act of renouncing or yielding. A constitution is not an act; the coward is defined on the basis of the acts he performs. People feel, in a vague sort of way, that this coward we're talking about is guilty of being a coward, and the thought frightens them. What people would like is that a coward or a hero be born that way.

One of the complaints most frequently made about *The Ways of Freedom*[1] can be summed up as follows: "After all, these people are so spineless, how are you going to make heroes out of them?" This objection almost makes me laugh, for it assumes that people are born heroes. That's what people really want to think. If you're born cowardly, you may set your mind perfectly at rest; there's nothing you can do about it; you'll be cowardly all your life, whatever you may do. If you're born a hero, you may set your mind just as much at rest; you'll be a hero all your life; you'll drink like a hero and eat like a hero. What the existentialist says is that the

---

1. *Les Chemins de la Liberté*, M. Sartre's projected trilogy of novels, two of which, *L'Age de Raison (The Age of Reason)* and *Le Sursis (The Reprieve)* have already appeared.—Translator's note. After this essay was translated, Sartre published a third volume, *La mort dans l'ame*, 1949 (translated as *Troubled Sleep*, 1951), and a fragment of a fourth, which was never completed.—Editor's note.

coward makes himself cowardly, that the hero makes himself heroic. There's always a possibility for the coward not to be cowardly any more and for the hero to stop being heroic. What counts is total involvement; some one particular action or set of circumstances is not total involvement.

Thus, I think we have answered a number of the charges concerning existentialism. You see that it can not be taken for a philosophy of quietism, since it defines man in terms of action; nor for a pessimistic description of man—there is no doctrine more optimistic, since man's destiny is within himself; nor for an attempt to discourage man from acting, since it tells him that the only hope is in his acting and that action is the only thing that enables a man to live. Consequently, we are dealing here with an ethics of action and involvement.

Nevertheless, on the basis of a few notions like these, we are still charged with immuring man in his private subjectivity. There again we're very much misunderstood. Subjectivity of the individual is indeed our point of departure, and this for strictly philosophic reasons. Not because we are bourgeois, but because we want a doctrine based on truth and not a lot of fine theories, full of hope but with no real basis. There can be no other truth to take off from than this: *I think; therefore, I exist.* There we have the absolute truth of consciousness becoming aware of itself. Every theory which takes man out of the moment in which he becomes aware of himself is, at its very beginning, a theory which confounds truth, for outside the Cartesian *cogito,* all views are only probable, and a doctrine of probability which is not bound to a truth dissolves into thin air. In order to describe the probable, you must have a firm hold on the true. Therefore, before there can be any truth whatsoever, there must be an absolute truth; and this one is simple and easily arrived at; it's on everyone's doorstep; it's a matter of grasping it directly.

Secondly, this theory is the only one which gives man dignity, the only one which does not reduce him to an object. The effect of all materialism is to treat all men, including the one philosophizing, as objects, that is, as an ensemble of determined reactions in no way distinguished from the ensemble of qualities and phenomena which constitute a table or a chair or a stone. We definitely wish to establish the human realm as an ensemble of values distinct from the material realm. But the subjectivity that we have thus arrived at, and which we have claimed to be truth, is not a strictly individual subjectivity, for we have demonstrated that one discovers in the *cogito* not only himself, but others as well.

The philosophies of Descartes and Kant to the contrary, through the *I think* we reach our own self in the presence of others, and the others are just as real to us as our own self. Thus, the man who becomes aware of himself through the *cogito* also perceives all others, and he perceives them as the condition of his own existence. He realizes that he can not be anything (in the sense that we say that someone is witty or nasty or jealous) unless others recognize it as such. In order to get any truth about myself, I must have contact with another person. The other is indispensable to my own existence, as well as to my knowledge about myself. This being so, in discovering my inner being I discover the other person at the same time, like a freedom placed in front of me which thinks and wills only for or against me. Hence, let us at once announce the discovery of a world which we shall call inter-subjectivity; this is the world in which man decides what he is and what others are.

Besides, if it is impossible to find in every man some universal essence which would be human nature, yet there does exist a universal human condition. It's not by chance that today's thinkers speak more readily of man's condition than of his nature. By condition they mean, more or less definitely, the *a priori* limits which outline man's fundamental situation in the universe. Historical situations vary; a man may be born a slave in a pagan society or a feudal lord or a proletarian. What does not vary is the necessity for him to exist in the world, to be at work there, to be there in the midst of other people, and to be mortal there. The limits are neither subjective or objective, or, rather, they have an objective and a subjective side. Objective because they are to be found everywhere and are recognizable everywhere; subjective because they are *lived* and are nothing if man does not live them, that is, freely determine his existence with reference to them. And though the configurations may differ, at least none of them are completely strange to me, because they all appear as attempts either to pass beyond these limits or recede from them or deny them or adapt to them. Consequently, every configuration, however individual it may be, has a universal value. *structural arrangement*

Every configuration, even the Chinese, the Indian, or the negro, can be understood by a Westerner. "Can be understood" means that by virtue of a situation that he can imagine, a European of 1945 can, in like manner, push himself to his limits and reconstitute within himself the configuration of the Chinese, the Indian, or the African. Every configuration has universality in the sense that every configuration can be understood by every man. This does not at all mean that this configuration defines man forever, but that it can be met with again. There is always a way to understand the idiot, the child, the savage, the foreigner, provided one has the necessary information.

In this sense we may say that there is a universality of man; but it is not given, it is perpetually being made. I build the universal in choosing myself; I build it in understanding the configuration of every other man, whatever age he might have lived in. This absoluteness of choice does not do away with the relativeness of each epoch. At heart, what existentialism

shows is the connection between the absolute character of free involvement, by virtue of which every man realizes himself in realizing a type of
mankind, an involvement always comprehensible in any age whatsoever
and by any person whosoever, and the relativeness of the cultural ensemble which may result from such a choice; it must be stressed that the
relativity of Cartesianism and the absolute character of Cartesian involvement go together. In this sense, you may, if you like, say that each of us
performs an absolute act in breathing, eating, sleeping, or behaving in any
way whatever. There is no difference between being free, like a configuration. like an existence which chooses its essence, and being absolute. There
is no difference between being an absolute temporarily localised, that is,
localised in history, and being universally comprehensible.

This does not entirely settle the objection to subjectivism. In fact, the
objection still takes several forms. First, there is the following: we are told,
"So you're able to do anything, no matter what!" This is expressed in
various ways. First we are accused of anarchy; then they say, "You're
unable to pass judgment on others, because there's no reason to prefer one
configuration to another"; finally they tell us, "Everything is arbitrary in
this choosing of yours. You take something from one pocket and pretend
you're putting it into the other."

These three objections aren't very serious. Take the first objection.
"You're able to do anything, no matter what" is not to the point. In one
sense choice is possible, but what is not possible is not to choose. I can
always choose, but I ought to know that if I do not choose, I am still
choosing. Though this may seem purely formal, it is highly important for
keeping fantasy and caprice within bounds. If it is true that in facing a
situation, for example, one in which, as a person capable of having sexual
relations, of having children, I am obliged to choose an attitude, and if I
in any way assume responsibility for a choice which, in involving myself,
also involves all mankind, this has nothing to do with caprice, even if no
a priori value determines my choice.

If anybody thinks that he recognizes here Gide's theory of the arbitrary act, he fails to see the enormous difference between this doctrine and
Gide's. Gide does not know what a situation is. He acts out of pure caprice.
For us, on the contrary, man is in an organized situation in which he
himself is involved. Through his choice, he involves all mankind, and he
can not avoid making a choice: either he will remain chaste, or he will
marry without having children, or he will marry and have children; anyhow, whatever he may do, it is impossible for him not to take full responsibility for the way he handles this problem. Doubtless, he chooses without
referring to pre-established values, but it is unfair to accuse him of caprice.
Instead, let us say that moral choice is to be compared to the making of
a work of art. And before going any further, let it be said at once that we

are not dealing here with an aesthetic ethics, because our opponents are so dishonest that they even accuse us of that. The example I've chosen is a comparison only.

Having said that, may I ask whether anyone has ever accused an artist who has painted a picture of not having drawn his inspiration from rules set up *a priori?* Has anyone ever asked, "What painting ought he to make?" It is clearly understood that there is no definite painting to be made, that the artist is engaged in the making of his painting, and that the painting to be made is precisely the painting he will have made. It is clearly understood that there are no *a priori* aesthetic values, but that there are values which appear subsequently in the coherence of the painting, in the correspondence between what the artist intended and the result. Nobody can tell what the painting of tomorrow will be like. Painting can be judged only after it has once been made. What connection does that have with ethics? We are in the same creative situation. We never say that a work of art is arbitrary. When we speak of a canvas of Picasso, we never say that it is arbitrary; we understand quite well that he was making himself what he is at the very time he was painting, that the ensemble of his work is embodied in his life.

The same holds on the ethical plane. What art and ethics have in common is that we have creation and invention in both cases. We can not decide *a priori* what there is to be done. I think that I pointed that out quite sufficiently when I mentioned the case of the student who came to see me, and who might have applied to all the ethical systems, Kantian or otherwise, without getting any sort of guidance. He was obliged to devise his law himself. Never let it be said by us that this man—who, taking affection, individual action, and kind-heartedness toward a specific person as his ethical first principle, chooses to remain with his mother, or who, preferring to make a sacrifice, chooses to go to England—has made an arbitrary choice. Man makes himself. He isn't ready made at the start. In choosing his ethics, he makes himself, and force of circumstances is such that he can not abstain from choosing one. We define man only in relationship to involvement. It is therefore absurd to charge us with arbitrariness of choice.

In the second place, it is said that we are unable to pass judgment on others. In a way this is true, and in another way, false. It is true in this sense, that, whenever a man sanely and sincerely involves himself and chooses his configuration, it is impossible for him to prefer another configuration, regardless of what his own may be in other respects. It is true in this sense, that we do not believe in progress. Progress is betterment. Man is always the same. The situation confronting him varies. Choice always remains a choice in a situation. The problem has not changed since the time one could choose between those for and those against slavery, for example, at the time of the Civil War, and the present time, when one can side with the Maquis Resistance Party, or with the Communists.

But, nevertheless, one can still pass judgment, for, as I have said, one makes a choice in relationship to others. First, one can judge (and this is perhaps not a judgment of value, but a logical judgment) that certain choices are based on error and others on truth. If we have defined man's situation as a free choice, with no excuses and no recourse, every man who takes refuge behind the excuse of his passions, every man who sets up a determinism, is a dishonest man.

The objection may be raised, "But why mayn't he choose himself dishonestly?" I reply that I am not obliged to pass moral judgment on him, but that I do define his dishonesty as an error. One can not help considering the truth of the matter. Dishonesty is obviously a falsehood because it belies the complete freedom of involvement. On the same grounds, I maintain that there is also dishonesty if I choose to state that certain values exist prior to me; it is self-contradictory for me to want them and at the same state that they are imposed on me. Suppose someone says to me, "What if I want to be dishonest?" I'll answer, "There's no reason for you not to be, but I'm saying that that's what you are, and that the strictly coherent attitude is that of honesty."

Besides, I can bring moral judgment to bear. When I declare that freedom in every concrete circumstance can have no other aim than to want itself, if man has once become aware that in his forlornness he imposes values, he can no longer want but one thing, and that is freedom, as the basis of all values. That doesn't mean that he wants it in the abstract. It means simply that the ultimate meaning of the acts of honest men is the quest for freedom as such. A man who belongs to a communist or revolutionary union wants concrete goals; these goals imply an abstract desire for freedom; but this freedom is wanted in something concrete. We want freedom for freedom's sake and in every particular circumstance. And in wanting freedom we discover that it depends entirely on the freedom of others, and that the freedom of others depends on ours. Of course, freedom as the definition of man does not depend on others, but as soon as there is involvement, I am obliged to want others to have freedom at the same time that I want my own freedom. I can take freedom as my goal only if I take that of others as a goal as well. Consequently, when, in all honesty, I've recognized that man is a being in whom existence precedes essence, that he is a free being who, in various circumstances, can want only his freedom, I have at the same time recognized that I can want only the freedom of others.

Therefore, in the name of this will for freedom, which freedom itself implies, I may pass judgment on those who seek to hide from themselves the complete arbitrariness and the complete freedom of their existence.

Those who hide their complete freedom from themselves out of a spirit of seriousness or by means of deterministic excuses, I shall call cowards; those who try to show that their existence was necessary, when it is the very contingency of man's appearance on earth, I shall call stinkers. But cowards or stinkers can be judged only from a strictly unbiased point of view.

Therefore though the content of ethics is variable, a certain form of it is universal. Kant says that freedom desires both itself and the freedom of others. Granted. But he believes that the formal and the universal are enough to constitute an ethics. We, on the other hand, think that principles which are too abstract run aground in trying to decide action. Once again, take the case of the student. In the name of what, in the name of what great moral maxim do you think he could have decided, in perfect peace of mind, to abandon his mother or to stay with her? There is no way of judging. The content is always concrete and thereby unforeseeable; there is always the element of invention. The one thing that counts is knowing whether the inventing that has been done, has been done in the name of freedom.

For example, let us look at the following two cases. You will see to what extent they correspond, yet differ. Take *The Mill on the Floss*. We find a certain young girl, Maggie Tulliver, who is an embodiment of the value of passion and who is aware of it. She is in love with a young man, Stephen, who is engaged to an insignificant young girl. This Maggie Tulliver, instead of heedlessly preferring her own happiness, chooses, in the name of human solidarity, to sacrifice herself and give up the man she loves. On the other hand, Sanseverina, in *The Charterhouse of Parma*, believing that passion is man's true value, would say that a great love deserves sacrifices; that it is to be preferred to the banality of the conjugal love that would tie Stephen to the young ninny he had to marry. She would choose to sacrifice the girl and fulfill her happiness; and, as Stendhal shows, she is even ready to sacrifice herself for the sake of passion, if this life demands it. Here we are in the presence of two strictly opposed moralities. I claim that they are much the same thing; in both cases what has been set up as the goal is freedom.

You can imagine two highly similar attitudes: one girl prefers to renounce her love out of resignation; another prefers to disregard the prior attachment of the man she loves out of sexual desire. On the surface these two actions resemble those we've just described. However, they are completely different. Sanseverina's attitude is much nearer that of Maggie Tulliver, one of heedless rapacity.

Thus, you see that the second charge is true and, at the same time, false. One may choose anything if it is on the grounds of free involvement.

The third objection is the following: "You take something from one pocket and put it into the other. That is, fundamentally, values aren't serious, since you choose them." My answer to this is that I'm quite vexed that that's the way it is; but if I've discarded God the Father, there has to be someone to invent values. You've got to take things as they are. Moreover, to say that we invent values means nothing else but this: life has no meaning *a priori*. Before you come alive, life is nothing; it's up to you to give it a meaning, and value is nothing else but the meaning that you choose. In that way, you see, there is a possibility of creating a human community.

I've been reproached for asking whether existentialism is humanistic. It's been said, "But you said in *Nausea* that the humanists were all wrong. You made fun of a certain kind of humanist. Why come back to it now?" Actually, the word humanism has two very different meanings. By humanism one can mean a theory which takes man as an end and as a higher value. Humanism in this sense can be found in Cocteau's tale *Around the World in Eighty Hours* when a character, because he is flying over some mountains in an airplane, declares, "Man is simply amazing." That means that I, who did not build the airplanes, shall personally benefit from these particular inventions, and that I, as man, shall personally consider myself responsible for, and honored by, acts of a few particular men. This would imply that we ascribe a value to man on the basis of the highest deeds of certain men. This humanism is absurd, because only the dog or the horse would be able to make such an over-all judgment about man, which they are careful not to do, at least to my knowledge.

But it can not be granted that a man may make a judgment about man. Existentialism spares him from any such judgment. The existentialist will never consider man as an end because he is always in the making. Nor should we believe that there is a mankind to which we might set up a cult in the manner of Auguste Comte. The cult of mankind ends in the self-enclosed humanism of Comte, and, let it be said, of fascism. This kind of humanism we can do without.

But there is another meaning of humanism. Fundamentally it is this: man is constantly outside of himself; in projecting himself, in losing himself outside of himself, he makes for man's existing; and, on the other hand, it is by pursuing transcendent goals that he is able to exist; man, being this state of passing-beyond, is at the heart, at the center of this passing-beyond. There is no universe other than a human universe, the universe of human subjectivity. This connection between transcendency, as a constituent element of man—not in the sense that God is transcendent, but in the sense of passing beyond—and subjectivity, in the sense that man is not closed in on himself but is always present in a human universe, is what we call existentialist humanism. Humanism, because we remind man that there is no law-maker other than himself, and that in his forlorness he will decide by himself; because we point out that man will fulfill himself as man, not in turning toward himself, but in seeking outside of himself a goal which is just this liberation, just this particular fulfillment.

From these few reflections it is evident that nothing is more unjust than the objections that have been raised against us. Existentialism is nothing else than an attempt to draw all the consequences of a coherent atheistic position. It isn't trying to plunge man into despair at all. But if one calls every attitude of unbelief despair, like the Christians, then the word is not being used in its original sense. Existentialism isn't so atheistic that it wears itself out showing that God doesn't exist. Rather, it declares that even if God did exist, that would change nothing. There you've got our point of view. Not that we believe that God exists, but we think that the problem of His existence is not the issue. In this sense existentialism is optimistic, a doctrine of action, and it is plain dishonesty for Christians to make no distinction between their own despair and ours and then to call us despairing.

Albert Camus
The Myth of Sisyphus

from *The Myth of Sisyphus*

The gods had condemned Sisyphus to ceaselessly rolling a rock to the top of a mountain, whence the stone would fall back of its own weight. They had thought with some reason that there is no more dreadful punishment than futile and hopeless labor.

If one believes Homer, Sisyphus was the wisest and most prudent of mortals. According to another tradition, however, he was disposed to practice the profession of highwayman. I see no contradiction in this. Opinions differ as to the reasons why he became the futile laborer of the underworld. To begin with, he is accused of a certain levity in regard to the Gods. He stole their secrets. Ægina, the daughter of Æsopus, was

Source: From *The Myth of Sisyphus and Other Essays*, by Albert Camus, translated by Justin O'Brien. Copyright © 1955 by Alfred A. Knopf, Inc. Reprinted by permission of Alfred A. Knopf, Inc.

carried off by Jupiter. The father was shocked by that disappearance and complained to Sisyphus. He, who knew of the abduction, offered to tell about it on condition that Æsopus would give water to the citadel of Corinth. To the celestial thunderbolts he preferred the benediction of water. He was punished for this in the underworld. Homer tells us also that Sisyphus had put Death in chains. Pluto could not endure the sight of his deserted, silent empire. He dispatched the god of war, who liberated Death from the hands of her conqueror.

It is said also that Sisyphus, being near to death, rashly wanted to test his wife's love. He ordered her to cast his unburied body into the middle of the public square. Sisyphus woke up in the underworld. And there, annoyed by an obedience so contrary to human love, he obtained from Pluto permission to return to earth in order to chastise his wife. But when he had seen again the face of this world, enjoyed water and sun, warm stones and the sea, he no longer wanted to go back to the infernal darkness. Recalls, signs of anger, warnings were of no avail. Many years more he lived facing the curve of the gulf, the sparkling sea, and the smiles of earth. A decree of the gods was necessary. Mercury came and seized the impudent man by the collar and, snatching him from his joys, led him forcibly back to the underworld, where his rock was ready for him.

You have already grasped that Sisyphus is the absurd hero. He *is*, as much through his passions as through his torture. His scorn of the gods, his hatred of death, and his passion for life won him that unspeakable penalty in which the whole being is exerted toward accomplishing nothing. This is the price that must be paid for the passions of this earth. Nothing is told us about Sisyphus in the underworld. Myths are made for the imagination to breathe life into them. As for this myth, one sees merely the whole effort of a body straining to raise the huge stone, to roll it and push it up a slope a hundred times over; one sees the face screwed up, the cheek tight against the stone, the shoulder bracing the clay-covered mass, the foot wedging it, the fresh start with arms outstretched, the wholly human security of two earth-clotted hands. At the very end of his long effort measured by skyless space and time without depth, the purpose is achieved. Then Sisyphus watches the stone rush down in a few moments toward that lower world whence he will have to push it up again toward the summit. He goes back down to the plain.

It is during that return, that pause, that Sisyphus interests me. A face that toils so close to stones is already stone itself! I see that man going back down with a heavy yet measured step toward the torment of which he will never know the end. That hour like a breathing-space which returns as surely as his suffering, that is the hour of consciousness. At each of those moments when he leaves the heights and gradually sinks toward the lairs of the gods, he is superior to his fate. He is stronger than his rock.

If this myth is tragic, that is because its hero is conscious. Where would his torture be, indeed, if at every step the hope of succeeding upheld him? The workman of today works every day in his life at the same tasks, and this fate is no less absurd. But it is tragic only at the rare moments when it becomes conscious. Sisyphus, proletarian of the gods, powerless and rebellious, knows the whole extent of his wretched condition: it is what he thinks of during his descent. The lucidity that was to constitute his torture at the same time crowns his victory. There is no fate that cannot be surmounted by scorn.

If the descent is thus sometimes performed in sorrow, it can also take place in joy. This word is not too much. Again I fancy Sisyphus returning toward his rock, and the sorrow was in the beginning. When the images of earth cling too tightly to memory, when the call of happiness becomes too insistent, it happens that melancholy rises in man's heart: this is the rock's victory, this is the rock itself. The boundless grief is too heavy to bear. These are our nights of Gethsemane. But crushing truths perish from being acknowledged. Thus, Œdipus at the outset obeys fate without knowing it. But from the moment he knows, his tragedy begins. Yet at the same moment, blind and desperate, he realizes that the only bond linking him to the world is the cool hand of a girl. Then a tremendous remark rings out: "Despite so many ordeals, my advanced age and the nobility of my soul make me conclude that all is well." Sophocles' Œdipus, like Dostoevsky's Kirilov, thus gives the recipe for the absurd victory. Ancient wisdom confirms modern heroism.

One does not discover the absurd without being tempted to write a manual of happiness. "What! by such narrow ways—?" There is but one world, however. Happiness and the absurd are two sons of the same earth. They are inseparable. It would be a mistake to say that happiness necessarily springs from the absurd discovery. It happens as well that the feeling of the absurd springs from happiness. "I conclude that all is well," says Œdipus, and that remark is sacred. It echoes in the wild and limited universe of man. It teaches that all is not, has not been, exhausted. It drives out of this world a god who had come into it with dissatisfaction and a preference for futile sufferings. It makes of fate a human matter, which must be settled among men.

All Sisyphus' silent joy is contained therein. His fate belongs to him. His rock is his thing. Likewise, the absurd man, when he contemplates his torment, silences all the idols. In the universe suddenly restored to its silence, the myriad wondering little voices of the earth rise up. Unconscious, secret calls, invitations from all the faces, they are the necessary reverse and price of victory. There is no sun without shadow, and it is essential to know the night. The absurd man says yes and his effort will henceforth be unceasing. If there is a personal fate, there is no higher destiny, or at least there is but one which he concludes is inevitable and despicable. For the rest, he knows himself to be the master of his days. At that subtle moment when man glances backward over his life, Sisyphus returning toward his rock, in that slight pivoting he comtemplates that series of unrelated actions which becomes his fate, created by him, combined under his memory's eye and soon sealed by his death. Thus, convinced of the wholly human origin of all that is human, a blind man eager to see who knows that the night has no end, he is still on the go. The rock is still rolling.

I leave Sisyphus at the foot of the mountain! One always finds one's burden again. But Sisyphus teaches the higher fidelity that negates the gods and raises rocks. He too concludes that all is well. This universe henceforth without a master seems to him neither sterile nor futile. Each atom of that stone, each mineral flake of that night-filled mountain, in itself forms a world. The struggle itself toward the heights is enough to fill a man's heart. One must imagine Sisyphus happy.

Karl Jaspers
Sources of Philosophy

from *Way to Wisdom*

The history of philosophy as methodical thinking began twenty-five hundred years ago, but as mythical thought much earlier.

The beginning however is something quite different from the source. The beginning is historical and provides those who follow with a mounting accumulation of insights. But it is always from the source that the impulsion to philosophize springs. The source alone lends meaning to present philosophy and through it alone is past philosophy understood.

This source is of many kinds. Wonderment gives rise to question and insight; man's doubt in the knowledge he has attained gives rise to critical examination and clear certainty; his awe and sense of forsakenness lead him to inquire into himself. And now let us examine these three drives.

Source: Karl Jaspers, "Sources of Philosophy," *Way to Wisdom*, translated by Ralph Manheim (New Haven, Conn.: Yale University Press, 1954), pp. 17–27.

First: Plato said that the source of philosophy was wonder. Our eyes gave us "the sight of the stars, the sun and the firmament." This "impelled us to examine the universe, whence grew philosophy, the greatest good conferred upon mortals by the gods." And Aristotle: "For it is owing to their wonder that men both now begin and at first began to philosophize: they wondered originally at the obvious difficulties, then advanced little by little and stated difficulties about the greater matters, e.g., about the phenomena of the moon, and those of the sun, and of the stars, and about the genesis of the universe."

Wonder impels man to seek knowledge. In my wonderment I become aware of my lack of knowledge. I seek knowledge, but for its own sake and not "to satisfy any common need."

In philosophical thought man awakens from his bondage to practical needs. Without ulterior purpose he contemplates things, the heavens, the world, and asks, what is all this? Where does it come from? From the answers to his questions he expects no profit but an intrinsic satisfaction.

Second: Once I have satisfied my wonderment and admiration by knowledge of what is, *doubt* arises. I have heaped up insights, but upon critical examination nothing is certain. Sensory perceptions are conditioned by our sense organs and hence deceptive; in any event they do not coincide with what exists in itself outside me, independently of my perception. Our categories are those of our human understanding. They become entangled in hopeless contradictions. Everywhere proposition stands against proposition. In my philosophical progress I seize upon doubt and attempt to apply it radically to everything, either taking pleasure in the sceptical negation which recognizes nothing but by itself cannot take a single step forward, or inquiring: Where then is there a certainty that rises above all doubt and withstands all critique?

Descartes' famous proposition, "I think, therefore I am," was for him a solid certainty, though he doubted everything else. For even a total fallacy in my thinking, a fallacy which may be beyond my understanding, cannot blind me to the realization that in order to be deluded in my thinking I must *be.*

Methodical doubt gives rise to a critical examination of all knowledge, and without radical doubt there can be no true philosophical thought. But the crucial question is: How and where has a foundation for certainty been gained through doubt itself?

And third: While I concentrate my energies upon the knowledge of things in the world, while I am engaged in doubt as a road to certainty, I am immersed in things; I do not think of myself, of my aims, my happiness, my salvation. In forgetfulness of my self I am content with the attainment of this knowledge.

This changes when I become aware of myself in my situation.

The Stoic Epictetus said, "Philosophy arises when we become *aware of our own weakness and helplessness.*" How shall I help myself in my weakness? His answer was: By looking upon everything that is not within my power as necessary and indifferent to me, but by raising what does depend on me, namely the mode and content of my ideas, to clarity and freedom by thought.

And now let us take a look at our human state. We are always in situations. Situations change, opportunities arise. If they are missed they never return. I myself can work to change the situation. But there are situations which remain essentially the same even if their momentary aspect changes and their shattering force is obscured: I must die, I must suffer, I must struggle, I am subject to change, I involve myself inexorably in guilt. We call these fundamental situations of our existence ultimate situations.[1] That is to say, they are situations which we cannot evade or change. Along with wonder and doubt, awareness of these ultimate situations is the most profound source of philosophy. In our day-to-day lives we often evade them, by closing our eyes and living as if they did not exist. We forget that we must die, forget our guilt, and forget that we are at the mercy of chance. We face only concrete situations and master them to our profit, we react to them by planning and acting in the world, under the impulsion of our practical interests. But to ultimate situations we react either by obfuscation or, if we really apprehend them, by despair and rebirth: we become ourselves by a change in our consciousness of being.

Or we may define our human situation by saying that *no reliance can be placed in worldly existence.*

Ingenuously we mistake the world for being as such. In happy situations we rejoice at our strength, we are thoughtlessly confident, we know nothing but our actuality. In pain and weakness we despair. But if we come out of this situation alive we let ourselves slip back into forgetfulness of self and a life of happiness.

Such experience however has sharpened man's wits. The menace beneath which he lives drives him to seek security. He expects his mastery of nature and his community with other men to guarantee his existence.

Man gains power over nature in order to make it serve him; through science and technology he seeks to make it reliable.

1. The term here translated as "ultimate situation" is *Grenzsituation.* This is a concept of central importance for the understanding of Jaspers' thought, as for the understanding of Existentialism. As the context above shows, the ultimate situations are the inescapable realities in relation to which alone human life can be made genuinely meaningful. Ultimate situations cannot be changed or surmounted; they can only be acknowledged.

But in man's domination of nature there remains an element of the incalculable which represents a constant threat, and the end is always failure: hard labour, old age, sickness and death cannot be done away with. Our dominated nature is reliable only in isolated cases; in the whole we can place no reliance.

Men band together in a community in order to limit and ultimately abolish the endless struggle of all against all; they seek to achieve security through mutual aid.

But here again there is a limit. Only if there were states in which every citizen stood to every other in a relation of absolute solidarity could justice and freedom be secure. For only then, if a citizen suffered injustice, would all others oppose it as one man. Such a state has never been seen. Those who have stood by one another in extremity and weakness have never been more than limited groups, and sometimes no more than a few individuals. No state, no church, no society offers absolute security. Such security has been a pleasing delusion of quiet times, in which the ultimate situations were veiled.

But there is a counterweight to the general unreliability of the world: there are in the world things worthy of faith, things that arouse confidence; there is a foundation which sustains us: home and country, parents and ancestors, brothers and sisters and friends, husbands and wives. There is a foundation of historical tradition, in native language, in faith, in the work of thinkers, poets, and artists. However, this tradition also gives no security, it is not absolutely reliable. For we encounter it always as the work of man; God is nowhere in the world. Tradition always implies a question. Keeping sight of the tradition, man must always derive what for him is certainty, being, the reliable, from his own primal source. But the precariousness of all worldly existence is a warning to us, it forbids us to content ourselves with the world; it points to something else.

The ultimate situations—death, chance, guilt, and the uncertainty of the world—confront me with the reality of failure. What do I do in the face of this absolute failure, which if I am honest I cannot fail to recognize?

The advice of the Stoic, to withdraw to our own freedom in the independence of the mind, is not adequate. The Stoic's perception of man's weakness was not radical enough. He failed to see that the mind in itself is empty, dependent on what is put into it, and he failed to consider the possibility of madness. The Stoic leaves us without consolation; the independent mind is barren, lacking all content. He leaves us without hope, because his doctrine affords us no opportunity of inner transformation, no fulfilment through self-conquest in love, no hopeful expectation of the possible.

And yet the Stoics' striving is toward true philosophy. Their thought, because its source is in ultimate situations, expresses the basic drive to find a revelation of true being in human failure.

Crucial for man is his attitude toward failure: whether it remains hidden from him and overwhelms him only objectively at the end or whether he perceives it unobscured as the constant limit of his existence; whether he snatches at fantastic solutions and consolations or faces it honestly, in silence before the unfathomable. The way in which man approaches his failure determines what he will become.

In ultimate situations man either perceives nothingness or senses true being in spite of and above all ephemeral worldly existence. Even despair, by the very fact that it is possible in the world, points beyond the world.

Or, differently formulated, man seeks redemption. Redemption is offered by the great, universal religions of redemption. They are characterized by an objective guarantee of the truth and reality of redemption. Their road leads to an act of individual conversion. This philosophy cannot provide. And yet all philosophy is a transcending of the world, analogous to redemption.

To sum up: The source of philosophy is to be sought in wonder, in doubt, in a sense of forsakenness. In any case it begins with an inner upheaval, which determines its goal.

Plato and Aristotle were moved by wonder to seek the nature of being.

Amid infinite uncertainty Descartes sought compelling certainty.

Amid the sufferings of life the Stoics sought the repose of the mind.

Each of these experiences has its own truth, clothed always in historical conceptions and language. In making these philosophies our own we penetrate the historical husk to the primal sources that are alive within us.

The inner drive is toward firm foundations, depth of being, eternity.

But for us perhaps none of these is the most fundamental, absolute source. The discovery that being can be revealed to wonder is a source of inspiration, but beguiles us into withdrawing from the world and succumbing to a pure, magical metaphysic. Compelling certainty is limited to the scientific knowledge by which we orient ourselves in the world. Stoic imperturbability serves us only as a makeshift in distress, as a refuge from total ruin, but in itself remains without content and life.

These three motives—wonder leading to knowledge, doubt leading to certainty, forsakenness leading to the self—cannot by themselves account for our present philosophical thought.

In this crucial turning point in history, in this age of unprecedented ruin and of potentialities that can only be darkly surmised, the three motives we have thus far considered remain in force, but they are not adequate. They can operate only if there is *communication* among men.

In all past history there was a self-evident bond between man and man, in stable communities, in institutions, and in universal ideas. Even the isolated individual was in a sense sustained in his isolation. The most visible sign of today's disintegration is that more and more men do not understand one another, that they meet and scatter, that they are indifferent to one another, that there is no longer any reliable community or loyalty.

Today a universal situation that has always existed in fact assumes crucial importance: That I can, and cannot, become one with the Other in truth; that my faith, precisely when I am certain, clashes with other men's faith; that there is always somewhere a limit beyond which there appears to be nothing but battle without hope of unity, ending inevitably in subjugation or annihilation; that softness and complaisance cause men without faith either to band blindly together or stubbornly to attack one another.

All this is not incidental or unimportant. It might be, if there were a truth that might satisfy me in my isolation. I should not suffer so deeply from lack of communication or find such unique pleasure in authentic communication if I for myself, in absolute solitude, could be certain of the truth. But I am only in conjunction with the Other, alone I am nothing.

Communication from understanding to understanding, from mind to mind, and also from existence to existence, is only a medium for impersonal meanings and values. Defence and attack then become means not by which men gain power but by which they approach one another. The contest is a loving contest in which each man surrenders his weapons to the other. The certainty of authentic being resides only in unreserved communication between men who live together and vie with one another in a free community, who regard their association with one another as but a preliminary stage, who take nothing for granted and question everything. Only in communication is all other truth fulfilled, only in communication am I myself not merely living but fulfilling life. God manifests Himself only indirectly, and only through man's love of man; compelling certainty is particular and relative, subordinated to the Whole. The Stoical attitude is in fact empty and rigid.

The basic philosophical attitude of which I am speaking is rooted in distress at the absence of communication, in the drive to authentic communication, and in the possibility of the loving contest which profoundly unites self and self.

And this philosophical endeavour is at the same time rooted in the three philosophical experiences we have mentioned, which must all be considered in the light of their meaning, whether favourable or hostile, for communication from man to man.

And so we may say that wonder, doubt, the experience of ultimate situations, are indeed sources of philosophy, but the ultimate source is the will to authentic communication, which embraces all the rest. This becomes apparent at the very outset, for does not all philosophy strive for communication, express itself, demand a hearing? And is not its very essence communicability, which is in turn inseparable from truth?

Communication then is the aim of philosophy, and in communication all its other aims are ultimately rooted: awareness of being, illumination through love, attainment of peace.

Paul Tillich
Being, Nonbeing, and Anxiety

from *The Courage To Be*

An Ontology of Anxiety

The Meaning of Nonbeing

Courage is self-affirmation "in-spite-of," that is in spite of that which tends to prevent the self from affirming itself. Differing from the Stoic— Neo-Stoic doctrines of courage, the "philosophies of life" have seriously and affirmatively dealt with that against which courage stands. For if being is interpreted in terms of life or process or becoming, nonbeing is ontologically as basic as being. The acknowledgment of this fact does not imply a decision about the priority of being over nonbeing, but it requires a consideration of nonbeing in the very foundation of ontology. Speaking of courage as a key to the interpretation of being-itself, one could say that this key, when it opens the door to being, finds, at the same time, being and negation of being and their unity.

Nonbeing is one of the most difficult and most discussed concepts. Parmenides tried to remove it as a concept. But in order to do so he had to sacrifice life. Democritus re-established it and identified it with empty space, in order to make movement thinkable. Plato used the concept of nonbeing because without it the contrast of existence with the pure essences is beyond understanding. It is implied in Aristotle's distinction between matter and form. It gave Plotinus the means of describing the loss of self of the human soul, and it gave Augustine the means for an ontological interpretation of human sin. For Pseudo-Dionysius the Areopagite nonbeing became the principle of his mystical doctrine of God. Jacob Boehme, the Protestant mystic and philosopher of life, made the classical statement that all things are rooted in a Yes and No. In Leibnitz' doctrine of finitude and evil as well as in Kant's analysis of the finitude of categorical forms nonbeing is implied. Hegel's dialectic makes negation the dynamic power in nature and history; and the philosophers of life, since Schelling and Schopenhauer, use "will" as the basic ontological category because it has the power of negating itself without losing itself. The concepts of process and becoming in philosophers like Bergson and Whitehead imply nonbeing as well as being. Recent Existentialists, especially Heidegger and Sartre, have put nonbeing (*Das Nichts, le néant*) in the center of their ontological thought; and Berdyaev, a follower of both Dionysius and Boehme, has developed an ontology of nonbeing which accounts for the "me-ontic" freedom in God and man. These philosophical ways of using the concept of nonbeing can be viewed against the background of the religious experience of the transitoriness of everything created and the power of the "demonic" in the human soul and history. In biblical religion these negativities have a decisive place in spite of the doctrine of creation. And the demonic, anti-divine principle, which nevertheless participates in the power of the divine, appears in the dramatic centers of the biblical story.

In view of this situation it is of little significance that some logicians deny that nonbeing has conceptual character and try to remove it from the philosophical scene except in the form of negative judgments. For the question is: What does the fact of negative judgments tell about the character of being? What is the ontological condition of negative judgments? How is the realm constituted in which negative judgments are possible? Certainly nonbeing is not a concept like others. It is the negation of every concept; but as such it is an inescapable content of thought and, as the history of thought has shown, the most important one after being-itself.

If one is asked how nonbeing is related to being-itself, one can only answer metaphorically: being "embraces" itself and nonbeing. Being has nonbeing "within" itself as that which is eternally present and eternally overcome in the process of the divine life. The ground of everything that is is not a dead identity without movement and becoming; it is living creativity. Creatively it affirms itself, eternally conquering its own nonbeing. As such it is the pattern of the self-affirmation of every finite being and the source of the courage to be.

Courage is usually described as the power of the mind to overcome fear. The meaning of fear seemed too obvious to deserve inquiry. But in the last decades depth psychology in cooperation with Existentialist philosophy has led to a sharp distinction between fear and anxiety and to more precise definitions of each of these concepts. Sociological analyses of the present period have pointed to the importance of anxiety as a group phenomenon. Literature and art have made anxiety a main theme of their creations, in contents as well as in style. The effect of this has been the awakening of at least the educated groups to an awareness of their own anxiety, and a permeation of the public consciousness by ideas and symbols of anxiety. Today it has become almost a truism to call our time an "age of anxiety." This holds equally for America and Europe.

Nevertheless it is necessary for an ontology of courage to include an ontology of anxiety, for they are interdependent. And it is conceivable that in the light of an ontology of courage some fundamental aspects of anxiety may become visible. The first assertion about the nature of anxiety is this: anxiety is the state in which a being is aware of its possible nonbeing. The same statement, in a shorter form, would read: anxiety is the existential awareness of nonbeing. "Existential" in this sentence means that it is not the abstract knowledge of nonbeing which produces anxiety but the awareness that nonbeing is a part of one's own being. It is not the realization of universal transitoriness, not even the experience of the death of others, but the impression of these events on the always latent awareness of our own having to die that produces anxiety. Anxiety is finitude, experienced as one's own finitude. This is the natural anxiety of man as man, and in some way of all living beings. It is the anxiety of nonbeing, the awareness of one's finitude as finitude.

The Interdependence of Fear and Anxiety

Anxiety and fear have the same ontological root but they are not the same in actuality. This is common knowledge, but it has been emphasized and overemphasized to such a degree that a reaction against it may occur and wipe out not only the exaggerations but also the truth of the distinction. Fear, as opposed to anxiety has a definite object (as most authors agree), which can be faced, analyzed, attacked, endured. One can act upon it, and in acting upon it participate in it—even if in the form of struggle. In this way one can take it into one's self-affirmation. Courage can meet every object of fear, because it is an object and makes participation possible. Courage can take the fear produced by a definite object into itself, because this object, however frightful it may be, has a side with which it participats in us and we in it. One could say that as long as there is an *object* of fear love in the sense of participation can conquer fear.

But this is not so with anxiety, because anxiety has no object, or rather, in a paradoxical phrase, its object is the negation of every object. Therefore participation, struggle, and love with respect to it are impossible. He who is in anxiety is, insofar as it is mere anxiety, delivered to it without help. Helplessness in the state of anxiety can be observed in animals and humans alike. It expresses itself in loss of direction, inadequate reactions, lack of "intentionality" (the being related to meaningful contents of knowledge or will). The reason for this sometimes striking behavior is the lack of an object on which the subject (in the state of anxiety) can concentrate. The only object is the threat itself, but not the source of the threat, because the source of the threat is "nothingness."

One might ask whether this threatening "nothing" is not the unknown, the indefinite possibility of an actual threat? Does not anxiety cease in the moment in which a known object of fear appears? Anxiety then would be fear of the unknown. But this is an insufficient explanation of anxiety. For there are innumerable realms of the unknown, different for each subject, and faced without any anxiety. It is the unknown of a special type which is met with anxiety. It is the unknown which by its very nature cannot be known, because it is nonbeing.

Fear and anxiety are distinguished but not separated. They are immanent within each other: The sting of fear is anxiety, and anxiety strives toward fear. Fear is being afraid of something, a pain, the rejection by a person or a group, the loss of something or somebody, the moment of dying. But in the anticipation of the threat originating in these things, it is not the negativity itself which they will bring upon the subject that is frightening but the anxiety about the possible implications of this negativity. The outstanding example—and more than an example—is the fear of dying. Insofar as it is *fear* its object is the anticipated event of being killed by sickness or an accident and thereby suffering agony and the loss of everything. Insofar as it is *anxiety* its object is the absolutely unknown "after death," the nonbeing which remains nonbeing even if it is filled with images of our present experience. The dreams in Hamlet's soliloquy, "to be or not to be," which we may have after death and which make cowards of us all are frightful not because of their manifest content but because of their power to symbolize the threat of nothingness, in religious terms of "eternal death." The symbols of hell created by Dante produce anxiety not because of their objective imagery but because they express the "nothingness" whose power is experienced in the anxiety of guilt. Each of the situations described in the *Inferno* could be met by courage on the basis of participation and love. But of course the meaning is that this is impossible; in other words they are not real situations but symbols of the objectless, of nonbeing.

The fear of death determines the element of anxiety in every fear. Anxiety, if not modified by the fear of an object, anxiety in its nakedness, is always the anxiety of ultimate nonbeing. Immediately seen, anxiety is the painful feeling of not being able to deal with the threat of a special situation. But a more exact analysis shows that in the anxiety about any special situation anxiety about the human situation as such is implied. It is the anxiety of not being able to preserve one's own being which underlies every fear and is the frightening element in it. In the moment, therefore, in which "naked anxiety" lays hold of the mind, the previous objects of fear cease to be definite objects. They appear as what they always were in part, symptoms of man's basic anxiety. As such they are beyond the reach of even the most courageous attack upon them.

This situation drives the anxious subject to establish objects of fear. Anxiety strives to become fear, because fear can be met by courage. It is impossible for a finite being to stand naked anxiety for more than a flash of time. People who have experienced these moments, as for instance some mystics in their visions of the "night of the soul," or Luther under the despair of the demonic assaults, or Nietzsche-Zarathustra in the experience of the "great disgust," have told of the unimaginable horror of it. This horror is ordinarily avoided by the transformation of anxiety into fear of something, no matter what. The human mind is not only, as Calvin has said, a permanent factory of idols, it is also a permanent factory of fears —the first in order to escape God, the second in order to escape anxiety; and there is a relation between the two. For facing the God who is really God means facing also the absolute threat of nonbeing. The "naked absolute" (to use a phrase of Luther's) produces "naked anxiety"; for it is the extinction of every finite self-affirmation, and not a possible object of fear and courage. But ultimately the attempts to transform anxiety into fear are vain. The basic anxiety, the anxiety of a finite being about the threat of nonbeing, cannot be eliminated. It belongs to existence itself.

TYPES OF ANXIETY

The Three Types of Anxiety and the Nature of Man

(1) Nonbeing is dependent on the being it negates. "Dependent" means two things. It points first of all to the ontological priority of being over nonbeing. The term nonbeing itself indicates this, and it is logically necessary. There could be no negation if there were no preceding affirmation to be negated. Certainly one can describe being in terms of non-nonbeing; and one can justify such a description by pointing to the astonishing prerational fact that there is something and not nothing. One could say that "being is the negation of the primordial night of nothingness." But in doing so one must realize that such an aboriginal nothing would be neither nothing nor something, that it becomes nothing only in contrast to something; in other words, that the ontological status of nonbeing as nonbeing is dependent on being. Secondly, nonbeing is dependent on the special

qualities of being. In itself nonbeing has no quality and no difference of qualities. But it gets them in relation to being. The character of the negation of being is determined by that in being which is negated. This makes it possible to speak of qualities of nonbeing and, consequently, of types of anxiety.

Up to now we have used the term nonbeing without differentiation, while in the discussion of courage several forms of self-affirmation were mentioned. They correspond to different forms of anxiety and are understandable only in correlation with them. I suggest that we distinguish three types of anxiety according to the three directions in which nonbeing threatens being. Nonbeing threatens man's ontic self-affirmation, relatively in terms of fate, absolutely in terms of death. It threatens man's spiritual self-affirmation, relatively in terms of emptiness, absolutely in terms of meaninglessness. It threatens man's moral self-affirmation, relatively in terms of guilt, absolutely in terms of condemnation. The awareness of this threefold threat is anxiety appearing in three forms, that of fate and death (briefly, the anxiety of death), that of emptiness and loss of meaning (briefly, the anxiety of meaningless), that of guilt and condemnation (briefly, the anxiety of condemnation). In all three forms anxiety is existential in the sense that it belongs to existence as such and not to an abnormal state of mind as in neurotic (and psychotic) anxiety. The nature of neurotic anxiety and its relation to existential anxiety will be discussed in another chapter. We shall deal now with the three forms of existential anxiety, first with their reality in the life of the individual, then with their social manifestations in special periods of Western history. However, it must be stated that the difference of types does not mean mutual exclusion. In the first chapter we have seen for instance that the courage to be as it appears in the ancient Stoics conquers not only the fear of death but also the threat of meaninglessness. In Nietzsche we find that in spite of the predominance of the threat of meaninglessness, the anxiety of death and condemnation is passionately challenged. In all representatives of classical Christianity death and sin are seen as the allied adversaries against which the courage of faith has to fight. The three forms of anxiety (and of courage) are immanent in each other but normally under the dominance of one of them.

The Anxiety of Fate and Death

Fate and death are the way in which our ontic self-affirmation is threatened by nonbeing. "Ontic," from the Greek *on*, "being," means here the basic self-affirmation of a being in its simple existence. (Ontological designates the philosophical analysis of the nature of being.) The anxiety of fate and death is most basic, most universal, and inescapable. All attempts to argue it away are futile. Even if the so-called arguments for the "immortality of the soul" had argumentative power (which they do not have) they would not convince existentially. For existentially everybody is aware of the complete loss of self which biological extinction implies. The unsophisticated mind knows instinctively what sophisticated ontology formulates: that reality has the basic structure of self-world correlation and that with the disappearance of the one side the world, the other side, the self, also disappears, and what remains is their common ground but not their structural correlation. It has been observed that the anxiety of death increases with the increase of individualization and that people in collectivistic cultures are less open to this type of anxiety. The observation is correct yet the explanation that there is no basic anxiety about death in collectivist cultures is wrong. The reason for the difference from more individualized civilizations is that the special type of courage which characterizes collectivism . . . , as long as it is unshaken, allays the anxiety of death. But the very fact that courage has to be created through many internal and external (psychological and ritual) activities and symbols shows that basic anxiety has to be overcome even in collectivism. Without its at least potential presence neither war nor the criminal law in these societies would be understandable. If there were no fear of death, the threat of the law or of a superior enemy would be without effect—which it obviously is not. Man as man in every civilization is anxiously aware of the threat of nonbeing and needs the courage to affirm himself in spite of it.

The anxiety of death is the permanent horizon within which the anxiety of fate is at work. For the threat against man's ontic self-affirmation is not only the absolute threat of death but also the relative threat of fate. Certainly the anxiety of death overshadows all concrete anxieties and gives them their ultimate seriousness. They have, however, a certain independence and, ordinarily, a more immediate impact than the anxiety of death. The term "fate" for this whole group of anxieties stresses one element which is common to all of them: their contingent character, their unpredictability, the impossibility of showing their meaning and purpose. One can describe this in terms of the categorical structure of our experience. One can show the contingency of our temporal being, the fact that we exist in this and no other period of time, beginning in a contingent moment, ending in a contingent moment, filled with experiences which are contingent themselves with respect to quality and quantity. One can show the contingency of our spatial being (our finding ourselves in this and no other place, and the strangeness of this place in spite of its familiarity); the contingent character of ourselves and the place from which we look at our world; and the contingent character of the reality at which we look, that is, our world. Both could be different: this is their contingency and this produces the anxiety about our spatial existence. One can show the contingency of the causal interdependence of which one is a part, both with respect to the past and to the present, the vicissitudes coming from our world and the hidden forces in the depths of our own self. Contingent does not mean causally undetermined but it means that the determining causes of our existence have no ultimate necessity. They are given, and they cannot be logically derived. Contingently we are put into the whole web of causal relations. Contingently we are determined by them in every moment and thrown out by them in the last moment.

Fate is the rule of contingency, and the anxiety about fate is based on the finite being's awareness of being contingent in every respect, of having no ultimate necessity. Fate is usually identified with necessity in the sense of an inescapable causal determination. Yet it is not causal necessity that makes fate a matter of anxiety but the lack of ultimate necessity, the irrationality, the impenetrable darkness of fate.

The threat of nonbeing to man's ontic self-affirmation is absolute in the threat of death, relative in the threat of fate. But the relative threat is a threat only because in its background stands the absolute threat. Fate would not produce inescapable anxiety without death behind it. And death stands behind fate and its contingencies not only in the last moment when one is thrown out of existence but in every moment within existence. Nonbeing is omnipresent and produces anxiety even where an immediate threat of death is absent. It stands behind the experience that we are driven, together with everything else, from the past toward the future without a moment of time which does not vanish immediately. It stands behind the insecurity and homelessness of our social and individual existence. It stands behind the attacks on our power of being in body and soul by weakness, disease, and accidents. In all these forms fate actualizes itself, and through them the anxiety of nonbeing takes hold of us. We try to transform the anxiety into fear and to meet courageously the objects in which the threat is embodied. We succeed partly, but somehow we are aware of the fact that it is not these objects with which we struggle that produce the anxiety but the human situation as such. Out of this the question arises: Is there a courage to be, a courage to affirm oneself in spite of the threat against man's ontic self-affirmation?

The Anxiety of Emptiness and Meaninglessness

Nonbeing threatens man as a whole, and therefore threatens his spiritual as well as his ontic self-affirmation. Spiritual self-affirmation occurs in every moment in which man lives creatively in the various spheres of meaning. Creative, in this context, has the sense not of original creativity as performed by the genius but of living spontaneously, in action and reaction, with the contents of one's cultural life. In order to be spiritually creative one need not be what is called a creative artist or scientist or

statesman, but one must be able to participate meaningfully in their original creations. Such a participation is creative insofar as it changes that in
which one participates, even if in very small ways. The creative transformation of a language by the interdependence of the creative poet or
writer and the many who are influenced by him directly or indirectly and
react spontaneously to him is an outstanding example. Everyone who lives
creatively in meanings affirms himself as a participant in these meanings.
He affirms himself as receiving and transforming reality creatively. He
loves himself as participating in the spiritual life and as loving its contents.
He loves them because they are his own fulfillment and because they are
actualized through him. The scientist loves both the truth he discovers and
himself insofar as he discovers it. He is held by the content of his discovery.
This is what one can call "spiritual self-affirmation." And if he has not
discovered but only participates in the discovery, it is equally spiritual
self-affirmation.

Such an experience presupposes that the spiritual life is taken seriously, that it is a matter of ultimate concern. And this again presupposes
that in it and through it ultimate reality becomes manifest. A spiritual life
in which this is not experienced is threatened by nonbeing in the two
forms in which it attacks spiritual self-affirmation: emptiness and meaninglessness.

We use the term meaninglessness for the absolute threat of nonbeing
to spiritual self-affirmation, and the term emptiness for the relative threat
to it. They are no more identical than are the threat of death and fate. But
in the background of emptiness lies meaninglessness as death lies in the
background of the vicissitudes of fate.

The anxiety of meaninglessness is anxiety about the loss of an ultimate
concern, of a meaning which gives meaning to all meanings. This anxiety
is aroused by the loss of a spiritual center, of an answer, however symbolic
and indirect, to the question of the meaning of existence.

The anxiety of emptiness is aroused by the threat of nonbeing to the
special contents of the spiritual life. A belief breaks down through external
events or inner processes: one is cut off from creative participation in a
sphere of culture, one feels frustrated about something which one had
passionately affirmed, one is driven from devotion to one object to devotion to another and again on to another, because the meaning of each of
them vanishes and the creative eros is transformed into indifference or
aversion. Everything is tried and nothing satisfies. The contents of the
tradition, however excellent, however praised, however loved once, lose
their power to give content *today*. And present culture is even less able
to provide the content. Anxiously one turns away from all concrete contents and looks for an ultimate meaning, only to discover that it was
precisely the loss of a spiritual center which took away the meaning from

the special contents of the spiritual life. But a spiritual center cannot be produced intentionally, and the attempt to produce it only produces deeper anxiety. The anxiety of emptiness drives us to the abyss of meaninglessness.

Emptiness and loss of meaning are expressions of the threat of nonbeing to the spiritual life. This threat is implied in man's finitude and actualized by man's estrangement. It can be described in terms of doubt, its creative and its destructive function in man's spiritual life. Man is able to ask because he is separated *from*, while participating *in*, what he is asking about. In every question an element of doubt, the awareness of not having, is implied. In systematic questioning systematic doubt is effective; e.g. of the Cartesian type. This element of doubt is a condition of all spiritual life. The threat to spiritual life is not doubt as an element but the total doubt. If the awareness of not having has swallowed the awareness of having, doubt has ceased to be methodological asking and has become existential despair. On the way to this situation the spiritual life tries to maintain itself as long as possible by clinging to affirmations which are not yet undercut, be they traditions, autonomous convictions, or emotional preferences. And if it is impossible to remove the doubt, one courageously accepts it without surrendering one's convictions. One takes the risk of going astray and the anxiety of this risk upon oneself. In this way one avoids the extreme situation—till it becomes unavoidable and the despair of truth becomes complete.

Then man tries another way out: Doubt is based on man's separation from the whole of reality, on his lack of universal participation, on the isolation of his individual self. So he tries to break out of this situation, to identify himself with something transindividual, to surrender his separation and self-relatedness. He flees from his freedom of asking and answering for himself to a situation in which no further questions can be asked and the answers to previous questions are imposed on him authoritatively. In order to avoid the risk of asking and doubting he surrenders the right to ask and to doubt. He surrenders himself in order to save his spiritual life. He "escapes from his freedom" (Fromm) in order to escape the anxiety of meaninglessness. Now he is no longer lonely, not in existential doubt, not in despair. He "participates" and affirms by participation the contents of his spiritual life. Meaning is saved, but the self is sacrificed. And since the conquest of doubt was a matter of sacrifice, the sacrifice of the freedom of the self, it leaves a mark on the regained certitude: a fanatical self-assertiveness. Fanaticism is the correlate to spiritual self-surrender: it shows the anxiety which it was supposed to conquer, by attacking with disproporionate violence those who disagree and who demonstrate by their disagreement elements in the spiritual life of the fanatic which he must suppress in himself. Because he must suppress them in himself he must suppress them in others. His anxiety forces him to persecute dissenters. The weakness of the fanatic is that those whom he fights have a secret hold upon him; and to this weakness he and his group finally succumb.

It is not always personal doubt that undermines and empties a system of ideas and values. It can be the fact that they are no longer understood in their original power of expressing the human situation and of answering existential human questions. (This is largely the case with the doctrinal symbols of Christianity.) Or they lose their meaning because the actual conditions of the present period are so different from those in which the spiritual contents were created that new creations are needed. (This was largely the case with artistic expression before the industrial revolution.) In such circumstances a slow process of waste of the spiritual contents occurs, unnoticeable in the beginning, realized with a shock as it progresses, producing the anxiety of meaninglessness at its end.

Ontic and spiritual self-affirmation must be distinguished but they cannot be separated. Man's being includes his relation to meanings. He is human only by understanding and shaping reality, both his world and himself, according to meanings and values. His being is spiritual even in the most primitive expressions of the most primitive human being. In the "first" meaningful sentence all the richness of man's spiritual life is potentially present. Therefore the threat to his spiritual being is a threat to his whole being. The most revealing expression of this fact is the desire to throw away one's ontic existence rather than stand the despair of emptiness and meaninglessness. The death instinct is not an ontic but a spiritual phenomenon. Freud identified this reaction to the meaninglessness of the never-ceasing and never-satisfied libido with man's essential nature. But it is only an expression of his existential self-estrangement and of the disintegration of his spiritual life into meaninglessness. If, on the other hand, the ontic self-affirmation is weakened by nonbeing, spiritual indifference and emptiness can be the consequence, producing a circle of ontic and spiritual negativity. Nonbeing threatens from both sides, the ontic and the spiritual; if it threatens the one side it also threatens the other.

The Anxiety of Guilt and Condemnation
Nonbeing threatens from a third side; it threatens man's moral self-affirmation. Man's being, ontic as well as spiritual, is not only given to him but also demanded of him. He is responsible for it; literally, he is required to answer, if he is asked, what he has made of himself. He who asks him is his judge, namely he himself, who, at the same time, stands against him. This situation produces the anxiety which, in relative terms, is the anxiety of guilt; in absolute terms, the anxiety of self-rejection or condemnation. Man is essentially "finite freedom"; freedom not in the sense of indeterminacy but in the sense of being able to determine himself through deci-

sions in the center of his being. Man, as finite freedom, is free within the contingencies of his finitude. But within these limits he is asked to make of himself what he is supposed to become, to fulfill his destiny. In every act of moral self-affirmation man contributes to the fulfillment of his destiny, to the actualization of what he potentially is. It is the task of ethics to describe the nature of this fulfillment, in philosophical or theological terms. But however the norm is formulated man has the power of acting against it, of contradicting his essential being, of losing his destiny. And under the conditions of man's estrangement from himself this is an actuality. Even in what he considers his best deed nonbeing is present and prevents it from being perfect. A profound ambiguity between good and evil permeates everything he does, because it permeates his personal being as such. Nonbeing is mixed with being in his moral self-affirmation as it is in his spiritual and ontic self-affirmation. The awareness of this ambiguity is the feeling of guilt. The judge who is oneself and who stands against oneself, he who "knows with" (conscience) everything we do and are, gives a negative judgment, experienced by us as guilt. The anxiety of guilt shows the same complex characteristics as the anxiety about ontic and spiritual nonbeing. It is present in every moment of moral self-awareness and can drive us toward complete self-rejection, to the feeling of being condemned—not to an external punishment but to the despair of having lost our destiny.

To avoid this extreme situation man tries to transform the anxiety of guilt into moral action regardless of its imperfection and ambiguity. Courageously he takes nonbeing into his moral self-affirmation. This can happen in two ways, according to the duality of the tragic and the personal in man's situation, the first based on the contingencies of fate, the second on the responsibility of freedom. The first way can lead to a defiance of negative judgments and the moral demands on which they are based; the second way can lead to a moral rigor and the self-satisfaction derived from it. In both of them—usually called anomism and legalism—the anxiety of guilt lies in the background and breaks again and again into the open, producing the extreme situation of moral despair.

Nonbeing in a moral respect must be distinguished but cannot be separated from ontic and spiritual nonbeing. The anxiety of the one type is immanent in the anxieties of the other types. The famous words of Paul about "sin as the sting of death" point to the immanence of the anxiety of guilt within the fear of death. And the threat of fate and death has always awakened and increased the consciousness of guilt. The threat of moral nonbeing was experienced in and through the threat of ontic nonbeing. The contingencies of fate received moral interpretation: fate executes the negative moral judgment by attacking and perhaps destroying the ontic foundation of the morally rejected personality. The two forms of anxiety provoke and augment each other. In the same way spiritual and moral nonbeing are interdependent. Obedience to the moral norm, i.e. to one's own essential being, excludes emptiness and meaninglessness in their radical forms. If the spiritual contents have lost their power the self-affirmation of the moral personality is a way in which meaning can be rediscovered. The simple call to duty can save from emptiness, while the disintegration of the moral consciousness is an almost irresistible basis for the attack of spiritual nonbeing. On the other hand, existential doubt can undermine moral self-affirmation by throwing into the abyss of skepticism not only every moral principle but the meaning of moral self-affirmation as such. In this case the doubt is felt as guilt, while at the same time guilt is undermined by doubt.

The Meaning of Despair

The three types of anxiety are interwoven in such a way that one of them gives the predominant color but all of them participate in the coloring of the state of anxiety. All of them and their underlying unity are existential, i.e. they are implied in the existence of man as man, his finitude, and his estrangement. They are fulfilled in the situation of despair to which all of them contribute. Despair is an ultimate or "boundary-line" situation. One cannot go beyond it. Its nature is indicated in the etymology of the word despair: without hope. No way out into the future appears. Nonbeing is felt as absolutely victorious. But there is a limit to its victory; nonbeing is *felt* as victorious, and feeling .presupposes being. Enough being is left to feel the irresistible power of nonbeing, and this is the despair within the despair. The pain of despair is that a being is aware of itself as unable to affirm itself because of the power of nonbeing. Consequently it wants to surrender this awareness and its presupposition, the being which is aware. It wants to get rid of itself—and it cannot. Despair appears in the form of reduplication, as the desperate attempt to escape despair. If anxiety were only the anxiety of fate and death, voluntary death would be the way out of despair. The courage demanded would be the courage *not* to be. The final form of ontic self-affirmation would be the act of ontic self-negation.

But despair is also the despair about guilt and condemnation. And there is no way of escaping it, even by ontic self-negation. Suicide can liberate one from the anxiety of fate and death—as the Stoics knew. But it cannot liberate from the anxiety of guilt and condemnation, as the Christians know. This is a highly paradoxical statement, as paradoxical as the relation of the moral sphere to ontic existence generally. But it is a true statement, verified by those who have experienced fully the despair of condemnation. It is impossible to express the inescapable character of condemnation in ontic terms, that is in terms of imaginings about the "immortality of the soul." For every ontic statement must use the categories of finitude, and "immortality of the soul" would be the endless prolongation of finitude and of the despair of condemnation (a self-contradictory concept, for "finis" means "end"). The experience, therefore, that suicide is no way of escaping guilt must be understood in terms of the qualitative character of the moral demand, and of the qualitative character of its rejection. Guilt and condemnation are qualitatively, not quantitatively, infinite. They have an infinite weight and cannot be removed by a finite act of ontic self-negation. This makes despair desperate, that is, inescapable. There is "No Exit" from it (Sartre). The anxiety of emptiness and meaninglessness participates in both the ontic and the moral element in despair. Insofar as it is an expression of finitude it can be removed by ontic self-negation: This drives radical skepticism to suicide. Insofar as it is a consequence of moral disintegration it produces the same paradox as the moral element in despair: there is no ontic exit from it. This frustrates the suicidal trends in emptiness and meaninglessness. One is aware of their futility.

In view of this character of despair it is understandable that all human life can be interpreted as a continuous attempt to avoid despair. And this attempt is mostly successful. Extreme situations are not reached frequently and perhaps they are never reached by some people. The purpose of an analysis of such a situation is not to record ordinary human experiences but to show extreme possibilities in the light of which the ordinary situations must be understood. We are not always aware of our having to die, but in the light of the experience of our having to die our whole life is experienced differently. In the same way the anxiety which is despair is not always present. But the rare occasions in which it is present determine the interpretation of existence as a whole.

Periods of Anxiety

The distinction of the three types of anxiety is supported by the history of Western civilization. We find that at the end of ancient civilization ontic anxiety is predominant, at the end of the Middle Ages moral anxiety, and at the end of the modern period spiritual anxiety. But in spite of the predominance of one type the others are also present and effective.

Enough has been said about the end of the ancient period and its anxiety of fate and death in connection with an analysis of Stoic courage. The sociological background is well known: the conflict of the imperial powers, Alexander's conquest of the East, the war between his followers, the conquest of West and East by republican Rome, the transformation of republican into imperial Rome through Caesar and Augustus, the tyranny of the post-Augustan emperors, the destruction of the independent city and nation states, the eradication of the former bearers of the aristocratic-democratic structure of society, the individual's feeling of being in the hands of powers, natural as well as political, which are completely beyond his control and calculation—all this produced a tremendous anxiety and the quest to meet the threat of fate and death. At the same time the anxiety of emptiness and meaninglessness made it impossible for many people, especially of the educated classes, to find a basis for such courage. Ancient Skepticism from its very beginning in the Sophists united scholarly and existential elements. Skepticism in its late ancient form was despair about the possibility of right acting as well as right thinking. It drove people into the desert where the necessity for decisions, theoretical and practical, is reduced to a minimum. But most of those who experienced the anxiety of emptiness and the despair of meaninglessness tried to meet them with a cynical contempt of spiritual self-affirmation. Yet they could not hide the anxiety under skeptical arrogance. The anxiety of guilt and condemnation was effective in the groups who gathered in the mystery cults with their rites of expiation and purification. Sociologically these circles of the initiated were rather indefinite. In most of them even slaves were admitted. In them, however, as in the whole non-Jewish ancient world more the tragic than the personal guilt was experienced. Guilt is the pollution of the soul by the material realm or by demonic powers. Therefore the anxiety of guilt remains a secondary element, as does the anxiety of emptiness, within the dominating anxiety of fate and death.

Only the impact of the Jewish-Christian message changed this situation, and so radically that toward the end of the Middle Ages the anxiety of guilt and condemnation was decisive. If one period deserves the name of the "age of anxiety" it is the pre-Reformation and Reformation. The anxiety of condemnation symbolized as the "wrath of God" and intensified by the imagery of hell and purgatory drove people of the late Middle Ages to try various means of assuaging their anxiety: pilgrimages to holy places, if possible to Rome; ascetic exercises, sometimes of an extreme character; devotion to relics, often brought together in mass collections; acceptance of ecclesiastical punishments and the desire for indulgences; exaggerated participation in masses and penance, increase in prayers and alms. In short they asked ceaselessly: How can I appease the wrath of God, how can I attain divine mercy, the forgiveness of sin? This predominant form of anxiety embraced the other two forms. The personified figure of death appeared in painting, poetry, and preaching. But it was death and guilt together. Death and the devil were allied in the anxious imagination of the period. The anxiety of fate returned with the invasion of late antiquity. "Fortuna" became a preferred symbol in the art of the Renaissance, and even the Reformers were not free from astrological beliefs and fears. And the anxiety of fate was intensified by fear of demonic powers acting directly or through other human beings to cause illness, death, and all kinds of destruction. At the same time, fate was extended beyond death into the pre-ultimate state of purgatory and the ultimate states of hell or heaven. The darkness of ultimate destiny could not be removed; not even the Reformers were able to remove it, as their doctrine of predestination shows. In all these expressions the anxiety of fate appears as an element within the all-embracing anxiety of guilt and in the permanent awareness of the threat of condemnation.

The late Middle Ages was not a period of doubt; and the anxiety of emptiness and loss of meaning appeared only twice, both remarkable occasions, however, and important for the future. One was the Renaissance, when theoretical skepticism was renewed and the question of meaning haunted some of the most sensitive minds. In Michelangelo's prophets and sibyls and in Shakespeare's *Hamlet* there are indications of a potential anxiety of meaninglessness. The other was in the demonic assaults that Luther experienced, which were neither temptations in the moral sense nor moments of despair about threatening condemnation, but moments when belief in his work and message disappeared and no meaning remained. Similar experiences of the "desert" or the "night" of the soul are frequent among mystics. It must be emphasized however that in all these cases the anxiety of guilt remained predominant, and that only after the victory of humanism and Enlightenment as the religious foundation of Western society could anxiety about spiritual nonbeing become dominant.

The sociological cause of the anxiety of guilt and condemnation that arose at the end of the Middle Ages is not difficult to identify. In general one can say it was the dissolution of the protective unity of the religiously guided medieval culture. More specifically there must be emphasized the rise of an educated middle class in the larger cities, people who tried to have as their own experience what had been merely an objective, hierarchically controlled system of doctrines and sacraments. In this attempt, however, they were driven to hidden or open conflict with the Church, whose authority they still acknowledged. There must be emphasized the concentration of political power in the princes and their bureaucratic-military administration, which eliminated the independence of those lower in the feudal system. There must be emphasized the state absolutism which transformed the masses in city and country into "subjects" whose only duty was to work and to obey, without any power to resist the arbitrariness of the absolute rulers. There must be emphasized the economic catastrophes connected with early capitalism, such as the importation of gold from the New World, expropriation of the peasants, and so on. In all these often-described changes it is the conflict between the appearance of independent tendencies in all groups of society, on the one hand, and the rise of an absolutist concentration of power on the other that is largely responsible for the predominance of the anxiety of guilt. The irrational, commanding, absolute God of nominalism and the Reformation is partly shaped by the social, political, and spiritual absolutism of the period; and the anxiety created in turn by his image is partly an expression of the anxiety produced by the basic social conflict of the disintegrating Middle Ages.

The breakdown of absolutism, the development of liberalism and democracy, the rise of a technical civilization with its victory over all enemies and its own beginning disintegration—these are the sociological presupposition for the third main period of anxiety. In this the anxiety of emptiness and meaninglessness is dominant. We are under the threat of spiritual nonbeing. The threats of moral and ontic nonbeing are, of course, present, but they are not independent and not controlling. This situation is so fundamental to the question raised in this book that it requires fuller analysis than the two earlier periods, and the analysis must be correlated with the constructive solution.

It is significant that the three main periods of anxiety appear at the end of an era. The anxiety which, in its different forms, is potentially present in every individual becomes general if the accustomed structures of meaning, power, belief, and order disintegrate. These structures, as long as they are in force, keep anxiety bound within a protective system of courage of participation. The individual who participates in the institutions and ways of life of such a system is not liberated from his personal anxieties but he has means of overcoming them with well-known methods. In periods of great changes these methods no longer work. Conflicts between the old, which tries to maintain itself, often with new means, and the new, which deprives the old of its intrinsic power, produce anxiety in all directions. Nonbeing, in such a situation, has a double face, resembling two types of nightmare (which are perhaps, expressions of an awareness of these two faces). The one type is the anxiety of annihilating narrowness, of the impossibility of escape and the horror of being trapped. The other is the anxiety of annihilating openness, of infinite, formless space into which one falls without a place to fall upon. Social situations like those described have the character both of a trap without exit and of an empty, dark, and unknown void. Both faces of the same reality arouse the latent anxiety of every individual who looks at them. Today most of us do look at them.

Selected Annotated Bibliography

The following bibliography is intended to be neither exhaustive nor definitive. It is a personal and extremely selective list of works of and on existentialism and phenomenology chosen to provide a wider context and to shed a deeper light on the fundamental philosophical and literary issues emphasized in this anthology. I have not entered philosophical works from which selections have been made for the text. Also, the list of entries, with one of two significant exceptions, does not include studies of individual philosophers.

One of the criteria used in the selection of entries on existential literature has been recentness of publication. For earlier criticism and commentary consult (1) Kenneth Douglas, A Critical Bibliography of Existentialism *(The Paris School),* Yale French Studies *Monograph No. 1 (New Haven, Conn., 1950); (2) Richard Lehan, "French and American Philosophical and Literary Existentialism: A Selected Checklist,"* Wisconsin Studies in Contemporary Literature, *Vol. I, No. 3 (Fall 1960), 74–88; and (3) the bibliography on Jean-Paul Sartre in* Yale French Studies *No. 30 (New Haven, Conn., 1962), pp. 108–119. The student of literature should also avail himself of the annual* PMLA *bibliographical supplements and* MLA Abstracts of Articles in Scholarly Journals, Abstracts of English Studies, *and the annual indices and occasional bibliographic supplements of such periodicals as* Partisan Review, Yale French Studies, Modern Drama, Contemporary Literature, boundary 2, Journal of Modern Literature, Mosaic, Tulane Drama Review (*now* The Drama Review), New Literary History, *and* Diacritics.

The editions given are, in most cases, the most accessible.

I. PHILOSOPHY AND THEOLOGY

Altizer, Thomas J., and William Hamilton. *Radical Theology and the Death of God.* Indianapolis, Ind.: Bobbs-Merrill, 1966. A controversial expression, in a series of essays on literature and pop culture, of the "Death of God" theology in America.

Barth, Karl. *Epistle to the Romans.* Tr. Edwyn C. Hoskyns. London: Oxford University Press, 1933. The interpretation of Paul's *Epistle,* written during World War I, which, in attempting to give existential immediacy to the Christian message generated the central issue of Christian existentialism: how to interpret Scripture so it speaks to man in the present. It is, thus, one of the fundamental sources of the renewed interest in literary hermeneutics.

Berdyaev, Nicolas. *Dream and Reality: An Essay in Autobiography.* New York: Macmillan, 1951. An autobiographical record of the development of Berdyaev's Christian existentialism, which is grounded in his radical interpretation of Russian Orthodoxy and in his sense of identity with Fédor Dostoevski.

Bergson, Henri. *Time and Free Will: An Essay on the Immediate Data of Consciousness.* Translated by F. L. Pogson. New York: Macmillan, 1910. In

433

its critique of the scientific impulse to spatialize (solidify) duration (the temporality of conscious states), this book is an important precursor of existential philosophy.

Binswanger, Ludwig. *Being-in-the-World: Selected Papers of Ludwig Binswanger.* Edited with Critical Introduction by Jacob Needleman. New York: Basic Books, 1963. This book contains the essential statements of Binswanger's *Daseinanalyse,* which constitute an existential corrective of frentic psychoanalysis from the point of view of his understanding of Heidegger's thought in *Being and Time.* It also includes an excellent account and evaluation of Binswanger's existential psychoanalysis by the editor.

Bonhoeffer, Dietrich. *Letters and Papers from Prison.* Translated by Reginald Fuller. Edited by Eberhard Bethge. London: William Collins, 1959. The moving meditations, written before his execution by the Nazis, in which Bonhoeffer works out his understanding of the role of the Christian in a world which has "come of age," that is, in which God is absent.

Buber, Martin. *I and Thou.* 2d ed. Translated by Ronald Gregor Smith. New York: Scribner, 1958. The great and influential meditation on the possibility of dialogue between man and man, and man and God, based on Buber's Hasidic roots.

Bultmann, Rudolph. "New Testament and Mythology." In *Kerygma and Myth: A Theological Debate,* edited by H. W. Bartsch. Translated by Reginald H. Fuller. New York: Harper Torchbooks, 1961. The controversial essay on "demythologizing" that is the Christian counterpart of Heidegger's de-struction of the Western philosophical tradition.

Cox, Harvey. *The Secular City.* New York: Macmillan, 1965. A brilliant analysis, written from a Christian point of view, of the rise of urban civilization and the decline of traditional religion that suggests the dangers and the potential inhering in this "coming of age" of modern man (as Bonhoeffer puts it).

De Beauvoir, Simone. *The Prime of Life.* Translated by Peter Green. London: André Deutsch and Weidenfeld and Nicolson, 1962. The second of a four-volume autobiography by one of the great women of our time, this work deals with the period in her life—and in modern European history—that witnessed the emergence of Parisian existentialism in the context of the fall of France and the Resistance.

De Unamuno, Miguel. *The Tragic Sense of Life.* Translated by J. E. Crawford Flitch. New York: Dover, 1954. Revealing the influence of Kierkegaard, this great book explores the human condition in terms of the tragic contradiction between the human desire for immortality and the existential reality of death.

Derrida, Jacques. "Differance." In *Speech and Phenomena and Other Essays on Husserl's Theory of Signs.* Translated with Introduction by David B. Allison and Preface by Newton Garver. Evanston, Ill.: Northwestern University Press, 1973, pp. 129–160.

_____. "Structure, Sign, and Play in the Discourse of the Human Sciences." In *The Structuralist Controversy: The Language of Criticism and the Sciences of Man,* edited by Richard Macksey and Eugenio Donato. Baltimore, Md.: Johns Hopkins Press, 1972, pp. 265–272. Both the above entries of the French Heideggerian attempt to lay the foundations for the deconstruction of the teleological (logocentric) philosophical (and literary) tradition by perceiving the "beginning" (origin) as the "absence of presence," that is, la differance.

Frankl, Victor E. *Man's Search for Meaning: An Introduction to Logotherapy.* New York: Washington Square Press, 1963. A moving autobiographical account of the author's experience at Auschwitz and how it contributed to his development of an existential psychotherapy.

Gadamer, Hans-George. *Truth and Method: Fundamentals of a Philosophical Hermeneutic.* London: Sheed & Ward, 1975. Based on Martin Heidegger's meditations on the temporality of human understanding, this important work in hermeneutics (interpretation theory) is becoming an influential point of departure for the critique of New Critical interpretation and the development of an existential/ phenomenological mode of interpreting literary texts.

Heidegger, Martin. *Discourse on Thinking.* Originally published as *Gelassenheit.* Translated by John M. Anderson and E. Hans Freund. New York: Harper Torchbooks, 1966. An expression, partially in dialogue form, of the kind of meditative thinking (letting be or letting Being be) the later Heidegger opposes to Western "calculative thought," which is characterized by the "will to power" of the things it addresses.

———. *Poetry, Language, Thought.* Translated with Introduction by Albert Hofstadter. New York: Harper & Row, 1971. A collection of beautifully translated essays on literature and art drawn from the period between 1935 and 1960 and grounded in the meditative thinking articulated in *Gelassenheit* (translated as *Discourse on Thinking*).

Husserl, Edmund. *Phenomenology and the Crisis of Philosophy.* Translated with Notes and Introduction by Quentin Lauer. New York: Harper & Row, 1965. Contains two seminal essays on phenomenology from the beginning and end of Husserl's career, "Philosophy as Rigorous Science" (1910–1911) and "Philosophy and the Crisis of European Man" (1935), both of which point critically to the metaphysical prejudice underlying Western science and, in opposition, stress the need to "return to the things themselves."

James, William. *The Varieties of Religious Experience: A Study in Human Nature.* New York: Longman's, Green, 1925. In attacking rationalism on behalf of individual experience, this American early modern work is a significant precursor of European existentialism. It also points to his latter *Essays in Radical Empiricism* (1912), which, in returning to the things themselves, participates in the emergence of phenomenology.

Jaspers, Karl. *Man in the Modern Age.* Translated by Eden and Cedar Paul. Garden City, N.Y.: Doubleday Anchor Books, 1951. Written in 1931 prior to the rise of national socialism, this work is an existential analysis and critique of the modern world's commitment to "technique and apparatus" and the dehumanized mass-man society it creates and nourishes.

Kierkegaard, Soren. *Either/Or.* Vols. I–II. Translated by O. F. and L. M. Swenson and Walter Lowrie, revised by H. S. Johnson. Princeton, N.J.: Princeton University Press, 1959. A pseudonymous critique of the aesthetic stage from the point of view of the existential ethical stage, where choices must be made.

———. *Repetition: An Essay in Experimental Psychology.* Translated with Introduction by Walter Lowrie. New York: Harper Torchbooks, 1964. A pseudonymous "novel" that enacts the existential deconstruction of the aesthetic perspective *aeterno modo.*

Laing, R. D. *The Divided Self: An Existential Study in Sanity and Madness.* Baltimore, Md.: Penguin, 1965. An existential study of schizophrenia, including case studies, based on a psychoanalytic theory derived primarily from Heidegger's *Being and Time.*

Macquarrie, John. *An Existential Theology: A Comparison of Heidegger and Bultmann.* New York: Harper Torchbooks, 1965. In the words of Bultmann's preface, "the author gives a picture of an 'existential theology' by showing how the hermeneutic principle which underlies my interpretation of the New Testament arises out of the existential analysis of man's being given by Martin Heidegger in his work, *Being and Time.*"

Marcel, Gabriel. *The Mystery of Being.* 2 vols. Translated by G. S. Fraser and Rene Hague. Chicago: Regnery, 1960. As the title suggests the essential concern of this major work of the Catholic existentialist theologian (and playwright), Gabriel Marcel, is the preservation of the *mystery* of existence from the rationalist impulse to objectify it, that is, to perceive existence as a problem solvable by the objective or disinterested observer.

Merleau-Ponty, Maurice. *Sense and Non-Sense.* Translated with Preface by Hubert L. Dreyfus and Patricia Allen Dreyfus. Evanston, Ill.: Northwestern University Press, 1964. Written between 1945 and 1947, these essays treat themes in the arts, ideas and politics from the point of view of Merleau-Ponty's phenomenology of perception and existentialism and provide a good introduction to his thought.

Nietzsche, Friedrich. "The Use and Abuse of History." In *Thoughts Out of Season,* Part II. *The Complete Works of Friedrich Nietzsche,* edited by Oscar Levy. Vol. V. New York: Russell & Russell, 1964. Basically an attack on "metaphysical" or Hegelian historical thinking, this little book provides an excellent introduction to Nietzsche's proto-existential thought.

Ortega y Gasset, José. *The Revolt of the Masses.* Translator anonymous. New York: Norton, 1957. A powerful and provocative proto-existential diagnosis of the emergence of man to public power in the modern world.

Robinson, John A. T. *Honest to God.* London: SCM Press, 1963. This controversial little book by the Anglican Bishop of Woolwich is a radical expression of the "death of God theology" in England and is grounded in the Christian existential thought of Paul Tillich and Deitrich Bonhoeffer.

Sartre, Jean-Paul. *Being and Nothingness: An Essay in Phenomenological Ontology.* Special abridged ed. Translated with Introduction by Hazel E. Barnes. New York: Citadel, 1964. Sartre's fullest expression of his existentialism prior to his "conversion" to Marxism, this book has been one of the most influential of this century.

———. *The Words.* Translated by Bernard Frechtman. New York: Braziller, 1964. Sartre's moving autobiographical account of his discovery of the problematics hidden in the relationship between Word and words, Being and language.

Strauss, Erwin W. *Phenomenological Psychology: The Selected Papers.* Translated, in part, by Erling Eng. New York: Basic Books, 1966. Reacting against the metaphysical presuppositions of behavioral psychology, these essays ground psychology in Husserl's phenomenological imperative to "return to the things themselves," that is, the situation of psychological investigation in the lived world (*Lebenswelt*).

Thévenaz, Pierre. *What Is Phenomenology? and Other Essays.* Edited with Introduction by James M. Edie. Translated by James M. Edie, Charles Courtney, and Paul Brockelman. New York: Quadrangle, 1962. Extremely lucid essays on the development of phenomenology from Husserl to Heidegger, Sartre and Merleau-Ponty; and on the phenomenological question of origins, the "point of departure."

Tillich, Paul. *Systematic Theology.* 3 vols. Chicago: University of Chicago Press, 1963. The most important and influential expression of Protestant existential thought written in this century.

II. ON EXISTENTIAL PHILOSOPHY AND THEOLOGY

Barrett, William. *Irrational Man: A Study in Existential Philosophy.* Garden City, N.Y.: Doubleday Anchor Books, 1958. Despite its limited reference to phenomenology, this study is still the best general introduction to existential thought in print. In pointing to its historical sources and showing its relationship with the literature, art, and science of our time, this book reveals that existentialism is more a mode of consciousness than a philosophical "system" of thought.

Blackham, H. J. *Six Existential Thinkers.* London: Routledge & Kegan Paul, 1952. Intended as "exposition, not criticism nor advocacy," this introduction, which was influential in introducing existentialism to English readers, presents excellent essays on Kierkegaard, Nietzsche, Jaspers, Marcel, Heidegger, and Sartre which both discriminate between each and attempt to show their relationships.

Catalano, Joseph S. *A Commentary on Jean-Paul Sartre's "Being and Nothingness."* New York: Harper Torchbooks, 1974. A useful—and readily accessible—guide to the reading and understanding of one of the most important—and difficult—works of existential thought.

Farber, Marvin. *The Foundations of Phenomenology: Edmund Husserl and the Quest for a Rigorous Science of Philosophy.* 3d ed. Albany: State University of New York Press, 1968. Written by a former student of Husserl, this difficult but authoritative book traces the development of Husserl's phenomenology from the beginning to the end of his career, offering on the way a critique of his master's tendency toward idealism in favor of his interpretation of phenomenology as a descriptive philosophical method.

Gelven, Michael. *A Commentary on Heidegger's "Being and Time."* New York: Harper Torchbooks, 1970. In "translating" Heidegger's forbidding technical jargon into direct language, this section-by-section interpretation becomes a valuable introduction to one of the most important philosophical works of the twentieth century.

Grene, Marjorie. *Introduction to Existentialism*. Chicago: University of Chicago Press, 1959. First published as *Dreadful Freedom* in 1948, this study (primarily on Kierkegaard, Sartre, Heidegger, Jaspers, and Marcel) is both a lucid and an articulate critique of "existentialism as the attempt at a new 'revaluation of values'."

Heinemann, F. H. *Existentialism and the Modern Predicament*. New York: Harper Torchbooks, 1958. Written by an existentialist philosopher with theistic leanings, this study constitutes a lucid exposition of existential thought and a critique of its limitations (the tendency to systematize existence) from the point of view of an existential "Philosophy of Response."

Kockelmans, Joseph J., ed. *Phenomenology: The Philosophy of Edmund Husserl and Its Interpretation*. Garden City, N.Y.: Doubleday Anchor Books, 1967. A valuable collection of basic readings tracing phenomenology from its origins in Husserl to Heidegger, Sartre, and Merleau-Ponty and suggesting the applicability of its methodology to the sciences of man.

Kuhn, Helmut. *Encounter with Nothingness: An Essay on Existentialism*. London: Methuen, 1951. An early but still valuable critical interpretation of the varieties of existential thought (including a discussion of the relation between existentialism and Husserlian phenomenology) written for the general reader from a Christian point of view.

Lee, Edward N., and Mandelbaum, Maurice. *Phenomenology and Existentialism*. Baltimore, Md.: Johns Hopkins Press, 1962. Focusing on diverse but central figures and topics in the existential/phenomenological movement in philosophy, this significant collection of essays by some of the foremost American commentators is addressed primarily to advanced students, but, in dealing with the basic issues, serves as an equally valuable introduction to these areas of philosophical thought and their problematic relationship.

Macomber, W. R. *The Anatomy of Disillusion: Martin Heidegger's Notion of Truth*. Evanston, Ill.: Northwestern University Press, 1967. An excellent exposition of Heidegger's version of phenomenology and how it relates to his ontology and existentialism.

Macquarrie, John. *The Scope of Demythologizing: Bultmann and His Critics*. New York: Harper Torchbooks, 1966. A study of Rudolph Bultmann's controversial demythologizing of Christianity and the theological problems his existential approach to the biblical texts generates, this book illuminates the basic ground of the radical theology of Christian existentialism. In the context of *A Casebook on Existentialism*, it also suggests the continuity between Heidegger's "destruction," Bultmann's "demythologizing," and Derrida's "deconstruction," and the recent efforts to develop a "postmodern"—existential/phenomenological—theory of interpretation of literary texts (hermeneutics).

Marx, Werner. *Heidegger and the Tradition*. Translated by Theodore Kissel and Murray Greene. Evanston, Ill.: Northwestern University Press, 1971. Decisive in Professor Marx's appointment as successor to the chair at Freiburg University formerly occupied by Husserl and Heidegger, this important book is an interpretation and extension of Heidegger's "destruction" of the Western metaphysical tradition.

Michalson, Carl, ed. *Christianity and the Existentialists.* New York: Scribner, 1956. An early but still important book of essays on the implications of humanistic and Christian existentialism for the arts and sciences of man. Especially valuable is Stanley Romaine Hopper's essay "On the naming of the gods in Hölderlin and Rilke," pp. 148–189.

Murchland, Bernard. *The Age of Alienation.* New York: Random House, 1971. A broad analysis of the meaning(s) of cultural "alienation," including a valuable account of its historical sources, and of the possibilities of "de-alienation."

Palmer, Richard E. *Hermeneutics: Interpretation Theory in Schleiermacher, Dilthey, Heidegger, and Gadamer.* Evanston, Ill.: Northwestern University Press, 1969. In pointing phenomenologically to some of the fundamental limitations of the New Criticism (the critical counterpart of early Modernist literature), this study suggests the potential importance of an existential/phenomenological hermeneutics for a "postmodern" understanding of literary texts.

Reinhardt, Karl F. *The Existential Revolt.* 2d ed. with an Appendix on Existential Psychotherapy. New York: Ungar, 1960. A standard account of existential thought (Kierkegaard, Nietzsche, Heidegger, Jaspers, Sartre, and Marcel) from a sympathetic Thomist point of view.

Roberts, David E. *Existentialism and Religious Belief.* New York: Oxford University Press, 1959. This book, which contains critical analyses of Pascal, Kierkegaard, Heidegger, Sartre, Jaspers, and Marcel is still the best (and most lucid) introduction to existentialism written from a Christian existentialist point of view.

Roubiczek, Paul. *Existentialism: For and Against.* London: Cambridge University Press, 1964. Presented with the predominantly empirical British philosophical tradition in mind, this book constitutes both an exposition of existential thought and a critique that attempts to reconcile the "objectivity" of science and the "subjectivity" of existentialism.

Schrader, George Alfred, Jr., ed. *Existential Philosophers: Kierkegaard to Merleau-Ponty.* New York: McGraw-Hill, 1967. An excellent (and accessible) series of interpretations of the whole work of Kierkegaard, Jaspers, Heidegger, Marcel, Sartre, and Merleau-Ponty by American specialists in existential philosophy. The book also contains useful bibliographies of the work of each figure studied.

Scott, Nathan J., Jr. *The Unquiet Vision: Mirrors of Man in Existentialism.* New York: World Publishing Co., 1969. Written from a Christian existentialist point of view, this is a lucid study of Kierkegaard, Nietzsche, Camus, Sartre, and Buber relating their biographies to their existential thought.

Spiegelberg, Herbert. *The Phenomenological Movement: A Historical Introduction.* 2 vols. The Hague: Martinus Nijhoff, 1960. A definitive and thus indispensable historical study of the development of phenomenology from its origins in Husserl and his contemporaries to Heidegger and others.

Zaner, Richard M., and Don Ihde. *Phenomenology and Existentialism.* New York: Putnam, 1973. A well-chosen collection of essays by the major figures of the movement that attempts to suggest the integral relationship between phenomenology and existentialism.

III. ON EXISTENTIAL LITERATURE

Abbott, H. Porter. *The Fiction of Samuel Beckett: Form and Effect.* Berkeley: University of California Press, 1973. A valuable introductory study of imitative form in Beckett's fiction, this book suggests the relationship between the crisis content, the open form, and the engaged response of the reader.

Barrett, William. *Time of Need: Forms of Imagination in the Twentieth Century.* New York: Harper Torchbooks, 1973. An important book that begins the task of discovering the formal imperatives (especially for the novel, but also for the other arts) of the reality undergoing radical change in our time.

Barth, John. "The Literature of Exhaustion." *Atlantic Monthly,* Vol. 220, No. 2 (August 1967), 29–34. In stressing the metaphor of the labyrinth as fundamental to the exhaustion of traditional fictional forms, this famous essay on the "postmodernism" of Borges and Beckett, is ultimately about Barth's own novels.

Beckett, Samuel, and Georges Duthuit. "Three Dialogues." In *Samuel Beckett: A Collection of Critical Essays,* edited by Martin Esslin. Englewood Cliffs, N.J.: Prentice-Hall, 1965. An important statement in dialogue form of Beckett's philosophical/artistic commitments.

Bernheimer, Charles C. "The Literary Space of Gogol's 'Overcoat.' " *PMLA,* Vol. 90 (January 1975), 53–61. This excellent essay serves as a valuable model for those wishing to approach texts in terms of exploring the relationship between existential content and literary form.

Bové, Paul A. "Cleanth Brooks and Modern Irony: A Kierkegaardian Critique," Paper No. 3, University Seminar in Postmodernism. Binghamton, N.Y.: Graduate Office, SUNY at Binghamton, 1975. Forthcoming in *boundary 2,* Vol. 4, No. 3 (Spring 1976). A persuasive critique of the New Critical (and early Modernist) commitment to closed forms based on the analogy of Kierkegaard's existential critique of the "ironic" stance of the "aesthetic stage."

Clive, Geoffrey. *The Broken Icon: Intuitive Existentialism in Classical Russian Fiction.* New York: Macmillan, 1972. An "ideological and philosophical rather than literary" study of Gogol, Dostoevski, Goncharov, Tolstoi, and Solzenitsyn, this book attempts to show that, more than the European philosophers, the nineteenth-century Russian novelist "grasped the ambiguities of Reason and Existence that continue to puzzle and haunt contemporary man."

_____. *The Romantic Enlightenment: Ambiguity and Paradox in the Western Mind (1750–1920).* New York: Meridian, 1960.

De Man, Paul. *Blindness and Insight: Essays in the Rhetoric of Contemporary Criticism.* New York: Oxford University Press, 1971. A brilliant and influential analysis of the prevailing methodologies of modern criticism from, broadly, the vantage point of phenomenological deconstruction.

Detweiler, Robert. "The Moment of Death in Modern Fiction." *Contemporary Literature,* Vol. 13 (Summer 1972), 269–294. A suggestive application of existential accounts (mainly Heidegger's) of the phenomenology of death and dying to a wide range of works of modern fiction.

Driver, Tom F. "Beckett by the Madeleine: An Interview." *Columbia University Forum,* Vol. IV (Summer 1961), 21–25. A moving insight into the existential sources of Beckett's fiction and drama.

_____. *The Sense of History in Greek and Shakespearean Drama.* New York: Columbia University Press, 1960. An extremely important—and unfortunately neglected—book distinguishing between the Greek and Shakespearean sense of time from a Tillichean existential point of view.

Ellman, Richard, and Charles Feidelson, Jr., eds. *The Modern Tradition: Background of Modern Literature.* New York: Oxford University Press, 1965. A useful source book of primary material from essays, letters, novels, and philosophy, that, together, suggest the continuities and differences of the intellectual and literary life of the twentieth century.

Esslin, Martin. *The Theatre of the Absurd.* Garden City, N.Y.: Doubleday Anchor Books, 1961. An early, but still useful account of the intellectual and artistic roots and the early development of the existential drama of the absurd.

Harper, Ralph. *The Seventh Solitude: Metaphysical Homelessness in Kierkegaard, Dostoevsky and Nietzsche.* Baltimore, Md.: Johns Hopkins Press, 1965. A sensitive analysis and critique of the varieties of existential solitude written from a Christian existential point of view.

Hassan, Ihab. *Radical Innocence: The Contemporary American Novel.* New York: Harper & Row, 1961. One of the best thematic interpretations of American fiction of the post-World War II decade (Styron, Mailer, Malamud, Ellison, Donleavy, McCullers, Capote, Salinger, Bellow, and so on) from a broadly existential point of view.

Heller, Erich. *The Disinherited Mind: Essays in Modern German Literature and Thought.* Harmondsworth, Middlesex: Penguin Books, 1961. A still important analysis of the consequences for modern Western man of the death of God by way of individual studies of such German writers as Goethe, Nietzsche, Burckhardt, Rilke, Spengler, Kafka, and Kraus.

Hoffman, Frederick. *The Mortal No: Death and the Modern Imagination.* Princeton, N.J.: Princeton University Press, 1964. An often brilliant analysis of the stylistic and metaphorical imperatives of the emergence of death as an primary concern of the modern imagination.

_____. *Samuel Beckett: The Language of Self.* New York: Dutton, 1964. See especially "The Underground Man: Background of the Modern Self," pp. 3–55, a valuable historical account of the emergence of the underground man as symbol of the modern existential predicament.

Holquist, Michael. "Whodunit and Other Questions: Metaphysical Detective Stories in Post-War Fiction," *New Literary History,* Vol. III (Autumn 1971), 135–156. Although this essay is not based specifically on existential ideas, its analysis of the distinction between the formal characteristics of the classic detective story and that of contemporary practitioners like Robbe-Grillet and Borges adds a significant dimension to the existential definition of postmodern fictional form.

Hopper, Stanley Romaine, and David L. Miller, eds. *Interpretation: The Poetry of Meaning.* New York: Harcourt Brace Jovanovich, 1967. First delivered as papers for the Third Consultation on Hermeneutics at Drew University, several of these essays offer valuable guidelines for existential/phenomenological reading of literary text. See especially the introduction by S. K. Hopper; Heinrich Ott, "Hermeneutics and Personhood," pp. 14–34; and Beda Alleman, "Metaphor and Antimetaphor," pp. 103–123.

Howe, Irving, ed. *The Idea of the Modern in Literature and the Arts.* New York: Horizon, 1967. A useful anthology of essential works of criticism and speculative thought that suggest the diverse impulses of Modernism, including a stimulating and even provocative, if sometimes uncertain, introduction that attempts to define "the Idea of the Modern."

Ionesco, Eugéne. *Notes and Counter Notes.* Translated by Donald Watson. New York: Grove, 1964. An important collection of notes and manifestos that suggest the existential grounds of the "absurdist" forms of Ionesco's drama.

Jameson, Fredric. *Marxism and Literary Form: Twentieth-Century Dialectical Theories of Literature.* Princeton, N.J.: Princeton University Press, 1971. A distinguished study of the new Hegelian criticism that, under the influence of phenomenology and existentialism, subordinates didactic content in favor of form in the dialectical analysis of literature and culture. The figures interpreted are the German thinkers, T. W. Adorno, Walter Benjamin, Herbert Marcuse, Ernst Block, Georg Lukacs, and the Frenchman, Jean-Paul Sartre.

Kaelin, Eugene F. *Art and Existence: A Phenomenological Aesthetics.* Lewisburg, Pa.: Bucknell University Press, 1970. Based on his previous study "An Existentialist Aesthetic: The Theories of Sartre and Merleau-Ponty," this book is a provocative effort to apply phenomenology to various kinds of aesthetic experience, though the methodology is sometimes more formal than an existential-phenomenology allows.

Kahler, Erich. *The Tower and the Abyss: An Inquiry into the Transformation of Man.* New York: Braziller, 1957. Still one of the best analyses of the predicament of modern man—the Tower (collectivity) and the Abyss (the questing self) —this sociological study draws heavily from existential writers and provides an authoritative background for the study of existential literature.

Kartiganer, Donald M. "Process and Product: A Study of Modern Literary Form," *The Massachusetts Review,* Vol. XII, Nos. 2 and 4 (Spring and Winter 1971), 297–328; 789–816. A suggestive essay on the definition of Modernism based on the distinction between open and closed forms.

Kaufman, Walter. *From Shakespeare to Existentialism.* Garden City, N.Y.: Doubleday Anchor Books, 1960. A well-known book treating the relationship between poetry and philosophy as it manifests itself in Shakespeare, Goethe, Hegel, Kierkegaard, Nietzsche, Rilke, Freud, Heidegger (of whom Kaufman is extremely critical), and Toynbee.

Kermode, Frank. *The Sense of an Ending: Studies in the Theory of Fiction.* New York: Oxford University Press, 1968. One of the most important of recent books on fiction, this study brillantly explores the perennial relationship between crisis (apocalypse) and literary form as it is revealed in the Western tradition from Plato through St. Augustine to Murdoch, Sartre, and Robbe-Grillet.

Kern, Edith. *Existential Thought and Fictional Technique: Kierkegaard, Sartre, Beckett.* New Haven, Conn.: Yale University Press, 1970. A valuable analysis of the formal imperatives of existential thought, though the author's general equation of the *kunstlerroman* (the novel about the artist writing a novel) with the existential stance generates debatable conclusions about existential literary forms.

Knott, Jan. *Shakespeare, Our Contemporary.* Translated by Boleslow Tabor-ski. Garden City, N.Y.: Doubleday, 1966. An often brilliant interpretation of the contemporaneity of Shakesepare's plays from a broadly absurdist point of view.

Krieger, Murray. *The Tragic Vision: Variations on a Theme in Literary Inter-pretation.* New York: Holt, Rinehart and Winston, 1960. An effort to reconcile the New Critical preference for closed forms with existential thematic "openness," this book treats such "existential" authors as André Malraux, Ignazio Silone, Thomas Mann, Franz Kafka, Albert Camus, Joseph Conrad, Herman Melville, and Fëdor Dostoevski.

Lebowitz, Naomi. *Humanism and the Absurd in the Modern Novel.* Evan-ston, Ill.: Northwestern University Press, 1971. An interesting defense of the hu-manistic novel against the antihumanism of the existential absurdists.

Lewis, R. W. B. *The Picaresque Saint: Representative Figures in Contemporary Fiction.* Philadelphia: Lippincott, 1961. Thematic analyses of the existential jour-ney of the modern picaresque hero as it is presented by Alberto Moravia, Albert Camus, Ignazio Silone, William Faulkner, Graham Greene, and André Malraux.

Miller, J. Hillis. *Poets of Reality: Six Twentieth-Century Writers.* Cambridge, Mass.: Harvard University Press, 1965. An often distinguished application of the "phenomenological method" of literary criticism (I would say Husserlian rather than Heideggerian) developed primarily by the French critic Georges Poulet to Joseph Conrad, W. B. Yeats, T. S. Eliot, Dylan Thomas, Wallace Stevens, and William Carlos Williams.

Murdoch, Iris. "The Sublime and the Beautiful Revisited." *Yale Review,* Vol. 49 (1959–1960), 247–271. An important critique of the "closed" forms of early Modernist "symbolism" and a plea for a "generous" literature of openness form a broadly existential commitment to freedom.

Olson, Charles. *Selected Writings.* Edited by Robert Creeley. New York: New Directions, 1966. An authoritative selection of Olson's prose and poetry that clearly suggests this important and influential American poet's commitment to "the things themselves"—and that "Negative Capability" which relates him to Heidegger and the phenomenologists.

Poulet, Georges. "The Phenomenology of Reading." Translated by Richard Macksey. *New Literary History,* Vol. 1 (October 1969). A theoretical account of the kind of "spatial" or logocentric (as opposed to temporal) phenomenology that underlies the criticism of the "Geneva School" (Poulet, Raymond Roussel, Jean-Pierre Richard, Jean Starobinski, and so on), sometimes called the "criticism of consciousness" or "criticism of identification."

Rosenberg, Harold. *Act and Actor: Making the Self.* New York: Meridian, 1972. Not a book of literary criticism strictly speaking, this group of essays is nevertheless of great value to the study of the relationship between existentialism and contemporary literary form in its exploration of "dramatic fictions within real and imagined situations," especially of the "politics of illusion dominant through-out the world."

Ruotolo, Lucio P. *Six Existential Heroes: The Politics of Faith.* Cambridge, Mass.: Harvard University Press, 1973. A sensitive thematic study of the positive existential "encounter with nothingness" as it is expressed in the protagonists of Virginia Woolf's *Mrs. Dalloway;* Graham Greene's *Brighton Rock;* William Faulkner's *Go Down Moses;* Ralph Ellison's *Invisible Man;* William Golding's *Lord of the Flies;* and Bernard Malamud's *The Fixer.*

Sarraute, Nathalie. *The Age of Suspicion: Essays on the Novel.* Translated by Maria Jolas. New York: Braziller, 1963. An expression of the loss of faith in the fixed and stable psychology of the hero of the "old novel," these provocative essays suggest possibilities for "a new novel" based on the ambiguities of character found in writers like Kafka and Dostoevski.

Sartre, Jean-Paul. *What Is Literature?* Translated by Bernard Frechtman. New York: Harper Colophon Books, 1965. The very famous—and still misunderstood—articulation of Sartre's theory of *"la littérature engagée."*

Scott, Nathan A. *The Broken Center: Studies in the Theological Horizon of Modern Literature.* New Haven, Conn.: Yale University Press, 1966. Distinguished essays on various aspects of modern literature written from a Christian existentialist (basically Tillichean) point of view. Especially useful in terms of the concerns of this book are "The Name and Nature of Our Period-Style," pp. 1–25; and "Mimesis and Time in Modern Literature," pp. 25–75.

Seiden, Melvin. "The Classroom as Underground: Notes on 'The Grand Inquisitor.'" *The Journal of General Education.* Vol. X (October 1957), 217–222. An interesting account of a teacher's engagement in the moral ambiguity of Dostoevski's text.

Spanos, William V. "Modern Drama and the Aristotelian Tradition: The Formal Imperatives of Absurd Time." *Contemporary Literature,* Vol. 12 (Summer 1971), 345–372. This essay attempts to show that the open forms of the drama of the absurd can best be understood by way of the analogy of the existential understanding of time and history.

_____. "Modern Literary Criticism and the Spatialization of Time: An Existential Critique." *Journal of Aesthetics and Art Criticism,* Vol. XXXIX (Fall 1970), 87–104. Approaching the American New Criticism from an existential point of view, this essay attempts to show that the formalist doctrine of the autonomy of a work of literary art is grounded in an impulse to transcend the anxieties of existential time.

_____. "'Wanna Go Home Baby?': *Sweeney Agonistes* as Drama of the Absurd." *PMLA,* Vol. 85 (January 1970), 8–20. An extended analysis of the form of T. S. Eliot's *Sweeney Agonistes* as antidetective play, using the existential distinction between dread and fear as point of departure.

Sypher, Wylie. *The Loss of Self in Modern Literature and Art.* New York: Vintage Books, 1964. A very general, but insightful analysis of the parallel disintegration of the "center" between contemporary arts (literature and painting) and post-Newtonian science (Bridgman, Heisenberg, and so on) and philosophy (Whitehead, Lupasco, Heidegger, and so forth).

Vernon, John. *The Garden and the Map: Schizophrenia in Twentieth-Century Literature and Culture.* Urbana, Ill.: University of Illinois Press, 1973. A provocative book of recent literary criticism, especially valuable for its existential/ phenomenological analysis and critique of the positivisitc "map-consciousness" and its dominance in the Western humanistic tradition. See especially Chapters 1 and 2: "The Garden and the Map" and "Objectivity, the Novel and Schizophrenia."

Wasson, Richard. "Notes on a New Sensibility." *Partisan Review,* Vol. XXXVI, No. 3 (1969), 460–476. Using Iris Murdoch's critique of symbolist and Hegelian "totalitarianism" as its point of departure, this valuable essay examines contemporary writers such as Robbe-Grillet, John Barth, and Thomas Pynchon to show that their rejection of early Modernist formalism constitutes a new affirmation of a literature of contingency.

Printer and Binder: Hamilton Printing Company
80 81 82 83 8 7 6 5 4 3 2